C000271678

Commentaries on the municipal & mercantile law of Scotland : considered in relation to he subject of bankruptcy. Volume 1 of 2

George Joseph Bell

The Making of Modern Law collection of legal archives constitutes a genuine revolution in historical legal research because it opens up a wealth of rare and previously inaccessible sources in legal, constitutional, administrative, political, cultural, intellectual, and social history. This unique collection consists of three extensive archives that provide insight into more than 300 years of American and British history. These collections include:

Legal Treatises, 1800-1926: over 20,000 legal treatises provide a comprehensive collection in legal history, business and economics, politics and government.

Trials, 1600-1926: nearly 10,000 titles reveal the drama of famous, infamous, and obscure courtroom cases in America and the British Empire across three centuries.

Primary Sources, 1620-1926: includes reports, statutes and regulations in American history, including early state codes, municipal ordinances, constitutional conventions and compilations, and law dictionaries.

These archives provide a unique research tool for tracking the development of our modern legal system and how it has affected our culture, government, business – nearly every aspect of our everyday life. For the first time, these high-quality digital scans of original works are available via print-on-demand, making them readily accessible to libraries, students, independent scholars, and readers of all ages.

COMMENTARIES

ON THE

MUNICIPAL & MERCANTILE

LAW OF SCOTLAND,

CONSIDERED

IN RELATION TO THE SUBJECT

OF

BANKRUPTCY.

BY GEORGE JOSEPH BELL, ESQ.
ADVOCATE.

IN TWO VOLUMES.

VOL. I.

EDINBURGH:
PRINTED FOR ARCH. CONSTABLE AND CO., AND MANNERS AND MILLER, EDINBURGH: AND SOLD BY LONGMAN HURST REES AND ORME, AND J. BUTTERWORTH, LONDON.

1804.

Printed by Alex. Lawrie and Co.

PREFACE.

Every Branch of National Jurisprudence may be considered as in itself complete; as forming a subordinate whole, in which may be perceived the systematic operation of peculiar principles. An institute explains the general outlines of the law, with the connexions and dependencies of its component parts. But, to exhibit a comprehensive view of the principles of each division; to show their application to the business of life; to explain them in the way, which those engaged in practice naturally wish for; requires, in each, a fuller history, and more minute illustration. In other countries, the different branches of Law have been made the subjects of separate treatises, and, in this manner, the whole science has been most successfully cultivated;—in France under her old establishment, in Germany, in Holland, and in England. In England, the effect of this may be observed, in the precision introduced into the various titles of the law; and in the facility with which men are enabled to acquire a knowledge of the particular department in which they may be interested, without the necessity of embracing, like professional lawyers, the whole circle of a science with which they may have little concern. In no country of Europe, perhaps, has the history and illustration of the national jurisprudence been more neglected by individuals, than in Scotland—in very few, I believe, will it be found more deserving of attention. Till the publication of Mr Hume's excellent Commentary,

tary, it was a very arduous task, to acquire a knowledge even of the criminal law; which is so highly interesting to all of us, as subjects, or as jurymen: and at this moment there is not one branch of our mercantile law, except Insurance, which has been made the subject of separate consideration. That, in a country, which has successfully begun the great career of commercial prosperity, such indifference should have been shown to the branches of jurisprudence connected with trade, is surprising. Even the regulations that have been adopted relative to Bankruptcy, and the peculiar principles of judgement, which, in every country, form the Bankrupt Law into a separate code, deeply interesting as they must ever be to those engaged in trade, are nowhere to be found embodied in one systematic view: They have hitherto lain blended in the great mass of our common and statute law.

From these considerations, I was first led to think, that no Scotish lawyer could better employ that leisure, which the intervals of his professional duties happily afford him, than in investigating, successively, the several branches of the commercial law of his country; and I was not without hope that I might be enabled to accomplish a part, at least, of this great undertaking. With a solicitude proportioned to the difficulty of the subject, I now submit to the public, a Treatise on the Law of Bankruptcy.

This subject I have been desirous to present in a form so simple, that my work may be perused with advantage by men unaccustomed to the study of the law, and may be easily understood by those who have been familiarized with other systems of municipal jurisprudence. I am well aware how difficult it must ever be, to free from the technical language of the profession a

subject

subject of this nature; and how little reason I have to indulge the hope, that, in the first attempt to digest into a regular system, a code of laws so complicated, I have attained that simplicity of explanation, which I know to be necessary. But, in the attempt I have made, even a partial success may be useful. I have endeavoured, in an Introduction, to give such preliminary views of the plan and spirit of the Common law relative to the recovery of single debts, as seemed likely to facilitate the explanation of the peculiarities of the Bankrupt Code: and, by a comparison with the analogous points in the law of England, I have, in some measure, prepared the reader for those contrasted views of the laws of Bankruptcy in both countries, which, if properly executed, must, I am satisfied, contribute to their mutual illustration.

The chief design of this work, however, is to present a full body of information for the use of the professional lawyer; to connect, in one systematical view, the peculiar rules and institutions of the Bankrupt Law of Scotland. How far I may be thought to have succeeded in this attempt, I am afraid even to conjecture. I have indeed subjected myself to a very high responsibility; but I know, how candid the Profession is, to which I address myself, and how sensible they will be of the difficulty of the task which I have undertaken.

Should this book be honoured with a perusal by any English lawyer, he will require no other apology for any misconceptions of the law of his country, than the general difficulty which every man must feel, in comprehending the peculiarities of foreign institutions, and in learning how those things,

things, which, in a theoretical view, appear to be evils and defects, are remedied and corrected in practice.

For the attempt to contrast the Laws of England and of Scotland, my best apology will be found in the spirit with which I have made the comparison. I have not been actuated by the vain ambition of contending for national superiority, which has been too much, perhaps, the fashion of our day; but I have ever regreted those prejudices, which have been entertained against many of our civil institutions—prejudices which arose at a time when the law of this country was rude and unimproved, and which we have taken too little pains to remove, after those causes ceased to operate, from which they originally sprung. These prejudices have perhaps been stronger against the Laws of Bankruptcy, than against any other department of our jurisprudence. Half a century has not yet elapsed, since our Bankrupt Law was in a state so imperfect, as to deter English merchants from investing capital in this country; as to oppose the best interests of Scotland; and to retard her progress as a nation. Now, it is grown into a system, of which we have no little reason to be proud; which, compared with the Bankrupt Codes of other States, will be found chargeable with as few imperfections, and entitled to boast of provisions as just, equitable and humane, as those devised by nations the farthest advanced in commercial enterprize. No Scotchman, who takes an interest in the welfare of his country, can be destitute of curiosity to know the steps of this rapid improvement: And no one can inquire into the subject, without feeling a lively gratitude to the Supreme Court of the kingdom, to whose wisdom and unceasing care, Scotland is chiefly indebted for the improvement of a branch of law intimately

mately connected with national prosperity. We shall afterwards have occasion to see, that, from the first dawn of the Bankrupt Law, down to the last statute which has brought the system so near perfection, every valuable improvement is to be traced to the suggestions of that Venerable Court, to which the Legislature has ever looked for instruction, in reviewing and altering the jurisprudence of the country. To the Right Honourable Judge, in particular, who presides in this Court with so much ability, the nation is under high obligations. When, upon the expiration of the first Sequestration Law, a formidable opposition was made to its renewal, he was entitled, by his long experience, his eminent talents, and extensive knowledge of the law, to take a leading part in the public discussion. At the solicitation of the first merchants in Scotland, he stood forth the successful defender of this statute, and of the mercantile interest, which seemed to be involved in its fate: and the improvements which, in framing the new act, were introduced by him, are acknowledged to have been of the very first importance. Since he has been called to preside in the Supreme Civil Court of his country, it has again been necessary to renew this important statute; and, on this occasion, he has shown how truly he feels that it is one of the high duties of the station which he fills, to forward the improvement, as well as to watch over the execution, of the Laws.

TABLE OF CONTENTS

OF

THE FIRST VOLUME.

INTRODUCTION.

View of the general Principles of the Bankrupt Law—General Outline of the Common Law of Execution for Debt, in England and in Scotland—Contrast of the Bankrupt Laws of the two Countries—Plan of the Work.

BOOK I.

OF BANKRUPTCY.

BOOK II.

OF THE LAWS DIRECTED AGAINST FRAUDULENT OBLIGATIONS AND CONVEYANCES.

BOOK III.

OF THE LAWS BY WHICH JUDICIAL PREFERENCES ARE EQUALIZED IN RELATION TO BANKRUPTCY.

CHAP.

BOOK IV.

OF THE PROCESSES BY WHICH THE FUNDS OF BANKRUPTS ARE DISTRIBUTED AMONG THE CREDITORS.

PART

PART THE FIRST.

Of the Processes by which the Property of a Bankrupt is converted into Money, and Distributed among the Creditors, independently of Sequestration and Voluntary Trust.

PART THE SECOND.

Of the Sequestration, or Process of Distribution of the Estates of those engaged in Trade or Manufactures.

PART THE THIRD.

Of the Distribution of the Estate of a Bankrupt, by Voluntary Trust and Accession.

INDEX

INDEX OF CASES.

c

* See Advertisement at end of this Index.

T.

U.

V.

W.

Y.

* See Advertisement, opposite page.

ADVERTISEMENT.

1 In the case of Whyte against Butter, p 37 & 38, the Court has, since those pages were printed, altered their judgement, and found, that Morison was legally made bankrupt: 25th November 1800.

2. The case, p. 171, 29th January 1794, is, M'Hutcheon against Welsh, not M'Kichen The case was finally decided 20th May 1794. The report of what the Court thought of the former case of Campbell against M'Gibbon, is correct

3. When that part of the book was written, which relates to the computation of the sixty days of retrospect, under the act 1696, c. 5, I was not aware of the ground upon which the case of Mercer had been decided in the House of Lords, and which affords so plain and satisfactory a rule for all such cases; viz 'That the terminus a quo 'mentioned in the act respecting deathbed, is descriptive of a period of time (viz. the 'day or date of the deed) which is indivisible; and sixty days after, is descriptive of 'another and subsequent period, which begins when the first is completed. The day 'of making the deed, must therefore be excluded; and the maker lived only fifty-nine 'days of the period required. Had he seen the morning of the subsequent day, the 'rule of law would have applied—Dies inceptus pro completo habetur; which makes 'it unnecessary to reckon by hours.' Dict Vol. III p 173 4—If this rule be applied, in the computation of the sixty days of bankruptcy, the same effect precisely will be produced, as in counting backwards, exclusively of the day on which the bankruptcy is completed: p 191.

4. In the case quoted p 364, I have omitted the name of the estate It was the estate of Kingsgrange

INTRODUCTION.

The Laws of Bankruptcy form, in every nation, a separate code, distinguished by peculiar principles and appropriate institutions. By the common law, creditors are regarded as insulated individuals; unconnected in interest with each other; bound to no co-operation in execution, and to no plan of common benefit. Under the Bankrupt Law, they are formed into a community: The inadequacy of the fund, from which they are to be paid, is made the ground of mutual forbearance; the accumulation of expensive and separate proceedings is prevented; and a general plan is devised for the recovery and distribution of the estate, at the common expence. The law, as it regards the person of the debtor, suffers as complete a change, under the bankrupt code, as that which regulates the proceedings against the estate. The right of perpetual imprisonment, which, at common law, is held to belong to the creditors of an insolvent debtor, is modified by more comprehensive and liberal views: And although the debtor who is guilty of embezzlement or fraud, is exposed to harsher restraints, and regulations more highly penal; he, who is innocent, but unfortunate, is relieved from prison, or discharged of his debt.

This

This peculiar system, however, is not of rapid growth. Humane, and equitable and beneficial as its spirit appears to us, it is beyond the conception, and inconsistent with the most natural feelings of a rude age. The processes, by which performance of obligations is to be enforced, are devised, at first, with a view merely to individual contracts, and to the single creditor who may have occasion to seek the aid of a court of justice. Society has made considerable progress, before men learn to extend their views beyond themselves, or acquire any notion of a communion, where the general welfare is best promoted by mutual sacrifices. At first, each creditor thinks himself entitled to recover, as he best can, the debt that is due to him; to call his debtor into court, and to put in force against him those processes of execution which the law has provided for his use, without inquiring whether there be other creditors: Or he quickens perhaps his exertions, from a dread lest others should get before him. It is not natural for such a man to think of a communion with those who never can occur to him but in the light of rivals. Ignorant of any title to preference, but priority of gift or of seizure, he is not prepared to acknowledge the justice of a rule, which communicates the benefit of his exertions to those who have been careless, while he has been vigilant; which recals from him, perhaps, what he has already obtained; or stops him, at least, from completing the attachment he has begun. This natural opposition to what, in after times, appears so equitable, directs the course and maxims of the law. Instead of leading towards forbearance, or paving the way for the introduction of equality among creditors, the early regulations of every state tend to sanction and confirm the right of individual execution. 'Jus civile vigilantibus scriptum

'est,'

'est,' was the maxim of the old Roman lawyers: And this was too consonant with the spirit of the people, to be rejected by those nations who rose upon the ruins of the Empire.

As society advances, and the intercourse of mankind extends, the narrow maxims and harsh practices of the old law, naturally give place, by degrees, to a more equitable and a milder spirit. The injustice and inexpediency of perpetual confinement for debt come to be felt and acknowledged, when the situations multiply which give rise to insolvency; and the sense of a common interest among creditors is gradually unfolded, as the occasions more frequently arise, in which they are called upon to divide an inadequate fund. The introduction of credit, the invention of bills of exchange, the multiplying dependencies of men upon each other, in the relation of debtor and creditor, ripen by degrees the principles, and introduce the spirit of the Bankrupt Law. To trace the history of commerce, or to discuss the dangers or advantages of mercantile credit, is not the object of this treatise. But, without entering upon the general inquiry, we may assume the following position, without danger of controversy—That credit is, with all its benefits, necessarily productive of frequent insolvencies. Amidst the mischances incident to mercantile speculations, even that relief which the happy expedient of insurance affords, and those occasional aids, which, in a country enjoying the blessings of a free, vigorous, and settled government, the Legislature is enabled, in times of danger, to bestow, do not prevent this system from proving fatal to numberless individuals; or even, when pushed too far, from leading to serious national distress. It is amidst these frequent insolvencies, however, that the great principles of the bankrupt law are fully established; that men feel, by experience, the absurdity and unjust consequences of the old maxims; that they come to take a moderate, equitable, and enlarged view of the effects of insolvency upon the common interests of all; and to acquire a just sense of the benefit to be derived from unanimity, and from an equal division.

In every code of bankrupt law, which thus grows up amidst the multiplying transactions of a trading country, two great points may be taken, as the fundamental principles into which the whole is resolveable. One is, that, from the moment of failure, the inadequate fund becomes the common property of the creditors;—the other, that, as insolvency may often proceed from misfortune alone, it is not only unjust, but inexpedient, and even hurtful to the creditors themselves, to deprive of his freedom, a person, who gives up all for the payment of his debts, and who may be able, when at liberty, to labour for his creditors, and for himself.

I. The first of these principles is the more extensive in its operation; and forms the ground-work of all the peculiarities of the bankrupt law, with respect to the right of the creditors, and the powers of the debtor, over the estate.

Thus, it is a direct consequence of this principle, that, from the moment of insolvency, the debtor loses the power of a proprietor, and becomes a mere negotiorum gestor for his creditors, in the management of the common fund; that he is bound to make a fair disclosure of his estate; that he is deprived of the power of gratuitous alienation, and his hands tied up from acts of generosity or gratitude. This is the fundamental principle of all those regulations, by which, in the bankrupt laws of various countries, provision is made for the examination of the bankrupt; for preventing direct or indirect embezzlement; and for annulling fictitious debts and voluntary conveyances without value.

A second consequence of the general principle is, that although, in the ordinary case, a debtor is bound to pay his creditors upon demand, or to give security to those who are suspicious of his credit, and urgent for payment; he cannot, after insolvency, thus agree to favour any one, without doing injustice to the rest, by encroaching upon a fund which is common to them all. This, again, is the great foundation of those laws, which have for their object, the restraining of insolvent debtors from constituting preferences—from making payments in contemplation of bankruptcy—or delivering goods as the equivalent of payment—or granting deeds of security, in favour of prior creditors, over any part of the estate. And such laws are defective or perfect, in proportion to the success with which this great and general principle is reconciled with the fair rights of those, who, ignorant of the debtor's condition, may have been induced to rely upon his credit.

A third consequence, deducible from the above principle, is, that as the debtor is stopped, by the constitution

of

of the common right, from bestowing preferences upon particular creditors; so, those individual creditors themselves ought to be prevented from acquiring preferences, by the use of separate diligence. With this view, a legal process ought to be open to the creditors, for immediately vesting in them, or in trustees, the insolvent estate, to be managed for the general behoof, converted into money, and distributed at the common expence. The perfection of this set of regulations, in any country, must depend upon the simplicity of the process—the ease with which it may be obtained—and the rapidity and economy with which the distribution under it may be accomplished.

Lastly, the general principle entitles each creditor to an equal share of the funds, unless any of them shall, previous to the failure, have acquired a preferable real right over some part of the estate or effects. It is not the intention of the Bankrupt Law, to take, as a fund of division, what does not really belong to the bankrupt, or what may be exhausted and covered by real securities; but to allow, as far as may be consistent with these preferable rights, a perfect equality among the creditors.

Thus, the common interest of the creditors, in the inadequate fund, is the great principle, which pervades and systematizes the whole regulations of the Bankrupt Law, in relation to the estate of the debtor, and his powers over it.

II. The other great principle, above laid down, bears reference rather to the condition of the debtor. It is a principle which ought to operate in all cases; for, though

though the trader is chiefly liable to be overtaken by sudden misfortune, other men are not beyond the reach of mischance; and if a debtor, although no merchant, can vindicate his failure from suspicion, and is willing to deliver up his whole estate to his creditors, he ought to be freed from prison. That the more frequent and unavoidable dangers of a merchant's condition, and the necessity of his acting much upon credit, entitles him to some distinction, is unquestionable; but this should consist, not in the punishment of other men, but rather in the absolute discharge of the fair trader himself. It is a point, even of public expediency, that an honest merchant, who has failed, should be enabled to recommence his trade, undepressed by the load of former debts, which he has already done every thing in his power to discharge. It is scarcely a hardship upon creditors to give this indulgence; since the chance of insolvency, so peculiarly incident to all mercantile transactions, must have entered into their calculation of risk.

These seem to be the leading principles of the Bankrupt Law, considered in the abstract. The particular regulations of each State must of course vary with the general spirit of the common law, and with the peculiarities of its ordinary institutions: But, however numerous or perplexing the rules and institutions of any code may at first appear, in these points they will be found to centre; and the system may fairly be estimated as good or bad, in proportion as effect is given or denied to these general principles.

It

It might be interesting, in this view, to examine the systems of Bankrupt Law eſtabliſhed in various nations—to inquire how far they accord with these abstract principles—and to what peculiarity any deviation is to be traced. But this is a large field of inquiry, into which I cannot presume to enter far. As it is of chief importance for us to understand the two systems of Bankrupt Law, which are established in this island—to see how far they agree, and where they differ from each other; it may be proper to restrict ourselves, in this preliminary inquiry, to these limits: and, that the illustration from comparison may be the more complete, that we may understand more fully the difference of spirit and of principle in each, it may be proper to begin with inquiring into the general points of contrast between the laws of England and Scotland, relative to the recovery of single debts; tracing afterwards the effect produced by this difference upon the respective codes of Bankrupt Law.

§ 1. *Of Judgement and Execution for the Recovery of Single Debts.*

i. Execution against the person, or against the property of a debtor, can take place only in consequence of the sentence of a Court, either pronounced in a contested action, or proceeding upon previous consent, dispensing with the necessity of an action.

To explain the judgement or decree, in contested actions, would require a review of the Jurisdictions and Courts of the two countries, and of their forms of action and of trial: and although such a comparison would, no doubt,

doubt, be very interesting, I found, as I proceeded in drawing it up, that it would far exceed the limits of an introductory discourse. It may be sufficient, then, without entering into this inquiry, to explain the nature of the consensual judgement; and to mark what effect the laws of either country give to a judgement or decree.

By the consensual decree or judgement, the expence and delay of trials are avoided; the course of justice greatly facilitated; and the punctual performance of contracts easily and quickly enforced.

In England, this judgement proceeds upon a formal warrant of attorney to confess; and is generally used where an action is begun, and the debtor arrested upon the commencing suit is willing, at the same time, to avoid expence, and to gain indulgence. He signs a warrant to certain attornies to appear in an action, at his creditor's instance, and to confess judgement; a condition being generally added, that execution is not to proceed till a specified day. This warrant being delivered to the creditor, he is entitled, under it, to enter up a judgement on the record; that is to say, to have it enrolled as a judgement in the rolls of court. This he may do during vacation, as well as in term time; the judgement being entered up as of the preceding term. Such judgement has precisely the same effect with one regularly pronounced in a contested suit.

In Scotland, the consensual decree is much more common. There is not required with us, as in England, a formal warrant of attorney to confess judgement; but every solemn

lemn obligation and contract has a clause incorporated into it, by which the obligor consents that the deed shall be recorded in the books of a court having jurisdiction, and that decree may thereupon be summarily issued. The holder of such a deed, has nothing more to do, than to present his deed to the clerk of court, who puts it up among the records, and gives an authentic copy of it, as recorded by consent; armed with a decree, as if actually pronounced by the judge. The great advantage of this plan, as facilitating the execution of obligations, and saving the necessity of proceedings at law, induced the Legislature of Scotland, in the end of the 17th century, to extend it to bills of exchange. By the 20th statute of the year 1681, and the 36th of 1696, it is provided, that foreign and inland bills of exchange, if regularly protested for not-acceptance, or not-payment, shall be the ground of summary diligence or execution, provided the protest, with a copy of the bill prefixed, be recorded within six months. A decree of registration is immediately given out, as in the case of an obligation bearing a clause of registration. And thus, the necessity of an action is saved, in all mercantile cases, where bills have been accepted.

There is a strongly marked distinction between the law of England and that of Scotland, in the effect given to a judgement. The English judgement, whether pronounced in a contested suit, or proceeding upon a warrant of attorney to confess, is held, if followed within a year by the proper writ of execution for attaching the land, to bind the defendant's lands, from the day of its being pronounced. And, although the freedom of commerce has required that the moveables should not remain thus

bound

bound for a year, it is established, that, from the moment of the proper writ of execution against moveables being delivered to the Sheriff for execution, the moveables also are bound. As a judgement debt has thus the effect of a real security upon the land, and, in some degree, of an attachment of the moveables, great care has been taken to ensure the recording of the judgement in the rolls of the Court which pronounces it, so that it may be open to public inquiry, like an heritable security in this country.

In Scotland, a decree has no effect in binding the debtor's property before execution. The completion of the actual execution, is the commencement of the effect of the decree; and although all extracted decrees are entered in a record (at least, in the Court of Session), by which they can easily be traced, this is not necessary as a record for public information, as in England.

ii. In comparing the English with the Scotish forms of execution for individual debt, in cases where there is no insolvency, it may be proper to consider, 1. Those by which security is obtained previous to judgement: 2. Those by which real property in England, and heritable in Scotland, is attached in execution: 3. Those by which personal funds are attached in execution: and, 4. Those which affect the person of the debtor.

1. In the law of Scotland, there are two forms of diligence, by which the whole property of debtors, both the heritable and the moveable which is in the hands of others, may be attached, at the commencement of an action, in security of the claim; and by which the creditor may also

constitute a security to himself, for debts which are payable at a future day certain, or even for contingent claims. These are called INHIBITION and ARRESTMENT. As it would be very inexpedient to expose to latent attachment, the money or moveables of the debtor in his own natural possession, these diligences do not give any security upon such property. Even the indiscriminate use of diligence against property in any situation, may be attended with very disagreeable consequences; and therefore, a creditor is, even in the proper use of these two diligences, subjected to the controul of the Court of Session, who give relief to the defendant, if the attachment be unnecessary or oppressive.

INHIBITION is a writ, in the King's name, by which the debtor is prohibited from disposing of his land, or heritable property, to the prejudice of the inhibiting creditor, and even from contracting debt, so as to affect his lands. The public, also, is prohibited from contracting with him for his heritable property, to the prejudice of the inhibiting creditor. This diligence enters into a public record, like an English judgement.

The ARRESTMENT IN SECURITY, is a writ in the King's name (or it may be issued also by an inferior court, in the form of a precept), by which the creditor is authorised to attach, in the hands of third parties, debts due by them, or moveables in their possession, belonging to his debtor. These are to be retained, unless relieved by caution, till the creditor can have his debt established by judgement, or till the term of payment arrive, or the contingency of the debt be purified; when the attached property

perty may, in an action of forthcoming, be adjudged over to the creditor arrester in payment of his debt.—Having provided these remedies for attaching in security the property of the debtor, the law of Scotland has denied to the creditor a previous attachment of his person; unless there be good ground for suspecting him of an intention to leave the kingdom, so as to disappoint his creditor of the right of personal execution.

In England, there is, in all actions, a previous arrest of the person; first, ad respondendum, to oblige the debtor to answer to the action; and, next, ad satisfaciendum, to keep his person in prison, as the subject of personal execution when sentence is pronounced. The debtor is to be liberated, only by finding bail for his appearance; the bail being merely nominal in cases below 10l., and 'good substantial bail' in all above that sum. But by the common law of England there is no right of previous attachment of the property, to serve as an ultimate security to the plaintiff, should his claim be supported by judgement of the Court. There are, indeed, local customs, by which this defect is supplied. In the city of London, for example, the plaintiff may sue out what is called a writ of FOREIGN ATTACHMENT, by which the goods of the debtor may be attached, as by an arrestment in Scotland; and a similar custom, I believe, exists in the township of Hull.

2. In contrasting the English and Scotish forms of execution against land for debt, the comparison must run between the adjudication and the elegit.

The

The ADJUDICATION is the only form of ordinary diligence by which heritable subjects in Scotland can be taken in execution. Originating in the brieve of distress, it was, at first, and even for some time after it assumed (under the name of apprizing) the form of a writ of execution, a safe and useful diligence, under which the Sheriff of the county sold the lands, and paid off the debt; or, with the aid of a Jury of neighbours, valued the lands, and gave off an equivalent to the creditor. The introduction of a power of redemption to the debtor, was fatal to the sale, and had the effect of confining the diligence to the other alternative, viz. the setting off an equivalent in land for the debt. From causes, which it would be improper here to detail, this form of execution came, by successive changes, to its present state. It is now an action of execution before the Court of Session, for having the debtor's lands adjudged over to the creditor, redeemably. The judgement is alternative: Either such a portion of land is adjudged to the creditor, as may be found equivalent to the debt: or, if the debtor do not choose to concur in the special adjudication, a general adjudication of his whole lands is pronounced. It may be sufficient to say of this diligence, that, from the moment the summons is executed, it creates a lien over the land, called, in law language, Litigiosity; so, at least, as to prevent the debtor from voluntarily alienating to the prejudice of the creditor: that, if the subject be simply heritable, the decree of adjudication completes the creditor's right; if it be of a feudal nature, the decree of adjudication is completed and carried into execution by the common feudal forms of infeftment. The adjudication, when thus completed, entitles the creditor to enter into possession,

possession, and to recover the rents; the estate being redeemable within ten years, in the general adjudication, and five in the special. During this term of redemption, the creditor must, when called upon, account for what he may, or might have drawn, and resign his infeftment, if the debt have been paid off. If any part shall still remain due, it must either be paid off, and the estate redeemed, or the power of redemption may be foreclosed, by an action for declaring the term expired.

In England, as in every other feudal kingdom, land was, for a time, banished from commerce; and the only execution competent against the debtor's estate, was, distress by seizure of moveables. The writ of LEVARI FACIAS entitled the Sheriff to levy the rents and profits of the debtor's lands, as well as his common moveables; and, if necessary, another writ (VENDITIONI EXPONAS) was issued to authorise their sale. But it was not till the thirteenth century, that land was in any degree open to execution for debt in England. In the reign of Edward I, a new kind of execution was introduced, which is thus explained by Sir William Blackstone: 'When the restriction of alienation began to wear away, the consequence still continued; and no creditor could take possession of lands, 'but only levy the growing profits; so that, if the defendant aliened his land, the plaintiff was ousted of his remedy. The statute *, therefore, granted the writ of 'ELEGIT, by which the defendant's goods and chattels are 'not sold, but only apprized, and all of them (except 'oxen and beasts of the plough) are delivered to the plaintiff, &c. If the goods are not sufficient, then the moiety,

'or

* 13 Edward I. c 18

'or one half of his freehold lands which he had at the 'time of the judgement given, are also to be delivered to 'the plaintiff to hold, till, out of the rents and profits 'thereof, the debt be levied, or till the defendant's inte'rest be expired.' † Thus, the ELEGIT differs materially from our adjudication; for the estate, or right which the creditor acquires in the real property of his debtor, is not, like ours, a right of property, redeemable like a mortgage, but merely a conditional right of possession, ceasing with the payment of the debt, but affording no means of carrying the real right of property to the creditor himself.

3. The personal funds of the debtor are, in Scotland, taken in execution by the POINDING OF ARRESTMENT IN EXECUTION; by the FIERI FACIAS and ELEGIT in England.

The POINDING of the Scotish law, was, like the adjudication, originally a part of the execution under the brieve of distress. Like the adjudication, also, it was gradually debased; and it was only when reformed in the reign of his present Majesty, that it regained its original purity. It consists, at present, of an adjudication of the debtor's moveable property in his own possession, followed by a public sale, under the judicial superintendance of the Sheriff of the county; the price being applied in payment of the debt due to the poinding creditor. The ARRESTMENT IN EXECUTION, again, may be described as a lien created over the personal property of the debtor, in the hands of a third party, in consequence of an attachment. The property thus attached, like that attached by the arrestment

† 3. Blackst. 318.

restment in security, is made effectual to the creditor, in the course of an action of forthcoming, against the holder of the fund, and to which the debtor is made a party: it concludes, that the arrestee should be ordered to deliver up to the arrester the debtor's property, or to pay over to him the debt.

The original writs for execution against moveables in England, were, the LEVARI FACIAS and FIERI FACIAS. The former contained, at first, a power only to levy the goods, not to sell them; though, afterwards, the Supreme Courts came to insert, in the writs of levari facias issued by them, a power of selling. The fieri facias contained a power of levying the goods and debts, and 'making' of them to the avail of the debt. In the execution of these writs, the Sheriff made the goods be valued, fixed an up-set price upon them, and exposed them to sale. But here, his power ended, if no purchaser appeared; and a new writ, called Venditioni Exponas, was necessary to authorise a sale for what the goods could bring. The elegit, as applicable to moveables, introduced the power of appraisement, in case of the property not finding a purchaser. The fieri facias, and the elegit, are now the great writs of execution against moveables in England; and, under them, the purposes of our poinding and arrestment are accomplished; debts being levied under them, and goods sold for payment, or appraised to the value, and delivered in satisfaction.

4. In contrasting the law of execution against the person, it may be proper to recur to what has already been observed, in speaking of attachments previous to judgement,

ment, viz. that in England, the arrest of the person is the commencing step of every action; while, in Scotland, such an arrest is an extraordinary remedy, and used only for preventing the debtor from leaving the country. But the two laws do not differ in this point more widely, than in the whole plan and spirit of the execution against the person.

In Scotland, personal execution cannot proceed, till after the debtor has been charged to pay the debt, and a certain number of days have been allowed him for obedience. His disobedience to this charge, is followed by a new writ, authorising his imprisonment. The danger of the debtor's taking advantage of the days of charge to make his escape, is prevented by a warrant to apprehend him, (where there is ground for suspicion), as 'in meditatione fugæ;' and by forcing him to find bail, as in England, to present himself in court: voluntary banishment is, of course, the alternative of his absconding. In practice, these have been found sufficient to preserve the rights of the creditors uninjured. When imprisonment does follow, it is held by the law to have no other object, than to enforce payment, and the discovery of funds: And, thus, execution against the person, does not preclude execution against the property; nor can we, in Scotland, see a debtor living with extravagance in prison, as in England sometimes happens.

Imprisonment, as established in the English law, is not, like that of Scotland, a method, merely, of enforcing payment, and the discovery of hidden funds: it is regarded as a satisfaction for the debt. The consequence is, that

that the creditor can proceed with no execution against the property; that, while his right is satisfied by the imprisonment of the debtor, the fieri facias and elegit must sleep; and that, consequently, the debtor may, in the mean while, live in prison luxuriously and extravagantly, with his funds untouched by execution.

Having thus, in a rapid review, contrasted the common forms of execution in the two countries, in cases where there is no insolvency, the comparison may here be shortly resumed.—A creditor in England may, upon bringing his action, secure the person of the debtor; or, if in London, he may, by special custom, have a previous attachment, to secure the moveables, as the subject of execution upon judgement. When judgement is given, he may choose whether to proceed against the person, or against the estate. If he prefer personal execution, he may immediately imprison the debtor, and confine him for life, unless the debt be paid. If he choose to proceed against the estate, he may sue out a fieri facias, and recover his debt by sale of the moveables: or, by an elegit, he may take, first, the moveables, by sale or appraisement; and, if these be insufficient, the half of the debtor's land, to be held till, from the rents, he procure payment.—In Scotland, the creditor may secure his debtor's person, previous to decree, only when he is meditating an escape from the country; but, in all cases, where his debtor's credit is suspicious, he may take an intermediate security, by attachment of the lands of the debtor, or of such of his moveable property as may be in the hands of a third party. After judgment, he may proceed against the lands, moveables, and person, at one and the same time. He may, by adjudication, acquire a judicial mortgage, which, after the term of redemption is expired, may be foreclosed: he may proceed against the moveable property by poinding, or by arrestment and forthcoming; and he may imprison the person of his debtor, in order to enforce payment of the debt.

Before leaving this subject, it is necessary to explain a peculiar kind of execution, which is known in both countries, viz. the writ of EXTENT at the instance of the Crown. This is a kind of execution which originated in England, and was introduced into this country, when, at the union of the kingdoms, the Revenue Laws were put upon the same footing over the whole Island. The Court of Exchequer was then established in Scotland, to take cognizance of all Revenue questions. It is properly an English court, proceeding in all the steps of trial, judgment, and execution, according to the forms of the English law. All debts due to the Crown, whether by bond and recognizance, or by judgment, are put to execution by a writ called an EXTENT, or EXTENDI FACIAS; which is directed to the Sheriff of the county; and orders him, not only to take the body of the King's debtor into custody, and keep him in prison, till the King be satisfied for his debt, but also to inquire, by a Jury, what lands, goods, debts, &c. the debtor has belonging to him; to appraise these to the full extent, and to seize them to the King's use till his debt be paid. By 33. Henry VIII. c. 39, the King shall, in thus suing out execution, have his debt preferred

ferred to every other creditor, who has not obtained judgment before the King commenced his suit.

§ 2. *General Contrast of the Bankrupt Law of England and of Scotland.*

In reviewing the bankrupt laws of England and of Scotland, we shall find this striking distinction between them—that, in England, the regulations relating to bankruptcy are strictly confined to traders; while, in Scotland, the bankrupt law includes all ranks of men. The illustration of this difference, is naturally the first point of the contrast; and it will be found to elucidate, in some degree, the spirit and genius of the common law of either country.

The English have ever been wedded to their common law. From the days of the Parliament of Merton, down to the establishment of the Inns of Court, and thence to the present hour, the 'nolumus mutari' has still been the favourite maxim of England. But, that dread of the arbitrary maxims of the civil law, which had been strongly excited by peculiar circumstances, and burst forth in the unanimous exclamation of the Barons of Merton, has perhaps operated to a bad effect in matters of municipal regulation. In the department now under review, it cannot escape observation, that, while England was growing great in political power and riches, and even in commercial enterprize, the aversion from change, still left creditors in full possession of all the old rights of execution against the estates and persons of their debtors. So late as the sixteenth century, the power of imprisonment remain-

ed

ed an unalienable and sacred privilege of a creditor in all cases; and the preference over the funds by priority of execution, was still the maxim and rule of the common law. It was in the 34th year of the reign of Henry VIII, that the first alteration was made upon the ancient jurisprudence. But this was an alteration suddenly made, to provide against evils which bore hard upon the rising commerce of the country, and could not, in its full extent, be applied to others than merchants, without overturning the whole system of the common law. To understand this fully, it may be proper to observe, how radical an alteration was required, in many essential points, to provide for cases of insolvency.

There were three great inconveniences, which the rigid maxims of the English common law necessarily produced, in their application to the dealings of a commercial country: 1. The want of an easy and simple method of procuring execution, or even intermediate security for debts by bill, &c. otherwise than in consequence of the judgement of a court, with all its necessary delays, and all the interruptions of vacations, was, to traders, an evil of great magnitude, where their debtor was insolvent. For, during the interval, the debtor could not be prevented from enjoying his property, and sporting with the interests of his creditors. To remedy this, was one great object of the English bankrupt statutes; and it was accomplished, by authorising a commission of bankruptcy to be issued, to have the effect of an immediate legal execution, depriving the debtor of all power over his property, and carrying it, at once, to his creditors, to be divided among them for payment. 2. Although, originally, imprisonment

sonment for debt was not in England, any more than with us, the right of a creditor; yet, this right had grown up, and been long established as a sacred privilege. The inexpediency, injustice, and cruelty, of exposing traders to such a punishment, without any discrimination between extravagance or fraud, and mere misfortune, and with no other limit to the endurance of the punishment, than the caprice of the creditor, could not fail to be felt and acknowledged. But against this evil, as no provision was made by the common law, the interposition of the Legislature was necessary to provide for the debtor's discharge. This formed another object of the bankrupt laws. 3. Although all fraudulent deeds are, at common law, ineffectual, it is a matter of no small difficulty, to guard against the frauds which, upon the eve of bankruptcy, a debtor may be tempted to commit. It was, with this view, found necessary, in England, besides subjecting the debtor to a new code of penal laws, to allow the creditors to take out the commission of bankruptcy in secret, that it might fall suddenly upon the debtor, and surprise him, while his schemes of fraud were not yet completed. But the severity of these laws, necessary, perhaps, in one view, afforded many opportunities for oppression. Under them, an innocent man, far from being insolvent, was exposed to the disgrace of having his shop locked up, and his name publicly stigmatized as a bankrupt, without any notice of his danger, or possibility of avoiding a blow, that was, perhaps, to destroy his credit for ever.

In all these particulars (and in many more, which it is not necessary to detail at present), a wide departure from the maxims and rights of the common law, was, in cases of insolvency, found to be necessary for the occasions of an enlarged commerce. But it was not to be expected that a system, which so completely outraged that law, in particulars so important, would be suffered, by Englishmen, to reach beyond the range of necessity which gave it birth. And thus, although, by the first statutes of bankruptcy, in Henry the Eighth's reign, the commission was not restricted, but made applicable to all ranks of men; when the law came to be renewed, in the thirteenth year of Queen Elizabeth, it was limited to merchants; and other persons were left to the rules of the common law, neither restrained by the energy, nor favoured with the indulgence of this peculiar code. It has in this way happened, that, in England, no system of equal rights has been devised for the creditors of those unconnected with trade: there is no restraint upon the diligence of individual creditors; there is no limit to the accumulation of expence: and the debtor is exposed to that continual imprisonment, which the notion of its being a satisfaction for debt, necessarily implies.

The circumstances of Scotland, and the spirit of her common law, have been more favourable to the establishment of such regulations for insolvency, as were universal in their application to all ranks of men. Our forefathers felt not that dread of the civil law, by which the English barons were actuated. Perhaps, this might be accounted for, from the peculiar circumstances of the nations at the time, and from the different ways in which that system was introduced into the two countries. But, however this may be, there is little room for doubt, that the institutions and

rules

rules of our municipal law have been much improved by the influence of the Roman jurisprudence; holding it, as we have ever done, to be, not the civil code of this country (though some have affected so to represent it), but a body of general jurisprudence, the rules of which were to be adopted, wherever they were sanctioned by views of expediency, and not inconsistent with our own institutions or peculiar customs. This spirit, by which our ancestors were disposed to adopt the regulations and principles of a highly improved code, wherever their own institutions were defective, and to borrow freely whatever was found equitable and just, according to the opinions of the first jurists that ever graced the world, has led to the gradual improvement of the Scotish jurisprudence. The law of execution for debt partook of this improvement; and, instead of continuing fixed and unaltered, as in England, modifications and amendments were gradually admitted, according to the exigencies of an advancing people. In this way, it happened, that, when the commerce of Scotland called for regulations adapted to cases of insolvency, the general disposition of the common law accorded better with the condition of the country, and prevented the necessity of violent remedies.

Instead of rigidly adhering, then, as the English had done (with the single exception of the warrant to confess judgement) to the old rule, which required a judgement in every case before execution could pass, the decree of registration, when introduced in Scotland, was soon applied to all cases of mercantile documents, as well as to formal bonds. This gave a rapidity of execution, the want of which the English sorely felt; and which, we have seen,

seen, it was one object of the commission of bankruptcy to supply. We adopted the remedy of inhibition from the Canon law, and that of the arrestment in security from the Civil, as improved in the institutions of France, where that law was most successfully cultivated; and in this way, we had already apt means for securing a creditor against his debtor's fraud, during the dependence of his action, or the necessary delay of execution. We soon saw the justice of the cessio bonorum of the Roman law, which gave fredom to the innocent debtor able to vindicate his failure from fraud, and willing to give up every thing to his creditors. These were the three prominent evils which called for so sudden an alteration of the law in England; and they were thus gradually remedied in the law of Scotland, while yet our commerce was in its infancy. When that commerce did begin to increase, and to require rules for insolvency, the only points still to be provided for, were, the suppression of frauds, and the equal, quick, and economical distribution of the estate. These were, indeed, long of being properly provided for; but when the regulations came to be necessary, full leisure was given for attending to the necessities of the whole people, as well as of traders.

Thus, the progress of the Scotish Bankrupt Law has been gradual and imperceptible; and we see little of that violent opposition between the common law and the new institutions, which accompanied and restrained every interposition of the Legislature of our neighbouring country. The common and the statute law, have been enabled to go hand in hand, till, at last, instead of leaving every case of insolvency, not strictly mercantile, to the imperfect and

unjust

unjust rules of the old common law, as applicable to the recovery of single debts, a double system of laws relative to bankrupts has been formed:—one branch of it, general and applicable to all cases of insolvency; the other peculiar, approaching nearly to the English institution, and applicable only to mercantile failures.

From this general idea of the progress of the two systems, it may be proper to proceed, next, to inquire into their characteristical and distinguishing features, as compared more minutely with each other, and with the view we have already taken of the spirit of Bankrupt Law.

The English code of Bankrupt Law was, from its first institution, intended to form a complete body of regulations for the insolvencies of traders. The Scotish has grown up, after a very different fashion. At first, there was no idea of forming a complete and peculiar code, for the regulation of insolvency. The evils of perpetual imprisonment, of embezzlements, of fraudulent preferences, and of individual executions, were remedied by partial provisions, when, in the progress of the country, they came to be felt as grievances, requiring legislative interposition; and it is no more than half a century since any systematic plan of general attachment and distribution has been devised.

I. When, in the reign of Henry the VIII, the commerce of England had risen to sufficient importance to call upon the Legislature for a set of regulations that should free the trader from the evils of the old law, a plan was devised, and thus reduced to form. A commission was named, consisting of the first judges of the land, to whom very unusual and extensive powers were given. 'Their 'powers were, to take orders and directions, at their own 'wisdom and discretion, with the bodies of insolvents, 'and with their real and personal estate; and to cause the 'said estate and property to be viewed, rented, and appraised, and to make sale thereof; or otherwise to order 'the same, for the satisfaction and payment of the creditors, in proportion to the quantities of their debts:' they were also vested with very high powers, for the prevention and punishment of frauds, concealments, &c. In the thirteenth year of Queen Elisabeth's reign, this system was altered. Instead of the commission being vested in the Judges, it was, by a long succession of statutes, ordered to be vested in such wise, discreet, and learned persons, as the Lord Chancellor should appoint. The whole code has, in the progress of two hundred years, been gradually ripened, till it has grown at last into a complete system, having the triple object of preventing frauds; of dividing equally and expeditiously the estate of the debtor; and of discharging him from his debts, in cases of fair insolvency.

1. Certain acts are defined, as indicative of bankruptcy; the commission of which, with the view of preventing frauds, is declared to vitiate all the bankrupt's future transactions; and to entitle (with certain precautions) any creditor to take out a commission from Chancery for vesting the bankrupt's estate in the hands of the commissioners, who order his shop to be locked, and himself to be taken into custody.

2. The commissioners, as a court of delegation from the Lord Chancellor, are the judges, before whom the affairs of the bankruptcy are conducted; the debts proved; the bankrupt examined; and the funds divided: their orders and decisions being subject to the review of the Lord Chancellor.

3. The immediate and active management is entrusted to assignees, chosen by the creditors themselves. And,

4. The creditors are formed into a deliberative body, to determine all questions of management, and to judge whether the bankrupt be entitled to a discharge; reporting their opinion to the commissioners and the Lord Chancellor.

Such is the general scope of the Bankrupt Law of England. But, low as the consideration is, in which the English law has regarded other men, when compared with traders, they have not been entirely neglected. A debtor, although not a trader, is entitled to the benefit of what is called the Lords Act—intended as a remedy against the endless imprisonment of the common law. By this act, a debtor, in prison for a debt under 300l., may petition the courts for liberation; and, on stating his condition, his funds and his debts, and conveying every thing to his creditors, he will be liberated. Had the law stopped here, it would have been indeed a gracious provision, almost equivalent to our law of cessio bonorum; but the benefit of the whole remedy is destroyed by a declaration, that if the creditor, who has the debtor in execution, shall object to his enlargement, and

and find security for payment of a maintenance to him, (a weekly sum not exceeding two shillings and four pence), he may detain him in prison.

There does not appear to be any provision in England for dividing the funds of a debtor who is not a trader under the bankrupt law. The creditors are left to contest their rights upon the footing of the common law, or to agree, as they best can, in the prosecution of common measures. The creditors are preferred upon the lands, according to the dates of their judgements, when duly followed by Elegit—the first in order receiving an exclusive right of possession of one half of the land—the next, a right, equally exclusive, of the half of what remains; and so on, till the whole be exhausted: while the moveables, in the same way, are bound to each creditor, in the order of the delivery of his fieri facias to the Sheriff.

In reviewing that part of the English law, which is properly called the bankrupt law, and which is restricted to traders, we shall find, that, when examined by the abstract principles which regulate all bankrupt laws, it is wonderfully free from defects; perhaps as near to perfection, as, in the ordinary course of human institutions, it is natural to expect. But the examination of particular points of the system, it will be more proper to reserve for occasional contrasts, in the body of the work, with the analogous points of the Scotish law.

II. The first dawn of bankrupt law in Scotland, is perceptible in a very remote age; for the cessio bonorum of the Roman law was adopted by us even so early as the

date

date of Regiam Majestatem. By this benevolent institution, a remedy is provided against the perpetual imprisonment of insolvent debtors, when honest, and willing to convey every thing to their creditors; and those grievances are prevented, of which the English have so often and so loudly complained.

But, though this gracious remedy against perpetual imprisonment, was established so early in Scotland, it was not till the seventeenth century, that our commerce began to grow into importance, and the attention of the Legislature to be turned to insolvency. The first statute which professed to regulate matters of this kind, originated with the Judges of the Court of Session. By an act or rule of that Court, in July 1620, (which was adopted by Parliament, and makes the statute 1621, c. 18.), an attempt was made to prevent all collusive donations by insolvent debtors to their friends and relations, directly or indirectly; as, by such deeds, in the first instance, it is, that a debtor naturally endeavours, on the eve of his failure, to save something for his future subsistence, and to provide for those in whose welfare he is interested. In this law, provision was also made against the unfair interference of a debtor, with a view to disappoint, by private conveyances, the begun diligence of his creditors. This was done, by declaring all such deeds reducible by him who should thus be disappointed.

However complete this law may have appeared, as a remedy for the evils then existing, the increasing commerce of the country soon pointed out several defects in it. Towards the end of that century, while our commercial

cial ardour was yet unchecked by the failure of the Darien Expedition; when our linen manufactures were extending with a most promising rapidity; when our commercial intercourse with England, as well as with foreign countries, was daily increasing; and when the exigencies of our trade called for the establishment of a national Bank: cases of insolvency became more frequent, and, from the sums which they involved, infinitely more important than had hitherto been known in the country. Frauds were daily practised, which the existing laws were found inadequate to repress. Where a debtor granted a deed of preference to a favourite creditor, although in the immediate prospect of bankruptcy, no remedy existed, but a proof, at common law, that the debtor was insolvent at the date of the deed, and that the receiver knew this to be the case. These intricate points of inquiry, gave occasion to many involved actions: and it was found, in these investigations, so difficult to come to any conclusive issue, that little progress was commonly made after vast expence and delay. The Court of Session, who found themselves daily called upon to decide questions of this kind, and saw the bad consequences which flowed from the want of a fixed principle in a matter of such importance, named a committee of their number to prepare a remedy for it. This was in 1694; and the fifth statute, which passed in the Parliament of 1696, was the result of their deliberations. By that law, an universal and precise rule was laid down; the character of bankruptcy was precisely defined; and, this point being fixed, a presumption of fraud was established against all deeds granted, within sixty days before, in favour of prior creditors.

Besides these provisions for the annulling of fraudulent deeds, a direct punishment was enacted against the bankrupts themselves. The statute of 1621, declared all bankrupts, &c. who should be guilty of fraudulent devices against their creditors, infamous, incapable of honours and dignities, benefices or offices, or of sitting as jurymen, or bearing witness in judgment: the statute of 1696, subjects all fraudulent bankrupts to be tried by the Court of Session, and punished with any punishment short of death: and the cessio bonorum afforded an indirect punishment, of great efficacy, since the debtor could not hope for liberation, but by vindicating his honesty and fair dealing.

Thus, the attention of the Legislature was first called to the frauds of bankrupts; and, without feeling the necessity of instituting a peculiar code of laws, it was natural to rest contented with such regulations as might give precision and force to the principles of common justice, in preventing the debtor from injuring the creditors, or unfairly preferring favourite individuals.

While these laws were required as remedies against the prevailing frauds by voluntary deeds, the necessity began to be felt of introducing equality among creditors doing diligence against the estate. This equality, from peculiar circumstances, was first established in the adjudication; the nation being left, for a long period, to struggle with the evils of the old rule, in diligence against moveables. It may appear, at first sight, that it would have been the natural, as it certainly is the best remedy for inequalities among creditors, to introduce, as in England, a general form of attachment and distribution; but this remedy was

not

not adopted in Scotland. As the laws against preference by voluntary deed, were introduced in the shape of partial remedies, unconnected with any general process of division; so it happened also with respect to the laws against preference by diligence or legal execution. Perhaps this may be accounted for, in the following manner. The commerce of Scotland being as yet scanty and unimportant, the diligence against moveables seemed of little importance, when compared with that against land. But there ever has been a great repugnance, in the Scotish Legislature, to allow the estates of landholders to be taken irrevocably in payment of debt, where it was possible to avoid it. This bias first established, and afterwards confirmed, the right of redemption allowed to a debtor whose estate was apprised or adjudged. In seeking, then, for a remedy against preferences by adjudication, it was, according to this view of the law, necessary to avoid any plan which should, like the English commission of bankruptcy, act as a general attachment of the estate, and vest in the creditors an irredeemable right to it. The plan fallen upon was, to allow the creditors to proceed with their adjudications, and to bestow upon all who should adjudge, within a year of the first, an equal right. So tender, indeed, was the Scotish Legislature of the landholder's right, that it was with considerable difficulty the Parliament was at last prevailed upon to sanction a form of action for judicially selling the lands of those who were absolutely insolvent, so that the price might be divided amongst the creditors. This, however, was at last done in the years 1685 and 1696.

A mode of distribution was in this manner established for the lands of debtors unconnected with trade; it consisted of two great branches, 1. An equality of rights among all creditors adjudging within a year of the first completed adjudication: and, 2. A process of judicial sale and division of the price, where the debtor was insolvent. In this form the establishment exists at the present hour.

Still, the old maxims were applicable to execution against moveables; and the rule of preference rested upon mere priority in execution. Not only was much opportunity thus given for constituting fraudulent preferences, and for collusion with the debtors; but, from the overstrained anxiety of creditors, upon the slightest alarm, to secure for themselves a preference, much unnecessary expence was incurred, to the prejudice both of the creditors, and of the debtor. It was not till the year 1754, notwithstanding the precedent in the case of adjudications, that even partial measures were adopted for securing equality among creditors doing diligence against the moveables. The Court of Session made an act of sederunt, in that year, establishing an equality of preference among all poinders and arresters, within a certain period of bankruptcy. But this was a mere experiment; and, upon the expiration of the act, which was in force only for four years, it was not renewed. This part of the law, therefore, fell back into its old state of imperfection: priority gave preference; and the slightest alarm opened all the sluices of a torrent of diligence; which brought ruin upon the debtor, and established the most unjust preferences among the creditors. In this most defective condition, the law continued till the year 1772. During that period, a spirit of commercial enterprize had arisen in the country, and a connexion so intimate had been formed with England, that the evils of the old law were doubly felt. This was the period, during which the house of Alexander & Co. of Edinburgh, pushed their dealings so successfully, as to become one of the first trading houses in Europe. It was the period, too, of Mr Fordyce's success in London; and by his establishment, there, of the English Companies of James Fordyce & Neal, Walpole Ellison & Co., and several other considerable houses, became intimately connected with many Scotish merchants and manufacturers. The Douglas Bank was established; and, in the sanguine imaginations of our countrymen, Scotland was going on with a full tide to national prosperity.

The Court of Session, who had formerly attempted, by a rule of Court, to provide against the evils of the law, saw the imminent danger to which, at this critical period, the country was exposed. With a wise precaution, they digested a set of regulations for bankruptcy, which was at length passed into a law: and it was fortunate for the country, that these provisions had been made: for, while Scotland seemed to be flourishing in youthful vigour, the disease had made a rapid progress, which was to threaten death to her existence as a trading nation. The increasing calls of a commerce, which had been forced beyond its natural level; the extraordinary sums required by merchants, and by speculators in agricultural improvement; and the ruinous resources, which it was found necessary to adopt, in order to supply the demand, brought on convulsions of national distress; and bankruptcy followed bankruptcy, in a melancholy and alarming succession. These confusions began

in

in June 1772; and not a week of June, July, August, September, or October, passed away, without the failure of some considerable house. The ruin of the Douglas Bank was now inevitable; and the credit of Scotland was shaken to the centre.

It was upon the eve of this universal confusion, that the Legislature passed the law, which had been so wisely prepared. It regulated the management and distribution of the personal estates of bankrupts in Scotland, and provided for the equalizing of preferences by execution. By this law, instead of the commission of bankruptcy, a form of sequestration was introduced; of which an Englishman may have some idea, by recollecting the sequestration of the Court of Chancery. Under this form, the Court of Session sequestrated the whole personal estate of the debtor (the real being left to the adjudication and judicial sale of the old law), to be managed by a judicial factor, and fairly divided among the creditors; and it was declared, that no arrestment nor poinding, within thirty days previous to the petition for sequestration, should give any preference, in the event of a sequestration taking place; the poinder being bound to deliver the goods poinded, or the price of them, if sold; and the arrester to deliver the arrested goods or debt to the factor, in order to be distributed among the creditors.

But in this first attempt to form a general code of Bankrupt Laws for regulating the disposal of the personal estate, perfection was not to be expected. Like the first plan of the English commission in Henry the VIII.'s time, it included all ranks of men: and, as in England, it was thought

thought proper to restrict their new code to traders, so it appeared to be necessary, in the renewal of the Scotish law, to separate the trading and manufacturing part of the community from other men. But, in doing this, the Legislature did not altogether neglect the bankruptcy of those unconnected with trade, nor leave them to struggle with the evils of the old law. They felt that traders are often deeply interested as creditors, and their credit much involved with men who themselves are not traders; and, in altering the law, a double remedy was introduced—one for traders, simple like that of England—another for common bankruptcies, supplying what had formerly been unprovided for, in relation to the preferences by diligence against moveables.

1. In excluding from the sequestration the bankruptcy of men unconnected with trade, it did not occur, that any new regulations for the heritable estate were requisite; but it was necessary, to devise some means for preventing, in the execution against moveables, those preferences which had, prior to 1772, been the cause of so much anxiety to creditors, and oppression to debtors. The plan adopted, was nearly similar to that of the act of sederunt 1756. By 23 Geo. III. c. 12. the bankruptcy of the debtor (as under the statute of 1696, c. 5.) was taken as the criterion of preference among arresters and poinders, instead of the date of presenting the petition for sequestration. All arrestments and poindings, within thirty days before, and four months after the bankruptcy, were put upon an equal footing; and, by the statute 33 Geo. III. c. 74. the period is still further extended to sixty days prior to the bankruptcy.

There

There are several forms of action, in which effect is given to these equalizing rules for diligence against moveables; but the most general is, that of a multiple-poinding, or action of double distress, in which the holder of the funds calls into the field every creditor who has a claim upon them, that the order of preference may be determined by the Court, the fund divided, and the holder of it discharged.

2. The mercantile system of Bankrupt Law in Scotland, though differing in form, and also, in many essential points, from that of England, is so far similar, that both seem to accord well with the great pervading principles of Bankrupt Law.

By the first statute in 1772, the plan of distribution, which included only the personal estate, was alternative—1. By the sequestration of the common law, a disputed estate is taken by the Court under its own management, and a factor appointed, accountable to the Court, for behoof of the parties interested: upon this model it was provided, that a petition should be presented to the Court of Session, praying that, after due notification to the debtor, his personal estate should be sequestrated, and put under the management of a factor to be chosen by the creditors, and who should act under the direction of the Court, in disposing of the estate; and the creditors were to be ranked, and the price distributed by a judgement of the Court. 2. As the expence and delay of these proceedings (which were all judicial) were very considerable, it was declared, that the creditors might choose, at a meeting to be held after

after the sequestration had been awarded, whether to continue the sequestration, or to appoint a trustee, and have the whole affairs managed extrajudicially. Many improvements were made upon this plan, both in 1783, and in 1793; but these it would be improper at present particularly to detail. It may be sufficient to observe, that the whole estate, real and personal, heritable and moveable, was included; and that the radical change made upon the spirit of the institution, was the combination of the judicial and private alternatives of the first law, into one consistent system of trust, and of judicial controul; so as to give all the advantages of a private trust, with all the benefits to be expected from the superintendance of a Court of law. The sequestration, as a general diligence, stops all individual proceedings, and gives an opportunity of having the estate managed, in the mean time, by a factor, till the creditors can appear and verify their claims, in order to elect a trustee. This election of the trustee finishes the sequestration, properly so called; and the judicial trust begins. The trustee is vested with the estate, and is the manager and distributor of the fund. In his management, he is assisted by three commissioners, elected by the creditors from their own body, as a committee of management; and their proceedings are subject to the constant superintendance of the whole creditors. In his character, of distributor of the estate, he acts not as the English assignee does, but as judge in the first instance, subject to the review of the Court of Session. It is his business to bring up the bankrupt for examination—to make up proper states of the affairs—to make objections to the claims of the creditors—to rank the creditors on the fund—and to strike the dividend. When the final distribution comes to

be

be made, the creditors themselves determine, whether the bankrupt be entitled to a discharge; or whether he is to be left to the remedy of the common law, the cessio bonorum, which, without discharging him of his debts, relieves him from imprisonment.

We shall afterwards, in the particular examination of this law for mercantile bankruptcy, have an opportunity of explaining all those provisions, for the mutual advantage of the debtor and of the creditor, which, by the moulding hand of the first legal and mercantile abilities of the country, have brought it to a degree of perfection, of which, as a nation, we have reason to be proud.

§ 3. *Plan of the Work.*

It is not possible to treat a subject, so complicated as the Scotish Law of Bankruptcy, according to that simple and clear plan, of which the English Bankrupt Law is susceptible. But I have endeavoured to make the Plan of the present work as simple as possible, consistently with a full explanation of the important points of our law and practice.

I. The object of the First Book is, to explain the character of a bankrupt, as defined by the statute of 1696, c. 5, and by the later statutes; to show how it differs from mere insolvency; and to distinguish what persons may, by the law of Scotland, be made bankrupt.

II. I proceed, in the Second Book, to consider the various descriptions of fraud, which, in the anxious moments

ments that precede a failure, the debtor is apt to commit; and to inquire into the remedies provided against them.

III. The THIRD BOOK is occupied in explaining the regulations by which preferences from the operation of legal execution are equalized, in relation to the bankruptcy.

IV. As the funds of the bankrupt are distributed in different ways, according to his situation, and the nature of his property, I have found it necessary, in the discussion of the processes by which the distribution is accomplished, and which form the subject of the FOURTH BOOK, to adopt a threefold division.

i. Those processes are explained, by which the funds of a person, unconnected with trade, are divided. The JUDICIAL SALE AND RANKING for converting the lands into money, and distributing the price among the creditors —the MULTIPLEPOINDING, or action of double distress, the most general form of distributing the personal or moveable estate—the FORTHCOMING, for making effectual against the arrester the funds attached in his hand—and the ACTION AGAINST POINDERS, for dividing what may have been taken by one creditor, in consequence of poinding.

ii. The SEQUESTRATION is next explained. This is the general process of attachment and distribution of the estates of mercantile bankrupts, analogous to the English commission of bankruptcy. And,

iii. The forms of conducting a voluntary division of the

the debtor's estate, under a private trust-deed, conclude this branch of the subject.

V. In the division of every bankrupt estate, there are three main questions for decision. 1. What are the distributable funds? 2. What are the admissible claims, and how are they to be ranked in relation to each other? And, 3dly, What are the rules by which the distribution is to be made? These points of inquiry dictate the plan and arrangement of the FIFTH BOOK.

i. In considering the distributable fund, it is necessary to distinguish the following particulars: 1. What part of the acknowledged property of the bankrupt is legally exempted from attachment by his creditors? 2. Of that which is, in its nature, attachable, what is to be considered as properly belonging to the bankrupt? And this leads to an inquiry into the completion of bargains and transferences by delivery, real, symbolical, or constructive. 3. Though constructive delivery is effectual to transfer property, when the price has been paid; where the price has not been paid, there is room for stopping the goods in transitu, before they have reached the actual possession of the purchaser: The doctrine of stopping in transitu, forms, thus, an important point in distinguishing the funds. 4. Property may sometimes be taken by creditors, as a part of the fund of division, though not strictly belonging to the bankrupt, if the bankrupt be allowed to have such collusive possession as may entitle the creditors to believe that he is the proprietor: Such possession, then, as bestows upon the creditors this right, must be distinguished from the legal possession of a trustee, factor, &c. 5. Another question, of no mean importance, remains to be discussed, in distinguishing the funds, viz. What difference shall be admitted between the bankrupt himself, and his creditors, in respect to exceptions competent against them, as coming into his place. And lastly, These points being fixed, the funds are to be laid out by the trustee, &c. for division, and the interest upon the various particulars stated, with the proper deductions on account of expences. An explanation of this completes the view of the funds.

ii. The claims of the creditors, which are to be ranked upon the fund, are arranged in this order:

1. Those claims which are covered by SECURITIES EXPRESSLY CONSTITUTED by voluntary deed, or judicial act. These, as they affect the heritable estate, may be either real, when the creditor has, by infeftment, acquired a feudal right; or personal, which are rather of the nature of an exclusion of other creditors, to make room for some real right constituted in the person of him who holds the personal security: such are, inhibition, consent to a preference, &c. Constituted securities, as they affect the moveable estate, are susceptible of a similar division. These securities are considered, 1. As liable to objection; and the objections are classed and arranged, which, in making up a state and order of ranking, every trustee must have in his eye: and, 2. The principle is laid down, upon which the preference in a competition is to be regulated.

2. The next class of claims, consists of those which are covered

covered by SECURITIES RESULTING FROM POSSESSION; as, hypothecs, compensation, and retention.

3. The last class consists of PERSONAL CLAIMS, of which some are privileged; as, funeral charges, wages, &c. Others unprivileged; as, simple claims of debt.

This intricate subject is closed, by a connected view of the rules of ranking, as deduced from the principles thus laid down; with explanations of the methods of stating the order of ranking.

iii. The last division of the Fifth Book has, for its object, to explain how, in the division of the fund, full effect is to be given to the rights of the several claimants, as settled by the order of ranking. It may at first sight appear, that this can include only such discussions as more properly belong to the profession of an accountant; but it will be found, that here, many of the nicest distinctions in law are necessary to bring out the true rights of the claimants.

VI. The punishment of a debtor, if fraudulent; or his liberation or discharge, if fair and honest; form a great object of the Bankrupt Law; and I have endeavoured, in the SIXTH BOOK, to explain the Scotish law upon these points. Beginning with an historical deduction of the law of imprisonment in Scotland, and a comparison with that of England, I have endeavoured to present a systematical view of this department, marking in succession—the indulgent delay previous to the arrest; the remedy of a warrant de meditatione fugæ, for preventing the abuse

of

of it; the relief against the hardships of confinement, by bills of health, and by the act of grace; the laws concerning protections, by personal privilege, privilege of time or place, and judicial act; and the provisions for the liberation of bankrupts by cessio bonorum, and for the final discharge of those connected with trade or manufactures.

VII. It seems to form no improper conclusion of this Treatise, to inquire, What are the mutual effects, which, in England and in Scotland, are given by courts of justice to the proceedings under the Bankrupt Laws of the sister kingdom.

BOOK

BOOK THE FIRST.

OF BANKRUPTCY.

CHAP. I.

Of Bankruptcy in general—History of the Laws, in which the Character of Bankruptcy is defined.

To distinguish, with precision, the legal characteristics of a bankrupt, ought to be the first object in this inquiry. The bankruptcy of the debtor bestows upon the creditors that common interest in his estate, from which, as from a first principle, I have endeavoured, in the introduction, to deduce the most important rules of this department of the law.

It may, at first sight, appear natural, that mere insolvency should be sufficient to give birth to this common interest in the creditors; for insolvency necessarily implies, that the debtor's funds are inadequate to the debts. But in no country has it been thought expedient to give so strong an effect to insolvency, unless when accompanied with circumstances of public notoriety, or with plain indications of a fraudulent design against the creditors. The deficiency of the funds may be accidental and momentary; it may be concealed from the world; it may even be totally unknown to the debtor himself; while he on the other hand may, by honest perseverance in trade, be able completely to retrieve his affairs and save his creditors. The law would justly be reprobated, therefore, which, upon mere insolvency, should interrupt or annul the transactions of a debtor, and, by stopping all his exertions, deprive his

his creditors, as well as himself, of every hope or chance of his recovery. It is indeed just, that an insolvent debtor should, from the moment of his insolvency, be regarded as the factor or negotiorum gestor of his creditors, rather than as an uncontrouled proprietor; and, upon this principle, if his affairs should not be extricated, all his deeds of mere gratuity ought to be objectionable at the suit of creditors: but his transactions ought not to be disturbed, nor his hands tied up from trade; neither should the payment of just debts be liable to challenge, nor even the securities be objectionable, which he may have granted to creditors innocent of any collusion. These stronger effects should be reserved for that more public and confirmed insolvency, which the Legislature of every commercial country has been careful, under the title of bankruptcy, to define.

Bankruptcy, as contradistinguished from mere insolvency, is an open and public declaration of failure; to the description of which, various circumstances may be required, according to the views of the Legislature, or the practice of the country. But the difficulty of fixing upon a proper definition of bankruptcy, lies not so much in the selecting of public marks, by which the failure is to be distinguished, as in the discovering of a sound principle, upon which the Legislature may proceed, in carrying back the effect of the bankruptcy for a term anterior to the actual failure. Such a measure is necessary, in order to annul those deeds of preference which the debtor may have granted in the immediate contemplation of bankruptcy, or those judicial preferences by execution or diligence which his confidential friends may have been enabled to acquire: without it, the establishment of any legal marks of bankruptcy would indeed be of little value.

The law of England is essentially different from that of Scotland, not only with regard to the persons whom it includes in the description of bankruptcy, and the steps of execution by which the bankruptcy is declared, but also with regard to those regulations by which the legal effects of the bankruptcy are carried back to a period prior to the public declaration.

1. It is only by a commission of bankruptcy, that, in England, a person can be declared a bankrupt. This is a special writ, constituting a court of commissioners for superintending the recovery and distribution of the funds of a trader who has failed; and it vests those commissioners with powers so extraordinary, and, in all its effects, runs so much counter to the common law, that the Legislature has permitted it to be issued only in cases of mercantile failure.

In Scotland, the Legislature has declared, that every insolvent debtor, who shall, upon personal diligence, be imprisoned, or forced to abscond, shall be considered as a bankrupt, to the effect of equalizing all the claims against his estate, of levelling all preferences obtained on the eve of bankruptcy by particular creditors, and of subjecting the whole funds to an equal division, according to settled forms. Thus, in England, traders only can be made bankrupt: in Scotland, no man whatever is exempted.

2. In carrying back the effect of the bankruptcy for a term anterior to the public declaration of it, the English and Scotish laws differ as remarkably, as in regard to the steps by which that public declaration is made.

In England, the object of the law seems to have been, to select for this purpose, circumstances which might fairly be held to infer the debtor's knowledge of his impending failure; or a design of defrauding his creditors to his own advantage, or to that of his favourite creditors. These acts of bankruptcy are, 1. The debtor's 'beginning to keep house,' so that he cannot be seen or spoken to by his creditors: 2. Departing from his dwellinghouse, or otherwise absenting himself, to avoid payment of debt: 3. Taking sanctuary: 4. Departing the realm, with a view to delay or defraud creditors: 5. Remaining in foreign parts for three months after proclamation, with a view to defraud creditors: 6. Escaping from an arrestment for a debt of 100l., or suffering himself to be outlawed. 7. Yielding himself to prison, although able to pay off the debt 8. Willingly and fraudulently procuring himself to be arrested, or his

goods

goods to be attached or sequestered: 9. Making any fraudulent grant or conveyance of lands, tenements, goods, or chattels: 10. Procuring a protection, except the lawful protection of privilege of Parliament: 11. Being arrested for debt, and lying in prison for two months, the first arrestment being the date of the act of bankruptcy: 12. Giving security, payment, or satisfaction to a creditor suing out a commission, for more than his just debt: 13. Neglecting to make satisfaction for a just debt of 100l. or upwards, after the service of legal process upon any trader having privilege of Parliament.—I. Cook, B. L. 94—129.—II. Espinasse, Law of Actions and Trials at Nisi-prius, 552.—The assignees, as vested with the bankrupt's estate, are entitled, under the statutes, to make effectual, as a fund for division among the creditors, not only all the property which stands in the debtor's person at the commencement of their right, but all that property also, which he has alienated since the first of these acts of bankruptcy took place. And to this rule there seem to be only these three exceptions: *First*, Where a debtor of the bankrupt has *bona fide* paid up his debt; *secondly*, Where a purchase has been made *bona fide* from the debtor; and, *thirdly*, Where creditors have received payment from the debtor in the course of trade, without knowing of the bankruptcy or insolvency: I. Cook, 593. I. Espinasse, 119. & *seq*.

In Scotland, the retrospective effect of the bankruptcy is settled upon a much simpler principle. It is assumed as a fair presumption, that for sixty days before public bankruptcy, the debtor must have had his failure in contemplation; and, upon this ground, the bankruptcy is held to have begun at that period, to the effect of entitling the creditors to challenge all voluntary securities, and to level all judicial preferences constituted within that term.

But it may be proper to enter a little more particularly into the history of the Scotish law on this subject. We shall thus perceive the difficulties which were thought to stand in the way of this institution, and how they were surmounted.

It

It was not till the end of the 17th century that the description of the Scotish bankrupt was fixed by law. Before that time, indeed, statutes had been directed against conveyances made by insolvent debtors to relations and confidents, with the fraudulent view of embezzling their funds; and against deeds intended to disappoint the execution or diligence already begun by individual creditors: but there was no provision against the constitution of unfair preferences. The dangerous period of the eve of bankruptcy, was left under the vague controul of the common law alone; so that unless a case could be made out of direct fraud, or unless it could be shown that the deed challenged was intended to stop and interrupt diligence, there was no remedy.

While the law continued in this imperfect state, the common and the natural plea of creditors, injured by any deed of preference, was, that it had been granted with a view to bankruptcy; and for the purpose of preferring the grantee, and making an unfair, fraudulent, and unequal distribution of the funds. But as an onerous and fair creditor, receiving a security on the voluntary offer of the debtor, or procuring it by threats of diligence, might have been perfectly innocent of any fraud, or even of any knowledge of the insolvency, it is plain, that mere insolvency could not afford a good ground for annulling, at common law, any such deed of preference. The necessity of a general rule was apparent; but to fix upon a criterion of notorious failure, was found a matter of extreme difficulty. The extension of commerce, however, and the more frequent recurrence of insolvency, its natural consequence, forced the Legislature to come to some determination on the subject; and a rule was at last established.

The great failure of Cockburn of Langton brought the question forward in a very formidable shape. 'The Lords (says Lord 'Fountainhall, 23d January 1694), this day advised Sir Thomas 'Moncrieff's reduction against the other preferable creditors of 'Cockburn of Langton; whereby he quarrelled all the corrobo-'rative securities granted by Langton in March 1690, on the 'noise of his breaking, to his personal creditors, viz. giving them

'her table

'heritable bonds, whereon they immediately took infeftment, 'and confirmed, and so were preferable to Sir Thomas's debt. 'His reason of reduction was, that though the act 1621 did not 'reach this case, yet fraud was regulate and determined from the 'common law; and many citations were adduced, proving that 'a notour bankrupt could give no rights in prejudice of his cre-'ditors, and that our decisions had gone on the same principles; 'as in Street and Mason's case, in 1673, and the Lady Tarsappie 'and Kinfawns, and many others: so that Sir Thomas needs 'say no more, save that Langton was a notour bankrupt at the 'time when he granted these bonds.' Answered, That our law 'knew no such definition of a bankrupt, unless incapacitate by 'diligence against him at his creditors instance.' The Court first supported, but afterwards reduced the deeds; and their delibera-tions are very interesting, as they show the gradual ripening of our bankrupt-law. 'The vote being stated, Whether Langton's 'being notour bankrupt and fled, at the time of his subscribing 'these corroborations, was a relevant ground in law to reduce 'them as fraudulent, the receivers knowing the report of his be-'ing broken at the time, albeit there was no diligence actually 'execute against him at the time, but very shortly after a deluge 'of hornings, &c.? the Lords, by a plurality, found that there 'was no law yet in Scotland whereupon the securities could be 'annulled, though granted by a notour bankrupt *in fuga et qui 'cessit foro*, and had taken sanctuary in the Abbey; seeing we 'have no standard whereby to render and declare a man bank-'rupt, save only diligence, &c. To this, some of the Lords '(he adds) were moved, because the creditors who got these cor-'roborations did rely so little thereon, that they betook themselves 'to the legal security by adjudication: others thought Langton 'was as effectually bankrupt then as now, and that no deed 'then done by him was to be regarded, unless the Lords would 'allow him to rank his creditors in the Abbey, by partial pre-'ference; and after one was redacted to that case, they thought 'all the creditors would come in *pari passu*. The Lords were so 'sensible of the defect of law in this point, that they named a 'committee, to propose an act of sederunt to fix when one is re-

'puted

'pute to be such a dyvour and bankrupt, as that afterwards he
'can do nothing that shall subsist in prejudice of any creditor;
'and that the marches may be so distinct and clear, that every
'man may know it, without leaving it to the arbitrement of
'judges.' I. Fount. 596.

The case came afterwards to be reconsidered, on a petition for Sir Thomas Moncrieff, 'when the Lords, by a plurality, the chan-
'cellor being present, altered their former interlocutors; and ge-
'nerally agreed in this, that a notour bankrupt could not gratify
'nor prefer one creditor before another. But they differed as to
'what they called a notour bankrupt, and whether the circumstan-
'ces alleged against Langton made him such, for some made a
'difference between one notourly bankrupt, and one notourly in-
'solvent. They acknowledged that Langton fell under the last of
'these two, when he granted the corroborative rights now quar-
'relled, but that nothing could make him a notour bankrupt but
'what the law had so declared, by diligences done against him,
'which was not at that time. At last the Lords fell on this con-
'descendence, that he had, before the granting of this right, fled
'to the Abbey, or absconded, and that many bonds and hornings
'were then given in against him to be passed and registered; that
'he disposed of his whole moveables, and it (the disposition) was
'intimated at the cross of Dunse; that he gave the corroborations
'over his whole estate, so they were like a *cessio bonorum*, and he
'broke suddenly and unexpectedly. These circumstances the
'Lords, by a vote of five against four, found to be sufficient to
'make him a notour bankrupt, and incapable, after that, to grant
'any heritable bonds.' 8th February 1691, I. Fount. 605.

It seemed to be fixed by this decision, that notorious and public insolvency was sufficient to bestow upon the creditors that common right in the debtor's funds, which it is the great object of the bankrupt law to render effectual. But another case occurred in the end of the same year, in which, although the debtor was insolvent, he was not notoriously so; and the question was, whether the creditors private knowledge of the insolvency was sufficient to make out a case, includable within the principle upon which that of Langton had been decided? This was a reduction raised by the creditors of Carlowrie against Lord Mersington and others, of an infeftment of relief granted by Skene of Halyards and Drummond of Carlowrie, after they were 'obærate and bankrupts, and had retired to the Abbey, and were under diligence by hornings and inhibition.' The case of Langton was cited, 'but it was contended, that there was a further qualification required in Langton's case, which cannot be subsumed here, viz. that he was then holden and repute bankrupt. The Lords thought it deserved a hearing in presence, that they might settle the limits of bankruptcy, where one should be utterly incapacitate to dispose or grant any rights or gratification in favour of one creditor before another.' When the cause came to be decided, 'the Lords found the above qualifications not sufficient to reduce, unless it were also offered to be proved that he was then held and repute a bankrupt.' The challenging creditors next founded strongly on the private knowledge of the creditor, that his debtor was bankrupt; but 'the Lords did not find private knowledge sufficient in this case.' 5th January 1695, I. Fount. 652—659.

In the Parliament which met in September 1696, the bankrupt law was an early object of attention; and by the fifth act of that Parliament, in order to settle the law upon this point, and at once to put an end to all the distressing questions concerning fraud, which had perplexed the courts for some years, a precise definition of bankruptcy was marked out, and many excellent regulations made for preventing the frauds of bankrupts. In this law the Legislature adopted the ideas which were so naturally suggested by the cases of Langton, &c. They fixed accurately the circumstances which were thought to be proper for indicating a total failure; but, sensible that such a definition could be of little use, unless assisted by an anticipating principle, that should serve as a preventive of fraud, they calculated backwards from the period of open and public bankruptcy sixty days; and, by a presumption of law, they fixed at that point the date of the bankruptcy.

We

We have seen, that the English law carries back the incapacity to the first act of bankruptcy, however distant, and however secret it may be. In Scotland, the incapacity is fixed to a precise day, two months before the public bankruptcy. The difference of the two laws consists not in principle so much as in form. The Scotish retrospective rule seems to have been derived from France, where it had long been established. With France, our connexion was in former days extremely close and intimate, while yet the sister kingdoms were unnaturally divided. We were fond of imitating the French institutions in the infancy of our jurisprudence; and, even so late as the year 1696, our lawyers were better versed in the laws of France, than in those of England. The common origin of the French and Scotish laws in that of Rome, gave a greater consistency to the spirit of the two codes; and it was natural perhaps that the French rule should by our lawyers be preferred to the English, which was connected with so peculiar a system. The French rule of incapacity for bankrupts was retrospective; but the retrospect was much shorter than that which was adopted in this country. It was a retrospect of only ten days; ours was extended to sixty.

The words of the statute are, 'Considering that, notwithstanding of the acts of Parliament already made against fraudful alienations by bankrupts, in prejudice of their creditors, yet their frauds and abuses are still very frequent: therefore, and for the better restraining and obviating thereof in time coming, it is statuted and declared, That for hereafter, if any debtor under diligence by horning and caption at the instance of his creditors, be either imprisoned; or retire to the Abbey or any other privileged place; or flee or abscond for his security; or defend his person by force; and be afterwards found, by sentence of the Lords of Session, to be insolvent; shall be holden and repute, on these three joint grounds, viz. diligence by horning and caption, and insolvency, joined with one or other of the said alternatives of imprisonment, or retiring, or flying, or absconding, or forcible defending, to be a notour bankrupt; and that from the time of his foresaid imprisonment, retiring, flying, absconding, or forcible de-

'fending;

'fending; which, being found by sentence of the Lords of Session, 'at the instance of any of his just creditors, who are hereby em-'powered to raise and prosecute a declarator of bankruptcy, his 'Majesty, with consent of the Estates of Parliament, declares all 'and whatsoever voluntary dispositions, assignations, or other 'deeds, which shall be found to be made and granted, directly or 'indirectly, by the foresaid dyvour or bankrupt, either at or after 'his becoming bankrupt, or in the space of sixty days before, in 'favour of his creditors, either for his satisfaction, or further secu-'rity in preference to other creditors, to be void and null.'

One class of cases was omitted in this legislative description of bankruptcy, and the omission has been supplied by the bankrupt statutes of 1783 and 1793. No person could come under the definition given in the statute of 1696, who was, by privilege or personal protection, exempted from imprisonment for debt: but as the meaning of the Legislature was to include, under the bankrupt law, every person who could have creditors, the late statutes have provided, that wherever it is impossible to comply with the requisites of the old statute, 'a charge of horning, with an arrestment (attachment of moveables or of debts) 'not loosed for fifteen days; 'or a poinding of any of the debtor's moveables; or an adjudica-'tion for payment or security, shall be equivalent to the imprison-'ment, &c. required by the act of 1696.'

Having detailed, at so great length, the history and general nature of the laws by which the description of bankruptcy has been settled, I shall, in what remains of this book, consider,

1. The particular ingredients in the character of a bankrupt, as established by the statutes; and,

2. The persons who are capable of being made bankrupt by the law of Scotland.

CHAP.

CHAP. II.

Commentary on the Definition of a Bankrupt, as delivered in the Statute 1696, c. 5, and in the 33 Geo. III. c. 74.

The definition of bankruptcy, as laid down in the statute 1696, c. 5, and in the late bankrupt statutes, includes these three ingredients:—1. Insolvency. 2. Diligence by horning and caption. 3. Imprisonment; or the eluding of it by absconding; retiring to the Sanctuary; or resisting the officer, or the equivalent for imprisonment in those cases where it is incompetent, namely, arrestment unloosed for fifteen days, poinding, or adjudication.

The slightest consideration will show the justice and wisdom of requiring the concurrence of these circumstances. There is not one of them that may not singly happen to any man consistently with his return into full credit; and the serious consequences of bankruptcy to the creditors, as well as to the debtor, must be a strong motive with every wise Legislature for increasing the caution with which they mark out any man as a bankrupt. Our Legislature, therefore, neglecting such elusory and ambiguous indications as could be afforded by any one of the above circumstances taken singly, refused to put its stamp of incapacity and bankruptcy upon any man, while yet there was a chance of his struggling through his difficulties, and emerging again to credit and responsibility.

The requisites of bankruptcy pointed out in the statute, I shall consider in their order.

1. Insol-

1. INSOLVENCY.

Insolvency is the most essential requisite to the character of bankruptcy in Scotland. It is indeed the fundamental circumstance upon which the whole proceeds; and the other circumstances selected by the Legislature, are to be taken merely as the evidence by which the insolvency is established to be irretrievable. It may perhaps be conceived, that these other circumstances should, of themselves, be sufficient to infer the insolvency; but, in a point of so much importance, the law has chosen to leave room for those cases which certainly may occur, of ultimate diligence without insolvency. It is natural to observe the marked distinction between the Scotish and English laws in this particular. To entitle the creditors to apply for a commission of bankruptcy in England, it is not necessary that the debtor should be proved to be insolvent: the proof of the act of bankruptcy establishes that fact by legal inference. The difference is perhaps to be accounted for from the radical difference in the nature of execution for debt in the two countries. In England, one object at least of the commission of bankruptcy, was, to supply the means of a rapid execution for debt, which the common law did not allow: for, at common law in England, no execution can proceed against a debtor, but in consequence of a regular action, followed by the judgement of a court, unless in those cases where a formal warrant of attorney to confess judgement has been granted. In Scotland, we have seen, that execution is much more accessible and rapid, in consequence of our clause of registration, and under the statute which allows summary execution upon bills of exchange; so that, in constructing our law of bankruptcy, there was no occasion for the same precipitation as in the English commission of bankruptcy. Delay is of less consequence; and time may be taken for considering deliberately the situation of the debtor, before declaring him a bankrupt. Accordingly, it is established in the law of Scotland, that unless a debtor be actually insolvent, as well as under the operation of ultimate diligence, he is not to be declared bankrupt, or deprived of the management of his

his affairs; but, on paying the debt for which he is distressed, he is free to proceed with his transactions as before.

The statute of 1696 empowers the creditors 'to raise and prosecute a declarator of bankruptcy, for the purpose of having it found, by sentence of the Lords of Session, that the debtor is a notour bankrupt.' This was the natural form of action, when there was no particular reduction in view, and when the creditors at large wished the bankruptcy to be declared; but it is a form which, in the present day, has fallen much into disuse. Insolvency is commonly tried in the course of a reduction either of voluntary deeds, under the statute 1696, c. 5, or of preferences acquired by diligence, under the late bankrupt statutes. In such cases, the insolvency is considered as a part of the reduction, in the form of common proof, or by remitting the case for investigation by an accountant. In the trial of insolvency, the question is, Whether, at the particular period specified, did the funds exceed or fall short of the debts? The investigation must of course vary with the circumstances of the case. Upon the supposition of a fair disclosure of all the materials necessary, the natural and the best method of ascertaining the fact, will in general be, to have recourse to an accountant, who may examine the books, call for the information necessary to explain them, and digest the whole materials into regular states of the debtor's affairs. The only thing that seems proper to this place is, to lay down such general rules as may be useful in solving the more general difficulties incident to such investigations.

1. One very obvious difficulty arises from the interest which some of the parties may have to conceal the state of the affairs. If the insolvency is to be tried with a view to the challenge of a particular deed, as granted without value; or if it is to be tried in combination with other circumstances, in order to establish a bankruptcy, for the purpose of reducing all securities granted within a certain period; in either of these cases, not merely the debtor, but all those who may be in danger of suffering by the establishment of the insolvency, will naturally be anxious to pre-

vent

vent the appearance of debts. On the other hand, the debtor may be anxious to conceal his funds for his own private use, after the confusion is over. Such concealments can be prevented only by strict investigations on the part of the creditors; and, in this unpleasant task, the books of a trader will, in general, form the most effectual means of detection. False sets of books may, indeed, be so artfully made up, that it will be difficult to detect the fraud: But to construct such books (checked, as a long course of transactions must ever be, by collateral evidence), requires so consummate a skill, that a careful examination scarcely ever fails to expose the real state of the fund.

2. Where there is no suspicion of concealment, it sometimes comes to be questioned, what funds are fairly computable as belonging to the debtor? The answer to this question ought properly to consist of an inquiry into those principles and rules of law which regulate the exemption of particular funds from legal execution: But to enter here upon an inquiry so extensive, would lead us too far from the inquiry in which we are more immediately engaged. I shall have occasion to discuss the subject fully hereafter; and at present, therefore, I leave the question upon this general rule, that nothing can fairly be reckoned as a part of the debtor's estate, with respect to his creditors, which is inalienable by him, or which the law prohibits creditors from attaching. Thus, in the case of Kerr of Chatto against Scott, the Court refused to admit, in the computation of the fund, an estate which was entailed under such conditions as to place it beyond the reach of creditors; I. Dict. 69 *.

3. It is impossible to lay down any precise rules for the valuation of the different kinds of property. The common methods of conducting the valuation, according to the custom of the trade, or nature of the property, must be adopted. Thus, the market price of land will naturally be taken as the best and fairest criterion of its

* Lord Kaimes quotes Forbes as his authority; but the case is to be found only in Forbes's Index.

its value, after making the proper allowance for the state of the leases, &c.; and this market price is best established by the evidence of gentlemen, or men of business, conversant with the value of land in that part of the country. This, accordingly, is the kind of evidence taken in judicial sales. The value of any commodity will naturally be appretiated according to the circumstances of the case, and the state of the market. The value of annuities, liferents, and other rights having a course of time, will best be ascertained from the market rate of a similar right, equally well secured; and this can easily be learned from the money brokers. There is an old case reported by Lord Stair, which was well decided upon such a question as this. Two liferent rights were to be computed. They had subsisted for twenty years, and a difficulty was started, whether, in estimating the debtor's solvency, the value of the burdens was to be computed according to the time they had actually subsisted, or according to the computation of probability, which must have been taken, had the question occurred at the point of time to which the inquiry was directed. 'The Lords would not sustain the burden 'of the liferents *secundum eventum*, but as they were worth when 'the deeds challenged were granted; and estimated the liferent of 'the elder to five, and of the younger to seven years purchase; by 'which there was, free, above 30,000l. Scots when the deeds were 'granted:' 11th December 1679, Mouswell's creditors, II. Stair, 720. It appears from Harcarse, (cccccii. 107), that an opinion was afterwards expressed by the Court, disapproving of this decision: and Lord Kaimes has, in his Dictionary, inadvertently stated that opinion as an actual reversal of it. But such a doubt can only be attributed to the unsettled notions of those days respecting the value of such rights. There was then no proper test by which to try the value of a liferent right; for neither were the chances of lives understood, nor had money-brokers, at least in this country, made the purchase and sale of life annuities a branch of traffic.

The value of a profession or trade it must ever be difficult accurately to ascertain; or rather, perhaps, where a debtor is going on in business, he cannot strictly be called insolvent, unless it can be made out that his situation was such as to disable him from proceeding, except by the sufferance of his creditors.

4. In reckoning the debts, every thing must be computed, which, if the creditors were then to receive their payment, the debtor would be obliged to pay. Therefore, it is not merely the principal sums, with interest, that are be to taken into the account, but the penalties in bonds, &c. at least to the amount of the actual expence which has already been incurred. On the other hand, in establishing insolvency as at a particular time, the interest which has actually fallen due, between that point of time, and the period when the question comes to be tried, with all the intermediate expences, is to be kept out of the statement. In the ranking of the creditors of Sir William Forbes of Monimusk, a question of this kind arose. The Court decided it the more solemnly, as it was one of the first that had occurred upon the great bankrupt-statute of 1696, and, as Lord Fountainhall says, 'it was to be the rule when 'the case occurred in time coming.' It was found, 'That, in the 'computation, no more was to be reckoned but the principal sums 'and annualrents then owing, with such penalties as were then 'incurred; but annualrents falling due after, or penalties incurred 'by hornings posterior, and accumulations arising from diligence 'led after it, none of these were to enter into the computa-'tion, *quoad hunc effectum*, to annul the heritable securities he 'gave at the time of his breaking, so as to make him insolvent at 'that period; and neither the *actio Pauliana* in the Roman law, nor 'our act against bankruptcy in 1621, go any further; and never 'made him bankrupt' (insolvent) 'who had sufficiency of means 'at the time to pay all his debts, though, afterwards, by the heap-'ing up of diligence, the debt came to exceed the estate.'—5th January 1712, II. Fount. 698.

5. Where there are joint obligants in a debt, it would be most unjust to load the estate of any one of them with the whole burden, unless the other obligants have engaged as cautioners merely, so as to have a claim of relief against the person whose insolvency is in question. That share only can properly be included in the list

of

of debts, which remains to be paid by the debtor, after deduction of the sums to be drawn from the other obligants. Thus, Bruce of Kennet had engaged, as cautioner with others, for Bruce of Clackmannan. On Clackmannan's failure, a trust-deed was made by Kennet, to which his creditors objected on the ground of his insolvency, &c. The insolvency was denied, unless upon the supposition of the whole debt being laid upon Bruce of Kennet; and this, it was maintained, could not be done while there were co-obligants in Clackmannan's debt. The Lords decided, 'That Bruce 'of Kennet could not be esteemed insolvent, till not only his e'state, but also those of the principal and co-cautioners were comput'ed, the whole being the subject of the creditors payment, as well 'as Kennet's estate considered alone.'—9th January 1696, I. Fount. 697.

The only other question which can occur concerning insolvency, as an ingredient in the description of a bankrupt, seems to be, Whether the insolvency is not to be judged of as at the date of the imprisonment and diligence by horning and caption? I have subjoined, in a note, a full statement of the case of Monimusk's creditors * already quoted, from which it will be seen, that this decision

* The question occurred in a conjoined action of declarator of bankruptcy, and of reduction of voluntary conveyances, under the statute 1696, c 5 The ground upon which the personal creditors of Sir William Forbes of Monimusk (the pursuers) rested, was, that Sir William being, in December 1707, under diligence by horning and caption, had absconded The defence was, that at the time of his absconding, he was not insolvent 'The statute 1696,' it was said, 'has very wisely fixed and determined the marks and characters of a notour bankrupt, they being, before that, very uncertain, and much in *arbitrio judicis*; and they are, horning and caption, imprisonment, or retiring to the Abbey, Cunzie-house (Mint), or any other sanctuary, or fleeing or absconding, or forcible defending and resisting, &c., but with these the act requires to be conjoined, insolvency so all the former, though concurring together, will not make him bankrupt, without (unless) insolvency, at the same time with the diligence, be likewise proven. Now, the personal creditors cannot subsume, that Monimusk, in December 1707, was insolvent, in so far as his estate is now, in the roup, proved to be worth 125,000l (at nineteen or twenty years purchase), and his debt then was not above 95,000l; so his estate then exceeded his debt in 30,000l And where a man has effects and means, either personal or real, to pay all his debts, and an exces[illegible]r and [illegible]ove, that man can never be declared bankrupt by the Lords

And

decision fixed it as a rule, that the computation of insolvency, under the statute 1696, must be made as at the time of the execution of the diligence; and that if insolvency cannot be proved to have

And so Monymusk, not being insolvent absolutely at the time he granted our heritable bonds and infeftments, though he, for securing his person, fled and absconded, within the sixty days of the seisines (which many sufficient men, at some pinch, are forced to do), he cannot be reputed insolvent, and our securities must stand good.'—To this it was answered, 'The real creditors do violence to the act of Parliament; by which it is evident, that the period for calculating the bankrupt's insolvency, is, not his condition at the time of his absconding or fleeing, but as it stands at the time the Lords find and declare him bankrupt. The act says, "If any debtor, under diligence by horning and caption, &c. be either imprisoned or retire, &c. *and be afterwards found, by sentence of the Lords, to be insolvent*, he shall be held," &c. Now, in this view, it is incontestible, that Monymusk's debts do far exceed the value of his estate, &c. Considering the present condition of the estate, by a retrospect to his first absconding, he was certainly insolvent when he gave these heritable bonds and infeftments, especially seeing the annualrents and penalties now computed, are not new contracted debts (which, it is acknowledged, would not enter in computation to make him a bankrupt, so as to quarrel their rights by these new contracted debts), but are native consequences, resulting from the original bonds due long before his breaking.'—In reply, the real creditors stated, 'That this arguing comes from a wrong application of the word *afterwards*, in the clause of the act cited, as if it were to be referred to the word *insolvent*, whereas, in true grammatical construction, it connects with the word *sentence*, and runs thus, "And afterwards found, by sentence of the Lords, to be insolvent." so that the insolvency must be at the time of absconding, and other requisite qualifications set down in the act, otherwise no creditor could be in security, seeing the debtor, though solvent at the time of his borrowing the money, might, by granting gratuitous deeds or securities, within sixty days, or granting bonds for debts contracted any time before declaration of bankrupt, turn insolvent, and thereby overturn heritable debts contracted while he was solvent; at which rate, the statute, designed for a further security to the lieges against the frauds of bankrupts, would turn to their prejudice; and a door be cast open to all imaginable frauds.'—'The Lords proceeded,' says Lord Fountainhall, 'the more deliberately, that it was the interpretation of a new act, and 'the fixing a period when the debtor is to be reputed insolvent, in order to quarrel 'his voluntary infeftments, Whether at the time of granting, or, as his estate is burdened by increasing annualrents, penalties, and accumulations, at the time he is declared, by the Lords decree, bankrupt? They found the computation must be, as 'the state of his debt and fortune was at his retiring, incarceration, &c.; and if his 'effects and estate were better than his debt at that period, then the infeftments he 'had given within the sixty days could not be reduced and annulled, though, *ex post facto*, his estate came to be overburdened with diligences,' &c; 5th January 1712, Personal Creditors of Sir William Forbes of Monymusk, II Fount. 692.

have at that time concurred with the other requisites, there is no legal bankruptcy under the statute.

II. DILIGENCE BY HORNING AND CAPTION.

The next thing required by the statute to make a person bankrupt, is, that he shall be under diligence by horning and caption; that is to say, that the necessary writs shall be taken out for proceeding to ultimate personal execution by imprisonment.

The law respecting imprisonment for debt, I shall have occasion to discuss in the last book of this work; but it may not be improper to anticipate the explanations there to be delivered, so far as to show the general nature and course of those writs of execution, which are, in this statute, appointed as requisites in the character of bankruptcy. Imprisonment for debt, originally forbidden by the law of Scotland, was introduced in two different ways. One kind of imprisonment was permitted by the Statute-Merchant, enacted for the encouragement of traders, and to promote the rise of cities and towns; and another form of imprisonment succeeded, by gradual steps, to the old ecclesiastical proceedings, by which the clergy had acquired, for their own jurisdictions, a power and efficacy in execution unknown to the civil courts of the country. 1. The imprisonment introduced by the Statute-Merchant proceeds upon a warrant, issued by the magistrates of burghs, called an act of warding; and this warrant is contained either in a judgement pronounced by the magistrates, or in a decree of registration, given forth from the court of the magistrates upon a clause of consent. 2. The imprisonment in other cases proceeds upon letters of horning and caption. Letters of horning are issued from the Court of Session. The warrant must be either a judgement of that Court, pronounced in an action, or a decree of registration, or a decree given in supplement of the judgement of an inferior court. The letters of horning are addressed to messengers at arms, ordering them to charge the debtor, within a

certain

certain number of days *, to pay the debt, under the pain of being denounced a rebel; for, as we shall hereafter see, it is only as against a rebel that the warrant of imprisonment proceeds. When the days of the charge are expired, the debtor is denounced a rebel; a ceremony once of most formidable efficacy, but now a mere form and prelude to the issuing of the caption. The horning, with the messenger's return of the charge, and of the denounciation of rebellion, is recorded in a particular register; and when the certificate of registry is indorsed upon it, the horning forms the ground of a new application, by bill, to the Court of Session, for letters of caption; and this is granted of course. The caption is also a writ in the King's name, passing under the signet, and charging messengers at arms to apprehend the debtor wherever he can be found within Scotland, and to call upon magistrates for assistance in apprehending and throwing him into prison.

As the object of the statute of 1690 was to mark out as bankrupts, those who should be under ultimate personal execution, imprisonment upon an act of warding should have been as good a criterion, it may be thought, of irretrievable insolvency, as that which proceeds upon caption. But the expressions of the law are precise, and the Court has always rigidly adhered to them. The question was directly tried in 1744; and the Court found, that a debtor imprisoned upon an act of warding, was not to be considered as bankrupt, in terms of the statute, although he was absolutely insolvent, the statute specially requiring caption. 13th November 1744, Snodgrass against Beat's Creditors, Kilk. 51.

But, with respect to one kind of horning, it came to be seriously doubted, whether it was meant to be included under the statute? Formerly, in cases where whole societies, corporations, or sets of men were liable to any demand, the common diligence was by general letters, which, without any citation or previous sentence, were

* The days of charge are fifteen, upon ordinary judgements of the Court of Session; six upon bills of exchange, and whatever number may be fixed by the deed (generally six) in decrees of registration.

were issued against all of that description, without mentioning their names; and authorised a charge for payment against any individual who fell under the class. Thus, general letters of horning were issued against landholders for payment of the land-tax; against heritors for payment of stipend, &c. When it is considered how very serious the evils of denounciation in our ancient law were, it will not seem wonderful that there should have been an anxiety to prevent such consequences, from following upon charges on general letters, issued of course, and without any previous notice to the persons against whom they were directed. By 1592, c. 140, one great evil was removed. Denounciation upon general letters was declared to be incompetent, so that the escheat could not fall upon such a warrant. 'No charges,' says the act, 'nor letters of horning shall be generally directed against all and sundrie, except it be against ane burgh, college, or community, whilk represents ane body; at the least, it sall not be leasom to denunce onie particular party to the horn upon sick general letters, except gif the said party be first lawfully and specially called to hear and see the said letters direct against him for a special and certain duty or fact,' &c. This statute did away a part, but not the whole, of the evil: for although it was not possible to subject a man unawares to the penalty of denounciation, it was still competent to imprison him by a caption proceeding upon the general letters, (III. Stair, iij. § 13.): and therefore, by 1690, c. 13, general letters were altogether prohibited, except, 1. for the King's revenue: 2. for ministers stipends upon decrees of locality: 3. upon decrees for poinding of the ground. And these are the only cases in which general letters are used in our day.

The first, and I believe the only case in which it was questioned whether general letters of horning and caption fell under the provision in the statute 1696, c. 5, occurred in the competition of the creditors of Andrew Walls, in 1702. Walls made a disposition of part of his funds to certain creditors, upon the 14th February 1700. Immediately after this, he left his place of residence for some weeks, and, on his return, was imprisoned. In a joint action of declarator of bankruptcy, and reduction of the disposition, it was objected by the holders

holders of the deed, that the caption produced, 'being only on 'general letters for the excise of brandy, is not equivalent to the 'diligence required by 1696, c. 5, which should be for some obliga- 'tion of debt, or on a decree; whereas, general letters are prohibited 'in the common cases by 1690, c. 13, and go of course, for any 'branch of his Majesty's revenue, against the best merchants in the 'kingdom, and can be no qualification of bankruptcy.' Answered, '1. The act of Parliament speaks of a horning and caption, 'without making any distinction; et ubi lex non distinguit, non est 'nostrum distinguere: 2. It is not horning and caption alone that 'infers the conclusion of bankruptcy, but it must be conjoined 'with insolvency at the time, and some of the alternatives of the 'said act, as his retiring to the Abbey, fleeing, absconding, forc- 'ing,' &c. The Lords 'repelled the defence, and found the horn- 'ing sufficient:' 25th July 1702, Man against Walls and his creditors; II. Fount. 156. Lord Fountainhall adds, 'The Lords were 'more circumspect in deciding this case, because it was among the 'first pursuits that have been founded on the late act of Parliament; 'and it was fit to clear the same for the future.'

The anxiety with which creditors contest every point that may be for their advantage, gave birth to many absurd pleas under the act 1696. Thus, it was questioned, (8th February 1705, Creditors of Cleland), whether one charge of horning, with caption, was sufficient; or whether, according to the true spirit of the statute, it was not neceſſary that there should be a concourse of diligence? 'But the Lords remembered (says Fount.) that, in the late case be- 'tween Man and Walls, 25th July 1702, they had found one horn- 'ing and caption sufficient,' and so, accordingly, they decided here: II. Fount. 266. Another question was made, equally absurd, namely, whether, in the view of a challenge of a deed of preference, it was not necessary that the diligence should have been taken out before the granting of the deed under reduction? The plain object of the act was to fix the point of bankruptcy for the general behoof, which being once ascertained in any particular case, the presumption of law took effect, that all deeds granted within the sixty days were to be held as made in contemplation of bankruptcy,

and

and to be annulled. Yet the Court 'inclined to think that the fly-'ing within the sixty days did not annul an assignation, unless there 'was horning and caption against the bankrupt *before* the voluntary 'deed:' 15th February 1698, Gray against Baird, I. Fount 824. Lord Fountainhall, however, was not satisfied with this decision: for he says, 'But the case being on a new act, deserves to be con-'sidered.'

The act of Parliament, in requiring diligence by horning and caption, as one of the requisites of bankruptcy, must be held to intend, that the diligence shall be regular and formal: for, although it is to effect a purpose just and expedient, that a person is made bankrupt by this law, in order to prevent him from constituting unfair preferences; yet as such preferences may be given to creditors who are in optima fide; nay, as indorsations of bills, assignations, and almost every other deed, are included under the rule, and are, in so far as the creditor who receives them is concerned, reducible, even though passed away, or transacted in the course of trade, and without suspicion; there must often be a strong, and indeed a very favourable interest, to oppose a bankruptcy being improperly declared. I do not mean here to enter into a discussion of the various objections that may be stated against hornings and captions; but shall only observe, that were I to venture upon a general rule, perhaps it should be this, that whatever objection would form a good ground for an action of wrongous imprisonment, if the caption were executed, would also be sufficient to prevent the diligence from bearing its part as one of the requisites of bankruptcy.

III. IMPRISONMENT, AND ITS EQUIVALENTS.

The third requisite in the statute, is IMPRISONMENT, or its equivalents of ABSCONDING, RESISTING, or TAKING THE SANCTUARY. The view of the Legislature in assuming these alternative circumstances, as summing up and completing the character of bankruptcy, it is not difficult to discover. They are acknowledgements the most positive and direct, that the debtor is unable to pay his debts;

and this acknowledgement is equally strong, whether the debtor suffer the disgrace of imprisonment, or choose to abscond, or to take sanctuary, as the only means by which he can avoid it. The acknowledgement implied in these acts taken by themselves, cannot indeed be considered as any thing more than that of a gross omission by the debtor, or of accidental derangement in his affairs, or of unforeseen disappointments in remittances, &c.; but, taken along with the other circumstances in the statute, insolvency and expired diligence, they may justly be considered as proofs of bankruptcy, and as the signal for measures being taken by the creditors to secure an equal division of the funds.

IMPRISONMENT.—In England mere imprisonment is not an act of bankruptcy. It must be either a fraudulent yielding to prison, for a true debt which the debtor is able to pay, or for a false debt raised up for the purpose; or, if the arrest be fair, the debtor must have lain two months in prison, without paying or finding bail for the debt. In Scotland, IMPRISONMENT is a plain mark of bankruptcy; for it takes place not suddenly, like the arrest of the English law, but after a fair warning to the debtor to call forth all his resources. If he cannot save himself from prison, and if he be at the same time insolvent, he is rightly to be considered as bankrupt.

There have been disputes concerning the nature of imprisonment, according to the true import and meaning of the Scotish statute,—whether it be necessary that the debtor be within the walls of a prison, or sufficient that he be actually in the custody of a messenger? In these questions, it is of importance to recollect, that while the great object of the statute was the prevention of fraud, the means adopted for this purpose were such, as to risk the greatest injustice to those creditors, who had received deeds from the bankrupt two months before, when perhaps he was in the fullest degree of credit and responsibility. If, therefore, the prejudice against fraud, on the one hand, should lead to a broad interpretation of the statute, this consideration should, on the other, tend much to limit and restrict it. The view of the Legislature undoubtedly

doubtedly was, that imprisonment, &c. should be considered as evidence of the debtor's inability to extricate himself; and the question should therefore come to issue upon that principle.

There is a material difference between the laws of Scotland and of England, in regard to imprisonment. As the English arrest is sudden, it has been thought necessary to give to the debtor the indulgence of a spunging-house (2 Geo. II. c. 22. § 1.) But as in Scotland imprisonment must be preceded by a charge to pay, and by the elapse of the days of law, no such indulgence as the English spunging-house has been thought necessary. An indulgence is indeed generally given by the messenger, that the debtor may make one last effort before entering the prison; but this is not to be considered as a suspension of the imprisonment. It is scarcely to be supposed that a man will allow the days of charge to pass idly away, without making an attempt to extricate his affairs, and provide for the demand. During that dreadful suspense, he sees bankruptcy before him with all its humiliating consequences; he knows, that if he can provide no means of payment, imprisonment will surely follow, unless he abscond, or take sanctuary. When he is actually arrested, therefore, the indulgence of his creditor, or of the messenger, in allowing him to remain out of prison for some hours, ought not to weaken the legal inference, that his affairs are completely deranged. It may often happen, too, that the delay to incarcerate is not an indulgence, but the effect of mere necessity. The debtor may be arrested far from a prison; or in sickness perhaps, and unfit to be removed; and it would be attended with the worst consequences, if the imprisonment should be held as incomplete till the debtor were lodged in jail.

But although it is not necessary that the debtor shall have been actually incarcerated, in order to establish his imprisonment, in the true sense of the statute of 1696; neither, on the other hand, is bare apprehension sufficient to satisfy the law. The debtor may be actually on his way to pay the debt, when he is arrested; or he may have sent a person with the money to the creditor, and in that very moment the officer may have come upon him. It may even

happen,

happen, that he has not received the charge, nor known of the danger in which he stood: he may have been from home at the time; the execution may have been given to a servant, and never been seen by him; and it may thus be necessary for him to beg a short indulgence, in order to send for money, with which to pay the debt, or for a friend to bail it.

The first question which occurred upon this point of imprisonment, was in the case of the creditors of Woodston against Colonel Scott of Commiston, in 1755. Mr Turnbull of Woodston, against whom a variety of hornings and captions had been taken out, was, on the 31st of March 1742, apprehended by a messenger upon a caption. He was detained a prisoner for that night, and part of next day, but never was taken to jail. He then paid the debt, and was liberated; and the question arose, whether, in the reduction of an heritable bond on the statute 1696, c. 5, this was imprisonment?* The Lords repelled the objections to the heritable bond; or, in other words, they found the debtor's having been in the custody of the messenger, not equivalent to imprisonment; 18th Feb. 1755, I. Fac. Coll. cxxxix. 306. But this decision was reversed

* It was pleaded on the one hand, That the statute being intended to assist the common law in preventing frauds, it was entitled to a liberal interpretation—that imprisonment is only a mark of bankruptcy, and so also are its equivalents, of retiring, fleeing, &c—that, in this sense, apprehension is in England equivalent to imprisonment; and, to escape from the house, or even from the arrest, of a constable, is to be guilty of breach of prison—that, in the same manner, in Scotland, a suspension will not liberate a debtor from the custody of a messenger—that if a messenger attempt to seize a debtor, and he escape, it is confessedly bankruptcy—and that it were strange, if, when he were actually seized, and happened to escape, that were not also bankruptcy. To this it was answered, That as a statute imposing a restraint upon the use of property, this act of Parliament 1696 ought to be strictly interpreted—that from this consideration proceeds that precision with which it limits the description of those whom it incapacitates—that it was the notoriety of the acts serving as a warning to all not to contract with the debtor, which pointed them out as proper marks of bankruptcy—that the remedy is violent which this law introduces, striking down all deeds, whether in security or in payment, which have been granted only two months before the bankruptcy—and that our law admits of no equivalent for imprisonment, since imprisonment, upon an act of warding, has been rejected as insufficient.

reversed in the House of Peers, where it was found, 'That Alexander Turnbull having been arrested, and actually in custody of the messenger, upon the caption at the suit of Sir William Ogilvie, was imprisoned within the true intent and meaning of the act of Parliament 1696.' This was followed as a leading decision in the case of MacAdam against MacIlwraith, 23d November 1771. In a later case, Fraser against Monro, a distinction was attempted, upon this ground, that Knowles the debtor, who had been twice apprehended, had remained the first time with a messenger in a public house, only till a bond of presentation should be written out; the next time, he had remained for three or four hours in a public house, when the whole debt, except 3l., was paid, and he was liberated; whereas, in Commiston's case, the debtor was in custody during the whole night, in which time no transaction can be presumed to have been going on. 'But the Court was clear to adhere to the decision of the House of Peers in the case of Commiston, as establishing a rule that ought to be permanent, and not arbitrary; and that, for the same reason, there was no room for going into a distinction as to the time or number of hours of a bankrupt's being in the messenger's custody; and therefore, they found the evidence sufficient, that at the time of granting the disposition challenged, Francis Knowles was bankrupt in terms of the act 1696.' 5th July 1774, Fraser against Monro: V. Fac. Coll. cxxi. 326.—The next case in which the question occurred, was that of Maxwell and others against Gibb; but in that case, there was neither actual incarceration, nor even a taking into custody. The execution of the messenger bore, that 'he had apprehended the debtor, but that, without imprisoning him, or taking him into custody, he had afterwards liberated him, on promise of payment.' The Court, distinguishing between this case and the former, 'repelled the reason of reduction:' 17th Nov. 1785, VII. Fac. Coll. ccxxxi. 359.—A similar decision had been given, 3d March 1768, Elliot against Scott, IV. Fac. Coll. lxvi. 306.—The last case upon the point, is that of M'Kellar of Dale, where it was proved, that from 1773 downwards to 1779, repeated instances had occurred, of creditors having ordered caption to be put in execution against M'Kellar; that messengers had frequently been looking for him; that sometimes he had got messengers to suspend the execution of the diligence, and sometimes had settled the debt; and, in particular, that on the 5th August 1776, M'Kellar was apprehended in the Grass-Market of Edinburgh—walked up the Lawn-Market with the messenger—and, after being in custody of the messenger for a short time, paid the debt, from a loan then negotiated by him, and which formed a claim upon his estate. The cause was very ably pleaded, and all the former cases fully examined and laid before the Court. The Judges were clear, that in this case there was distinctly an imprisonment within the meaning of the statute: 1st March 1791, M'Math against M'Kellar's trustees.

Such being the nature of the imprisonment required, the next point of inquiry is, by what evidence it is to be established? whether it be necessary to have a return by the messenger to establish the fact, or, whether other evidence will not be received? There seems to be only one case, in which any difficulty can arise, respecting the evidence of imprisonment, viz. where the debtor has been liberated without having ever been confined in a gaol. Where he has been actually in prison, the books of the prison will afford good evidence. An execution returned by the messenger, would be the proper evidence in the case of an imprisonment without having entered a gaol; but executions are seldom returned; and sometimes, it is even the interest of the incarcerating creditor, to keep out of sight all evidence of the imprisonment. Where his harshness, for example, has been the means of extorting from the debtor a deed of preference, which would be cut down by the bankruptcy being established within sixty days, he will not readily be brought to disclose evidence of a fact so destructive to his right. Some other evidence must therefore be resorted to; and the law permits circumstantial evidence to be received. In the case of Cleland's creditors, 8th February 1705, the Court found 'all these alternatives, viz. that the debtor was either imprisoned, or had retired 'to a privileged sanctuary, or absconded, or forcibly defended his 'person against the messengers, each of them relevant separatim, prout de jure;'—that is to say, that it should be competent,

by

by every species of evidence, to establish these several points: II. Fount. 266.—In the case of Richmond against the trustees of Charles Dalrymple, the question was very fully discussed. The Court expressed an unanimous opinion, that there was no ground for supposing the execution of a messenger essential to the proof of the facts respecting a bankrupt's imprisonment, which might be equally well established by parole testimony; but as, in this case, the evidence was deemed inconclusive, (the circumstances proved not amounting to imprisonment in the sense of the statute), the Lords adhered to Lord Stonefield's interlocutor dismissing the reduction: 14th January 1789, VIII. Fac. Coll. liv. 95.—This case is held to have settled the question: and in the subsequent case of M'Kellar in 1791, although the point was pleaded, it passed in silence upon the Bench, the Court finding the imprisonment established, although the evidence was only circumstantial, or prout de jure, as our law terms it.

FORCIBLY DEFENDING.—This is a circumstance which can admit of no ambiguity. The evidence of it ought naturally to be, the attestation of the messenger and witnesses in an execution or return. It will be observed, that it is not to any penal effect, as in deforcement, that this fact is to be established; but to the mere civil effect of ascertaining that the debtor resisted imprisonment, and would have been imprisoned but for that resistance. The same strictness of evidence should not, therefore, be required here, as in a question of deforcement; and although it be the most natural way for the messenger to stamp the fact by the sanction of a public instrument, there being no probable interest in the creditor to destroy or withhold the execution; yet, even in this case, there seems little reason to doubt, that the Court would admit a proof prout de jure; as the diligence and execution cannot be in the hand of any creditor but the user of it: and accordingly, this we have seen to be the decision in the above case of Cleland's creditors in 1705.

ABSCONDING.—In comparing the law of England and of Scotland upon this point, we must recur to that fundamental difference of principle which has already been marked. In England, any absence which hinders or delays a creditor in his payment, entitles him to the privilege of the statute execution of a commission of bankruptcy, instead of an action at common law *. But as, in Scotland, there are means provided for the rapid recovering of debt by individual creditors, without resorting to so rigorous and general a kind of execution as a commission of bankruptcy, the conduct of the debtor is more favourably and coolly judged of; and no absconding is sufficient to render him bankrupt, which does not infer an acknowledgement of inextricable confusion and insolvency. Every appearance of absconding is not to be received as evidence: but the debtor is admitted to give such explanations as may relieve him from the severe effects of the legal inference to be drawn from that fact. When a debtor retires to the Abbey, his being there can admit of one interpretation only: but he may, by business, by duty, by the calls of affection, have been obliged to leave home for a time; and it were extremely cruel and unjust to subject him, on account of such an accident, to a declarator of bankruptcy.

Two questions may arise upon absconding: 1. There can be no doubt that the messenger's return of execution, stating that, after a thorough search, the debtor could not be found, is good evidence, prima fronte, that he has absconded; and that, unless opposed by contrary evidence, it must be held as sufficient to authorise a declarator of bankruptcy. But what facts will entitle a messenger to return such an execution? Is it enough that the debtor is not at home? In a man of good credit, this circumstance is nothing; for business may have called him abroad: but, in an insolvent debtor, such absence from home is more suspicious, and was found sufficient, in one case, to infer, presumptione juris, an absconding under the statute 1696.—A messenger reported, in his return of execution, that he had searched for Thomas Bushby in his

* Perhaps this view of the law is more properly applicable to the older opinions, than to the more modern doctrines; for although, in three cases stated by Mr Cook, B. L. 94. 5 the intent was disregarded, and the fact of delay held to be sufficient; yet I am informed, that, in a later case, these judgements have been disapproved of, and a fraudulent design absolutely required.

his dwellinghouse, without being able to find him. The Court found, 'That Thomas Bushby, by the execution of search produced, fell under the description of the statute 1696.' It was 'observed on the Bench, That the absence of a debtor from his 'dwellinghouse, at a time when he is notoriously insolvent, will 'create a presumptio juris of absconding: not being, however, a presumptio juris et de jure, it may be elided by a contrary proof.' 9th August 1785, Spedding against Hodgson and Donaldson: VII. Fac. Coll. ccxxix. 356.—But perhaps, to sanction so strong an inference as that of absconding, there ought to be some other circumstance reported than mere absence; as the lateness of the hour, or the apparent concealment or ignorance of the domestics of what has become of the debtor. Thus, in the case of Ross against Chalmers, 25th June 1782, the search was made between eleven and twelve at night, and the proof of absconding held to be complete. This might perhaps surprise an Englishman, should he overlook the very different inferences drawn from the fact of absconding in the two countries. In England, the law looks to the delay of payment, and so holds a denial or absence from his house, at an hour when business is transacted, as inferring an act of bankruptcy in the debtor; but absence or denial, at an hour when no business is done, as insufficient to found such a conclusion. Thus, Lord Hardwick held eleven o'clock at night to be a very improper hour for creditors to call, and that a man's denying himself at such an hour, would not make him bankrupt. I. Cook, B. L. 96.—But, with us, the law looks not so much to the delay of the creditor's payment, as to the imprisonment, or to the absconding in order to avoid imprisonment, for founding the inference of a total inability in the debtor to extricate himself. And as absence from home, at any hour when a search may lawfully be made, is evidence of absconding, the later the hour is, the better always must the evidence of absconding be. In the case of Young against Grieve and others; 'the circumstance of a debtor not being found at his dwelling-'house by a messenger ready to execute a caption against him, and 'of his family not giving information whither he had betaken him-'self, were construed to be an absconding under the statute:' 4th July 1783, VII. Fac. Coll. cxi. 175.—From such circumstances, absconding may fairly be inferred; for although a man, even while insolvent, may be forced abroad, without any intention of eluding the diligence of his creditors, yet nothing should ever hinder him from leaving notice of the place where he may be found, or the time when he is to return home.

2. Although the messenger's return of execution is *prima facie* evidence of absconding, the Court has always allowed a proof in explanation of the cause of the debtor's disappearance. This is, in justice, due to every man, that he may escape a consequence so ruinous as that of bankruptcy. Much caution, however, should be used in examining the apology made by the debtor. The statute 1696 was made for the prevention of frauds; and it is plain, that often, by the gain of a day or two, a deed, made in the prospect of inevitable bankruptcy, may be put beyond the statutory term, and validated. Absconding upon a plausible pretence, may sometimes be a part of the fraud; and while, on the one hand, it is the duty of every creditor, using diligence for the purpose of making a debtor bankrupt, to be very cautious in establishing a clear and unambiguous absconding; it is the duty of the Court, upon the other, to weigh, with jealousy and doubt, every thing brought forward by the debtor in explanation of his absence. The execution of a caption is no sudden or unforeseen act: the debtor is first charged with horning, so that he knows the very day when the caption will be executed, and ought to be particularly cautious of being from home, without giving accurate information where he is to be found. In the competition of Cleland's creditors, in 1705, the debtor endeavoured to take off the effect of an execution of search, by a proof of his going freely to kirk and market for more than sixty days after granting the deed; but it was proved, that he saw the messenger coming, and hid himself in his house, and that the messenger searched for him, and could not find him. The Court found that he had absconded, in terms of the act: II. Fount. 266. In the case of Finlays against Aitchison and Moffat, 21st January 1767, the execution bore, "that Romanis' house had been broken open, and a search made, but he could not be found; and that there was reason to believe, he had made

made his escape by a back door.' A proof was allowed, the result of which was, that Romanis was not at home when the search was made; that the messenger, being refused access, broke open the door, and on searching did not find him. It was pleaded, that Romanis' absence from home that night being purely accidental, can infer no intention of eluding diligence. 'The Lords found no sufficient evidence to show that Romanis had absconded in terms of the act 1696.' But the next case implies the best comment upon this decision. The debtor's house was searched between eleven and twelve at night, and he was not found. A proof was offered, that he had that day left his house for the purpose of visiting his wife, who resided with her father; but the Court rejected it. 'They seemed,' says the reporter, 'to be of opinion, that the execution of such a search was of itself conclusive evidence of the debtor's having absconded, and could not be redargued by the proof here offered:' 25th June 1782, Ross against Chalmers, VII. Fac. Col. xlix. 78.

The most effectual way of absconding, is to leave the country. Where that is done, without any view of escaping from diligence, as in the case of an officer marching with his regiment, it is not to be deemed absconding, the case comes under the rule established by the late bankrupt statutes respecting debtors who are abroad. Where, without any public call of duty, or pressing necessity, a debtor leaves the country, law will hold it as an absconding. Thus Andrew Brown, a sailor and merchant, went abroad apparently in the way of his business, before caption was taken out against him. It was made a question, Whether he was to be considered as having absconded? On the one hand, it was said, that business carried him away. On the other, that his motive was not discernible, being actus animi; but that going away after horning, though before caption was raised, and staying away no less than two years, evince a design of eluding diligence, which he knew to be in dependence against him. The Lords sustained the reduction. 29th June 1737, Davidson against Brown, Clerk Home, lxiv. 112.

RETIRING TO THE ABBEY.—Retiring to the sanctuary is made equivalent to imprisonment, because it sets at defiance all attempts to imprison the debtor, and infers the strongest acknowledgment of insolvency, and of a design to avoid diligence. It is clear that for twenty-four hours the protection is complete without booking. From the moment therefore of taking the sanctuary, it is fair in the law to infer that acknowledgment which was intended by the selection of imprisonment and its equivalents as marks of bankruptcy. In the ranking of Castle-Somervil, it was tried, Whether a debtor, having taken lodgings in the Abbey, without having his name marked in the books, fell under the description of the act 1696? And 'the Lords, being generally of opinion, that it was not necessary to bring a man under the qualifications of the act, that he should be marked in the clerk's book, found it proved that James Somervil was notour bankrupt.' 3d December 1751, Dickson, II. Falc. cclvi. 292.

5. EQUIVALENTS INTRODUCED BY THE LATE STATUTES.—It was not till within these few years, that care was taken to supply the palpable defect in the statute of 1696, which excluded from the description of bankruptcy all those who were out of the country, or who, by reason of personal privilege or protection, were exempted from horning and caption and imprisonment. The remedy was first provided in the statute, 23 Geo. III. c. 18. § 1.; and these provisions are renewed in the statute, 33 Geo. III. c. 74, § 2. in these words: 'In all actions and questions arising 'upon the construction and effect of an act of the Parliament 'of Scotland, made in the year 1696, c. 5. intituled, "An act "for declaring nottour bankrupts,' when the debtor is out of 'Scotland, or not liable to be imprisoned, by reason of privilege, or personal protection, a charge of horning executed 'against him, together with either an arrestment of any of his 'effects not loosed or discharged within fifteen days, or a poinding 'executed of any of his moveables, or a decree of adjudication of 'any part of his estate, for payment or security of debt, shall, 'when joined with insolvency, be sufficient proof of notour bank'ruptcy, and from and after the last step of such diligence, the

'said

'said debtor, if insolvent, shall be holden and deemed a notour
' bankrupt; and every person, whether he be out of Scotland or
' not, whose estate shall be sequestrated under the authority of
' this present act, shall also be holden and deemed a notour bank-
' rupt in all questions upon the said act of 1696, from and after
' the date of the first deliverance on the petition to the Court of
' Session for awarding the sequestration.'

It has upon this new rule been doubted, whether it applied to the case of a person who had, before caption was taken out against him, retired to the sanctuary. Morison was, upon 7th March 1795, charged, in virtue of *letters of horning*, to make payment of a debt of 45l.; on the 15th May he retired to the sanctuary, and on the 20th May, the creditors, instead of taking out a caption against him, poinded his effects. The late bankrupt statutes give to creditors who shall summon the poinder, a right to participate in the goods poinded, provided the poinding has been executed within sixty days of bankruptcy: and Whyte, a creditor of Morison, wishing to take the benefit of this law, brought an action against the poinding creditor. The point in question was, whether it was necessary, in terms of the statute of 1696, to show that Morison was under diligence by horning and caption? or, whether it was not enough that a poinding had been executed of his moveables, as he was a person under the privilege of sanctuary? There was some difference of opinion on the Bench. It was stated to have been decidedly the intention of the framers of the law, to include this case; and, even should the words not be thought to express that intention clearly, the true interpretation of the clause, and the nature of the situation, were argued upon as sufficient to bring it under the law; for it is as absurd to apply for a caption against a person in the Abbey, as it is to take one out against a peer. It was, on the other hand, maintained, that whatever may have been the intention of the framers of the law, the Court were, as Judges, bound to interpret *it* as *it must have struck the nation* at large, who made it the rule of their proceedings; that, in this view, the act did not appear to include the case, 1. Because there was no occasion for a new provision where there was no defect;

and

and although there was a defect in the old law, in so far as respected peers, and those under personal protection, or out of the country, caption being incompetent against them, there was no defect in the law, as applicable to the case of a man in the sanctuary; since a caption might be taken out against him; his continuance in the sanctuary after caption, being sufficient to infer bankruptcy. 2. Because the sanctuary cannot be considered properly as a personal protection; it is only a local exemption; merely temporary, and depending upon the will of the debtor himself. The Court found Morison not to be bankrupt; 21st May 1800, Whyte against Butter: but the case stands in the roll for reconsideration.

It seems to be a question of some difficulty, whether it be necessary that the diligence, by a charge, with an adjudication, or an arrestment unloosed for fifteen days, shall be at the instance of the same person, or whether it be enough to establish the bankruptcy, if it can be shown that there existed at the same time a charge of horning, and an adjudication, or arrestment, though on separate debts. Both the spirit and the expression of the act seem to require, that the diligence necessary to make a man bankrupt in this way, shall be at the instance of the same creditor. The Legislature meant to provide for the situation, where it was impossible, under the old law, to make a debtor bankrupt, and to give a remedy, by which a creditor, wishing to render him bankrupt, might accomplish it without the necessity of apprehending him upon a caption. But, in order to fix upon a man the inference of irretrievable insolvency, the law seems to require the evidence of ultimate diligence, followed up as far as it can be carried by any one creditor. Now, it may happen that a creditor may have adjudged, or may have arrested the goods of a debtor, without any idea of rendering him bankrupt; and at the same time, another creditor may have charged him with horning, but equally without any intention of rendering him bankrupt. It may also happen, that the debtor may have allowed the arrested fund to remain from choice, and not from irretrievable insolvency; rather choosing that it should go in payment of the debt for which it has been attached: and, above all, it may easily happen, that the estate of a solvent debtor may be adjudged. The inference of bankruptcy, therefore, from these diligences concurring in the hands of different creditors, does not appear to be so strong as the law had in view, in establishing this character of bankruptcy. The expressions of the law seem also to countenance the idea of the diligence there pointed out, being a train of diligence at the instance of the same creditor. They are, that 'a charge of horning executed against the debtor, together with either an arrestment of any of his effects not loosed, &c., or a poinding executed of any of his moveables, or a decree of adjudication of any part of his estate for payment or security of debt, shall, when joined with insolvency, be sufficient proof of notour bankruptcy, and from and after the *last step of such diligence*, the said debtor, if insolvent, shall be holden and deemed a notour bankrupt:' § 2.

These additional provisions do not seem to require any further commentary; for they are clear and distinct in pointing out what is to be held as sufficient to make the debtor bankrupt.

These are all the statuteable ingredients of bankruptcy; and from the moment that insolvency, diligence by horning and caption, with imprisonment, or any of its equivalents concur, the debtor is publicly bankrupt. But, before leaving this subject, one point remains to be discussed. The chief use of establishing a bankruptcy against any man, is to afford to the creditors means of legal redress against the constitution of unfair preferences within the preceding term of sixty days; and therefore, it is a point of great importance to fix what is to be held as the precise date of the bankruptcy.

The date of the bankruptcy depends entirely upon that of the imprisonment, absconding, &c. as concurring with insolvency and previous diligence; and no difficulty can arise on the subject, but from an accidental or fraudulent ambiguity in the date of these

acts.

acts. 1. I have already taken occasion to observe, with regard to imprisonment, that it may sometimes be the interest of the creditor to conceal the imprisonment altogether. The same interest may lead him to conceal, if possible, the date of it, even when it has been discovered that the debtor was incarcerated. If the debtor was actually in jail, the books of the prison will afford evidence, at least of the time of his entry; for every prisoner's name is entered in a register when he first comes into the jail. It must remain with the creditor, having that point fixed, to make the due inquiries at the messenger and witnesses, in order to have proper evidence of the time of the debtor's apprehension; for, whatever doubts may be entertained concerning the effect of bare apprehension, when not followed by imprisonment, this at least is clear, that when imprisonment does follow, the first touch of the messenger is the completion of the bankruptcy. The evidence of the messenger and witnesses will fully establish the fact of apprehension. If the debtor never has been in jail, both the fact of the imprisonment, and the date of it, must be of much more difficult proof. But all that can, with propriety, be delivered upon the subject here, is, that the creditors, whose object it may be to establish these things, must exert themselves to find the best evidence which the nature of the case affords; and they may consider themselves as fully entitled to the benefit of a circumstantial proof on the occasion. 2. The date of the debtor's taking sanctuary, is much more easily established, than that of his imprisonment or apprehension. As the Sanctuary affords no protection, ipso jure, for more than twenty-four hours, a debtor, who is really absconding, will be careful to have his protection recorded within that time. 3. Resistance and absconding, are naturally followed by a regular execution, which fixes the point of time at which they took place. In both cases, the messenger is, for his own justification, and that of his cautioners, called upon to return an execution; and, in the case of absconding, the search being generally made for the very purpose of establishing a bankruptcy, an execution is made out to fix the date. 4. Some doubts may occur with respect to the equivalents introduced by the statute 33 Geo. III.

It

It has not been decided, whether, in the case of an arrestment used against an absent or privileged person, and not loosed for fifteen days, the bankruptcy shall be held as completed at the time of using the arrestment, or upon the fifteenth day after. But the spirit and intention of the statute seem to establish, that the fifteenth day should be taken as the date of the bankruptcy; for it is then only, that there is room for that legal inference of absolute incapacity to proceed, which the statute assumes as the completion of the bankruptcy.

RESTORATION FROM BANKRUPTCY.

In order to complete the view of this subject, we must inquire, whether Bankruptcy, once established, can be done away? This inquiry includes two questions. 1st, What power the incarcerating creditor has, to destroy or discharge his diligence, to the effect of cleansing the debtor from bankruptcy? 2dly, Whether returning solvency can purge away the taint of bankruptcy, while any of the debts remain unpaid? There have been several cases upon this question of restoration. A few years after the statute of 1696, it was contended, in the competition of Cleland's creditors, that the debt whereupon the diligence proceeded, being paid off before the granting of the deed in question, the diligence was extinct, and could not be founded upon in the reduction. The question was not decided, the Court having only ordered the evidence of its payment, before the said deed, to be produced, reserving the question upon the effect of that evidence: 8th February 1705, II. Fount. 267. But the question came to a decision, in the case of the creditors of Mrs Campbell of Rachan, in 1743. Mrs Campbell was rendered bankrupt upon the 17th February 1728, having been imprisoned upon a caption, while utterly insolvent. Six months afterwards, she made a minute of sale of a house in Edinburgh; and, in a reduction of this sale upon the statute 1696, c. 5, the question was, Whether Mrs Campbell was bankrupt at the date of the minute? On the one hand, the debt and diligence had been paid off and discharged; but, on the other, Mrs Campbell still remained insolvent; so that it was the fairest case that could have occurred for the decision of the question of law. A hearing in presence was appointed; for the Court was much divided. The Judges previously fixed the point in dispute, and upon which they wished to hear counsel, to be this, 'Whether a person, being 'once notour bankrupt in terms of the act 1696, still continues 'a notour bankrupt, by construction of the act, though the debt in 'the caption, upon which he was imprisoned, be paid, the cap-'tion discharged, and he set at liberty? or, Whether it be neces-'sary that he continue under diligence, as well as continue insol-'vent?' After a full discussion, it was decided, 'That the 'debt upon which the imprisonment proceeded, being paid, and 'so the person not under caption at the time the deed quarrelled 'was granted, the case did not fall within the act of Parliament '1696.' 9th February 1743, creditors of Mrs Campbell of Rachan against Henry, Kilk. 49, Clerk Home, 370. Viewing the question according to the notions of our day, it cannot require much consideration to perceive, that this decision is erroneous. But I forbear making any remarks upon it; for, in the next case which occurred, it was well considered, and condemned as a bad decision. Johnson was imprisoned upon a caption on the 16th August 1745: he was liberated four days afterwards, on giving an heritable security to the incarcerating creditor, with an obligation to pay the debt in a month, and a proviso, that, at the end of that time, the creditor should be entitled to use his caption again, if the money was not paid. The caption was not again put in execution, and for two years the debtor went on with his trade, although really insolvent. A reduction was then brought, of a certain deed granted prior to the imprisonment, and also of the heritable bond granted to the incarcerating creditor. A proof of the insolvency was allowed; when the debts appeared to be 1300l., and the funds no more than 700l. or 800l. After an inquiry into the circumstances of Rachan's case, the Court, at first, bowed to the authority of that decision. They supported both deeds, although the minority stated that the precedent was not applicable to the deed granted prior to the bankruptcy. But, afterwards, they altered the judgement, de-

[illegible]

approved of the decision in Rachan's case, and found both deeds reducible upon the statute 1696. The remarks of Lord Kilkerran upon this case, are in themselves so valuable, and give so much information concerning the views of the Court, in pronouncing the decision, that I shall make no apology for quoting them entire. 'The Lady Rachan's case,' says his Lordship, 'had too much regard paid to it, at pronouncing the former interlocutor. As it was but a single decision, or rather a single interlocutor never brought under view, so, the point thereby determined was not necessary to the decision of the cause; as the security which the Lady had granted, was given by her as cautioner for a third party, which, at the same time, was found not to fall under the statute. But, what is more material, the plurality came now to think it a wrong judgement. That all the three requisites must concur at the time when the deed quarrelled is granted, may be at least intelligible, in the case of actual imprisonment. it is really not intelligible in other cases, particularly in the transient act of forcibly defending. But the substantial argument against that judgement, was this, That the act of Parliament was to fix the bankruptcy at a precise period, namely, the imprisonment. A man may, for many years, be under horning and caption; and he may, during the same period, be also insolvent. but the statute does not proceed, upon these, to declare him notour bankrupt. But when, to these, any of the other alternatives are superadded, which are, imprisonment, without distinction, whether it last for an hour, or a year; retiring to a sanctuary, also without distinction how long he continues in it, forcibly defending, suppose it to be but one act; this fixes the party to be a notour bankrupt from that moment. Nor can the statute otherwise admit of a sound meaning, when it is not conceiveable how otherwise the sixty days before or after the bankruptcy can be computed, than by supposing the bankruptcy fixed to a precise point: The three requisites must once concur; but, if they once concur, he must for ever be held bankrupt, quoad all and each of his creditors, who are such at the period fixed by the statute for his bankruptcy; and no after incident by the creditors, at whose instance he was imprisoned, liberating him from pri-

'son,

'son, or even discharging the debt, can deprive them of the right 'of reduction competent to them by the statute: and, were not 'the statute to be so understood, the creditor using diligence, 'would have the sole power over the bankrupt, and, by consenting 'to his liberation, or discharging his diligence, could put an end 'to the right of other creditors, contrary to the very intention of 'the statute.——And whereas it had been argued, in the case 'of Lady Rachan, that it were absurd to suppose, that one who 'had once been bankrupt, and had thereafter acquired an opulent 'estate, should nevertheless be supposed to continue all the while 'bankrupt; and that all rights, in that time, granted by him, 'should be reducible, as granted by a bankrupt;—it was answered, 'There was no absurdity in it; for the statute makes no provision 'for the creditors that became such after the bankruptcy: and if 'they neglect to obtain payment of their debts, while their debtor 'continues to be in good circumstances, they have themselves to 'blame. It has only been omitted to observe, that, in the pre-'sent case, some of the Lords were moved with the hardship it 'would be, to make a creditor's own diligence defeat the security 'he had obtained by it, which was Dirleton's case, who, by his 'imprisoning the debtor, procured the heritable bond. But, how-'ever such reasoning might be proper for the Legislature, it was 'improper for a court of law. The law hath said, that if an in-'solvent debtor, under horning and caption, shall be imprisoned, all 'securities granted by him to his creditors shall be void, whether 'to the creditor at whose suit he is imprisoned, or to another, 'and the law must take its course:' 9th November 1750, Earl of Hopeton and others, creditors of Johnson, against Nisbet of Dirleton and Innes; Kilk. 59. See also Kaimes's Rem. Dec. 241.

The only other case in which this question has ever occurred, is that of M'Kellar in 1791. M'Kellar was, on the 5th August 1776, rendered bankrupt. The debt upon which the caption had proceeded, was paid, and M'Kellar transacted his affairs as usual; but he remained insolvent down to 1779, when the deed under challenge was granted. This was proved by periodical states of his affairs.

affairs. The Court held M'Kellar to have been bankrupt in 1776, from which state he had not recovered at the date of the bond of corroboration. It was observed from the Bench, that when a man becomes bankrupt in terms of the act, he must remain so, till his affairs be extricated, and he regain a state of solvency. A creditor who does diligence, and so renders the debtor bankrupt, acts not for himself; but every other creditor acquires a right, of which he cannot be deprived by the person at whose instance the diligence proceeded. The consequences which follow imprisonment, are pleadable by all the creditors. Were it otherwise, very bad effects might ensue; for, supposing a person to have been rendered bankrupt on diligence, which proceeded for a trifling debt, and a creditor, in a large sum, to have purchased up this debt and diligence; such creditor might then dispose of the diligence at pleasure: he might acquire preferences from the debtor, discharge the diligence, and so defraud every other creditor. But this cannot happen, as the law stands; for the bankruptcy gives a jus quæsitum to each creditor. It was also observed, That when a person has been rendered notour bankrupt, the effect of it can be taken off only by solvency, by cessio bonorum, or by discharge from his creditors. This man was bankrupt when the diligence was used; and the progressive states of his affairs show, that they were daily more and more involved.—1st March 1791, M'Math against M'Kellar's trustees.

By these decisions, it may be regarded as fixed, that after the whole circumstances of bankruptcy have once concurred, and a debtor has been rendered bankrupt, in terms of the statute, there is a jus quæsitum constituted in each of his creditors, to have that bankruptcy declared; and the character remains upon the debtor while he continues insolvent. The law of England, in this matter, is different. 'An act of bankruptcy, if once fairly com-'mitted, can never be purged, even though the party continue to 'carry on a great trade. If, indeed, the act be doubtful,' (as a great many of the English acts of bankruptcy may be), 'then cir-'cumstances may explain the intent of the first act, and show it

' not

'not to have been done with a view to defraud creditors; but if, after 'a plain act of bankruptcy, a man pays off, and compounds with all 'his creditors, he becomes a new man.'—I. Cook, B. L. 129. The law of Scotland requires insolvency, as the great ingredient in the mixed character of bankruptcy; all the other requisites being taken only as marks of the publication of that insolvency. Without insolvency, they are nothing; and therefore, when a man recovers his solvency, and his creditors have it in their power to obtain their payment, each, by his own individual measures, law holds the debtor to be no longer a bankrupt.

CHAP.

CHAP. III.

OF THE PERSONS WHO MAY BE MADE BANKRUPT.

WHEN we are told, that in England no man can be made bankrupt but a trader, we should remember, that the term, Bankruptcy, has in that country a meaning very different from that which it bears in Scotland. Bankruptcy, in England, is a character which bestows upon the debtor himself privileges unknown to the common law, and to the enjoyment of which the misfortunes of trade have alone been thought sufficient to entitle him. But, in Scotland, bankruptcy is a character which bestows no privilege upon the debtor; which is intended merely for the benefit of the creditors; and to secure them against the creation of unfair preferences. The principle upon which it rests, is therefore universally applicable; and the character is confined to no one rank or class of men. Every one in Scotland who may be insolvent, may also be made bankrupt.

Persons are, in the view of the law, either individual or corporate; and, in this order, I shall consider them, with relation to the present question.

1. OF INDIVIDUALS.—*Keeping in view the intention of the law*, in declaring a person bankrupt, and that, as the law now stands, creditors may have this benefit, in cases where ultimate personal diligence

ligence is incompetent, it will not seem in any degree repugnant to humanity or justice, to say, that a pupil, an idiot, or a lunatic, may be rendered bankrupt. In England this cannot be; because these persons are incapable of engaging in trade. In Scotland also, till 1783, it would have been absurd to have spoken of making such persons bankrupt; because, prior to the sequestration act of that year, the only effect of bankruptcy was, to tie up the debtor's hands from making deeds of unfair preference; and, by natural incapacity, pupils, idiots, and lunatics, are deprived of the power of granting deeds. But, since it is now declared, that bankruptcy shall have the effect of introducing an equal ranking of all poindings and arrestments, used within sixty days before, and four months after the bankruptcy, there may be a very strong necessity for having bankruptcy declared, even against such helpless beings.

A person under age, or non compos mentis, is incapable of personal obligation; but he may, by his tutors or curators, have taken up the succession of a predecessor; and the claims upon him, in that character, may be made the subject of diligence against his estate. Against his person, no diligence can proceed. It were inconsistent with every principle of humanity and justice, to permit personal execution against those who are incapable of any civil act; and accordingly, all that is harsh and personal in the diligence of our law, is taken away, when such a person is concerned. Nothing is left to the creditor, but those powers of attaching the estate, which are necessary for the purposes of justice: 1696, c. 41. We shall afterwards have occasion to show, that this statute, which exempts minors from imprisonment, was merely declaratory of the common law; and that the rule is equally applicable to the case of all who naturally, or by disease, labour under mental incapacity. In cases of exemption from imprisonment on account of mental incapacity, the bankruptcy must be constituted in the way pointed out in the late statutes, either by adjudication, or by poinding, or by arrestment unloosed for fifteen days.

But there is another class of persons, concerning whom a similar doubt may be moved, viz. married women. The general

rule

rule of the law of Scotland is, that a married woman is not capable of incurring personal obligation, and consequently is exempted from personal diligence for debt. In cases where there has been no separation, personal diligence has been uniformly found incompetent against married women, unless for enforcing performance of an act within their own power. Neither has a married woman any power of contracting personal obligation, even with her husband's concurrence, so as to bind herself during the marriage: (8th December 1761, Menzies; 10th December 1772, Watson; 23d February 1791, Harvey and Fawell); nor can even the fines imposed upon a wife, or the damages found due by her, authorise diligence against her person during marriage: (5th December 1738, Pain, Kilk. 256; 19th February 1790, Chalmers against Douglas). But the Court, sensible of the hardship of preventing married women, whose husbands have left the country, from engaging in trade for their maintenance, have authorised diligence against them, as the only means of giving them credit. In the case of Churnside against Currie, 11th July 1789, 'the husband having left Scotland in bankrupt circumstances, the wife entered into trade, in order to maintain herself and her children. Being charged with horning for payment of a bill of exchange, she suspended, upon the ground that a married woman is not liable to personal diligence.' 'This plea, however,' says the reporter, 'was utterly disregarded, as inapplicable to a case like the present, where the debt had been contracted by a wife in her own name, while her husband was out of the kingdom. To refuse the ordinary legal compulsitors in such circumstances as these, would, it was observed, in the end prove hurtful to the women themselves, by preventing them from gaining a livelihood in trade, at a time when their husbands could not afford them any support.' The bill of suspension was refused by the Lord Ordinary, and the Court affirmed this judgement: VIII. Fac. Coll. lxxviii. 141. The law respecting the bankruptcy of married women, may be reduced to these propositions. 1. That in the common case, a married woman cannot be made bankrupt. 2. That when there is a separation, and the wife acts as a single woman, and, entering into trade, is in that character trusted, and contracts debt, she may be the subject of personal execution, and can be made bankrupt; and this rule holds still more strongly, when the husband has left the country.

With regard to all other individuals, whether they be liable to diligence; or privileged, as peers and members of the House of Commons; or under personal protection from imprisonment; they may all be made bankrupt, either in the way pointed out in the statute of 1696, or by the means prescribed in the statute of 1793, taken notice of in the last section.

2. OF CORPORATE BODIES.—Corporate bodies are in law considered as persons; whether they be associated by public authority, or united merely by private agreement, as trading companies. When a community is established by public authority, it has a legal existence as a person, with power to hold funds, to sue, and to defend: (Ersk. B. 1. tit. 7. § 64). It must, of consequence, be subject to diligence; and, although personal execution cannot proceed against this ideal and legal person, so as to subject him to the bankruptcy of the statute 1696, c. 5.—(June 1747, Shoemakers of the Canongate, Kilk. 52.)—yet there seems to be no reason for doubting that, under the new law, a community may be made bankrupt, by a charge with adjudication, poinding, or arrestment unloosed. The particular manner of executing such diligence, must depend upon the constitution of each incorporation: and, upon this head, much instruction is to be received from the case of Dalrymple of Waterside against Miss Bertram, 23d June 1762. The question in that case respected the validity of an arrestment used in the hands of the British Linen Company; and the general doctrine to be drawn from the case, seems to be, that, in citing a corporation, or using diligence against them, the legal method is, to execute it against the representatives in a body, when they are met for managing the affairs of the incorporation, or by executing it against each of the governors or representatives personally and separately: Kaims' Select Decisions, cxcviii. 263.

Trading

Trading companies, established by private agreement among individuals, are also in law regarded as persons, and held to be liable to diligence and bankruptcy. Ultimate diligence raised against all, or against any one of the partners, for a copartnership debt, is sufficient to render the company bankrupt. And upon this ground, by the sequestration law, a company in that condition, or their creditors, may apply for sequestration, as in the case of an individual who has been rendered bankrupt: 33. Geo. III. c. 74. § 18.

BOOK

BOOK THE SECOND.

OF THE LAWS DIRECTED AGAINST FRAUDULENT OBLIGATIONS AND CONVEYANCES.

INTRODUCTION TO BOOK II.

I PROPOSE now to consider those statutes, and those rules of the common law, by which the voluntary conveyances and obligations of the debtor, to the prejudice of his lawful creditors, are detected and restrained. In this book, I do not intend to take notice of the more indirect methods of bestowing preference, by facilitating the operation of the diligence of one creditor, and interrupting the progress of others, or by intimating to particular creditors an approaching failure, which the world may have no reason to suspect, and thus enabling them to take the priority in execution. These form the subject of the next Book: At present I restrict myself to voluntary deeds.

The frauds which debtors may accomplish by means of voluntary deeds, seem to be reducible to three classes. The FIRST comprehends all those devices by which a debtor fraudulently diminishes the funds that ought to be equally distributed among his creditors. Under this class are included, the concealment and embezzlement of effects, for the purpose of withdrawing them from the reach of creditors—conveyances made, without value, to relations, or to confidential friends—and fictitious debts, raised up for the unfair purpose of enabling the feigned creditors to draw a dividend, and unduly to influence the management of the bankruptcy. A SECOND class of frauds, comprehends all those deeds, by which the debtor attempts to counteract legal execution, when begun by particular creditors. And a THIRD class comprehends all those voluntary conveyances and deeds, which are intended for securing, in the view of a total bankruptcy, a larger share to particular creditors, than in justice they ought to receive.

For repressing these various kinds of fraud, there are two classes of remedies; one, of a corrective nature, directed against the person in whose favour the right is granted, and having for their object the voidance of that right; another, penal, directed against the debtor himself. The penal remedies are, the refusal of a discharge to the debtor, or even of a liberation from prison, and, in flagrant cases, trial and punishment as a criminal before the Court of Justiciary. The corrective depend upon two great principles, which should naturally regulate the course of our inquiry concerning them.

1. The embezzlement of the funds is prevented by laws, which proceed on this plain principle, that, from the moment of insolvency, the debtor becomes a mere trustee for his creditors, and can neither defeat the diligence which individuals may have begun, nor give a donation out of the common fund.

2. The principle upon which the law has restrained the granting of voluntary deeds, for the purpose of bestowing preferences upon particular creditors, is somewhat different. It will be readily admitted, that such preferences, when concerted with the bankrupt by creditors apprised of his situation, are fraudulent; while it must also be allowed, that, in many situations, a creditor may fairly and honourably stipulate for a further security. To draw the line of distinction, to fix, in cases where the evidence must be ambiguous, the point at which the bona fides ends, and the collusion begins, must at all times be a matter of extreme difficulty; and we have already seen, that it was chiefly with a view to the solution of this difficulty, that the Legislature, in the year *1696*, settled a precise description of bankruptcy, to serve as a ground of presumptive fraud against deeds prejudicial to the creditors.

The

The two principles which have now been generally explained, point out the natural divisions of this Second Book. I shall consider,

1. The frauds which require only that the debtor should be insolvent, not that he should be actually bankrupt, in order to give effect to the legal remedy.

2. The frauds against which the establishment of the character of bankruptcy was intended to provide, and the particular nature of the remedies which flow from that provision. And,

3. The penal remedies against the frauds of bankrupts in general.

CHAP. I.

OF GRATUITOUS CONVEYANCES AND FICTITIOUS DEBTS.

THE frauds practised by insolvent debtors, for the purpose of embezzling their funds, seem to be chiefly of two kinds. 1. Where a conveyance is made directly to a confidential friend, without any value received for it; and, 2. where fictitious debts are constituted for the purpose of enabling the debtor indirectly to draw a dividend from his own estate, and to influence the deliberations of the assembled creditors; or of throwing the management into the hands of the debtor, or of his friends. Happily, in this country, we have had few instances of the latter and more complicated of those devices. In England, it seems to be of almost daily practice; and we find the English writers giving detailed accounts of fraudulent bankruptcies, conducted with every appearance of fairness, and so as almost to bid defiance to detection. Whether it be wise thus to point out the road of guilt, I shall not determine; but this country scarcely affords those opportunities which seem to be requisite to the success of such accomplished villany.

It is in all laws a general rule, that when fraud is detected, redress is to be given. To entitle themselves to the benefit of this rule, creditors must rely greatly upon the vigilance with which they watch all the motions of the bankrupt, and observe every expedient by which he may attempt to accomplish his unfair purposes. But in this difficult task, they are not left entirely without assistance:

assistance: in the code of every commercial nation, there are certain legal presumptions of fraud, which, independently altogether of the secret purpose of those concerned, serve as safeguards to the true creditors. To this the law of Scotland has not been inattentive.

After a person becomes insolvent, he cannot in justice be permitted to give away his funds in mere gratuity. While in full capacity, and free from debt, there can be no question of his power to bestow his property as he pleases; or to bind himself for the payment of money, without any consideration, but that of mere kindness and affection. But from the moment that his funds are covered by his debts, his powers of gratuitous disposal are at an end; he becomes then the trustee, or rather the negotiorum gestor of his creditors, he may, as long as he is permitted, continue his trade, with the intention of gaining for his creditors and for himself, as any prudent man would do; but his funds are no longer his own, to be given away as caprice or affection may dictate. Here, then, we find the great and first general principle which is to act as an auxiliary to the creditors of an insolvent debtor in the detection of fraud. When this principle is acknowledged, the creditors have no longer to dive into the secret plans and fraudulent views of their debtor, and of his friends; but to direct their inquiries to this point alone, Whether was this man insolvent when he granted this deed, or constituted this debt against himself; and whether did he act thus, without a valuable consideration?

In the law of Rome, that great fountain of jurisprudence, from which the legislatures of modern Europe have drawn so largely, this general principle was fully acknowledged. 1. At common law, a mere donation was revocable, at the suit of creditors, if granted by an insolvent debtor, and to their prejudice. 'If' (says the great Ulpian) 'a donation be given, the question is not, whether the donee knew it to be a fraud upon creditors, but whether the creditors be defrauded? Nor does he, though ignorant of the fraud, seem to be injured, since he is only deprived of

'his

'his gain, not made to suffer a loss. Those who unknowingly 'receive gifts from one insolvent, will be liable to an action to 'the extent of their gain, but no further *.' 2. But this was not all: Conveyances, though good at common law, if onerous, were often made instruments of fraud: to remedy which, the Prætor published an edict, called the Prætorian Edict 'DE ACTIONE PAU-'LIANA,' by which he declared, that he would give an action in equity to the creditors, or their curator bonis, for the revocation of all deeds which were, to the knowledge of the receiver, prejudicial to creditors.

It was in France that the Roman jurisprudence was preserved most pure. A general law was made, to annul all deeds done in defraud of creditors, directly, or indirectly †, but it was not specified what should be considered as a deed in defraud of creditors; and the general rule received its interpretation from the Roman law. 'When the property in question was acquired by a third party by onerous title, it was liable to restitution, if the receiver was participant in the fraud (conscius fraudis); when, by gratuitous title, restitution was competent, without participation in the fraud ‡.'

In England, a law was made in the reign of Queen Elizabeth, of precisely the same kind with the French ordonnance, providing for

* 'Si cui donatum est, non esse quærendum, an sciente eo, cui donatum, gestum sit 'sed hoc tantum, an fraudentur creditores? Nec videtur injuria affici is, qui ignoravit, 'cum lucrum extorqueatur, non damnum affligatur. In hos tamen, qui ignorantes ab 'eo, qui solvendo non sit, liberalitatem acceperunt, hactenus actio erit danda, quatenus 'locupletiores facti sunt: ultra non.' Digest Lib. xlii tit. 8 l. 6 § 11.

† The edict of Henry IV in 1609, and the 4th art of the 2d title of the ordonnance of 1673, 'declarent nuls tous transports, cessions, ventes & donations des biens 'meubles & immeubles, faits en fraude des creanciers, & qu'ils soient rapportez à la masse 'commune des effets.'

‡ 'Si le debiteur,' says M Pothier, 'lorsqu'il a fait passer à un tiers, la chose 'qu'il s'etoit obligé de me donner, n'etoit pas solvable, je pourrois agir contre le tiers 'acquereur, pour faire rescinder l'alienation qui lui en a eté fait en fraude de ma creance, 'pourvu qu'il ait eté participant de la fraude (conscius fraudis) s'il etoit acquereur à titre 'onereux, s'il etoit acquereur à titre gratuit, il ne seroit pas meme necessaire pour cela 'qu'il eut eté participant de la fraude.' Trait des Oblig § 153 tom. 1. 65.

for the annulling of all false conveyances and obligations, but without declaring specifically what should be held to be objectionable, or whether mere gratuity in the conveyance should entitle the true creditors to relief. 'For avoiding and abolishing of all feigned 'covenous, and fraudulent testaments, gifts, grants, alienations, con-'veyances, bonds, suits, judgements, and executions, as well of 'lands and tenements as of goods and chattels, which have been 'and are devised, &c. to the end, purpose, and intent, to delay, hin-'der, or defraud creditors and others, of their just and lawful ac-'tions, suits, deeds, &c. it is enacted, That all and every feoff-'ment, gift, grant, alienation, bargain and conveyance of lands, &c. 'which are made for any intent or purpose before declared or ex-'pressed, shall be deemed and taken to be clearly and utterly 'void, frustrate, and of none effect.' 13 Eliz. c. 5.—But it was soon found necessary to make the law more precise; and accordingly, in 1604, a statute was made, declaring all voluntary deeds, granted without a valuable consideration, to be unavailable against creditors. This statute (1 Ja. I. c. 15. § 5.) provides, 'That if any who hereafter is, or shall be a bankrupt, shall con-'vey or procure, or cause to be conveyed, to any of his children, 'or other person or persons, any manors, &c. or transfer his debts 'into other mens names, except the same shall be purchased, con-'veyed, or transferred, for or upon marriage of any of his children, 'both the parties married being of the years of consent, or for 'some valuable consideration, it shall be in the power and autho-'rity of the commissioners, &c. to bargain, sell, &c. in as ample 'a manner as if the said bankrupt had been actually seised or pos-'sessed thereof, or the debts were in his own name, &c. and that 'every such grant, &c. of the said commissioners, or of the great-'er part of them, shall be good and available, to all intents and 'purposes in the law, against the offender or offenders, and his 'heirs, &c. and against all other persons claiming by, from, or 'under such offenders, or such said other persons, to whom such 'conveyances shall be made by the said bankrupt, or by his means 'or procurement.'

In Scotland, not only has the general principle, which, under the Roman law, annulled all gratuitous deeds made in prejudice of creditors, been acknowledged and received, but a special statute has been enacted for the purpose of giving a greater force to the principle, and rendering it more efficacious. As it is, in truth, scarcely less difficult to prove the gratuitous nature of a deed, than to prove the fraudulent intention of the parties, the Parliament of Scotland endeavoured to remove this difficulty, by assuming, as the ground of a legal and presumptive fraud, the most prominent circumstances of suspicion. Thus, it is likely that a near relation, or one in the confidence of an insolvent person, will be apprised of his situation before it is known to the public, and the presumption is natural, which, upon the debtor's failure, holds a deed granted to such a person, to have been made with a bad design, or collusively. Again, the first step of diligence taken by a creditor, is a warning to the debtor to disappoint it, by bestowing preferences upon his favourites: This, too, is a situation which calls for attention, and, if left without a remedy, the value of legal diligence would be impaired. With these circumstances in view, the Legislature of Scotland, not contented, as the Legislature of England and France seem to have been, with acknowledging the general principle, has established presumptions, of great use in practice; presumptions, which make the law itself the guardian of the insolvent's funds, and of the rights of the creditors at large. This was the object of the statute 1621, c. 18. It has two branches.—By the first branch, as settled in a long course of decisions, every deed granted to a near relation, or to a confidential friend, after the existence of debts, is to be held as granted after insolvency, and without value; unless the holder of the deed shall prove the contrary:—while the general principle of the common law is left, unassisted, to operate against those deeds which, without the aid of presumption, can be proved to fall under it. The second branch of the statute protects, against all voluntary conveyances by the insolvent debtor, the right of proceeding to completion with diligence once begun.

In the further prosecution of this subject, I shall, in the first place, consider those cases, in which the creditors are assisted by the statute made in 1621, and, afterwards, those which are left to the disposal of the common law, to be brought under the influence of the general rule, by an investigation into the particulars of the value given for the deed, or the circumstances from which the debt may have arisen.

SECTION I.

COMMENTARY UPON THE FIRST BRANCH OF THE STATUTE 1621, C. 18.

THIS early statute, we owe to the Judges of the Court of Session; for it was first enacted as a rule of Court, or act of sederunt, in July 1620; and was adopted and confirmed in Parliament, by the 28th chapter of the year 1621.

I have subjoined, in a note, the words of the statute,* from which it will appear that the regulations introduced by it, as a check upon gratuitous conveyances, were simply these.

1. That

* 'Our Sov. &c ratifies an act of the Lords of Council and Session, of which 'the tenour follows: The Lords of C and S understanding, by the grievous and just 'complaints of many of his Majestie's good subjects, that the fraud, malice, and fal- 'hood of a number of divours and bankrupts is become so frequent and avowed, and 'hath already taken such progresse, to the overthrow of many honest mens fortunes 'and estates, that it is likely to dissolve trust, commerce, and faithful dealing amongst 'subjects, whereupon must insue the ruine of the whole estate, if the godlesse deceites 'of those be not prevented and remedied, who, by their apparent wealth in lands and 'goods, and by their show of conscience, credit and honestie, drawing into their hands, 'upon trust, the money, merchandize, and goods of welmeaning and credulous persons, 'do no wayes intend to repay the same, but either to live ryotously, by wasting of other 'mens substance, or to enrich themselves by that subtil stealth of other mens goods, 'and to withdraw themselves and their goods forth of this realme, to elude all execution 'of justice, and to that effect, and in manifest defraud of their creditors, do make 'simulate and fraudful alienations, dispositions, and other securities, of their lands

1. That all conveyances made to any conjunct or confident person, without true, just, and necessary causes, should, if done after the

'reversions, teyndes, goods, actions, debts, and others, belonging unto them, to their 'wives, children, kinsmen, alleyes, and other confident and interposed persons; without 'any true, lawful, or necessary cause, and without any just or true price interveining in 'their said bargaines, whereby their just creditors and cautioners are falsly and godlesly 'defrauded of all payment of their just debts, and many honest families likely to 'come to utter ruine.' After this formidable enumeration of frauds, the act proceeds in these words: 'For remedie whereof, the said Lords, according to the power 'given unto them by his Majestie and his most noble progenitors, to set down orders 'for administration of justice, meaning to follow and practice the good and commendable laws, civil and cannon, made against fraudful alienations in prejudice of 'creditors, and against the authors and partakers of such fraud; Statutes, ordaines, and 'declares, that in all actions and causes depending, or to be intended by any true creditor, 'for recoverie of his just debt, or satisfaction of his lawful action and right, they will 'decreet and decern all alienations, dispositions, assignations, and translations whatsoever, 'made by the debtor, of any of his lands, teyndes, reversions, actions, debts, or goods 'whatsoever, to any conjunct or confident person, without true, just, and necessary 'causes, and without a just price really payed, the same being done after the contracting 'of lawful debts from true creditors, to have been from the beginning, and to be in all 'times comming, null, and of none availe, force nor effect, at the instance of the true 'and just creditor, by way of action, exception, or reply, without further declarator. 'And in case any of his Majestie's good subjects (no wayes partakers of the said fraudes) 'have lawfully purchased any of the said bankrupt's lands or goods, by true bargains, for 'just and competent prices, or in satisfaction of their lawful debts, from the interposed 'persons trusted by the said divours; in that case, the right lawfully acquired by him 'who is no wayes partaker of the fraude, shall not be annulled in manner foresaid; but 'the receiver of the price of the said lands, goods, and others, from the buyer, shall 'be holden and oblished to make the same forthcomming to the behove of the bankrupt's 'true creditors, in payment of their lawful debts: And it shall be sufficient probation 'of the fraud intended against the creditors, if they, or any of them, shall be able to 'verifie, by write, or by oath of the party, receiver of any security from the divour or 'bankrupt, that the same was made without any true, just and necessary cause, or 'without any true and competent price; or that the lands and goods of the divour and 'bankrupt, being sold by him who bought them from the said divour, the whole, or 'most part of the price thereof, was converted, or to be converted to the bankrupt's 'profit and use. Providing alwayes, that so much of the said lands and goods, or prices 'thereof, so trusted by bankrupts to interposed persons, as hath been really payed or 'assigned by them to any of the bankrupt's lawful creditors, shall be allowed unto them, 'they making the rest forthcoming to the remanent creditors.' Then follows that part of the statute relating to begun diligence, (which forms the subject of the next chapter), and imposing penalties upon the debtors who shall be guilty of these frauds.

the existence of lawful debts, be null, at the instance of the creditors injured.

2. That it should be sufficient evidence of the fraud, if the creditors were able to prove, by the writ or oath of the receiver of the deed, that it was made without an onerous cause.

3. That the right of one purchasing bona fide from the confident and interposed person, should not be null; but the interposed person should be liable to the creditors of the bankrupt for the price received; and the purchaser should make, whatever part of the price remained unpaid, forthcoming to the creditors.

The ambiguity of expression which unfortunately prevails in this statute, led to many doubts and questions. It does not contain a simple or clear explanation of the remedy, which it was intended to bestow; and, in the interpretation of it, judges have been even forced to do some violence to the expressions. That something more was intended, than was reached by the simple rule of the common law, must at all times have been evident; but it was not easy to say, with precision, what that was. Two presumptions have, in the subsequent interpretation of the statute, been held as auxiliaries of the common law, viz. That in all challenges, after insolvency, of deeds granted to conjunct and confident persons, subsequent to the challenger's debt, 1. The insolvency should, presumptione juris, be carried back to the date of the deed; and, 2. The gratuitous nature of the deed should also be presumed. But it was not at first, that this view of the law was acknowledged; on the contrary, there were expressions in the statute, which seemed to oppose, at least, the latter of these propositions.[t] I shall not, however, stop to explain how the interpretation came to be settled; because this will best appear in the course of the commentary upon the statute. It is enough, in this place, to have intimated, that such was at last fixed to be the import of the law.

In the further prosecution of this subject, I shall inquire, 1. What creditors are entitled to the benefit of the statute?

2. What deeds are liable to be challenged? and, 3. What is the effect of the challenge when successful?

I.—1. In considering the title to challenge, under the statute, the first question naturally is, Whether it be necessary that the challenger's debt be prior to the deed challenged?

It may at first sight appear, that as, in a competition, no preference is given to a prior creditor over a posterior, merely on account of the priority of his claim, and, independently of judicial or voluntary security; there ought to be no distinction between them, in respect to the right of challenging gratuitous deeds, under the statute 1621. But, on second thoughts, we shall be inclined to correct this notion, and to acknowledge, that there is room for distinguishing, in this question, between the favour due to a prior creditor, and that to which a posterior creditor is entitled. One presumption, to the benefit of which a prior creditor has been admitted, is, that of the debtor's insolvency at the date of the deed challenged. But, how shall a posterior creditor be allowed to avail himself of this presumption, when his own transactions with the debtor, at a subsequent period, show him to have been acting as a solvent man? To the benefit of this presumption, therefore, a posterior creditor has not been thought entitled; but no further is his right to challenge the gratuitous deeds of his debtor in any shape abridged. That a posterior creditor is thus excluded from the benefit of the statute, is not very clearly expressed in the statute itself; but it has been generally so understood and interpreted. Mr Erskine says, That "creditors whose "debts are contracted after the alienation made by the debtor, "though they have no aid from the statutes (of 1621 and 1696), "are not excluded from the remedies competent to them by the "common rules of law." B. 4. tit. 1. § 44.

In ascertaining the priority of the challenger's debt, one very strange doubt was moved in the last century, whether a debt was

to

to be held as of the date of its origin, or of that of its establishment, by a written voucher, or by decree? The question first occurred in the case of Pollock against Pollock, where the Court found 'debts constituted by witnesses, to be effectual from the time of 'contracting, and not merely from the time of probation or sen-'tence, to take away any posterior deed of the debtor, done with-'out a cause onerous.' 21st January 1661, I. Stair, 587. 8. A question, somewhat similar, occurred in the great case of Street and Mason, 27th July 1669; but it differed from that of Pollock in one particular: there was a bond granted in liquidation of the debt, bearing it to have been for 'merchant ware;' and witnesses were admitted to prove the particular times at which the merchandise was furnished. I. Stair, 645. 6.

Where there is no distinction in time, between the origin of the debt and the voucher of it, the common rules of law, respecting dates, must have place. The statute 1681, c. 5. is indeed very defective in providing evidence of the dates of deeds; since the date is contained in the testing clause, which, in most cases, is written out after the witnesses have subscribed: but, in the eye of law, a deed so executed, is considered as good and legal evidence of its date, till shown to be false. The date which it bears, is therefore to be held as the true date of a document, executed in terms of the statute 1681, whether we speak of the deed challenged, or of the voucher of the challenger's debt. But where the deed is holograph, and is not executed before witnesses, it is held in law not to be evidence of its date, and to be exposed, in all questions, to the most unfavourable presumption in this respect.

But it is not always the date, merely, that is regarded as the criterion in this question; for a deed is, in such cases, to be considered as really of the date of its delivery. If, therefore, the challenger can prove, that the deed under challenge was not a delivered deed, till after the existence of his debt, he will, I apprehend, sufficiently vindicate his title to the privileges of the statute. In this question of delivery, however, the presumption in

the

the common case is, that a deed found in the hands of the grantee, and conceived in words of present alienation or obligement, is delivered of the date it bears; though, where a father makes a deed to his children, a different rule is admitted, and the burden of proving the delivery, lies upon the children. 14th November 1676, *Inglis against Boswell*, *Dirleton*, cclxxxiv. 187.

As neither acceptances nor indorsations of bills are, in general, dated, it may be doubted what date is to be assigned to them in questions of this kind. 1. As to an acceptance, it was questioned, in the case of Man against Walls, 25th July 1702, II. Fount. 156, whether it was of the same date with that of the bill itself? The bill, and the disposition quarrelled, bore the same date; the acceptance bore no date. It was argued, that a bill, 'being a mandate, 'constitutes no debt till acceptance, which can only be known 'by the protest, and that is posterior to the disposition.—Answer-'ed, The acceptance wanting date, must be held as of the date 'of the bill, seeing both drawer and accepter dwelt in the same 'town; and it might have been easily presented and accepted 'within an hour after being drawn.—The Lords did not sustain 'the presumption, that the acceptance was of the same day's date 'with the bill, unless it were otherwise proved, and found that 'the drawer was not creditor, till acceptance; and which, being 'posterior to the disposition, he had no interest to quarrel the 'same, which could be done only by anterior creditors, unless he 'could astruct and fortify his bill, by some grounds of debt owing 'by Walls to him prior to the same.' When, afterwards, the question came forward, by what evidence this was to be established? the challenging creditor offered to prove, by witnesses, that he had delivered to Walls, certain parcels and quantities of merchant goods prior to the date of the bill, and which was the cause of granting it; and he also offered to bring forward those who had the custody of Walls' books, from which it would appear that he was creditor prior to the deed challenged. 'The Court consider-'ed, that in adminiculations and astructions of this nature, they 'did not require a full and positive probation: and that where a 'bond is quarrelled, as granted on deathbed, or as being holo-

'graph,

'graph, and so presumed to be in lecto, as not proving its own 'date, they used to sustain a reply, offering either to prove an 'antecedent ground of debt prior to sickness; or that the writ was 'seen and read by severals before contracting the sickness where-'of the grantor died; and that both these are in use to be proved 'by witnesses. Therefore, the Lords repelled the objection, and 'allowed the witnesses to be received; but would not permit him 'both to prove by them, and likewise to call for writs, unless it 'were quoad distinct articles; and therefore ordered him to elect 'any of the two he pleased, but not to make use of both, quoad 'the same points.' II. Fount. 158.—2dly, As to indorsations, a case occurred, upon the act 1696, respecting an indorsation; in which the creditors contended, that as it could not prove its own date, (for in this case the indorsation was dated), it must be held as granted within the sixty days. But the Court seeing no suspicion of unfairness in the transaction, and that, if they did not take the date affixed to the indorsation, as the true one, it must come to the legal presumption, that the indorsation was of the same date with the bill, they repelled the objection: 15th May 1794, Thistle Bank against Leny. This would intimate, that the legal presumption is for the indorsation being of the date of the bill; and, so far, there seems to be a contrariety in these decisions. But this apparent incongruity, may perhaps be thus reconciled: Although, in bills, the natural presumption should be favourable for them, yet, as they are the most dangerous of all modes of defrauding creditors, the circumstances in which they have been granted or conveyed, will, in all challenges brought against them by creditors, be examined with scrupulous accuracy; and the holder, if not in the condition of an onerous indorsee, be obliged to give every information that may lead to a knowledge of the true date. In a case under the act 1621, I should hold, notwithstanding Walls' decision, that where the challenger founds upon a bill, either drawn in his favour, or indorsed to him, the presumption must be, that the acceptance or indorsation is of the date of the bill.

But although it is only to a prior creditor that the benefit of the presumption of insolvency, reared up by the statute, properly belongs, there seems to be good ground for thinking that, to the other presumptions of the statute, even a posterior creditor will be entitled, provided he can make good the evidence of insolvency at the date of the deed. The presumption of gratuity, does not indeed seem to rest so much upon the statute, as upon the common law: and in the case of a posterior creditor, who has been deceived by the debtor, and who, in challenging a deed in favour of a confident or conjunct person, can establish the previous insolvency of the granter, in which the challenger has, by a continuance of the fraud, been involved, the ground of the presumption is as solid, as in the case of a prior creditor.

2. The date being settled, what kind of debt will entitle the challenging creditor to the benefit of the statute?

All creditors, in conditional debts, have a right to reduce deeds granted to their prejudice at the insolvency; for their debts will be as completely due on the existence of the condition, as if the debt were pure. The only difference is, that when a reduction is pursued by a creditor whose debt is conditional, the effect of the decree of reduction is suspended till the purification of the claim. These cases are considered at large by Sir George M'Kenzie, in his Observations upon the statute 1621, c. 18. p. 31. 5. and the principle upon which he puts the law, is a plain and sensible one,— that 'although personal actions for payment, are not competent to 'such creditors, before the day or the condition exist; yet they may 'obtain declarator, that, notwithstanding of such fraudulent rights, 'their bonds shall be effectual to them, and their debtor's estate 'liable to them, and to execution at their instance, as if those 'rights were not granted; and, upon the matter, reductions are 'nothing else but declarators to the effect foresaid.'

Gratuitous creditors are also entitled to challenge posterior gratuitous deeds; for as donations granted by a man, with full power over his property, confer, unless revocable, a good right upon the donee, not to be taken away by the mere whim of the donor, the donee is, in every proper sense, entitled to the character of a creditor,—

ditor.—Sir George M'Kenzie, in speaking of this case, seems to think, that although this be good law, ' yet the great reason why ' the statute was introduced, seems wanting here, since the credi- ' tor does not lend out his money, in this case, in contemplation of ' his debtor's estate. '—But this does not seem to be the principle of the statute. The true principle, is one which is by no means wanting in the case of a gratuitous creditor. It is, that the grantor of the challengeable right, is bestowing gratuitously a fund which really does not belong to him, but which his creditors have a title to claim, to the full extent of his obligations to them.

II. The next subject of our inquiry is, What are the circumstances necessary to infer fraud against any deed, so as to entitle the creditors to reduce it? And here it may be proper to take notice of what has been blamed by Lord Kames as a gross imperfection in this act. His Lordship speaks of this act, as if it were confined to the case of actual fraud *. But in this he seems to have misapprehended the spirit of the statute. It speaks indeed of fraud—its very object is the suppression of the daily frauds which then prevailed; but it defines, at the same time, what is the particular fraud against which a remedy was proposed. It declares, that deeds granted to conjunct and confident persons, without onerous causes, and in prejudice of prior debts, shall be reducible. This is not therefore a regulation confined to actual and criminal fraud, but extended as far perhaps as a statute should go.

In order to bring the discussion of this subject into as simple a form as possible, I shall begin with the case of a deed which still remains with the first holder. The case of a purchaser from the grantee, will afterwards be considered.

There are three things required by the statute to the reduction of a deed under it—that the grantee be a conjunct or confident person—

* Principles of Equity, B 3. c 5 Vol II p 218.

person—that the deed be granted without value, and without a necessary cause—and that the granter be insolvent at the time of making the deed. As the first of these gives birth to the presumption against the deed, in regard to the other two; it may be proper to follow this course in the statement of them—considering, in the first view, what is the character of conjunct and confident, pointed out by the law—the other two circumstances being taken up in the shape of defences urged in support of the deed.

1. CONJUNCT AND CONFIDENT PERSONS.—In guarding against frauds by embezzlement, the most natural jealousy arises against those who, from the ties of blood, or from their intimate friendship and confidential communications with the bankrupt, may be supposed to sympathize with his distress, and to wish to assist him in his schemes. It is with peculiar propriety, therefore, that they are taken notice of in this statute as objects of a presumptive fraud. Transactions of this kind are not to be managed by a debtor, with any prospect of success, without concealment, so planned as to elude direct detection.

A CONJUNCT PERSON is one who, by his alliance to the debtor, stands within the range of suspicion of a participation in his schemes; and, as law must ever proceed upon general rules, it stops, in this matter of bankruptcy, at that point where, in other cases, the presumption of a biassing affection is fixed. In a witness, and in a judge, there must be impartiality; and, for our natural weakness, law has made allowance, by forbidding any one to be called upon in either of these capacities, where his near relation is concerned. As the same presumed affection which deadens the sense of justice, or sways from the impartiality of truth, may well be supposed capable of misleading a person into a participation in devices for saving his friend, the Court has, in all these questions, applied the same test. Thus, it being made a question, whether a step-son was conjunct, 'although there uses to be little amity between 'such relations, yet the Lords thought them conjunct persons; 'for they could not marry, nor be witnesses nor judges of each o'ther:' 15th January 1695, Mercer against Dalgarno, I. Fount. 659.

659.—The question next occurred, respecting uncle and nephew-in-law. The Court found them not conjunct, because not hindered to judge in each others causes, by the 13th act of the 3d Parl. of Charles II.; 8th February 1712, Lord Elibank against Adamson and Callander—Forbes, 586. A brother-in-law was found to be conjunct, under this statute; 18th June 1712, Scott against Kerr, II. Fount. 739 In a note by Lord Fountainhall, I. 67. it is said, that 'it was debated before the Lords, (6th December 1679), whether a cousin-german, or a cousin once removed, receiving a disposition from a bankrupt, is to be reputed such a conjunct person as is meant by the act 1621; for they may marry together; and the relation, as to the design of the act of Parliament, must stop somewhere.'—'It is affirmed (he continues) that the Lords found a cousin-german such a conjunct person.'—And this seems almost to be confirmed by the decision, Sinclair against Dickson, 22d June 1680, where a deed being challenged, the narrative bearing onerous causes, was maintained to be sufficient evidence in support of the deed; a cousin once removed not being a conjunct or confident person. The Court ordered the holder to support the narrative by what evidence he could bring, reserving the effect of that evidence for future judgement · II. Stair, 773 —It does not appear what the ultimate decision was, or what evidence was brought.

A CONFIDENT PERSON is not so easily defined; nor is it settled, by any long established test, who are included under this description. The principle applies to every intimate and confidential friendship. It seems to apply to servants, to factors, to confidential men of business; and Sir George M'Kenzie quotes a case (which however I cannot find in the books of reports) where an ordinary agent was found to be such a confident person: 26th June 1672, Moubray against Spence—Observations on the Statute 1621, p. 68.

The proof of this confidential situation, or of an alliance by kin, sufficient to bring a person within the description of conjunct, must of course ly upon the challenging creditor. It is the very ground of his reduction, and the foundation of that presumption of

K fraud

fraud which the holder of the deed is bound to overcome.' In what way the effect of this presumption is to be removed, I now proceed to inquire.

The defence against the reduction must be, either that the deed was necessary, or granted for a valuable consideration; or that, at the time of making it, the grantor was solvent. And in considering these two points, I shall have the best opportunity of shewing how they came to be classed as defences against the reduction, instead of being considered as grounds of reduction, which the challenger was bound to make good.

I. The inquiry with respect to the first of these defences, naturally divides itself into two branches: *First*, What are the circumstances, which, if proved, will infer such a necessity, or such a valuable consideration, as shall save the deed from reduction? And, *Secondly*, By what kind of evidence are those circumstances to be established?

All that it seems requisite to say upon the import of the expression 'NECESSARY CAUSES' in the statute, is to be found in Lord Kilkerran's report of the case of Grant of Tillifour, 9th November 1748. 'On this occasion,' says his Lordship, 'there was some 'reasoning among the Lords, upon the construction of the act '1621, wherein they agreed, that the words, "necessary causes," 'are in practice thus understood: That though the words, "true, "just, and necessary causes," would appear, as they stand, to be 'conjunctive, they have always been considered as disjunctive; so 'that, if either the deed be granted in consequence of a previous 'obligation, or, though there be no such previous obligation, if 'the deed be granted for a true and just cause, it is not reducible.' —P. 55.

But the legal description of an onerous deed, as opposed to one that is gratuitous, will require to be more fully detailed. For the sake of more clear discussion, I shall consider those deeds, first, which bear no reference to any former obligation; and, afterwards, those which are more complicated in their nature, as grounded upon some antecedent debt.

1. In the common case of a transaction entirely new, bearing no reference to any former obligation or engagement, the question must in general turn upon the fact, whether value was actually given, or upon the adequacy or inadequacy of the value. In point of fact, a fair and satisfactory explanation must be given of the onerous cause, whether the deed challenged be of the nature of a conveyance, or of a debt: and, upon this point, nothing further can, à priori, be said, since every case must depend upon its own circumstances. As to adequacy of value, there is not, at common law, in Scotland, as there was in Rome, an actio quanti minoris; but the reduction of a deed as in fraudem creditorum, produces nearly the same effect in cases of insolvency; for, where the value given is inadequate, there can be no doubt, that, to the extent of the inadequacy, it is a conveyance granted in prejudice of creditors, without a just and true cause.

But there are several cases of a peculiar nature, in which the inquiry is not a question of fact, or an estimate of value but, whether the consideration, upon which the deed proceeds, be not sufficient to support it, although it cannot strictly be said that value, in the common meaning of that term, was bartered for the right bestowed.

Thus, where a person enters into a cautionary engagement for another, without receiving any valuable consideration or recompense, he acts gratuitously; and, if the principal debtor fail, the holder of the obligation claims, as a creditor of the cautioner, for a sum which must be paid without remuneration. Yet such an obligation, though granted for no true, just, or necessary cause, and without a just price really paid, is not to be regarded as gratuitous, in the meaning of the statute. It may indeed be called gratuitous, so far as the cautioner is concerned; but it is most onerous,

so

so far as the creditor, who receives the security for his debt, is interested. Without a specific charge of fraud, then, there does not appear to be any ground for doubting, that the receiver of a cautionary obligation is safe from any attempt, by the creditors of the cautioner, to deprive him of his security, on pretence of the deed having been gratuitous on the part of their debtor. Nay, it may be said, that there is even a kind of value given for such an obligation, since the cautioner and his creditors have a claim of relief against the principal debtor, for whom the security was interposed.

Another example of onerous deeds, for which, in strict language, it cannot be said that any value is given, are, the PROVISIONS in ANTENUPTIAL MARRIAGE CONTRACTS whether to the wife, or to the children.

Without regard to the tocher or dower which the wife brings, the provisions stipulated to her, in an antenuptial contract, entitle her, if they be in the form of an obligation, to the character of an onerous creditor; or to the character of an onerous holder of a right, if they contain conveyances in security of those provisions. But, onerous as those rights are, the Court will reduce even an antenuptial provision to a wife, if it be exorbitant. Thus, in the case of Duncan against Sloss; Sloss having settled a large jointure on his second wife, an objection was moved by a child of the first marriage, upon whose provisions it encroached. It was admitted, that, in many cases, the Court had restricted postnuptial contracts; but the onerous nature of an antenuptial contract, was maintained as sufficient to secure it from alteration. The Court, however, restricted the jointure to a rational extent, in the same manner as if it had been granted in a postnuptial contract: 8th February 1785, VII. Fac. Coll. cxcvii. 310.

In all questions with regard to the onerosity of antenuptial provisions to children, it will be remembered, that the existence of the children is in a manner conditional; as it is only upon a compliance with the stipulations urged in their favour by those, who, upon their existence, will be interested for them, that the contract

is

is entered into, from which they are to spring. The provisions made to children in such a contract, are therefore most onerous. But it will depend very much upon the terms of the contract, whether the children, upon their existence, will be entitled to the character of creditors of their father, or of mere heirs, to whom the claims of creditors will be preferable. This is a question, upon which I cannot enter at present. The distinctions will be found well laid down in the case of the creditors of Napier against his children, 24th July 1696, and 17th June 1697, I. Fount. 729—776.; and that of the children of Mactavish against his creditors, 15th November 1787, VIII. Fac. Coll. ii. 5, as opposed to the cases of Sir Robert Preston's children against his creditors, 15th July 1691; Mrs Lyon against the creditors of Easteroglc, 24th January 1724, I. Kames 122.; the creditors of M'Kenzie against his children, 2d February 1792, VIII. Fac. Col. cciii. 427.

2. Having considered the cases in which the deed stands by itself, without reference to any prior obligation, we now advance to a question of greater nicety. There cannot be a doubt, that, if the deed be granted in fulfilment of a proper legal obligation, it is not to be held as gratuitous, or subject to reduction upon the statute. It is onerous; since, even upon the former obligation, the receiver might have claimed as a creditor:—it is, in the sense of the act, as already explained, necessary; and therefore safe from reduction. But the question is not easily solved, where the obligation is of a less perfect kind; a natural obligation, for example, or one merely civil. Cases of this kind occur most frequently upon family settlements, where creditors challenge a postnuptial deed of provision granted in favour of a wife or of children; and where the defence is, that the deed is in implement of the natural obligation incumbent upon a husband and a father. An investigation into the decisions of such cases, will illustrate the effects of the less perfect obligations, in supporting deeds against this statute.

POSTNUPTIAL PROVISIONS TO WIVES, stand in a very different situation, in respect of onerosity, from those which are antenuptial. In the latter case, the marriage itself is contracted upon the security

of

of the provision stipulated in the contract. In the former case, the wife has, without any stipulation of security, united her interests with those of her husband, and may be presumed to have taken the risk of his good and of his bad fortune. But though such be the distinguishing features of each of these cases, both of them admit of qualifications. In the case of an antenuptial contract, we have seen, that the wife's provisions are not supported, if immoderate: and the same principle must, of course, operate where a postnuptial deed is made in implement of an antenuptial agreement. On the other hand, although, where there is no antenuptial contract, the wife seems to have taken the risk, her claim, in natural justice, to an aliment of some kind, has been held sufficient to support a moderate postnuptial provision.

That a postnuptial deed is supported completely by an antenuptial contract, unless in so far as the provision is exorbitant, the following case will show. Mrs Brown received an infeftment in liferent, of her husband's whole estate. In a competition of creditors, Sir James Stansfield objected fraud, as the infeftment had been granted after the contracting of debts. Mrs Brown maintained her right, upon the ground of its having been granted in implement of an anterior cancelled contract of marriage, which the deed itself bore. It was replied, that the bond cannot prove, against creditors, that it was in fulfilment of a former deed. The Court decided, that although 'the narrative of the bond of provision does not 'prove that there was an anterior contract having the equivalent 'provision, this alledgeance was relevant to be proved, to sustain 'the provision against any personal debts anterior to the contract 'of provision: but found this provision reduceable, in so far as it 'was exorbitant; and valid, only in so far as it was competent for 'such persons, according to the condition of the husband's estate 'and the wife's tocher; and ordained the same to be condescended 'on and instructed.' 19th January 1676, Sir J. Stansfield against Brown, II. Stair, 401.

That where the postnuptial deed rests upon the natural obligation merely, the Court holds the marriage itself to be an onerous consideration,

consideration, to the extent of a moderate provision, these cases sufficiently establish. After Sir James Campbell had contracted debts beyond the value of his estate, he married. There was no contract; but, by a postnuptial bond, he gave an annuity of 100l. to his lady, besides a house and other conveniences; and, upon the precept of sasine, she was infeft. This bond was challenged on the statute 1621. 'Some of the Lords were of opinion, that 'where a woman marries without a contract, upon the faith of 'the legal provision, any postnuptial provision is a gratuitous deed, 'and, as such, reducible at the instance of prior creditors, and 'that, were it otherwise, there were nothing to hinder any man, 'who had married without a contract, after he knew himself in-'solvent, to settle a provision on his wife, preferable to all his per-'sonal creditors.' But the opinion which prevailed was, 'that 'marriage itself is an onerous cause, which yet will not be sufficient 'to sustain the provision, any farther than what may be a moderate 'subsistence; for so far only the husband is under obligation. And 'as to the case supposed, of a husband's settling a provision upon 'his wife, after he knew himself become insolvent; even in that 'case, it was thought the provision might be sustained, to the ef-'fect of a subsistence.'—'But, be that as it may,' continues Lord Kilkerran in his report, 'the present case was thought different. 'As, in the supposed case, there is more an appearance of fraud 'than in the present case, where there was no change of the hus-'band's circumstances, between the marriage, and the time of grant-'ing the provision; and as it was not controverted, but, at the mar-'riage, he might have granted a provision, it was thought to be 'straining too hard, to say he could give more thereafter, although 'no change had happened in his circumstances.'—The Court 're-'stricted the lady's bond of provision and infeftment to 50l. year-'ly, in full of all she could claim by the said bond.' 26th July 1744, Kilk. 51. In this case, almost all the principles are explained, upon which decisions, respecting postnuptial deeds in favour of wives, have been pronounced.—See the cases of Walker against Polwart, 19th June 1635; Durie 767. 11th January 1738, Robertson against Handyside.

If the natural obligation, incumbent upon a husband, to provide for the maintenance of his wife, be thus sufficient to validate and render onerous a moderate provision, although postnuptial, and subsequent to the giver's insolvency; there seemed to be little room for doubt, that where an antenuptial provision had been given, but rendered by the diligence of creditors ineffectual, the wife was entitled to have recourse to a postnuptial provision granted to her, in the form of a liferent right over some of her husband's property. The Court would not listen to the challenge of the creditors, and found the infeftment in liferent not to be reducible upon the statute 1621. 17th February 1738, Sir Rod. M'Kenzie against Monro; I. Dict. 71. In a case very similar to this, the wife having claimed both provisions, the Court held the liferent right to be, in a question with creditors, a security merely for the previous provision. 14th February 1778, Campbell against Sommervil; VI. Fac. Coll. xvi. 29.

POSTNUPTIAL PROVISIONS TO CHILDREN, are, like those to wives, either in implement of the natural obligation which lies upon a father to aliment his children, or in fulfilment of a prior obligation. 1. Where a deed of provision is granted after the contracting of debts, and where, against a challenge by creditors, the sole defence is, that the deed is in implement of the father's natural obligation to provide, there can be no doubt that the deed must fall, and cannot be supported against creditors. The children must follow the condition of their father, and can claim provision and support from him, only according to the measure of his ability. Accordingly, it was found, that even where a contract of marriage bore an obligation on the father to aliment his daughter, till the stipulated term for the payment of her provision, this obligation, being only exegetical of his natural obligation, could produce no effect against creditors: 13th February 1736, Falconer—I. Dict. 34.—In the case of Johnson against Arnold, the Court found a postnuptial provision given to a daughter, reducible at the instance of a creditor whose debt was prior to its date or delivery: 22d July 1668—I. Stair, 557.—Mr Erskine expresses the rule in this way: 'Provisions to children already existing, are, in the judgement of

'law,

'law, gratuitous, and, of consequence, may be annulled, in a 'competition with creditors, if the grantor was not solvent.' IV. i. 34. Perhaps it would have been more accurate, had he said, that 'postnuptial provisions to children are, in the judgement of 'law, gratuitous,' &c. 2dly, Where the provision, granted to a child, is fortified by an anterior obligation, it must depend entirely upon the nature of that obligation, whether the subsequent provision is to be regarded as onerous. There is no doubt, that a man who is solvent, and in full capacity, can so bind himself in favour of his children, as to make any deed, afterwards deemed necessary for the fulfilment of that obligation, onerous, in a competition with creditors. It will however be observed, that, on the one hand, the propriety and expediency of leaving to a father the full administration of his funds, and, on the other, the opportunity of defrauding creditors, by means of latent deeds granted to children, operate so strongly, that the deed must be clearly and precisely conceived, which is to vest a child with the character of creditor; restricting his father's freedom of acting, and of incurring debts. Hence the presumption must, in such cases, ever lie against deeds of provision. But, where those deeds are fair, and conceived in proper form, they will have the effect of validating, as onerous deeds, those executed in implement of them, though after insolvency, and the existence of debts. The most common case is, where, in the marriage-contract, a provision is appointed for the children; and the general rule of decision in such a case is, that where the sum is not due till the father's death, the children have a mere spes successionis; it being only where the provision is made to vest during the father's life, that it is considered as a debt, and held sufficient to authorise diligence by the child for procuring implement of it; or to give support, in a question with creditors, to any subsequent deed of implement granted by the father: 24th January 1724, Mrs Lyon against the creditors of Easter-Ogle, I. Kaims 122.—2d February 1792, Creditors of M'Kenzie against his children, VIII. Fac. Col. cciii. 427. But it is not only by the stipulations in a marriage contract, that a wife or children may acquire the character of onerous creditors. A father may, by bonds or deeds of provision granted after marriage, and during his solvency, bestow upon them this right; so that, afterwards, it may stand as the safeguard of a conveyance made when he is insolvent, and which, unless so fortified, would fall under the statute: but, as such prior deeds can be granted only while the father is in full solvency, (6th January 1677, Creditors of Mouswell—Dirl. No 418.), law will presume that the deed was dated after insolvency, and require evidence to support it.

Before leaving this subject, I may take notice of one class of cases, of a mixed nature, between a provision to a wife, and provisions to children. In contracts of marriage, it is frequently stipulated, that the wife shall have a certain provision, to be restricted on the existence of children. Several cases of this kind have occurred, in which competitions have arisen between the creditors and the children, for the sum arising from the restriction. In the case of Erskines against Carnegie and Smith, the wife was provided to the liferent of the whole property, but, 'in case there 'were children surviving, to be restricted to one half.' The Court found the jointure to be exorbitant, and the restriction fraudulent, and preferred the creditors. 23d December 1679, II. Stair 726.— I should conceive the grounds of this decision to have been, 1. The exorbitance of the provision, which would have prevented it from being supported, even to the wife; and, 2dly, That the provision to the children having been merely in case of their survivance, they could be regarded only as heirs, not as creditors of the father. In a subsequent case, where the wife was provided to a liferent annuity of 300 merks out of her husband's lands, and, 'per 'verba de præsenti,' renounced conditionally, on the existence of children, '100 merks of the annuity in their favour, secluding all 'others from the benefit thereof,' there arose, between an adjudger, after the father's death, and the children, a question, to whom the benefit of the restriction should accrue? In the argument, the distinction was taken between this case, and that of a restriction conceived in favour of the heirs of a marriage, which is held to accrue to the creditors. The Court seems to have proceeded on the idea of the provision to the wife being effectual, as moderate, and the restriction being so expressly exclusive, that the creditors could have no right under it; 'they found this provision so ex-'pressly exclusive, that they preferred the children to the credi-'tors:' 1st July 1703, Reid against Whitsom and Rutherfords, II. Fount. 185.

Having now seen what deeds are considered as gratuitous; we have next to inquire, by what evidence the onerous consideration, of a deed, granted to a conjunct and confident person, is to be established?

As the presumption against deeds to conjunct and confident persons, is rather of a negative, than of a positive nature, the deed being only not held as onerous, some little difficulty occurred at first, where the deed itself bore onerous causes, whether that was not to be held as sufficient to counteract the negative presumption? Thus, in the case of Riddoch against Young, the Court found such a clause insufficient to support a deed in favour of a son, without the aid of other evidence of an onerous and lawful cause. 9th March 1629, Durie 882. See also 12th February 1670, Napier against Gordon, I. Stair 671; Lady Lucy Hamilton against Boyd, 15th July 1670, Ib. 697, and Whitehead against Lidderdale, 29th November 1671, II. Stair 13.—A distinction was indeed taken in a subsequent case, between a narrative bearing onerous causes in general, and one bearing a sum instantly borrowed. The Court decided, that a disposition by an insolvent person to his brother, bearing sums instantly borrowed, could not be taken away but by the disponee's oath, while onerous causes in general must be otherwise instructed: 28th November 1673, Campbell—Gosford. But this decision, as it does not appear to be grounded upon solid principle, so, it seems to be the only one which points to such a distinction. In the subsequent case of Stansfield against Brown, 19th January 1676, II. Stair 401, a narrative in a postnuptial contract of marriage, bearing that it was granted in implement of a price, was found not to be sufficient evidence. And Lord Fountainhall, at the beginning of the year 1682, in his Journal,

his

has the following note—'The Lords are now constantly in use to 'force conjunct persons, as brothers and brothers-in-law, uncles 'and nephews, to astruct (establish) the onerous cause of their 'debts, otherwise than by the assertion of the bond itself, or of 'their own oath.'—Still, however, the point was not understood to be settled: and, in the case of MacLerie against Glen, it was objected to a bond, that, being to a brother, it cannot be held as onerous, merely upon its own evidence. The inconvenience and danger of stopping, by such a decision, all trade between near relations, was insisted upon. 'The Court found, that there might 'be cases, where bonds among relations might prove, if dealings 'in commerce appeared; but that the bond in this case is not pro-'bative, unless it were, by other evidents and documents, astruct-'ed and adminiculed:' 5th December 1707, II. Fount. 400. *

It may be held, then, as established, that, in deeds to conjunct and confident persons, the narrative is not considered as sufficient evidence to remove the presumption of the deed being gratuitous, although, as we shall afterwards see, it is held sufficient for this purpose, where the deed is in the person of a stranger. It scarcely requires to be added, that where the narrative bears gratuitous causes, it is considered as confirming so strongly the presumption of gratuity, that the law holds it as ultimate evidence of no valuable consideration having been given.

The statute, in speaking of the evidence with regard to the consideration of the deed, makes use of the terms 'oath and writ 'of the party receiver;' and advantage seems to have been taken of these expressions, to contend, that if, in addition to the narrative of the deed, the holder's oath were given in proof of onerosity, the evidence would be complete. This is a palpable perversion of the expressions of the statute. It never was, by that statute, intended to give the holder of the deed the benefit of his own oath; that being held out merely as one mode of proof to which the

* See also the case of the Duke of Buccleugh against his grandfather's creditors, 8th July 1757, II. Fac. Coll. xl. 71.; M'Niel against Livingston, 14th February 1758, Ib xcix. 178.

the creditors might resort. But, in some cases, this sort of evidence was actually admitted, at least to the effect of overcoming the legal presumption of fraud. In considering these cases, it may be taken as the reconciling principle of the varying decisions, that wherever the presumption arising from the mere connexion of the parties, was alone to be overcome, the narrative, fortified by the holder's oath, was received as sufficient; but, wherever any additional circumstance appeared, indicative of unfair dealing, other evidence was deemed necessary *.

It is a matter of some nicety to discriminate, in cases where proof is necessary, what ought to be regarded as sufficient evidence of value. Where shall we stop? If there be fraud, fraud takes a thousand shapes; and, though it were proved that money had been paid—though a cancelled bond were shown—still the doubt recurs, is it not possible that these might have been contrived, in order to correspond with, and support, the fraudulent deed? Such questions must, in general, depend upon the balancing of evidence, and of presumptions. Were any rules to be given upon the point, perhaps they might run thus: 1. That such evidence as would be sufficient in an action of constitution of the debt, will be sufficient to establish value, in a question upon this statute: and, 2dly, That where a previous obligation is founded on, as the onerous cause of a deed, that obligation must be proved, either to have been itself onerous, or to have existed at a period when the granter was solvent, or at least prior to the date of the challenger's debt.

Where the onerous cause is simple, as, the payment of money, the delivery of goods, &c. the necessity of proving the fact circumstantially, must be apparent. The testimony of witnesses is not, in our law, received as evidence of the payment of money; but

* See, on the one hand, the cases of Skene against Beatson, 17th January 1632, Durie 611.; Nisbet against Williamson, &c. 22d June 1642, Durie 895, Grey against Chiesly, 4th July 1711, Forb 516.—And, on the other hand, the cases of Auld against Smith, 29th January 1629, Durie 418., Glen against Binnie, 24th November 1626, Durie 235.

but it is held as evidence of the delivery of commodities of any kind. It is a natural ingredient in such a proof, to show some state of the funds of the holder of the deed, where there is any strong ground of suspicion or doubt; and, in general, it may be laid down, that witnesses are competent in all circumstantial proofs. See Duff and Brown against Forbes of Culloden, 15th December 1671, II. Stair 25.*

The existence of a former deed, indicative of an onerous cause, may be proved, and yet it may happen to be in no better a situation than the deed challenged: that is to say, it may have been granted during the insolvency of the grantor. Thus, a bond, upon which adjudication had followed, was objected to, as granted to a brother. The holder fortified the narrative, which bore former cancelled bonds, by production of the bonds. This was contended not to be good evidence; and much was said upon the opportunity which the admission of such evidence would give for fraud. Answered, Where any suspicious circumstances accompany the appearance of such relative deeds, the presumption may still be continued; but, in the common case, where there is no concealment of the retired deeds, and no close connexion in time between the granting of the first and of the second or innovating deed, it were of bad consequence to commerce, to reject such evidence. The Court found the disposition, as to its onerous cause, sufficiently instructed by the production

* Besides the general point, of the competency of witnesses in a circumstantial proof, there was another question decided in the case of Culloden. The holder of the deeds being called upon to prove its onerosity, produced bonds which were due at granting the deed in question, but had been cancelled. The debtor's name was taken away, but the names of the witnesses remained; and an offer was made to prove, by their oaths, that the bonds were true debts, and unpaid at the date of the deed challenged. The debtor also in these bonds, and grantor of the deed challenged, acknowledged the bonds. ---It was objected, That no connexion was proved between the bonds and the deed challenged. Answered, It is to be presumed, unless the bonds shall be proved to have been paid aliunde. The disponee's oath was found sufficient to establish the connexion between the bonds and the disposition: II. Stair 25.

See in Kilkerran, p. 441, a case, where a bond of relief, by an insolvent debtor to his brother, was supported upon the evidence of the creditors who got the brother's security, &c. 13th February 1745, Carlyle against Mathison.

tion of the anterior bonds to which it relates; unless it be offered to be proved, that the grantor was insolvent, or holden and repute bankrupt, at the time he granted those bonds which are the cause of the subsequent disposition: 22d February 1711, Rule against Purdie, II. Fount. 640.* Lord Kilkerran, in his report of the case of M'Kies against Agnew, 18th January 1739, lays it down as a general rule, arising out of that case, that, 'where a right is 'quarrelled upon the act 1621, as granted without an onerous cause, 'and anterior bonds are produced for instructing thereof, there is 'no necessity also to instruct the onerous cause of these bonds; 'though, had these bonds been the deeds quarrelled, the onerous 'cause of them must have been instructed:' Kilk. 440. The authority of so sound a lawyer as Lord Kilkerran, is not to be questioned lightly; but, great as my respect for him is, I never have been able to reconcile this opinion (for he does not detail the case) with the principle of the statute. I should rather have been inclined to consider this shape of the rule as more accurate; 1. That if the documents, produced in fortification of the deed challenged, be anterior to the date of the challenger's debt, they will have the effect (as in Rule and Purdie's case) of making the challenger a posterior creditor, and forcing him, in order to succeed in his challenge, to prove insolvency, &c. as at the date of the documents. 2. That if they be not anterior to the challenger's debt, they leave the challenger in as full possession of the legal presumptions, as if these documents had been the original object of his challenge, and the holder must prove, either solvency in the grantor at the date of the documents, or onerosity in the debt.

II. The second defence to be urged against a reduction on the statute of 1621, is, that the grantor was SOLVENT at the time of making

* This case was thought a very difficult one. 'Some thought it hard, that the 'debtor, making a show of wealth in lands and goods, with conscience, credit, and 'honesty, should insnare a simple credulous neighbour, by drawing his money into his 'net; and then make a disposition of his land to his own brother, depending on a bond 'which is itself posterior to Rule's debt, who was his lawful creditor before the contrivance made up between the two brothers. The Lords saw evident inconveniences on 'both sides: but, after balancing the arguments hinc inde, they sustained the '[illegible] disposition with the quality of his [illegible] onerous.' II. Fount. 640

making the deed. The obvious intention of the Legislature was, that where insolvency exists at the time of the challenge, the burden of proving that the grantor of the deed was, at the time of making it, solvent, should rest upon the holder; and that the creditor who makes the challenge, should not be held to establish the insolvency as at that time. But the words of the statute are in one sense ambiguous. They leave room for maintaining, that something more, than the establishment of a mere presumptio juris, of insolvency and of fraud, was intended by the Legislature; and that if the challenger can show his debt to be prior in date, the deed being granted to a conjunct and confident person, this is sufficient to insure success to his challenge; against which a proof of solvency can be no defence. The expressions of the statute are, 'That in all actions, &c. to 'be intended by any true creditor for recovery of his just debt, or 'satisfaction of his lawful action or right, they' (the Lords of Session) 'will decree and decern, all alienations, &c. made by the 'debtor, of any of his lands, &c. to any conjunct or confident 'person, without true, just, and necessary causes, and without a 'a just price really paid, the same being done after the contracting 'of lawful debts from true creditors, to have been from the beginning, and to be in all times coming, null and of none avail, 'force nor effect, &c.' But, when it is remembered that this law is directed only against frauds, and that no fraud can be charged against a deed granted during solvency, even though in its nature gratuitous, it will be acknowledged, that, according to the true import and scope of the law, a proof of the grantor's solvency, at the granting of the deed, is a good defence. The contests upon this point, however, were not soon settled.

The first case in which the question was moved, was that of Lady Borthwick against Goldilands, 5th March 1629; where it was decided, that solvency was a good defence against the challenge: Durie 432. Again, in 1675, the question was very solemnly argued, and deliberately decided. A person had entered into a contract along with his wife and his sister-in-law, by which he conveyed, in consideration of a certain counter conveyance, the right which, by his marriage contract, he had acquired in his wife's estate. This deed

was

was challenged by the husband's creditors; and defended, 1. on the ground of its being onerous, 2. on the ground of the solvency of the grantor at the time of making the deed. 'The Lords, upon debate 'at the Bar, and amongst themselves,' (says Lord Dirleton), 'did 'find, that debtors might dispose of a part of their estate by way 'of gift, and without an onerous cause, if they retained as much, 'and more than satisfy their creditors: And therefore they found 'the defence relevant, that the debtor had as much estate, besides 'the fee of the said tenement, as would satisfy the pursuer's debt.' 30th June 1675, Clerk against Stewart, Dirl. cclxxxviii. 139.* The question

* I have subjoined Dirleton's report of the debate, and of the opinion of the minority of the Court upon this case, because it is to be considered as the most solemn determination of a question which, though now held to be at rest, was once very keenly contested. I disregard all that was said upon the first defence, with which, at present, we have no concern —'It was alleged,' says Dirleton, 'that the act of Parliament did militate only in the case of dyvours, and dispositions granted by them, 'whereas the pursuer's debtor was a person of credit for the time, according to his quality, and had sufficiency of means and estate aliunde, that might have satisfied the 'pursuer's debt, the time of the said last contract, and thereafter, so that the said contract being valid ab initio, it could not be taken away, upon pretence that, thereafter, 'the husband became insolvent; seeing it cannot be said that the husband did intend to 'defraud his creditors, or that there was any fraud upon his part.' The reply was— 'Although the case of bankrupts, and their fraudulent practices, mentioned in the said 'act, being so frequent, did give occasion and rise to the same, yet it appears evidently, 'by the said act, that it was intended that debtors should not be in a capacity to give 'away any part of their estate, in prejudice of their creditors, to any person, in so 'far as the dispositive words of the act are in these terms—'That in all causes at 'the instance of a true creditor, the Lords will decern all alienations and rights 'made by the debtor to any conjunct person, without true, just, and necessary causes, 'and without a just price really paid, the same being done after contracting of lawful 'debts from true creditors, to be null, without further declarator.'—'And the said act 'does not bear, that all rights made by BANKRUPTS should be null, it being hard to 'give a character and definition of bankruptcy, so that diverse questions may arise anent 'the notion of bankrupt, and what debtor should be esteemed bankrupt, and therefore, 'for cutting off the same, the act is conceived in the terms foresaid, and annuls dispositions made by bankrupts without an onerous cause. And the Lords, by the statute (act of sederunt) 'ratified by the said act, do declare, that they intend to follow and 'practise the laws, civil and canon, made against fraudful alienations in prejudice of creditors; and, by the civil law all rights and deeds made and done in prejudice of creditors, 'without

question was, however, moved again, at the distance of only two years, when a similar decision was pronounced. It was a case of a postnuptial provision to children, challenged by creditors. 'The 'Court found the defence for the children relevant, viz. That 'their father, at the time of granting the bond for their provision, (which, as postnuptial, was, of course, in the judgement of law, gratuitous), 'had a liferent estate besides, out of which the credi- 'tors might have been satisfied *.' 6th January 1677, Creditors of Mouswell against the Children; Dirl ccccxviii. 205.—A long list of cases might be cited, in which the question was decided in the same way; but this does not seem to be necessary. It is now set- tled,

'without an onerous cause, are null, and may be rescinded, actione Pauliana. And the 'law doth presume, praesumptione juris, that they are fraudulent, being prejudicial to cre- 'ditors, ex eventu et re, who are not obliged to say that they are fraudful, concilio, which 'is in animo, and hardly can be proven.'—The opinion of the minority is thus preserved to us: 'Some of the Lords were of opinion, that the case being of so great consequence 'as to the preparative,' (as a precedent), 'it was fit to be thought upon, and urged 'these reasons: 1. That the words and letter of the law appear to be clear against deeds 'done by debtors without an onerous cause: 2. Though our law were not clear, yet, 'in cases of that nature, where we have not a municipal law nor custom to the con- 'trary, we ought to follow, though not the authority, yet the equity of the civil law, 'which is received everywhere, where there is no custom to the contrary, especially 'seeing it is declared by the said statute, that the Lords are to follow the civil and ca- 'non law made against deeds and alienations in prejudice of creditors: 3. It is hard to 'put creditors to dispute the condition of their debtors, the time of making donations, 'and whether they had effects and sufficiency of estate to satisfy their debt, notwithstand- 'ing the said deeds, which may be unknown to the creditors: it being sufficient to say, 'that the deed was without an onerous cause, and that the debtor became insolvent: '4. If a debtor should become insolvent ex post facto, though, at the time of the do- 'nations, the residue of his estate might have satisfied the debt, it is more just and rea- 'sonable that a donator, who has a lucrative title, should rather suffer ex eventu, than 'a creditor.'

* In this case, also, Dirleton states the ideas of the minority: 'This decision, 'being also by the major part, seemed hard to others, who thought that a debtor could 'do no deed in prejudice of his creditors, without an onerous cause; and though the 'father might be looked upon, at the time of granting provision to his children, as in 'a good condition, and therefore the creditors to be secure, and needed not to do dili- 'gence; yet if, thereafter, he should become insolvent, the loss ought to be upon the 'children, and not the creditors: and that it being a principle, that a debtor can do 'nothing

tled, that, on the one hand, wherever the debtor is insolvent at the time of the challenge, there is a legal presumption of insolvency at the date of the deed, if granted to a conjunct and confident person, and challenged by a prior creditor: (5th August 1783, Creditors of Cult against the younger children, VII. Fac. Coll. cxvii. 182.) And, on the other, that the deed will be completely supported, by a proof that the grantor was solvent at the time of making it.

We have now considered, very fully, all the circumstances which the statute requires in the deed challenged; and the result of our inquiry is, That, if a deed be granted in favour of a conjunct or confident person, and posterior to the contraction of debt, nothing can save it from reduction, under the statute 1621, but evidence of an onerous consideration; or of solvency, either at the time of the challenge, or at the date of the deed.

No observation is necessary concerning the form or nature of the deed. The principle of the law strikes at every possible form and shape of conveyance, or of obligation, by which a right belonging to the debtor, and which is legally capable of being converted to the payment of his just creditors, is transferred, or by which a feigned debt is raised up, to rank along with just creditors. Negative, as well as positive acts of diminution and embezzlement, are included under the law. The allowing an unjust decree to pass, or the omission of a good defence, are as fully objectionable, as the granting of a bond, or accepting of a bill without value. 'In 'laws introduced for the obviating of cheats,' says Sir George M'Kenzie, 'extensions, from the same principles, are most neces-

'sary;

'nothing in prejudice of his creditors, without an onerous cause, it is certainly both 'fraud and prejudice that he should not pay his debt, but should give away to his child-'ren that part of his estate which the creditors might have affected. and inhibitions 'being only in these terms, that the party-inhibiter should do no deed in defraud of the 'creditors, it might be pretended, by the same reason, in reductions ex capite inhibi-'tionis, that the party-inhibiter did nothing in defraud or prejudice of the pursuer, in 'respect, at the time of the granting the bond or right craved to be reduced, he had 'effects and sufficiency of estate besides.'

'say; because the same subtile and fraudulent inclination which 'tempted the debtor to cheat his creditors, will easily tempt him 'likewise to cheat the law, if the wisdom and prudence of the 'judge did not meet him wherever he turned.' Observ. &c. 22.

It remains only to be considered, What difference is produced on the question, by the circumstance of the right, constitued in favour of the original holder, being transferred to a stranger?

The statute, in providing for the case of a stranger, purchasing, bona fide, the right granted to a conjunct or confident person, declares, that it shall not in his person be annulled. The remedy provided to the creditors in that case, is a claim against the purchaser for the price, if not paid; or, if paid, an action against the receiver of the price, to make it forthcoming. The words of the statute limit the privilege of freedom from reduction, to the case of a purchaser, and allow no such favour to an adjudger. The reason of this is, that a purchaser pays his money, trusting to the records, or to the fair face of his seller's titles: an adjudger takes only such security as he can get: the right, which happens to be in his debtor, he adjudges 'tantum et tale' as it stands in him. These principles are well stated by Sir George M'Kenzie, in giving an account of the case of Jack against Jack, July 1666 *. This case was

* 'I have heard it debated, that though a third person, who acquires a right from 'the person interposed for an onerous cause, be not liable to this action; yet a com-'priser, comprising this right from the interposed person, had no such privilege; as, for 'instance, a right made by one brother to another, without an onerous cause, is re-'duceable: and therefore, if one of the creditors of that brother, to whom the right was 'made, should comprise the right so made to him; it was alleged, that as this right 'would have been reduceable in the person of the first acquirer, if it had continued with 'him; so it would have been reduceable from the compriser, and that for these reasons '1. A compriser comprises only, omne jus quod in debitore erat, tantum & tale, and 'therefore, since it was reduceable in his debitor's person, it ought to be so in his, even 'as it had been reduceable from his creditor, ex capite inhibitions, aut interdictions, '&c.

was debated, but not determined; and ' divided the opinions of very ' able lawyers' The question was decided, consistently with the above principles, in a very strong case which occurred in 1680. One disponed lands to a brother-in-law, who, in consequence of the conveyance, was infeft publicly, and entered into possession. A creditor of the disponee apprised those lands from him, and was infeft; and, betwixt him and the disponee his author, the lands were, for twenty-eight years, peaceably possessed. Long after this apprising, a creditor of the person who disponed the lands, apprised them, and, ' in a competition,' says Lord Fountainhall, ' between these two appprisers, (Pitmedden having reported), the ' Lords preferred the posterior appriser, because he had apprised ' from the disponee; unless the appriser from him, who got the ' disposition, would instruct the onerous cause of his author's ' rights, otherwise than by the narrative of his disposition; be- ' cause, being inter conjunctas personas, law presumes it simulate, ' unless the onerous cause be instructed.'—' This interlocutor,' continues his Lordship, ' offended many; and the Lords resolved ' to reconsider it: for, 1st, What if he' (the disponee) ' paid ' him' (the disponer) ' money for it over the table? Or, 2dly, ' That they had retired and cancelled the account, they being ' both

' &c. 2 The express words of the privilege given by this paragraph, does not meet ' this case, for the words run thus " If any of his Majesty's good subjects shall, by " lawful bargains, purchase." But so it is, that he who comprises, cannot be said to ' purchase by way of bargain. But, though a comprising be a legal disposition and assig- ' nation, yet it is a sale by the Judge, and not a purchase, or contract amongst the ' parties 3 This case seems not to fall under the reason of the act, for the act pri- ' vileges such as, having a good security, do, in contemplation of that right, (which ' for ought they can know, is sufficient), lay out their money, and so follow the faith ' of that right in the first constitution of their debt But the compriser lent his money ' to his debitor, without shewing that he relied upon the right now quarrelled, but, ' finding thereafter that he could not recover his debt, he comprised any thing he could ' find 4 If this were allowed, it would open a wide door to fraud, for rights might ' be made to confident persons, and then might be comprised, which any creditor ' might be induced to, whereas few would adventure to buy originally those rights, as ' said is This case was debated in July 1666, betwixt Jack and Jack, but was not ' decided and it did divide the opinions of very able lawyers' Observations on 28th Act, 23d Parl James VI p. [illegible] 'both merchants; how could the preceding onerous cause be 'proved? 3dly, An appriser, who is a singular successor, can- 'not be master of the writs, by which the onerosity of his author's 'disposition can be astructed, especially after twenty-eight years, 'and that they have peaceably possessed during all that time: 4thly, 'Some thought brethren-in-law not so near conjunct persons, yet 'they were found, even before this, conjunct, as to the design of 'this act of Parliament 1621 against bankrupts.'—'The Lords' (he adds in a nota-bene) 'afterwards mitigated this interlocutor,' but in what degree, or upon what principle, he does not explain: 24th January 1680, Kerr, I. Fount. 76.

As it is effential that the purchaser, in order to be clear of the challenge, should 'in no ways be partaker of the fraud,' wherever it appears that he knew the circumstances, he will be liable, as 'a partaker,' to have his right reduced. Therefore,

1. If the deed express the connexion of the parties, and the gratuitous nature of the right; as this gives complete information to a purchaser, of the two great circumstances from which fraud is to be inferred, and puts him on his guard to inquire well, before trusting his money on such security, it will be reducible: 6th February 1672, Hay against Jameson, II. Stair 63.

2. When the deed mentions only one of these circumstances; where, for example, it appears, ex facie, to be gratuitous, or to be granted to a conjunct person; still it would seem, that the same decision must be given against the purchaser. Thus, in the case of Lesly against Lesly's creditors, 15th June 1710, Forb. 409, the Lords found, 'that a disposition granted to a brother-in-law, does 'not prove the onerous cause thereof; and that, the same bearing 'the relation between the disponer and Lachlan Leslie, that they 'are brethren-in-law, Lachlan's creditors are in no better condi- 'tion than he; and therefore must instruct the onerous cause of 'the disposition, otherwise than by the narrative of the writ itself.' It is very true, that, in this case, the question occurred with adjudgers, and not with purchasers. The Court, however, does not

appear

appear to have put the decision upon the footing of this distinction, but seems rather to have wished to keep to the general ground, as stated above. The same decision was pronounced, in the case of Spence against Dick's creditors, 28th November 1693, I. Fount. 572. See also the case of Lyon against the creditors of Easter-Ogle, January 1723, I. Dict. 75.

As to the evidence by which the mala fides of the stranger purchasing is to be established, where the deed itself does not bear it, much is to be learned from the case of Allan against Thomson, 9th January 1730. The first disponer, in that case, was brother to the disponee, and the second disposition was granted, by the original disponee, to his daughter and her husband; but the deed did not mention the alliance. It was argued, on the one hand, that the daughter and her husband could not be ignorant of the connexion between the father and the uncle: on the other, it was contended, that, although they had known the connexion, there was no evidence of their knowledge that their father's right flowed from the uncle. 'The Lords, in respect there was no evidence that the 'defender was in the knowledge that Charles Sangster's right flow- 'ed from William his brother, assoilzied.' I. Dict 75.

When it is considered, that even a gratuitous deed to a relation is good, if the grantor be solvent, it will appear, that the presumption should go no further against the purchaser, even where the deed bears the connexion between the grantor and receiver, than to infer a necessity, on his part, of inquiring into the circumstances of the grantor of the first right. If his circumstances were supposed to be good; if the general understanding was, that he was solvent; there appears to be no good ground for reducing the purchaser's right. It cannot be supposed that a stranger, bargaining for a right, can either have the opportunity of knowing, or can effectually inquire into, the affairs of the maker of the original deed: he will naturally think himself perfectly free to enter into a bargain with the disponee, without any danger or challenge, unless where insolvency appears, or where creditors are proceeding with diligence against the disponer. The case of Spence against Dick's creditors, is instructive upon this point. 'The Court determined 'this day,' says Lord Fountainhall, 'that it was not relevant, to 'reduce a singular successor's right, that he saw, by the tenor 'and progress of the writs, that his author was a conjunct person 'to the first disponer, unless he also knew, or might have known, 'that the first disponer was at the time a bankrupt: and though 'he acquires for onerous causes, yet he is particeps fraudis, if he 'knew that the disponer, without an onerous cause, was bankrupt 'at the time he made the disposition: and that participation of 'fraud in singular acquirers, was not so strictly to be understood, 'as to be restricted only to him, who was upon the contrivance 'and design of defrauding creditors, but also ought to be extend- 'ed to any who knew him then to be bankrupt, seeing that know- 'ledge was sufficient to put him in mala fide. For the Lords 'thought it not enough, that the right was granted to a son, or other 'conjunct person; and, though it bore to be for onerous causes, 'yet law justly presumed it to be gratuitous, unless the conjunct 'person, the receiver of it, instructed its cause aliundè than by its 'own narrative; but, further, required a second qualification against 'the singular successor acquiring from that conjunct person, that 'he knew him' (the original disponer) 'to be then broke: and, 'because private knowledge cannot be well proved, especially 'where the parties are dead, it must be elicited from circumstan- 'ces, or witnesses deposing that he was then generally holden and 'reputed a notour bankrupt by all; for it is not yet clearly decided 'what makes one a bankrupt;' (the statute 1696 had not yet passed): 'whether diligence against him; or that he is obæratus a- 'bove his estate; or that cessit foro, and has fled: for the Lords 'did not incline to reduce all gratuitous dispositions by fathers to 'their children, unless it were instructed, that the father was be- 'fore, or by the making thereof, rendered bankrupt: for many 'estates were bruiked by extraneous persons, who bought from 'sons having right by such dispositions: and donations are not 'quarrellable, unless the donor was thereby rendered insolvent: so 'that if a conjunct person be denuded, and receive a price, the 'buyer from him is secure, unless they prove that the conjunct 'person's author was then bankrupt when he disponed to his rela-

'tion,

'tion, as well as that it was gratuitous, and without any onerous 'adequate cause.'—I. Fount. 572.

After a long lapse of time, the situation of a singular successor becomes more favourable, independently altogether of the running of prescription against the challenge. The lapse of a long time, should naturally take away the presumption of a fraudulent design. Thus, in the above case of Spence against Dick's creditors, it was found unnecessary for the holder of the deed, after the expiry of forty years, to bring any other evidence of the onerous cause, than that of the deed itself; and this, independently of the plea of prescription; for there had been interruptions. The same decision was given in the case of Guthrie against Gordon, 2d February 1711, after a period of fifty-eight years, Forbes, 492.; 18th January 1749, Blackwood of Pitreavie, Kilk. p 56. In the case of Elliot against Elliot, more than forty years had elapsed: 10th November 1749, Kilk. 58 In these cases, and particularly in the last, the distinction was drawn, between prescription, and the effect of the mere lapse of time in overcoming the presumption. In none of the other cases, was there room for the plea of prescription; and in the last, the Court, by taking up the above point, (of which there was thought to be no doubt), got quit of the difficulty arising from the danger of loosening the faith of the records, by admitting interruptions of prescription in such cases.

III. The effect of this reduction, must be explained here, slightly, although I shall hereafter have occasion, in treating of the principles of ranking, and especially of the effect of partial and personal securities, in the division of a bankrupt's funds, to discuss the subject more fully.

The operation of this statute, considered as a law of insolvency, ought to have been general; and the effect of any reduction, under it, available to the whole creditors, by restoring the part alienated, to the general fund, so as to be divisible among the creditors, according to their respective rights; or, at least, so as to be affectable by every creditor, equally with any other unalienated part of the debtor's funds. But, at the time that the law was enacted, no such general plan was thought of, for regulating the interests of creditors, or the division of an insolvent estate. The statute was little more than a declaration of the common law, or rather of the principles of equity; by which, every creditor who felt himself encroached upon, might apply to the Court for redress, against any voluntary alienation. 'Such is the effect of a reduction on this 'act,' says Lord Kilkerran, 'as to be profitable only to the re'ducer; and, even to him, only where he has affected the subject, 'the nullity introduced by the statute, being, not a simple nullity, 'but only a nullity, to the effect of giving access to the creditor re'ducer to affect the subject.' Kilk. p. 48.

SECTION II.

OF FRAUDULENT EMBEZZLEMENT OF FUNDS, AS REDUCIBLE AT COMMON LAW.

HAVING now considered the statute, by which, in this country, creditors are assisted in vindicating their funds from embezzlement by the confidential friends and near relations of the bankrupt; we return to the general rule of the common law. It is here, that the creditors must be threatened with the greatest dangers; those which, being less suspicious in appearance, are less easily to be guarded against. An insolvent debtor, capable of engaging in frauds against his creditors, will naturally avoid such devices as may throw the burden of the evidence upon the holder of the deed. He will grant conveyances to strangers, whom he may gain to his interest: he will rear up fictitious names, to be the apparently fair holders of claims, or of securities against him, and against his estate: but he will avoid all his relations; he will take care to employ, in such a service, none of his confidential friends. To these dangers, nothing stronger can be opposed, than the general rule already explained, viz. That, upon evidence shown, of the feigned nature of the debt, or of the want of a valuable consideration for the right conveyed, the creditors will prevail in reducing the one, or in excluding from the competition the other. No presumption can be reared up against deeds, fair and onerous in appearance, which, although made after insolvency, are granted by a man who is still going on in trade, and who is not deprived of his power of alienation, for, under such a presumption, though the guilty might be detected, the honest creditor might happen also to suffer. Indeed, so far was this carried at one time, that it was held, by some of our older lawyers, that, if the grantee was not a conjunct or confident person, under the statute, the deed was not liable to challenge as gratuitous. 'Since the clause of 'the act' (says Sir George Mackenzie) 'annuls only deeds done 'to the prejudice of creditors, in favour of conjunct and confident 'persons; it would seem, that such rights, when made to others, 'not conjunct nor confident, are not reduceable: and yet, de 'praxi, (in practice), all rights made to any persons whatsoever, 'without an onerous or necessary cause, are reduceable by the statute; and our law considers the difference between deeds to conjunct and confident persons, and to others, only in reference to 'the way of probation, so that those must prove an onerous cause, 'while the others need not.' Observ. on 28th Act, Parl. 23d, James VI. p 7^.

But although there be no ground for a presumption against deeds apparently onerous, and in favours of strangers, similar to that which the law has reared up against those made in favour of confident and conjunct persons; care ought to be taken, on the other hand, that the difficulty of checking such deeds, be not too much increased. Mr Erskine has delivered a doctrine, upon this subject, which seems to require some qualification. 'In a deed,' says he, 'in favour of a stranger, the narrative, expressing an onerous cause, is sufficient, per se, to support the deed, unless its 'onerosity be disproved by the writing or oath of the grantee,'

IV.

IV. i. 35. If this doctrine be rigidly true, there is some reason to fear, lest much room be left for fraud; lest the difficulties of detection be made so great, that insolvents may be empowered to cheat their creditors without impediment. If it be enough, to protect a device of this kind from challenge, that it bears the semblance of an onerous deed—that it is expressed in the body of the deed, that value has been given for it; and if no other proof is to be admitted against such a deed, but the acknowledgement of him who holds it, and claims under it; no bankrupt can be at a loss to execute his most fraudulent designs. But, upon what ground does this doctrine rest? Such deeds are reducible upon a principle of common law; and, in all challenges upon fraud, at common law, the general rule must hold, that a circumstantial proof is admissible. Mr Erskine rests his doctrine upon a case, decided in the last century, that of Trotter against Hume, 22d June 1680. But I should be inclined to object, that, even if the case went the full length of sanctioning Mr Erskine's doctrine, an early decision ought not perhaps to be entirely trusted to, in a question of this kind; and that it does not appear, to me, that the decision affords a solid ground for the doctrine that is rested upon it.

1. Frauds of this kind naturally increase with the extension of commerce, and the more frequent recurrence of insolvency; and we have already had occasion to see, that, in 1680, the trade of this country was so backward, as not yet to have led to a precise definition of the character of bankruptcy. The expediency of putting a strong check upon fraud, could not therefore at that time be fully understood: and as Mr Erskine refers for his doctrine to a decision, not to a law; as that decision, too, is grounded on the common law alone; it ought not to be taken as a precedent, without large allowances for the times in which we live, when compared with simpler, if not more virtuous days.

2. But I should question, whether the precedent, cited by Erskine, were sufficient to support his doctrine. It was not, at that time, well settled, what the effect of the statute of 1621 was; and frequently, deeds, which were not truly included, were objected

to,

to, as, upon the footing of the statute, with the view of throwing the burden of proving the onerous cause on the holder. Thus, in 1665, an attempt of this kind was made in the case of a bond, bearing to be for borrowed money, where the creditor was neither conjunct nor confident; it was unsuccessful:—Monteith, 28th June 1665, I. Stair, 288. In Trotter's case, the grantee was dead; the challenge was brought against his heir; and the objection was, that the deed, bearing, as its consideration, 'sums of 'money paid and undertaken, conform to an inventory;' it was the duty of the disponee's heir to produce that inventory, and to justify the payments, not only to have been made, but to have been just and subsisting debts. The heir defended himself upon the narrative, as sufficient to support the deed, without any inquiry into the nature of the debts paid off, or any production of the inventory; and the Court 'found the narrative of the disposition, of 'undertaking the debts, did astruct the cause onerous, the buyer 'not being a conjunct or confident person; and would not oblige 'the buyer's heir to produce the inventory, or instructions there-'of, even so far as extant.' (22d June 1680, II. Stair, 772.) But if it be supposed, that the inventory, in that case, had been recorded, so as to be within the reach of the challenger, or that, instead of an inventory, the debts had been enumerated in the deed; and that the creditors, in these debts, had appeared, claiming upon the estate, with their documents undischarged in their hands: is it to be conceived, that the Court would have refused such evidence of the onerous cause in the deed being all a fiction? And yet, if such evidence would have been received, Erskine's doctrine is not sound, in restricting the evidence to the oath or writ of the receiver of the deed.

There seems to be no doubt, that a deed, which expresses an onerous consideration, is subject to an inquiry, conducted upon the footing of common evidence. A case was decided, on the very same day with that of Trotter's, in which the deed challenged bore, as its consideration, 'sums of money, and other causes and 'considerations.' It was argued, That a narrative of 'other causes 'and considerations,' implies only love and favour: and the

Court

Court ordered the holder of the deed to explain the cause of granting, that they might judge of it: (22d June 1680, Sinclair; II. Stair, 773.) The doubt, therefore, whether creditors may reduce a deed, bearing expressly onerous causes, by evidence of a slighter kind, than the acknowledgment of the holder, rests entirely upon the presumption in favour of a formal and legal deed. But, although the general rule of law is, that a written deed is not to be cut down by parole evidence, an exception must be admitted, wherever fraud appears. In the case of Fordel against Monteith of Carriber, as reported by Dirleton, 'the Lords found, 'that albeit writ cannot be taken away, but by writ directly, and 'that a disposition could not be taken away, but by a renunciation, or some other writ, where there is no question as to the 'validity or formality of the same; yet, it may be taken away by 'a reduction ex capite metus et doli, et minoris ætatis, and lesion; and that, in such pursuits, the reasons, being in fact, and 'libelled either upon force, or circumvention and fraud, are probable by witnesses.' (Dirl. ccccxxxii 213)—Although a debtor is not, therefore, in the common case, entitled to object to the creditor, that his bond was granted without value, unless he shall establish his objection by the debtor's oath, or written acknowledgement; yet, where a deed has been granted by a person insolvent, against whose acts there is a natural presumption of fraud, the creditors would surely be admitted to investigate the circumstances prout de jure, as we call it, by every kind of proof which can be useful in the detection of a train of fraudulent conduct. To oppose the express declaration of a deed, that value was given, is difficult, as a negative cannot be proved. But, indirectly, it may be proved, in particular cases; and the law will not scruple to admit the evidence. The law, introducing sequestrations in mercantile bankruptcies, provides for the examination of the debtor, and those who are of his family, or connected with his business. Such a power of inquiry, has appeared to be peculiarly necessary in these bankruptcies; the transactions of a merchant affording daily opportunities of committing frauds, inscrutable by any common means. A well conducted inquiry of this kind, may often lead to the train of circumstances, by which the fictitious nature of of a deed, apparently onerous, may be proved; and wherever circumstances, thus discovered, are sufficient to disprove the narrative of the deed, they will themselves be held capable of parole proof. The examination of the grantee, previous to a reference of the matter to his oath, may help also to complete the tissue of facts.

If, by legal evidence, the creditors shall be able to show insolvency, on the one hand, and want of value, on the other; they will have done enough to secure a reduction of the deed, under the common law. It does not appear to be necessary, that they should prove a fraudulent design in the debtor, and a collusion or participation on the part of the receiver of the right; for it is to save them from a proof, so difficult, that the general rule is established, by which the debtor is prevented from granting deeds to the prejudice of his creditors.

But there is another case, to which, hitherto, we have paid no attention; and which yet gives rise to a question of much importance. A debtor, who is solvent, makes a gratuitous conveyance, or grants a bond, or accepts a bill, without value, and afterwards becomes insolvent: Is such a deed reducible? The act of 1621 gives the aid of presumption, in order to establish insolvency in the grantor, and gratuity in the deed; but the case, now proposed, is one, in which there is no insolvency at the date of the deed, and in which the gratuitous nature of the deed is supposed to be open and avowed.

So far there is a difference between this case, and that of a deed granted after insolvency, that here, the debtor being, at the time of making his deed, in no shape deprived of his natural powers as proprietor; not being a trustee merely for his creditors, but the free master of the balance, at least, of his fortune; there appears to be no ground for a reduction, unless the deed, under challenge, shall appear to have been kept latent, to deceive posterior creditors; or unless a direct participation, in a fraudulent design, can be actually proved against the holder of the deed.

Several instances of challenges of this kind, occurred at an early period; and will be found very instructive. But, before entering upon the detail of them, I may take notice of an argument drawn from the statute, as barring all such reductions. It was said, that the statute was intended to root out all fraudulent gratuitous deeds; and, that the exclusion of posterior creditors from it, was equivalent to a total denial of action to such creditors. But this plea was uniformly rejected. It was held, that this statute cleared up, so far as it went, the principles of reductions on the head of fraud; but that it left those cases, which it did not specially include, to the guidance of equity and the common law.

The first case of a reduction, by a posterior creditor, of a deed granted during solvency, is, that of the creditors of Pollock, 21st January 1669, I. Stair, 587.; where, a bond having been granted by a father to a son, it was objected to, as a deed that was kept latent, while the creditors were induced to go on, bona fide, to contract with the father. It was answered, That there was no room for reduction here, on the statute 1621, as the bond, objected to, is prior to the debts of the challengers: and that there was no ground for reduction at common law, since the bonds had been delivered; since creditors may guess that children will naturally be provided; and since there is no legal obligation or necessity to publish deeds like those in question. 'The Lords would not sustain the reduction, upon the act, nor upon the general ground, that posterior debts were preferable to all bonds of provision; but ordered a condescendence of fraud.' The condescendence accordingly was put in, containing these articles: 1. That the son was forisfamiliated, and sufficiently provided for, before. 2. That the bond was not payable till after the father's death, and bore no interest. 3. That the deed was kept latent, and the debts all contracted within a very short time after the bond, which was within a year of the grantor's death. There was some argument upon the nature of the evidence; the one party contending, that the act 1621 had exhausted all the cases of presumptive fraud, leaving no ground of reduction at common law, but actual fraud, to be prov-

ed

ed by oath or writing; the other maintaining the necessity for presumptive frauds being established by circumstantial evidence. 'The Lords found, the matter of fact, and circumstances alleged, 'relevant to infer a presumptive fraud and contrivance between 'the father and the son, which did ensnare the creditors who 'continued to trade; and, therefore, reduced the same, as to the 'creditors, and preferred them, &c. They did not find the 'grounds, that this was a gratuitous deed, and to be considered, 'at best, *only* as revocable by the father, relevant to prefer a pos-'terior onerous obligation to a prior gratuitous; and they were 'chiefly moved, because of the inconvenience to creditors, acting, 'bona fide, with a person trading and repute in a good condition, 'and where, in eventu, his estate is not sufficient both to pay his 'creditors and this bond; for, if it had been sufficient for both, 'they would have come in pari passu, having both done diligence 'within the year.' I. Stair, 602.

The next that occurred, was the great case of Street and Jackson against Mason, towards the end of the last century.—Street and Jackson were creditors of James Mason, in consequence of a train of mercantile transactions and correspondence. Mason, after *this correspondence* had begun, and continued *for some time*, gave to his son a conveyance of his lands of Powbeath and others. A reduction was raised, by Street and Jackson, of this conveyance, as fraudulent; and an inspection of Mason's books, and investigation of his transactions, was ordered. From the report, it appeared, that although, at the date of the deed, the balance due was inconsiderable, yet the train of transactions and correspondence had been uninterrupted. From this report also, Mason seemed, at the time of granting the deed, to have had no other visible estate, and to have been under great difficulties. Mason had, as much as possible, concealed the conveyance, and always acted as proprietor of the lands conveyed; and although the deed appears to have been recorded, the son's name was the same with the father's; so that even the record was not a distinct intimation of the conveyance. The Court reduced the deed, as fraudulent, granted without any sufficient means, and concealed from his creditors*. 2d July 1673, II. Stair, 197.

The

* In this case, I have thought it right to put down here, an analysis of the argument, with the full judgement of the Court.

It was maintained for the CREDITORS, 1 That the final result of the correspondence, must be stated as at its commencement, so as, in the fair interpretation of the statute 1621, to make them anterior creditors. 2 That there should be an exuberant trust between merchants, else there is an end to commerce; and, by this rule, the Court has generally decided in commercial questions, so as to make our laws consistent with the laws and customs of other nations, and with the interest of commerce;—a continued account, for example, saves from the triennial prescription. 3 By the laws and customs of nations, and the common law, although actio Pauliana was competent only to anterior creditors, yet the rule was extended (as in common sense it should be) to posterior creditors, wherever there are indications of fraud 4 Mason had never any means to purchase land, but must have done it with the money of his creditors, and so they have a good right to a declarator, that the son's right must be burdened with the debts.—MASON ANSWERED, 1 That the conveyance was recorded 2 The actio Pauliana was given to posterior creditors, only where the receivers were participes fraudis, and there was no opportunity in Rome, as with us, to discover, by the records, fraudulent deeds 3 The grantor was not at the moment debtor to Street and Jackson; and the statute 1621 is the only rule, and not extendible beyond its enactment REPLIED:—In Rome, the insinuatio donationum, was more solemn than our recording. but the recording, here, is nugatory, in so far as it could be an intimation to creditors, since the son's name is the same with the father's; and (as appears from the report) all believed that the father continued propritor In the civil law, it is only to onerous deeds that the rule applied, by which the actio Pauliana was refused, without evidence of participation: in gratuitous deeds, fraus in eventu was enough—'The Lords having considered the debate, and the writs and testimonies produced, They found, that there was a trust and correspondence between Street and Mason elder, begun in 1660, and constantly continued till the furniture and bonds, whereupon this pursuit was founded, and likewise, that the same correspondence was begun between Jackson and Mason, a day before Mason's disposition to the son, and a month before the son's seisine; and that Mason did produce no count-book, to insruct that he had any means to purchase this land for his son, and pay his creditors, or any means to satisfy the pursuer's debts, but that he was commonly looked upon as having no such estate. And therefore, the Lords found the reasons of reduction sufficient, upon this gross fraud and contrivance, viz That the disposition by the father to his son, was done by a merchant, who carried on a public trade and correspondence, and could have no rational intent, but to deceive the pursuers, being strangers, and his correspondents; the son being an infant, and no obligement upon the father to infeft him, neither being provided for his marriage, nor for a stock, when he were of age, and being almost the father's whole estate,

'and

The next case is, that of Reid against Reid of Daldilling Reid of Daldilling disponed his estate to his son, in fee; afterwards, he borrowed money; and, upon his death, his creditors being unable to affect the estate or the heir, (as he having been infeft before then debt existed, and so was neither heir nor lucrative successor post contractum debitum), brought a reduction upon the ground of fraud. ' The Court found the reason of reduction, by the circum-' stances condescended on, relevant to infer fraud, and to reduce ' the deed, in so far as prejudicial to posterior creditors, viz. that ' the infeftment was granted to a son when an infant; and that the ' contract of marriage provided the son only to be infeft as heir, ' and not in fee; and that the father continued to act as fiar, and ' not as liferenter; and that the registers were out of the country, ' the time of borrowing of those debts ' 4th December 1673, Reid; II. Stair, 234.

It is clear from these cases, not only, that, wherever fraud can be actually proved, it will authorise a reduction of the deed, but that it may be inferred from circumstances. No classification of such circumstances into legal presumptions, can well be delivered; and it must ever, in some degree, be an arbitrary and jury question. But it is proper to observe, that mere gratuity in the bestowing of the right on near and confidential connexions, (which are the grounds of the presumptive fraud under the statute), are not sufficient to infer fraud at common law: that the decisions of the Court have never gone further than to throw the onus probandi of solvency upon the holder of the deed, where the connexion between the parties has been very close and intimate, and where the deed was of a latent and undiscoverable nature. Thus, in the case of the creditors of Marshall against his Children, ' The Lords thought it ' unjust, to put creditors to expiscation and inquiries into their ' debtor's

' and more than he had free, without reservation of the father's liferent, or power to ' burden, and the father carrying himself constantly as proprietor And they reduced ' the disposition, and declared Mason infamous, for so great a fraud, but they did not ' decide severally upon any of the grounds, either upon account that these debts were ' to be drawn back to the first trust,' (commencement of the correspondence), ' or ' upon any other account, but upon [illegible] II. [illegible].

'debtor's solvency, where he gave latent bonds of provision to his 'children: and, therefore, preferred Marshall's creditors to his 'bairns, both of the first and second marriage; and would not bring 'them in pari passu with the creditors:' 24th December 1709, II. Fount. 546. In the case of Inglis against Boswell, this addition-al principle co-operated towards a similar decision, that deeds, granted to children, and still in the father's hands, although, in the common case, they are presumed to be in his custody for the benefit of the children, are, in a case of this kind, to be held as undeliver-ed, to the effect of inferring a revocation of the provision by the contracting of future debt: 14th November 1676, Dirl. cccLXXXIV. 187.

But where the relationship is not of this close nature, the onus pro-bandi is left upon the challenger. Thus, in the case of MacChristian against Monteith, a disposition by a nephew to an uncle, not com-pleted by seisine till after diligence was begun by a posterior credi-tor, and therefore charged as kept latent for fraudulent purposes, was preferred, in competition with an adjudging creditor: 10th February 1709, II. Fount. 490.

Wherever the deed is kept intentionally concealed, or care is taken to present to the public eye the appearance of no conveyance having been granted, it has been held (as is most natural) a cir-cumstance indicative of some sinister design, and sufficient to ground a presumption of fraud. In the case of Ardblair against Wilson, a bond having been granted for love and favour, payable after the grantor's death, the Lords found, 'That the said bond, 'being granted without an onerous cause, to be paid, in manner 'foresaid, after the grantor's decease, could not prejudge posterior 'creditors, who were in bona fide to lend their money, notwith-'standing any such latent deeds or bonds.' Dirleton remarks, that 'this decision seems to be hard, seeing it was lawful, both to 'the grantor and receiver of the said bond, to grant and receive 'the same: and the said donation being lawful ab initio, could not 'become thereafter unlawful by any deed of the grantor. And 'fraud cannot be pretended, but where creditors or others, the

'time

'time of the granting such bonds, were prejudged; unless it did 'appear, by some specialty and circumstance in the case, that there 'had been a design to cheat and circumveen those who were to 'lend their money, by granting and settling, upon the relations of 'the debtor, his estate, and thereafter to get into his hands his 'creditors means, whom he was not able to satisfy; which was 'found in the case of Mason and Pollock, and was not alleged in 'this case.' 24th January 1677, Dirl. ccccxxxviii. 214.

These notes of Dirleton's, express the opinion of a sound lawyer. They do not absolutely oppose the judgement given in this case; but they show, that the decision goes as far in favour of creditors, as law and sound principle will admit. The above opinion seems to contain the whole doctrine which can safely be delivered upon the subject. 1. That a person solvent, and in full power, may effectually give to one, who is in bona fide to receive: 2. That a conveyance by a solvent person, cannot, by a separate and posterior transaction, lose its effect, unless there be fraud in it from the first: and, 3. That fraud cannot, in such cases, be presumed, unless there be circumstances indicating a design to mislead and deceive creditors into a confidence in the debtor, by keeping the conveyance secret, till the transactions betwixt the debtor and them be concluded. With this doctrine, the above mentioned case of Marshall's children (24th December 1709) concurs. And in the case of Robertson's creditors against his Children, a bond of provision, kept latent, and never known till the father broke, was reduced, on the prosecution of posterior creditors. This decision did not proceed upon the idea of its being an undelivered deed, and so, not fairly established to be prior; for the children offered to prove the delivery. The case is reported shortly by Lord Fountainhall, (vol. I. p. 497.), and more at length by Lord Harcarse, (No. 218.)

CONCLUSION OF CHAP. I.

It may not be improper to sum up, in one view, the remedies afforded, by the law of Scotland, against those gratuitous deeds, by which the funds of an insolvent debtor may be fraudulently diminished. All cases of this kind, are provided for, either by the first branch of the statute 1621, c. 18., or by the common law.

1. Under the statute, are included, all cases where a creditor, of an insolvent debtor, can show that a deed has been granted to 'a 'conjunct or confident person,' after the contracting of his debt. Such deeds are reducible by this act, unless the holders of them shall establish that the deed was granted for onerous causes, or that the debtor was solvent at the time of making it.

2. By the common law, all deeds are reducible at the pursuit of posterior creditors, which, being granted to a conjunct or confident person, without a valuable consideration, can be proved to have been made after the insolvency of the grantor.

3. Those deeds which are granted in favour of strangers, who, neither by their confidential connexion, nor by their alliance in kin with the debtor, can be presumed participant in his unfair practices, are, at common law, reducible, if it can be established that the deed was granted without value, and after insolvency.

4. Even deeds granted during solvency, are reducible, when gratuitous; either if the challenger can prove a direct participation, on the part of the grantee, in a fraudulent design to injure creditors; or, if he can show that the deed has been kept concealed, so as to induce creditors, ignorant of the right, to trust the debtor.

CHAP. II.

Of Conveyances, to the prejudice of Individual Creditors, who have begun Execution against the Debtor's Estate.

Having considered those limitations, which, with a view to prevent a debtor from lavishing or embezzling the funds, have been imposed upon his usual powers, we now proceed to the Second Class of limitations, the object of which is, to protect, against deeds and conveyances in favour of particular creditors, the diligence which others may have already begun, for affecting the debtor's estate.

It was not till the year *1696*, that a general law was made, for securing to creditors a remedy against deeds of preference granted in contemplation of bankruptcy. But, in the same statute which has already, in the first chapter, occupied so large a share of our attention, the Legislature endeavoured to provide against the debtor's interfering, to disappoint individual creditors, in their lawful exertions to attach his funds. Unfortunately, this statute was constructed, without much attention to distant consequences; and we shall frequently have occasion to regret the obstructions, which, in a more advanced age, it opposed to the improvement of the bankrupt law. It entitled an individual creditor, who had begun execution, to persevere, even in opposition to deeds granted for the general

general benefit, and to establish for himself a preference over every other creditor who was behind him in the race of diligence.

To understand precisely what the Legislature did, in the second branch of the statute of 1621, it is necessary to attend to the state of the common law at that period. By the common law, large provision had already been made for the protection of creditors, who had commenced their diligence against the debtor's estate; and it was the object of the statute, which we are now considering, to strengthen and extend that protection, according to the supposed exigencies of the state of insolvency. The protection afforded, at common law, to a creditor doing diligence, was of two kinds. 1. If his claim was not yet ascertained; or, if he had reason to fear, that, before he could obtain the necessary writs, the debtor might take means for placing his property beyond the reach of execution; he had the remedy of inhibition, by which the lands might be attached—and that of arrestment, upon which such of the moveables might be attached, as were in the possession of others than the debtor himself. 2. If his debt was ascertained, and he was ready to proceed to execution against the debtor's property, he might have ordered a messenger, with a warrant of apprising in his hands, to proceed to the debtor's land, to search for moveables, as the first subject of execution; and, failing them, to proclaim publicly upon the lands, and at the market-cross of the jurisdiction, that the lands were, against a certain day, to be apprized for the debt. From the moment of such proclamation, or denounciation (as it was called), the lands were held to be attached, as a subject, not to be alienated, till the apprizing should be completed. As to moveables, the creditor was, at that time, (though not now), entitled to proceed, at once, and without any previous charge against the debtor, to poind such of them as were in the debtor's own hand; or he might, in the same sudden manner, have attached them by the diligence of arrestment, differing little, in its form, from the arrestment used upon unliquidated debts.

Thus, if the creditor chose to proceed at once to execution against his debtor's lands or moveables, there was little opportunity for

for the debtor to disappoint him. But there was another course, which was more commonly taken, though, happily, in these days, we know its effect only from our law books. When imprisonment came to be admitted, as a method of recovering civil debt, it proceeded upon the idea of rebellion; which, when established by denounciation, was followed by the falling of the escheat, or forfeiture of the debtor's moveables, and, if the debtor continued a year and day in rebellion, with forfeiture of his liferent right to his lands, &c. As the right of the King's donee of forfeiture, was burdened with payment of the debt in the horning, on which the rebellion proceeded; creditors were led to prefer diligence by horning, to execution against the estate. But the law was defective in protecting this diligence; for no attachment of property was held to begin, by a mere charge upon letters of horning, as in the case of diligence directed against particular subjects.

Such was the state of the law, when, in 1620, the new regulation was thought to be necessary for the case of insolvency. The opportunities that remained open to the debtor, for disappointing begun diligence, appeared to the Judges, who prepared the act of sederunt afterwards adopted by the Legislature, to be well deserving of attention. But, in providing against the evil, the only remedy which the state of the country seems then to have allowed, was, merely, an extension of the principle upon which, at common law, diligence was already, in some degree, protected. It was therefore enacted, That 'if, in time coming, any of the said di-'vours, or their interposed partakers of their fraud, shall make 'any voluntary payment, or right, to any person, in defraud of the 'lawful and more timely diligence of another creditor, having served 'inhibition, or used horning, arrestment, comprizing, or other law-'ful means, duly to affect the divour's lands, or price thereof, 'to his behoof; in that case, the said divours, &c. shall be holden 'to make the same forthcoming to the creditor, who, being pos-'terior to him in diligence, hath obtained payment, by partial 'favour of the debtor, or of his interposed confident, and shall 'have good action to recover, from the said creditor, that which 'was voluntarily paid in defraud of the pursuer's diligence.'

In thus extending the safeguard of legal diligences, there was great danger that the Legislature should sacrifice some of the most important rights of the public; for, even the doctrine of an attachment by litigiosity, at common law, has been held, by our lawyers, to be pregnant with much injustice to bona fide creditors. Until it be seen, how, under this statute, the interest of the public was, by the interpretation of the Court, reconciled with that of the creditors, whom it was the object of the law to protect, we cannot understand the spirit and effect of the statute; and therefore, before proceeding to the detail, I shall make a few general remarks upon this subject.

It is in the point which has just been hinted at, that the great difficulty of all laws, restraining the common powers of individuals, is found to lie. In the Roman law, so much regard was paid to bona fides, on the part of creditors receiving payment, or transacting with the debtor, that they were safe, till the missio in possessionem; when the estate, being publicly put under a curator for the creditors, all bona fides was necessarily precluded. Sir George M'Kenzie says—'Our law has equalled diligence done 'by horning, inhibition, &c. to the missio in possessionem of the 'Roman Magistrate.' Observ. on 18th act of 23d Parl. of Ja. VI. p. 149. But, in what respect have the precautions, which made this rule safe, been attended to in our law? It does not seem, indeed, to have been ever conceived, that the statute applied to the case of new transactions, entered into in the course of commerce. The uniform interpretation has been, that it included only the case of deeds granted without value, or payments and securities to former creditors *. Neither has it ever been held to cut down payments to a creditor in cash. (Kilk. 62.) But the injustice which a prior creditor may suffer, who has bona fide received even a security from the debtor, and finds it unavailing, may be very great. Let it be supposed, that a creditor has insisted for payment,

* 28th June 1665, Monteith, I. Stair, 288.—25th January 1681, Bathgate against Bowdon, II. Stair, 841.—8th February 1681, Nielson; II. Stair, 856; IV Ersk. iv. 37.—9th March 1781, Blackie against Robertson, VI Fac. Coll. part 9. h. 90.

payment, and threatened diligence; and that, to appease him, the debtor has granted a security, in consequence of which, he has given up his intention of proceeding to execution. If he be afterwards forced to relinquish the security thus fairly acquired, and this, not that it may become a part of the common fund of division, but that it may serve as a fund of payment to an individual creditor, who, perhaps, by diligence secret and quite unknown, may have entitled himself to the benefit of the statute; the receiver of the security has reason to complain of hardship and injustice. Many a struggle was maintained for such an interpretation of the statute, as should prevent these evils; and, at last, with some degree of success.

There were only two ways, in which the interest of the public, and that of the creditors doing diligence, could, under this statute, be reconciled;—either by requiring, as an ingredient in every reduction of a voluntary deed, under this statute, that the diligence of the challenging creditor should have advanced so far, as, of itself, to be an intimation to the public, of the inchoated right of the creditor; or by making the reduction competent in no case where the debtor was not notoriously insolvent, or known by the holder of the deed to be so.

1. To require the diligence to be advanced so far as to serve for a public intimation, would have been to render nugatory the very intention of the statute; for, already the common law had done this, by the protecting power which accompanied the commencement of the various diligences. The Court of Session, therefore, uniformly rejected all attempts to restrain the operation of the law, in this respect. Thus, mere citation of the debtor in an inhibition, even without publication, was held sufficient to entitle the creditor to have his diligence protected by the statute. Gartshore against Sir James Cockburn; Harcarse, DCXXXIX. 176 *. 9th January 1696, Bruce of Kennet's creditors, I. Fount, 698. Again, a mere charge of horning was held sufficient to support a reduction under

* Lord Kames has erroneously put this down in his Dictionary, as a decision upon the mere point of litigiosity. Vol. I. p. [illegible].

under the statute. 21st January 1686, Chaplain against Sir Geo. Drummond; I. Fount. 396.

2. But, to require that the holder of the deed should be apprized of the insolvency of the debtor, in order to entitle the creditors to reduction, was truly consistent with the spirit, though not, perhaps, strictly according to the words, of the statute. When this was first tried, however, in the case of Milne of Carriden, it was rejected. 'The Lords found, that a charge of horning satisfied 'the terms of the act of Parliament, and therefore sustained Carriden's reduction, he proving Sir William Nicolson's insolvency 'at that time, though his condition was not then so propaled '(public) as to make him holden and repute a notour bankrupt, 'the standart being but lately fixed by the act of Parliament, containing a notour bankrupt's marks and definition.' 19th November 1697, Milne of Carriden against Sir William Nicolson's Creditors; I. Fount. 796.—But although this first decision pointed strongly against the opinion, that notorious insolvency was necessary to found a reduction under the statute, the succeeding cases have fully established this to be the rule. In the case of the Royal Bank against Kennedy of Glenour, &c. certain deeds were challenged, as granted after a charge of horning. 'The Lords found, 'that the assignation fell under the compass of the act 1621, against rights in defraud of anterior creditors, unless the assignees 'should prove, that, at the time of his granting the assignation, 'he was holden and reputed to be solvent.' 24th February 1709, II. Fount. 497.—This judgement loosened, a little, what seemed to be established in the case of Milne of Carriden; for it amounted to a decision, that a belief of solvency, founded upon the debtor's being held and reputed solvent, would be sufficient to sustain the deed. The next case that occurred, was still stronger.—Tweedie sold a stock of sheep to Din, for which he got his bond. He did diligence on the bond, by horning, upon which denounciation followed, and registration. On attempting to poind, Tweedie found that the sheep had been delivered over by Din, to satisfy some of his prior creditors; and, to this effect, the receivers gave evidence, in an action for redelivery brought against them. Tweedie claim-

ed

ed the sheep, upon the footing of the act 1621. 'The Lords 'found insolvency of the common debtor, with horning and de-'nounciation against him, not relevant, per se, to give the pur-'suer the benefit of the last clause of the act of Parliament 1621, 'anent bankrupts, unless the common debtor had been commonly 'reputed bankrupt, or that the pursuer can qualify that the de-'fenders were some way partakers of the fraud.' 7th June 1715, Tweedie against Din and others; Dalr. cxlii. 196.; Bruce xcii. 109 *.

The conclusions, then, which I should be inclined to draw, respecting the general scope and spirit of the statute, are these: 1. That it authorises the reduction of all voluntary deeds, granted after such diligence shall have been begun, as law has appointed for the attachment of the subject conveyed, provided the debtor was insolvent at the date of the deed. And,

2. That if the holder of the deed shall be able to establish, that the insolvency was secret, and in particular, unknown to him, the reduction will not be successful

Having said so much, in general, I shall, in what remains to be explained of the subject, follow a similar arrangement with that which I observed in the commentary on the first branch of the statute,—considering, 1. the title of the creditor who pursues the reduction, and the nature of the diligence which he must have commenced, 2. the deeds which are struck at by the act, and, 3. the nature and effect of the reduction.

1. TITLE

* This decision may no doubt have proceeded, in some measure, upon the idea of a payment being a more favourable case for the creditor, but it will be observed, that lawyers never seem to have conceived, that a payment, by delivering of moveables, is entitled to the same favour with a payment in money Kilk p 63. And, as a general decision upon the statute, this of Tweedie's seems to rest upon good and solid ground.

I. Title of the Challenging Creditor.

The title necessary to the challenger of a deed, upon this branch of the statute, rests upon these three points: 1. He must be a creditor, who has begun to use such diligence as would, if not interrupted, legally affect the subject alienated. 2. The diligence must be regular and formal, so that, if concluded, it would not be liable to any objection that should prove fatal to it 3. The diligence must have been prosecuted in due course, and without any unfair or improper delay. These I shall consider in their order.

1. The words of the statute, seem almost to restrict the remedy, to the case of creditors who have attached the heritable estate of the debtor. The enumeration does indeed include diligences of both kinds; inhibition, comprizing, horning, and arrestment: but it is followed by this apparently restrictive conclusion—'or other lawful 'means, duly to affect the divour's lands, or price thereof.' This ambiguity makes it necessary to remark, in the outset, that as the statute, in its whole scope and intention, plainly holds out a remedy to creditors of all kinds, doing diligence against any part of the debtor's funds; so it has been uniformly interpreted by the Court. Reductions have been sustained, of conveyances of moveables, as well as of conveyances of heritage.

Another doubt arose, upon the interpretation of the act, viz. Whether it was necessary that the creditor, who brought the challenge, should be able to state himself, as in a course of diligence, legally to affect the subject of that conveyance? or, whether (to use the words of Sir George M'Kenzie) 'any of the diligences, alluded 'to in the statute, should be a sufficient ground, promiscuously to 'quarrel any disposition?' From Sir George M'Kenzie's remarks, it would appear, that those who contended for the promiscuous right of reduction, rested strongly upon the fulness of the provision, which was already made, at common law, for securing each particular diligence, once begun. But the opposite opinion has been held

the

the better of the two. It has Sir George M'Kenzie's support Observations, &c. 155, & seq. And Mr Erskine (IV. 1. 39.) lays it down, in very express terms, 'That the diligence ought to be 'of that nature, or kind, which is proper to affect the right questioned.'

The proper diligences against land, are, inhibition and adjudication, as coming in place of apprizing The inhibition is not a complete diligence, till it be executed against the debtor, and against the public, and duly entered in the record, but, from the moment of its execution against the debtor, the right of reduction, under the statute, begins. This was decided, in the cases already mentioned. The adjudication needs no assistance from the statute; for it is not held a begun diligence, till citation; and, with citation, the litigious quality begins, at common law. It is natural to conclude, from what has been said, that no creditor will be heard in a reduction of any heritable right, unless he can state himself as having begun, either an inhibition, or an adjudication. On turning over the older decisions, however, we find innumerable instances, of hornings being held sufficient for this purpose. We can distinctly trace these judgements to one of two principles, either that the horning was a necessary step previously to some comprizings, (M'Kenzie, p. 160); or that, as the direct manner of inferring rebellion of the debtor, (in which, if he continued for year and day unrelaxed, his heritable property fell to the Crown), it was, in one sense, an heritable diligence. There is no case to be found, since the abolition of escheat as a consequence of civil rebellion, in which, upon the footing of this statute, a reduction was ever tried, of an heritable right, by a creditor who had merely denounced his debtor upon a horning: whence a very strong indirect conclusion arises against the relevancy of such a challenge, and to this doctrine Mr Erskine seems to add the weight of his authority, (IV. i. 39.) But I apprehend, that wherever a charge of horning is a necessary or proper step of diligence, previous to an adjudication, the creditor using it, might, even at the present day, claim the benefit of the statute. We have one example of such a charge, in an old case.—Murray of Kellor bought

certain

certain lands, by minute of sale. The seller, disregarding his obligation, sold to another, also by minute. Keillor charged the obligant, on horning, to implement the sale to him: but the obligant took this as the warning for him to complete the second purchaser's right. Keillor brought a reduction on the act 1621; and the Lords sustained the horning, as sufficient to entitle Keillor to the benefit of the statute. 18th July 1677, Murray against Drummond, II. Stair, 543.

Arrestment and poinding are, since the abolition of escheat, the legal diligences for affecting moveables. But, in general, the first step taken by a creditor, before proceeding to any diligence against particular funds, (unless the debtor's circumstances appear to be very desperate), is, to charge him, upon the horning, to pay. This, indeed, is a step absolutely necessary, before he can proceed to poind; but arrestment may be used, the moment after the warrant is issued from the signet. Is a creditor, then, who charges his debtor upon the horning, protected by the statute against conveyances of moveables? The expression in the statute, is strong in favour of the affirmative: but, at that time, the horning was, by means of the escheat, a direct form of execution; and in the numerous cases of the older law, the decisions can be traced to this principle. Mr Erskine, in speaking of this subject, says, 'Though the late statute, 20 Geo. II. 50. has for ever discharged 'the casualties of single and liferent escheat, consequent upon the 'denounciation, at the horn, of rebels, in any civil debt or obligation; so that, now, denounciations can neither affect heritage nor 'moveables, except upon delinquencies: yet letters of horning 'continue to be a legal warrant for poinding the moveables of 'debtors in a civil obligation: and therefore, a voluntary right of 'moveables, granted by the debtor to a creditor, after a charge 'given to him, upon letters of horning, by another creditor, may 'be voided at the suit of the creditor charger.' (IV. i. 39.) Mr Erskine has not here expressed himself with perfect clearness. He leaves a material question unresolved: Whether a charge of horning can sanction the reduction of a conveyance, where the subject is is not poindable, but attachable only by arrestment? A horning, with a charge, can be regarded as the beginning of execution, only in the view of poinding; and, upon that point, Mr Erskine rests his opinion. It is not necessary, as a harbinger of arrestment; and I should be much inclined to doubt, whether it could found the reduction of an assignation of debt. No harm would be done to the creditor, and no remedy refused to him, by such a decision; since the common law entitles him to use at once his arrestment. Neither can it be said, that this begun diligence is disappointed, since the charge of horning is no step towards any form of execution, by which the subject could be affected. On the contrary, by neglecting to arrest, which he has in his power, and by using a charge, which can be necessary only in the view of diligence of another kind, the creditor tacitly declares his intention of disregarding the arrestable fund.

2. The second point to be considered, relative to the challenger's title, is, the regularity of his diligence. It is not enough, that he has begun that sort of diligence, which the law has appointed, for affecting the subject conveyed, he must also be able to show, that, so far as he has gone, his proceedings are so correct and regular, that, if carried on to completion, they would have formed an unobjectionable and valid right. This is not the place, in which an examination of objections to diligence can be entered into; far less, any principles explained, that can be useful, in estimating the effect of such objections. Afterwards, it will be necessary to enter generally into this subject, when treating of the principles and rules, by which trustees are to regulate themselves, in dividing the funds among the creditors. I shall stop here, only to intimate one distinction, viz that, in adjudications, very different effects are given to objections. Some, are fatal to the diligence altogether, annulling and destroying it; others, have only the effect of limiting the adjudication to a mere judicial security or mortgage, depriving it of its capacity of being declared an absolute right of property, after the expiry of the term of redemption. The title to reduce a conveyance, as prejudicial to an adjudication, must follow this distinction,—be excluded by an objection which

would be fatal to the diligence; but not by an objection, whose sole effect would be, to restrict it, from an absolute right, to a mere security.

3. As it is plain, that a debtor's hands cannot, with any regard to justice or expediency, be for ever tied up, by the secret bond of inchoated diligence, a creditor must, in the view of this law, bring the diligence to completion, within a moderate and proper time, otherwise he will lose the benefit of the reduction.

In the case of Mr Drummond, treasurer to the Bank of Scotland, against Kennedy of Glenour, the effect of a delay in diligence, was very fully considered. There had been an interval of five months between the charge and the denounciation; during which interval, an assignation had been granted by the debtor. The user of the diligence, argued strongly upon the words of the statute, as requiring only that horning should be used, not that it should be completed; for, then, it would not need the aid of the statute. The assignee answered, That, by inchoated diligence, the statute understands diligence begun, and duly carried on, without delay. And although, in reply, it was said to be inexpedient, in a trading country, to hurry on the diligence of creditors, rather than to allow a short time for the debtor to extricate himself; 'the Lords 'refused to sustain the reduction; in respect that, albeit the pur- 'suer had used horning, by a charge, before the assignation; yet 'he had not connected and completed his diligence, by denouncia- 'tion, five months thereafter.' 9th July 1709, Forbes, 343.— A delay of four months was found to take away the benefit of the statute: November 1688, Young against Kirk, Harcarse, clvi. 35. And, in Duff of Kilmuir's case, an assignation having been granted three months after a charge of horning, though the reduction was not brought for eight years, the assignation was sustained: 22d July 1742, Duff against Bell's Representatives, Kilk. 48.

The pursuer of a reduction, on this statute, must therefore be able to show, that his diligence is prior to the deed challenged;— that it is of a kind which, if not interrupted, would duly have

affected

affected the subject conveyed;—that it is liable to no fatal objection;—and that there has not been, in the prosecution of it, any undue delay,—a delay, of even a few months, being sufficient to cut down the right of challenge.

II. DEEDS LIABLE TO CHALLENGE.

The expressions, by which the deeds, liable to challenge, are described in the statute, are these: 'Any voluntary payment, or '*right, to any person, in defraud of the lawful and more timely di*-'ligence of another creditor.' But, these seemingly comprehensive words, have been held not to apply to acts which, at first sight, they seem directly to include: Thus, payments in cash, though made to prior creditors, are not reducible; nor bargains fairly entered into for value, though to the complete disappointment of the challenger's diligence. Necessary deeds are, by the very expression of the act itself, saved from reduction. It will be proper, first, to consider these exceptions.

1. PAYMENT.—With respect to the exception of payments in cash, from the rule of this statute, it will be sufficient to give the detail of a case upon the point, as reported by Lord Kilkerran. Forbes, a creditor of Farquhar's, arrested, and obtained a decree of forthcoming, for 94l.; which was all that the arrestee acknowledged to be due, and which the arrestee offered to pay, for a discharge of all he owed the common debtor. Forbes not only refused this, but, being thus led to suspect that the arrestee owed more than he had acknowledged, he imprisoned the common debtor. While he was proceeding with this, the arrestee pressed him for the discharge he had formerly solicited; and, at last, threatened, that with the money he had in his hands, for the purpose of paying the arrester, he would pay others of his creditors. and this threat he fulfilled, by paying the money to some of his own creditors. These payments were challenged by Forbes, on the acts 1621 and 1696. 'The question turned upon the con-'struction of the act *1621*,' says Lord Kilkerran; and, after quot-

ing

ing the words, he says, 'The words are strong, and, at the first 'view, would appear to comprehend payment made in numerata 'pecunia; and no case can occur, more favourable for this con- 'struction, than the present, where the payment was maliciously 'made. Nevertheless, as there is no instance, where a payment, 'in pecunia numerata, has been found to be affected by any of the 'statutes concerning bankrupts, nor has any of our lawyers ever 'said so: so, these words in the statute, "having served inhibition," '&c. "or used other lawful means to affect the divour's lands," '&c. were thought to limit the statute, so as only to concern con- 'veyances of subjects which may be affected by such diligences; 'notwithstanding of the reply, that, even taking the statute in the 'strictest sense, a debtor's ready money, as well as his other ef- 'fects, is affected by horning and denounciation, as, at the date 'of the statute, it fell under his escheat, which is burdened with 'the debt in the horning; as, properly, the escheat affected nothing 'to the creditor, although the Crown was, by special statute, sub- 'jected to the debt; and that the subjects, which the statute sup- 'poses to be affected, are only the debtor's lands, or his goods, or 'the price thereof, none of which comprehended his ready money: 'and, as none of the statutes do restrain him from spending or 'squandering his ready money, it would have been strange to 'have restrained him from giving it to his creditors.' The infe- rior Judge had assoilzied the defenders, that is, had sustained the payments. To this, the Lord Ordinary adhered, and the Court confirmed the judgement: 26th January 1751, Forbes against Bremner, &c. Kilk. p. 62. 3.—'There was no occasion,' Lord Kilkerran adds, 'in this case, to determine what the case would 'be, of payment made by delivery of moveables; though it was 'mentioned, in the reasoning, as a thing not to be doubted, that 'such payment would fall under the statute.'

But, under the principle of this exception of payment, there is no exemption to creditors who have received conveyances, although, out of the subject conveyed, they have subsequently received payment. The first case, in which such a defence was attempted against a reduction on this statute, is reported at great length,

length, (though, to say the truth, not very clearly), by Lord Stair. The whole case seems to lie here:—That a creditor, having used horning against the common debtor, in 1648, obtained a gift of his escheat in 1652; that his competitor had not used horning, till 1649; and that he had proceeded no farther with diligence, but got an assignation to certain bonds, from which he received payment. Between these two creditors, a competition arose. The creditor, who had received payment, strongly urged the danger to commerce, if a creditor, receiving payment, should be forced, by the operation of secret diligence, to make restitution. and the peculiar hardship of this case was much dwelt upon, the creditor receiving payment being a foreign merchant, and creditor for the price of wines furnished. But 'the Lords found, that Veitch, 'who stood in right of the horning, in 1648, against the com-'mon debtor, and the gift of escheat taken and declared in 1652, 'could not be prejudged by the rebel's voluntary assignation; but 'that the same was null: and though payment had been obtained, 'on that assignation, it was liable to repetition, in respect there 'was sufficient evidence and probation adduced, that Sanderson 'was bankrupt and insolvent.' Veitch against Pallet, 11th November 1675, II. Stair, 366. Yet see the case of Lady Ricarton against Gibson, 9th July 1709, Forbes, 344. & seq.

NOVA DEBITA.—Although the words of the statute seem to include all deeds granted to the prejudice of prior diligence, yet, as they are declared to be only such deeds as are granted 'in de-'fraud' of the previous right, they have been held, not to include new transactions. Commercial expediency calls for such a decision; and the interpretation, in this way, has been uniform. Lord Stair says, in his report of the case of Veitch against Pallet, 'In 'this judgement, there is nothing to hinder commerce, by buying 'from bankrupts, or rebels, goods, for present money delivered to 'them, or by any permutation, without fraud, for, in these cases, 'the bankrupt does not become debtor, nor the buyer creditor. 'But, in sales upon trust, a merchant, whether a foreigner or 'Scotchman, behoves to run the hazard of his debtor's condition 'and estate, who cannot prefer him, becoming once creditor, to

'the

'the more timeous diligence of other creditors, the debtor being 'bankrupt, and not able to pay them all.' II. Stair, 367.—He lays down the law explicitly in favour of purchasers for a fair price, (I. Stair, Inst. ix. 15. p. 86.)—And, in the cases mentioned below *, this was fully established. Mr Erskine also lays down the rule, upon the authority of these cases, (IV. i. 37.) And in the case of Blackie against Robertson, 9th March 1781, the reduction was sustained, on the ground of fraud, as distinct from the rule of the statute. 'It has been found,' says the reporter, (alluding, it would appear, to the case of Brugh against Gray), 'that 'a voluntary disposition, for a price instantly paid, and not for 'anterior debts, fell not under the statutes 1621 and 1696· in 'like manner, that voluntary securities, granted for money in'stantly received, were not affected by these statutes, (Ersk. loc. 'cit.) In this case, it appears, from a proof, that the sums, for 'which an heritable security was granted by the bankrupt, had 'been advanced by a favourite creditor, through an interposed 'person, in order to prefer that creditor, by making payment to 'him of the money so advanced. The transaction being thus 'evidently calculated to elude the statutes, the Lords reduced the 'security.' VI. Fac. Coll. part ii. li. 90.

NECESSARY DEEDS.—The expression 'voluntary,' in the statute, is plainly exclusive, in the *first* place, of all such deeds as are not properly the act of the debtor, but merely the completion, by the creditors, of a right formerly granted, but imperfect: and, *secondly*, of all deeds which the debtor is bound in law to grant.

In the case of Hunter of Muirhouse, a competition arose between the personal creditors of Mr Hunter, and certain creditors who had received heritable bonds, on which infeftment had followed. The objection was, that the seisines were not taken till after Muirhouse's bankruptcy, after a charge of horning against him, and after the creditors knew that he was broken. 'The 'Lords

* Nelson, 8th February 1681, II. Stair, 856. Bathgate, 25th January 1681, II. Stair, 841. Monteith, 28th June 1665, I. Stair, 288. And Brugh of Tinmouth against Gray, 1st January 1717, Bruce xiv. 60. bound up with III. Fac. Coll.

'Lords found, there did not arise any hypothec, or jus reale, to 'the personal creditors, on Muirhouse's bankruptcy, so as to impede those, who had heritable bonds, to take infeftment upon 'their precepts of seisine, even though they had charged with 'horning before the completing their rights by infeftment; seeing 'the act of Parliament 1621 discharges the debtor, after diligence 'inchoate against him, to do any voluntary deed or ratification to 'their prejudice. But here was no deed of the debtor, who had 'given the heritable bonds long before; and the creditors might 'uti jure suo quandocunque; and the act anent registration, in '1617, did not lay any such necessity upon them, or prescribe a 'time, in which they ought to have taken infeftment; and that 'the creditors cannot be repute interposed persons for the debtor, 'seeing their precepts were procuratories and mandates in rem 'suam; and there was no sufficient evidence of fraud, in their 'delaying to take their seisines; or in their doing so, when they 'heard Mr James was dying, and under incumbrances.' 16th December 1696, Creditors of Hunter of Muirhouse, I. Fount. 688. 743.

Respecting deeds actually granted by the debtor, but, in justification of which, a plea of necessity may be stated, Sir George M'Kenzie argues strongly, that all deeds, granted by the debtor, to which he was not actually compelled, should be objectionable, notwithstanding any previous obligation to grant them. (Observ. &c. 149. 153.) But it does not appear that this doctrine is admitted. Lord Kilkerran says, in reporting the case of Grant of Tillifour, 9th November 1748; 'On this occasion, there was some 'reasoning among the Lords, upon the construction of the act '1621; wherein they agreed, that the words, "necessary causes," 'in the act 1621, are, in practice, thus understood, that there be 'a previous obligation to grant the deed—that, though the words, "true, just, and necessary causes," would appear, as they stand, 'to be conjunctive, they have always been considered as disjunctive: so that, if either the deed be granted in consequence of a 'previous obligation, or, though there be no such previous obligation,

'tion, if the deed be granted for a true and just cause, it is not 'reducible.' Kilk. 55. 6.

These exceptions leave, under the influence of the statute, all deeds, granted by the debtor voluntarily, and to a prior creditor, or without value, whether they are deeds of security, or deeds of conveyance.

It is against deeds of conveyance, that the statute seems principally to have been aimed--deeds, by which any part of the debtor's funds was withdrawn from those of his creditors, who had actually begun diligence. Securities are in the same situation: they are to be regarded as conveyances merely: but if the subject conveyed, or given in security, be one, over which no diligence can extend, the statute cannot sanction a reduction. An alimentary fund, for example, cannot be attached by creditors: the person who holds it may, however, spare some part, to pay a particular creditor: but, as no other can say, that, in this way, his right is encroached upon, or a subject given away, over which he could have extended his execution, he does not seem to have an interest to challenge or object to the deed.

An obligation, is no direct conveyance: but, by an obligation, a debtor may so facilitate the operations of a particular creditor, as to enable him to attain a preference, by priority of diligence. Is it, then, competent, under the statute, to object to such deeds? We shall afterwards see, that, under the statute of 1696, all deeds of obligation, granted within sixty days of bankruptcy, so as to give to a prior creditor an advantage, which, without the debtor's interference, he could not have enjoyed, are reducible. But the act 1696, is a general and equalizing law, by which every deed is levelled, whose effect is to raise one creditor to a preference over the rest. The statute, now under consideration, is different. It looks only to the interest of one single creditor, not to that of the whole mass;—it favours the growth of preferences;—it gives, to a liquidated debt, a favour over those which are unliquidated, and, yet, may be equally just. Unless the words of the statute, then, forbid

forbid any latitude of interpretation, it seems not inconsistent with the principles of equity, that the debtor should be permitted to acknowledge, by bond, or other form of voucher, debts which are justly due by him, so as to give the creditors in them, a fair chance for equality, with others, who are accidentally better situated in this respect. The words of the law, seem not to include deeds of this kind; for payments and rights, in defraud of diligence, are the only deeds which are forbidden. But the Court have interpreted the law otherwise: and they seem to have proceeded upon this principle, that an insolvent debtor ought to do no deed, by which the situation of his creditors may be affected, but to leave every thing to the operation of the law. The first case, in which the question occurred, was, that of Scott against Bruce, in 1788. One creditor had executed a poinding, and another, in order to entitle himself to a participation, had no resource, but to make the debtor bankrupt. As he could not, however, do this, without having his debt constituted, he applied to the debtor, and got from him a bill, upon which he raised horning and caption, and made the debtor bankrupt, within the time prescribed in the late bankrupt statutes. The poinding creditor brought a reduction of the bill and diligence, upon the statute 1621, as granted after the commencement of that diligence, which he afterwards completed by poinding. The bill, &c. were reduced: 19th January 1788, Scott against Bruce.—This is a very strong case; for, here, the object of the deed was, to secure that equal division, which the law is so anxious, in the statute 1696, and, in the late sequestration acts, to accomplish.—In a case, still later, this decision was confirmed —A bond of corroboration, upon which adjudication was led, with the intention of coming in equally with other adjudications, (according to the rule of pari passu ranking), was challenged, as a voluntary deed, in prejudice of prior diligence,—having been granted after the first effectual adjudication had been completed, and a process of ranking and sale raised. Some of the Judges were a good deal moved by the hardship to the creditor, (who had time, in this case, to have led an adjudication independently of the bond), and by the object of the documents having been, not to give him a preference over other

 creditors,

law, and according to those rules of distributive justice, by which the rights of the creditors of bankrupts must be determined, all deeds, which assign to individuals a larger share of the fund, than, in the general division, they ought to receive, are frauds against every other person who has a claim upon the estate.

The difficulty, and, in many cases, the impossibility, of discovering fraudulent designs, has led, in every commercial country, to the establishment of some general and comprehending law, for the purpose of securing creditors, as far as the interests of commerce could allow, against preferences bestowed in contemplation of bankruptcy. It plainly cannot be sufficient for such a purpose, that the bankrupt should suffer a loss of power, only from the moment of his public failure. It is necessary to carry back the effect of the bankruptcy, so as to include all those acts which, on the eve of his failure, the debtor may have been busy in performing, for the advantage of those whom he has wished to favour. It is in this particular, that the bankrupt laws of various countries seem most essentially to differ: and that law must be the most perfect, which best reconciles the interests of the public with those of the creditors.

In England, as I have already taken occasion to remark, the property of the bankrupt is vested in the assignees under the commission, by relation back to the first act of bankruptcy. 'The 'legal effect,' says Mr Cook, 'of an act of bankruptcy committed 'by a trader, is, to put it in the power of the commissioners, to 'divest the property of the bankrupt by relation, which may go 'back to a great length of time, and avoids all acts done by the 'bankrupt, without regard to the fairness or fraud of them;—so 'that a sale of goods by the bankrupt, after the act of bankruptcy 'committed, is a sale of the assignees' property, for which they 'may maintain trover;* and it is the same, as to the payment of 'money.

* Trover, is 'an action which lies, where one man gets possession of the goods of 'another, by delivery, finding, or otherwise, and refuses to deliver them to the owner; 'or sells or converts them to his own use, without the consent of the owner, for which 'the owner, by this action, recovers the value of his goods.' II Espinasse, N P 538.

'money. But the rigour of this rule has been relaxed by the Le-
'gislature, whereby it is provided, that the relation to the act of
'bankruptcy, shall not extend to the prejudice of any debtor of the
'bankrupt, who paid his debt to the bankrupt truly, and bona
'fide, before he shall understand or know that he is become a
'bankrupt; or to purchasers, for valuable consideration, unless the
'commission is sued out within five years from the bankruptcy;
'or to payments bona fide made to the bankrupt in the course of
'trade, without knowing that he is become bankrupt, or in in-
'solvent circumstances.' I. Cook, B. L. 593.—Whether this law be, in all its provisions, consistent with commercial expediency, I shall not presume to inquire. I cannot venture to express, what I fear might be a rash conclusion, with respect to a law so essential in this department, and which has so long regulated the practice of a nation eminent in jurisprudence, and in commerce, like England. But it is natural, on such an occasion, to regret, that the great men, who have written on the law of England, have never condescended to draw the comparison between their own institutions and ours. Indeed, a Scotchman will feel perhaps something like indignation, when he sees how little the English writers, in general, have thought it worthy of them to become acquainted with our law; and that, on questions, where an assimilation of the laws is of infinite importance, they have recourse to the ordinances of foreign countries, for analogies, rather than to those of Scotland. Sir William Blackstone, for example, in treating of the very point now under review, runs a parallel between the law of France, and that of England; entirely neglecting the institutions of the sister kingdom, though they not only regulate the bankruptcies of this end of the island, but must often decide, in the course of these bankruptcies, upon much mercantile capital of Englishmen.

In his contrast of the English and French laws, Sir William Blackstone has not scrupled to give the preference to that of England. He seems however to have regarded the French rule of 'relation for ten days precedent to the act of bankruptcy,' as absolute and universal, striking down every possible deed, and ad-

mitting

mitting of no qualification or exception. I shall not enter, here, into any discussion of the French law, nor attempt to explain how this rule was qualified in practice; but I would observe, that the Scotish law, in adopting the form of the French rule, and extending it from a term of ten to one of sixty days, will be found to have reconciled the law with essential justice, and the interests of trade,—by exempting from the general rule, not only those cases which, in England, are excluded, but others, which expediency seems equally to point out as exceptions.

It was by that statute, which has already been the subject of commentary in the first Book, that the Legislature of Scotland provided, against the frauds of bankrupts, a remedy, beyond the reach of the common law. Creditors were, before this, protected, at common law, against every possible form which fraud could assume; but, to entitle them to this protection, they were bound to give evidence of the fraud. This statute established a presumption of fraud, with a view to save creditors from the necessity of a difficult and expensive investigation, and to comprehend every possible device, by which, upon the eve of bankruptcy, preferences could be voluntarily bestowed;—the injustice and hardship, naturally flowing from such a comprehending law, were corrected, by exceptions, as far as the spirit of the institution could allow. I have endeavoured already to detail the history of that statute; to show the distracting scenes of litigation, which arose from the want of a general rule, saving creditors from the necessity of inquiring into actual fraud; and to point out how naturally the involved failures, which occurred towards the end of last century, fashioned the law into that particular shape which it has assumed. I shall not here enter into that subject more fully, nor indulge in any speculation on the nature and effect of the law; for this will best be understood, from a clear explanation of the points which it involves.

It seems scarcely necessary, after what has been said, to observe, that this statute, intended to save creditors from expensive and difficult investigations concerning actual fraud, was not, by any

means,

means, intended to preclude the operation of the common law, where fraud could be directly established. Many cases remained unprovided for by this statute, which it would have been of the worst consequence to have left without a remedy. This chapter seems naturally, therefore, to divide into two Sections the one will consist of a commentary on the statute; the other will contain an exposition of the common law.

SECTION I.

COMMENTARY ON THE STATUTE 1696, c. 5. AGAINST PREFERENCES CONSTITUTED BY VOLUNTARY DEED. *

To comprehend, fully, the object and effect of this statute, it is necessary for those, who have been accustomed to the jurisprudence of England, to observe well that essential difference, which has already been hinted at, between the plan and spirit of the two laws, in respect to challenges 'by relation to the bankruptcy.' The great principle

* After the description of a bankrupt, which I quoted as the subject of commentary in the first Book, (p 11) the statute proceeds thus: 'His Majesty, with consent of the 'Estates of Parliament, Declares all and whatsoever voluntary dispositions, assignations, 'or other deeds, which shall be found to be made and granted, directly or indirectly, by 'the foresaid dyvour or bankrupt, either at, or after his becoming bankrupt, or in the 'space of sixty days of before, in favours of his creditors, either for his satisfaction, or 'further security, in preference to other creditors, to be void and null Likeas, it is 'declared, That all dispositions, heritable bonds, or other heritable rights, whereupon 'infeftment may follow, granted by the foresaid bankrupts, shall only be reckoned, as 'to this case of bankrupt, to be of the date of the seisin lawfully taken thereon, but 'prejudice

principle of the English law is, that the assignee's right operates, universally, against all conveyances and deeds done after the first act of bankruptcy. In Scotland, on the contrary, every deed done by the debtor, at whatever period, is good, unless it be proved to be fraudulent, or unless it have been made within sixty days before the bankruptcy, and in favour of a prior creditor. The consequence of this difference is—that, in England, (independently of the exceptions of the later statutes), neither can the debtor pay a debt, nor can he even receive payment, to the effect of discharging those who are indebted to him; while, in Scotland, payments to the bankrupt, being in no shape deeds of preference in favour of creditors, and payments by him, not being includeable in the term 'deeds,' are both effectual:—that, in England, as the whole funds are the lawful property of the assignees, from the first act of bankruptcy, they cannot even be sold, effectually, by the debtor, for a fair price, but may be recalled from the purchaser, he being left to claim as a creditor; while, in Scotland, a sale, or new transaction of any kind, for full value, is effectual, because it, in no shape, is a deed of preference to a prior creditor.

The full effect of the general principle adopted in the English statutes, has undergone, we have seen, considerable restriction, to fit it for the practice of a commercial country. Payments to the bankrupt, when bona fide, and without notice of the bankruptcy, have been declared unimpeachable: 1 Ja. I. c 15. § 14. Payments received from him, in the course of trade, for goods sold, or for bills due, have also been, in similar circumstances, saved from recal, (19 Geo. II. c. 32. § 1.); and a fair purchase, for value delivered, has been

'prejudice to the validity of the said heritable rights, as to all other effects, as formerly 'And because infeftments for relief, not only of debts already contracted, but of debts 'to be contracted for thereafter, are often found to be the occasion or covert of frauds, 'it is therefore further declared, That any disposition, or other rights, that shall be 'granted for hereafter, for relief or security of debts to be contracted for the future, 'shall be of no force, as to any such debts that shall be found to be contracted after 'the seisin, or infeftment, following on the said disposition or right, but prejudice to the 'validity of the said disposition and right, as to other points, as accords.'

been declared secure, unless a commission of bankruptcy shall have followed within five years: 21 Ja. I. c. 19. § 14. In Scotland, all these things were fully provided for, without any direct interference of the Legislature to declare them: and it shall be a chief object of this Section, to explain how, in interpreting the statute, doubts had arisen on these points, and how they were removed by the decisions of the Court.

1. OF NEW TRANSACTIONS.

It is a question, which has been contested with great heat, Whether new transactions are comprehended under the law? To this point, I shall first turn my attention.

As the view of the Legislature, in enacting the statute of 1696, was to afford a remedy against deeds executed by bankrupts, for the purpose of bestowing preferences; so, this intention is expressed, in very clear terms, in the statute itself. The description of the deeds, to which it was meant to apply, is in these words—'All and whatsoever voluntary dispositions, &c. which shall be found to be 'made and granted, directly or indirectly, by the said dyvour or 'bankrupt, &c. IN FAVOUR OF HIS CREDITORS, either for his' (their) 'SATISFACTION OR FURTHER SECURITY, IN PREFERENCE 'TO OTHER CREDITORS.' These words contain an express declaration, that, to bring the deed under the law, it must be granted to a 'CREDITOR,' and it must give him a preference over 'OTHER 'CREDITORS.' But a person with whom the debtor enters into a new contract, which is begun and finished as one act, whether it be a sale of land or of goods, or even a loan of money upon security, is in no sense a creditor at the time of entering into the transaction; nor does the right granted by the bankrupt, in such a transaction, bestow a preference upon one creditor, to the prejudice of the rest. That a debtor may more easily accomplish his fraudulent schemes, by having cash, instead of unwieldy property, at his disposal, is true; but the act of converting the property, is no fraud. The creditors can suffer only from the bad use which their

debtor

debtor may make of his opportunities; and the bona fide dealer ought not to be made participant in the fortunes of a man, in whom he has never trusted. Accordingly, in the very first case which occurred, the Court found the statute inapplicable to a new debt. The question arose upon an indorsation; and the Court found that the act of Parliament could not apply, unless 'the pursuer proved 'the indorsation to have been made, not for present value, but in 'satisfaction or security of a prior debt.' 16th January 1713, Campbell of Glenderuel against Graham, Dalr. xcvii. 136. Forb. 646.

This is now the settled doctrine of the law, although certain doubts, which arose in cases of a complicated nature, have seemed occasionally to obscure it. The grounds, upon which it rests, are well and shortly explained by Lord Kilkerran, in reporting the case of Johnson against Burnet & Hume, 29th January 1751. 'The 'Court,' says he, 'considered, that the statute was only meant 'to supply the defects of the act 1621, and to prevent the debtor's 'giving securities to some, in prejudice of his prior creditors; that 'he, nevertheless, remains to have power to exercise all other acts 'of ordinary or extraordinary administration; and therefore may, 'however notour bankrupt, borrow money, and grant securities for 'the same; or he may sell his land for a just price paid, whereof 'no creditor can complain, as the bankrupt's funds are not thereby 'lessened.' Kilk. 65.

But, although the general doctrine is thus clear, it requires some discussion, to explain, what particular transactions have been considered as falling under the description of 'nova debita.'

1. No title to land, in Scotland, is complete, till seisine has been taken upon the conveyance. It may be possible, in some cases, to take seisine on the same day that the conveyance is granted; but, in general, there must be some interval. Of this, advantage has frequently been taken, to rear up an interpretation of the statute, that might prove fatal to securities on land. To explain this, it may be proper to anticipate, in some degree, a matter that will

will be fully discussed hereafter. In order to give to creditors, as much as possible, the advantage of the term of sixty days, it has been provided, that a conveyance of land shall be held not to be of the date of its being granted, but of the date of the seisine, or public act, by which it is completed. 'All dispositions, &c. 'whereupon infeftment may follow,' says the statute, 'shall only 'be reckoned to be of the date of the seisine lawfully taken there-'on.' Now, upon this clause, it was argued, that, being intended for the benefit of the creditors, and not of the holder of the deed, it must have the effect, in all questions on the statute, to make the security, or real right, be considered as of the date of the seisine, while the money advanced in consideration of it, is, of course, held to constitute a debt, from the moment of advance. The effect of this subtilty, if sanctioned by the Court, would have been, to have included, within the statute, every transaction, however fair and onerous, in which an advance was made, previous to the completion of the security. But, after many variations of opinion, the Court have at last settled, that such a case does not fall within the rule.

When the question first occurred, the opinion of the Court was much unsettled, with respect to the exclusion of new transactions from the statute; and the judgements were chiefly regulated by the opinion, which prevailed at the time, upon this principal question. These early decisions, therefore, I shall not detail; but merely refer to them, that the reader may have it in his power to examine them. 1st January 1717, Brugh against Gray; Bruce, xlv. 60 *.—29th January and 12th December 1717, Grant against Duncan, Dalr. clxviii. 232; clxxviii. 244.—19th January 1726, Chalmers against Creditors of Craig of Ricarton; I. Kaimes, xix. 186.

In this last case, of Craig of Ricarton, the principal question, with respect to the exclusion of new transactions from the statute, was settled in the affirmative: and, in the next case that occurred, the

* The collection to which I here refer, is bound up with the 31 vol of the Faculty Collection.

the pure question, of an exception founded upon the subtilty with respect to the date of heritable conveyances, came to trial.

In the great bankruptcy of Lowis of Merchieston, the following case arose.—Two heritable bonds were granted by Lowis of Merchieston, to Colonel Charteris of Aimsfield: one, dated 3d March 1718; the other, 22d November 1721. But seisine was not taken on either, till December 1727; several years after the dates of the bonds, and within sixty days of Merchieston's bankruptcy. Much litigation took place upon the question, Whether, laying the statute out of view, the bonds had not been granted for prior debts, the old documents having been cancelled? But it was found, that there was no proof of this; so that the question came to rest upon the statute alone: and the footing upon which it was pleaded before the Lord Ordinary, was, 1. That the securities were to be held as of the date of the infeftments, and within sixty days of bankruptcy: 2. That as this presumptive date was not introduced in favour of the creditor infeft, so as to give him a privilege as if his contract with the bankrupt were of the date of the seisine, but in favour only of the other creditors, and in pœnam of him who kept up his seisine latent, the deed was to be considered as granted of the date of the seisine, and in security of a prior debt, originating at the date of the bond. The Lord Ordinary (Newhall) decided, 'That both the bonds, bearing date so many years before 'Merchieston's bankruptcy, fell under the statute 1696; in regard 'the infeftments thereupon were not taken by the Colonel till 'within sixty days of Merchieston's bankruptcy, according to the 'disposition of the said act; and that the clause of the said act, 'making the securities to be considered as of the date of the in-'feftment, was noways introduced in favour of the creditor infeft, 'to give him the privilege, as of a new debt then contracted of 'the date of the infeftment, but was introduced only in favour of 'the co-creditor, and in pœnam of the creditor infeft, who had 'kept up his precept of seisine latent; and, therefore, that both 'the first bond, as to its whole sums, and the second bond, falls 'under the act of Parliament 1696, and are reducible upon the 'said act.'—This judgement, it will be observed, did not proceed,

like

like those in the former cases, upon the question, Whether a new transaction, within the sixty days, was subject to reduction under the act? That question, on the contrary, was taken for granted in the negative; and the point determined, was merely this, Whether, in pœnam of concealed securities, the act did not authorise a splitting of the security from the bond, so as to bring the case under the description of a disposition, &c. for an old debt? *

The

* This case is nowhere reported, but in the Dictionary; and therefore I subjoin the argument.—Mr JOHN FORBES, in a petition for Colonel Charteris, the holder of the security, argued against the admission of any penal distinction (which was not expressed in the act) between the case of a novum debitum, the security for which is completed, unico contextu, within the sixty days—and the case of a transaction taking place before the sixty days, the seisine upon which is taken within them. The validity of a security of this kind, within the sixty days, is implied, and is indeed necessary, for supporting the commerce of the country. The security of the records depends upon it; for, otherwise, no man could safely lend money, though the records should show a free and unincumbered estate; since personal debts may exist, on which the borrower may be made bankrupt in sixty days, when the security must fall. Now, when the bond is, by the act, drawn forward to the date of the seisine, the debt must be held as contracted of that date; at least, there is no foundation, in this statute, for a different conclusion. The act of 1696, as well as that of 1621, applies only to the case of securities for prior debts. The whole of the act 1696, when taken together, as well as the precise words, show this. The provisions are against securities for debts already contracted, on the one hand, and debts to be contracted, on the other; and the second clause of the act, relating to the date of the deed, must be interpreted to refer only to the deeds already mentioned in the act, viz. securities for prior debts.

DUNDAS of ARNISTON, (afterwards Lord President), for the Creditors, contended, That the clause, declaring the date of the seisine to be the date of the security, is quite general, without any distinction between old and new debts, it being intended to prevent persons, in collusion with their debtor, from taking securities, upon which infeftment might follow, and keeping them latent, till the debtor (having induced others to lend him money) could hold out no longer, when the infeftment might be taken, and the creditors deluded. Without this provision, the statute is defective and useless. The plain intention of the Legislature was, to declare, that, at whatever time the debt might be contracted, the security should be held as of the date of the seisine, and a fraud presumed from the keeping of the precept latent. Thus, creditors have an opportunity of bringing matters to a stop, when they see securities given: and the creditor

The Court adopted the very words of Lord Newhall's judgement, admitting the distinction, and reducing the deed: and, upon a petition and answers, they adhered. 19th June 1731, Trustees for the creditors of Lowis of Merchieston against Colonel Charteris of Aimsfield; I. Dict. 86.—Sess. Pap. Adv. Lib.

The

creditor has himself to blame, if he do not instantly take seisine on his security. He entraps nobody, when he takes infeftment immediately; but every thing is reversed, and the presumption of collusion is strong, where he does not instantly take his infeftment. It is a security for a novum debitum, in the one case---for an old debt, in the other And if the law favours a new debt, he who takes infeftment immediately, is entitled to that favour · he who delays it, is not

Upon this argument, the Court adopted the very terms of Lord Newhall's judgement.

FORBES of CULLODEN (afterwards Lord President also) wrote a petition against this judgement, and ARNISTON again wrote the answer —In the petition, Forbes argued, 1. That the case of a fair purchase, was not within the range of the statute · and he assimilated the case of an heritable security, for money advanced, to a purchase. it is the purchase of a redeemable right to lands. The purchaser, in either case, is no creditor, till the transaction is finished, and the deeds delivered The law annuls not all dispositions: that would have been unjust, inexpedient, and hard —it annuls those only, which are made to creditors And, that no doubt can be entertained, that this word 'creditor' is applied only to anterior creditors, is plain, from what follows ---since a disposition, for ready money paid, is not in satisfaction, till that instant, the creditor has nothing to ask; and an heritable bond is no satisfaction · ---nor are these deeds in further security, for the acquirer has no prior security. A disposition, or heritable bond, then, exchanged for cash within the sixty days, is not challengeable under the words of this law. 2 Then, how does the second clause of the act strike? This second clause is a mere execution of the first, and is clearly dependent on it; and the expression must be very strong indeed, to bring a case within it, which fell not within the first. But, on the contrary, the words limit the second clause to the case of the first one The provision is to operate, only as to the case of a bankrupt disponing in security of a prior debt. There may be inconveniency, in a purchaser, or lender, omitting to take his infeftment: but this is not the inconveniency, against which the statute is pointed It might prevent frauds, to force them instantly to take seisine but the law says not so If such a law be fit, it should be enacted: but never can any such new law affect this case And it is the universal practice, not only for purchasers, but for creditors on heritable bonds, to defer taking seisine, (especially if the money is not to lie long), till the debtor's circumstances be suspected

There

The decision, pronounced in the case of Scott of Blair's creditors, against Colonel Charteris, confirmed the judgement in the above case.—The question arose, upon a conveyance granted by Scott of Blair, as cautioner for Lowis of Merchieston, to Colonel Charteris: and the only difference between this case and the last, was, that Merchieston was infeft, and gave an heritable security, containing precept of seisine, on which the seisine followed: whereas, Scott was not infeft, but, having right to an heritable debt, by assignation, on which he never had been infeft, he conveyed it, with assignation to the unexecuted precept. Lord Newhall (Ordinary also in the former case), and, afterwards, the Court, found, 'That this case did not fall under the act; because, whatever 'might have been the intent of the statute, the words respect only the cases where infeftment is necessary to denude the bankrupt: and, where it goes this length, it has a most valuable effect, but cannot, by construction, be extended further than the 'words will bear.' January 1734, I. Dict. 86.—See also, 25th November 1735, Mathieson's Creditors against Smith.

These decisions proceeded, not upon the ground that the statute was, in any shape, applicable to a security purchased by a present advance; but that the second clause of the statute was intended, in every case, to prevent creditors, in possession of securities, from keeping them latent; and that, being intended for the general benefit, in opposition to the creditor holding the security, it was to have the effect of splitting the real right from the obligation, and bringing the case under the description of a security given for a former debt. But all those subtleties were swept away by the decision in the case of Home of Manderston, which occurred about

There was nothing new in the argument for the creditors They refuse Aimsfield's interpretation of the second clause, as merely applicable to the first—maintain the expression, 'this case of bankrupt,' to be general, including all competitions on bankruptcy—and repeat their assertion, that the law is elusory, unless this be held as a provision applicable to all cases of dispositions, &c whether for old or new contractions. Why (they argued) should it be in pœnam only of those getting security for a new debt, when the fault, the evil consequences to other creditors, the presumption of collusion to entrap, is as strong in the case of a person entering into a new transaction?

bout twenty years after those of Merchieston, &c. and to which I have already referred, in speaking of the general point.

Home of Manderston became cautioner for Thomson, in a cash-account, and received, in security, a disposition from Burnet, a friend of Thomson's, containing an assignation to an unexecuted procuratory of resignation. Burnet having, about six months after, become bankrupt, Manderston executed the procuratory, and took infeftment. A creditor of Burnet challenged the security, on the act 1696. There were two questions: 1. Whether the statute applied to the case of a conveyance, where seisine was not necessary to divest the debtor? 2. Whether, as a novum debitum, this transaction was not without the rule of the statute? It is unnecessary to detail the argument at the Bar upon this last point, (which is all that we have any thing to do with at present); for it was taken up on the Bench; and every thing valuable in it, is detailed by Lord Kilkerran, in stating the opinions of the Judges. The Court 'found, that the case did not fall under the act of Parliament 1696.' But they did not fix upon what point they rested their judgement. Lord Kilkerran, in stating their opinions, after giving a review of the cases of Duncan, of Ricarton's, and of Merchieston's creditors, in which he states the first and the last, as having proceeded upon an opinion, that the act was intended to force a creditor, holding a security, to publish it, whether the transaction was old or new, and upon the idea of a splitting of the security from the obligation, he adds—'But this construction 'appearing to be altogether imaginary, and to have no foundation 'in the statute, the Lords were now unanimous,* that the statute 'did not reach nova debita. They considered, that the statute was 'only meant to supply the defects of the act 1621, and to prevent 'the debtor's giving securities to some, in prejudice of his other prior 'creditors—that he, nevertheless, remains to have power to exercise all other acts of ordinary or extraordinary administration, 'and therefore may, however notour bankrupt, borrow money, and

* Lord Kames, in his report, says, 'Elchies dissented, on the authority of Merchieston's case.'

' and grant securities for the same; or he may sell his land, for a ' just price paid, whereof no creditor can complain, as the bank- ' rupt's funds are not thereby lessened. But, to suppose the clause ' in the statute, which enacts, that the dispositions or assignations ' shall be held to be of the date of the seisine, did extend to such ' nova debita, were to suppose, what nobody ever dreamt of, that ' the statute was intended to restrain the commerce of borrowing ' money by bankrupts; for, as the clause makes no distinction, ' whether the seisine be taken recently, or not, a creditor, who ' lends his money upon heritable security, during the running of ' the sixty days, would lose his preference, though he took his in- ' feftment without delaying an hour, as there must always be some ' interval between the date of the bond, and the date of the sei- ' sine: and, to add but one consideration more, the most sanguine ' advocates, for extending the statute to nova debita, can have no ' pretence for understanding it to comprehend irredeemable dispo- ' sitions for a price paid; and surely, if the statute had been in- ' tended to oblige creditors, even for nova debita, not to defer ' taking their seisines, or, in pœnam, to be subject to that certifi- ' cation in the statute, it must have, with equal reason, done the ' same, with respect to seisines upon irredeemable dispositions.' 29th January 1751, Johnson against Burnet and Home of Man-derston, Kilk. p. 63.; Kames' Rem. Dec. cxx. 246.; II. Falconer, clxxxix. 227.

I shall mention only one other case, in which the judgement, settling the point as above, was strongly confirmed. By antenup-tial contract of marriage, between James Milne and Marjory Finlay, he, for the causes therein specified, disponed to her the liferent of a house and garden; and the deed contained a precept of seisine. James Milne was not infeft; and no infeftment was taken on the contract for two years. In the mean while, Milne contracted debts, and, within sixty days of his bankruptcy, the liferent was properly completed, by seisine being taken in Milne's favour, and another seisine upon the contract of marriage. A reduction was brought, of this deed in favour of the wife, as falling under the statute 1696, c. 5. Lord Craig, Ordinary, refused to reduce the deed; and

and a petition, against his judgement, was unanimously refused, without answers. 12th November 1798, Mitchell against Finlay.

Thus, it may be regarded as a settled point, that no objection can be taken, on the statute, to securities granted of the date of the advance, although the seisine should not happen to be taken till within the sixty days before bankruptcy.

2. There seems to be still less reason to believe, that a conveyance of moveables, made in consideration of a sum advanced, is to be held as a security for a former debt, merely because the last act of its completion was posterior to the moment of the advance. The case of this kind, most nearly analogous to those which we have been considering, is, that of an assignation to a bond, or other personal ground of debt. It is not a complete transference of the claim, so as to be effectual, in competition with creditors of the assignor, doing diligence, or getting a second assignation, unless intimation of the conveyance has been made to the debtor; and this has given rise to the doubt, whether the conveyance is not to be held as of the date of the intimation? But it is now settled, that, when the intimation is made, it has relation back to the date of the conveyance, and that the date of the conveyance is the date of the real right. This question was tried in the case of Hay against Sinclair & Co., and so decided. Sinclair & Co. obtained, from a debtor of theirs, an assignation to certain shares in a mercantile adventure, in security of certain debts previously due, and of a sum of money, which they advanced to him at the date of the assignation. This deed was dated in January, it was not intimated till October; and, within sixty days after the intimation, the assignor was rendered bankrupt. The trustee for the creditors of the assignor, objected to this, as a security constituted within the sixty days; and the question was, whether the conveyance was to be held as of the date of the intimation, or as of the date of the assignation itself? The Court sustained the assignation, as not included under the rule of the statute: 8th July 1788, Hay against Sinclair & Co., VIII. Fac. Col. xxviii. 45.

The

The principle of this decision, I apprehend to be applicable to all cases of securities, which require a separate act to complete them. Thus, if a bill be drawn by a merchant upon his correspondent, in favour of one who advances money for it, strictly speaking, it is neither a security, nor a conveyance, till accepted by the drawee: yet, the date of the acceptance being posterior to the advance, will not entitle the creditors of the drawer to challenge it, as a security for a prior debt. In the same way, if money be borrowed, upon the security of a vendition of a ship which is at sea, the vendition is not complete, without taking possesion, but the delay of this act of completion, till the arrival of the vessel, will not alter the lender's condition, nor endanger his security upon the statute, as granted for a prior debt.

It is a very different question, whether, in any of these cases, the creditors of the person borrowing, or a trustee, under a sequestration of his estate, could prevent the lender from completing his conveyance, and would be preferable to him, if prior, with the completion of their rights, and diligence? I shall have an opportunity of showing, hereafter, that of this there can be no doubt; but, in a question, whether the security can be cut down, after it has been actually completed, there seems to be as little doubt, that the statute of 1696 has no application.

3. In the cases already discussed, the debtor is supposed to have done his part, in completing the right of the person to whom the transference is made. The taking of seisine on the heritable securities—the intimation of the assignment—the procuring acceptance of the bill—the taking possession of the vessel—are all acts, to be accomplished without the further interference of the bankrupt: but the question is more difficult, where any thing is required to be done by the bankrupt himself, in order to make the right effectual. Perhaps the distinction may lie here; that wherever the bankrupt interferes, only to do that which both parties understood had been done at first, and upon the faith of which understanding, alone, the money was advanced, the act is not objectionable, nor such as can entitle creditors to separate the security from the advance; but,

but, where he does that, which both parties were sensible he had not done at first, and which he only bound himself to do, it is objectionable.

Of the former, we have an example, in the case of More against Allan, where, a merchant, in this country, having drawn a bill on his correspondent in London, for the amount of a cargo consigned, raised money, on the faith of that bill being accepted. The consignment was, however, rejected, and acceptance refused; upon which, the cargo was given over to another house, upon whom a new bill was drawn, and put into the hands of the lender, in place of the original one. This new bill was challenged, on the act 1696, as given in satisfaction of a prior debt; but the Court refused to sustain the action. The case is stated very fully in the judgment of the Lord Ordinary (Armadale). He found, 'That about 'the middle of March 1796, Messrs Sinclair & Williamson consigned a cargo of wheat, belonging to them, to Mr Claud Scott, 'merchant in London, and indorsed the bills of lading thereof to 'Mr Scott: That, upon the 16th March 1796, Messrs S. & W. 'drew a bill, for 1000l. Sterling, upon Claud Scott, to whom the 'foresaid cargo of wheat was consigned, and indorsed said bill to 'the defender Mr Allan, for value given of that date: That, upon the 18th March, Messrs S. & W. drew another bill for 1200l. 'upon Claud Scott, the consignee to the foresaid cargo of wheat, 'and indorsed said bill to the defender Mr Allan, for value given 'of that date: That the value of the cargo of wheat, exceeded the 'amount of the foresaid bills; and, that these two bills were 'drawn by S. & W. upon Claud Scott, and indorsed to the defender Mr Allan, in the view of the consignment of said cargo: 'That Claud Scott, the intended consignee, refused to receive the 'consignment of the cargo of wheat, made to him by S. & W., 'and likewise to accept the said bills, drawn upon him, and indorsed to the defender. That the foresaid cargo of wheat, and 'the bills of lading thereof, were thereupon given to Mr Alexander Ross, of London, who, upon 29th March 1796, accepted 'two bills, drawn by S. & W., one for 1000l., and the other for '1200l., which were indorsed to the defender, in lieu of the two

'former

'former bills drawn upon Mr Scott, the intended consignee.'—Sinclair & Williamson were rendered bankrupts in the beginning of April. In these circumstances, the Lord Ordinary decided, 'That the two bills last granted, ought not to be consider-'ed as a security falling under the act 1696.' To this judgement, the Court adhered, by refusing a petition, without answers: 23d January 1800, More, trustee for Sinclair and Williamson's creditors, against Allan.—Upon the same principle, perhaps, might such a case be decided, as that of Smith and Pickering was, in England; where a bill of exchange was delivered over for a valuable consideration, but the debtor forgot to indorse it. It was found, that he might indorse it, after an act of bankruptcy. In Scotland, had the debtor been applied to, in such a case, to indorse a bill, on which he had thus raised money, is there not reason to believe, that the case would have been held not to fall under the statute 1696?

But in the other set of cases, where the parties are sensible that the security was not at first completed, and where the advance is made on the faith of its being afterwards granted, it can scarcely be said, that the lender of the money is more than a personal creditor merely. In one sense, it is true, the security makes, in such a case, a part of the original transaction, or rather of the communing of parties, but still the act of Parliament seems to apply. In the cases of this description, which have occurred in the Court, two grounds of argument have been taken in support of the security: FIRST, that the transaction is to be held as continuous, the security and advance of money being the counter considerations for each other: and, SECONDLY, that a security granted in consequence of such previous obligation, is not (as the act requires a challengeable deed to be) 'voluntary.' These pleas are naturally so mingled and interwoven with each other, that, although I had intended to reserve any remarks upon necessary deeds, for another part of the discussion, it will be more natural, perhaps, to consider the point here.

Although the statute of 1696 does not, like the English statutes of bankruptcy, vest a right in the creditors, or a trustee for them, as at the commencement of 'the term of relation,' it was evidently intended to take away all power from the debtor, of interfering to alter the rights of the creditors, within the sixty days. The view of the Legislature seems to have been, that wherever a person stood, at the commencement of the appointed period, as a mere personal creditor, whether the debtor's obligation to him was to pay money, to deliver goods, or to grant a deed, he should have nothing to expect, but from the operation of law; and that it should be unlawful for the bankrupt to interfere, or to grant a deed which might have the effect of bestowing a preference upon one, to the prejudice of the rest. There is, in truth, no essential difference, in respect of personal credit, between the condition of a creditor to whom the bankrupt has bound himself to grant a deed, and him to whom he is bound to pay money. They are both personal creditors merely: the faith of the debtor is trusted to in both cases: the aid of the law stands equally ready for enforcing either obligation. If a person have lent money, trusting, not to the borrower's personal credit, but to a real security, which is either complete, or the completion of which is in his own power without any necessity for the borrower's interfering, he is safe; provided he completes it before other creditors use diligence to attach the subject, or complete their conveyances before him. But if he have lent his money upon a mere promise, or personal engagement, that a security shall be granted; how is he entitled to greater favour, than one who has lent his money, or allowed it to remain with the debtor, upon an express obligation, that the money shall be paid at a particular day? Both of them trust to the personal credit and good faith of the borrower, and run the risk of his bankruptcy, and of the loss of power to perform his personal engagements, which is naturally consequent upon it. It would therefore appear, that the expression 'voluntary,' in the statute, is properly opposed merely to judicial; and that no act of the bankrupt, which gives a preference to a particular creditor, is, upon pretence of the debtor being under an express obligation to grant it, exempted from the rule of the statute.

Of

Of those cases, in which an obligation to grant a security has been held insufficient to exempt it, when actually granted, from the rule of the statute, the first is, that of Eccles against the Creditors of Merchieston. In that case, the narrative of an assignation bore, as the consideration, money instantly advanced: but it having been referred to the assignee, whether it was not in security of a prior debt? he declared, that, when he lent his money, it was covenanted, that he should have an assignation, as part of his security; but that, when the money was lent, and the bond written out, the assignation was not written, and was not delivered to him, till about a week afterwards:—'The Lords found, that the assignation falls 'under the sanction of the act of Parliament:' 4th February 1729; Dict. vol. 1. p. 83. *

The next case of this kind, was Houston and Company, of Glasgow, against Stewarts. Stewarts interposed their credit for Maxwell, who agreed to give them heritable security for their relief; and accordingly wrote them a letter, desiring them 'to 'employ any writer they pleased, to draw out an heritable bond of 'security, on my subject, any way you and he agrees, for the sum 'of 60l., and this shall be your security till that is done.' The title-deeds were also put into the hands of Stewarts, but the heritable bond was not made out and executed, till within the sixty days of Maxwell's bankruptcy. A reduction was brought upon the statute; and the defence was, that this was one and the same transaction, from beginning to end; that there was, here, an advance of money, upon the faith of a security, stipulated for, and agreed to; and that the security, granted under an express obligation, could not be considered as voluntary.—The Court supported the security: 20th February 1772, V. Fac. Coll. ix. 14. †

There

* In Nisbet of Northfield against Cairns, a debtor proposed to borrow 1500l on heritable security. It was advanced, in three payments, by the lender's agent, who had been instructed to find a hand for it; and, some months afterward, the security was completed within sixty days of the debtor's bankruptcy. The security was challenged; but I do not know the judgement of the Court. Winter 1771.

† This case is frequently quoted, but always disregarded as a precedent. In one case, to be afterwards taken notice of, (16th November 1799, M'Lean against Primrose),

the

There is another case reported upon this point, which is as little entitled to be relied on as that of Houston & Co. That is, the case of Spottiswood against Robertson Barclay; 19th November 1783, VII. Fac. Coll. cxxii. 193.

I have frequently heard the first Judges on the Bench, express disapprobation when that case was quoted to them. One judgement was, indeed, pronounced in it, sustaining an heritable bond of annuity, granted by a husband, within sixty days of his bankruptcy, in respect of a prior obligation to grant it, contained in his marriage contract. But the Judges were much divided in opinion; and a hearing, in presence, was appointed, for the purpose of solemnly reviewing and settling the question. It never came again to trial, having been compromised. But, if I can judge, from the incidental opinions, which I have heard, of two Judges, in particular, (one of whom sat upon the Bench at the time, and another was Counsel in the cause), there is much reason to believe, that the ultimate decision would have been very different from the first judgement.

The question came to trial, however, in the course of Brough's bankruptcy, in two different cases. In the one, (with Messrs Duncan & Jollie), an heritable security was given by Brough, for relief of a cautionary obligation undertaken for him: there was an interval of a month, before the granting of the security; but it had been stipulated, at the first, and was the condition of the cautioner's engagement. In the other case, (with Messrs Spankie & Jollie), there was, as in Houston's case, a written obligation, in which there was this clause: 'And, seeing I agreed to give you 'an heritable security, in relief of said sum, previous to your con- 'senting

the Lord Ordinary (Meadowbank) accompanied his judgement with a note, reprobating this judgement in Houstoun's case. 'That decision,' says his Lordship, 'is clearly contrary to principle; since an obligation to grant a preference, cannot constitute an 'actual preference on an heritable subject, in a question with other creditors: and 'accordingly, it is one of those decisions which are frequently quoted, and as often 'disregarded, by the Court.'

'senting to join me in said bill, I oblige myself to do so according-
'ly over my property in Register Street; and that, as soon as
'the proper writings can be made out.' This letter was of the same date with the cautionary engagement, but the heritable security was not granted till within the sixty days.

On the first of these cases, it was observed, on the Bench, that 'there could be no difficulty whatever. The debt to the Bank, 'was contracted in March, and the heritable bond not granted till 'May. During the interval, Messrs Jolly and Duncan had only 'a personal claim of relief against Brough. the heritable bond, 'therefore, being clearly a further security, falls under the act:' and so the Court unanimously found. On the second case, it was said from the Bench, that 'the above judgement, in the case of 'Houston & Co. against Stewarts, was erroneous. Till the heritable 'bond was granted, Messrs Spankie & Jolly were mere personal 'creditors; and it is contrary to the principle of our law, as laid 'down, both by Lord Bankton, and M'Kenzie in his Commentary 'on 1621, that an obligation to grant an heritable security, 'should entitle the bankrupt voluntarily to fulfil it, after he falls 'under the retrospect of the act 1696.' And in this case, also, the Court unanimously sustained the objections: 5th June 1793, Trustees of Brough against Duncan & Jollie, and against Spankie & Jollie, IX. Fac. Coll. lvii. & lviii. 123. 126.

Another case was decided lately, which, although not a solemn decision, may be taken, as illustrating and confirming the judgements in Brough's. John M'Lean, merchant in Leith, was in the right of an heritable bond, and his right was duly completed by infeftment. This bond, with the conveyance, and the two infeftments, he deposited with Sinclair & Williamson, to whom he was due 300l., it being intended to convey the security regularly to them, for which purpose, a scroll of the conveyance was made out. Mr Primrose was prevailed on to advance the 300l. to Sinclair & Williamson; and the heritable bond and infeftment were deposited with him, and the scroll of the conveyance delivered to

him,

him, to have it extended in his own favour. The conveyance was not, however, completed, and M'Lean became bankrupt. A trust-deed was executed; and, at a meeting of the trust-committee, M'Lean stated the transaction, and expressed his anxiety to have the conveyance completed. The committee ordered evidence to be produced, of the advance, and of the agreement at the time, and of the lodging of the writings, and they required an opinion from a lawyer or conveyancer, that Mr Primrose was entitled to the conveyance. An eminent lawyer was consulted, who gave the opinion quoted below *. The conveyance was not, however, executed. Mr M'Lean refused to do it, and Primrose brought an action against him, for having him ordered to implement his obligation, by granting a conveyance. Appearance was made for Mr M'Lean alone, not for the creditors; and his defence resolved into this, That he had informed the committee of Mr Primrose's demand—that, without their orders, he could not grant the deed—and that, by doing so, he would risk the benefit of the cessio bonorum, for which he had applied. The Sheriff pronounced judgement against M'Lean. The cause was brought into the Court of Session, and Lord Meadowbank, as Ordinary on the bills, 'remitted to the Sheriff, to alter 'his interlocutor, and to assoilzie Mr M'Lean.' Upon a petition against this judgement, being presented, the Judges seemed to be of

* 'I think, there is sufficient evidence, that the memorialist (Primrose) paid the money to Sinclair & Williamson, on the faith of Mr M'Lean's granting an assignation to the heritable bond: and, in particular, I refer to the delivery of the heritable bond and infeftment to the memorialist, the payment of the money to Sinclair & Williamson; the scroll of the assignation to them; and the written declaration of Sinclair & Williamson, and Mr M'Lean. In this situation, I think, that Mr M'Lean, and Mr Nairn, (the trustee), may be compelled to grant the conveyance demanded by the memorialist. My reason for thinking so, is, that Mr M'Lean was under an obligation to grant the conveyance, previous to the trust; and nothing has since happened, to bar his implementing that obligation. The act 1696, does not apply to a conveyance of the heritable bond and infeftment, by Mr M'Lean, to the memorialist, granted under the circumstances of this case, which seems exactly to resemble that of Houston & Co against Stewarts, 20th February 1772, where the Court assoilzied from a reduction, brought by creditors, of an heritable bond, granted by a common debtor within sixty days of his bankruptcy, and refused a petition against that interlocutor, with answers.'

of opinion, that, where the creditors of a bankrupt oppose such an action as this, the bankrupt cannot be compelled to grant a deed, which, if he granted without compulsion, would convict him of fraud, and be reducible, under the statute 1696, but, as the only opposition was on the part of M'Lean, the Court returned to the Sheriff's interlocutor: 16th November 1799, M'Lean against Primrose.

It seems to be a legitimate conclusion, from these decisions, that it will not entitle a security to exemption from the statute, that the holder of that security stipulated for it, at advancing the money. He must be able to show, that the exchange of the security, for the money, or other consideration, was simultaneous—that it was one and the same transaction—and that, at no period, did he trust to the mere personal credit, or good faith, of the bankrupt.

4. Where the security is granted, not to the creditor in a prior debt, but to a cautioner, who becomes bound to that creditor, is this to be regarded as a security given for a new debt, or as in nothing different from a security to the creditor himself? Thus, Swinton was debtor to Sir William Forbes & Co.—a demand was made upon Swinton, and he offered, in security, a vendition of a ship—Sir William Forbes & Co. refused this, and Swinton then applied to Mr Campbell, who agreed to interpose his credit with Sir William Forbes & Co., on receiving, as a security for his relief, a vendition to Swinton's ship—Swinton was made bankrupt three weeks after this transaction. 1. Mr Campbell contended, against the claim of Sir William Forbes & Co, that his obligation depended on the efficacy of the vendition; and that he could not, therefore, be forced to pay, till that previous question were determined. The Court found, that Sir William Forbes & Co. had no concern with the efficacy of the vendition. 2. Then the validity of the debtor's acceptance was challenged. It was found a good acceptance. 3. Another question remained, but it was properly a question between the general creditors and the cautioner,

viz.

viz. the validity of the vendition, as a right, granted in security of the cautioner's claim of relief. But this question never received a judicial decision; it was compromised: 19th February 1790, Trustee for Swinton's creditors against Sir William Forbes & Co. In the papers in this case, reference was made to the case of Grant of Artamford against Grant of Carron; but that was a case in which no new cautioner was interposed. The circumstances were these: Artamford being creditor to Carron for 1500l., received 500l. in cash; and having occasion for the balance, the following transaction took place—The sum of 2000l. was borrowed from Mr Innes by Carron; and Artamford became his cautioner, on receiving an heritable security in relief over part of Carron's lands, called Allochie. On the day the 2000l. was received, Artamford got payment of the balance of his debt, being 1050l.; and Carron having become bankrupt within the sixty days, Artamford was obliged, as cautioner, to pay the 2000l.; and claimed in Carron's ranking upon his heritable security in relief. An objection was stated to him, so far as concerned the 1050l.; and the Court found the heritable bond of relief struck at by the act 1696, in so far as extends to the sum of 1050l., with interest, for which Artamford was antecedently creditor to Carron; reserving the effect of the personal obligation of relief: Summer Session 1788. *

In the case of Brough's trustee against Duncan & Jollie, 5th June 1793, quoted above, we have seen, that a security was given, in relief, to cautioners; but it was not granted till some time after the cautionary engagement was undertaken, and, consequently, was not properly a case of novum debitum. An attempt was indeed made, to bring it to the case of a new debt, by saying, that the security was originally stipulated for, and made a part of the new transaction·

* In the ranking, a question occurred, which will demand particular attention hereafter, viz. Whether, in claiming as an adjudging creditor on the whole estate, under the personal obligation of relief, Artamford was entitled to rank for the full sum, without deducting what he had received under the preferable security? or, whether his claim on the adjudication was not to be restricted to the balance? The Court ranked him as an adjudger on the general estate of Carron, without deduction of what he had drawn in consequence of his heritable bond over Allochie. 2d March 1791.

transaction: but this was unsuccessful, and there was no decision on the point, whether such a deed, granted to a cautioner, would have been considered as a security in a new transaction, if it had been made at the time of the cautioner's engagement.

The last case, in which this question occurred, was, that of the Trustees for Monteith's creditors against Douglas of Mairs, &c. The case was shortly this: Monteith being indebted to the Dutchess of Douglas in 2500l., her trustees agreed to supersede diligence against him, on his procuring security for 1250l. He applied to Mr Douglas, and others, and they became bound for the 1250l.; Monteith disponing to them, in security, a house in Glasgow, worth 500l. Seisine was taken and recorded, on this disposition, on the 17th October 1785; and Monteith was made bankrupt on the 7th December, fifty-two days after the seisine. A reduction was brought on the act 1696. The Court first reduced the deed; but afterwards, they supported it: 10th December 1794, Monteith's Trustees against Douglas. *

5. The

* On the abstract question, some of the Judges thought the statute applicable: In which opinion, they seem to have proceeded upon these grounds 1 They allowed, that, in form, the debt, so far as the cautioner was concerned, was a new debt; since it was, by his cautionary engagement, that he first became debtor. and that, in this view, the statute did not apply. But, 2dly, they said, that the act provides against indirect, as well as against direct securities, and this is plainly nothing else than an indirect security, and must be included It was admitted, that a case might be supposed, of an indirect preference, brought about by means of a security, which, yet, would not fall under the act; as, where one borrows money, and, with that money, pays off prior creditors, for the lender has no concern with the application of the money But, where a man becomes cautioner, the natural question is, Why cannot you as well give the security directly to the creditor, without any interposition? The answer is, 'That may be struck at by the act, if I be rendered bankrupt in sixty days; but this comes to the same thing in the main, and the act cannot trouble us' This is, in short, the very form of transaction which the law prohibits, under the description of an indirect security. These Judges, in short, considered a decision, which should exclude this case, as equal to a repeal of the statute.

The Judges, who thought the act inapplicable to the case, seemed to rest their opinion upon the effects to commerce, and the injustice to cautioners, with which an

opposite

5. The last question, which deserves attention, on this point, (and it is, indeed, of great importance), is, Whether the transactions, indorsations, draughts, &c. &c of merchants, carried on in the course of trade, and without any suspicion of fraud, down to the bankruptcy of one of them, fall under the act? This question, I speak of, as very important; because, should the act apply, it is less possible (if, indeed, it be in any shape possible) for the most upright dealers to avoid the effects of the statute. In a cautionary engagement, the very transaction implies suspicion, but the rapidity of mercantile transactions, allows no time for deliberation or inquiry.

A question, nearly of this kind, occurred in the Bankruptcy of James Stein of Kilbagie. Stein had a cash-account with Sir William Forbes & Co., and the transactions upon it went on regularly to the day of Stein's failure. Stein failed on the 28th February 1788, when the balance due, on his cash account, was 34,636l.

opposite judgement must be attended Bankers do not like heritable securities, they prefer good personal obligations When they give a cash account, and, rejecting heritable security, desire personal, it is natural for the person getting the credit, to offer, to those who engage as his cautioners, that security which the banker rejects · so, the affair is settled. But the cautioners die, and new ones are demanded—the new cautioners require heritable security, and it is given them. Why should this be more objectionable than the other? The thing happens every day; new cautioners come into cash accounts, and new securities are granted. There may be cases, where fraud can be proved, and, when proved, it authorises a reduction; but, upon the general question, whether the act applies to reduce such a security as this, given on such an occasion, there can be no doubt The act is against securities given to prior creditors for anterior debts: but this is not a security given to a prior creditor, directly or indirectly. no security is given over the debtor's estate; the creditor can avail himself nothing of the security given to the cautioner. That there is a defect, and possibility of evading that law, may be true, but that is for the Legislature to consider, not for a Court

Such were the different opinions on the abstract question But one Judge, of high respectability, moved a distinction, in this case, founded upon the facts of the case, as indicative of the total absence of fraud. To this, however, the other Judges would not agree. They held, that the act 1696 was made, as a rule, to preclude the necessity of inquiries into fraud, and, for this purpose, established a presumption of fraud, not to be got the better of by any proof Although, therefore, in cases which do not fall under this presumptive rule, if fraud can be proved, it must annul the transaction; yet, no proof of fairness can rescue those cases, which do fall within the description, from the penal effects of the statutory rule.

34,636l. 11s. 10d Sterling. In security of this balance, the Company held bills, that had been deposited by Stein, and those of them which had been deposited within the sixty days of the bankruptcy, amounting to 18,158l. Sterling, were challenged, under the act; although, within the same period, no less than 38,599l. of advance had been made by Stein.

But the decision, in this case, went entirely upon the specialty, that the payments within the sixty days, had not only equalled, but even exceeded the value of the indorsations, so that, instead of a preference, or advantage, being given to Sir William Forbes & Co., they would, if restored to their situation as at the commencement of the sixty days, have been great gainers. David Stewart, trustee for Stein's creditors, against Sir William Forbes & Co.; 1. Ma. 1791.

To a question of this kind, in England, the statute of 19 Geo. III. would, in all probability, be held to apply. One great object of that statute was, to remove from objection the daily acts of merchants, in the course of trade and, although the expression seems to restrict the law to the case of payments in money, there seems to be little question entertained, in the English courts, that payments, by draughts and indorsations, would come under the statute. *

From this long deduction, it appears that the statute is confined to deeds granted in satisfaction, or security, of former debts. and, so strictly is it applied to securities of that description, that

* In the case of Hawkins & Penfold, Lord Hardwick said—' There is an express ' proviso in the act of Parliament, which indemnifies creditors in receiving money for ' their debts, though after an act of bankruptcy, if no notice; and there is no dif- ' ference between an actual payment of money, in satisfaction of debts, and indorsing ' bills of exchange, provided the money was received on them, before the commission ' issued; for I should take that as only a medium of payment, and no more; other- ' wise, it would be very hard.' 2 Vezey, 550.

that the shortest interval between the advance of money, and the granting of a security not originally stipulated, or relied on, is fatal to the preference. In the bankruptcy of Bertram Gardner & Co., a case occurred, in which this principle was strongly acknowledged.—A large advance was made, by the Royal Bank, to Bertram Gardner & Co., at a time when they were exerting themselves to avoid the bankruptcy which afterwards overtook them. This advance was made at 10 o'clock in the morning. In the course of that forenoon, the Bank began to fear for the credit of the house; and, having insisted for security, Bertram Gardner & Co. deposited bills with them, to a large amount. This was challenged, upon the statute, as the constitution of a security for a prior debt. When the cause came into Court, it was the general opinion of the Judges, that the security was objectionable, in so far as it applied to prior advances; upon understanding which, the Royal Bank, at once, renounced any claim upon these bills, as a security for the prior advance; so that the question did not come to judgement: July 1796, Mr Hotchkis, trustee for the creditors of Bertram Gardner & Co., against the Royal Bank.

Having seen, from this investigation, that the statute does not apply to new transactions, it is natural to inquire, in the next place, whether it be held to include every deed, which bestows an additional security for a prior debt. In the view of this inquiry, deeds may be divided into those which import a conveyance of some part of the debtor's funds, in satisfaction or security; and those which amount only to an obligation, or acknowledgement of debts.

I. DEEDS OF CONVEYANCE.—The words of the statute are so clear, that no question can be made, whether dispositions to heritable subjects, or heritable bonds, or assignations to heritable securities, fall under it, if given in satisfaction or security of former debts, and within sixty days of bankruptcy. But, with respect to conveyances of moveables, doubts have arisen: for the Court having settled,

settled, that payments in cash do not fall under the words of the law, and are not included in its scope and intention, it has been contended, upon the analogy of this case, that the delivery of goods, and the indorsation of bills, must also be exempted from the rule. The consideration of these cases, will clear up this part of the law.

1. PAYMENT, being the natural and proper way of extinguishing debt, law considers it as so favourable, that it is hardly to be recalled. Where, indeed, there is fraud in the transaction, it will be reduced; but, as no creditor can be said to act unfairly, or unjustly, in exerting himself to procure payment of his debt, and even in redoubling these exertions, in proportion to his fears for the credit of the debtor, it must be acknowledged, that it were extremely hard, if a creditor, after having demanded and received his own money, and employed it on commerce, or squandered it, perhaps, so that no wreck of it remained, should be forced to repay it. In securing payments, received bona fide from a bankrupt, the law of Scotland has gone further than in England has been thought safe. In respect of payments by the bankrupt, the only exception, which the English law admits, to the general right of the assignees, is, of money paid on bills of exchange, and money paid for goods purchased in the course of trade. I have subjoined the words of the statute *; the effect of which is concisely and clearly stated

* 'Whereas,' says the 19 Geo II c 32 § 1. 'many persons, within the 'description of, and liable to the statutes concerning bankrupts, frequently commit secret acts of bankruptcy, unknown to their creditors, and other persons, with whom, 'in the course of trade, they have dealings and transactions, and, after the committing thereof, continue to appear publicly, and carry on their trade and dealings, by 'buying and selling of goods and merchandizes, drawing, accepting, and negociating 'bills of exchange, and paying and receiving money, on account thereof, in the usual 'course of trade, and in the same open and public manner, as if they were solvent 'persons, and had not become bankrupts And whereas the permitting such secret acts 'of bankruptcy, to avoid and defeat payments, really and bona fide made, in the 'cases, and under the circumstances above mentioned, where the persons receiving the 'same had not notice thereof, or were privy to such persons having committed any act 'of bankruptcy, will be a great *discouragement to trade and commerce, and a prejudice* to credit in general, No person who is, or shall be, really bona fide a creditor 'of

ed by Espinasse. 'It confines strictly to the terms of it, all 'dispositions of his property by the bankrupt; so that, after an 'act of bankruptcy committed, he can only dispose of his property in the regular course of trade, as, by paying for goods when 'delivered, or bills of exchange, or notes, when regularly due.' I. Espin. N. P. 121.—In Scotland, the Legislature was averse to risk the embarrassments and interruptions to trade, which the recalling of payments, fairly received by creditors, might occasion; and, therefore, left the case of payment entirely out of the statute of 1696, to be judged of at common law, according to the circumstances of each particular case †. In Scotland, a creditor, who, by threats, or by actual diligence, has recovered payment of a just debt, is safe from any recal of the money, under this statute; and may confidently employ it in trade, without fear of being obliged to repay it. But, in England, it has been thought sufficient, to expose the case, unprotected, to the operation of the assignment, that a bill was not paid when due, but a short delay given, at the expiry of which, the money was paid, (which the Court of King's Bench was clearly of opinion, was not a payment made in the course of business, and, so, not protected by the statute). Vernon v. Hall, 2 Term. Rep. 640.—And judicial proceedings against the bankrupt, to enforce payment, are held equally to exclude the case from the exception. Bradly v. Clark, 5 Term. Rep. 198.

In

'of the bankrupt, for, or in respect of goods really and bona fide sold to such bank- 'rupt, or for any bills of exchange really and bona fide drawn, negotiated, or accept- 'ed, by such bankrupt, in the usual and ordinary course of trade and dealing, shall 'be liable to refund, or repay to the assignees of such bankrupt's estate, any money, 'which, before the suing forth of such commission, was really and bona fide, and, in 'the usual and ordinary course of trade and dealing, received by such person, of any 'such bankrupt, before such time as the person receiving the same, shall know, under- 'stand, or have notice, that he is become a bankrupt, or that he is in insolvent cir- 'cumstances.'

† It may be proper here to observe, that, by the late sequestration statutes for mercantile bankruptcy, it has been declared, that, 'after the date of the first deliverance upon the petition of sequestration, all payments made by the debtor to any of 'his creditors, shall be void and insufficient to the receivers, in the event of a seque- 'stration taking place; and the trustee shall be entitled to recover the money so paid, 'as part of the bankrupt estate.' 33 Geo. III. c 74. § 29.

In the interpretation of the English rule, respecting payments in the course of trade, it is natural to hold the delivery and indorsation of bills as payment; for these are the most frequent payments which a merchant makes in the course of trade. Hawkins & Penfold, 2 Vezey, 550.* But the Scotish statute of 1696, in taking no notice of payment, has used words which include every form of deed, or document, draughts and indorsations, as well as conveyances of land. The negative exception, therefore, can apply only to payments in money. Strictly speaking, nothing is to be considered as money, but the legal circulating coin of the country, which the law holds to be a proper tender for payment; but, in the question at present under consideration, there seems to be little room for doubting, that a payment in Bank notes, navy bills, goldsmiths' notes, &c. which are commonly paid and received as cash, would be held as a payment in money.

There have been few cases of payment brought under challenge, upon the statute of 1696, because the question in the abstract has never been understood to admit of doubt; and the few cases which do appear in the books, plainly shew, that the challenge has never been thought to have a chance of success, but when supported by suspicious circumstances, or some admixture of fraud, nay, even in circumstances of strong suspicion, payments have been sustained. Thus, in the case of Forbes against Bremner, already taken notice of, † the creditors seem to have been urged to the challenge, chiefly by the irritated feelings, so natural to men abused as they had been: and it was unsuccessful, though resting chiefly upon the statute of 1621, which expressly includes 'voluntary 'payments.'—Another case occurred, in 1760, of a challenge made to a payment: but the near alliance of the parties, gave room for strong suspicion of collusion; and, to that, the creditors seem chiefly to have trusted. Mr Strachan, finding his affairs in disorder, and being debtor to his sister, in a bond of 250l., raised money, by discounting bills, and paid her the principal and interest, and

* See above, p. 161

† See above, p. 123.

and broke within the sixty days. The creditors challenged the payment, and urged, very strongly, the connexion of the parties, and their living in family together, as evidence of a collusion to their prejudice. A proof was allowed; and the facts, now stated, were established. But 'the Court found, that the payment made to 'Rachel Strachan, the defender, does not fall under the act 1696.' 1st August 1760, Bean against Strachan, II. Fac. Coll. ccxliii. 443 See also IV. Ersk. i. 41. in fin.

2. Let us now turn to the cases, which it has been attempted to assimilate to that of payment; viz. the delivery of goods, in satisfaction, to a creditor,—and the indorsation of bills of exchange.

DELIVERY OF GOODS.—If the delivery of goods, in satisfaction, or security, of a former debt, were not challengeable, under the statute of 1696, much of the force of that statute, in preventing undue preferences, would be lost. But the statute, which is directed against all dispositions and conveyances, strictly and literally includes this case; for it is by delivery, without writing, that almost all transferences of moveables are made. This is not a case, which, like payment, was intentionally left out of the statute, or which, in the spirit of the law, can be regarded as an exception.

In the first case that occurred, upon this question, under the act 1696, Forbes of Craigie having delivered several articles, in satisfaction and payment, to some of his creditors, another creditor challenged these conveyances, upon the act 1696, and argued, that the expression, 'disposition, assignation, or other deed, made 'and granted,' could apply only to written conveyances; whereas, this was a delivery of goods, de manu in manum. It was answered, That not only does the reason of the law include the case, as it is directed against fraud, but the words also apply; for the expression, 'deed,' does not necessarily imply writing. The preceding act, of this year, for example, in regulating 'deeds' granted on deathbed, includes alienations of jewels, &c. on deathbed,

as

as heirship, though not conveyed by writing. 'The Lords sustained the challenge:' Dalrymple, cxxvii. 184.* It was only a few months after this, that, in the case of Din and Tweedie, upon the act 1621, the Court refused to reduce a transfer of moveables, unless fraud, or participation, were proved.† But still, in all cases upon the act 1696, the Court sustained the reduction. Thus, in 1728, Butter having, within sixty days of bankruptcy, delivered to Taylor, lint, dales, &c. to the value of 70l., and paid, in cash, 30l., as the balance of 100l., for which Taylor was creditor to him by bill, a reduction was brought, on the act 1696. There was, besides the general question of law, a question of fact, arising from the nature of the debt; but that was reserved. '‡ The Lords found, that the delivery of the goods fell under the 'act 1696, and that the defender was liable to restore them, or 'their

* This is the judgement, as reported by President Dalrymple, but, in the subsequent case of Smith and Taylor, to be immediately taken notice of, it was agreed, on both sides, (and the decree pronounced in this case of Forbes's was there produced), that the judgement bore, 'that the act 1696, anent (concerning) notour bankrupts, 'comprehends the case, of a merchant delivering goods to another merchant, or others, 'his creditors, within sixty days of his being bankrupt, in payment or security of debts 'due before the sixty days.'

† See above, p. 116.

‡ As this case is to be found reported only in the Dictionary, I have here detailed the argument, from the papers in the Advocates' Library. In support of the reduction, it was argued, That the intention of the act 1696, was, to put it out of a debtor's power, in a state of bankruptcy, to prefer favourite creditors, by making over his effects to them; and to reserve every thing for the operation of diligence. If the transfer of moveables be left out of this provision, the law is very imperfect. But, as the law ought to be a universal remedy, so, its expressions bear, all and whatsoever dispositions, assignations, and other deeds, &c., i. e. dispositions to lands—assignations to bonds and personal rights—and other deeds whatsoever—seem intended to include all the indefinite ways of transferring moveables, the only kind of alienation not included under the other two: and this view of the law, is supported by the above case of Forbes.

ANSWERED, (as in the former case), That deeds can signify only written conveyances: and, a general expression, subjoined to particulars, takes its interpretation from those particulars: That it never could be the intention of the law, to include the delivery of moveables, since this would render trade unsafe, and stop the commerce of moveables; for moveables pass from hand to hand; and n r an need inquire further, 'their value; and preferred the arresters; and found, that the defender comes not in pari passu' 19th January 1728, Smith against Taylor, I. Dict. 83.--A similar decision was pronounced in a late case, where the circumstances were particularly strong. Thomas Turnbull being debtor to Johnson, prevailed on his brother George to join in a bill to him. Finding his affairs in disorder, he put a quantity of wool into his brother's hands; and he, as cautioner, satisfied Johnson, by conveying this wool to him in payment; and the bill was delivered up. The transaction was challenged, and the Court reduced it. The reporter says, 'The Court seemed to consider the specialties of the case, as of no importance; and, in general observed, that if the plea, of goods having been delivered in solutum, and not in security, were to 'be

than, whether he got them in a fair way of delivery, whereas, in other cases, a man must know the condition of him he contracts with There is no difference between the present case, and the case of a purchase, fairly made from the bankrupt by the creditor, *for money paid over, which money should be immediately returned, in payment of a* prior debt. Neither the sale, nor the payment, in such a case, are objectionable If any fraudulent design, it is easy to make a third party purchase. If every thing is fair, and the creditor acts bona fide, it cannot be, that the act should annul a sale, to reach a creditor receiving payment bona fide The Roman law reduced transactions where there was fraud: so does ours But this, in question, is merely a presumptive fraud, extended by statute to written deeds, which are the deeds of importance, but not applicable to the easy transmission of moveables, passing from hand to hand. The decision in Forbes's case, is, no doubt, unfavourable to this argument; but it is single, and against the spirit of Tweedie and Brown's case. At all events, if the act shall be thought to apply; still, *it must operate only to the effect of introducing an e*quality—making the creditor, who receives the goods, be ranked on an equal footing with the creditor who challenges. Equality is the very principle of the law.

REPLIED. 1. In our law, whatever it may be in England, facts and deeds are reciprocal terms. but all alienations, and transmissions of property, comprehend the transference here objected to; and these are properly deeds, whether with, or without writing. 2. No injury can fall upon commerce; since a fair purchaser, for a price, cannot be affected by the statute—an exemption, which cannot be extended to securities for prior debts. Indorsations to bills, are most favoured by commerce; yet they fall under the law, when granted for a prior debt As to the case of a sale, intended to pay the creditor's debt, it would be reducible as simulate. 3. If the partial deed of the bankrupt be once set aside, there is no ground, upon which this creditor can stand, in opposition to Smith, who has done legal diligence. The goods remain in bonis of the bankrupt, subject to such diligence as has been led against them 'be admitted, in support of such a conveyance, it would be easy, 'in any case, to evade the salutary regulations of the statute '1696.' 25th June 1783, Young against Johnson, VII. Fac. Coll. cix. 172.

BILLS have been assimilated to the case of payment, apparently with more reason than the delivery of goods. Bills are the money of a trader—the instruments of his commerce, with which he naturally makes his payments, and manages all his transactions, they are, in law, considered as bags of money. A debtor may gratify a favourite creditor, either by drawing a bill in his favour, upon some of his debtors, or by indorsing to him a bill, which stands in his person. But, if the act do not strike at such deeds as these, it is plain, that a trader has it in his power upon the eve of bankruptcy, and within the sixty days, to distribute, among his favourite creditors, the whole of his circulating capital, except the goods which he has actually in his warehouse: nay. these also may be thus disposed of, if he choose to sell them, and take the bills for the price, payable to the creditors. It were, therefore, a great imperfection, if the statute did not include such deeds: but the words are fully adequate to include them; and the spirit of the act is strongly applicable. The act strikes against 'all dispositions, 'assignations, or other deeds, made and granted, &c in favour of 'creditors, either for satisfaction or further security, in preference 'to other creditors' and a bill, whether an original draught in the creditor's favour, or an indorsation to a draught, in which the bankrupt is creditor, is strictly and properly an assignation, for satisfaction or security, in preference to the other creditors.* I defer speaking of promissory notes, or acceptances, by the bankrupt, till I come to consider acknowledgements of debt, and deeds of corroboration; for they are to be regarded more in the light of mere documents of debt, than as assignations or conveyances; since

* It will be remembered, that, here, we are speaking only of bills, indorsed, or delivered in payment of prior debts---not those which are negotiated in the course of trade, and for a present advance This is a case, which we have seen not to be included in the statute.

since they give no preference over a particular fund, their worst effect, as contributing to a preference over other creditors, being, to facilitate the diligence of the holders.

The question concerning draughts, seems first to have occurred in the competition among the creditors of Balfour, in the year 1700. Durward had got a draught from Balfour, for 50l, upon Wilson, who accepted it; but, before payment, an arrestment was used in Wilson's hands, and a reduction was raised, of the draught, as within the sixty days. The holder of the bill argued, that bills are bags of money, and that the commerce of them cannot be clogged by latent objections. The creditors answered, That all this was very well, provided the bill was for a present advance, or for goods sold at the time; but, when given to a creditor, in payment or security of a former debt, a bill falls under the act, as well as any other deed; and, if it did not, this method would be adopted by all bankrupts, for preferring their favourites. 'The 'Lords found bills included within the act of Parliament, as well 'as other assignations, unless they bore value received, or were 'so proven,' &c. II. Fount. 86.—The only scruple that remained, is thus expressed by Lord Fountainhall: 'The great inconvenience, 'by this interlocutor, is, that it puts parties to prove the onerous 'cause of their bills, which may be a retardment to the currency 'of trade.'

Thirteen years afterwards, the question occurred again, in the case of an indorsation, made by a debtor to his creditor, within sixty days of bankruptcy. The case was very fully argued, and, upon the part of the holder, chiefly on this ground, that, as bills are deemed, by law, to be exempt from all latent objections, and especially from compensation, on account of the drawer's or indorser's debt, so, the objection, on the act 1696, ought not to have effect against them, since, in fact, it resolves into a compensation and latent objection of this kind. The Court decided, 'That the 'act of Parliament 1696, concerning bankrupts, takes place, if the 'suspender prove, that the indorsation was for satisfaction or se-'curity of a prior debt, and not for present value received:' 16th January

January 1713, Campbell of Glenderuel against Graham [illegible] Forbes, 646. Dalrymple, xcvii. 136.

Another case occurred, at a much later period. Fle[illegible] dorsed two bills to Campbell and M'Gibbon, who were his [illegible] tors. Another creditor, before the [illegible] of the sixty [illegible] dered him bankrupt, and challenged the indorsations. Th[illegible] above quoted, were founded on, as decisive of the question [illegible] were opposed, upon the old ground, that one [illegible] indorsee [illegible] free from all latent exceptions. 'The Lord Ordinary (Monb[illegible] 'found the bills subject to be reduced, upon the act of [illegible] 1696; and the defenders liable to repeat (pay back) the [illegible] 'of them, which they had received, for behoof of the [illegible] 'and the whole creditors of Fletcher.' A distinction appe[illegible] have been hinted at, upon the Bench, (which has since, [illegible] been disapproved of), between the case of a creditor, d[illegible] a distance, and one at hand, receiving a payment by an [illegible] tion. 'The Court,' says the reporter, 'considered cas[illegible] 'kind, as different from those in which the debtor [illegible] 'live at a great distance from each other, and where [illegible] 'could not easily be made, except by the indorsation of [illegible] 'that case, the bills would not have fallen under the ac[illegible] 'But, to sustain such indorsations as the present, made [illegible] 'neighbour to another, it was observed, might tend, in a [illegible] 'measure, to defeat the purpose of the statute.' 10th A[illegible] 1780, Campbell against M'Gibbon and Campbell, VI. Fac C[illegible] cxxv. 230.—This is a distinction, which seems to be sanctione[illegible], in some measure, by one of the principles upon which payment, in cash, is supported, but it is rather arbitrary. It seems to throw loose, what ought either to be held as a general rule, upon the statutory presumption, or left altogether open to the presumptions and evidence, which each case would naturally afford. Accordingly, I understand, that, in a case decided 29th January 1794, M'Kechen against Welch, the Court disapproved of this distinction, and held the rule to be general, in its application, to all indorsations whatever. This case is not reported.

Upon this question, then, it may safely be concluded, that draughts, by a bankrupt upon his debtor, in favour of a prior creditor; or indorsations, to such creditor, of accepted bills, in the hands of the bankrupt, are, in the sense of the act of Parliament, assignations, in security or payment, in preference to other creditors, and so reducible, if within sixty days of the bankruptcy.

II. OBLIGATIONS AND ACKNOWLEDGEMENTS OF DEBT.—Diligence, against the person or estate of the debtor, can proceed only in consequence of the judgment of a court. But we have already had occasion to see, that, in Scotland, it is not necessary to the obtaining of a judgement, upon which execution may pass, that the creditor should raise an action, and go through all the forms of judicial proceedings. A bond, containing a clause of registration, or a promissory note, or acceptance, which, by statute, may be registered, entitle the creditor to have immediate execution, as if judgement, in a formal action, were regularly obtained. When a debtor falls into suspicious circumstances, those of his creditors, whose claims against him stand upon open account, unvouched, naturally wish, if they cannot obtain payment, to procure, at least, a voucher of their debt; upon which, after such delay as may be agreed upon, they can, at once, proceed with execution. To grant such a voucher, is an act of justice to the individual creditor, which, if refused, he can, by an action, enforce. It is an act of prudence, in the debtor, as it saves him, and his funds, from the expence of judicial proceedings. But, although such an act, is not properly a conveyance or security, since it gives no real right over any part of the fund; it enables the creditor to accelerate his diligence, to proceed instantly with his attachments, to take the start, perhaps, of other creditors, or to put himself upon a level with those who have already done diligence, and who would have enjoyed a decided preference, but for this interference of the debtor. It is a question of great importance, whether the statute 1696, in declaring every deed objectionable, which, directly or indirectly, bestows a preference, strikes against deeds of this kind—mere vouchers and acknowledgements of debt.

Whatever

Whatever may have been the opinion of lawyers formerly, upon this interesting question, it seems now to be settled, and at rest; for the Court has fixed, in two very late cases, that a bankrupt can do no act, by which the situation of his creditors may be altered. I shall, therefore, proceed to state these decisions, and to add a few remarks, with the view of pointing out the extent and effect of the rule thereby established.

The first case, in which the question was tried, is that of Cowan against Mansfield's Trustees, in 1762; and, at that time, the objection appeared to the Court, in a very different light from that in which it has been lately viewed. Bruce had indorsed a bill to Mansfield, which Mansfield having re-indorsed, he was, upon failure of the accepter, obliged to retire it: upon this, Bruce accepted his draught for the principal sum, interest, exchange, &c. By concert, in order to try the question, Bruce was held as bankrupt within the sixty days; and the bill, having been made the ground of an arrestment, was challenged, as falling under the act 1696. The creditors argued, That there can be no doubt of this being a bill for a prior debt; and that it is a deed, which, though not directly a conveyance or assignation, is indirectly the same thing as enabling the creditor to do diligence. The holder of the bill replied, That three ingredients are necessary to bring any case within the statute: 1. That the deed import alienation: 2. That it be granted for a former debt: 3. That it be in preference. None of these hold here. There is no alienation, direct or indirect; there is no security granted, but a mere voucher given, which, of itself, can bestow no preference: and, as to the facilitating of diligence, an action could have been raised, in a few hours, and an arrestment used, independently of the bill. The Court preferred the holder of the bill. 7th January 1762, Cowan against Mansfield's Trustees, III. Fac. Coll. lxxiv. 167.— I shall only remark, upon this case, that there was, in the accumulation of principal, interest, charges, exchange, re-exchange, &c. into a principal, an obvious, and an undue advantage, given by the new bill, which could not have been obtained by the operation of the law alone.

In the case of Swinton's Creditors against Sir William Forbes, which has already been quoted *, an objection of this kind was moved to a bill, accepted by the debtor, within sixty days of bankruptcy. Swinton was due several sums, by bill, to Sir William Forbes & Co. The Company insisted for payment, and received an acceptance, from Swinton, indorsed by a gentleman of undoubted credit. The Lords found, that the granting of the promissory note, by the bankrupt, did not fall under the statute of 1696; and a reclaiming petition was refused, without answers. 19th February 1790, Trustee on Swinton's estate, against Sir William Forbes & Co.

The next case, upon the subject, is, the well known case of M'Math against M'Kellar's Trustees. The right objected to, was, an adjudication, in the person of M'Math, proceeding upon a bond of corroboration, granted by M'Kellar, within sixty days of bankruptcy. This bond included, 1. Debts due originally to M'Math's father, as well as debts to himself; and so saved confirmation: 2. Debts, the term of payment of which were not yet arrived 3. Accumulations of principal, interest, and expences, on the debts. The objections rested on these points: That a bond of corroboration, or other deed of acknowledgment, is an indirect conveyance, as enabling the creditor to proceed with diligence, more rapidly, than, in the common course of law, he could have done; and that, here, the claim of the creditor was, by the accumulation of interest, expences, &c. increased beyond the reach of any legal operation. The case was argued with great ability, and the decision intended to be a solemn settlement of a very important point. The objection was sustained, and the provisions of the statute found to strike at the bond of corroboration.—I shall not detail, here, the argument stated at the Bar, but endeavour to compress, into as concise a form as possible, the reasons upon which the Court seemed to proceed.—1. It was agreed, that a bankrupt is no otherwise deprived of the capacity of granting deeds, than as he interferes with the interests of the creditors.—2. Upon the validity of the bond of corroboration, so far as the debt was thereby enlarged,

and

* Page 160 & seq

and a penalty superadded, it was, on all hands, agreed, that, where this was done, to an extent which could not have been attained by the operation of legal diligence, it was objectionable.—3. With respect to those accumulations, which might have been effected by legal diligence, although it was, at first, the opinion of several of the Judges, that a bond of corroboration could not be objected to, yet, it seems, at last, to have been agreed, that every accumulation, not made by law, should be challengeable; and that interest upon interest should be struck off, when it arose by a voluntary accumulation.—4. The only other question, then, was, Whether such a document of debt could validly stand in place of a legal constitution of the claim by action, or save to the creditor the delay and expence of completing a title by confirmation, &c.? Upon this point, the opinions of the Court were much divided. Those of the Judges, who denied the application of the statute to such a case, proceeded upon these grounds: They considered the frauds of bankrupts, as resolving into two classes; the fraudulent increase of debts, and the fraudulent distribution of the funds. The first of these, they considered as provided for by the act 1621, and the common law. When, therefore, the act 1696 came to be enacted, there was no occasion to guard against the admission of false debts, and the fraudulent increase of true debts; but the object of the act was, to prevent the bankrupt from giving securities to particular creditors over the fund from which all should be paid: and the words of the act, they held sufficient to prove, that the intention of the Legislature was, to prevent a dilapidation of funds, not to stop the fraudulent increase of debts. The mere acknowledgement of a debt, therefore, which is truly due, or the renewal of a personal obligation, unattended with any transference or right over the funds, in preference to other creditors, cannot fall under the statute. It saves to the creditor the expence of proceedings at law: it supplies the place, perhaps, of a title, which it would cost much money and time to make out: it brings a creditor, whose debt, though most onerous, is still unvouched, to an equal footing with others: But, in all this, a deed of this kind is fair, just, commendable; not fraudulent, but such as justice calls for, and law would enforce. No doubt, a debtor may be partial, and

and refuse to one creditor, what he grants to another; but this would make a case of fraud, which, wherever it can be established, the Court will correct.—The Judges, whose opinions favoured the application of the statute, took another view of the question. The great object of the bankrupt statute 1696, they held to be the establishing of a general presumption of fraud, with a view to crush it, and leave no possibility of committing it. At common law, deeds are reducible, if fraud can be proved; but this law defined fraud, and dispensed with the necessity of investigating the ever-changing circumstances of fraudulent transactions. As fraud may arise, says the Legislature, if such and such deeds be permitted; therefore, we declare such deeds to be ineffectual, if executed within sixty days of bankruptcy. All deeds, therefore, which may be a cover to fraud, are struck at by this statute. Bonds of corroboration, and deeds of a similar kind, may be instruments of fraud, by enabling a creditor to accelerate his diligence, and get the start of others. The debtor may act fraudulently, in refusing them to one, while he grants them to others; nay, from its mere secrecy, the acknowledgement of a debt may be fraudulent: whereas, a legal constitution by action, being public, would have given intimation to the other creditors to take similar steps. In short, the purpose of the act is, to avoid all questions of actual fraud, in such cases, and to make a rule, which may stifle fraud. The principle, that a bankrupt cannot alter the situation of his creditors one iota, was strongly inculcated in the case of Fairholms, and assented to in the great retention cause, Harper against Faulds.

Such were nearly the different grounds of opinion, in this solemn deliberation. The case was decided by a narrow majority, 1st March 1791, M'Math against M'Kellar's Trustees.

As a strong confirmation of this decision, I quote the case, which I already detailed under the second branch of the statute of 1621, the Creditors of Thomas Dunbar against Sir James Grant *. The statute of 1696 did not indeed apply; but 'a great 'majority of the Court was of opinion, that a bankrupt ought to 'execute

* See above, p. 129, 130.

'execute no deed, by which the situation of his creditors is affect-'ed; and that it would be dangerous to support any deed of that 'nature.' The deed objected to, was a bond of corroboration IX. Fac. Coll. lxi. 133.

In estimating the effect of the statute, as thus interpreted, it is proper to examine, how, upon the eve of bankruptcy, preferences may be acquired, and how they are to be prevented. On the one hand, a creditor, who receives a voucher, enabling him instantly to proceed with diligence, may adjudge the heritable estate, or poind, or arrest the moveable funds; and if allowed, uninterruptedly, to proceed with his diligence, he must, of course, acquire a preference. On the other hand, creditors, who have received securities from the debtor, or who hold vouchers or decrees entitling them to proceed with diligence, may [illegible] for themselves a preference over all who have only open claims. So stood the common law, giving preference to priority; and, while it stood so, the refusal of a voucher, to a creditor, might, in one situation, be an act of justice to the rest, and, in another, a gross act of injustice to that individual—in the one case, it might prevent him from acquiring a preference; in the other, it might prevent him from guarding himself against the attempts of others. But, as the law now stands, an equalizing of all such preferences, is brought more within the reach of creditors. Under the sequestration law, if an individual creditor, having obtained a bill or bond from his debtor, be proceeding with his diligence, any of the creditors may, by applying for sequestration, level it at once: and, on the other hand, a creditor, by open account, may apply for sequestration, without any voucher of his claim, and so reduce all preferences which other creditors may be attempting to establish. In common bankruptcies, the remedy, though not so perfect, is sufficient to prevent much inconvenience, from the above rule, in practice. 1. In reducing a voluntary conveyance, we have seen, that it is necessary to render the debtor bankrupt within sixty days of its date: this, a creditor, by open account, can scarcely, it is true, accomplish, in his own person, unless by means of a voucher from the debtor, however insolvent the debtor may be; for he must first bring his action, then obtain a judgement, then raise his horning, give his charge, wait its expiry, raise his caption, and execute it: but it seldom can happen, that others should not be interested to reduce the preference, whose debts may enable them to take measures for doing so. 2. In reducing preferences, by diligence; a creditor, by open account, can scarcely be excluded from the pari passu preference of adjudgers, since a year is allowed, after the date of the first effectual adjudication, for any creditor coming in; and, within that time, his action of constitution, adjudication, &c. may easily be raised and where other creditors are proceeding with diligence against the moveables, by poinding or arrestment; though it is only by rendering the debtor bankrupt (as in the case of voluntary preferences) that equality can be established; yet, in this case also, other creditors will always be found, who have an interest, and are ready to make the debtor bankrupt. If that be done, the creditor, by open account, can run no risk; for he may arrest, the instant he raises his action; and although he must have a decree, before he can summon the poinders to communicate the benefit of their diligence, he has a period of six months, in which to accomplish this. Thus, there does not appear to be much danger of unjust preferences, on either hand, by refusing to allow debtors the power of granting obligations and vouchers for former debts. Indeed, the only danger seems to arise from the possibility of the debtor not being made bankrupt in due time: but it is scarcely credible, that there should be an insolvency at all, in which certain creditors are endeavouring to acquire preferences, without some one being ready to take the proper measures for securing himself, and his fellow creditors, from loss.

Before leaving the consideration of those deeds which are objectionable under the statute, I must take notice of a class of deeds, neither, on the one hand, to be regarded as proper deeds of conveyance, nor, on the other, to be classed with obligations and acknowledgements of debt. These are deeds, by which a link in

A

a defective conveyance is supplied. Thus, in the case of the creditors of Watson against Cramond, Mr Watson had granted to Cramond a bond of relief, on which infeftment was taken, more than sixty days before the bankruptcy; but Watson had not been served heir, and gave, within the sixty days, a procuratory for serving himself heir.*—The service proceeded after he was actually in the Abbey, and, by accruing to Cramond's right, made it good. The creditors objected to the procuratory, that it was a deed granted within the sixty days, in order to validate a security in favour of a prior creditor, and establish for him a preference over the rest. Answered, This is not a deed in favour of a particular creditor;—it is a step taken for the benefit of the whole, as tending merely to the making up of that title, which may be beneficial to all; and the advantage derivable from it by Cramond, is a mere consequence of the legal accretion. 'The Lords found, that Mr Watson's 'posterior infeftment did accresce' (accrue) 'to Mr Cramond, and 'therefore repelled the nullity objected.' 31st July 1724, Edgar, 117. Four years after this, a case, of nearly the same kind, occurred, and the same decision was given. Johnson of Gratney had succeeded as substitute in a deed of settlement, but had never taken infeftment. He granted rights of annualrent † to the Duke of Queensburgh, and other creditors; and they were infeft, though his titles were not yet completed. Other creditors afterwards adjudged; and the debtor, to prevent further diligence, made a trust-disposition, for behoof of his creditors, in which he gave a preference to the

* In order to render these cases intelligible to those unacquainted with Scotish law, it is necessary to explain a peculiarity in that law. It is not in Scotland, as it is, at this day, in the English law, (II Blackst. 209), and as it was formerly in France, (4 Denizart, Collection de Jurisp. actuelle, 451), where the title of an heir is completed by the mere act of the law. Certain forms are necessary, in Scotland, to vest the right in the heir. In feudal property, he must be acknowledged by the superior, or proved by the verdict of a Jury, (called a service), to be the heir entitled to succeed; and his right must be completed by seisine. In the same way, personal property is vested in the the executor, by a sentence of the Commissary court, called a confirmation: and, in neither case, have conveyances granted by the heir, or executor, unentered, any effect till his own title be completed, so as to accrue to the conveyance.

† A right of annualrent was the old form of security for money over land; the nature of which I shall shortly explain, in the next Chapter.

the Duke of Queensburgh, &c. Seisine was taken in Johnson's person, as substitute in the deed under which he had succeeded; and then the trustees took infeftment upon the trust-disposition. The heritable creditors argued, 1. upon the trust deed; 2 upon the accression of the infeftment in Johnson's person, to their prior heritable securities. 'The Lords found, that the infeftment could 'not accresce' *(accrue)* 'in regard the adjudication upon special 'charges between the infeftment of annualrent, and infeftment in 'favour of the Colonel, which alone gave him the real right, were a 'mid impediment; and therefore preferred the adjudgers.' Then certain personal creditors adjudged. They took up the two questions also; but we shall concern ourselves only with the validity of the seisine in Johnson's favour, considered as an act accruing to the prior heritable securities.

The adjudgers pleaded, that, as accretion depends upon a fiction of law, making the new right acquired by the author, in consequence of his seisine, to be, as it were, of new disponed, there can be no accretion where the author is not in a condition that would have allowed him validly to dispone. They therefore contended, that the procuratory, as a deed, directly or indirectly, creating a preference, is reducible. It was answered, That the taking of seisine in the debtor's person, is only the completion of that right through which all must claim: That it is strange to object to an easy and little expensive way of completing the right, when, in another way, only at greater expence, the same object might have been attained; especially when the only object of such opposition is to do injustice to creditors, who have long since received the securities which they hold, and who have not deluded others, but published their rights, from the first: That an inhibition could not have stopped the debtor from completing his titles; for the completing of the titles is of the nature of an acquisition, not an alienation, though it may happen to produce an eventual good effect on rights already granted to creditors; nay, that the debtor could have been forced to complete his right, notwithstanding an inhibition: That the act 1696 can have no stronger effect, than an inhibition, in this respect: and that this is no alienation, but a just and necessary deed,

deed, meant for the benefit of all the creditors, who would have been in a much worse condition, had their debtor died in a state of apparency. 'The Lords repelled the objection, and preferred the 'annualrenters;' thus deciding, that the statute of 1696 has no effect against such an act, to prevent its accruing to the securities formerly granted to creditors. February 1728, Creditors of Graitney competing, I. Dict. 83. Sess. Pap. Adv. Lib.

Such are the forms of deed, which are comprehended under this statute, as liable to challenge. But a most essential part of the objectionable character of the deed remains still unexplained. It must be a deed, granted either 'after the grantor's becoming bank-'rupt, or in the space of sixty days of before.'

In commenting upon this part of the description in the statute, we have to inquire into the method of computing the sixty days of retrospect, as relative to the date of the bankruptcy, on the one hand, and to that of the deed challenged, on the other. But, as I have already taken occasion, in the First Book, to comment, pretty fully, upon the date of the bankruptcy, and nature of the evidence by which it is to be ascertained, I have now only to explain the law with regard to the date of the deed, and the computation of the term.

I. Date of the Deed.—The Legislature, in framing the statute of 1696, and giving to the bankruptcy a retroactive power, conferred upon the creditors, not merely an eventual benefit—a right to reduce all deeds, which should be found to have been granted within that period; but the true spirit and intention of the law was, to put into their hands an active instrument, by which, upon hearing of a deed of preference, they might be enabled to take measures for rendering the debtor bankrupt, to the effect of striking down the security, thus constituted to their prejudice. Such a law as this must be perfect, in proportion to the means afforded to the creditors, of learning what deeds have been granted

by

by the debtor:—it must be imperfect, and exposed to evasion, in proportion to the possibility of a debtor constituting preferences secretly. By the law of Scotland, no deed is effectual against land, or other heritable property, without being entered in a public register, open to all the world. If, in the case of heritable deeds, then, the time of registration had been assumed as the date, in questions upon the act 1696; and, if it had been possible to contrive a harmless criterion, of a similar kind, for deeds concerning moveables, there could scarcely have been a possibility, of an insolvent debtor eluding the vigilance of his creditors, or constituting unfair preferences, to their prejudice. The legal term of sixty days, would then have begun to run, only from the moment of publication of the deed; and the creditors would have had it fully in their power, to act as their own protectors and guardians. But, unfortunately, at the date of the bankrupt law, the records were not reduced to a settled and orderly system, so that, even with regard to heritable conveyances, they were not thought of, as the criterion of the date: and it is perhaps impossible, consistently with the interests of commerce, to permit any similar incumbrance, upon transactions or conveyances concerning personal property. I shall endeavour, as concisely as possible, to explain the rule, with regard to the dates of the various kinds of deeds.

1. Although the Legislature did not adopt the registration, as the criterion of the date of heritable securities, the principle upon which they proceeded, naturally led them to require something more public than the execution of the conveyance itself, which might, for a long time, be kept latent. The seisine is, in some degree, a public ceremony; since it must be taken in open day, and by a notary, before two witnesses. It is upon the seisine, too, that the security absolutely depends for its effect, as a conveyance of heritage; the deed not being held in law as complete, till seisine have passed. It was therefore natural to adopt the date of the seisine, rather than that of the conveyance itself, as the point of completion of the security, in the view of the statute of 1696. Accordingly, the statute bears, that 'all dispositions, heritable 'bonds, or other heritable rights whereupon infeftment may fol-

'low,

'low, granted by the foresaid bankrupts, shall only be reckoned, 'as to this case of bankrupt, to be of the date of the seisine law'fully taken thereon, but' (without) 'prejudice to the validity of 'the said heritable rights, as to all other effects, as formerly.' It is very obvious, that seisine, although, in some degree, entitled to the character of a public act of completion, can very easily, in most cases, be concealed, and accordingly it happened, that, in bankruptcies, latent infeftments were daily brought forward, to the utter exclusion of creditors. Many expedients were tried, to get the better of the rule established by the statute. The first, and most natural attempt, was this:—Immediately after the passing of the bankrupt act of 1696, the attention of the Legislature had been called to the state of the records. It had formerly been required, that every heritable conveyance should be recorded; but the law was much evaded: and, by a statute passed in the same year with the law now under consideration, it was declared, that no seisine should have any effect against third parties, unless recorded *. Creditors took advantage of this statute, to maintain, that the date of the registration was now made the only effectual date, in all questions with third parties; and that, in the interpretation of the bankrupt law, the date of the registration should be considered as substituted, in place of that of the seisine itself. The first case in which this plea was maintained, occurred in 1715; but the Court adhered strictly to the words of the bankrupt statute, and found the date of the seisine, not that of the registration, to be the rule. 17th February 1715, Inglis against Dr Menzies; Dalrymple, cxxxvii. 189.; Bruce, lxxiii. 88.—The question was again tried, so late as the year 1782 The date of the seisine was beyond the sixty days; the date of the registration was within them. The late Lord Hailes, as Ordinary, 'having considered 'the

* 'Our Sovereign Lord,' (says the statute), 'considering, that, unless seisines, 'and other writs and diligences appointed to be registrate, be booked, and insert in the respective registers appointed for that effect, the lieges cannot be certiorate thereof, 'which is the great use and design of this registration: Therefore, &c no seisine, &c. 'shall be of any force or effect, against any but the grantors, and their heirs, unless it 'be duly booked, and insert in the register' 1696, c 18

'the words of the act 1696, and the decision in the case of the 'creditors of Menzies, in the year 1715, found, that the deeds 'under challenge were not reducible under the act 1696:' and this judgement the Court affirmed. 13th December 1782, Douglas Heron & Co. against Maxwell; VII. Fac. Coll. lxxvi. 117.—Thus, the Court of Session left this class of cases precisely upon the footing of the statute of 1696, although the Judges have often expressed their conviction, that the date of the registration ought to be made the rule of decision. Perhaps it may appear proper to the Legislature, when the bankrupt law comes to be renewed, that this alteration ought to be made upon the rule.

But although, in the cases now taken notice of, the words of the statute 1696, c. 5, applied too strictly, for the Court to permit this argument, from the statute of registration, to have any effect, there was another case, in which more room seemed to be left for liberal interpretation.—A conveyance, made to a superior, is completed by the mere resignation ad remanentiam, without seisine. It was therefore contended, in such a case, that, as the bankrupt law speaks only of the date of the seisine, and here there was no seisine, the registration should, according to the 18th chapter of 1696, be held as the regulator of the date. The Court, however, found, 'That if the debtor was bankrupt within sixty 'days of the date of the instrument of resignation ad remanen-'tiam, the deed fell under the act 1696 *.' 7th November 1749, Dickson, &c. Creditors of Castle-Somervel, against Mitchell; Kilk. p. 57.

Thus,

* 'The ground,' says Lord Kilkerran, 'upon which the Court proceeded, was, 'that where lands are disponed to a superior, the resignation ad remanentiam is truly 'the seisine, though it goes by a different name; what is called the instrument of sei-'sine, on a precept contained in a disposition to a third party, being called an instru-'ment of resignation, where a disposition is to a superior, containing procuratory of 'resignation ad remanentiam. And, as the date of the disposition, containing such 'procuratory, cannot be the period from which the sixty days run, in respect of the 'clause in the statute, which declares, that all dispositions shall be reckoned, as to this 'case of bankrupt, to be of the date of the seisine lawfully taken thereupon, so, as 'little could the registration of the instrument be the period, as, even in seisines, pro-'perly so called, the time of the registration thereof is not respected.'

Thus, it was fixed, that the date of the disposition, on the one hand, and the date of the registration of the seisine, on the other, were to be laid out of view, in all questions upon the act 1696, c. 5.; and, that the date of the seisine, or of the instrument of resignation ad remanentiam, was the invariable rule, in all questions respecting heritable securities granted by a debtor, feudally vested, in favour of a prior creditor.

But, another set of questions, respecting the dates of heritable securities, arose upon this part of the statute. The date of the seisine was declared, by the statute, to be the date of the deed, only in the case of 'dispositions, &c. whereupon infeftment 'may follow, granted by the foresaid bankrupt.' Yet it was natural to doubt, 1. Whether this rule was intended to apply to a disposition, granted by a debtor, who had not himself been infeft, and where the disponee's infeftment, of course, must have proceeded upon the unexecuted procuratory, or precept, assigned to him by the disposition? and, 2. Whether it was to apply where the debtor himself was infeft, but had granted a disposition, without procuratory or precept, upon which no infeftment could follow, without an adjudication in implement? Upon the first of these questions, the judgement of the Court varied exceedingly, in consequence of very unsettled opinions, respecting the fundamental question of law, Whether a debtor, holding a personal right to lands, be completely divested by a disposition, without seisine? To this question, which was at last settled in the negative, by the judgment in the well known case of Bell of Blackwoodhouse, * we shall, hereafter, in treating of funds, have occasion particularly to attend: but the only express and pure decision of the point, now under consideration, was prior to that decision, and proceeded entirely upon the idea, that a debtor was completely divested, by the disposition, of a right merely personal. This was in the case of the trustee for the creditors of Scott of Blair, against Charteris of Amisfield,

* 22d June 1737, Bell against Gartshore, Clerk Home, No. 102, 1 Dict. [illegible]

Aimsfield, in January 1734; * and there is every reason to believe, that, had the question again come to judgement, after the decision in Bell of Blackwoodhouse's case, it would have been decided the other way, and the date of the seisine found to be the rule.

In the case of a disposition, granted by a debtor infeft, but containing no procuratory nor precept, the rule of the statute seems,

* Scott of Blair, conveyed to Charters of Aimsfield, in security, an heritable bond, which stood in his person by conveyance, but, upon which, infeftment had never followed. This security remained latent for several years; till, Scott of Blair having become bankrupt, Aimsfield took infeftment, in virtue of the assignation to the precept of seisine. The creditors of Blair challenged the security, on the statute 1696, c. 5, and contended, that the date of the security, was to be held as regulated by that of the seisine, not that of the assignation. The question came before Lord Newhall, who decided, that 'this case did not fall under the act of Parliament 1696.' The creditors petitioned the Court. They PLEADED, That the statute has made no distinction between rights completed by infeftment, and those on which no infeftment has passed; for the words are general—'All dispositions, &c. whereupon infeftment may 'follow.' But it is not the words, alone, of the statute, that strike against such a conveyance; the spirit of the act directly opposes it. It is as much a fraud, to give a disposition of an estate, which is vested only by a personal right, in the debtor, as if infeftment had followed. The disposition is equally an alienation, equally affects the creditors; equally sweeps away the debtor's funds. The fraud is as great, by the not taking of the infeftment, for infeftment would have given an alarm to the creditors, to attend to their interests.—It was ANSWERED for Aimsfield, 1. The words of the statute do not apply, for a conveyance, of this kind, is not the deed on which infeftment is taken: It is taken on the original precept, and the heritable bond, containing that precept, was not granted by the bankrupt. The conveyance by the bankrupt, is a personal right merely, on which no seisine can be taken. The act, as inducing a presumption contrary to fact, must be strictly interpreted. 2. But the spirit, also, of the act, is against the challenge: It was intended to protect creditors, who, trusting to the records, lent their money to one visibly possessed of a fortune, to prevent the granting of latent rights, which, by the taking of seisine, might be, in a moment, reared up into effectual securities. But Mr Scott was not infeft: his only right was personal, and it is not upon the infeftment, that Aimsfield's preference stands. He would be preferable, independently of the seisine; and it is useful only, in a competition with another seisine.—REPLIED. Aimsfield could not take infeftment, but upon the deed granted by the bankrupt; so that the case falls expressly under the words of the act. And, as to the effect of the conveyance, without seisine—1. Although it be held, now, that a personal right to lands, on which infeftment has not followed, is fully conveyed by a disposition, without infeftment, yet, formerly, the first infeftment gave the preference,

seems to be strictly applicable, for, in this case, it will be observed, that the argument used by the holder of the disposition, where the debtor is not himself infeft, has no application. Creditors, seeing the debtor infeft, are entitled to trust to the records. The debtor

ference, though on the second disposition, and, as the statute has not distinguished between dispositions, to be completed by infeftment, and those which need none, it cannot be restricted 2. But, till seisine, Aimsfield's right was not complete, for if, after the disposition to Aimsfield, the procuratory, or precept, had been executed in favour of Mr Scott, and he had conveyed to one who got the first seisine, he would have been preferred, or, if creditors had adjudged, and charged, the personal disposition from one, afterwards taking infeftment, would have been good for nothing---DUPLIED. An infeftment was not necessary, to constitute a preference, in favour of Aimsfield, over the other creditors of the bankrupt, for, without seisine, all the right the bankrupt had, was conveyed If the bond had been assigned, by Scott, to another than Aimsfield; by him to another, and so round, till, after going through several hands, it had come, at length, into Aimsfield's person, who had taken infeftment, Would the challenge have been good, founded on the date of the seisine? No But the direct conveyance is really not different, in point of law The difference, where the right is real, and where it is only personal, lies here---that, where only personal, an assignation completes the conveyance of all the debtor's right, without any seisine--where real, there must be a procuratory and precept; and the seisine, that is to divest the one, and invest the other, must proceed upon that deed: and, in the latter case, it would only be the taking of the infeftment, that would complete the right of the receivers, and constitute the preference over the creditors But, it is admitted, that, without infeftment, the personal right is conveyed This always was our law, so that an infeftment, on a second disposition, from one having only a personal right, would have no effect, in preferring the second disposition.

'The Court found, That this case does not fall under the act; because, whatever 'might have been the intent of the statute, the words respect only the cases where infeftment is necessary to denude the bankrupt; and, when it goes this length, it has a 'most valuable effect, and cannot, by construction, be extended further than the words 'will bear' January 1734, Scott of Blair's creditors, against Charters of Aimsfield, Dict 86---Sess Pap Adv Lib.

To this case, I shall subjoin a notice of another, in which the line of distinction was drawn---In the ranking of Lowis of Merchiston's creditors, certain heritable bonds were challenged, as falling under the act, in consequence of the seisine being within the sixty days. Though the bonds themselves were of an old date, they were granted in the course of the same transaction which gave rise to Scott of Blair's case. They came before the same Lord Ordinary; and he so far distinguished, between that case and the case of the assignation, as to hold the statute applicable to the former, and not to the latter See the case detailed above, p 142 & seq debtor is clearly not divested by the mere disposition; the creditor who receives the disposition, can depend only upon his seisine for security; and this seisine, though not expressly warranted by the disposition, nor resting upon it solely, must be regarded as proceeding on it, since it proceeds under the authority of a legal step, taken in implement of what that disposition necessarily implies.

It is to be expected, that, in the next bankrupt law, an end will be put to all these questions, by establishing, as the general rule, that registration of the deed, or act, by which the conveyance is completed, shall be the regulator of the date, in challenges upon the statute of 1696.

2. But questions have also arisen, respecting the dates of conveyances of moveables; and these, I now proceed to explain.

DEBTS are conveyed by ASSIGNATION, and the assignation is held to be complete, only when it has been intimated to the debtor. Now, although the statute made no exception to the rule, that the date of the conveyance itself, should regulate the computation of the sixty days, excepting only in the case of seisine, the idea was not perhaps unnatural, of extending the spirit of this exception, to the case of assignations; for, when the act speaks of 'dispositions, assignations, &c. made and granted,' it may well be understood to mean, complete and effectual deeds, having the force of conveyances; which an assignation has not, till intimated. The debtor himself, and his heirs, are, indeed, barred, by personal exception, from objecting to the conveyance; but it has no effect, in competition with any other diligence, or voluntary right, completed before it. Till intimation, the assignation is an unfinished, ineffectual conveyance; and therefore, independently of any idea of publication to the creditors at large, an assignation seems hardly, even under the words of the act, to entitle the creditor to found on it as a conveyance, till it be intimated. In the case of Hay against Sinclair & Co., already quoted upon another point, the Court found the date of the assignation, not that of the

intimation,

intimation, to be the rule. 8th July 1788, Hay, VIII. Fac. Coll. xxviii. 45. When, in the bankrupt acts of 1783 and 1793, so much care was taken, to prevent the acquisition of partial preferences, by means of arrestment and poinding, within sixty days of the bankruptcy, it is to be regreted, that no notice should have been taken of this case of assignations; but it was probably omitted from the multiplicity of other important matters, that pressed upon the attention of the Legislature, in framing these statutes. In the case of Buchan against Farquharson, decided 24th May 1797, the Lord President took occasion to observe, that this was an omission in the statute, and that, he thought, the rule ought to be extended to the competition of assignations, as well as to arrestments and poindings, and, it is probable, that such will be the case, in the new statute.

CONVEYANCE OF MOVEABLES.—The contract of sale is complete, from the moment of full consent; but the property is not transferred, till tradition. If, for example, a bargain be struck in a market, though the sale is completed, the creditors of the seller may, even after the price has been paid, affect the subject by diligence, prior to actual delivery; or the seller may stop it, in transitu, where the price is unpaid. The same thing takes place, where one merchant, for instance, writes to another, that he has a quantity of grain, or other commodities, on hand, which he offers for sale at a certain rate, and his correspondent sends a commission for a parcel. The sale is complete; but the property untransferred. In a question, then, under the act 1696, Whether is it the date of the contract, or that of the delivery, that is to be the rule, in computing the sixty days? Considering the principle of the law, as directed against fraud, it is to the date of the contract that it should be held to refer; for it is then that the parties engage themselves; and that, if there be fraud in the contract, it must have been devised. The delivery is an act, to which the seller is previously bound, and in which, consequently, there can be no fraud. Considering the analogy of other cases, upon the interpretation of this statute, and, particularly, the above decision, respecting the date of an assignation, the conclusion will be the same,

same, that it is not the final completion of the transference, but the date of the contract, that should be taken as the rule; though there is no doubt that, in all questions of competition, the date of the delivery, is the point of completion. Whether the retaining of possession, may not form a circumstance, indicative of fraud, at common law, is another question, of which I shall have occasion to treat hereafter.

INDORSATIONS OF BILLS, are not, in general, dated. In the case of Smith against Home, 5th December 1712, Dalrymple, xciii. 130, it was held, on the Bench, and not much controverted, that if an indorsation be without date, it is to be considered as of the date of the bill. In the case of the Thistle Bank against Leny, 15th May 1794, a question arose upon an indorsation, which, though it bore a date, yet, being in the handwriting of the indorsee, was objected to, as incapable of proving the date. It was contended, that, in these circumstances, the conveyance must, as in dubio, be held to have been within the sixty days. Evidence was produced, to show, that the indorsation could not be antedated. It was remarked, upon the Bench, in support of the objection, that, by means of an indorsation, the act 1696 might be very easily evaded. But, to this, it was thought a sufficient answer, that the danger struck equally both ways; for, if the consequence of repelling the objection, was to give an easy method of evading the act, the sustaining of it, might throw loose transactions, settled by indorsations, not only during the period of sixty days, but even for years, preceding the bankruptcy. The majority of the Court came to this opinion, that as the date of the indorsation, if that be taken as the rule, was beyond the sixty days; and if the date affixed to the indorsation, be thrown aside, as there was nothing to prevent the Court from following the legal presumption, and carrying back the date to the earliest possible term, they must, in either view, hold the transmission as not falling under the act.—This case, then, teaches us, 1. That an indorsation, if dated, is to be held as of that date, till the contrary be proved: and, 2. That if it be not dated, the legal presumption is, that the indorsation was made at the date of the bill.

II.

II. COMPUTATION OF THE SIXTY DAYS.—Having seen how the date of the bankruptcy, on the one hand, and the date of the various kinds of deeds, on the other, are ascertained, the next point of our inquiry is, how the statutory period, of sixty days, is to be computed?

The rule of this computation seems to be this: That it is to be reckoned backwards, and exclusively of the day upon which the diligence is completed—that the first day is to be reckoned from the midnight preceding the completion of the diligence, by imprisonment, &c.—and that all deeds, granted after the sixty-first midnight from the completion of the diligence, must fall under the act.

The computation of periods, has given occasion to much debate and subtilty in our courts. Respecting the computation of the sixty days, under the law of deathbed, for example, several questions have arisen: and any one, who wishes to see what has been argued, upon either side of this question (which would have delighted the hearts of the schoolmen, and which indeed formed one of their favourite points of discussion), will do well, to examine the papers in the case of Mercer against Sir John Ogilvy, 10th December 1793. But, the rule to be drawn from the decision, in that case, and in the few questions which have occurred relative to diligence, I apprehend to be, that which has been stated above: For, 1. In Mercer's case, it was fixed, that the maxim, dies inceptus pro completo habetur, applies not to any case, in which time is computed by days; but only where a day is adjected, in majorem evidentiam of the expiry of a greater period. 2. In the case of Margaret Blair against the Town of Edinburgh, it was fixed, that the day does not run from noon to noon, (as it does in navigation reckoning), but, consistently with the common understanding of the country, from midnight to midnight. The Court, in that case, subjected the Magistrates, for having freed a debtor, on the act of grace, after twelve o'clock of the tenth day from the intimation; 11th November 1704, II. Fount. 238. 3dly, It is not only the common understanding, in citations and charges, that the calling

calling of the action or denounciation, cannot proceed till after the midnight of the last day of the citation or charge; but this understanding and practice, is grounded upon a decision, so old as the time of Colvil, in 1581; where it was found, that 'the last 'day of an execution of horning, "cedit debitori;" although, in 'computing, de momento, the whole six days were complete, 'some hours before the last day runs out.' December 1581, Menzies.

The statute, which is now under review, though, in many respects, excellent, is imperfect, when viewed according to the notions of our day. In particular, the exclusion, from the benefit of the reduction, all creditors, whose debts are posterior, in date, to the deed challenged, is inconsistent with the spirit and views of the bankrupt law. In this respect, we are less fortunate than our neighbours of England. The English Legislature, in their statutes of bankruptcy, aimed, from the first, at the establishment of a general system of distribution; they declared the fund to consist of every property in the bankrupt, after the first act of bankruptcy they admitted, to an equal share, in the division of it, every creditor, whose debt was contracted previously to the issuing of the commission; and thus, all had the benefit of the measures, taken by the assignees, for recovering the alienated funds. But, in Scotland, the Legislature were called upon to guard against fraudulent preferences, before the nation was ripe for a system of general distribution. Commerce had not, in the end of the last century, advanced so far, among us, as to lead to any peculiar institution for her accommodation; and the same unwillingness, which, to this day, in England, prevents the adoption of a general plan of distribution, in the failures of those unconnected with trade, was, at that period, sufficient, in Scotland, to bar the introduction of it in any case. The statute of 1696 was constructed at this unfavourable period. Connected with no plan of division among the creditors—but intended merely to prevent a debtor from injuring, by his voluntary acts, those to whom he had already engaged himself; it is not surprising, that, in this law, the rights of those,

who

who might become creditors after the granting of the deed, should have been overlooked. And although, in judging of such a statute at the present day, it is natural to wish, that its expressions were capable of an interpretation, which might include posterior creditors; the Judges of the Court of Session, duly distinguishing between the powers and duties of a Court of law, and those of a Legislature, have forborn to alter, what, they were decidedly of opinion, was the express declaration of the Parliament of 1696.

The first case, in which the point was questioned, occurred within six years after the date of the statute; and there seems to be every reason for believing, that the doubt would not have been stirred, at least so soon, had it not been exceedingly questionable in that case, whether the debt of the challenging creditor was posterior to the date of the deed, or not. The chief question, there, was, Whether a bill, dated on the same day with the deed challenged, was to be held as accepted of that date, or as not accepted till afterwards, and consequently as posterior? And it was natural, in seeking arguments to support the right of challenge, in so peculiar a case, to stumble upon a plea, which would not otherwise have been stated. The circumstances of the case were these:—Man raised an action of reduction, on the statute of 1696, of a conveyance, granted by Walls, to several creditors, in prejudice of him, a prior creditor. He was opposed, on the ground, that he was no prior creditor, since his bill, being dated the same day with the deed, and the acceptance not being dated, it was to be presumed posterior. Man contended for the priority of his debt; but argued, further, that, even were it not prior, he was entitled to challenge. The Lords found Man not to have been a creditor, till acceptance; and 'which, 'being posterior to the disposition, he had no interest to quarrel 'the same, which could only be done by anterior creditors, un-'less he could astruct and fortify his bill by some grounds of 'debt owing by Walls to him, prior to the same.' II. Fount. 156. 7. This decision is very strong against the right of posterior creditors; for, not only was the bill dated on the very same day with the disposition, but, Lord Fountainhall says, 'the Lords 'were the more circumspect in deciding this case, because it was 'amongst the first pursuits that have been founded on that late 'act of Parliament; and it was fit to clear the same for the fu- 'ture.'

So much was the question considered as at rest, by the declaration of the statute, and this deliberate interpretation of it, made at a time when those very men were on the Bench, by a committee of whom the law was prepared, that it was not, till near a century afterwards, that it was moved again. This was in the case of Robertson Barclay against Lennox of Woodhead.

In July 1778, Roberton of Bedley granted, in security, an heritable bond, to Mr Lennox, one of his creditors. Infeftment was not taken till the 28th May 1779, and, within the sixty days, Bedley was made bankrupt. A reduction was brought by Robertson Barclay, who became a creditor, between the date of the bond, and the date of the seisine. Several points, respecting the bankruptcy of Bedley, were discussed: but what concerns us, at present, is the plea stated, by Lennox, in bar of the reduction, viz. 'Even supposing his heritable security were, in general, found to 'be liable to challenge upon the act *1696*; yet, such of the cre- 'ditors, whose debts were contracted after the date of the secu- 'rity (i. e. after the 4th July 1778, when the heritable bond was 'granted), cannot be entitled to claim the benefit of that act.' The Court found the date of the seisine to be the rule; and 'sus- 'tained the objection to the claim of preference, so far as the 'debts of the objecting creditors were contracted prior to the date 'of the seisine; but found, that the creditors, whose debts were 'contracted subsequent to the date of the seisine, were not entitled 'to object to that preference.' This last part of the judgement is omitted in the printed report of the case, though it appears, from the papers, to have been the words of the decree. 19th November 1783, Robertson Barclay against Lennox, VII. Fac. Coll. cxxiii. 195 *.

However

* In support of the plea of exclusion of posterior creditors, it was ARGUED, that the acts 1621 and 1696 were (like the edict of the Roman Prætor, 'quæ in fraudem cre- 'ditorum

However consistent these decisions may be, with the words of the statute of 1696, and with the views entertained by the Legislature,

'ditorum facta sunt ut restituantur') made for the benefit of anterior creditors alone: That the act 1621, in its first branch, restricts the provision to the case of voluntary alienations, after the contracting of lawful debts; while the act 1696 is meant to repress securities given in prejudice of creditors, and declares all deeds of preference to other creditors, (that is, in preference to those who, being creditors at the time, are injured by the alienation), to be null: That it could never be the intention of this act, to provide for the security of future creditors, so as to cut down, in their favour, securities granted to prior onerous creditors, and the heritable bond, in question, cannot be said to be granted in prejudice of creditors who had not then lent their money.

In ANSWER to this argument, the creditors never thought of contesting the general point, whether, supposing the debt posterior, they had a right to challenge it under the act. They seem to have admitted that, and confined their argument entirely to that part of the statute, which brings the date of the security to that of the seisine; and as the seisine, on the heritable bond objected to, was posterior to the right of the creditor who made the challenge, the objection stated to him could have no foundation.

In REPLY to this argument, it was very ingeniously stated for Mr Lennox, that this clause, relating to the date, was not general, but to be explained by what goes before. The law is laying down a rule for preventing securities to the prejudice of creditors. That rule is, that all deeds granted to their prejudice, after bankruptcy, or even within sixty days before it, shall be null; and it is declared, that it shall be sufficient, if the seisine be dated within the prescribed period. But still, in all the various cases, the challenger must be able to state himself as a prior creditor; since, if his debt was posterior to the deed, the deed could not be granted in prejudice of it. This clause, in short, was meant to form a circumstance in the computation of the sixty days, not to change the nature of the title to challenge. If a bond be granted in security by one owing no other debt, it is not a security in prejudice of other creditors; it is the same thing, as to them, with a security for a new debt; and the delay to take seisine, should have no other effect, in this question, than the Court has found it to have in cases of nova debita: the latency of the security can have no worse effect. (See Howston & Co's case, and the still stronger case of Douglas Heron & Co.) Suppose that a person, having only one creditor, gives him an heritable security over lands in Orkney, on which it is impossible to take seisine for a month perhaps: no law can strike against this: no creditor is hurt by it: before the seisine can be taken, the grantor borrows money—squanders—and at last is made bankrupt, within the sixty days of the infeftment; it would be a hard law, that cut down so fair a security. There is no fraud in contracting the first debt, or giving the security for it, while there is no other creditor in existence; but it would be grossly fraudulent, and highly unjust, if, by contracting after debts, perhaps by connivance, to make himself bankrupt, the debtor could thus void the security he had granted. Sess. Pap. Adv. Lib.

ture, at that time, the rule, which is thus settled, is productive of consequences inconsistent with the spirit of the bankrupt law, as now established. We shall afterwards, in considering the rules of division, have occasion to observe the effects of this rule. At present, all that it is proper to observe, is, that although the estate of the bankrupt ought to form a general fund of division, among all those who are his creditors at the date of his bankruptcy; yet, by the operation of this law, those who have been fortunate enough to become creditors before the date of a deed, which is stigmatized and reduced as fraudulent, enjoy a decided preference over those whose debts are posterior to that date.

OF SECURITIES FOR FUTURE DEBTS, AND OF THE MANNER OF SECURING A CASH ACCOUNT HERITABLY.

We have now seen the gradual progress of our statutes against frauds: first, the rude and imperfect remedies of the statute 1621, and afterwards, in 1696, the establishment of a presumptive fraud, respecting all deeds done in prejudice of creditors, within sixty days of bankruptcy. But the remedy would have been imperfect, had the Legislature stopped here. There had arisen, in those days, a form of security, for debts to be afterwards contracted, which would have furnished ample room for the evasion of the statute 1696, c. 5. This form of security had arisen, in direct opposition to the plain principles of the Scotish law: but, so common had it become, that it was thought necessary, by a clause in the statute, to provide against the dangers which it threatened. In order to explain the nature of this security, the evils which were dreaded from its use, and the remedy provided by the statute, it may be proper to give a short sketch of our heritable securities for debts.

Our voluntary securities upon land, for debt, are few in number, and very simple in principle. They are strictly reducible to two; the wadset, and the heritable bond. And the principles, upon which they depend, are two also · FIRST, That the real right of the creditor, or jus in re, is constituted by the feudal form of seisine: SECONDLY, That the security, or burden, must precisely appear in the record.

1. The wadset was, in its original form, a conveyance of land, in impignoration to the creditor, for payment of a sum lent. The right of the creditor was secured by seisine. He entered into possession, or drew the rents; and his right was at an end, only when the total sum of advance was repaid. This form of security, though little in use now, was once the most common of all: for, amidst all its inconveniences, it had this advantage, that, under the cover of it, more easily than under that of any other security, the canonical prohibitions against the taking of interest could be eluded. It is needless to trace the steps of the progress, by which creditors came to elude, and debtors to permit the elusion of this prohibition: we have only to attend to the nature of the security which was used. At first, then, the right of the wadsetter, or creditor, was that of a proprietor, qualified by a condition of redemption, declared in the deed. Afterwards, the disposition to the creditor, and the condition of reversion to the debtor, were expressed in different deeds; and then the creditor became, in appearance, an absolute proprietor of the debtor's lands, but liable to a personal right of redemption in the debtor. This personal right, when taken to the debtor, and his assignees, could be assigned by the debtor, and the right of the assignee was completed by intimation to the creditor: or, the right of redemption could be renounced, in favour of the creditor himself, and then his right became absolute: or, if the debtor required a further advance, and the creditor was willing to make it, a partial renunciation, to that extent, of the right of reversion, (which obtained the strange name of an Eik, or addition to the reversion), enlarged the creditor's security, so as to include the new debt. But as, in the wadset, the creditor's right was ex facie absolute, and the right of reversion merely personal, it became necessary, on the one hand, to secure the reversers, or proprietors, and their heirs, assignees, and creditors, against the possibility of a bad use being

being made, of the apparently absolute right, which was held by the wadsetter, or lender, and, on the other, to secure strangers against the secret claims of the reversers, or borrowers. These two objects were accomplished by the statutes 1469, c. 27, and 1617, c. 16, declaring reversions to be real rights, effectual against singular successors, and ordering them to be recorded, for publication.—Gradually, from this time, the wadset came again to be expressed in one deed; and, when this security is used at the present day, it is executed in the form of a contract.

2. Besides the wadset, there was another very ancient mode of borrowing money upon land, viz. upon the security of a right to an irredeemable annuity payable from it. This was called an infeftment of annualrent. Strictly speaking, neither this form of security, nor the rent charge, (which was little else than this, deprived of its feudal form of seisine *), were entitled to the name of a security; since they were proper purchases, of an irredeemable and annual payment from land. But they were, with the wadset, the only forms of security once in use. Gradual approaches were, however, made, in the use of this form, to the modern form of our heritable security. Conveyancers, even prior to the abolition of the canon law, ventured to introduce, into their annualrent rights, a clause of redemption; which, of course, converted them into impignorations of a rent, as the wadset was an impignoration of the land itself. and, after the Reformation, the deed was furnished with a counter part to this clause of redemption, viz. a power of requisition by the lender. The next step of the progress

* There is much plausibility in Mr Ross's notion, (Vol II p. 324.), that the infeftment of annualrent preceded the rent charge, and was, in this country, the mode of constituting securities, analogous with the subinfeudations, which were used, for the same purpose, in England, before the statute 'Quia Emptores' that the seisine of the former security was dropped, upon the enactment of the statute of Robert III, against subinfeudations; (the same progress taking place in England, on the like restraint, by the statute 'Quia Emptores'): and that the security which, in consequence of that statute, appeared, for a short time, in the form of a rent charge, afterwards, as this law fell into disuse, gradually resumed its pristine form of an infeftment, securing the creditor in an annual sum, payable from the debtor's lands.

gress was, to introduce, instead of the power of redemption and requisition, a proper personal bond, to accompany the annualrent right, and, in consequence of which, the principal sum might be recovered. By degrees, the deed was converted into the present form of an heritable bond; in which the debtor not only binds himself, personally, to repay the money, as in a common bond, and, in further security, infefts the creditor in an annualrent, payable out of the lands; but gives infefment in the lands themselves, for security of the principal sum, redeemable at any time, upon payment of that sum, and interest. By this right, the creditor has a real security for the sum of debt actually due at the date of infeftment, and for the interest, as it arises, and he has a power of entering into possession, or recovering the rents. If he do enter to the possession, he is obliged to account for the sums which he receives; and his security is extinguished, in proportion to the amount of his intromissions or payments; subsisting only for the balance.

Such are the general features of our proper heritable securities for debt; and their application to the case of money presently advanced, or of debts formerly subsisting, is plain and natural. But occasions were to arise, when something else was necessary. The advantages of our modern cash accounts, may teach us to conceive, how ardently men, who were in want of occasional supplies of cash, and who, at the same time, preferred the borrowing of money to the sale of their land, should have longed for a form of security, under which a creditor, having the command of money, should have no scruple of making occasional advances, or of relieving them from such pressing debts as they might, at any time, be called upon to pay. In seeking to apply the forms of the common securities to such an occasion, the only one that seemed in any degree fitted for the purpose, was the wadset. But, in its proper shape of a mutual contract, or even of an absolute conveyance, qualified by a bond of reversion, made real under the statutes 1469 and 1617, even this form of security was ill adapted for such an occasion, for the wadset can become a cover for a future debt, only by an ' eik to the reversion,' recorded and made real, in terms of

law,

law. There was, however, one form of wadset, which suggested a kind of security, not unfit for the occasion. The separation of the disposition and right of reversion, showed the possibility of using the form of an absolute disposition, qualified by a personal back-bond; the absolute right being thus established in the creditor, so that no one deriving right through the debtor, could have a claim for restitution, until a balance should be struck, and paid up to the creditor. But it will not be wondered at, that such a security should not have been adopted into common use, when it is considered, how unwilling any proprietor must have been, to grant an absolute conveyance of his estate; by which he must not only have ceased to appear in the world as proprietor of it, but (being unprotected by the acts 1469 and 1617) must have left it entirely in his creditor's power to convey his estate away from him, for ever. Lawyers and conveyancers, therefore, set themselves to torture the old forms of security, into a compliance with the wishes of their employers. The wadset, they made to cover future debts, (as in M'Dowal of French's case, to be immediately detailed), by taking it, at once, for sums advanced, or to be advanced. The annualrent right, being the purchase of a rent, redeemable on payment of the purchase money, was not so easily convertible into a security for future debt; but it was made to serve the purpose, by a declaration, (as Dallas informs us), that all other debts and engagements should be settled by the debtor, before the power of redemption should be open to him.

To bend the stubborn form of the heritable security to this new use, for which it was not originally calculated, other means were taken. As a security for a precise sum, this form must be limited by the actual extent of what is due at the giving of the seisine, since there can be no security where there is no debt: it must, of course, be extinguished, too, by payment or intromission, and cannot be tacitly revived. But as such a security was always thought competent for a cautionary engagement, or (in the language of our law) capable of securing an obligation of relief, advantage was taken of this, and the heritable right given in security, and 'for relief of all sums, debts, engagements, and cautionaries.'

This

This appears, from Lord Stair's report of the case of Inglis, (vol. II. p. 527.) to have been a common security, towards the end of the last century.

These securities in relief, were stopt in their effect, as covers to future debts, by the intervention of infeftment, in favour of another creditor, as in the case of M'Dowall of French against Sir John Rutherford, where a security, by wadset, for sums advanced, or to be advanced, was found preferable, in a competition with other heritable securities, only for such sums as were advanced at the date of the other infeftments being made public: 19th January 1715, Bruce, xxv. 39. But, notwithstanding this qualification, all such securities were pregnant with mischief, and became the instruments of the most detestable frauds. By their means, prior to the act 1696, a debtor could, with perfect ease, have evaded the provisions of the act 1621; for he had no more to do, than to grant a deed, such as either of those now described, while yet diligence had not begun against him; and then, when diligence began, his disponee busied himself in paying off favourite creditors, neither the debtor himself, nor the creditors, being entitled to have the land restored, without accounting with him for all the money he had paid out for the debtor. When, by the act 1696, it was enacted, that the debtor could give no deed of preference within sixty days of his bankruptcy, the efficacy of the enactment was in danger of being nugatory and useless, if such securities were still suffered to exist,—if a person holding a deed of security for relief of all sums and engagements, &c. were permitted to pay the favourite creditors of the bankrupt, and to cover his claim by the previous security. Therefore it was provided, that, 'because infeftments for relief, 'not only of debts already contracted, but of debts to be contracted 'for hereafter, are often found to be the occasion and cover of 'fraud; all dispositions or other rights that shall be granted for 'hereafter, for relief or security of debts to be contracted for the 'future, shall be of no force, as to any such debts that shall be 'found to be contracted after the seisine or infeftment following 'on the said disposition or right; but prejudice to the validity of 'the said disposition or right, as to other points, as accords.'

By this part of the statute, the Legislature confirmed and cleared the plain principles of the feudal law. This has been delivered as the opinion of the greatest of our feudal lawyers of the present age. It was laid down, both in the case of Sir G. Abercrombie, and in that of Pickering, (to be afterwards more particularly taken notice of), that the giving of heritable securities for future debts, was a practice that had grown up in direct violation of every feudal principle, and that the statute did nothing more than declare the common law.

But even this declaration of the Legislature might have been nugatory, had it been lawful to grant a security on land, for an indefinite sum; as the common opinion was, till the decision of the House of Lords, in the case of Cuxton, &c. followed by the Court of Session as a rule, in the case of M'Lelan's creditors, in 1734,* and in later cases. Since the year 1734, it has been held, that no such security is competent by the law of Scotland: Stein's Creditors against Newnham & Everet, 14th November 1789, affirmed in the House of Peers, 25th February 1791; and more directly, between the same parties, 1st February 1793; where this was the judgement of the Court—'Upon the report of Lord Swinton, Find 'the conveyance granted by James Stein, &c. to be an indefinite 'security; and therefore, that it cannot be sustained, so as to 'create a preference to Messrs Newnham Everet & Co., in a question 'with the other creditors of James Stein.'—And this judgement was affirmed in the House of Peers, 10th March 1794.

Thus, two points were fixed: 1. That no effectual heritable security could be given for an indefinite sum; and, 2. That the security, even where the sum was definite, could cover only the debt actually subsisting at its date. The sole question that seemed to remain, was this, What is to be considered as a subsisting debt, in the view of the statute? Whether is it necessary, that there should be

* These cases I shall hereafter detail, at some length; for, though perhaps the most important desisions in our law, they are no where to be found, but in the short notice of Mr Erskine, (E. iii. 50.), and in the Dictionary

be an actual advance of money, at the date of the seisine, in order to validate the security? The first case of this kind, was, that of Dempster against Lady Kinloch. Dempster was creditor in an heritable bond for 20,000l. Scots; but only 8735l. had been advanced at the date. For the balance, he bound himself by a backbond, 'payable at Whitsunday then next, or any subsequent term of 'Whitsunday, upon a premonition of forty days.' and it was declared, 'That if the advance already made, with others thereafter to be required, should not extend to the said sum of '20,000l., then the heritable bond, with what should follow thereon, should be restricted to what should be truly paid and advanced 'of the said 20,000l., and no further.' The cause turned entirely upon the point, Whether it was to be held, that the whole sum was, in the sense of law, advanced? The Court were 'all agreed, 'that, taking it as an absolute obligation for the 11,269l. not advanced, that could have been affected by a creditor of Sir James's, 'it would have been secured by the infeftment, no less than if it 'had been advanced at the date of the bond, *nothing being more* 'ordinary, than to make up a part of a sum, by a bill or bond, 'for a balance. But, on the other hand, considering it as an obligation, which could not have been affected by a creditor, but 'an obligation, pendent upon the will of Sir James, whether he 'would require the money, or not, there was as little doubt, that 'the security was to be restricted.' The Court understood the obligation, first, as absolute, and therefore sustained the security: afterwards, they held it to be merely arbitrary, and restricted it in the competition: Kilk. p. 393-4. Lord Kames, in his report, says, that Lord Elchies supported the opinion, that this was a proper debt, to the full extent: while 'Arniston, and 'the other Judges, held, that the back-bond did not constitute a 'debt; that no action of debt could ly upon the back-bond, but 'only an action to create a debt, or to lend money; and that, 'when Dempster advanced the money, it was not paying a debt 'due by him, but, on the contrary, it was lending money, and 'creating a debt:' 13th June 1750, Kinloch against Dempster, Kames's Rem. Dec. cxv. 223. Resting the question, then, upon the principle which prevailed in this case, it may be taken as a

point

point fixed, that, wherever an absolute and irrevocable obligation is granted by the holder of the security, the debt is to be held as advanced, and the security as effectual.

The statute provides, that no security shall be effectual, for any money advanced after the date of the seisine. If this is to be strictly interpreted, it may lead to very severe and unjust consequences, in many cases. A creditor, who lends money on security, is safe, only when he sees an infeftment taken, and recorded, prior to any other. In strictness, therefore, no creditor will ever advance his money, prior to the date of the infeftment; and, in cases, where the lands ly in a distant part of the country, it may be long after the date of the seisine, before the security can be brought to him, in this complete form. Does he incur the danger, then, of any objection under the statute, by insisting, that the transaction shall be managed in this way? This question was very solemnly decided, in the case of Sir G. Abercrombie against Sir James Norcliffe. The transaction, from which the question arose, was, a loan of 5000l. by Sir Robert Abercromby to Sir James Dunbar. The bond was made out, and seisine taken, in November 1774; and the whole 5000l. was not paid up till Spring 1775. In the ranking of Sir James Dunbar's estate, this security was objected to; and a very full inquiry was made into the circumstances of the transaction, from which it appeared, that, although there was no absolute and written obligation upon the creditor, to complete the loan, the agreement was for a loan of 5000l., to be paid by the retiring of different bonds, bills, &c. due by the grantor of the security, and of which the lender received a list; that these sums were accordingly paid up, that the security was deposited in the hands of a man of business, till the whole sum should be advanced; and that, on the last part of the sum being paid, it was delivered up to the creditor. The Lord Ordinary (Swinton) drew a distinction. He sustained the bond 'as effectual, for all sums advanced, or bills, or other obligations, granted by the lender to the 'borrower, which, previous to the taking of the seisine, the lender 'either took up, or for which he granted his own obligation to the 'creditor: but, as to all sums advanced, debts paid, or obligations 'granted,

'granted, by the lender to the borrower, after the day on which 'seisine was taken, he found the security ineffectual.'—His Lordship, in this judgement, gave precise application to the principles established in the above mentioned case of Dempster against Kinloch. But, when the question came before the Court, they took it in another point of view. They viewed the transaction as indivisible; the sum, as one loan, which, from peculiar circumstances, took some time to be paid up; and the security, as not effectual, till, by delivery of the deeds, after the whole money was advanced, it came into the power of the lender. They held, that, to interpret the statute so judaically as the creditor contended for, was, to put an end to heritable securities in Scotland; that the law, which declared a lender's safety to depend upon a recorded infeftment, could never mean to forfeit his security, merely because he insisted on seeing the deeds thus completed, before he made any advance; and, that the true intention of the statute, was, to strike down general securities, and deprive a debtor of the power of contracting new debts, under the cover of an old security. They, therefore, altered the Lord Ordinary's judgment, and repelled the objections to the security. 30th July 1789, Sir G. Abercromby against Sir James Norcliffe, and other creditors of Sir James Dunbar.

But although the statute of 1696, might have been evaded more easily, had not all this care been taken to prevent securities from being constituted for debts to be afterwards contracted; yet these provisions were, in one respect, productive of unfortunate and unforeseen consequences. They formed a complete obstacle to the constituting of a security, on land, for a bank credit, or cash-account. By a cash-account, the trader has, on the one hand, a power to draw upon the banker, to the value agreed upon, and, on the other, the sums drawn out, are paid up by the daily profits of his trade. The debt is in a state of continual fluctuation. To-day, the bank may have paid out the whole sum of the credit; to-morrow, again, it may be all repaid; and, the third day, the whole may be drawn back. The beneficial effects of these operations, are

now

now universally acknowledged; and it was an object of much importance, to apply heritable security, in this manner, to the active purposes of trade. But, those who sought the attainment of this object, found two obstacles in the way. 1. As, from the nature of an infeftment in security, nothing can be considered as secured under it, but what has actually been advanced, or expressly and irrevocably engaged for by the lender; and, as it is not the purpose of a bank credit, to transact an immediate loan, but to enable a person to draw out money, as he may have occasion for it, in trade; it is impossible, viewing the matter, either upon the principles of the feudal law, or as fixed by the statute, to give to the banker a real security, for a sum not advanced. The parties may, indeed, get over this objection. The person, who receives the credit, may draw out the whole sum at once, and deposite it again. But, this device would expose the security to another objection, which shall immediately be taken notice of.—Another expedient might be fallen upon. The banker might grant an absolute and irrevocable obligation, to pay the whole sum when demanded, and so entitle himself to be considered as a creditor for the whole sum. But, then, he would, in this way, not only renounce his power of recalling the credit, when he might wish to do so, but he would also destroy the true character and use of a cash-account; because, his letter of credit would then cease to be personal to him who obtained it; and, any of his creditors would have it in their power to attach the amount in the banker's hands, as the proper fund of their debtor. How far this would be a departure from the true character and use of a cash-account, it is needless to explain. 2. The other obstacle alluded to, is one which strikes at the very root of heritable securities, as applicable to such a purpose. An heritable security is extinguished by intromission, or payment; and, when extinguished, in whole or in part, the infeftment, and heritable right, are, to that extent, purged away. The debtor himself is, therefore, reinvested with the real right; and it can leave his person, only in consequence of a new conveyance. But, the very object of a cash-account, is, to permit the person who receives it, to draw out, or pay in money, as his hands may be full, or as his necessities may require.

To

To remove these objections, against the use of heritable securities, in cash-accounts, was, at one time, the object of much solicitude. The matter has been, within these few years, settled by a statute, which has supplied the omission of the old law, and given the sanction of the Legislature to this application of the heritable security. In one sense, therefore, it is now of less importance, to trace the progress of the decisions upon this question. But, still, this may be not uninteresting, as the inquiry may illustrate, in some degree, the mercantile progress of the country, and as the opinions maintained in the course of the discussion, may be useful, with relation to that part of the rule which has not been altered.

In 1772, the ruinous expedient, of drawing and redrawing bills of exchange, brought this country to the brink of ruin; and though, by temporary expedients, the evil day was kept off for a while, it came, at last, attended by terrible bankruptcies in England and in Scotland. The credit of all the Scotish houses, was rapidly falling, along with the decline of the Douglas Bank; and, to avoid a general failure, the attention of all ranks was directed to the discovery of funds of credit. In particular, much deliberation was bestowed upon the possibility of applying the heritable bond to the security of bank credits. The greatest lawyers of the time were consulted; and I have heard the late Lord Justice-Clerk M'Queen say, that they fairly confessed themselves unable to devise a way, in which this could be effected. At this period, the partners of the house of Alexander, of Edinburgh, (one of the most considerable mercantile houses in Europe), were possessed of extensive estates in the West Indies, and of an estate in Scotland; and they contrived to make this property a kind of prop to the credit of all the Scotish houses. Among other expedients, they, with the aid of Messrs Walpole of London, prevailed upon the Bank of England, on the faith of securities over their estates in the West Indies, and in Scotland, to give them a credit to a large amount. At the time that this agreement was entered into, there were lying in the Bank of England, discounted, under the acceptance of Messrs Glyn & Halifax, of London, who had stopped payment, bills to the amount of 47,000l., besides acceptances, to a very large amount, by Messrs Johnston & Smith, of Edinburgh, also discounted for Messrs Alexanders. The agreement was, that the Bank of England should continue to discount the bills of the Messrs Alexanders, for any sums not exceeding (with the above) 160,000l. This credit, which, in Scotland, would have been managed by the means of a cash-account, is managed, according to the common practice of the Bank of England, by discount. The bills are drawn at short dates; and, when they fall due, other bills are drawn, and discounted, for the same sum. It was in this way, that this transaction was managed. The two houses, of Walpole & Ellison, and Walpole Clerk & Bourne, agreed to be guarantees; and a collateral security, over their West Indian, and their Scotish estates, was to be given by Messrs Alexanders. This agreement was settled in July 1772. In August 1773, the heritable security was granted over the estate of Clunie. Prior to the granting of the heritable security, the transactions had proceeded on the faith of the mutual obligations of the parties. The discounts had been made, and the bills retired, regularly; one set of bills being discounted to retire another, and the deficiency, or interest discounted, being always paid up; till, on the eve of granting the security, the advances had mounted up to 6800l. above the maximum of 160,000l. This excess was paid off; and the advance stood at the stipulated maximum, when the heritable security was completed, on the 13th August 1773.

There was little question, that the security, in this case, was not liable to the objection, of having been granted before the advance of the money. The chief questions which arose, were, 1. Whether it was a security for a definite sum? and, 2. Whether the discounting of new sets of bills, to retire the old, having proceeded after the date of the security, as it did before, the security was not extinguished by payment, or novation at least? *

'The

* THE BANK OF SCOTLAND, AS A CREDITOR, ARGUED, 1. That this was a general security, for an indefinite operation of discounting; limited as to the maximum, but that maximum fixed so high above the value of the estate, that it was scarcely any limitation

'The Lords repelled the objections made to the real security, 'on which the Bank of England claimed their preference in the 'ranking.'

tion at all. On the face of the security, the amount of the debt, at any one period, was quite uncertain, and could appear only from an investigation into private transactions, and, if such a security is admitted, it sets at defiance all inhibitions, and posterior infeftments—every future debt comes to be covered by it. 2. That not only is it the principle of the common law, fortified by the act 1696, that an heritable security is extinguished, past the possibility of revival, by payment;—but, here, the retiring of one set of bills by another, gave the debtor, who held the retired bills, an opportunity of deceiving purchasers, or lenders of money, into a belief, that the whole was paid off. A bond of corroboration hurts not the original document of debt: they both remain with the creditor, and subsist together. But, if a first bond, heritably secured, be given up, and cancelled, and a new bond given, taking no notice of the former existence of the debt; the first bond is extinguished, and the heritable security, its concomitant, expires along with it. The heritable security, in the present case, was not the original and proper constitution of the debt, the bills being collateral vouchers of it—but the reverse: the bills were the original constitution—the heritable security merely collateral: without the bills, the disposition is nothing. Bills cannot be considered as corroborative vouchers, all subsisting and hanging together, through the whole period of a discounting connexion. Bills are not like bonds. The debt and the bond are independent of each other. The debt subsists all along, unchanged, however the written voucher may be renewed, or corroborated. But, in a bill, the debt and voucher are hardly separable. Two bills, for the same sum, are different debts, indorsible, and for which the accepter would be liable. He must have the one extinguished, therefore, before the new one be granted. The Company relies, thenceforward, not upon the first bill, or the diligence that may have been done on it, but upon the second bill alone. The indorsers upon the first bill are liberated; and the diligence, by horning, arrestment, &c. extinguished for ever. An inhibiter, or adjudger, would not have been permitted to rank, if the bill, on which he had proceeded, had been retired, or renewed. The specialty pleaded here, viz. that there was, in the original agreement, a stipulation for a renewal of the discounts, which connected the whole succession of bills together, as parts of one and the same transaction, is not enough: for if, without such stipulation, the heritable security would have been extinguished, on the retiring of the first set of bills, as no longer applicable to a prior advance, the question comes to be, Whether, by a stipulation of this kind, the act 1696 can be dispensed with? The creditors concluded, with stating the decision, the Duke of Norfolk against the York Building Company annuitants, (Kames's Sel. Dec. 1. 1.), as establishing, even in the case of a bond, the doctrine contended for, viz. That where one bond had come in place of another, the heritable security, applicable to the first bond, was extinguished.

THE BANK OF ENGLAND ANSWERED, 1. The heritable security is granted in implement of a mutual obligation, by which the Bank of England was bound, by ac-

'ranking.' 1st March 1781, Governor and Company of the Bank of Scotland against the Governor and Company of the Bank of England;

ceptance of the bond of security of the Alexanders, to discount to the value of 160,000l The advance was to be posterior; but the obligation to make it by discounting, absolute and, if the Bank had stopped discounting, Messrs Alexanders might have recalled their security This takes the case out of the line of an indefinite security and makes the security good, even although the advance had not been actually made at the date of the seisine. The rule against indefinite securities, never has been applied, where the maximum is fixed The record showed the estate burdened with 160,000l The great extent of this maximum rather shows, that no one should have trusted to the security of that estate, since no probable reduction could bring the debt down to its value It is right, that every man should have it in his power, to use his estate is a fund of credit Here, there was not a general power, of including all debts under the security, the Bank was permitted to apply it only to bills drawn, accepted, and indorsed, by houses particularly specified. Every debt is subject to diminution, by partial payment; and, here, the maximum being fixed, the worst was known A security in relief is quite indefinite, both as to the extent, and existence of any claim, yet it is good. So is an infeftment for a jointure, where its existence is made to depend on the state of the family All these are sustained, on the plain principle, that the records show the worst of them 2 The act 1696 is strictly interpreted it applies, properly, only to cases of fraud In many cases, subsequent advances are supported, as covered effectually by the real security—as in cautionary engagements, &c But, here, the money was all advanced. and, as to the retiring of the bills by new discounts, it is nothing A debt, and its voucher, are quite distinct First, second, and third bills of exchange, do not multiply the debt Bills are as completely capable of separation from the debt, as bonds The loss of the voucher, or its destruction, does not extinguish the debt. The present loan was, from the first, meant to be permanent —a provision was made, for periodical discounting, to carry it on—heritable securities were provided—and the loan was never to exceed a certain sum. The loan is permanent: the vouchers must, from the practice of the Bank, be fluctuating.---Suppose this a proper heritable bond, for 160,000l instantly advanced, but that Messrs Alexanders were to place deposites, of equal value, in the hands of the Bank, as additional securities, subject to such alterations as parties should choose: this, confessedly, would have been good: yet this was just the case The bills were the deposites, in additional security—bags of money—or the pledged credit, at least, of Messrs Walpoles---which, by no change, could operate the smallest extinction of the debt A new set of deposites redeemed the old ones, and stood in their place The personal bond narrated the agreement of the Bank to make the advance; and, by acceptance, the Bank confirmed that. Had the advance been specified to be made in their own notes, or cash, the receipts for these would have been, merely, the voucher of the performance of the obligation The same thing might have been proved by the books

England; VI. Fac. Coll. part II. sh. 72. The report does not state the ground of decision; but it appears to have been, that, as the security was given for a sum actually advanced at the time, the mere renewal of the vouchers was not to be taken as payment, to the effect of extinction.

In this case, the question did not strictly relate to the security of a cash credit (on which account, I have detailed it more fully); but in several cases which have occurred since the above decision was pronounced, the heritable bond has been found inapplicable to a proper cash account.

Thus, in Pickering against Smith Wright & Gray, in 1788, Smith Wright & Gray, having opened a cash account in favour of James King, he, for their security, granted a simple heritable bond for the sum of 2500l., on which infeftment was taken; and this bond was qualified by a separate deed, in which Smith Wright & Gray acknowledged, that this sum had not been advanced, but that the bond was intended as 'a security for such payments as 'they already had made, or should thereafter make, during the 'currency of a cash account which they had opened in King's 'favour.' King operated on this credit, and afterwards became bankrupt; and, on the face of the account, the balance stood much against him. Pickering, as trustee for his creditors challenged the security. Here, then, the two objections occurred, 1. That the debt, was not a subsisting debt at the date of the security; since it neither was advanced, nor absolutely and irrevocably engaged

of the Bank, &c. Here, that the debt was constituted, as originally stipulated, and that it subsists still, is proved by the clerk of the Bank. The debtor having the retired bills, is nothing. If a bond be given up, on the granting of a corroborative bond, still the debt subsists; although the debtor may thus have it in his power to show the original documents, apparently retired. Here, the security referred, not to a particular set of bills, but to a future discount, and no one could be deceived, by seeing one set of bills retired. As the debt, here, rested on the original obligation, if any case of diligence is to be taken, (as an inhibition), it must be taken as proceeding upon that obligation, not upon the bills. In the York Building Company's case, not only were the documents changed, but the annuities were taken to different creditors, and on lives.

gaged for, so as to be attachable by creditors: and, 2. That the constant fluctuations of a cash account, are inconsistent with the nature of a real security. It was observed, on the Bench, that so salutary 'an enactment as this (the act 1696), ought not to be 'narrowed in its construction. Far from introducing any inno-'vation, it does no more than confirm the doctrine of our feudal 'law. The loan of the money was essential to the constitution of 'the right in question. But it is absurd to conceive this right 'continually fluctuating between existence and non-existence, ac-'cording as the money, during the currency of the cash account, 'should have been paid, repaid, and paid again; the creditor being, 'of course, the vassal one day, the next not so; the third, a se-'cond time vassal, and so forth.' The Court sustained the rea-sons of reduction of the heritable bond, so far as respected the sums advanced posterior to the date of the seisine thereon. 16th January 1788, VIII. Fac. Coll. xiv. 25.

In the ranking of Stein's creditors, the question again occurred. Stein interposed his credit for Buchanan & Co.; and, in order to procure for them a cash account from Newnham Everet & Co., he conveyed to those gentlemen an heritable bond, standing in his person, for 1200l.; and this, in pledge, as an additional and collateral security for the more certain reimbursement of such sums of money as should be drawn from them, 'by orders or draughts 'of the said Messrs Jo. Buchanan & Co., or by their receipts, ac-'cepted bills, or promissory notes, granted by them, or by letters 'addressed by them to the said Messrs Newnham Everet & Co., 'in consequence of, and upon the faith of the said credit, or cash 'account, over and above what of the proper cash or value, be-'longing to the said Messrs Jo. Buchanan & Co., which may 'happen to be lodged with, and put to the credit of the said ac-'count current, in the books of the said Messrs Newnham Everet '& Co,' &c. And Newnham Everet & Co. are taken bound to make just accounting and payment to Messrs Buchanan & Co., by credit on the account, or, failing that, to Stein, of the sum of 1200l., so conveyed in security, or for such part as they shall have received from the debtor in the heritable bond. Both Stein

and

and Buchanan & Co. became bankrupt, by which time, the draughts far exceeded the 1200l. It will occur, from what has been already stated, this security was liable to two objections; 1. That it was indefinite in the debt to be secured: 2 That it could not subsist for the sums advanced after its date. Only the last of these questions came to trial in the first action: the other was afterwards brought forward, in consequence of a remark that fell from the present Lord President, who, in reporting the cause to the Court, as Lord Probationer, said, that, independently of the date of the advance, the security, as granted for an indefinite sum, was, in his judgement, illegal, agreeably to the decision of the House of Lords, in 1734.

The question, respecting the advances after the date of the security, came to be tried upon the 14th November 1789; when the case of Pickering was founded on, and the point of law well argued, not only in papers, but at the Bar. The Lord Ordinary had found, 'that the infeftment, for the security of Newnham & 'Co., could not avail them for any sums paid, or obligations un-'dertaken by them, posterior to the date thereof.' To this judgement, the Court adhered; and an appeal was entered. The point of law was fully argued before the House of Lords, the history of the act discussed, and the cases analized. Their Lordships (25th July 1791) affirmed the judgement of the Court of Session. Then the trustee brought forward the plea, founded on the indefinite nature of the security, as striking against even the prior advances. The chief defence, in bar of this ground of reduction, proceeded upon the nature of an heritable bond, considered as a separate estate. The objection to indefinite securities on land, is, that the land itself is indefinite in value, and the extent of the burden cannot appear. But an heritable bond is limited in value, and, if conveyed in security, it must be presumed, that the burden equals the sum conveyed. This is, at least, the maximum; and the less the debt is found to be, so much the better for the creditors. If the security had borne to be for advances, to the extent of 12,000l., it would have been unobjectionable for all advances prior to seisine: but, as it is a right to 12,000l., out of land

conveyed

conveyed in security of whatever advances should be made, it is precisely the same thing. This distinction was denied on the other side. An heritable bond, is an heritable estate, in every feudal view; and the objection is, that an uncertain debt is made a burden upon a certain estate. The Court, 'upon the report of 'Lord Swinton, found the conveyance, granted by James Stein, 'of the heritable bond, by Robert to James Stein, over the lands 'of Kincaple, belonging to Robert, was an indefinite security, 'and therefore cannot be sustained, so as to create a preference 'to Messrs Newnham Everet & Co., in a question with the other 'creditors of James Stein.' 1st February 1793, IX. Fac. Coll. xxii. 45. And this decision was affirmed in the House of Lords, 10th March 1794.

By the decisions already quoted, it was fully established, that an heritable security cannot be made to apply directly to a cash account. But one other question remained to be tried on the subject, Whether the same effect might not be produced by the interposition of a cautioner, who should become directly bound to the Bank, and for whose relief an heritable security might be granted? A case of this kind occurred, in the ranking of Brough's creditors (so fertile in cases upon this statute); and it was decided, that a security, granted to the cautioner, was in no better situation than that granted to the creditor directly. Brough, in June 1788, obtained a cash credit from Sir William Forbes & Co. for 500l., on a joint bond by him and Mr Selby. Of the same date, Brough granted a bond of relief to Selby, binding himself 'to 'free, relieve, harmless keep, &c. him and his heirs, of and from 'payment of the contents of the said bond, or any part thereof, 'with all cost, expences, &c. through his having become cau'tioner as aforesaid; and, for that effect, to deliver up the said 'bond cancelled, or to report a valid discharge thereof,' &c. And, in further security and relief, he sells and dispones to him a house in the New Town: infeftment followed immediately. This credit was used for some time; and, when Brough's affairs went into disorder, it was found, that, on the 9th June 1789, he was due 539l., which Selby paid up, and claimed relief, under the

the heritable security. His claim was objected to, and the question came before the Court. Lord Dreghorn, Ordinary, decided in favour of Selby; and founded his judgement upon the distinction between this case, and that of a direct security to the Bank. 'Having considered the objections, &c., and, in particular, that, 'in the bond of relief, John Brough, the principal debtor, is 'bound to relieve, harmless and skaithless keep, R. Selby, the 'cautioner, from the payment of the contents of the bond of 'credit; and, for that effect, to deliver it up to him cancelled, 'or report a valid discharge thereof, duly registered, against the 'term of Whitsunday then next; repels the objection.' But when the cause came before the whole Judges, they viewed the matter differently. Holding it as a fixed point, that an heritable security was not, in the first instance, applicable to a cash account, they would allow no distinction in favour of this secondary manner of performing the same operation. They considered the cautionary obligation as an accessory, which must follow the principal, and can be in no better situation; and they held the words of the act, (as striking against all deeds, in security and relief of engagements), to be invincible. They accordingly, with the exception of the Lord Ordinary, preferred Selby, in virtue of his infeftment, 'only for the sums that could be instructed to have been 'advanced by Sir William Forbes & Co. to Brough, at the date of 'the infeftment.' 2d March 1791, Brough's Creditors against Selby.

Out of this reserved part of the cause, arose another question, viz. Whether advances made, prior to the date of the cash-account, were to be held as included under it, and, consequently, as a prior debt, in the view of the security. This was a question of fact, rather than of law; and the Judges were all of opinion, that Selby was liable for 402l., which stood against Brough, on his cash-account, at the time the joint bond was executed. The only difference of opinion, turned upon the effect of subsequent payments by Brough, in extinguishing the security, past the power of revival. In the judgement, it was 'found, that Brough did, upon 'the 17th June 1783, owe Sir William Forbes & Co. the sum of '402l. 16s., upon a current account; and that Selby having, in

'consequence

'consequence of the bond of credit thus subscribed by him and 'Brough, become chargeable with the said sum; therefore, the 'sum must be understood to have been covered by the infeftment, 'taken next day upon the bond of relief granted by him to Brough.'

But, a new reservation was necessary, in order to come regularly to a discussion of the other point, viz. the effect of the operations on the account, in extinguishing the real security: and, accordingly, the Court 'remitted to the Lord Ordinary, before further 'procedure, to hear parties upon this point, whether the subse- 'quent operations of the said John Brough, in drawing out, or 'paying in money to Sir William Forbes & Co., ought to have the 'effect of extinguishing or diminishing the preference competent 'to the heirs of the said Robert Selby, under the said infeft- 'ment?'—I believe this case never came to a decision.

But, although it was thus, by a train of very deliberate judgements, established, that no debtor could give a proper security, over his heritable estate, for a future debt, or for a cash-account; it was always possible to have effected this object indirectly, by means of one of the forms already explained, viz. an absolute conveyance, qualified by a back-bond. A proprietor has it always in his power, unless prevented by insolvency, to convey his estate, even for gratuitous considerations; and, where he chooses to convey it, for the purpose of borrowing money, (a back-bond being taken from the disponee), the only right which remains in his person, or of which his creditors can avail themselves, is, that of redemption, under the back-bond, or of calling on the disponee to account. Such a deed may be objectionable, on the statute of 1621, or upon the statute 1696, if the granter be bankrupt, (at least in so far as it is not a conveyance for a novum debitum); but it is not affected by that clause of the statute, which is directed against future debts, and which, we have the first authority for saying, can be considered only as a declaration of the principles of the feudal law. The first case, in which the question was tried, is, that of Riddel against the creditors of Niblie;—where, Jamieson having disponed his lands of Langside to Niblie, he was infeft, and, of the

the same date, granted a back-bond, declaring, that no price had been paid, but that the infeftment was meant to subsist as a security for certain debts of Jamieson, then in the person of Niblie, and for such other debts as Niblie should thereafter transact with Jamieson's creditors, the Court, 'in respect this was not an infeftment in relief or security, but an absolute disposition to the 'property, sustained the same, to the extent of the debts due by 'Jamieson to Niblie, at whatever time contracted.' 16th February 1782, Riddel against creditors of Niblie, VII. Fac. Coll. xxxiii. 54.

The judgement in this case of Niblie, has been frequently confirmed since, and declared, by the first of our Judges, to form a point fixed, and at rest. Before proceeding to detail these cases, however, I would premise, that, wherever the back-bond is recorded in the register of seisines, or produced judicially, the absolute disposition becomes, from that moment, a restricted estate in the person of the disponee. The operation of this principle, will be seen in the two following cases.

Mr Stewart agreed to advance to Sir James Cockburn, the sum of 4400l. Sterling, on a conveyance to the heritable office of Usher, and to the lands of Bingham. The disposition was to be absolute, qualified by a back bond. Accordingly, on the 9th of May 1777, Mr Stewart advanced to Sir James Cockburn, 3000l of the money, for which Sir James granted his bond, in the English form; and, on the day following, an absolute disposition of the above subjects was executed in favour of Mr Stewart. Of the same date with the disposition, Mr Stewart gave his missive, binding himself to execute such a deed as Andrew Stewart Esq should direct, for reconveying the subjects, on payment of the money advanced in virtue of the disposition. Mr Stewart was infeft in the office of heritable usher, on the 3d of June 1777, and in the lands, on the 4th. On the 7th of the same month, the seisine was duly recorded. On the last of these dates, that is, on the 7th, when the seisine was put on record, the remaining 1400l, which completed the sum of 4400l, was advanced, for which 4400l, Sir James Cockburn granted his bond. On the 24th June, Mr Stewart, as had been agreed upon, granted a formal back-bond to Sir James Cockburn. In this deed is narrated, the transaction, the absolute disposition, and the bonds which had been granted by Sir James: It is then acknowledged, that the disposition, though conceived as an absolute and irredeemable conveyance, was granted merely in security of the two sums of 3000l. and 1400l. Sterling; and that the subjects stood vested in Mr Stewart, only as an additional security, to enable him to operate his payment: Mr Stewart is bound, on receiving payment of principal, interest, and expences, to denude, and to reconvey the subjects to Sir James, and, in the mean time, to account for their produce: It is also declared, that Mr Stewart shall have liberty to sell; and he binds himself to account to Sir James for the price. This back-bond was recorded in the register of seisines, on the 30th June 1777. Sir James Cockburn's affairs having gone into disorder, and his estate having been brought to sale, Messrs Drummonds, who had acquired right to Mr Stewart's debt, produced, as the ground of their claim, the above absolute disposition and infeftment in Mr Stewart's favour, with a conveyance of them to the claimants. To this claim, it was objected by the common agent, That, from the conveyance by Mr Stewart to Messrs Drummonds, and also from the back-bond, it appeared, that the disposition by Sir James Cockburn, was granted, as an additional security, for the sum of 3000l., and for the sum of 1400l. Sterling; and, that this last sum, having been advanced after the date of Mr Stewart's infeftment, it fell under the act 1696, c. 5, by which, all infeftments, for posterior debts, are declared to be ineffectual. The Lord Ordinary found, 'That the disposition 'granted by Sir James Cockburn to Mr Stewart, and the infeft-'ment following thereon, though, ex facie, absolute and irredeem-'able, are instructed, by the relative missive and back-bond, to 'have been truly granted for security of money advanced by Mr 'Stewart to Sir James, partly prior, and partly posterior, to the 'date of the infeftment: Found, That, in a question with Sir 'James Cockburn's other creditors, the said disposition, in so far 'as granted in security of a debt contracted after the date of the 'infeftment, is, by the act 1696, ineffectual, and of no force: 'Therefore, Sustained the objection to the interest produced, and

'preference

'preference claimed, for Messrs Drummond, as standing in the 'right of Mr Stewart, in so far as respects the sum of 1400l, be-'ing the money advanced after the date of the infeftment' This judgement having been brought under review by the claimants, the Court altered the Lord Ordinary's judgement, and supported the claim. 2d March 1791, Campbell, &c. creditors of Sir James Cockburn, against Messrs Drummonds.

As, in this case, the creditors had the reserved estate completely in their power, in consequence of the registration of the back-bond, no advance, made afterwards, could have been covered by the security. But this appears more fully, from the case of Keith against Maxwell.—An absolute disposition was granted by Syme to Maxwell, qualified by a back-bond. The debt was 6000l., which had originally been due by Syme to Mr Constable. The back-bond was not recorded; but, in a reduction of the absolute disposition, by a creditor of Syme's, it was produced, and the right of Constable, as in security of the 6000l., fully explained. Syme paid a great part of his debt; continued his business; and having, in 1788, procured a cash-account from Sir William Forbes, Mr Maxwell became his cautioner, and received, in relief, a bond from Syme, in which he declares the disposition and infeftment, in the person of Mr Maxwell, as trustee for Mr Constable, a subsisting security in his person for the 6000l, and for this new engagement. A question arose between Maxwell, and the trustee for Syme's creditors, who objected to this security for the cash-account. The Court reduced it, on the ground, that the right was, in the former action, established to be, not an absolute right of property, but a conveyance to Maxwell, as trustee for Constable, to the extent of securing the 6000l. 8th July 1795, Keith against Maxwell.

Thus, then, the law stood, respecting securities for future advances, and cash-accounts, at the renewal of the bankrupt statute in 1793. It was competent, to secure a cash-account, or a future advance, only by an absolute disposition, qualified by a back-bond, and,

and, even in this form of security, if the back-bond was recorded, (without which, the borrower had only a personal security for the redemption of his land), it brought the case precisely to the same point, as if the security had been attempted in the ordinary way. The expediency of an alteration in this branch of the law, so far, at least, as respected cash-accounts, was evident; and a clause was introduced into the new law, for the purpose of allowing heritable securities to be granted for them. 'Whereas,' (says the 12th section of the statute), 'by an act of the Parliament of Scotland, in the year '1696, c. 5. intituled, "An act for declaring notour bankrupt," it 'is, inter alia, declared, That any dispositions, or other rights, 'that shall be granted for hereafter, for relief or security of debts to 'be contracted for the future, shall be found of no force, as to 'any such debts that shall be found to be contracted after the seisine or infeftment following on the said dispositions or rights: 'And whereas, cash-accounts or credits, granted by banks or bankers, were not, at that time, in use, but have since proved very 'beneficial to commerce; and whereas it would tend, not only 'to the further benefit of commerce, but also of agriculture and 'manufactures, if part of the before recited act were repealed, so 'far as to make it lawful for persons possessed of lands, and other 'heritable property, to grant security thereon by infeftment, for 'the payment of cash-accounts, or credits, to be granted to them: 'Therefore, be it enacted, by the authority aforesaid, That it shall 'and may be lawful, for any person or persons, possessed of lands, 'or other heritable subjects, and desiring to pledge the same in security of cash-accounts or credits, to grant securities upon their 'said lands, or other heritable estate, containing procuratory of 'resignation, and precept of seisine, for infefting any bank, or 'bankers, or other persons, who shall agree to give them such 'cash-accounts or credits, provided the principal and interest, 'which may become due upon the said cash-accounts or credits, 'shall be limited to a certain definite sum, to be specified in the 'security: And it is hereby declared, That it shall and may be 'lawful, to the person, to whom the said cash-account or credit 'is granted, to operate upon the same, by drawing out, and paying in, such sums, from time to time, as the parties shall settle

'between

'between themselves; and that the seisines or infeftments, taken
'upon the said heritable securities, shall be equally valid and ef-
'fectual, as if the whole sums advanced upon the said credit, had
'been paid, prior to the date of the seisine or infeftment taken
'thereon; and that any such heritable security shall remain and
'subsist, to the extent of the sum limited, or any lesser sum, un-
'til the cash-account, or credit, is finally closed, and the balance
'paid up and discharged, and the seisine renounced.'

Provided, then, that the principal sum, and interest which may become due upon the account, shall be limited to a certain definite sum in the security, the two obstacles, that formerly stood in the way of granting a real security for a cash-account, are removed—a prior advance is declared unnecessary, on the one hand; and, on the other, the danger of extinguishing the real security, by replacing the advance, is taken away. Thus, the effect of all the objections, competent by common law, and under the statute of 1696, against fraudulent deeds of preference, either directly, or by means of securities for future debts, are reserved—while provision is made against the possibility of interrupting cash-accounts.

SECTION

SECTION II.

Of Deeds of Preference, granted in Contemplation of Bankruptcy, but which, not being included under the Statute, are reducible at Common Law.

Before the passing of the statute of 1696, creditors were, in challenging deeds of preference, left unassisted by any legal presumption. A direct proof of fraud, or, at least, the establishment of such facts, as might give birth to suspicions, and probabilities, and arbitrary presumptions of collusion, was necessary to their success; and, in the cases which immediately preceded the passing of the statute, we have seen into what disheartening labyrinths of inquiry creditors were in danger of being led. The view of the Legislature was, to strike off, at once, all these perplexities, and to establish a general and overruling law, which might supersede the necessity of recurring to proofs, or to arbitrary presumptions of collusion. But, on the one hand, there is no reason to believe that this statute was intended to deprive creditors of their remedy at common law, where fraud could actually be proved; and it is a natural consequence, on the other hand, of establishing so ample a provision, that challenges, at common law, ought to be restricted to cases, in which either a design of evading the statute shall appear, or where the debtor shall be proved to have had bankruptcy in contemplation, and the creditor receiving the security, to have participated, mala fide, in the unfair preference.

The frauds, at common law, by which undue preferences may be constituted in contemplation of bankruptcy, seem to be reducible to two great classes—one, comprehending all those devices by which the words of the statute may be eluded, in cases includeable within their spirit—another, comprehending all those preferences,

ences, which are reached, neither by the words, nor by the spirit, of the statutes.

§ 1. OF DEVICES FOR ELUDING THE STATUTES.

It is scarcely possible to lay down rules for cases of this kind. The discernment, and sound discretion of our Judges, must be exerted, according to the circumstances of each particular case, to detect, from circumstantial evidence, and fair legal presumptions, what is meant to be concealed, and, with proper regard to the bona fides of the individual, to give full operation to those rules of equality, which it is the great intention of the laws of bankruptcy to establish among creditors.

1. It is clear, that, where the debtor and creditor can be proved to have combined, for the purpose of evading the statute, the preference will be reducible. Thus, a security was reduced, where, under the appearance of the security having been granted for a fair price, it was proved, that the sums for which it was given, were advanced by the creditor himself, through an interposed person, in order to enable the debtor to pay off his debt. 9th March 1781, Blackie against Robertson, VII. Fac. Coll. Part II. li. 90.

2. Where, even without the debtor's co-operation, a creditor contrives to bring matters into such a shape, as to give birth to a preference in his own person, it will be reduced. Thus, Provan & Co. bought goods from Marshall, to the value of 236l.; and, when called upon for the price, or bills at six months, which they had engaged for, they defended themselves, by setting off bills of Marshall's, indorsed to them by Hamilton & Co., to whom, in return, they had granted a bill for the amount of the indorsations. There was some doubt respecting the date of the sale. If posterior to the indorsation, then, as Provan & Co. would have been creditors to Marshall at the date of the sale, and as Marshall was made bankrupt within sixty days, the sale would have been struck at by the statute, as a security to Provan & Co. for a prior debt. and of this, all the Judges were clear. But if, on the other hand, the indor-

sation was posterior to the sale, then, although the case fell not under the statute 1696, it was exposed to challenge, as a device to give security to Hamilton & Co.; Provan & Co. getting right to their debt, for the purpose of compensating, or setting off the debt due by them against it. The Court gave judgement for the price of the goods, refusing to admit the compensation, or set off. One of the Judges dissented; being of opinion, that if the sale preceded the indorsation of the bills by Hamilton & Co. to Provan & Co., it was to be considered as a fair transaction. Provan & Co. stated, that there was no collusion, Marshall & Co. having purchased their bill, by the indorsation of Marshall's, only because they had money to transmit to Manchester, where Provan & Co.'s name was better known. But the rest of the Judges were decidedly against supporting the transaction. 'The act 1696, it was observed, being 'made to repress fraud, and, as every possible device would be fal-'len upon to evade it, the most liberal interpretation should be 'given to it. The presumption of law arising from it, is, that a 'person foresees his bankruptcy sixty days before it occurs; and 'therefore, all securities granted by him, for prior debts within 'that period, are annulled. But, if the transaction in question 'were sustained, a person, even within a few days of insolvency, 'might defeat this salutary regulation, merely by informing a fa-'vourite creditor of his situation, and desiring him to assign his 'debt to some friend, to whom he had sold goods equal to its a-'mount, for the price of which he would be entitled to plead com-'pensation upon the debt thus assigned. Although, therefore, in 'the present case, there was no evidence of the bankrupt's being 'privy to the transaction between the two defenders, yet it was 'too dangerous, in point of precedent, to be supported. Indeed, 'independently of the badness of its general tendency, it is clear, 'from the whole circumstances attending this transaction, that the 'indorsation of the bills arose from an apprehension of Marshall's 'bankruptcy; and, on that account, it was an improper accom-'modation by Provan & Co. to Hamilton & Co., especially as the 'former had previously entered into an agreement with Marshall, 'to grant him their own bills for his goods, from which they were 'not entitled to depart:' 21st January 1794, Marshall's trustees

against

against Provan & Co. IX. Fac. Coll. xcv. 212. The perusal of this case, will show what infinite delicacy of judgement would be requisite in drawing the line of fraud, beyond which, all arrangements or conveyances should be considered as reducible, while all within it should be held unobjectionable and effectual. This will serve as the best apology for pushing the inquiry no further.

§ 2. OF PREFERENCES NOT INCLUDED WITHIN THE STATUTE.

In considering the preferences, which are includeable neither within the words, nor within the spirit of the statute, there may seem to be room for distinguishing between those constituted by a form of transaction, which the act was not intended to affect; and those constituted by such a deed as it would have reached, if within the appointed term. The statute puts an instrument into the hands of creditors, by which, on hearing of a preference by deed, they may level it, in rendering the debtor bankrupt; and we have already seen, how difficult it must ever be to conceal deeds of preference from creditors. But, where the transaction is of a kind which the statute leaves untouched, the creditors cannot, by rendering the debtor bankrupt, guard against the intended preference. There is more occasion, therefore, in this latter case, for every possible aid which can be afforded by legal presumptions and inferences, in eking out the evidence of mala fides, on the part of the creditor receiving the preference; while, in the former case, a court will naturally feel more reluctance in cutting down a preference which has existed unchallenged for two months; and be less apt to favour the general creditors, in weighing the evidence upon which the challenge is supported.

How far such a distinction would be admitted, or what effect might be given to it, in the weighing of evidence, it does not become me to say; for I do not find, in the decided cases, any fixed points, which can be taken as illustrative of it. Indeed, the judgements on fraudulent preferences at common law, have been so few, or, at least, so few of them are preserved to us, that it would be presumptuous in me to hazard any general doctrine on the subject:

 and

and I venture to state the following propositions, rather as points which seem to be settled, than as comprising the doctrine of this part of the law.

1. There can be no doubt, that where a creditor receives payment, or has a security constituted in his favour, in preference to other creditors, the preference so bestowed will not be effectual, though beyond the sixty days, if both the debtor and the creditor shall be proved to have known, that bankruptcy and a general division of the funds, were inevitable.

2. Dispositions omnium bonorum, to an individual creditor, or to a certain number, either expressly excluding other creditors, or tacitly refusing the benefit of the deed to those who are known to the disponees to be creditors, have been taken as securities, so palpably unfair, that they can bestow no preference. In support of this position, many cases might be quoted, prior to the statute of 1696; but I shall content myself with referring to those which have been decided since. Thus, a disposition, by a tenant, of 'the corn crop upon his possession, and all and whole his horse, 'nolt, and sheep, and other goods and gear, of whatever kind, 'pertaining and belonging to him,' was found to be ineffectual to bestow a preference on the disponees: 25th February 1737, Cramond against Bruce & Hervey. And the case of the Dutchess of Buccleugh against Sir James Sinclair, determined in December 1728, may be taken as a kind of negative confirmation of the same point. For there, the objection to a disposition, in security, was repelled, on this ground, that it did not bear to be a disposition omnium bonorum, but was merely a disposition of a particular subject,' which might or might not be the whole property of the debtor. I. Dict. 67.

3. Where the debtor gives a security unasked, it is, at least, a circumstance, strongly indicative of a design to secure the creditor, to whom it is given, against some approaching confusion; and where this is done by one, who afterwards proves bankrupt, it founds a kind of presumption of mala fides, and participation, on the

the part of the receiver. But it would scarcely seem, that this alone would be held sufficient. In the only case, which appears, in our books, of this complexion, there was joined with this circumstance, another, which seems to have had some influence, viz. that the securities were completed in a secret and unusual manner, such as must have excited suspicion in the creditors; and that the creditors were ignorant of the preferences which were bestowed upon them; so that they could not have trusted to them, or acted on the faith of them. The case, to which I allude, is, that of Grant against Grant of Tillifour. These were the circumstances. Grant of Tillifour, being debtor in a great sum to Sir A. Grant, secretly executed three heritable bonds, in favour of his other creditors, and took infeftments on them, without the privity of the creditors, as was clearly proved. Of these securities, Sir A. Grant brought an action of reduction, founding both upon the statutes and upon the common law. Neither of the statutes applied; for there was no diligence, to afford room for the statute 1621; and no bankruptcy, in terms of the act 1696, within sixty days of the deed. 'The Lords found, that the heritable bonds of corroboration were fraudulent, devised, and made, with intent to prefer the creditors therein named, before Sir A. Grant; and therefore reduced the heritable bonds, so far as to subsist only, and be ranked, pari passu, with Sir A. Grant.' 10th November 1748, Sir A. Grant against Grant of Lurg; Kames's Rem. Dec. 167.—On looking into the Session Papers, I find Lord Kames's original note of the judgement, in these terms: 'The Lords were all of opinion, that the acts of Parliament had nothing to do with the matter; but they considered the dispositions, granted to the creditors, executed in a hidden way, to be fraudulent, and therefore reduced the same, to the effect of bringing in Sir A. Grant pari passu.' Sess. Pap. Adv. Lib.

4. Where the debtor contrives to make such an arrangement, as to enable favourite creditors to acquire a preference, and they take advantage of the opportunity, the Court have refused to sustain the preference, although the transaction by which the arrangement was made, could not be objected to, or reduced. Thus, Gillespie, an

insolvent

insolvent debtor, was apprehended upon caption, and liberated; but, thinking it full time to dispose of his property, he sold his farm and stocking for full value. It does not appear, what his intention, in this, really was; but, in effect, the transaction enabled some of his creditors, better informed of his situation than others, and, in particular, some who had one of his sons bound along with them, to acquire a preference over the price, by diligence. The other creditors challenged the preference so acquired. The sale was obviously not objectionable in itself; and so the Court 'did 'not reduce it, as to the purchaser; but, as to the creditors, they 'did reduce it, to the effect of ranking all, pari passu, upon the 'price.' 6th July 1754, Brown against Murray; Kames's Sel. Dec. lxv. 85.

CHAP.

CHAP. IV.

Of the Penal Remedies against the Frauds of Bankrupts.

The difficulty of detecting the frauds by which a bankrupt may prefer particular creditors, or facilitate the embezzlement of his funds, and the consequent imperfection of those laws, the object of which is to redress the evil, when it shall be discovered, have led, in all countries, to remedies, of a penal nature, against the frauds of bankrupts; that the fear of discovery and of punishment may deter from the practice of this secret crime. In this country, the plan of trial and of punishment for fraudulent bankruptcy is, perhaps, as complete as it can well be, consistently with the nature of a public and general law.

There seem to be three faults in the institutions of other countries, with regard to the punishment of fraudulent bankruptcy. 1. Although imprisonment be a part of the common execution, which an individual is entitled to use in order to enforce payment of his debt, it is unjust to continue it in cases of insolvency, where the debtor is innocent, and gives up all to his creditors; it ought to be reserved as a punishment for those who are guilty of fraud. And yet, in England, there is, in this respect, no distinction, except in mercantile bankruptcies, between the villain and the honest man: they are equally subjected to perpetual imprisonment, at the caprice of their creditors. 2. Even where the Legislature has given

given (as in mercantile cases in England) the benefit of a discharge to a fair debtor, the creditors are generally made the sole judges, whether he shall receive that benefit. But, on the one hand, the creditors may be irritated and unjust in their determination; and, from their judgement, there is no appeal: On the other hand, there is much reason to think, that, in the liberal disposition of such a meeting, or in the backwardness which most men feel to be the means of inflicting perpetual imprisonment, frauds of great enormity may sometimes be passed over. 3. Where such frauds have been committed as are proper objects of investigation and punishment in the criminal court, few choose to be the accuser; and, for want of an accuser, the criminal goes unpunished.

In Scotland, if I am not deceived, all these evils are guarded against, by a well-balanced system of provisions. 1. Imprisonment for debt, is with us, as in England, a part of the ordinary execution for enforcing payment; but it is limited, in point of severity, by the law of cessio bonorum, which entitles a debtor to freedom from prison, (though not to a discharge of his debts), on proving his honesty, to the satisfaction of the Court of Session. Here, therefore, is established a tribunal, by which the frauds of every insolvent debtor may be punished with imprisonment, and the innocent man released. 2. In mercantile bankruptcies, the law, with respect to the bankrupt's discharge, is precisely the same with that of England; but we have an advantage over them in this—that, with us, the creditors are, in their deliberations on the bankrupt's conduct, less under restraint than they can be in England: they may, with less compunction, refuse the discharge, without having their generosity abused, by the fear that perpetual confinement shall follow, as the consequence of that decision; since the debtor has still, at common law, his remedy, by cessio bonorum, to save him from perpetual imprisonment, without depriving his creditors of their claims upon him, should his embezzled funds make their appearance. 3. Either an individual creditor, or the Lord Advocate, in the course of his duty, as public prosecutor, may bring the debtor to trial, as a fraudulent bankrupt, under the laws to be

immediately

immediately detailed. This is the very institution which is proposed by a French author, as necessary for supplying the defects of the former law of France. 'Si on ajoutoit,' says he, 'une loi, qui 'confieroit au fisc, le soin de poursuivre la punition de la banque-'route frauduleuse, comme de l'un des delits publics qui cause le 'plus de desordre dans la societé, on parviendroit à mettre le 'commerce à l'abri de l'un des orages qu'il redoubte le plus.—C'est la 'crainte de l'action de la partie publique, en France, & en Hollande, 'qui fait qu'on n'y voit, presque jamais, de banqueroute frauduleuse 'de la part des comptables.*—On peut en conclurre, que si la partie 'publique prenoit, par le seul devoir de sa charge, le même interêt 'dans les banqueroutes frauduleuses etrangeres aux deniers publiques, 'ou previendroit, ou detroiroit, presque entierement, ce fleau, qui 'repand tant d'inquietude sur les operations des negocians, & qui 'resserre les limites de commerce. †'

The Judges of the Court of Session, with that regard for the public interest which has ever distinguished their proceedings, feel often for the situation of individuals averse to a public prosecution; and when, in the course of a cessio or other process, they meet with fraudulent and reprehensible conduct on the part of a bankrupt, they recommend it to his Majesty's Advocate to bring the proper trial.

After these introductory remarks, a very few words will serve to explain the penal statutes, against the frauds of bankrupts. I shall not say more, at present, with respect to the discharge, or cessio bonorum, and the restraint thereby imposed upon fraud. I reserve the consideration of these subjects for that part of the work, in which, I propose to treat of the disposal of the debtor's person.

DESCRIPTION

* The reader need scarcely be informed, that this refers to the laws against insolvent debtors to the fisc or public treasury, who were subject to the trial and punishment, here proposed to be adopted, in common bankruptcies.

† Les Interêts des Nations de l'Europe developées, relativement au Commerce.

DESCRIPTION OF THE CRIME.—It is a delicate matter, to settle the limits of fraudulent bankruptcy; and, even the Court itself has been averse to deliver any opinion or judgement, which might circumscribe, within the bounds of a definition, a crime, so infinitely varied in its shapes. 'What should be thought fraudulent 'bankruptcy, in order to punishment,' says Lord Kilkerran, in reporting the case of Forresters, 'was, in general, observed to be 'a matter of some delicacy:' Kilk. 55.—Mr Hume, in his excellent commentary on the criminal law of Scotland, has described it as 'the wilful cheating of creditors by an insolvent person, or, 'one who conducts himself as such; whether this be done by 'withdrawing his effects for his own use and behoof, or for that 'of others, whom he is disposed unduly to favour.' II. Hume Com. 402.—That part of the statute of 1621, c. 18, which relates to the punishment of frauds, is expressed in general terms of description, unless it be held to refer to all the acts and deeds forbidden in the former part of the statute. * The statute of 1696, c. 5, is also general. But, presumptive fraud, though, under these statutes, sufficient to found a reduction of a deed made in prejudice of the creditors, will not be sufficient to infer punishable guilt against the debtor. Contrivance, and fraudulent design, must be proved, such as to leave no doubt of a criminal intention.

In the case of Mason, (detailed above, p. 106.), the Court declared him infamous, from a conviction that his whole conduct was fraudulent, and that he had been guilty of concerting, and endeavouring to execute, a scheme for defrauding his creditors of his funds. In the case of Forresters, the elder of two brothers having, for some years, carried on a small trade in the pedlar line, between Glasgow and England, gradually introduced a younger brother,

* 'Finally, the Lords declare all such bankrupts and dyevours, and all interposed 'persons, for covering or executing their frauds, and all others who shall give council 'and wilful assistance unto the said bankrupts, in the devising and practising of their 'said frauds and godless deceits, to the prejudice of their true creditors, shall be reputed 'and holden dishonest,' &c

For the rest of the statute, see p 63 & 113.

brother, who found means to purchase, on credit, large parcels of goods from merchants, and went off to England, and broke. Some time afterwards, the two brothers returned to Glasgow, when the younger brother, the bankrupt, proposed a composition of 7s or 8s per pound; and his brother offered to be surety for him. Some suspicions of a concert having arisen, they were apprehended, and examined, and, at last, the fraudulent scheme fully proved. The Court not only found the elder brother liable for the debts, but punished them both, the one as principal, the other as accessory. Lord Kilkerran says, that, although the Court were averse to say, in general, what should be held fraudulent bankruptcy; 'in this 'case, the circumstances were too strong to admit of a doubt, 'though none of those concurred, which the act 1621 mentions; 'as what were not mentioned with a view to limit the evidence to 'these, but as instances at the time most frequent, and which 'gave rise to the law.' 23d July 1748, M'Kenzie against Forresters, Kilk. 54.

TRIAL.—The trial of fraudulent bankruptcy is committed to the Court of Session. 'If any person,' says the statute of 1696, c. 5, 'shall, for hereafter, defraud his creditors, and be found, by 'sentence of the Lords, to be a fraudulent bankrupt, the degree of 'his fraud shall also be determined by the same sentence.'

The prosecution is brought, not before the Lord Ordinary, as a common action, by summons, but before the whole Court, by petition and complaint; 10th August 1765, Syme against Steel, IV. Fac. Coll. xxviii. 50.; and this complaint must either be prosecuted by the Lord Advocate, as public prosecutor; or must, at least, have his concurrence; Ib.: the Crown being interested, that no trial for a crime shall proceed, without due notice being given to the officer appointed to watch over the public interest in this respect; II. Hume, Com. on Crimes, 403.—III. 198.

PUNISHMENT.—By the statute 1621, c. 18, it is declared, that those who are guilty of fraud against their creditors, 'shall be re'puted and holden dishonest, false, and infamous persons, inca-

 'pable

'pable of all honours, dignities, benefices and offices, or to pass 'upon inquests or assizes, or to bear witness, in judgement, or 'outwith, in any times coming.' The statute of 1696, c. 5, after ordering that the Court of Session shall determine the degree of the fraud, proceeds to declare, 'that the person guilty, shall not 'only be held infamous, infamia juris, but also be by them punished 'by banishment or otherwise, death excepted, as they shall see 'cause.'

'The ordinary course,' says Mr Hume, 'has been, by sentence 'of pillory, as in the case of James Wauchope, 4th February 1757, 'and of James and George Keltie, 14th February 1776; but, in 'more aggravated cases, such as, that of George and Robert Fo-'resters, the pannel has been adjudged to be transported beyond 'seas:' II. Hume, Com. 402.

BOOK

BOOK THE THIRD.

OF THE LAWS BY WHICH JUDICIAL PREFERENCES ARE EQUALIZED IN RELATION TO BANKRUPTCY.

INTRODUCTION TO BOOK III.

It is late, in the progress of a nation, before the true principles of the Bankrupt Law are understood or acknowledged, before the right of persisting, with his individual diligence, which, at first, is held to be the indisputable right of each creditor, yields to the notion of a common interest. It gives way, in very different degrees, according to the rapid, or the gradual advancement of the country, and affords, perhaps, one of the surest criterions by which to judge of the progress of commerce.

In a nation, whose progress is gradual and slow, it will naturally happen, that, as the intercourse of men extends, and credit, and debts, and insolvency, become frequent, rules will be introduced for regulating the rights of creditors concurring in execution; and for preventing, by an equalizing rule, those accidental or collusive preferences, which arise to individuals, from greater vigilance or better information. But such partial provisions cannot long be sufficient; more general and comprehensive remedies must be devised, such as may prevent the accumulation of individual diligences, and lead, at once, to a general attachment for the behoof of all the creditors, and to an equal division of the common fund.

Such has been nearly the progress of the Bankrupt Law of Scotland. We can distinguish the two sets of provisions, by which the inequalities of the ancient common law have been corrected: One, consisting of the partial remedies against preferences by priority; unconnected with any general process of division, and having merely the effect of equalizing the concurring diligences of individual creditors;—another, comprehending those general forms of attachment and distribution, by which the attempts of individual creditors to acquire preferences, are rendered ineffectual, and the estate converted into a divisible form, and distributed equally among the whole creditors. I shall follow this division, in treating the subject—considering the former set of provisions, in this Book—the latter, and more perfect, in the next.

There is a wide distinction between the Scotish and the English law, in the preventing of judicial preferences upon the estates of insolvent debtors.

1. In England, such preferences fall under that single and comprehensive rule, by which the right of the assignees, under the commission of bankruptcy, is carried back to the first act of bankruptcy, without regard to any preference, voluntary or judicial, constituted after that time. 'All judgements, statutes, and 'recognizances,' says Mr Cullen, 'whether affecting lands or 'goods; attachments by the custom of London, or any other 'place, obtained, or made after an act of bankruptcy; and all exe'cutions or extents, not served and executed till after that time, 'though proceeding upon judgements, &c. obtained before it, are 'avoided as against the assignees *.' In Scotland, a particular rule is established, for the equalizing of each diligence, independently of any general process of division, and suited to the peculiar nature of the diligence itself. Thus, in the adjudication, all creditors, who concur within a year from the date of the diligence first completed, are put upon an equal footing. In the diligence against moveables during the debtor's life, the equalizing rule bears reference to the date of the bankruptcy; all creditors, concurring in arrestments and poindings, or taking those steps which the law has appointed, being declared equal. And in diligence done against

* Principles of the Bankrupt Law, by Archibald Cullen, Esq. p. 242.

against moveables after death, all who claim within six months, are entitled to an equality.

2. The English rule is confined to the case of mercantile failures; there being, at common law, no remedy against preference by priority, where the debtor is not a trader. The Scotish rules are equally applicable to all conditions; the debtor's circumstances making no alteration upon the right of the creditors.

In considering the laws, by which, independently of any general process of distribution, equality is established among individual creditors concurring in diligence, I shall take into view, 1. The diligence, by which lands, and other heritable property, are affected; and, 2dly, That by which moveables are attached. And although it will be necessary to present the reader with a previous explanation of the various diligences, that the equalizing rules provided for each may be clearly understood, I shall forbear entering here into many of those more minute explanations, relative to their nature and effects, which will be necessary in treating of competitions, in a subsequent part of the work.

CHAP.

CHAP. I.

Of the Diligence by which Lands and other Heritable Property, is affected, and of the Laws by which Concurring Adjudications are equalized.

Of the two diligences against heritable property, which have already been generally explained in the introduction to this work, the adjudication alone is subject to an equalizing law. The inhibition has been left unrestricted, with all the rights which, at common law, it is capable of conferring. In this chapter, therefore, it is to the adjudication alone that we have to attend. I shall first endeavour to present a general view of the progress and nature of the simplest form of the adjudication; and to explain clearly the changes necessary upon this diligence, in order to adapt it to the variations of the debtor's circumstances, or the nature of the debt: and then I shall proceed to consider the laws by which equality is established among adjudgers, as applicable to all the varieties of the diligence.

SECTION I.

General Idea of the Progress and Nature of the Simple Adjudication for Debt, and of the Varieties of the Diligence.

Although diligence against land, as now established in Scotland, is entirely different from that which was practised under the Roman law, it may not be improper to begin this sketch of the subject, with a general view of the Roman execution; that we may observe the changes, to which the peculiarities of the feudal system gave birth.

In Rome, judgements were put to execution, under the immediate superintendance of the judge who pronounced them, or of the judge or magistrate within whose jurisdiction the subject of execution lay. For this purpose, at the distance of four months after sentence (which period was allowed for voluntary obedience), an action was instituted, called Actio Judicati; in which the judge first issued his warrant to seize, as a judicial pledge, the moveables, and, within eight days, to sell them for payment of the debt; and afterwards, if there was a deficiency of moveables, he authorised the immoveable property to be seized, and delivered, in pledge, to the creditor, or put under the care of a factor or curator. At the end of two months, if the debt was not extinguished, he authorised the land, &c. to be sold publicly, and the debt to be paid from the price, the balance being delivered over to the debtor. Dig lib. xlii tit. 1. De re Jud. l. 15. & 31.; Cod. lib. viii. tit 34 De Jure Dom. impet. l 3.—At first, there seems to have been no remedy, where purchasers did not offer for the lands; but afterwards, an alternative was introduced, by which the property might be adjudged over to the creditor, to the value of his debt. Cod. lib. viii. tit. 23. Si in causa Jud. pig. l. 2. & 3.

This regular system of judgement and execution, was, in the feudal kingdoms, much disturbed and interrupted. And, although this is not the place, in which to enter upon that curious and interesting part of the history of modern Europe, which relates to the origin and settlement of regular jurisdiction and obedience to the civil courts; it may not be improper to touch upon one or two of the leading features, in order to explain the changes which arose in the forms of execution.

I do not stop to inquire into the nature of the original jurisdiction of barons, or counts, or sheriffs, nor into the confusion and surcease of justice, which arose from the repledging of defendants by powerful lords, to their own courts. It is unnecessary for me, in the present inquiry, to pass that period which is well illustrated and known, when these confusions began to be dispelled, and regular jurisdiction and obedience to be restored. This was accomplished by express delegations of the Royal jurisdiction; from which there could be no repledging. These delegations, both in England and in Scotland, were made by brieves, issued from the King's Chancery. They were directed to sheriffs, or other officers, to whom the King was pleased to commit the cause *: They constituted a jurisdiction pro re nata: and they contained also a warrant, by which the jurisdiction they created might command respect—a warrant to attach or seize the moveables of the debtor, in order to enforce attendance, and to be the subject of execution. For a long time, execution was, in both countries, confined to moveables; but, at last, it was extended, though in very different degrees, to land.

In England, a writ of execution, called ELEGIT, was, in the reign of Edward I, invented, for the attachment of land, and it is the only form of execution by individual creditors against land, at this day. It gives to the creditor possession of one half of the debtor's land, to be delivered over to him by appraizement; but it in

* In Quoniam Attachiamenta, we find it enacted, as one of the great advantages of the process upon brieve, 'Quod tollit a Barone curiam suam de homine suo qui 'taliter fuit implacitatus,' c 47 § 11.

in no shape authorises, either an absolute and irredeemable sale of the land, or even a redeemable transference of it.

It seems to have been prior to the beginning of the thirteenth century, that the execution against land for debt was first introduced into the practice of Scotland. In the time of Alexander the II., who began to reign in 1214, we find it established by express statute, that, if there be no moveables, 'Vicecomes et Ministri Regis 'præmoneant debitorem, ante levationem curiæ, quod in defectu 'mobilium, vendere tenetur terras et possessiones debitoris, infra 'quindecim dies, ad satisfaciendum creditori. Quod si debitor, 'per se, non fecerit infra quindecim dies, Vicecomes et Ministri 'Regis vendant illas terras et possessiones debitoris, secundum 'consuetudinem regni, quousque fuerit creditori satisfactum de 'summa principali cum damnis expensis et interesse. Et vicecomes 'infeodabit emptorem, per chartam regis si de rege tenentur. Et si 'de Barone tenentur, et ipse easdem emere voluerit de jure videtur 'habere,' &c —Stat. Alex. II. c. 24. *

At this time, it will be observed, that the sale, or, failing a sale, the transference, of the goods or land to the creditor, was absolute and irredeemable. But, in 1469, a statute was passed, which produced a most important alteration upon the execution against land. There was given to the debtor a power of redemption, within seven years. In this statute it is enacted, that 'quhair the debtour hes 'na movable gudes, but hes landes, the Scheriffe, before quhom the 'said summe is recovered by the brieff of distress, sall gar sell the 'land, to the availe of the debt, and pay the creditour, swa that 'the inhabitantes of the said lands be not hurt nor grieved for their 'lordis debtes. Neverthelesse, it sall be leiffull to the person that 'aught the land, first to redeeme and quite out the samin again, 'within seven zeires, payand to the byer the money that it was 'sauld for, and the expences made on the overlorde for charter, 'saising,

* It has been well observed by Mr Ross, (vol. I. p 408), that 'the execution 'against land was thus both earlier and more complete in Scotland than in England.' Edward I, under whom the elegit was introduced, began to reign in 1272, Alexander the II. about sixty years before.

'saising, and infeftment: and the said redemption and lowsing to 'be maid within seven zeires, or not.'—'And gif there cannot 'be foundin a byer to the said lands, the Scheriffe of that schire, 'or ony uther whair he (the debtour) hes land, sall cheese of the 'best & worthiest of the schire, and least suspect to onie of the 'parties, to the number of threttеene persons, and apprize the 'said landes, and assign to his creditour, to the availe of the 'said summe, within sex moneths after the said summe be recovered 'before the Scheriffe. † And als, the overlord sall receive the cre-'ditour, or ony other byer, tenant till him, payand to the overlorde 'a zeires mail, as the land is sett for the time; and failzing thair-'of, that he tak the said land till himself, and undergang the debts.' 1469, c. 37.

Thus, in the middle of the fifteenth century, the execution against land was by law established in the alternative form of a sale or transference. But this sale, as well as the transference, was not pure. it was qualified with a right of redemption. It was not to be expected, therefore, that the sale should be very successful: a purchase of a redeemable right is not eligible, even in these days, when money is more plentiful; and, in the early times of which we speak, it must have been still less so. The consequence was, that the power of selling the lands was, in reality, nothing more than a name; that it was gradually dropt altogether; and that the diligence came to be restricted to a redeemable transference of an appraised portion of land.

For some time, the appretiation was conducted with that degree of attention and care, which its importance deserved. Balfour (Comprizing, c. 3. p. 402.), and Sir George M'Kenzie, (Observ. 5th Parl. Ja. III. c. 37.), have preserved some notes of the rules of appretiation, followed in these inquests. But, fair and equitable as the apprizing was at first, it soon declined into a most oppressive diligence. The remote cause of this declension, is to be looked for, in that complete revolution in the forms of our judicial

† That is, within six months after judgement has been pronounced for the debt.

dicial proceedings, which was occasioned by the institution of the College of Justice. Upon this event, the brieve, under which causes were formerly tried, fell into disuse; and, instead of it, a writ, called a Summons, was introduced; which, being followed by a judgement, or decree, was put to execution, in virtue of letters issued in the name of the King, called Letters Executorial. Those directed against land, had the special name of Letters of APPRIZING. They were issued, only upon judgements of the Court of Session; either pronounced in an action originally depending there, or given forth in confirmation of a Sheriff's judgement, and for the purpose of extending execution beyond his territory. They were, at first, directed specially to the Sheriff, within whose territory the lands to be apprized lay; but, afterwards, to messengers at arms, with power to act as sheriffs, pro re rata, wherever execution should be necessary. After this practice, of addressing the executorial letters to messengers, as sheriffs in that part, was fully introduced, the apprizing (in consequence of causes, which it is unnecessary here to investigate) fell entirely into the hands of the messengers,—men, ignorant and irresponsible.

When the whole ceremony of apprizing, came thus into private managment, instead of continuing under judicial superintendance, every thing went into disorder:—the sale gradually vanished—the intimation to the public, which was, at first, most carefully made, fell into neglect—the appretiation itself was carelessly done—and the lands were assigned over to the creditor, at monstrous undervalue. It was, at last, thought to be more fair and just, to transfer the whole ceremony to Edinburgh, where men of skill and impartiality might more easily be procured, to sit as a jury upon the rights of the parties. But, in this stage of the declension of this diligence from its ancient purity, the expence of bringing up witnesses, to prove the value of the lands, gradually put an end to the appretiation altogether; and the creditor was allowed to enter upon a general redeemable right to the whole lands; of which, during the term of redemption, he drew the rents, without accounting. His right was completed, if the property was feudal, by charter and seisine—if not feudal, by the execution of the apprizing.

In this barbarous state, the execution against land continued for a century. To the debtor, the injustice and hardship were intolerable; for, the possession being allowed to go for the interest of the money, inability to discharge the debt, within the years of redemption, was inevitably followed by the loss of the estate, however great the disproportion of its value above the debt: and many families in Scotland, had to deplore the loss of their estates in this way. But, to posterior creditors, the injustice was equally glaring. If, indeed, it happened, that a posterior creditor was able to pay off the first apprizer's debt, during the term of redemption, he was entitled to step into his place: but, if he was unable to do so, he had nothing better to expect, than the debtor himself had; and was forced tamely to see the property, which should have afforded him the means of payment, irredeemably transferred to a prior creditor, at an undervalue.

It is very true, that, in form, the apprising bore, hitherto, an alternative of a sale, and of a transference: but, to have given the full value of this alternative, it would have been necessary to restore the irredeemable sale, which, both in the Roman law, and with us, in early times, was the chief part of the execution against land for debt. This might have redressed, at once, all these evils. But, to such a measure, the Legislature had a strong repugnance. Commerce had not yet advanced far among us; the necessity was not so pressing as it afterwards became; and the strength of Parliament being with the landholders, against the moneyed men, no remedy was ever proposed, which could shake the established right of redemption. The Legislature turned themselves a thousand ways, rather than consent to the demolition of this right.

When a remedy could no longer be denied to the evils of the general apprizing, the Legislature began to take measures for admitting subsequent apprizers to a communication of the benefit.

The

The first step taken, was in 1621, when Parliament declared, that all intromissions, by apprizers or adjudgers, with the rents of the lands, above the value of the interest of their debts, should be imputed, pro tanto, in discharge of the principal sum, (1621, c 6. & 7) But this remedy was not sufficient. Still, the evils of a preference, by priority of apprizing, were great. They are well painted, in a statute passed in the middle of the last century. 'Oftentimes,' says this statute, 'creditors, in regard they live at 'a distance, or, upon other occasions, are prejudged and preveen-'ed, by the more timeous diligence of other creditors, so that, 'before they can know the condition of the common debtor, his 'estate is comprized, and the posterior comprizers have only right 'to the legal reversion, which may, and doth often prove ineffec-'tual to them, not being able to satisfy and reduce the prior ap-'prizings, their means and money being in the hands of the com-'mon debtor' The remedy adopted for those evils, was this. 1. All apprizings, led before, or after and within year and day of, the first effectual apprizing, were brought in upon an equal footing, or 'pari passu,' as if one apprizing had been led for the whole. 2. The first effectual apprizing was defined to be, that upon which the first feudal right was completed by seisine, or charge against the superior. 3. The expence of the first effectual apprizing, was made a common burden, to be defrayed by all who should claim the benefit of it 1661, c 62.

So far as creditors were concerned, this was, in some measure, a remedy for the evils, against which it was directed. but, something more was necessary, to secure the debtor himself from injustice With this view, an alteration was made upon the form of the diligence. Instead of letters of apprizing, the Legislature, by the statute 1672, c. 19, ordered execution, against land, to proceed by adjudication; which was a new form of action before the Court of Session This action was to be of the nature of an amicable suit, in which, dropping even the form of the alternative sale and apprizing, the debtor should appear as defendant in the action; produce the title-deeds of his estate, concur in a fair trial, for ascertaining the value of the land; and in setting off, to be adjudged to the creditor, subject to a power of redemption, a quantity of land, precisely equivalent to the debt, and a fifth part more, in consideration of taking land for money. After all this was done, the debtor was to renounce the possession of the part thus adjudged to the creditor, and consent to the transference, under a power of redeeming within five years. As this new form was intended for a relief to the debtor, from the hardship of the general right acquired by the old apprizing, and proceeded upon the idea of the debtor's concurrence in this measure, for his own benefit, the Legislature thought it not unjust, to leave those, who did not choose to take the benefit of it, to all the evils of the former law. This was not, indeed, in the original plan of the statute; for Sir George M'Kenzie tells us, that 'this act came into Parliament, simply in 'these terms,' (viz. that adjudication for the principal annualrents, and a fifth part more, should be substituted for apprizing), 'but 'it being strongly urged, by the lawyers, burgesses, and other 'members who were moneyed men, that it was most unreasonable, to force the creditor to take land, unless the debtor should 'produce to him a good progress and security; for, both to be 'forced to take land, and yet to want a sufficient right thereto, 'was altogether unreasonable: Therefore, the Parliament ordained, That, if the debtor did not compear, and produce a sufficient 'progress, and renounce the possession, the creditor might adjudge the whole estate, as formerly he comprized it.' (Observations—2d Parl. Cha. II. Sess. 3 c. 17.)—For this purpose, it was ordered, that adjudications for debt, should contain an alternative of a special and a general adjudication. The special adjudication was the remedy already explained. The general, was in the nature of a penal alternative, in which no trial was to be taken, of the respective values of the land, and of the debt—no allotment of a precise portion to the creditor; but a general and indefinite adjudication, pronounced (as in the degenerated form of the apprizing) for the principal sum, interest and penalty, without including, like the special adjudication, a fifth part more. The penal nature of this execution, induced the Legislature, however, to lengthen the term of redemption, and make it equal to double the time allowed in the special adjudication. It may, perhaps, at first sight, appear strange, that, almost from the first moment that this boon was granted to debtors, down to the present day, it has been neglected, and the penal and general adjudication preferred. But the explanation of this is, 1. That, even in the least involved case that can be supposed, the debtor has an advantage, by the general adjudication; as the term of redemption is of double length, and as the general possession, which it entitles the creditor to take, of the whole lands, is burdened with an obligation, strictly to account for every farthing of the rental—while, in the special adjudication, the value of the land and of the debt being supposed equal, the creditor's possession goes for the interest. 2dly, It must commonly happen, that the debtor's affairs are so much involved before adjudication is begun against him, that it is not easy, perhaps impossible, for him to clear off the incumbrances, and give the adjudger an unexceptionable title.

Thus, the adjudication against land came to assume a shape, nearly similar, in the manner of proceeding, to the actio judicati of the Roman law. Instead of execution by apprizing, a proper action of adjudication was introduced, which, although in form an action, differs entirely from the action for debt. It is, properly, an action of execution; and cannot proceed, unless the debt has been already constituted, and its precise amount ascertained, by a judgement, or, at least, by a legal written voucher. The summons of adjudication, after stating the debt, and the debtor's refusal to pay, cites the statute of 1672, and concludes, FIRST, That as much of the debtor's estate, as may be equivalent to the debt and interest, and a fifth part more, as accumulated into one principal sum at the date of the decree of adjudication, shall be adjudged to the creditor, redeemably, in security and payment of the debt; and that the debtor shall, for that purpose, appear, produce his title-deeds, consent to the adjudication, and renounce the possession: Or, SECONDLY, That a general adjudication of all and sundry the lands, &c. shall be made to the creditor; redeemable, on payment of the sums of money, penalty, and interest, but without any addition of a fifth part more.

Upon this summons, the debtor is cited to appear, and defend himself; and the action proceeds (with particular forms of intimation, &c.) to decree. The alternative form of the summons, is thus, we see, preserved; but the only use that is ever made of the special alternative, is, to procure a delay in the pronouncing of the decree of adjudication. For, though there are not, I believe, more than two or three instances of the special adjudication, since the year 1672, when they were introduced, it still is the privilege of the debtor to deliberate, whether he shall not comply with the alternative.

The decree pronounced by the Court, adjudges the lands, &c. to the creditor, redeemably, and orders the superior to receive him as vassal. It is accompanied by an abbreviate, or abridged statement of the decree, containing the names of the creditor and of the debtor, the full enumeration of the debtor's subjects adjudged, and the words of the decree of adjudication. This is signed by the Judge who pronounces the decree, and must, within sixty days of its date, be recorded in a register appointed for the purpose.

The decree of adjudication supplies, in law, the want of a voluntary conveyance from the debtor, and is, in its effect, precisely equivalent to it. All property, therefore, which is of an heritable nature, and requires, to its transmission, nothing more than a simple conveyance from the holder, is fully vested in the adjudger (redeemably) by the decree of adjudication alone. But property of a feudal nature cannot, according to the maxims of the law of Scotland, be transmitted, by the mere conveyance of the proprietor. It is necessary that there should be a feudal entry of the acquirer, as vassal; and this, in the case of a general adjudication, is to be attained only, by applying to the superior to enter the adjudger as his vassal, instead of the debtor. The law has provided means for forcing an entry, should the superior be unwilling; and the superior's charter of adjudication, followed by seisine, completes the right of the adjudger; a right which, like the English mortgage, is redeemable. The term of redemption in the special adjudication, is five, and, in the general adjudication, ten years. The adjudication

tion is then convertible into an absolute right of property, by an action for declaring the legal term of redemption to be expired, or the mortgage foreclosed, as an English lawyer perhaps would say.

It has already been shortly stated, that an apprizing was declared, by the statute of 1661, to be rendered effectual and complete, in all questions with other apprizings, by a charge against the superior, without the necessity of having the diligence crowned with infeftment; and the same rule was, of course, applied to the general adjudication, when it was substituted in place of the apprizing. A signature presented in Exchequer, when the Crown is superior, or general charge of horning against superiors, at the market-cross of Edinburgh, pier and shore of Leith, when the superior of the fee is a subject, are at this moment sufficient to render the adjudication effectual, in all questions with concurring adjudgers. But this point I shall fully discuss in a subsequent Section.

Having now traced, historically, the diligence of adjudication, and presented a general idea of its nature, in the most simple case; I shall, next, endeavour to give a clear view of the varieties in the form of the adjudication. Adjudications are generally divided into common adjudications—adjudications for debita fundi—and adjudications in implement. And of these, I shall speak in their order.

§ I. OF COMMON ADJUDICATIONS.

There are three cases, in which it may be necessary for a creditor to lead a common adjudication for his debt. 1. Where the debtor is alive, and the estate to be adjudged is his own property right. 2. Where the debtor has succeeded to an heritable estate, but has not hitherto completed his titles to it. And, 3. Where the debtor has died, leaving an estate.

1. ADJUDICATION OF PROPERTY VESTED IN THE DEBTOR.

This is the simplest species of the adjudication; and as it is the form, which, in the preliminary sketch of this diligence, I have had in view, I trust that no further explanation, with regard to it, will be necessary.

2. ADJUDICATION OF PROPERTY, TO WHICH THE DEBTOR HAS SUCCEEDED.

The difficulty of this second case, arises from a peculiarity of the Scotish law of succession. The right of the heir, in Scotland, is not completed by the mere operation of law. Certain forms are necessary, both to enable the heir to convey, voluntarily, the property to which he succeeds, and to entitle his creditors to attach it.

The estate descendible to the heir, consists of subjects vested feudally, or of subjects not feudally vested in the ancestor; and these are carried to the heir, by different forms of investiture *.

1.

* As this is a curious, and an important point, in the law of Scotland, and very necessary to be understood, in order to comprehend the varying forms of our adjudications, I have thought it right to enter a little more fully into it, here, than I could have ventured to do in the text.

The feudal investiture, which formerly was, in all the kingdoms of Europe the sole form of transferring lands, either to purchasers, or to heirs, still continues in Scotland. We do not, indeed, retain the oath of fealty, and the feudal ceremonies, for the military spirit of the institution is gone: but still, seisine, or the delivery of the fee, symbolically, in the name, and by the warrant, of the superior, is an essential solemnity in every transmission of land, whether to an heir, or to a purchaser, and a notarial instrument, reciting the ceremony, and recorded within two months from its date, is a necessary part of the title by which the land is held An heir is thus entered, and feudally invested, either in consequence of the voluntary charter of the superior, proceeding on his own private knowledge; or under a charter, proceeding upon the verdict of a Jury, declaratory of the heir's right, and which the superior is bound to receive, as the legal evidence of that fact The former method of entry, is called a Charter, or Precept of Clare Constat, from the first words of the superior's acknowledgement, the latter, is called an Entry by Special Service. In the entry by service, a brieve is directed for the trial of the special facts necessary for establishing the heir's title to succeed to

the

1. If the property was vested, by seisine, in the ancestor, the heir either obtains an entry, voluntarily, from the feudal superior, by

the particular lands in which his predecessor died vested, and the verdict of the Jury contains a precise answer to each. These are the forms of entry to property of a proper feudal nature, and which have been vested feudally in the person of the ancestor. But some further explanation is necessary with respect to that property which is not transmissible by seisine; or which, in the person of the ancestor, was not feudally vested.

The favour of the Scotish law, has ever leant towards the heir, and, in order to enable him to support the family dignity, or to accomplish himself for his military duties, many things have been assigned to him in the succession, which are not of a feudal nature, which require no entry by the superior, no service to invest them in the heir's person. For many ages, indeed, the heir of line, and the successor to the fee, would naturally be the same; and the investiture in the fee would, of consequence, be held as a sufficient legal declaration of the title by which the heir had right to the inferior parts of the succession. But, when alienation was introduced into the feudal law, the heir would often find, that the fee had been disposed of, or sometimes the heir of provision or destination would be a person different from the legal heir. The established mode of proving the heir's title, by the verdict of a Jury, before allowing him any active right to lands, seems to have led, insensibly, to the practice of establishing, by a service, the right of the heir, even in cases where no feudal entry was to be demanded; and we accordingly find this to have been the practice of the law. The special service for completing the heir's title to the fee, necessarily included the general title of heir; and when, to carry inferior rights, in cases where there was no fee to be transmitted, the establishment of the general title was necessary, the old brieve was taken out, and an answer returned to this point alone, leaving the other counts, or heads of the brieve, unanswered. Thus, two kinds of service were established, and are used in practice at this day; the special service, for the purpose of completing the heir's right to particular lands, including necessarily a general service, and the general service, intended for the establishing of his right to those parts of the heritable succession which did not require seisine.

It is natural to believe, that the institutions of France, and of England, both of them subject to the feudal law, must have been somewhat similar in respect to the entry of heirs, to those which have now been explained. But whatever it may have been in former times, the feudal investiture and seisine, which has been retained in the Scotish law, has been, for a long course of years, dropt by them. Mere occupancy, the apprehending of actual possession, is the only seisine requisite, in either of these laws, for investing an heir in the full and real right to the land of his predecessor. Thus, Judge Blackstone, in speaking of succession, lays it down, that a bare right, or title to be entered, or otherwise seised, is not sufficient to make an ancestor, to whose succession an heir may enter. 'He must be the last person actually seised thereof.'

But

by precept of clare constat; or he purchases a brieve, gets himself served heir in special as to that property, and, upon the retour of the verdict, proceeds to force the superior to grant him a charter, upon which he is infeft. 2. If the property be feudal, but the ancestor have neglected to take seisine, a general service puts the heir precisely in his place; and he proceeds to complete his title,

But this seisine is not a feudal ceremony like ours. It is 'notoriety of possession' merely; 'which notoriety of possession, has succeeded in the place of the ancient feudal 'investiture, whereby, while feuds were precarious, the vassal, on the descent of lands, 'was formally admitted in the Lord's court, as is still the practice in Scotland, and 'there received his seisine, in the nature of a renewal of his ancestor's grant, in the 'presence of the feodal peers; till, at length, when the right of succession became in-'defeasible, an entry on any part of the lands within the county, (which, if disputed, 'was afterwards to be tried by those peers), or other notorious possession, was admitted 'as equivalent to the formal grant of seisine, and made the tenant capable of trans-'mitting the estate by descent:' II. Black 209 In France, the same thing happened Anciently, in France, as in other feudal kingdoms, land was transferred only by actual investiture from the superior; but, in almost all the provinces, this custom was dropt, and even transferences to purchasers came to be completed without seisine 'Le 'plus grand nombre des nouvelles coutumes, en negligeant l'ancien usage, ont admis 'pour principe, que la propriete des immeubles peut etre transferre par la seule conven-'tion, sans qu' il soit besoin d'ensaisinement pour operer l'expropriation La saisine, 'autrefois si necessaire, est devenue absolument voluntaire dans ces coutumes.' IV. Denisart, Collect de Decisions, &c relative à la Jurisprudence Actuelle, 451

The forms which have been already explained, as necessary for establishing the right of the heir in Scotland, to such heritable subjects as were feudally vested in the predecessor, and to the unfeudalized heritage, left one case unprovided for. When the rigour of the feudal law was a little abated, and when the title of a vassal came, instead of one deed reciting a single continuous act of entry, to be divided into the charter and the seisine, it frequently happened, that a vassal, though possessed of a charter, with a warrant to take seisine, delayed the taking of it, and died unvested The same thing also happened in the case of purchasers of lands; the purchaser dying with an unexecuted procuratory of resignation, or precept of seisine, in his person. These warrants were, as mandates, held to fall by the death of the mandatory; and, till towards the end of last century, it was only by expensive proceedings that the heir of such a person could complete his titles, or force his superior to give him an entry But, by statute 1693, c. 35, it was declared, that a general service should entitle an heir to take seisine upon the unexecuted warrants of infeftment left by the ancestor; and these warrants were also declared assignable and adjudgeable by creditors It is scarcely necessary to observe, that this law has no application to the case of a precept of clare constat, which is strictly personal.

title, by executing the procuratory of resignation, or precept of seisine—the warrants under which a feudal investiture is bestowed; or, if the ancestor's title contained neither of these warrants, he proceeds to supply their place, by adjudging in implement. 3. If the property be heritable, but not feudal, the general service is a complete title.

Now, to apply this to the subject of the present inquiry—A creditor, whose debtor has succeeded to heritable property, can have no difficulty in adjudging, if the debtor choose voluntarily to take up the succession: for, 1. When he has served himself as heir in general, all the property, unvested by seisine in the ancestor, is open to adjudication by his creditors;—the unfeudalized subjects being carried by the adjudication alone; the personal titles to the feudal subjects being also carried by the adjudication; and the adjudger being equally well entitled, as the heir himself would have been, to complete his feudal investiture, upon the unexecuted warrants for seisine. 2. When the debtor has served himself heir in special, and, so, completed his feudal title, by seisine, to lands in which his predecessor was vested, the case, as to the adjudger, is the same as if the debtor had been originally proprietor of the estate. Even where the heir has not been infeft, but, having served heir in special, has charged his superior to enter him, the creditor may proceed to adjudge, as if the title were complete 25th November 1629, Dickson; Durie, 469.

But the difficulty was, to find a remedy, where the debtor did not enter to his ancestor's estate. There was a time, when no remedy for such a case seems to have been known—when the refusal, or non-compliance of the heir, with the request of his creditors, that he should take up the succession, and enable them to attach it, was irremediable by the creditors. In 1540, a statute was passed, which afforded a remedy, though not so much intended for the case which is at present under consideration, as for the benefit of the creditors of the ancestor, attaching his estate, for their payment, after his death. By this statute, it was enacted, that the creditor should be entitled to apply for the King's letters, charging the

the heir, after the expiry of a year from the ancestor's death *, to enter to the property within forty days; under the declaration, that, if he failed to do so, apprizing should proceed of the lands; and that this should have 'als great strength, force, and effect, 'as if the said heir were entered thereto, and the said apprized 'lands to be holden of the immediate superior thereof; providing 'always, that it sall be leasom' (lawful) 'to the said heirs, and 'their successors, to redeem the said lands within seven years,' &c. 1540, c. 106.—But doubts came to be entertained, whether this statute authorised the remedy to be used by the creditors of the heir, as well as by those of the ancestor. To remove these doubts, a declaratory statute was enacted, in 1621, ratifying the above— 'With the addition and explanation following, That the same 'shall be extended unto debts owing by any person himself, as 'well as to those which are addebted by his predecessor; for the 'which debt, it shall be as lawful for a creditor to charge any per-'son to enter heir to his predecessor, and with the like certifica-'tion, as if the predecessor had been debtor therein; whereupon 'comprizing may follow, in manner specified in the said act:' 1621, c. 27.

The want of the service, is thus supplied by this statutory certification. The form, by which this effect is produced, is so fully described in the statute, that a less minute explanation seems to be necessary. The creditor, upon production of his grounds of debt, obtains a warrant from the Court of Session, for letters of special charge. These letters are issued from the signet; and, proceeding upon a narrative of the debt, and of the heir's refusal to enter, to the disappointment of the complainer's diligence, they authorise messengers at arms to charge the debtor to enter heir in special to the predecessor, in the lands, or other subjects particularly enumerated, and to complete his right thereto within forty days, to the effect that the complainer may obtain execution, by adjudication, for the sums specified. The certification, if he fail, is, that

* A year is allowed to an heir, to determine, whether he shall enter to his predecessor's estate, and, so, subject himself for his debt. See afterwards, p. 259, Note.

that the complainer shall be allowed to proceed with his diligence, as if the debtor were actually entered. Where the property, to which the debtor has succeeded, was feudally vested in the predecessor, this charge can be complied with only by the heir getting himself served heir in special in the lands. Where it is unfeudalized property, or property standing only upon a personal right, a general service is sufficient. This leads necessarily to a small variation in the form of the charge; and a distinction, in name, accompanies it; the one being called a special charge, the other a general-special charge. The general-special charge, although it points only to a general charge, contains a specification of those subjects which are to be adjudged by the creditor, and which must be thus enumerated, to give effect to the certification.

The heir is not obliged to answer to these charges, nor, consequently, can the statutory certification take effect, before the expiry of the annus deliberandi, unless it can be shown, that he has already assumed the character, by possessing the estate, or granting conveyances of it. *

After the days of the charge are expired, (provided the heir has already assumed the representation of his predecessor, or the year has elapsed), the creditor is entitled to proceed with his adjudication. It differs in nothing, neither in its nature, nor in the proceedings, from the adjudication in the simple case: and the right of the creditor is to be completed just in the same way as if the debtor had served heir in special; that is to say, the creditor executes his general charge against superiors, if there be no voluntary securities

* This long delay, although undoubtedly very inconvenient, is not so dangerous as it may at first sight appear to be; since there is a legal preference given to the creditors of the deceased, using diligence against the estate any time within three years from his death, over the creditors of the heir, (1661, c. 24), and since none other of the heir's creditors can get their diligence forward any faster. There no doubt is one danger, viz. that the heir may voluntarily grant a conveyance to some one of his creditors, to the prejudice of those of his own creditors who mean to adjudge, and whose hands are tied up by the law. But there is, in the diligence of inhibition, an effectual remedy against such a fraud: for an inhibition strikes against all voluntary conveyances, not only of subjects vested in the debtor, but of those which shall afterwards be acquired by him.

securities to be dreaded, and which may make seisine necessary to the creditor's security; or, after charging the superior, he proceeds, in the proper form, to obtain an actual entry by seisine, if that be necessary, in order to enter into competition with other real rights.

But the debtor may wish to renounce the succession entirely; and not even to suffer that implied and legal service which the statute has declared to be the result of a special charge unanswered. And the doubt has been moved, Whether a renounciation be competent in such a case? This indeed is a doubt as old as the time of Lord Durie. Six years after the passing of the statute of 1621, (by which the law of special charge was declared applicable to the heir's own debt, as well as to the ancestor's), it was questioned, in a case between the Laird of Carse and his brother, Whether a renounciation was, in such a case, competent? The debt being established by a registered obligation, the Laird of Carse was charged, under the statute 1621, c. 27. to enter heir in special of his father, to certain lands. The Laird suspended, and gave in a renounciation, which was opposed. The Lords found, that he might lawfully renounce to be heir. 23d March 1627; Durie, 294.

Were such a question to occur at present, there seems to be reason for thinking, that renounciation would not be allowed. We shall have immediate occasion to consider the case of an heir called upon to take up the succession of his ancestor, for no other purpose than to facilitate the payment of that ancestor's creditors. Between that case, and the case now under consideration, there is a very broad distinction. No man can be forced to undertake, for the benefit of others, to whom he owes no duty, a succession which implies burdens; but when a succession has opened to a person who is owing debts, he cannot be allowed to renounce that succession; for that were, in other words, gratuitously to bestow upon the next heir, property to which his creditors are entitled. Another main distinction between the cases is this, that, in the former, as we shall see by and by, the creditors of the ancestor are not deprived of the fund, by the refusal of the heir to enter, although his compliance might have facilitated their operations: for law entitles them

them to proceed directly against the hæreditas jacens, or unvested property, itself, as coming in place of their debtor; whereas, in the case of a debtor succeeding to property, his heirs can have no way of reaching it, but through him. A renunciation, in the former case, is therefore of little consequence; in the latter, it deprives the creditors of the fund, which ought to be open to them. Perhaps some distinction might be made between the case where the succession were free and unincumbered, and that in which the debts of the ancestor should appear to exceed the value: as no man can be forced to borrow money to pay his debts, or, what is worse, to take, for the payment of his own debts, a share of an estate, which is already, in justice, the property of others.

3. Adjudication of the Debtor's Property after his Death.

The natural method of recovering payment of debt, after the debtor is dead, is, by applying to his heir. Should he refuse to pay, the next object of the creditor will naturally be, to attach, in the hands of the heir, whatever property the ancestor may have left; or, if the heir's titles be not completed, to force him to his election, whether to take up the succession, or to leave it at the disposal of the law, for the benefit of the creditors. We have already seen, that the law has provided a method of calling upon the heir to enter; and there could have been no hesitation in making this remedy absolute, without leaving to him a choice, had it not been for one principle, admitted in the law of Scotland, which the English law does not acknowledge, viz. that an heir, who enters to the succession of his ancestor, becomes personally liable for all his debts. *

If

* In the law of Rome, and in that of all the nations of Modern Europe, who have adopted the principles of the Roman jurisprudence, the entry to the succession of a person deceased, is equivalent to the assumption of his person. The heir succeeds to all the rights, active and passive, of the predecessor: he is proprietor of all that belonged to him, and debtor in all his debts. The hardship of this universal representation, this liability to all the predecessor's debts, however much exceeding the amount

of

1. If the heir choose to enter to the estate of his ancestor, and to complete his titles to it, the creditors of the ancestor proceed to have their debts fixed upon him, as representing their debtor. This is done, either voluntarily, by bond, &c. on the part of the heir; or, judicially, by the judgement or decree of a court. The creditors then proceed to adjudge the estate, as if the heir had been

of his estate, led, in the Roman law, to the establishment of some very important rules, for the protection of the heir. 1. It was necessary that he should declare, either expressly, by 'aditio hæreditatis,' or tacitly, by 'gestio pro hærede,' that he accepted of the succession. 2. He was not required to make this declaration, till a year after his predecessor's death, being allowed this term to make his inquiries, and to deliberate upon the propriety of risking the representation. And, 3. If, at the end of that time, he should not be satisfied of his safety, he was entitled to enter heir 'cum beneficio inventarii,' to make up an inventory of the property to which he succeeded; and, beyond the extent of this inventory, he was not liable.

In France, where the Roman law was much regarded, the provisions for this case were, in essence, the same. There was only this difference in form, that the right of the legal heir was held to be vested in him, from the moment of his predecessor's death, so that, a renounciation was necessary, to clear him from the consequences of the succession, and relieve him from the debts of the ancestor. It was only the heir by institution, who was required to declare his acceptance.—'L'heritier, est celui qui succede à 'tous les droits actifs et passifs du defunt, par consequent, à tous ses obligations, 'toutes ses dettes. Il n' est pas tenu des dettes comme d' un charge des biens auxquels 'il succede, mais il en est tenu comme successeur, non pas seulement des biens, mais de 'la personne meme du defunt; c'est à dire, de tous ses droits personels actifs et passifs, 'et par consequent, de toutes ses dettes meme au de-là de la valeur de ses biens.' Pothier, Traite des Successions, 230.—'Suivant le droit Roman' (says he in another place) 'la succession qui etoit deferee à un heriteur, ne lui etoit pas acquise jusqu'à ce 'qu' il l' eut acceptee.—Au contraire, suivant notre droit Francois, une succession est 'acquise à l' heriteur, qui la loi y appelle de l'instant meme que elle lui est deferee, et 'avant qu' il en eut encore la moindre connoissance; c'est à dire, de l'instant de la 'mort naturelle ou civile du defunt, qui a donnee ouverture à sa succession.—C'est [illegible] 'signifie cette regle de notre droit Francois, le mort saisit le vif,' &c. Ibid. 126.

In Scotland, the law is the same with that of Rome, and of France, in giving the heir a year to deliberate, and in subjecting him to an universal representation, unless where the entry is made by inventory: but it agrees with the Roman, rather than with the French law, in requiring a formal entry by the heir. Indeed, it would appear, that, in Scotland, even more than in Rome, a formal entry, as heir, is necessary. The passive representation may, indeed, be incurred tacitly, by 'gestio pro hærede,' but the heir has not a full active title, without a formal entry, as I have taken occasion [illegible] to explain.

been originally their debtor, and the proprietor of the estate: and they have this peculiar privilege over the creditors of the heir himself, that their adjudications, if dated within three years of their debtor's death, give them a preference upon the ancestor's estate.

2. If the heir, either tacitly, or by express act, assume the general succession; if he behave as heir, and, taking the benefit, render himself liable, as representative, for his ancestor's debts, the creditors of the ancestor, founding upon that representation, bring their actions of constitution; and, upon obtaining decrees, transferring the ancestor's debts against him, they proceed, as I have already had occasion to describe, and force the heir to complete his titles, in order to validate the adjudication of the property. They charge him, upon a special, or a general-special charge, according to the nature of the subject; and, as he cannot, in such a case, be allowed to renounce the succession, having already assumed it in general representation, he must either enter, or, the certification of the statute 1540, c. 106, will supply the place of an actual entry, and enable the creditors to proceed, as if the heir were served in special.

3. If the heir have not assumed the representation, then the creditors of the ancestor are to take measures for obliging him to declare his election. This is done, by means of a charge to serve himself heir in general to the debtor, otherwise to be held as heir. This charge cannot, however, be given with effect, till the annus deliberandi be expired; the heir not being obliged sooner to declare what his resolution may be. The general charge gives the heir forty days for obedience; and it has been settled, that the charge may be given, so that these forty days shall run along with the annus deliberandi: 19th June 1628, M'Culloch; Durie, 376.

Whether the heir choose to answer this charge, or not, the creditors of the ancestor may, immediately after the expiry of the forty days, proceed with their action of constitution, for the purpose of transferring the ancestor's debt against the heir. The heir may, in this action, appear, and answer the charge, by renouncing the succession: but, if he do not, judgment is pronounced against him,

him, as lawfully charged to enter heir to his ancestor. If he appear, and defend himself against the debt, upon any plea, as in right of the ancestor; this is an assumption of the passive title, in respect to that particular debt; but it will not give a right to other creditors, to make h universally liable: 10th December 1674, Auchintoul, Dirl. cxcix. 88.; 20th January 1675, Carliac, Dirl. ccxxiii. 104.—Neither of these passive titles, in short, reach further than the special debt in question; but, as to that debt, they subject the heir, in his person, and in his own estate, as well as in his right to the estate of his ancestor. If the decree on the general charge, however, be in absence, the heir will be allowed to suspend it, on producing a renounciation; at least, to suspend it, in so far as it subjects him, or his estate, for his ancestor's debts. No limitation of such right of suspension will be admitted, unless some of the heir's creditors have attached the ancestor's estate; in which case, the heir must clear off the debt, before his renounciation will be admitted: III. Ersk. viii. 93.—The debt being fixed against the heir by this decree, when he has not chosen to renounce the succession, the creditors, of course, proceed to charge him to enter in special; either upon the special, or upon the general-special charge, as the subject is feudal, or simply heritable. The special charge cannot be given, till the decree of constitution be pronounced; because, 'the special charge is a part, 'and preparation for the execution of a sentence, and so cannot 'precede the sentence.' And, on this ground, a comprizing, following on a special charge, raised and executed before the decree of constitution, was found null: 15th February 1627, Earl of Cassillis; Durie, 274.—Yet it is no objection, that the special charge was executed before extracting the decree of constitution, it having been actually pronounced: 1st December 1738, Creditors of Catrine, Kilk. 119. It is by the decree of constitution, that the debt is fixed upon the heir; and therefore, it is proper and regular to recite that decree in the letters of special charge: but the omission of this, founds no objection against an adjudication, provided the decree was actually obtained before raising the letters: 10th December 1751, Sir Thomas Maxwell, II. Falc. ccxlvi. 301.

4. Thus, it is plain, how the creditors of the ancestor are to proceed, where the heir enters, or where he is silent. But, where he chooses to renounce, the proceeding is somewhat different. The estate of the ancestor being then abandoned by him who has the right of succession, the creditors must be entitled to attach it for their debt. Upon production of the renounciation, all personal conclusion against the heir is discharged, and the heir absolved from the action; but, decree is pronounced, simply, to the effect of declaring the amount of the debt which is to be a burden on the succession. This is called, a decree ' cognitionis causa contra hæ-' reditatem jacentem et bona mobilia;' and, after it has been pronounced, a summons of adjudication is raised, calling upon the heir, and all others having interest, to hear and see the lands, &c. adjudged to belong to the creditor, in payment of his debt. The decree of adjudication, thus pronounced, has the same effect with the common adjudication for debt. It entitles the creditor to complete his right by infeftment, and to enter into possession. This adjudication was first declared redeemable by posterior creditors, in 1621. By c. 7. of that year, posterior creditors, either of the ancestor, or of the heir, may redeem. Prior to that act, it was doubted, whether the heir himself could; but it is thereby fixed, that he cannot, unless minor at the date of the renounciation. The method of redeeming, if he wish to do so, is, to grant a trust-bond, on which the trustee, adjudging, may redeem: II. Ersk. xii. 49.

Of the forms of attaching the estate of a deceased debtor, that in which the heir takes up the succession, and that in which he subjects himself to the diligence authorised by 1540, c. 106, were regular and known forms of diligence by appriling, in 1672; and, when the Legislature, in that year, substituted adjudications before the Court of Session, instead of the old form of appriling, the adjudications, in these cases, were, along with the simple adjudication for debt, included in the law. The third kind of diligence, ' contra hæreditatem jacentem,' never appeared in the form of an

apprizing,

apprizing, but, from the first, in the shape of an action, for adjudging the hæreditas jacens to belong to the creditor. When the Legislature, then, substituted adjudications in place of apprizings, and declared the Court of Session the only competent judicatory for these substituted adjudications, it did not mean (at least so it has been decided *) to include adjudications contra hæreditatem jacentem; and they, accordingly, have always been held competent before the Sheriff, as all apprizings formerly were. This is the first peculiarity that deserves notice, in the adjudication contra hæreditatem jacentem. A second is, that, in adjudications contra hæreditatem before the Sheriff, there is no absolute provision for recording or publishing. The abbreviate of the adjudication, which enters upon the record, is a mere substitute for a form which was in observance while execution against land proceeded by apprizing. An allowance, or decree, in confirmation of the apprizing, was written out on the back of the apprizing, by authority of the Court of Session, to serve as a warrant for letters of horning, &c. against the superior; and these allowances, or decrees conform, were entered on the record. When adjudications were introduced, the abbreviate was ordered in place of the allowance, (Regulations 1695, Art. 24.) But there never was any decree conform, or allowance, pronounced upon adjudications contra hæreditatem jacentem. They never had the form of apprizing, but were, from the first, proper actions of adjudication, in order to the execution of which, against the superior, a separate, and accompanying action, was at first raised; and afterwards, a conclusion for a decree against the superior, was thrown into the summons of adjudication contra hæreditatem jacentem itself. When abbreviates, therefore, were introduced instead of allowances, by the Regulations 1695, art. 24, adjudications contra hæreditatem jacentem, were not included. This omission, in so far as regarded such adjudications, when led before the Court of Session, was supplied by the additional regulations 'concerning the Session,' 1696, art. 3.; but the remedy extended not to those which proceeded before the Sheriff. It has, indeed, been the practice, to have abbreviates signed by the Sheriff, and to record

* 4th Januar, 709, Ker against Primrose, Forb. 297.

record them, like the abbreviates of the Court of Session, in the register of adjudications; but the Judges have thought themselves entitled to go no further, than to refuse issuing letters of horning against superiors, when this has been omitted. Thus, in the case of Murdoch King, 14th December 1742, an application was made by King, for horning against superiors. The warrant produced with the application, was, the Sheriff's precept, included in the decree of adjudication. The Court thought it dangerous to give horning, so as to raise up into the first effectual, an adjudication, for the recording of which, there was no provision made by law; and, under the influence of this reason of expediency, they found, that there was sufficient ground for refusing the bill of horning, upon the incompetency of the Sheriff's precept against the superior: Kames's Rem. Dec. xxxiv. 53.—Kilk. 9.

§ 2. OF ADJUDICATION UPON DEBITA FUNDI.

The adjudication for personal debt, becomes a real right, only, in consequence of the seisine which follows upon it. But adjudication may be led for debts which are already made real upon the estate, and which form, independently of any adjudication, preferable claims upon it. The purpose of leading an adjudication, in such a case, is, not to give the debtor further security, or even to obtain payment of the real debt, but to accumulate the debt, with its interest, into a capital bearing interest. In so far as concerns the real debt, and interest due on it, these adjudications are preferable to all others; or, to speak more correctly, leading an adjudication for them, does not deprive them of their natural preference as real debts *. but the adjudger has no preference over other adjudgers, for the interest of the accumulated sum in his adjudication; since it is not a real, but merely a personal debt, being interest upon interest.

Debita fundi, which thus are entitled to a preference over all adjudications, are such as form a real burden upon the lands, whether constituted

* They are expressly excepted from 1661, c 62.

constituted by law, or by agreement. Debts secured upon land, by heritable bond, with the interest upon them,—debts forming burdens, by reservation,—the duties due to the superior,—all are real debts, entitling the holders of them to preference. But, in order to raise the interest due upon arrears, into a real debt, or debitum fundi, so as to be the ground of a preferable adjudication, it is necessary to use the diligence of 'poinding the ground.' This is an action, in which the proprietor of the ground, and tenants, are called, and which concludes for decree and warrant to poind the moveables on the lands, and adjudge the ground right, in payment of the arrears due. This converts the arrears into a principal sum, bearing interest, and really secured. An adjudication following on this, and accumulating the arrears which have been the subject of this diligence, bestows a preference for the interest of the accumulated sum, as being now converted into a real debt: II. Ersk. viii. 37. It does not seem to be necessary to have a decree of constitution against the heir, in order to found an adjudication on a debitum fundi; for letters of poinding of the ground, proceed without any constitution, upon merely calling the apparent heir for his interest; (2d January 1667, Oliphant, I. Stair, 422.): and the poinding of the ground is a direct warrant for the adjudication.

§ 3. OF ADJUDICATION IN IMPLEMENT.

The adjudication in implement is, not a mode of execution for debt, but a form of legal diligence, by which the want of a complete voluntary title is judicially supplied to those who hold an effectual obligation entitling them to demand it. It is not, and in its nature cannot be, subject to any rule of communion with other creditors. It is to be considered, merely, as the completion of the form of a transference already constituted in part, and which the proprietor had bound himself to complete. Like a voluntary transference, then, this adjudication bestows a real and a preferable right, from the date of the seisine which follows on it. Sir George M'Kenzie, Observ. 1. Parl. Cha. II. c. 62.—12th December 1677, Lady Fraser, II. Stair, 577.

The

The adjudication in implement is led against the grantor of the imperfect title himself, if alive, in the same manner as a common adjudication for debt. The summons recites the transaction, and concludes for decree of the Court, adjudging the lands, &c to the pursuer, in implement. If the adjudication is to be led against his heir, the previous forms of a general charge, action of constitution, and either special charge, or adjudication contra hæreditatem jacentem, must be observed, as the heir shall renounce, or be silent. The adjudication contains, of course, no reversion, and admits of no pari passu preference.

This adjudication is to be completed, by obtaining an entry from the superior. It was once doubted, whether the superior was obliged to enter such an adjudger; but these doubts are now at an end. The effect of a charge to the superior, depends entirely upon the force of the statute, in a common adjudication for debt; and it has no influence at all, except against co-adjudgers. It seems, therefore, extremely doubtful, whether any effect would be given to a mere charge upon an adjudication in implement. It has indeed been found, that where no step was taken to complete the first adjudication in implement, a second, with a charge against the superior, was entitled to a preference: 21st June 1704, Sinclair, Dalr. xlix. 62 : but this is not be taken implicitly, as settling that a charge gives security to such an adjudger. It seems indisputable, that, in competitions with voluntary securities, such a charge could be no bar to seisine, nor entitle the adjudger to a preference. Neither could it stand against an adjudication for debt, completed by infeftment, after the date of the charge. Neither does there seem to be any ground for thinking, that the second adjudger in implement, with the first infeftment, would not be preferable.

From the above view of the various kinds of adjudications, it will appear to what extent, and in what shape, the regulations of the statute 1661, introducing equality among adjudgers, applies to them. The adjudication in implement plainly was not of a nature to admit of communication. The adjudication for real debts, or debita fundi, was also (in so far as related to the real debt) of an incommunicable nature. And, in the case of concurring diligence by the creditors of a deceased debtor, and those of his heir, the equalizing rule necessarily received a modification, in consequence of the established preference allowed to the creditors of the deceased, upon diligence within three years of their debtor's death. In the next section, I shall proceed with the commentary upon the statutes.

SECTION II.

COMMENTARY ON THE STATUTES BY WHICH EQUALITY IS INTRODUCED AMONG ADJUDGING CREDITORS.

THE statutes, by which equality is established among adjudgers, are these: 1. By 1661, c. 62, the 'pari passu preference' was first introduced, at a time, when the diligence against land was in the shape of apprizing. 2. By 1672, c. 19 adjudications are introduced, in place of apprizings, and declared to confer the same rights on the adjudging creditor, on the other creditors, and on the debtor. 3. By 33 Geo. III. c. 74, § 10. & 11., certain provisions are made for the improvement of this law, in particular, by lessening the number of adjudications, and the expence of the proceedings, and by defining, more clearly, what shall be held as the first effectual diligence, to regulate the competition. I have printed, in a note, the statute of 1661 *: the provisions supplemental to that statute, will be explained in the course of the discussion.

In

* 'And because oftentimes creditors, in regard they live at distance, or upon o'ther occasions, are prejudged and prevecned, by the more timeous diligence of other 'creditors, so that, before they can know the condition of the common debitor, his 'estate is comprised, and the posterior comprisers have only right to the legal reversion, 'which may, and doth often prove ineffectual to them, not being able to satisfie and 'redeem the prior comprisings, (their means and money being in the hands of the com-'mon

In treating this subject, I shall distinguish two cases: 1. Where the debtor is alive; and, 2. Where he has died, during the course of the adjudications.

§ 1. OF THE PARI PASSU PREFERENCE IN THE ORDINARY CASE.

DESCRIPTION OF THE FIRST EFFECTUAL ADJUDICATION.

As adjudication is the legal diligence for affecting all property which law considers as heritable, whether it be vested by feudal titles or *not*, two cases may be distinguished in this inquiry. 1. What is to be held as 'the first effectual adjudication,' when the right, though heritable by succession, is not of a feudal nature? And, 2. What is an 'effectual adjudication,' where the estate is of a feudal nature?

I. Although the plain intention of the Legislature, in passing the statute of 1661, was to make a general law for preventing any individual creditor from acquiring, merely by the accident of better information, or perhaps by fraudulent collusion, an unfair preference

' mon debtor): Therefore, it is statute and ordained, That all comprisings, deduced ' since the 1st day of January 1652 years, before the first effectual comprising, or after, ' but within year and day of the same, shall come in pari passu together, as if one ' comprising had been deduced and obtained for the whole respective sums contained in the ' foresaids comprisings: And it is declared, that such comprisings as are preferable to ' all others, in respect of the first real right and infeftment following thereupon, or the ' first exact diligence for obtaining the same, are, and shall be holden, the first effectual ' comprising, though there be others, in date, before and anterior to the same: And ' the foresaid benefit given and introduced hereby, in favours of these whose comprisings ' are led within the time, and in manner foresaid, is only granted and competent, in ' the case of comprisings led since the 1st day of January 1652 years, and to be led ' after the date of thir presents, and for personal debt only, without prejudice always, ' of ground annuals, annualrents due upon infeftment, and other real debts, and debi- ' ta fundi, and of comprisings therefore, of lands and others affected therewith, which ' shall be effectual and preferable, according to the laws and practick of this kingdom ' now standing: And it is also provided, that the creditors having right to the first ' comprising, except as is above excepted, shall be satisfied, by the posterior comprisers ' claiming the benefit foresaid, of the whole expence disbursed by them, in deducing ' and expeding the said first comprising, and infeftment thereupon preference over his fellow creditors;' so strangely was the statute expressed, that very serious doubts were entertained, whether it did not apply exclusively to apprizings of complete feudal rights, leaving those estates, which were not feudally vested, to the old and unequal rule of the common law. The act bears—' That such ' comprizings as are preferable to all others, in respect of the first ' REAL RIGHT AND INFEFTMENT following thereupon, or the first ' exact diligence for obtaining THE SAME, are, and shall be holden, ' the first effectual comprizing, though there be others, in date, ' before and anterior to the same.' In a case which occurred towards the beginning of this century, the first adjudgers of an heritable bond, upon which the debtor had not been infeft, objected to the claim of posterior adjudgers within year and day, that they were not entitled to the benefit of the pari passu preference provided by the statute; which is declared applicable only to the apprizings and adjudications of real rights, whereupon infeftment has followed. But the Court found ' the clause general, and that ' it comprehended all apprizers: and therefore, they brought in ' pari passu all who had adjudged within year and day of the ' first:' 26th June 1705, Stewart of Pardovan against Stewart of Torrence, II. Fount. 278.; Dalr. lxiii. 81., Forb. 16. A similar decision was given, where the land adjudged was not feudally vested in the debtor, his right continuing personal, upon a disposition with procuratory and precept unexecuted: December 1725, Sir Thomas Moncrieff against Moncrieff's Creditors. And, again, where the debtor had a disposition to land, without procuratory or precept: 27th June 1734, Falconar's widow against Creditors. In the case, also, of personal bonds, heritable by succession, the pari passu preference has been admitted; 19th November 1734, Jackson against Drummond: although once it was refused, February 1729, Sir J. Sinclair against Gibson. It, therefore, is well established now, that the rule, of equal ranking among adjudgers, applies to all cases of adjudication for debt: II. Ersk. xii. 30.

It need scarcely be laid down, that, in the adjudication of unfeudalized subjects, as there can be no seisine, the right of the creditor

is

is perfect, from the date of the decree, provided it be duly recorded within the sixty days. Ersk. loc. cit.

II. Where the estate to be adjudged, is of a feudal nature, that completion of the diligence which, according to the statute of 1661, is sufficient to make an adjudication be held as the first effectual for regulating the pari passu preference, would have no effect in competition with voluntary securities or conveyances. In the latter case, nothing short of an actual investiture, by seisine, is to be depended on; but, in the former, the statute has declared it to be sufficient, if the creditor has done diligence for forcing the superior to enter him. This it may be proper shortly to explain. It has already been stated, that a decree of adjudication is equivalent to a conveyance from the debtor, with procuratory of resignation in favorem creditoris; and that the adjudger is entitled, under his decree of adjudication, to apply to the superior for a charter, upon which seisine may follow. Long before superiors were bound to receive voluntary purchasers, creditors were entitled to demand an entry. Even so early as the time of Alexander II, the superior had his choice, of taking the land himself, or entering the creditor as vassal: (Stat. Alex. c. 24. § 5. & 7.) By statute 1469, c. 37. it was expressly enacted—'that the overlord sall receive the creditor, 'or ony other buyer, tenant till him, payand to the overlord a 'zeires mail, as the land is sett for the time; and, failzing thereof, 'that he tak the land till himselfe, and undergang the debt.' This legal obligation upon the superior to enter the apprizer, was, in ancient times, inforced by diligence, proceeding against the superior, upon the decree conform, or allowance of the apprizing the predecessor of the abbreviate. At that period, the common diligence for enforcing performance of obligations ad factum præstandum, was by letters of four forms. They consisted of four different charges, given by officers of the law, under the authority of four warrants successively issued; and increasing, in severity of requisition, to the last. In the common case, of an obligation ad factum præstandum, the last of these charges denounced against the debtor, in case of disobedience, all the penalties which the law had appointed for the punishment of rebellion. In the diligence upon the apprizing, the penalty was not so terrible: it was only this, that if the superior should not, in compliance with the requisition, enter the adjudger, the creditor should be allowed to go to the next superior, and receive an entry from him; and so successively up to the Crown, who never refuses a vassal. To prevent superiors from unjustly granting an entry to one adjudger, and refusing it to another, that statute, which established the communion among adjudgers, declared, that diligence against the superiors should be sufficient to complete the adjudication, in so far as respected that competition. The statute describes the first effectual adjudication to be—'that upon which infeftment 'shall first have followed, or the first exact diligence for obtaining 'the same.' But many questions arose upon the interpretation of this statute. It was often doubtful, what should be held as exact diligence for obtaining an infeftment. In the simple case, indeed, it was not questioned, that a charge to the superior was sufficient, or the presenting of a signature in Exchequer, where the Crown was superior. But there was an infinite variety of cases in which the simplicity of this rule was disturbed: and although the Legislature, in 1793 *, swept away all these perplexities, perhaps the spirit and effect of that statute cannot otherwise be so well understood, as by a review of the questions which arose under the former law. Besides, questions of this kind may still occur, where the first adjudger feels it necessary, on account of the possibility of his being opposed by voluntary securities, to complete his diligence by infeftment.

1. As the law, in admitting the charge to the superior to be a due completion of the diligence in all questions with co-adjudgers, proceeded merely on the ground, that the creditor could do no better, and that such a regulation was necessary, to prevent the rights of creditors from being exposed to the caprice or injustice of the superior: it followed, that wherever the creditor could complete his adjudication without applying to the superior, the reason of the law did not apply, and the charge should not be held

as

* Statute 33. Geo. III. c. 74. § 11.

as an effectual completion. Thus, where the debtor's right to the estate adjudged, continued upon a naked disposition, personal, and uncompleted by infeftment, the creditor had another way of completing his right, than by going to the superior. 1. If the disposition contained an unexecuted warrant for infeftment, the adjudger, as in the debtor's right, could proceed at once to complete his title, by taking seisine on the precept; and, in order to do so, he was entitled to have the aid of a court, to procure exhibition of that warrant: and accordingly, adjudications thus completed, were, in competition with those completed by a charge, held to be the first effectual: 6th December 1695, Dewar against French, I. Fount. 684.; 22d June 1791, Peirce against Limond, VIII. Fac. Coll. App. No. 2. 2. If the debtor's right contained no warrant for seisine, as the creditor might adjudge in implement, so, in this case also, the charge to the superior was held not to be the legal method of completing the adjudication: 27th June 1734, Falconar's Widow, I. Dict. 19.

2. Many difficulties arose, where the titles of the superior were incomplete. As a superior unentered has, in the eye of law, no feudal character, a charge against him, to enter a vassal, was nugatory; and our best lawyers required, to the completion of the adjudication, a charge also against the superior, to get himself entered in the superiority, that he might be in a capacity to receive the vassal. * This question, of the necessity of charging the superior

* In order to force an entry from the superior where his titles were not completed, a law had been enacted, in 1474, against the fraudulent lying out of superiors unentered, to the prejudice of their vassals. By the statute it is declared, that if the superior do not enter to the superiority, within forty days after requisition to do so, he shall lose the superiority during his life. Hope, in his Minor Practics, explains the procedure, under this statute, to have been by a special charge, issued from the Court of Session, ordering the superior to enter within forty days, upon which (if the superior did not obey) a summons was raised against the superior, and against his superiors, for having his tinsel (loss) of the superiority declared, and his superior ordered to infeft the vassal: a similar process being necessary upwards to the Crown, (tit. IV. § 26, 27.) As to apprizers, the process was precisely similar. Hope says, 'If the superior be not 'infeft himself in the superiority, in-that case, the superior must be charged to enter to

 'the

superior to enter, came to be discussed in the ranking of Keı e[illegible]. In the competition, respecting the Lands of Little-Mill, between Mr Pierce and Mrs Ross, both parties mistook the state of the titles, and made up their adjudications erroneously. These lands had been held feu of Lord Cathcart by Mrs Crawford. She had conveyed them to William Ross, and he infeft himself base upon his disposition. After his death, his brother Hugh Ross paid his debts, and took steps for vesting his right in himself, as creditor, but he never was infeft. Thus, it will be observed, that there was a superior remaining interjected between Lord Cathcart and William and Hugh Ross, viz. Mrs Crawford; for William Ross's disposition was base. But Hugh Ross, overlooking this circumstance, obtained a disposition from Lord Cathcart, and, upon the procuratory, resigned in the hands of the Crown, and, upon the Crown charter, infeft himself and his son. Now, two of his creditors followed different plans in adjudging. Mrs Ross having adjudged, applied for a Crown charter of adjudication; and was thereupon infeft. Mr Pierce thought he had taken effectual means for attaching the property, by charging Mr Ross, as superior under his Crown holding, to enter him as adjudger. But the Court found, that neither of these creditors had effectually adjudged the property; since the charge ought to have been given to the heirs of Mrs Crawford, the interjected superior. On the Bench, it was said by one of the Judges, that a charge given to the proper superior to enter the adjudger, would be held (although his titles were not complete) to make an effectual adjudication; but a different opinion prevailed, viz. That where the superior is unentered, it is necessary, first, to charge him to enter, and then to charge him to receive the adjudger. The creditor is bound, before going to the Crown, who refuses none, to take every proper measure for forcing the superior to complete his titles. This opinion not only rests upon the solid ground, that a charge against the superior to enter the creditor is inept, since the person charged is not the feudal superior; but it

is

' the superiorit[illegible] within forty days, conform to the order before expressed, in the form
' introduced in favour of vassals, by act of Parliament of King James III. [illegible] tit. [illegible] § [illegible]'
And St Martins details the practice, in his System of Stiles. Part I. p. 91.

is supported, as we have seen, by the authority of one of our oldest and best lawyers, and sanctioned by the practice which the other lawyers of his time approved of and directed.

3. Another class of difficulties arose respecting the completion of adjudication, where the creditor adjudging, was himself the superior. Lord Stair thought, that, in such a case, no seisine was necessary, (III Stair, Inst. ii. 23), but Mr Erskine shortly and ably refuted this doctrine, and showed it to have proceeded upon a mistaken notion, with regard to the nature of the feudal consolidation, (II. Ersk. xii. 29)

4. Difficulties multiplied, in a most distressing degree, where base rights had been constituted, and the titles and connexions of parties were not clear. Thus, in the case of McKenzie of Redcastle, a question occurred, respecting the proper method of making an adjudication of a base right effectual, where the disponee was dead. Redcastle being infeft, as a Crown vassal, disponed to his son with procuratory and precept, and died. The son was infeft base, and never made his right public by confirmation or resignation. His creditors did diligence, by adjudication, against the superiority as in hereditate jacente, and against the property; and a competition arose among them, for the quality of first effectual. The superiority clearly was in hæreditate jacente of Redcastle; the property in his son. There were three ways in which it was conceived that the adjudications ought to be made effectual: 1. By the adjudgers obtaining, in Exchequer, a charter of adjudication of the superiority, and then, as superiors, giving infeftment to themselves in the property: 2. By throwing into the signature of adjudication, a clause of confirmation of the base right, so as to enable the creditors to take seisine on the adjudication, as if the right were consolidated. 3. By charging the heirs of Redcastle to enter, and infeft the adjudger in the property. The last of these methods would, no doubt, have been effectual, upon the principles stated above in Kerse's case, but it was excluded here, by the second method, which had been taken before, and which all agreed was good. As to the first, it was universally thought,

thought, that it gave no right to the property; and the only question was, Whether, as it preceded the second, it did not serve as a mid impediment to the confirmation? But the Court found it did not; and that although it made the first effectual adjudication, quoad the superiority, it precluded not the confirmation, as making the first effectual against the property. 1st June 1791, M'Kenzie against Ross & Ogilvie, VIII. Fac. Coll. clxxxiii. 371.

I have enumerated these difficulties, and endeavoured shortly to explain the nature of the cases which arose for decision, that the necessity of that rule which was introduced by the statute of 1793, may be the better understood. Even in the most simple case which I have taken notice of, where the vassal had not taken seisine on the disposition, the adjudger could not complete his adjudication, without possession of the disposition; and this he might find great difficulty in recovering. In the more complicated, it was necessary for the creditor adjudger, in order to proceed with safety, to have the most masterly assistance to direct him what step to follow, in the peculiar situation of the feudal titles of his vassal, or of the superior; and even the materials for such deliberation, he could not be expected to have at command. Of this distressing uncertainty, the case of Murdoch against Cheslie may be taken as an illustration; where the debtor appeared to be fully vested in the feudal right, and several creditors proceeded, in completing their adjudications, upon that idea; but, a strict investigation having shown, that there was an essential flaw in his title, other creditors took steps for forcing him to complete a proper title, and were preferred. 29th January 1766, IV. Fac. Coll. xxiii. 56.

The same strictness is still required, where the adjudication is to come into competition with other real rights—with heritable securities or dispositions: but, in competitions between adjudgers, expediency demanded, that another rule should be taken, a method of completing the diligence more within the reach of a creditor, and less exposed to the collusion and fraud of the debtor, or of his superiors. It was therefore enacted, by the 33 Geo. III. c. 74.

§ 11.

§ 11. 'in order to fix more clearly, in time coming, what diligence 'is necessary to make an adjudication effectual, that the presenting 'of a signature in Exchequer, when the holding is of the Crown; 'or the executing of a general charge against superiors, at the 'Market Cross of Edinburgh, and pier and shore of Leith, when 'the holding is of a subject; and recording an abstract of the said 'signature, or the said charge, in the register of abbreviates of 'adjudications; shall be held, in all time coming, as the proper 'diligence for the purpose aforesaid.' In the interpretation of this law, a difficulty may be stated, Whether it can be held to apply to the case of a superior adjudging the property of his vassal? On the one hand, there does seem to be a sort of absurdity, in a person charging himself, by horning, to do an act which is within his own power; but, on the other, the view of the law evidently was, to form a general rule for all cases; and, without regarding the peculiarities of situation, or the person or state of the superior, to make a general charge, recorded, supply all deficiencies. There is a possibility, at least, that a superior may be mistaken as to the titles of his debtor, and that, in giving an entry to himself, he may be as far from the true line, as if he had no connexion with the property: there may be interjected superiors, of whom he knows nothing, and therefore the general remedy should be open to him, as to others.

The first effectual adjudication, once constituted, is the criterion of the pari passu preference, or equalizing rule of the statutes. It becomes, from that moment, not merely a diligence, belonging exclusively to the individual who uses it; but a general diligence, in which every creditor, who afterwards adjudges, has an interest. In this view, it is not entirely at the disposal of the individual; its quality, of effectual, remains, to sanction and complete the other adjudications, although the debt upon which it proceeds may have been paid off, and the adjudication, of course, extinguished as an individual diligence. Thus, a first effectual adjudication having been extinguished, by payment of the debt, an adjudger,

adjudger, within year and day of it, contended for a preference over those who were beyond the year and day. The other adjudgers, on the contrary, maintained, that, by the extinction of the first adjudication, the second became the first effectual, so as to entitle the creditors, who adjudged within year and day of it, to come in pari passu. But the Court found, 'that the posterior 'apprizers could not come in with him who was within the year 'of the first apprizing.' 13th December 1672, Street against the Earl of Northesk, II. Stair, 133. See also 28th January 1676, II. Stair, 407., and 7th November 1679, Straiton against Bell, II. Stair, 704.

Another question, of great importance, is, What the effect shall be, of any nullity or objection, which may be stated against the first effectual adjudication, in altering the rule of competition among the adjudgers? With a view to this question, the objections that may be stated against an adjudication, may be divided into these two classes: FIRST, Such as affect the adjudication itself; and, SECONDLY, Such as affect only the steps used for completing it.

1. An adjudication, it will be remembered, is a diligence, which, after the expiry of the term of redemption, admits of being converted into an absolute right of property; while, during that term, it operates as a real security. The law distinguishes, in judging of the effect of objections to adjudications, between these two qualities. Objections of a very slight kind are sustained to take away the effect of the adjudication, as leading to the constitution of an absolute conveyance; while none, but those of a more serious nature, are held to injure it as a security. This distinction is followed in judging of the effect of any objection to the first effectual, considered as the criterion of preference among the adjudgers. When the objection is of such a kind, as only to restrict the adjudication to a security, it is not held sufficient to destroy the quality of first effectual; as the Court decided in the case of Sinclair against the Earl of Caithness, 8th December 1781, VIII. Fac. Coll. xi. 20. But if the objection had been of a kind that would

would have annulled the adjudication, the quality, of first effectual, would have fallen along with it *.

2. As to the effect of objections to the steps taken for completing the adjudication, there is one case, which, in part at least, clears the question. In the ranking of Kerse, a competition arose between Mrs Pierce and Mrs Ross, who had both obtained charters of adjudication from the Crown. Mrs Ross's signature was first presented; but the seisine, which followed upon her charter, was reduced, on account of the misnomer of an instrumentary witness. The Court found, that the presenting of the signature, by Mrs Ross, made her the first effectual adjudger, the reduction of the seisine affording no good objection to her right. 1st February 1793, Pierce against Ross.

The same decision would, no doubt, be given in the case of a charter and seisine from a superior, if preceded by a charge; but it may be doubted, whether, if no charge happened to be given, and the seisine, following upon a voluntary charter, should be annulled, the quality of first effectual would fall? I apprehend that it would: since, in that case, there would be neither a full completion of the right of the adjudger at common law, nor a compliance with the requisites of the statute, introducing the equivalent of a charge. And, in favour of this opinion, every reason might be pleaded, which can flow from the equalizing spirit of the law, since the only effect of denying the quality of first effectual, would be, to avoid preferences, and to extend the pari passu ranking to creditors, who, by the lateness of their diligence, might otherwise have been entirely cut off.

The Period of Communion

Having examined the character and requisites of the first effectual adjudication, we next proceed to inquire into the nature and precise

* In a subsequent part of this work, I propose to consider the effect of the various objections in annulling or restricting adjudications, and to that part I refer, for any further enquiries on the subject.

precise extent of the equalizing rule established by the statute. That rule is, That all adjudications, which are prior to the first effectual, and all those which, being posterior to it, are stated within year and day of the pronouncing of the decree, are to be brought in equally, or pari passu. The expression of the act, to this effect, seems to be clear; and yet it has given rise to doubts. The statute bears, 'That all apprizings, &c. BEFORE the first effectual 'apprizing, or AFTER, but within year and day of the same, shall 'be brought in pari passu.' Lord Kames, in his Dictionary, states a case (which, however, I have not been able to find in the Reports), where an attempt was unsuccessfully made to limit the pari passu ranking, even as to prior adjudgers, to the term of a year and day. '21st December 1680, Forbes,' I. Dict. 17.

1. The year and day, within which it is necessary for every adjudger to obtain his decree of adjudication, in order to entitle him to an equal share, begins to run, not from the moment of completing the seisine, or the diligence, by which the first effectual adjudication is completed, but from the date of the decree of adjudication. The first case, in which this point was fixed, and which is always referred to, as the leading case, is, that of Balfour against Douglas: in which an apprizer, having remained uninfeft till after the expiry of the term of redemption, and having then taken infeftment, another creditor apprized, and claimed a pari passu preference with him, as being within year and day of the infeftment by which the first apprizing was rendered effectual. The question was very fully discussed, and the Court 'preferred 'the first apprizer, and excluded the second; and found, that the 'year is to be reckoned from the date of the first effectual ap-'prizing *, and not from that of the diligence whereby it becomes 'effectual.' 4th July 1671, I. Stair, 747.—A similar decision is thus stated by Lord Fountainhall: 'The Lords found, the coming 'in of posterior apprizings pari passu with the first, must be cal-'culated year and day from the date of the first apprizing, and 'not

* The expression should have been, 'from the date of the first apprizing that is 'rendered effectual.'

'not from the date of the infeftment.' 27. July 1678, I. Fount. 12. 'This was decided,' he adds, 'in the same way, 4th July 1671 *.'

2. In computing the term, the year and day is to be reckoned, not by the number of days which go to make up a year, but by the return of the day of the next year that bears the same denomination. This rule was settled so long ago as 26th January 1681; when, a competition having arisen among certain adjudgers of the estate of Bangour, an attempt was made to exclude the Lady Bangour, whose adjudication was dated 31st July 1680, while the first effectual was dated 30th July 1679. The Court decided, 'That 'the year was not to be counted by the number of days, but by 'the return of the day of the same denomination of the next year; 'and therefore admitted the Lady Bangour's adjudication to a pari 'passu preference.' II. Stair, 842.—Sir G. M'Kenzie says, That, in this question, as in all others where a day is adjected to a larger term, 'Dies inceptus pro completo habetur.' (Observ. 1 Parl. Charles II. c. 62.) If the meaning of this be, that the expiry of the year excludes an adjudication from the pari passu ranking, and that, if dated on the day after the expiry of the year, the adjudication must be postponed; it may be observed, that the only decision upon the point contradicts this—for, in Lady Bangour's case, the first effectual was dated 30th July 1679, and hers on the 31st July 1680. I should rather be inclined, were I to attempt any explanation of this rule, to say, that when a term is appointed, within which a thing must be done, the maxim, 'Dies inceptus 'pro completo habetur,' is properly applicable to the commencing day of the term;—where, on the contrary, a term is appointed, beyond which things must have continued in a particular state, the maxim properly applies to the concluding day of the term. In the former case, it makes the term begin to run on the day following that upon which the act takes place; whereas, in the latter, the term begins instantly to run; and the commencement of the day after the completion of the term, indicates the expiry of it. This distinction seems to be necessary, in order to give, in either case, the fair benefit of the assigned term.

* This is the case from Stair, quoted above.

OF THE PUBLICATION OF THE FIRST EFFECTUAL ADJUDICATION.

The equalizing rule would be of comparatively little advantage to creditors, if careful provisions had not been made, for bringing the first effectual adjudication to their knowledge. But the record of adjudications, on the one hand, and the regulations, for publishing the proceedings in the Court of Session, on the other, seem to provide sufficiently for this.

1. I have formerly hinted at the rule, by which the recording of the abbreviates of adjudications is required. But if the publication of the diligence stood upon this rule alone, it would be imperfect: there seem to be cases, where the recording of the abbreviate is not absolutely necessary. The statute 1661, c. 31. which first established, by Legislative authority, the necessity of recording the allowance of the apprizing, did not require it under the sanction of nullity. * On the contrary, it was held, 1. That a comprizing, though not recorded, was still entitled to the benefit of the pari passu preference under the subsequent law, c. 62. of that year: 17th July 1668, Stuart against Murray, M'Kenz. Observ. 2. Parl. Cha. II. c. 31. And, 2. That infeftment fully supplied the want of the recording of the comprizing: M'Kenz. loc. cit. III. Stair, Inst. ii. 25., II. Ersk. xii. 26. The statute 1672, c. 19. introducing adjudication, ordered the allowance to be registered, in the same manner, ' and under the same certification with the ' allowance of apprizings.' And the 24. art. of the Regulations 1695, appointing abbreviates instead of allowances, requires their registration, ' conform to the act of Parliament anent the recording ' of apprizings.' It will thus appear, that where infeftment can be obtained without a charge to the superior, the adjudication may be the first effectual, without having been recorded; and it will be

* All apprizings were ordered to be registered within sixty days after the date thereof, with certification, ' that, if they be not allowed and recorded within the said space, ' any other apprizing, though posterior in date, yet, if it be allowed and recorded be- ' fore the prior comprizing, the same shall have preference according to the date of the ' allowance and record; but' (without) ' prejudice to any further diligence, by in- ' feftments or charges against the superior, according to the priority or posteriority ' thereof, prout de jure.'

be remembered, that the year begins to run, not from the completing of the real right, but from the date of the decree. And, if an adjudger be entitled to the benefit of the pari passu preference, although his diligence has not entered the record, there can be little danger in a cunning creditor trying the experiment. The adjudication contra hæreditatem jacentem before the Sheriff, has regularly no abbreviate, and, consequently, is not null, though unregistered. 14th December 1742, King; Kilk. 9.

2. But the provisions, for publishing the proceedings in the Court of Session, act as a strong security against the chance of the year and day expiring, without being known to the other creditors. There is a fictio juris, that all proceedings in courts are public; but the notoriety of adjudications rests not upon this fiction, so often fallacious and unjust. FIRST, The rolls of Court are printed, for the use of all the practitioners, forming a record of every action which comes into Court. SECONDLY, A minute-book is kept by the clerks of Court, in which all the important proceedings, in every cause, are daily entered: This book is also printed and distributed weekly, for the use of the practitioners, and forms another record, easily consulted, in which an adjudication must appear. THIRDLY, It is provided, 'That the 'Lord Ordinary, officiating in the Court of Session, before whom 'the first process of adjudication against any estate, for payment 'or security of debt, is called, shall ordain intimation thereof to 'be made in the minute-book, and on the wall, in order that any 'other creditor of the common debtor, &c. may be conjoined in 'the decree of adjudication.' This is sanctioned with a declaration of nullity, if the intimation shall be omitted, 33 Geo III. c. 74, § 10.

PROVISIONS FOR ABRIDGING THE PROCEEDINGS IN POSTERIOR ADJUDICATIONS, AND RENDERING MORE EFFECTUAL THE PARI PASSU PREFERENCE.

It is a favourite object of the bankrupt law, to establish equality among creditors; and, to promote this desirable end, in the use of the diligence of adjudication, creditors have not only received the aid of the equitable powers of the Court of Session, but the Legislature has interposed, to establish such regulations as could not be reached by those equitable powers. The old law of pari passu preference among adjudgers, has been assisted in three different ways: 1. By interpositions of the Court of Session, as a court of equity; 2 By statutory provisions, for diminishing the number and expence of adjudications, considered as unconnected with any process of general attachment and division; and, 3dly, By bestowing upon the general processes of distribution, which form the subject of the next Book, the effect of a common adjudication for all the creditors.

I. In considering the equitable interpositions of the Court of Session, it is proper to remember, that, while the establishment of equality is an object of much favour, the term allowed for creditors to come in, is very long; and that the most ample provisions are made, for intimating the first adjudication to the public. Although, therefore, every proper aid will be given to posterior adjudgers, in order to bring them within the term, the Court have ever regulated themselves, in all such questions, by the rules of a sound discretion, and paid due regard to every essential form of legal diligence.

The interference of the Court may be necessary, either in the action of constitution of the debt, which is a necessary forerunner of the adjudication where the creditor holds no written voucher, or in the adjudication itself.

1. In the action of constitution, they may be called upon to interfere, on three different occasions:—to dispense with the ordinary term for the debtor's appearance in Court—to prevent the debtor from delaying the decree, by the discussion of his defences—and to dispense with the usual intimations, subsequent to decree.

It is essential to the very existence of an action, and the validity of any order or decree to be pronounced by the Judge, that a proper intimation should be given to the defender, to appear in Court. The Judges have never held themselves entitled to dispense with

with this essential part of the action, nor conceived, that any decree, pronounced where it was omitted, could be legal or effectual. But there are cases, in which equity has permitted the Judges to dispense with a part of this form; and they have not scrupled to do so. The common form, in all actions, is, to cite the debtor to appear, at two different days. Formerly, these citations were given upon separate summonses—the act for the second citation, being pronounced under the jurisdiction which attached to the debtor, upon the expiry of the first term. But, while matters continued on this footing, a second citation was held to be essential, only where the debt was not established by written evidence, and where a proof, by witnesses, was necessary. After the union of the two summonses, the double diet of appearance was still kept up: but, as formerly, the second was not held essential, where the debt was established by writing; and this rule is held strictly to apply to the present state of the proceedings. According to this view, the Judges considered themselves as entitled to dispense with the second diet of appearance, in a case, where the debt against the ancestor of the defender was constituted by writing; and where the defender, having given in a written renounciation to be heir, decree cognitionis causa was pronounced. 16th November 1794, Cannan against Greig; IX. Fac. Coll. cxxiii. 302.

The Court have, in order to favour the pari passu preference, thought themselves entitled to cut short the debate upon the merits of the action, and all litigation between the parties; reserving to the defender the full effect of all his defences, as objections contra executionem. This is is an interposition which equity sanctions; for the defender is in no shape injured by the decree, while an enormous evil may arise to the pursuer, from the delay.—Sir John Sinclair brought an action against Patrick Sinclair, for the balance of an account. While his action was depending, another creditor adjudged; and, there being a likelihood of a long investigation of accounts, between Sir John and Sinclair, the Court authorised decree to be pronounced, reserving all objections contra executionem. 26th January 1792, Sir John Sinclair against Sinclair.

All

All decrees, acts, and important steps of proceedings in the Court of Session, are inserted in a minute-book, for the information of all concerned; that, during the dependence of an action, the practitioners shall be duly apprized of every step that is taken by the adversary; and that every person, against whom judgement is pronounced, shall be enabled to take measures, if he shall be so advised, for bringing the judgement under review; or for complying with it, without the disgrace of diligence being issued against him. By act of sederunt, 20th January 1671, it is provided, 'That no act or decreet done, either in the Inner or Outer-House, 'shall be extracted,* until 24 hours elapse after the same is read 'in the minute-book.' It may sometimes be of importance, to dispense with this delay, especially as the act of sederunt, 5th June 1725, appoints the reading of the minute-book to begin on the sixth sederunt or court-day of each Session. The Court, therefore, in particular cases, grant dispensations, permitting the decree to be instantly extracted. Is not such dispensation justifiable, in all cases where the decree is merely for constitution of a debt, on the same principle which has induced the Court to reserve the consideration of defences? Thus, in the above mentioned case of Sir John Sinclair, the pursuer, after he saw adjudications begun by other creditors, raised an action of adjudication, during the dependence of the constitution, and petitioned the Court to decern in the constitution, and allow his adjudication instantly to proceed. The Court remitted to the Lord Ordinary, to pronounce a decree in the action of constitution; to dispense with reading in the minute-book; and to call the action of adjudication, and pronounce decree in it; reserving all defences. Some years afterwards, the Court allowed a decree of constitution cognitionis causa, to be extracted, without abiding the course of the minute-book, that the person obtaining the decree, might get within the year: 24th February 1795, Common Agent in the ranking of Polquhairn, against Corrie, IX. Fac. Col. clx. 366.—At the same time, it should be observed, that the Judges were much moved, by the consideration, that,

* The extract of a decree in the Scotish courts, is analogous with the exemplification of a judgement in England

that, here, the only person interested in the judgement had renounced, and that no one could have appeared, to bring it under review.

2. In the adjudication itself, the Court also interferes, to abridge the unessential forms.

The Court interfered, to dispense with the second diet of compearance in a posterior adjudication; on this principle, that the debt being established by writing, (which must always, of course, be the case in adjudications), and the benefit of the alternative of a special adjudication, which alone could have required a proof, being forfeited to the debtor, by his having allowed a first adjudication to pass against him, it was not an action which required, according to the old rule, a second diet: 17th July 1761, Hamilton against Blackwood, III. Fac. Coll. xlviii. 101.

The defences against adjudication will be reserved, to be stated as objections, wherever prejudice can arise from delay; and this, even in a first adjudication, Kilk. 8.—But, as the privilege of the special alternative cannot be reserved in this way, the debtor is entitled to take a day for producing his titles, unless he shall have renounced his privilege, by already allowing a general adjudication to pass. It is seldom that there can be any interest in hastening on a FIRST adjudication: but it may happen: as, where the adjudger is a creditor of the ancestor, and the three years of preference are nearly expired. The Court refused, in such a case, to dispense with the alternative. 13th December 1776, Pedie petitioner, IV. Dict. 149.

II. The Legislature has endeavoured, in the two statutes of 23d and 33d Geo. III, to diminish the number, and lessen the expence of concurring adjudications, by regulations, beyond the reach of the equitable interference of the Court of Session. The object of these provisions has been, to make the intimation of depending adjudications more complete, and to enable posterior adjudgers to be conjoined in the decree, instead of each leading a separate adjudication. But, as several questions have arisen on these laws, it is proper to consider them particularly.

By the 23d Geo. III, c. 18, it was provided, 'in order to lessen the number of adjudications, and, consequently, the expence upon a bankrupt estate, that the Lord Ordinary officiating in the Court of Session, before whom any process of adjudication is called, shall ordain intimation thereof to be made in the minute-book, and on the wall, in order that any creditors of the common debtor, who may think proper to adjudge his estate, and are in readiness for it, may produce the instructions of their debts, and be conjoined in the decree of adjudication; and a reasonable time, not exceeding twenty sederunt days,' (court-days), 'shall be given for that purpose, unless there be any hazard from a delay, which the Court, or the Lord Ordinary, shall judge of.' 23d Geo. III. c. 18. § 5.—The object of the Legislature, in this enactment, seems to have been, that every adjudication brought into Court, should be intimated, (where there was no danger from delay, and of which, the Lord Ordinary was to judge), that each might, in its turn, be the means of contributing to the general design of lessening the number of separate diligences. But the practice, under this statute, was extremely loose, and gave occasion to several questions. The intimation, in posterior adjudications, was generally omitted; and, when the lawyers came to the Bar, and stated, that 'this was a posterior adjudication,' the Lord Ordinary pronounced decree of adjudication at once, without ordering intimation. But, as the appearance of an adjudication in the weekly rolls, was a kind of intimation, other creditors frequently came to the Bar, with their grounds of debt prepared, and were conjoined with the adjudger, at the first calling of the cause, and where no intimation had been made. In the ranking of Redcastle, objections were taken to both these practices. Several adjudications within year and day of the first, had been led without any intimation; and with some of them were conjoined, creditors, who had produced their grounds of debt at the Bar. Three points

were

were questioned: 1. Whether the want of intimation, in the posterior adjudication, was not a nullity, under the statute? 2. Whether the conjoined creditors were to be considered as having legally adjudged? and, 3. Whether some relief was not to be afforded to postponed creditors, who, if intimation of each adjudication had been made, would have been apprized of the necessity and opportunity of producing their grounds of debt? These questions were very fully discussed. On the first of them, the Court found the want of intimation, no good objection to the posterior adjudications; and that the Lord Ordinary, having power to dispense, must, in all cases, be supposed to have virtually dispensed with the form. On the second question, the objecting creditors endeavoured to show, that the great view of the Legislature, in appointing intimation, was, that the intimation might supply the place of citations, &c, by the creditors who should apply to be conjoined; and that no conjunction could therefore be lawful, which was not preceded by intimation. But this view of the matter, the Court did not regard. They held the conjunction by the Lord Ordinary, under the powers given him in the statute, to be effectual, as an adjudication to the creditors who were conjoined. And, as to the third point, the Court had no difficulty in deciding, that no relief was to be given, since these creditors ought to have come in before. De Roveray and others, against M'Kenzie and others, March 1793.

This decision was immediately followed by the statute of the 33d Geo III. (passed on the 17th June 1793); and the law was considerably altered, in two essential points. 1. Intimation was made necessary only in the first adjudication and, 2. It was required, that a creditor, applying to be conjoined, should not only have his grounds of debt ready for adjudging, but, that he should also have his summons of adjudication libelled and signeted. But it was left ambiguous, whether conjunction was to be allowed, in any other adjudication than the first. The words of the statute are—' And, in order to lessen the number of adjudications for ' debt, and consequently the expence to all parties, and to facili' tate the pari passu preference of creditors in similar circum-

'stances, be it enacted, That the Lord Ordinary officiating in 'the Court of Session, before whom the first process of adju-'dication against any estate, for payment or security of debt, is 'called, shall ordain intimation thereof to be made in the minute-'book, and on the wall, in order that any other creditors of the 'common debtor, who, at the next calling of the cause, can 'show that, although they have not executed their summonses of 'adjudication, they are, in other respects, by the nature of their 'grounds of debt, and steps taken by them, in condition to pro-'ceed in adjudging their debtor's estate, may produce the instruc-'tions of their debts, with summonses of adjudication, libelled 'and signeted, for the purpose of their being conjoined in the de-'cree of adjudication, twenty sederunt days being allowed for 'such intimation, before the cause can be called a second time; 'and, if any of these forms shall happen to be omitted, the said 'adjudication shall be null and void, without prejudice to the va-'lidity, and order of ranking of posterior adjudications, accord-'ing to the rules of law.' § 10.

Although, under this statute, there seems scarcely to be any authority for conjoining, in posterior adjudications, creditors, producing summonses of adjudication, with the grounds thereof, the spirit and intention of the law, certainly was, to lessen, by means of conjunctions, the number of separate diligences. And the practice, which began under the old statute, has been continued under this new one, of conjoining creditors, whether the adjudication in dependence was a first, or a posterior one. The only alteration has been, that the summons of adjudication, as well as the grounds of debt, have been required, as the title to such conjunction. Upon the words of the statute, objections have been taken, in several rankings, to the claims of creditors thus adjudging by conjunction. How the point will be decided, it becomes not me to anticipate; but I may be allowed to remark, that, while the statute does not expressly give to the Lord Ordinary those powers which were bestowed upon him by the 23d of the King, and which had much influence on the decision in De Roveray's case; the strong tide of practice, and the hardship of reducing creditors, who, trusting to such

such adjudications by conjunction, have lost the opportunity of coming within the year, will naturally have much regard paid to it.

I formerly took occasion to observe, that nullities in the first effectual adjudication, may be fatal to it, considered as the criterion of the pari passu preference. But where a creditor comes forward under the late statute, in consequence of the first adjudger's intimation, and is conjoined in the decree, he cannot be hurt, I apprehend, by any defect in the first adjudger's diligence. The completion of the combined decree, by a charge against superiors, will make any one of the conjoined adjudications an effectual diligence, though all the rest, that are conjoined with it, should be null. To give any other interpretation to the statute, would not only defeat the very object of the Legislature, since no creditor would rest his debt upon the diligence of another, but it would have the further effect, of converting the second adjudication into the first, and subjecting it to a fatal objection, as not being intimated in terms of the statute.

§ 3. EFFECT OF THE DEBTOR'S DEATH UPON THIS PARI PASSU PREFERENCE.

In considering this question, it may be proper to distinguish between the case, where the creditors of the deceased debtor alone are in the field, and that in which the creditors of the heir are also competing.

1. Where the creditors of the deceased debtor alone are in the field, some of them having adjudged during his life, and others not till after his death, it may be taken as a fixed point, that an adjudication deduced against the heir, for the ancestor's debt, or proceeding upon his renunciation of the succession, is entitled, if within year and day of the first effectual adjudication, to be placed on an equal footing with those led against the ancestor himself, during his life. The case of Sinclair against the Earl of Caithness, 8th December 1731, has settled this point. The question was discussed by the first lawyers at the Scotch Bar.—Innes of Sand-

side

side had led an adjudication, and rendered it effectual, during the life of Sinclair of Assery. There were other adjudgers, after year and day; and their object was, to have Sandside's adjudication held as not the first effectual; by which means, they would have come in pari passu with each other. They tried several objections; but all having been repelled, they rested here at last—that an adjudication, led during the ancestor's life, could not regulate the competition of those which were deduced against his heir. Thus, the whole question came to be discussed, Whether the adjudication before and after the debtor's death, for his own debts, could be conjoined, under the rule of the act 1661, c. 62? The Court found Sandside's adjudication to be the first effectual, making it the criterion of the pari passu preference: VII. Fac. Coll. xi. 21.

But a difficulty occurs here. The heir is entitled to refuse answering the charge to enter, till the expiry of the annus deliberandi. In this way, the term of the pari passu preference may expire, before the posterior adjudgers can obtain their decrees, and, so, the benefit of the equalizing rule be denied to them. This difficulty was stated in the above case, and thus answered — Such an inconvenience and injustice 'might be rectified, by allowing the diligence of the other creditors to proceed within the 'year, in the same manner as when the heir, in favour of particular creditors, has renounced the benefit of the annus deliberandi.' (III. Ersk. viii. 55.) And the reporter adds this note to the case: 'N. B.—All the Judges who spoke, declared 'their opinion, that a creditor, in danger of losing his preference, 'by the death of his debtor, after an effectual adjudication had 'been led by another creditor, would obtain relief, in the way 'suggested by the respondents.'

2. Where there is a competition between the adjudging creditors of the ancestor, and those of the heir, there is a statutory preference given to all the ancestor's creditors, who shall, within three years after his death, use diligence to affect his estate: 1661, c. 24. Before the expiry, then, of the three years, the creditors of the heir are not entitled to lead adjudications, so as to be effectual in compe-

tition

tition with those led by the ancestor's creditors, within that period: but if the three years have been allowed to expire, without any adjudication on the part of the ancestor's creditors, the distinction between the two sets of creditors is gone, and they are all to be ranked as if they were the creditors of the same debtor.

It seems to be a question of some difficulty, however, whether a completed adjudication, by a creditor of the ancestor, within the three years, should serve as the first effectual, to a creditor of the heir. I should rather apprehend that it would not; but that a creditor of the heir adjudging, must make his own adjudication effectual. The statute 1661, not only supposes a common debtor, but proceeds upon the very idea, that the case would have admitted of one adjudication being led, for all the creditors entitled to the benefit of it; 'as if' (says the act) 'one adjudication had been 'led for the whole of the respective sums contained in the adju-'dications, equally preferable, by virtue of this act.' By the statute 1661, c. 24, the estate of the ancestor is preserved for his own creditors doing diligence within the three years, and, although the creditors of the heir are not obliged to remain inactive for this long period, yet, if they do proceed to diligence within the three years, they do it in a character, and upon a footing, totally different from that in which the creditors of the ancestor act.

CONCLUSION OF CHAP. I.

Such being the laws establishing equality among adjudging creditors, it follows, as a consequence, that all adjudications which do not fall within them, which are not led till after the expiry of the year and day from the first effectual, are left to the old rule of preference, by priority of date. It is not necessary for such adjudgers to take infeftment, or to give a charge to the superior, in order to complete the postponed adjudication, (II. Ersk. xii. 33): and each, in his order, acquires a preference upon the residue of the estate, after satisfying prior adjudgers, according to the date of his decree of adjudication.

CHAP.

CHAP. II.

Of Diligence against Moveable Property, by individual Creditors,

and

Of the Laws establishing Equality among them.

In considering the laws, by which equality is established among the creditors of a bankrupt doing diligence against his moveables, I shall follow nearly the same order, as in discussing the adjudication; only it is more necessary to distinguish between the diligence used during the debtor's life, and that which is used after his death. The provisions for equalizing diligence against moveables during the debtor's life, have been introduced purposely with a view to bankruptcy: the only provisions which secure equality in the diligence after death, had no such situation in view.

SECTION I.

Of Diligence against Moveables during the Debtor's Life, considered independently of any Competition.

The nature of the Scotish diligence, against the moveable or personal estate of the debtor, during his life, differs considerably from that of England. In England, execution proceeds, against the personal estate, by the writs of Fieri Facias, or Elegit, issued upon the judgement of a Court, as their warrant. In Scotland, there are three forms of execution,—the Poinding—the Arrestment in Execution—and the Arrestment in Security. The general description of these diligences, is this:—1. The creditor may, after charging the debtor to pay the debt, in the judgement or decree, have his moveables poinded, or seized in execution; and either sold for his payment, or delivered over to him at an apprizement, if no purchaser appear. 2dly, He may, immediately after judgement, attach, by Arrestment in Execution, those moveables which are in the possession of another than the debtor, or those debts which are due to him: and, 3dly, If his debtor's circumstances be suspicious, he may, even before sentence, attach, by Arrestment in Security, the debts due to the debtor, or the moveables belonging to him and not in his own possession.

I shall proceed with the detail of the particular diligences, according to this order.

§ 1. Of Poinding, considered as an Individual Diligence.

When poinding proceeds, in execution of a judgement of the Sheriff, it is by precept from him, directed to his officers, that the

warrant

warrant is given: when it proceeds upon a judgement of the Court of Session, whether that judgement be pronounced in a cause tried there; or given forth, in common course, upon a registered deed; or pronounced in confirmation of the judgement of an inferior court, and for the purpose of extending the execution beyond the territory of that court; it is, by a writ, or letters of poinding passed under the King's signet, and running in his name. Although I have said, that poinding proceeds upon a special warrant, both in the Sheriff-court, and in the Court of Session, it may be proper to observe, that the precept of the Sheriff, and the letters executorial from the signet, both include a warrant for arrestment, as well as for poinding. The letters of poinding, indeed, make now (since the statute 1696, c. 29) a part of the writ, or letter of horning and poinding, which contains warrants for all the execution competent against the person, and against the moveable estate.

No poinding, whether it proceed upon the precept of the Sheriff, or upon the King's letter, can be executed till the debtor has been charged to pay the debt, and the time has expired, which law allows for the debtor's voluntary obedience. Even under the brief of distress, a certain number of days was allowed after judgment, for complying with the judgment of the Court, before execution could proceed against either the land or the moveables. These were called the days of law; and they might safely be indulged to the debtor, at a time when the Sheriff could attach his property as a security for the debt. A similar indulgence, to a much greater extent, was given in the Roman law: the *actio judicati* could not be begun till four months after sentence. In France, although there does not appear to have been any appointed period for compliance, it was necessary, before proceeding to execution against either the lands or moveables, 'avoir mis le debiteur auparavant en demeure 'de payer.' (I. Denisart, 508; Pothier, traité de la proc. civil. 174, 210.) In England the law is very different: at one time, the *fieri facias* bound the moveables from the date of the writ, although that may have been nearly a twelvemonth before the execution; and, even at the present day, it operates as an universal attachment from its delivery to the Sheriff. Although, in our old law, fifteen

fifteen free days, after sentence, were allowed for compliance, and the execution against the goods levied under the brief of distress, did not proceed till after the expiry of that period; there was no warning to the debtor necessary, as in the Roman law by the 'actio 'judicati,' and in the French law by the 'commandement.' After the institution of the College of Justice, and the introduction of poinding upon special writs of execution, the days of law were still respected: but there was no charge to the debtor to pay: the pronouncing of sentence, was thought sufficient intimation to him; and, after the expiry of the days of law, the execution of the poinding proceeded of course. The hardships of this practice, must have become every day more palpable, as the trade of the country increased. A man might be totally ignorant of the sentence pronounced against him, even though he had appeared in Court by his attorney, and, in decrees in absence, or by default, he could not know of his danger. While thus dreaming on in security, this ruinous and disgraceful diligence might have been executed against him. These evils were sorely felt, and are well described in the preamble of the statute which reform the practice. By 1696, c. 4. it is enacted, that no poinding shall proceed, till the debtor has first been charged to pay, and the days of the charge have expired. The legal evidence of a compliance with this requisite, is the messenger's return of execution of charge. The debtor may legally oppose the execution of a poinding, unless the messenger shall be able to produce, not merely the horning as his warrant, but also the execution of charge; or, in the inferior court, the execution of a charge upon the precept or decree. And although the creditor poinding, is obliged, by the late statutes, (independently of the bankruptcy of the debtor), to admit to a conjunction with his poinding, another creditor who is ready to poind, yet he or his messenger may refuse to do so, unless such evidence shall be produced. Indeed, if the messenger should admit a creditor to a conjunction, where the days of his charge are not expired, or where, although they be expired, the messenger's return of the execution of charge is liable to a good objection, the employer of that messenger is not bound to submit to the conjunction; but may afterwards object, and prevail in excluding the creditor so admitted. The messenger acts as sheriff in

 that

that part; and the creditor is entitled to redress, if he have judged amiss. This doctrine is strongly illustrated by the judgement on a late case, where a messenger, having admitted a creditor to a conjunction, whose execution of charge was of an erroneous and indeed impossible date, the Court held these three points to be clear 1. That the messenger's decision in this matter was not irreversible: 2. That it was necessary, in order to procure conjunction, to produce legal evidence, that the charge had been given, and that the days were expired: 3. That the execution of a messenger, is an actus legitimus, which must be perfect at the time it is first produced in judgement, and cannot afterwards be corrected or supplied by another. 2d June 1797, Hogg against M'Lellan.

In considering the nature and form of poinding, I shall not trouble the reader with a detail of the evils of the old law, since they are now happily redressed by the late sequestration laws: I shall confine my attention to this improved state of the diligence. It may only be observed in general, that the old poinding might not improperly have been called an irredeemable adjudication of the property of the debtor's moveables to the creditor, at a value put upon them by the messenger, and by appretiators chosen by him. The messenger came to the house of the debtor, seized his goods, made them be appretiated, carried them to the Market Cross of the jurisdiction; and there, after a revisal of the appretiation, proclaimed an offer of return to the debtor, or to any one in his name, at these values; and, if none appeared, the messenger declared and adjudged them to belong to the creditor, at the value put on them and this adjudication by the messenger, as proved by his return of the execution, or by instruments taken in the hands of a notary, was the completion of the poinding, operating as a direct and irrevocable transference of the property from that moment. (III. Ersk. vi. 25.)

Poinding, as new-modelled by the late statutes, is not an adjudication of the goods to the creditor, at a value put upon them by men of low characters, retainers of the messenger. A fair and public sale is provided, under the order of the Sheriff of the county; insuring

insuring to the unfortunate debtor a fair value for his property. To reconcile the interests of the creditor and of the debtor; to give to the one, security against his diligence being disappointed, while to the other is given all the benefit of arranging the sale in the way most likely to be productive, it is fixed, 1. That after the goods are apprized, they shall be offered to the debtor or his friends; and, on their refusal to take them, they shall be adjudged by the messenger (the adjudication completing the real right of the creditor), and then a return shall be made to the Sheriff, that he may give such orders concerning the sale, as may seem most prudent: 2. The debtor continues in possession, but the creditor has a real right not to be disappointed. The statute provides, that 'in 'future the messenger, or other officer employed in executing a 'poinding for debt, shall leave in the hands of the debtor, a sche-'dule of the poinded goods, and note of the apprized value (one 'apprizement being in every case sufficient); and shall forthwith 'report his execution of poinding to the Sheriff, or other Judge 'Ordinary, who shall give directions for selling the goods poinded 'by public roup, after such publication, at such time and place as 'circumstances may require.' The goods are allowed to remain in the debtor's hands, it being declared, 'that any person who intro-'mits with, or carries off the goods in the mean time, in order to 'disappoint the poinding, shall be liable in double the apprized va-'lue thereof.' 33 Geo. III. c. 74, § 5.

In considering the application of this diligence *, these three principles seem to comprehend the whole doctrine: 1. That this is the only diligence competent against those moveables, which are in the debtor's own possession, 2. That it is a diligence co-operative with arrestment against those of the debtor's moveables, which are in another's possession; and, 3. That it affects only corporeal moveables, not debts.

1. Although,

* In this short view of the diligence against moveables, I intend only to indicate the general principles which regulate the application of the poinding, and of the arrestment. The more minute discussion of the subject, I reserve for that part of the work, in which the [illegible] to the various diligences are to be reviewed.

1. Although, at one time, arrestment was held to be competent even in the debtor's own hands, this doctrine has been given up for more than a century, during which period (in the words of Sir James Stewart), 'the habilis modus, of affecting moveables in a 'debtor's own hand, has been only by poinding.' (Ans. to Dirl. p. 10)

2. Poinding was originally the sole execution against moveables Arrestment has taken its place, in cases of debt due to the person against whom the execution is taken out; but, in all other respects, it leaves the poinding uninjured. Both diligences are competent against moveables, in the possession of another than the debtor, even in the creditor's own hand—19th July 1678, Tillicoultry, I. Fount. 10.; and in this the distinction between them lies, that the poinding is a perfect diligence, operating at once as a transference of the debtor's property to the poinder; but it cannot proceed till after the expiry of the charge: arrestment, on the other hand, is an imperfect diligence, requiring a decree of forthcoming to complete it; but is competent the instant that decree is pronounced, or even before decree. We shall afterwards have occasion to see, that after one creditor has used arrestment; another, having his diligence ready, and his charge expired, may at once proceed to poind, and thereby carry a complete right of preference over the arrester. There is one kind of moveable property, however, which is understood not to be liable to poinding Neither ships themselves, nor goods on board of ships, are held, in practice, to be capable of being poinded; arrestment being supposed the only proper diligence for attaching them. Lord Bankton cites a decision to this effect—Feb. 1760, Cochran, III Bank p 521. But I have not been able to find the report of any such case, and Lord Bankton gives nothing of the circumstances. Perhaps, this opinion respecting ships, arose from the necessity, under the old law, of carrying every thing poinded to the Market Cross; though the rudder should have been sufficient, like the coulter of a plough.

3. Debts were formerly levied, as well as moveables, upon the poinding, as they are at this day in England levied under the fieri

facias.

facias. But the lawful diligence for attaching them now, is the arrestment, nor has the poinding been used in this way during the whole of the 18th century.

The poinding may be opposed by the debtor, or by the true owner, if the goods do not belong to the debtor, or by the possessor of the goods, though they be the debtor's, provided he can plead a right of lien over them. 1. The debtor himself may oppose the poinding, upon the ground of any objection to the regularity of the diligence, which appears ex facie—as the want of an execution of charge—the prematurity of the poinding, &c.—or he may oppose, on the ground of the property not being his. This, however, he must prove by clear evidence; his declaration, or even his oath, cannot be taken as sufficient. 2. The true owner of the goods may appear, and, claiming the goods, oppose the poinding. This he may do, any time before the sale of them; and, now, it is of less consequence whether he appear at first, since the goods are not taken away, as formerly, to the Market Cross, but are left in possession of the holder, till the Sheriff shall order a sale. The proprietor producing a written title, the messenger must stop, unless there be some palpable objection to the deed. If there be no deed, then the oaths of the claimant, and of the debtor, will be taken by special interrogatory, or the messenger will, I apprehend, be obliged to take upon oath, such evidence as the owner shall offer to him. In the law of France, it was necessary to have both the oath of the debtor, and that of the claimant; and it was also necessary that they should be sufficiently unconnected, to validate their testimony in each other's favour; if not, the claimant must have offered other witnesses, or evidence of some other kind, in support of his property. (Pothier, p. 186.) 3. Those who have a lien over the goods, are not to be deprived of it by poinding; they may, therefore, oppose the poinding, and stop it from proceeding to any effect injurious to them. Thus, a landlord of a house, or of a farm, may oppose a poinding of his tenant's furniture and stocking, for he has a hypothec over them, which no one coming in the debtor's right can disappoint. If caution be offered for the whole rent, the landlord cannot stop the poinding. So; it m

every

every other case where a lien is competent to the possessor—a factor, for his general balance—an artificer, for the value of the labour bestowed—a carrier, or shipmaster, for the carriage and freight: But I apprehend that they could not prevent the poinding from going on the length of an adjudication by the messenger, under burden of their rights, to the effect of constituting a real right in the creditor over the residue of the goods, after satisfying the lien. Thus, a poinding may proceed suspensively, although the possessor of the goods may have, upon contract, a right to possess for a certain term; as in the case of Davidson—where, a house having been subset with furniture, a creditor of the person who gave the sublease, proceeded to poind the furniture: it was before the late reformation in the form of executing poinding; and the Court found, that the poinding might proceed, and that the possessor was obliged to submit to the temporary inconvenience of allowing the furniture to be carried to the Market Cross, '*although the poinding could not have its full effect, before* '*the right of possession expired.*' 11th December 1784, Davidson, VII. Fac. Coll. clxxxii. 286.

This may suffice, as an explanation of the nature, operation, and effect of poinding, considered as an individual diligence. The doctrines which belong to it, considered as in communion with other poindings—and the rules adopted, by the bankrupt statutes, for equalizing the claims of creditors attempting, by the use of this diligence, to acquire preference over their fellows—will more properly be explained, after considering the arrestment.

§ 2. OF THE ARRESTMENT AND FORTHCOMING, CONSIDERED AS AN INDIVIDUAL DILIGENCE.

I shall, in considering the diligence of arrestment, take the two forms of it separately; but, in the following short notice of the introduction of this writ into our practice, it will be necessary to attend to both.

There

There seem to be strong reasons for believing, that the arrestment, in security, was first adopted by us; and that our familiarity with the use of this diligence, and its peculiar fitness for the levying of debts due to the debtor, at last introduced the arrestment in execution.

In the Roman law, execution proceeded under the superintendance of a judge, in a regular actio judicati. He first ordered the moveables to be seized, and sold; next, he disposed of the lands; and, lastly, he ordered the jura incorporalia, the debts and claims of the debtor, to be made effectual against those who were bound for them, and the sums, thus raised, to be applied in payment of the debt. In France, although the form of execution against corporeal moveables was less solemn, the execution against the jura incorporalia proceeded, as in the Roman law, under the direct superintendance of the judge. The officer arrested or stopt in the hands of the debtor, the sum which he owed to the person against whom the execution was directed; by intimating to him, that the claim was in the hands of justice, and summoning him to appear, along with the person to whom the money was due, that they might hear the debt adjudged over to the prosecutor. This form of execution, was called, 'Saisie arret,' and was completed by the sentence adjudging over the debt *.—When our ancient national form of proceeding, by brief and distress, was abolished, and, with the institution of the College of Justice, the spirit of the Roman law was introduced into our judicial proceedings, it was not unnatural, that the forms of execution already established in France, from which country the whole of the new institution was borrowed, should be adopted. This was the more promoted by the two following circumstances. FIRST, The contempt of our Sheriffs for all their ministerial functions. Originally, under the writ of poinding, as under the brieve of distress, the Sheriffs levied the debts, as well as seized the goods, of the debtor; but when they abandoned all those duties to messengers, the necessity of following the French practice, at least in the levying of debts, became very palpable. SECONDLY, The suspension of poinding,

* Pothier, Trait. de la Proc. Civ. p. 19[illegible]

till the expiry of the days of law, and the danger of an intermediate dissipation of the funds, called loudly for some form of attachment. Such an attachment had been established, we have seen, in France, both before and after sentence; and, after trying the effect of inhibition, it would appear, that, at last, the two remedies established there, had been directly imitated by us: the 'simple arret' of that law, was adopted by us, under the name of arrestment on the dependence, and, in some measure, supplied the want of the attachment previous to sentence, formerly competent on the brief of distress. The 'arret et execution,' gave us a model for the arrestment in execution, by which a creditor might be guarded against the frauds practicable during the running of the days of law.

I. OF THE ARRESTMENT AND FORTHCOMING IN EXECUTION.

The arrestment in execution, thus introduced, for laying an attachment instantly upon the effects of the debtor in the hands of others, came soon to be considered as the only kind of diligence, by which the debts due to the debtor could be levied. At this day, its application is to these two cases alone—1. Where moveables are in the possession of another than the debtor; and, 2. Where personal debts are due to him. It is, in form, an arrestment; in essence and reality, a poinding. As a poinding, it cannot be discharged upon bail—as an arrestment, it must be followed forth by an action of forthcoming, the transference of the real right being completed only by the decree of forthcoming.

1. The great distinction between the arrestment in execution, and the arrestment in security, is, that the latter may be taken off or loosed upon bail; the former cannot, without payment or consignation. And the reason of the distinction is, that, in the former case, a decree of a court has already passed, either by consent, or in an action ordering execution to proceed; while, in the latter, it is a question, whether such authority shall ever be obtained. Although, therefore, arrestment may be obtained upon any written voucher of debt, that is, an arrestment in security merely, and

not

not an arrestment in execution, which can proceed upon no other warrant but the decree of a court. A sheriff or magistrate may, upon an obligation capable of registration for execution, or in an action, give warrant to arrest, as well as to poind. These warrants will have full effect within their jurisdiction; and, by an application to the Court of Session, a supplementary warrant will be given for arrestment, in any part of Scotland, in the same way as if the original decree had been pronounced by the Court of Session.

The warrant for arrestment, is given in a very few words. The King's letters of horning and poinding, order the messenger, 'in Our name and authority, to fence, arrest, apprize, compel, 'poind, and distrinzie, all and sundry the readiest moveables, 'goods, gear, debts, and sums of money, pertaining and belong-'ing to the said A. B.' In the precept of inferior judges, the words of the warrant of arrestment are equally sparing. In each, the word ARREST is the whole warrant, and, indeed, includes all that the messenger can do. When he has arrested, his power is at an end, and it is only by the judgement of a court, that the spell can be broken. The terms of the execution of arrestment are these: The messenger 'fences and arrests, in the hands of 'the said C D. the sum of Sterling, less or more, due 'and addebted by him to the said A. B. or to any other person or 'persons, for his use or behoof, by bond, bill, &c. &c., with all 'and sundry goods, gear, &c. belonging to him, all to remain in 'your hands, under sure fence and arrestment, at the instance of 'the said complainer, ay and while' (until) 'he be completely sa-'tisfied and paid of the sum of Sterling of principal, and ' of expences, and annualrent thereof.'

The form of execution is a matter of importance, as, upon the regularity of it, the diligence must often depend. I do not mean to enter at large into the subject here; but it may be proper to take notice of the following rules: FIRST, That where the arrester is an individual, the forms prescribed by the act 1540, c. 75, must be observed. It is not an obsolete law, but in viridi observantia; in so much, that, in the case of Fraser Reid & Sons against Lancaster

& Jamieson, it was sustained as a good objection to an arrestment, 'That the copy was left for Mr Coats within his counting-house in 'Glasgow, he being a single or private merchant, and his counting-'house in a different street, and at a considerable distance from 'his dwelling-house:' 14th January 1795. This judgement proceeded upon a very careful search into the practice, and therefore seems to be one which may be relied on in future. SECONDLY, The practice is different, with regard to a Company: their counting house is regarded as the residence of the Company; and an arrestment executed there, seems to be effectual. In the hands of a Corporation, or Society, arrestment may be executed when they are met for the dispatch of business, or against the representatives of the Society, separately and individually: 23d June 1762, Dalrymple against Bertram, Sel. Dec. cxcviii. 263. THIRDLY, Where the arrestee is a pupil, the arrestment must be used in the hands of his tutors and curators; if a minor, it may be used either in his own hands, or in those of his curators, III. Ersk. vi. 4 —21st February 1738, Binning against M'Doual, Cl. Hume, lxxxix. 142.

As to the time of executing an arrestment, it was found, in Grant & Jones, that an arrestment, bearing to be used between 12 o'clock and 1 in the morning, was effectual to establish a preference over one used next morning between 5 and 6. Kilk. p 45. I. Falc. 83.

When the debtor to the arrester's debtor is not in the country, the form in arrestment (as in all other diligence) is to execute, at the market cross of Edinburgh, pier and shore of Leith. But this, although uniformly practised in arrestment, might, till lately, have been all done, without its ever coming to the ears of the debtor, so as to warn him of the danger of paying to the original creditor. To remedy this imperfection, it is enacted by the last bankrupt act, § 4, That no arrestment, executed thus, 'shall be held to 'interpel a person, out of Scotland, from paying to the original 'creditor, unless proof be made, that he, or those having authority 'to act for him, were previously in the knowledge of such arrest-'ment having been used.' Where the subject to be arrested is

on

on board of a ship, or otherwise situated within the precincts of the jurisdiction of the High Court of Admiralty, an application must be made to the Judge Admiral, for his concurrence, before the arrestment can be executed. this is obtained, of course, upon production of the horning.

By this execution, the attachment is made; and the next part of the diligence is, to make it effectual in contributing to the payment of the debt: this is done by the forthcoming. The action of forthcoming has two objects: 1. To ascertain the property in possession of the arrestee, or the debt due by him to the arrester's debtor: and, 2 To have that property sold, for the arrester's payment, as in a poinding; or the debt adjudged to belong to him. This action is brought before the Judge Ordinary of the place in which the arrestee resides, or before the Court of Session. An action of forthcoming may be brought in the inferior court, although the arrestment has proceeded on letters of horning, and, on the other hand, the action may be brought before the Court of Session, though the arrestment has been laid on by the Sheriff. It may also be brought in the Court of Session, though the arrestment be laid on by the Court of Admiralty. 22d May 1637, Finnie, Durie, 842. These points seem always to have been settled. But doubts were entertained among our older lawyers, whether, an arrestment being laid on by the warrant of an inferior judge, it was competent to bring the forthcoming before another inferior judge, in case of the debtor removing into another jurisdiction. Prior to Lord Stair's time, the views of our lawyers seem to have been very narrow on this point They denied the competency of such an action: but he laid down the true principle, that all jurisdiction centres in the King. and his commands, begun to be executed in one jurisdiction, may be completed in another, to which the debtor has removed, provided the judge shall be acting only within his own territory (III. i. 24) Still the practice was very unsettled, till a case occurred, which gave the Court an opportunity of confirming the reasoning of Lord Stair. 23d June 1710, Dalrymple, Forb. 415. III. Ersk. vi 15

The

The action of forthcoming naturally comes to be raised, only when, with his diligence in his hand, the creditor has found a person holding funds of his debtor, against whom he may use arrestment. But it has been found not incompetent to raise the action of forthcoming, even before the arrestment was executed, that so the citation on the summons might be given immediately after the imposing of the arrestment, and as little time lost to the creditor as possible. 7th January 1704, II. Fount. 210.

The parties to the action of forthcoming, are, the arrestee and his original creditor. * It is against the former, that the decree of forthcoming is to be directed. The latter is called to attend to his interest, to prevent a decree of forthcoming from going out in favour of one who is no true creditor of his, or for a greater sum than is due. The only defences which it is competent for the arrestee to set up, are, that he is not debtor to the arrester's debtor, and holds no property of his; or, that he has a lien over the property which he holds: or, that the arrestment or forthcoming is informal, (in which case, the decree will not save him from a claim at the instance of the original creditor); or, that other arrestment or diligence is used in his hands for the same sum, so that he may be in danger of being obliged to pay twice. † It is the business of the original creditor alone, to object to the claim of the arrester; and if he do not appear to do so, the arrestee has no right nor interest to take up the plea.

The first object in this action is, to prove that the arrestee holds property of the debtor, or is due money to him, and to what amount. For this purpose, all the channels of evidence are open to the arrester; and if he can in no other way succeed, he may

make

* If the original creditor do not live within the jurisdiction in which the arrester resides, he must be summoned by a writ of supplement from the Court of Session.

† In such a case, the proper remedy is by process of multiplepoinding, or double distress, in which the arrestee states, that there are several claimants upon the fund in his hand, and concludes, that they should be called into Court to dispute their preference, so that he may pay safely to him having best right, under deduction of the necessary expence of his calling them into Court. Of this action, see afterwards, Book IV. part i. chap. ii.

make a reference to the oath of the arrestee. If the general fact shall be acknowledged, the amount is next to be ascertained, and, according to the nature of the fund, the proceedings will vary. If the fund be of the nature of a debt, then the decree of forthcoming will ordain that debt (at least as much of it as shall be necessary) to be paid over to the arrester. If the fund consist of moveables, the arrestee will be ordained to produce them, that they may be sold, as in a poinding. 17th February 1735, Muirhead against Corrie, I. Dict. 54.—III. Stair, Inst. i. 35.—III. Ersk. vi. 17.

The following rules seem to regulate the whole doctrine of the application and use of arrestment. 1. It is inapplicable to obligations which are not of a pecuniary nature. 2. It is the sole diligence for attaching personal debts. 3. Against goods which are in the possession of another than the debtor, it is a co-operative diligence with poinding. And, 4 It cannot be used, unless the fund to be attached is in the possession of another than the debtor.

Upon the effect of the diligence, I would here observe, 1. That the arrestment, considered independently of the equalizing law, establishes a lien over the fund attached, in favour of the arresting creditor, provided it be regularly followed by decree of forthcoming; and that this lien, although it is not strong enough to exclude a poinding from carrying off the goods, gives a preference to the arrester over all the other creditors arresting after him, although they should, by some accident, have got the start of him in the decree of forthcoming. 2. That the decree of forthcoming is, from its date, a complete adjudication, needing neither intimation, nor delivery, to make it perfect, but carrying full right to the arrester, from the moment of pronouncing the decree, a right, of which even the execution of a poinding, before delivery of the goods to the arresting creditor, cannot deprive him. 3 That the force of an arrestment lasts only for five years *. If action of forthcoming

* By statute 1669, c. 9 it is enacted, 'That all arrestments to be used hereafter 'upon decrees, registered bonds, dispositions, or contracts, not pursued and insisted on 'within five years after the laying on thereof, [illegible]

coming be not raised within that time, the arrestee may safely pay, or deliver to his original creditor. Even within that period, an undue delay in the bringing of the action of forthcoming into court, or in the conducting of it, when brought, will entitle another arrester to take the preference.

II. OF THE ARRESTMENT AND FORTHCOMING IN SECURITY.

Having so fully explained the nature and effect of the arrestment in execution, it will be sufficient, in considering the arrestment in security, to point out the differences in its form, nature, and effect.

The arrestment in security, proceeds upon a precept from an inferior court, or upon letters of arrestment, issued from the signet, by warrant of the Court of Session. As formerly observed, in speaking of the arrestment in execution, where the subject to be arrested lies within the jurisdiction of the Court of Admiralty, the arrestment must either proceed, by precept from the Judge-Admiral, or be sanctioned by his concurrence.

The production of the obligation, if, ex facie, legal and effectual, will be sufficient to procure a warrant for letters of arrestment, till caution shall be found. The warrant for arrestment on the dependance, is issued, of course, upon production of the depending process. Formerly, it was doubtful, whether there should be strictly and properly an action depending, to authorise the granting of such warrants? And although, in one case, the court supported an arrestment, under a Sheriff's authority, contained in the precept or summons on which the action proceeded, this was chiefly on the ground, that such was the practice in the Sheriff-court: 21st February 1730, Oliphant, Kilk. 46. The practice in the Court of Session, never sanctioned the issuing of arrestment, till a summons was produced, executed. It is plain, that, in many cases, this might give room for disappointing, altogether, the creditor's intention of arresting, by allowing the debtor to withdraw all his arrestable funds: and therefore, in the late sequestration act, it is provided, that, 'in time coming, letters, or precepts of arrestment, bearing to be upon a depending action, may be granted, summarily, upon production of the libelled summons.' It is also declared unnecessary, either that the summons should be executed, or the debt liquidated at the date of the arrestment, provided these and all other necessary steps are taken, without any undue delay.

I. The first difference, worthy of observation, between the arrestment in security, and the arrestment in execution, is, that the former, being an act of common execution to enforce payment, is competent against the funds of the debtor, whatever his state of credit may be, while the arrestment in security is an extraordinary remedy against the failing condition of the debtor, not to be applied where his credit is unsuspected and entire. The inhibition, which is a diligence having a similar object of security, is under the controul of the Court of Session, by whom, any improper and oppressive use of it will be restrained. In the same way, the arrestment in security is under the controul of the court by which it is issued, whether the inferior court, or the Court of Session. In a commercial country, this embargo upon a man's floating capital, his goods and his money, may be attended with the worst effects upon his credit: it may stop the whole circle of his transactions—interrupt the supplies on which he may have depended for paying his bills—and, in a thousand ways, lead to very unpleasant consequences. There are two remedies:—One is, that this kind of arrestment shall be taken off altogether, if there be no good ground of alarm; and the other, that, in all cases, it may be loosed upon bail.

1. If the debt be future, and no change have taken place in the situation of the debtor, after the time of entering into the contract on which the diligence is taken out—no possibility of alleging that he is vergens ad inopiam—no diligence proceeding against him by other creditors; the Court will take off the arrestment, without caution or consignation. When a contract is entered into, or an obligation granted, it is to be presumed, that the creditor demands

all the security which he deems necessary, and receives all that it may be convenient for the debtor to give; beyond which, he would not have consented to go. To force the debtor thus, by the operation of an arrestment, to find bail or caution, or to lock up his property, while yet the debt is not due, is a breach of the contract; an alteration of the terms on which the parties have settled; an occasion of great interruption and confusion to the debtor, to which no court ought to subject him; and from which, unless his credit shall have become worse, he is entitled to relief. The same reasoning applies to contingent debts. Even in those claims, which, ex hypothesi of the arrester, are due, but which, not being liquidated, require an action to establish them, the arrestment will be loosed, unless the condition of the alleged debtor be suspicious: for, on the one hand, it is not yet proved that there is a debt existing, upon which the funds of the defendant ought to be arrested, and his transactions interrupted; and, on the other, the creditor, by not taking a document in such a form as could admit of summary diligence, may justly be held to acknowledge that he did not look for such premature security, unless his debtor's credit should appear to be failing. Another argument should have some weight in this matter. It is a privilege of the Court of Admiralty, in all maritime causes, to arrest the property of the defendant, till caution shall be given judicio sisti et judicatum solvi, that is, not only that the defendant shall appear, but that he shall pay whatever shall be adjudged against him. If arrestment on the dependance were to be allowed in all cases, looseable only upon caution, no pursuer could want this privilege, of making the person, against whom he claimed, find caution for his full debt. It is a more precise and effectual ground of relief against arrestment in security, that the arrester is already secured, either in consequence of other diligence, as inhibition, adjudication in security, &c. or by caution, or by rights of lien or compensation.

2. But where the arrestment is legally used, and such as cannot be removed on the ground of oppression, the debtor is entitled to relief, on finding bail for the value of the property arrested; or, if that exceed the arrester's debt, to the extent of that debt. But

this

this privilege is given, only where the arrestment is in security, or on the dependance, not where it is in execution.

Arrestment is loosed, by applying to the Court of Session for letters of loosing arrestment. The application is by bill, along with which the caution is specified. It is the business of the clerk of the bills to be satisfied of the sufficiency of the bail: 1617, c. 17.—the Lords modifying, *ex arbitrio*, the sum for which caution is to be given, where the debt is not liquid: 4th July 1739, Heriot, *Kilk.* 37. When the caution is received, and the bond recorded, warrant is given for the letters of loosing arrestment. They are issued from the signet, and contain authority to messengers at arms to loose the arrestment; which is done, by leaving with the arrestee a notice in writing to that effect, specifying the authority under which the messenger acts, and by intimating to the arrester, in writing, that the arrestment is loosed.

Mr Erskine holds the goods or debt to be still subject to forthcoming, if in the arrestee's hands when the arrester obtains his decree: III. Ersk. vi. 13. For this he quotes a decision, which proceeded on the ground, 'that the caution found in loosing arrestments, is overlie and insufficient:' 7th February 1665, Grahame, I. Stair, 265. But, on comparing the obligation on the clerk who receives the security, as then, and as now established, (21st June 1626, L. Balmerino, Durie 204.; IV. Stair, Inst. iii. 10.; M'Kenzie, Obs. Ja. VI. P. 22. c. 17), and recollecting the hardships arising, in a commercial country, from the stopping of goods, and interrupting of contracts, there seems to be room for doubting of this doctrine. The arrestee must be called in the action of forthcoming brought against the cautioner, the cautioner being liable no further than to the extent of the sum due by the arrestee: Durie, 204. 267.: but the cautioner is not entitled to the *beneficium discussionis*: Ib.

II. The second material distinction, between an arrestment in execution, and an arrestment in security, is, that the former prescribes in five years from its date; the latter, in five years from

 the

the date of the decree of constitution, or from the term of payment of the debt, if used upon a future debt: 1669, c. 9.

III. The third material distinction relates to the effect of the diligence. A creditor, arresting in execution upon a pure debt, is entitled to rank, in competition with other creditors, for his whole debt, and to draw the whole, or whatever dividend may belong to him, instantly: A creditor, in a future debt, can rank only for the balance, after deducting the interest to the term of payment: And a contingent creditor is entitled only to security, not to payment; to consignation of the dividend, which shall, upon just principles, be found to belong to his claim; or to caution, that it shall be paid on the existence of the condition.

SECTION II.

COMMENTARY ON THE LAWS ESTABLISHING EQUALITY AMONG CREDITORS DOING DILIGENCE AGAINST THE PERSONAL OR MOVEABLE ESTATE.

To one who considers the strange and unjust consequences of permitting priority in execution to bestow preference, and that, till within these forty years, the law of Scotland knew no check upon this rule, so far as the moveable or personal property was concerned, it will scarcely appear surprising, that foreigners should have imbibed a strong prejudice against our law. Till the memorable year 1772, not only was each creditor entitled to proceed with his diligence, regardless of his fellows, and to claim the reward of his alertness, by ranking before all who were later in execution than he; but, unfortunately, those laws which had been made in the last century, for repressing fraud, extinguished all possibility of relief against these evils. Before the law of a country has publicly acknowledged the principle of communion among the creditors, and provided rules for enforcing it against those individuals who would selfishly scramble for their own advantage, an honest debtor, or, who feels himself to be insolvent, will anticipate the execution of interested individuals, by conveying his funds to a trustee, for the general benefit. But, unfortunately, this could not be done in Scotland. By the second branch of the statute of 1621, a creditor, who had taken the first step of his diligence, could interrupt and prevent such a trust-conveyance, though to the general behoof; and, by the statute of 1696, c. 5, any creditor might, by rendering the debtor bankrupt, destroy such a conveyance, so far as it could prevent individuals from acquiring preferences by legal execution. The effect of these statutes completed the injustice of the old maxim, thought to be so peculiarly appropriated to the law of diligence—Vigilantibus non dormientibus jura subveniunt.

While matters continued in this barbarous state, the opportunities of fraud and collusion between debtors and their favourite creditors, were numerous, and the execution of their schemes scarcely to be prevented. But there were other consequences, which must have been felt severely. The slightest rumour against the credit of a debtor, must have been productive of a torrent of diligence, dangerous even to the most solvent merchant. There was no time for inquiry or accommodation; but each creditor, alarmed with the thoughts of exclusion, rushed desperately on to execution. It is a curious fact, which I have frequently heard mentioned by those who were engaged in business prior to the 1772, that, on the eve of an insolvency, every person who could be procured was busied in the offices of well employed writers, day and night, completing warrants of poinding and arrestment upon all the debts which could admit of it; that they might be all executed at one moment, so as to secure an equality, and prevent the selfish operations of creditors, who were disposed to act against the common interest. How precarious must, then, the condition of a trader have been! How distressing that of a well-disposed and liberal creditor! How sore the oppression upon commercial exertion! How strong the obstacles against strangers wishing to connect themselves with the merchants or manufacturers of Scotland!

In

In 1754, an attempt was made by the Court of Session to remedy the most prominent of these evils. An act of sederunt was made, in which, after explaining the motives of their interposition, the Judges laid down certain rules, by way of experiment, for securing equality among the creditors of bankrupts doing diligence against the moveable estate. 'The Lords, &c. considering,' says this act, 'the manifest abuses committed in poinding, &c. and the 'great injustice done to the creditors of notour bankrupts, by the 'preference given to arrestments and poindings, according to their 'dates; that, by such arrestments and poindings, the moveable 'and personal estate of the bankrupt comes to be carried off by the 'favourite creditors of such bankrupt, and by those creditors who 'first come to the knowledge of the circumstances of the bankrupt, 'before his other creditors who live at a distance, and who are 'not favoured by the bankrupt, can have any knowledge of the 'circumstances, or can discover his effects:' Therefore, they declare, 1. That all arrestments of a bankrupt's effects, within sixty days before his bankruptcy, or within four months after, shall be preferable pari passu, as if one arrestment: 2dly, That second arrestments shall be granted summarily upon a dependance, and even upon unliquidated debts: 3dly, That all poindings within sixty days before, or four months after bankruptcy, shall also be preferred pari passu: 4thly, That to give room for the benefit of this pari passu preference, all arrestments and poindings shall be registered in the Sheriff-clerk books of the bankrupt's residence within twenty days; and, if there be no post-office in either the shire where the diligence was executed, or in that where the debtor resides, or where the course of post between them is more than six days, the registration within twenty days in the shire of Edinburgh, shall be sufficient, arrestments being held as of the date of the registration: And, 5thly, That the first poinder, or arrester, shall be entitled to deduction of the expence. 10th August 1754.

Unfortunately, the Court had their eyes open to too many defects, and wished, in this act of sederunt, to remedy them all. The consequence was, that, in practice, some part of it seems to have failed. In particular, merchants still complained of the ac-

cumulation

cumulation of diligences, which this act tended not much to diminish, and, when the act expired, (for it was enacted only for four years), it was not renewed. Thus, matters returned to their old footing. For fourteen years, the nation continued to struggle with this unimproved and unjust state of the law; till at last, in 1772, a remedy was introduced, by the sequestration law. This law did much to put a stop to the evils of preference by individual diligence, and to the accumulation of proceedings, which was thought the greatest defect in the act of sederunt. It applied to every debtor, whether a trader or not. It was a form of general attachment, vesting the estate in the hands of the Court of Session, to be delegated by them to a factor chosen by the creditors for managing the common fund, and for having it divided among all the creditors. Not only did the sequestration act as a general attachment, superseding all individual diligences, but it was declared, that no individual, arresting or poinding thirty days before, should have any preference. The defects of this system, were strongly founded upon, in 1783, as reasons for abandoning the plan altogether; and the sequestration law had nearly shared the fate of the act of sederunt of 1752: but, strong representations of the evils of the old law, in mercantile cases, led to the re-enactment of the sequestration law, in mercantile bankruptcies; while a remedy was provided for other cases, upon a plan somewhat similar to that of the act of sederunt of 1754.

By the statute of 1783, it was declared, that all arrestments, within thirty days before, or four months after, bankruptcy, should be ranked pari passu; and that no poinding within the same period, should give any preference; all creditors, having liquid grounds of debt, or decrees, and summoning the poinders within the four months, being entitled to have their proportion, after deducting the expence of the poinding. The statute of 1793 makes only this alteration on the rule, that, instead of thirty days before bankruptcy, the period shall be sixty days; and the poinder shall have, besides his expence, a preference of 10 per cent. on the price of the poinded goods.

In

In commenting upon this law, it is necessary to take notice of a question of considerable importance, which has of late years been moved, respecting the rights of future and contingent creditors. It has been doubted, whether, at common law, such credi-ditors, arresting in security, can, in a competition, stand against those who have arrested upon decrees in execution. If they cannot, they are utterly excluded from the benefit of this law of pari passu preference; a consequence so unjust and inexpedient, that it is not easily to be admitted. That arrestment in execution is competent, on future and contingent debts, none have ever pretended to deny. It is only their effect in competition, which has been thought questionable. This doubt has received support from Mr Erskine's authority, (III. Ersk. vi. 18.), and has been thought to be sanctioned by the law of England, which, even at present, excludes contingent debts, and did, till the 7th Geo. I, exclude also future debts from the commission of bankruptcy. But Mr Erskine seems not to have sufficiently attended to the effect of insolvency; and the English law proceeds upon a peculiarity unknown to ours.

There is no express law nor decision in Scotland, which can thus condemn the future or contingent creditor to the hardship of utter exclusion. The question is therefore open to discussion, on principle; and, not only does equity dictate, that these classes of creditors should not be excluded, but, both in the civil law, on which so much of our common law is founded, and in the laws of all those countries which have followed the Roman jurisprudence, their right to be included is well established.

1. In a question which does not presuppose insolvency, neither the future, nor the contingent creditor, can prevent a creditor in a pure debt, from recovering payment;—so far the rule, of preferring a creditor having 'parata executio,' is well founded. But, where the debtor is insolvent, the competition assumes the nature of a general distribution, from which, if any be excluded, he is for ever deprived of his debt. If Mr Erskine's opinion could be supposed applicable only to the former case, it would be unobjectionable—if extended to the latter, it is pregnant with injustice, as exclud-

ing

ing even the holders of bills at short dates. But an arrestment in security, presupposes insolvency, since that alone can justify it. If the law mean any thing, therefore, in providing for the security of future and contingent creditors in such a case, it must follow up the provision, by protecting the arrestment against the other creditors.

2. In Rome, not only was an arrestment competent upon a future and contingent debt, (Voet, lib. ii. tit. iv. § 20), but it was also established, that, in the distribution, a future creditor was entitled to a share, proportioned to his debt, after the proper discount; and a contingent creditor, to security for payment, when his obligation should be purified *.

3. This law was followed in Holland, as Voet informs us; and in France, where an enlightened system of jurisprudence was established on the foundation of the Roman code, the rule was similar. The principle is well explained by M. Pothier. Of future debts, he says, 'Le terme accordé par le creancier au debiteur, est 'censé avoir pour fondement la confiance en sa solvabilité; lors 'donc que ce fondement vient à manquer l'effet du terme cesse. 'De là il suit, que lorsque le debiteur a fait faillite, & que le prix 'de ses biens est distribué entre les creanciers, le creancier peut 'toucher, quoique le terme de sa dette ne soit pas expiré.' Traité des Oblig. vol. 1. p. 99.—Of contingent debts, he speaks thus: 'Quoique le creancier conditionel n'ait encore aucune droit avant 'l'accomplissement de la condition, neanmoins il est reçu à faire 'tous les actes conservatoires du droit qu'il espere avoir une jour.' Ib.

* Si debitoris obæratí bona, curatore dato, auctione publica intervenientibus hastæ solennibus distractæ fuerint, etiam creditori in diem vel sub conditione liberum est suum debitum profiteri, et de protopraxia cum cæteris ejusdem debitoris creditoribus disputare, ut, si debitum in diem certum sit, illud ipse suo ordine recipiat, deducto inde repræsentationis seu præsentis solutionis emolumento, in quantum juxta jura vulgata plus accipit qui statim, quam qui post tempus accipit; sin conditionale sit, ei suum jus prælationis aut concursus cum cæteris creditoribus assignetur, executionem habiturum, cum conditio debiti extiterit, adversus eos, qui ex puro debito, sed debiliori jure munito, suum reciperunt sub cautione de reddendo, si qui emerserint potiora jura habentes. Voet, lib. v. tit. i. § 28.

Ib. p. 95.—By the French law, as by the Roman, the future creditor is allowed a share proportioned to his debt, after the proper discount; the contingent creditor is entitled to security for payment of the share accruing to him, should the condition be purified *.

4. The law of England has not acknowledged these principles. There is not in England, at common law, as with us and the other nations who have followed the Roman jurisprudence, any legal provisions for intermediate security, during the dependence of an action, or prior to the term of payment. The writ of execution follows the judgement, and therefore must abide the emergence of 'a cause of action,' which may found the judgement. This peculiarity has been fatal to the claims of future and contingent creditors at common law. When the statute execution of a commission of bankruptcy was introduced, it was intended to come in place of the ordinary execution; and therefore could not, without an express declaration, be held to include creditors, who, at common law, were entitled to no judicial interference in their favour. See Caldwell *v.* Clutterbuck, II. Strange, 867.; Tailor *v.* Mills, Cowp. 525. It sometimes happens, that a general admiration of the great system of English law, operates so strongly with the best intentioned men, as to prevent them from distinguishing, in particular cases, whether the rule, which they admire, proceeds from a peculiarity in the system, or is a point of the mercantile law, fixed by the decisions of Juries of merchants, with the assistance of enlightened Judges. Perhaps something of this kind has happened in the case we are now discussing. But let any one read the preamble of the ſtatute 7. Geo. I. c. 31. and observe how inconsistent the peculiarity of the English common law, with respect to future debts, was found to be with the best interests of commerce, and the

* Lorsque le debiteur a fait faillite, et que le prix de ses biens est distribué entre les creanciers, le creancier (quand un terme a eté accordé) peut toucher, quoique le terme de sa dette ne soit pas expiré. C'est encore une difference entre le terme & la condition · car le creancier conditionel, en ce cas, n'a pas droit de toucher, mais seulement d'obliger les autres creanciers, qui toucheront, à s'obliger de rapporter à son profit, si par la suit la condition existe. Pothier, vol. 1. p. 99.

the plainest principles of mercantile jurisprudence; and he will learn to trust less to such analogies, and to be more reconciled to the general spirit of our own common law.

From this deduction, it seems to be no rash conclusion, that, under an arrestment in security, a future creditor is entitled to rank for his debt after the proper discount, and a contingent creditor to insist either for consignation of his legal proportion, or at least for security that his share shall be paid, on the condition being purified. Mr Erskine has said, 'An arrestment, whether on a dependence, or on a decree, or whether laid on for debts not yet due, or for debts already due, are all of the same kind, and lay an equal foundation for the arrester's preference:' III. Ersk. vi. 18. Had he stopped here, he would have delivered what seems to be the true doctrine of the Scotish law. In adding the qualification, that, at the time of the competition, such arrestment cannot stand against an arrester having 'parata executio,' unless the term have arrived, or the condition been fulfilled, he seems to have spoken loosely, and without sufficiently attending to the effect of insolvency.

In proceeding to explain the rules established by the statute, we shall first consider the measures which ought to be pursued, in order to stop any threatened preference. For the due attainment of this object, two things seem to be necessary. In the FIRST place, that the diligence, by which such preference can be acquired, should be made so public, as to put the other creditors upon their guard, and give them an opportunity of taking measures for establishing an equality: and, SECONDLY, That when the diligence does come to their knowledge, they shall be furnished with means of preventing the intended preference, easily, and at little expence.

In the first of these views, there is a marked distinction between the rule now established, and that which was framed by the Court of Session in 1754. Where an arrestment, or poinding, proceeds upon a warrant from the Court of Session, passing under the signet, it may, indeed, by extreme-diligence of inquiry, be discovered in the signet rolls; but, even this may be attended with some difficulty, as only the surname is set down. Where they proceed upon the precept of an inferior court, they never can be traced, or open to observation; at least, so it must be with arrestments; though, now, all poindings being ordered, by the bankrupt law of 1793, to be reported to the Sheriff, they may be traced perhaps in this way. To remedy this secrecy of diligence, we have seen, that, by act of sederunt 1754, a record was ordered to be kept in the sheriffdom where the debtor lived; and, in it, all diligences, by arrestment or poinding, were required to be inserted within twenty days, under the penalty of being held, if not recorded till after expiry of that term, as of the date of their recording, not of their execution. By keeping their eye upon this record, creditors could at once discover, what proceedings were going on against their debtor. But this plan has not been adopted by the Legislature; perhaps from a dread, lest a record of this kind might occasion much distress, and expose the most solvent men to the attacks of alarmed creditors. Whatever the reason may have been, creditors are left, under the statute, to judge of their debtor's credit, from other circumstances than a record of diligence.

In order to prevent the diligence of an individual from bestowing a preference, two things are necessary, under this law. 1. The debtor is to be rendered bankrupt; for it is the circumstance of his bankruptcy, that brings matters to a level. Where a number of creditors concur in the wish to prevent preferences, there can be no difficulty in rendering the debtor bankrupt, provided he be insolvent. If there be no insolvency, the equalizing law has no application; but each creditor is left to his individual exertion, for procuring payment. The bankruptcy must follow within sixty days of the using of the diligence, the effect of which it is intended to prevent. The exprssions of the statute are, 'That all arrestments, which shall have been USED for attaching, &c. within 'sixty days prior to bankruptcy, &c. shall be ranked pari passu:' —and, 'That no poinding of the moveables belonging to the 'bankrupt,

'bankrupt, USED within sixty days before the bankruptcy,' shall give a preference to such poinder: c. 74. By the expression, 'USED,' in these two passages, I apprehend (though I do not know that it has been so decided) that the delivery of the execution of arrestment to the arrestee, in the one case, and, in the other, the adjudication by the messenger, and the leaving of the schedule of poinding in the hands of the debtor, is to be understood; and that, calculating backwards from the date of the bankruptcy, all arrestments, which shall not have been completed by the delivery of the arrestment to the debtor, and all poindings, in which the messenger shall not have made the adjudication prior to the commencement of the sixtieth day, shall be subject to the law. There can be no difficulty in ascertaining these dates; for the executions of the messengers express them; and, in computing the term, the same rules will be applicable, as in the reduction of voluntary conveyances under the statute 1696, c. 5.* 2. But it is not enough, that the debtor be rendered bankrupt. The other creditors must either proceed to apply for a sequestration, (where that can be done), or they must, within four months after the bankruptcy, use such diligence as the law entitles to a communication with that already used. If the creditor, whose preference they wish to prevent, has used an arrestment, all those who mean to take the benefit of the law, must, if their debts be established by voucher, apply for letters of arrestment; and, if their claims are still unvouched, they must bring an action, and take out letters of arrestment on the dependence, (which are granted of course, upon production of the libelled summons), and afterwards proceed, without undue delay, to have their debts liquidated. If a poinding have been begun, the other creditors must take care to have their debts liquidated by voucher, or by decree, and, within four months, summon the poinder.

There is one peculiarity in the pari passu preference of poindings, of which it is proper here to take notice. It has been thought reasonable, that the poinding creditor, who, in consequence of this statute, shall be called upon to communicate to others, part of

* See above, p. 191.

of what he has received, should be allowed some consideration for the hardship of being obliged to make restitution. This allowance has been fixed by the statute, at ten per cent. on the price or apprized value of the poinded goods, to be applied in payment of the poinder's debt, preferably to the other creditors, besides payment of the expence of the diligence.

It seems scarcely necessary to observe, that the statute has left all diligence against moveables, by poinding and arrestment, not used till after four months have expired from the date of the bankruptcy, to 'rank with one another, according to the former law 'and practice:' § 3. & 6.

SECTION III.

OF DILIGENCE AGAINST MOVEABLES, AFTER THE DEBTOR'S DEATH, AND OF THE LAWS ESTABLISHING AN EQUALITY AMONG THE CREDITORS OF DECEASED DEBTORS.

BEFORE explaining the methods, by which the creditors of deceased debtors can prevent undue preferences from being acquired by priority of diligence, it will be necessary (more perhaps than with respect to diligence during life) to show the general course and nature of the proceedings, by which debts are recovered after the death of the debtor.

§ 1.

§ 1. OF DILIGENCE BY AN INDIVIDUAL CREDITOR, AGAINST MOVEABLES, AFTER DEATH, CONSIDERED INDEPENDENTLY OF COMPETITION.

In England, the estate of the deceased is, in the person of the executor, liable to direct execution for the testator's debts. 1. If an action have been begun against the testator, and he die in the course of it, it is transferred against the executor, by a writ called SCIRE FACIAS; and the judgement proceeding against him, goes to execution, as if he were the original party: 2. If the defendant die after judgement, the judgement is revived against the executor, by a writ of scire facias in the court in which the judgement is entered up: and, 3. If fieri facias be actually taken out against the testator, before his death, it is effectual, and may, without any revival, be put to execution against the executor: (Farrer v. Brooks, II. Crom. 105.) The Sheriff, in all these cases, may proceed to execution against the goods in the hands of the executor, as if still in the hands of the original party: (I. Sellon, Pr. of King's Bench and Common Pleas, 528. & II. 190—196.) But, against the estate and effects of the executor himself, the creditors of the testator can have no execution; for, there is not in England, as in Scotland, a passive representation. It is necessary, before it be possible to subject the executor's own estate, that he shall be proved to have wasted the executry funds; which is done, either under a writ of inquiry, called a DEVASTAVIT, or by bringing an action of debt against the executor, upon the judgement obtained during the testator's life, and suggesting, in that action, a devastavit. Upon the waste being proved, judgement proceeds against the executor, de bonis propriis: II. Sellon, 198—9. If none of the testator's kindred will take out the administration, a creditor may, by custom, do it, in order to procure his payment: III. Blackst. 505.

In Scotland, the law is, in some of the above points, nearly similar. Thus, if the defender in an action die during its dependance, it may be transferred against his representatives, so as to give the decree the same effect against them, as if they had been the original parties.

parties. Again, if no person will enter to the succession, a creditor is allowed to do so. But the Scotish law differs essentially in all the other points: For, in place of regarding (as the English law seems to do) the effects as a part of the ancestor's estate untransferred, and lying ready for execution, while the executor himself is not to be touched; the Scotish law considers the effects as belonging to the executor; as forming one common mass with his original property; and, of course, as exposed to execution only through his person; while he himself is personally regarded as the debtor in the debts of the testator, as representing him by a passive obligation, which the English law does not acknowledge. It follows from this, 1. That a judgement against the debtor can authorise no execution against his executor; but a new action must be raised, to fix the debt personally upon the executor as representative, and so liable for the debt. 2. A poinding expires, if not completely executed before the debtor's death: (20th June 1765, Earl of Morton, IV. Fac. Coll. ix. 212,—215). And, 3dly, A warrant for arrestment falls by the debtor's death; although, if executed before it, the action of forthcoming may be brought against the heir: 21st Dec. 1738, Earl of Aberdeen; Clerk Home, cx. 176.; Kilk. 35.

To explain these points of the Scotish institutions more particularly, something must be premised of the general course of the proceedings, by which moveable succession is vested.

Upon death, the moveable estate, or executry, falls under the jurisdiction of the Commissary Court, the successor of the Bishops, or Consistorial Court. In this court, the title of any one claiming the office of executor is examined; a preference, according to established rules, given to the person whom law deems to have the best right to it; and, after the choice is fixed by a decree (which, however, is unnecessary, where an executor has been named by testament), the right to the administration of the estate is completed by a sentence, authorising the executor to sue for, possess, and administer the whole, for the behoof of all concerned. This is called a CONFIRMATION. Now, there are two situations, in which the succession may stand; Either the next of kin, or the executor

named

named by the deceased, may have completed his titles, and assumed the administration: Or, 2dly, the administration may remain untaken up. And, for the use of a creditor desiring execution in either of these two situations, there are different remedies.

1. An executor nominate, or dative, is, when confirmed, a trustee for the heirs, legatees, and creditors of the deceased. His confirmation proceeds upon an inventory lodged by him, of the executry; and, for the faithful administration of which, he gives security. In proceeding against the executor, a creditor is not entitled, as in England by the scire facias, to revive his warrant of execution; but he must raise an action against the executor for payment of the debt. It would appear, that, formerly, a decree obtained in such action, was regarded as of somewhat of the nature of a decree of forthcoming upon an arrestment, and held to bestow a preference, not only from the date of the decree, but even from the date of the citation in the action: (July 1723, Gray against Callendar, I. Dict. 207.) And although the idea of allowing this effect to a decree against an executor, was so far given up, that the preference was not held to begin with the date of the citation (15th Feb. 1738, Græme, I. Dict. 207.—19th Feb. 1742, M'Dowal—and 21st July 1742, Johnston, Kilk. 176.); still the decree was long understood to give a preference. But it is now settled, (by the case of Russel against Simes in 1791), that while the fund continues undistributed in the hands of the executor, a decree in favour of one creditor, gives no preference over others, provided they have interpelled the executor from payment by a summons. Should the executor himself happen to be a creditor, the confirmation is held to be to him a diligence for the recovery of his debt. As an action and judgement against himself were absurd, he is entitled to pay himself by retention, (19th Dec. 1740, Lord Napier, Kilk. 172.—21st Dec. 1744, Kilk. 175.); and this even to the effect of securing him in relief of engagements undertaken for the deceased.

In order to understand clearly the nature of the diligence, by which the creditors are to make their rights complete, it is necessary to observe the situation in which the funds may be placed under

der the management of the executor as trustee.—1. The funds may be untouched by the executor. No diligence done by his own creditors, can be preferable to the creditors of the defunct over these funds; for he is trustee merely: and if he should be dilatory in realizing the fund, and paying it, the creditors may proceed to diligence, by arrestment and poinding, against the fund, and by personal execution against the executor. 2. If he have obtained bonds from the debtors of the deceased in his own name, no assignation granted by him, of these bonds, can be effectual to his own creditors, against the creditors of the deceased challenging; though, if bills be granted to him and indorsed, they will be good against the indorsees. No diligence by creditors, to whom the bonds, &c. may be assigned, will establish a preference over the executry creditors: 16th Dec. 1674, Kilhead.—II. Stair, Dec. 293.—III. Stair, Inst. viii. 71. 3. If he should have received payment of the executry fund, he may be forced, by diligence against his own estate or person, to pay it to the executry creditors; and, on his failure, recourse may be had against the cautioner in the confirmation.

Such is the law of diligence against an executor, for the fund given up in the inventory. But there may be subjects omitted in that inventory; or, those which are included in it, may be valued too low. For this, there are too remedies: Either the creditor may bring an action against the executor, for the value of the subject omitted, if the intromission with it can be proved (24th July 1639, Inglis); or, he may apply to the Commissary, to be himself appointed 'executor ad omissa vel male appretiata.' To this application, the executor must be made a party; and, generally, the only effect of it is, to make the omitted effects be added to the confirmation, so as to form a part of the fund.

2. If there be no executor confirmed, a creditor of the deceased may apply to be appointed executor, to the effect of administering to so much of the property, as may be sufficient for paying off his debt: (Act of Sed. 14th Nov. 1679.) This diligence is completed by the confirmation; for the decree dative, which precedes the confirmation, and finds the creditor entitled to the office, has no effect

in

in vesting any real right in the creditors: 23d Jan. 1745, Carmichael, I. Falc. 50. The confirmation vests the real right in the creditors, and forms the criterion of competition. In Cust against Garbet & Co., 8th March 1775, an assignation was intimated between eight and nine in the morning, of 30th October, the confirmation being dated on that day. The Court, 'in respect it appeared, from the instrument of intimation produced, that the same 'was made to the acting partner and manager, at the Carron 'Co.'s office, between the hours of eight and nine in the morning, 'of 30th October 1771; and that it is not denied, that the hour of 'cause, in the Commissary Court, is not till eleven o'clock in the 'forenoon; Found, that the assignation, in favour of the said Benjamin Cust, was completed by the said intimation, before any step 'was or could be taken upon the edict, in the confirmation in favour of Garbet & Co.; and therefore preferred Cust for his interest produced:' 8th March 1775.

3. It is competent to apply for confirmation as executor creditor, only where the debt is liquidated; where it is not, another course is necessary. By 1695, c. 41. it is provided, 'That in the 'case of any depending cause or claim against a defunct, the time 'of his decease, it shall be leisom to the pursuer of the said cause 'or claim, to charge the defunct's nearest of kin to confirm executor to him, within twenty days after the charge given; which 'charge, so execute, shall be a passive title against the person 'charged, as if he were a vitious intromitter, unless he renounce; 'and then the charger may proceed to have his debts constituted, 'and the hæreditas jacens of moveables declared liable by a decree 'cognitionis causa; upon the obtaining whereof, he may be decerned executor dative to the defunct, and so affect his moveables 'in the common form.'

4. Where the funds are to be affected, not by a creditor of the ancestor, but by a creditor of the executor himself, the above quoted statute provides, 'That the creditors of the nearest of kin 'may either require the procurator-fiscal to confirm and assign to 'them, under the peril and pain of his being liable for the debt if

'he refuse; or they may obtain themselves decerned executors da-'tive to the defunct, as if they were creditors to him; with this 'provision always, that the creditors of the defunct, doing diligence 'to affect the said moveable estate, within year and day of the 'debtor's decease, shall always be preferred to the diligence of the 'said nearest of kin.' 1695, c. 41.

§ 2. COMMENTARY ON THE ACT OF SEDERUNT, 28. February 1662, BY WHICH A PARI PASSU PREFERENCE IS ESTABLISHED IN DILIGENCE AGAINST THE MOVEABLE ESTATE OF DECEASED DEBTORS.

The rule of the common law, which bestows preference upon priority in execution, produced, among creditors doing execution after the death of the debtor, consequences as unjust as those which were so grievous in the common case. The remedy provided against them, so far differs from that which is directed against the inequalities of diligence during the debtor's life, that the latter has a reference to the debtor's bankruptcy, the former a reference to his death.

The death of a debtor is an event, which naturally calls upon his creditors to apply for payment of their claims. If priority of demand entitle the creditor to priority or preference in payment, the little opportunity which creditors, especially those at a distance, may have, of knowing that their debtor is dead, gives to his friends, and those connected with him, or living near him, a most unjust advantage over others. But, when this situation is duly considered, it will be found unjust and illegal, even at common law, for an executor to pay to the first claimants, without regard to the number who are behind, or the adequacy of the fund. An executor enters upon the administration, according to an inventory; and is entitled to no other character, in regard to the creditors, but that of a trustee, bound to recover the fund, and to distribute it fairly. But, so far had these principles been forgotten, or overlooked, in the old law, that an executor was thought entitled to pay, without hesitation or inquiry, the debt of any creditor who

had

had obtained decree against him in that character. A similar injustice was practised, in the granting of confirmations to creditors; though these are evidently encroachments upon the office of trustee for the general behoof, and ought never to have been granted, without such intimation being given to all concerned, as might have enabled them to take measures for their safety. To correct these evils, a law was enacted by the Commissioners of Cromwell, in which it was provided, 'That, hereafter, there be 'no executor creditors decerned and confirmed to any defunct, 'until half a year be passed after the defunct's decease; and that 'no decree for payment be extracted against any executor, for six 'months after the defunct's death; and that all creditors, who 'shall use diligence against the executor, within the said six 'months, shall come in pari passu with others, that have decrees 'ready to extract:' 1654, c. 16. & 18.—These laws expired with the Commonwealth; but their justice was strongly impressed on the minds of the nation: and, as points of common law, which required only to be declared and regulated, they were re-enacted, by the act of sederunt of the Court of Session, 28th February 1662. This act declares, 'That all creditors of defunct persons, using 'legal diligence at any time within half a year of the defunct's 'death, by citation of the executors and intromitters with the de'funct's goods, or by obtaining themselves decerned and confirm'ed executor creditors, or by citing of any other executor credi'tors confirmed, the said creditors using any such diligence before 'the expiry of half a year, as said is, shall come in pari passu 'with any other creditors who have used more timely diligence, 'by obtaining themselves decerned and confirmed executor cre'ditors, or otherwise:'—and 'the creditors using posterior dili'gence, shall bear a proportional part of the charges waired out 'by the executor creditor first decerned and confirmed, before he 'have any benefit of the inventory confirmed; and that it shall 'be lawful to the said creditor, to obtain himself joined to the said 'office of executry.'

Thus, as there is a pari passu preference established, for all adjudications within year and day of the first effectual, so, under

this

this act of sederunt, there is a pari passu preference established, of all claims against the executry of a deceased debtor, legally notified, by citation, within six months after death. But there is one marked distinction between these two rules of pari passu preference.—that which is established for adjudications, is absolute, and exclusive of all creditors who have not obtained decree within year and day;—that which is provided for claims upon executry, is not exclusive, but leaves room for creditors to apply after the appointed term is expired, and to obtain a share of the fund, if still undivided. This distinction arises, from the very constitution of the two rules. The one is a statutory rule; and the point from which the term runs, is intimated to the public by the record: the other is a rule of justice merely; moulded into shape by the old law of Cromwell, and by the act of sederunt of the Court of Session; and intended only to secure, at all events, a delay of the division, long enough to allow creditors to make their claims, but unarmed with any penal consequence, should the funds, by accident, remain undivided, after the elapse of the appointed term.

I shall restrict what I have to say, by way of commentary on this act of sederunt, to three points.

1. On the supposition of diligence, by poinding or arrestment, having been begun against the debtor during his life; How are his other creditors to proceed after death, in order to prevent the effect of these diligences?

If the debtor had been rendered bankrupt during his life, the matter does not seem to be attended with much difficulty. The statute, producing the pari passu preference of arrestments and poindings, provides, that every creditor, having liquidated grounds of debt, or a decree for payment, and summoning the poinder within four months from the date of the bankruptcy, is entitled to a proportional share; and that all arrestments, used for attaching the effects, within the four months, are entitled to be ranked pari passu, as if one arrestment had been used for them all. Now, it seems to follow, 1. That where the creditor has a liquid document,

ment, or a decree against the deceased debtor, he has a right, notwithstanding the debtor's death, to summon the poinder to communicate the benefit of his diligence. It is not clear, whether this can be done without citing the executor: but there seems to be some reason for concluding that it may; since the poinded property is not part of the executry. It is transferred to the poinder; and a creditor who claims, under the above law, a communication of the benefit, claims it as a part of that property, which the bankruptcy has rendered common to all the creditors; which, if he do not claim, the poinder will get, undivided; and of which, at all events, the executor can draw no share. 2. Where the creditor has no written or judicial constitution of his debt, he must immediately proceed to constitute it against the executor, as representing his debtor; and he seems to be entitled, under a decree against the executor, to all the privileges of a creditor holding a liquid document against the deceased; in particular, to the same communication of diligence which such a creditor has a right to claim. The analogy of the case of Sinclair against the Earl of Caithness, respecting the pari passu preference of adjudications led before and after death, seems to establish this beyond a doubt. That, and other cases upon adjudications, would also seem to fix, that, to avoid the injustice of throwing such a creditor beyond the appointed term, his decree would be allowed to pass, reserving all objections contra executionem. 3. Where an arrestment has been used, the creditors who wish to take the benefit of the statute, must bring their action against the executor, and arrest upon the dependance. The fund arrested is clearly a part of the executry, although attached; and arrestment on the dependance of an action of constitution, against the executor, seems to be completely competent to give the creditor the benefit of the statute.

But, if the debtor have not been made bankrupt during his life, and some of his creditors have poinded or arrested, there does not appear to be any remedy, by which the other creditors can, after his death, insist for a pari passu preference; since no man can be declared a bankrupt after he is dead; and the law provides no other medium for equalizing the diligence.

2. The

2. The next case to be taken, is, where the debtor has died, while yet there has been no diligence used by his creditors; and the question is, How the creditors are to preserve their rights over the funds left by the deceased? By the act of sederunt, they are protected against distribution of the fund, till the expiry of the six months from their debtor's death; and they are, during that time, to acquire a share in the division, in the following ways: FIRST, If an executor have been confirmed, an action must be raised against him, by each creditor, or by a trustee for a number of them concurring, to save expence; and the citation, in that action, constitutes the claim, as a debt to be paid from the executry, if it shall ultimately be sustained: SECONDLY, If there be no executor confirmed—or if he have not taken up the whole executry—or if there be only a confirmation by one individual as executor-creditor; the creditor wishing to have the benefit of the law, must get himself confirmed executor-creditor; or must cite the executor-creditor within the six months. The creditors, who have taken these measures, are entitled to a share of the executry fund; a part of the expence, if there has been a confirmation as executor-creditor, being deducted from their claims.

Beyond the six months, there is no protection to creditors who have not appeared; but if the fund be not distributed, a citation, by one of the creditors, is a sufficient interpellation of payment, and fully entitles him to be included in the division.—Thus, Litster died on the 2d September 1788. On 15th January 1789, Russel, a creditor of Litster's, brought an action against his widow, who had been decerned executrix; and, on 11th March, he obtained decree in absence. Other creditors raised an action, by Simes their trustee, on 9th March 1789, but did not obtain decree till December; having been opposed by the executrix. The funds were still in medio; and the executrix raised a multiplepoinding, that the preferences might be decided, and that she might pay safely. The Judges were unanimously of opinion, that, while the funds are undivided, every creditor, who cites the executor, has a title to a share; although the six months should have expired, and although the

the other creditors should have obtained decrees within that term: Russel against Simes, 1791.

3. As to the creditors of the executor himself, they are not entitled to compete with those of the deceased, who shall have done diligence within a year from the death of the testator; but, after that period, the fund is open to both sets of creditors.

CONCLUSION OF BOOK III.

We have thus considered the provisions against the preferences of the old law, independently of any general process for the attachment and distribution of the whole estate. We have seen, that, considered as a branch of the bankrupt law, this system of provisions is exceedingly imperfect; that there still remain some possibilities of unjust preferences being acquired by individuals; but, above all, that the levelling of those preferences can be effected only by an accumulation of expence, which leads often to the inevitable ruin of the debtor, and, in cases of insolvency, consumes much of the fund of division. We shall have occasion, in the next Book, to inquire how far relief is afforded against these evils, by the processes of general distribution.

BOOK THE FOURTH.

OF THE PROCESSES BY WHICH THE FUNDS OF BANKRUPTS ARE DISTRIBUTED AMONG THE CREDITORS.

INTRODUCTION TO BOOK IV.

THE object of this Fourth Book, is to explain the legal processes which the law has appointed, for calling the creditors of a bankrupt together, converting his estate into money, and dividing it among them.

To the speculative lawyer, choosing to disregard the natural progress of human affairs, it may seem a task of no mighty difficulty, to construct a simple and effectual plan for the accomplishment of these objects. He might think himself entitled to assume, what, in a commercial age, would, no doubt, be readily granted and acknowledged, that the funds of a bankrupt are no longer his own, but the property of his creditors; and that, to avoid the expence of individual proceedings, this general right is to be, as quickly as possible, vested, by legal forms, in the creditors, or in a trustee for their behoof, so that it may be managed, disposed of, and divided as a common stock; and, upon these data, he might proceed to rear his plan. But it is not in this way that such institutions arise. It is neither to be expected, that a plan, formed upon these simple principles, should be the product of an early age; nor is it to be looked for, that, in the institutions of more improved times, a Legislature is totally to neglect, or rudely throw aside, the remedies which, in the progress of a country, have gradually suggested themselves against the evils of the old law.—We have examined, in the Third Book, the more imperfect provisions of the Scotish law against preferences by priority of diligence:

diligence: we have seen, how gradually they arose, and how, at last, they were reduced to a system, independently of any process of general division. We shall find, in the same way, that the various forms of general division arose in a gradual manner—improved in their progress—accommodated themselves to the state of the country, and the general analogy of the law—and took such root, in their connexions with other institutions, that, with all their peculiarities, it was necessary to retain them. The task of the Legislature, in these more improved times, has been rather to bring these old institutions to accord with the true principles of the bankrupt law, than to despise and totally supersede them.

In England, it is by the statutes of bankruptcy alone, that any legal provision is made for dividing the estates of insolvent debtors; and as those statutes apply only to traders, the property of the rest of the nation is left, in this respect, to the unreformed rules of the common law.

In Scotland, the process of distribution of the estate of merchants is as simple, and as effectual, as that of England; while the bankruptcies of other men are not neglected. For although our sequestration, in mercantile bankruptcy, had no existence till within these forty years, the law has, in other cases, (not satisfied with the provisions, already explained, for preventing unjust preferences), further provided processes of general distribution, by which the creditors may be called into the field of competition—the estate put under management—and the whole fund divided among those who shall prove their right to a share.

The enumeration of the forms of distribution, will point out the plan of this Book.

1. In common bankruptcies, that is to say, where the debtor is not a trader, his lands, and other heritable property, are divided in the action of RANKING AND SALE; while his moveable, or personal property, after being affected by the legal diligence of poinding,

poinding, arrestment, &c. is distributed in the actions of FORTHCOMING or MULTIPLEPOINDING.

2. In mercantile bankruptcies, the estate is attached and divided in the SEQUESTRATION—analogous with the English Commission of Bankruptcy. And,

3. In all cases, a plan of distribution, by VOLUNTARY TRUST-DEED, may be adopted; to which, there are now, comparatively, fewer obstacles than once there were, since the chance of preferences, acquired by priority of execution, is almost extinguished.

PART

PART THE FIRST.

OF THE PROCESSES BY WHICH THE PROPERTY OF A BANKRUPT IS CONVERTED INTO MONEY, AND DISTRIBUTED AMONG THE CREDITORS, INDEPENDENTLY OF SEQUESTRATION AND VOLUNTARY TRUST.

THIS subject naturally takes a twofold division—The first, comprehending the Sale and Distribution of the Heritable Estate—The second, the Distribution of the Moveables, or Personal Estate.

CHAP. I.

OF THE JUDICIAL SALE OF LANDS, AND RANKING OF THE CREDITORS UPON THE PRICE.

THE statute which introduced equality among adjudgers, left them exposed, during the term of redemption, to all the confusions of a divided possession. It was to remedy the evils of this state of things, that the action of judicial sale and ranking was introduced; by which any of the creditors, who held a real security

rity over an estate inadequate to the debts of the proprietor, was empowered to bring it to a public sale, and to have the price divided.

In entering upon the explanation of this institution, it may not be improper to state, shortly, the analogous regulations of the Roman and French laws; because, there is every reason to believe, that from them ours were borrowed. Afterwards, I shall endeavour to elucidate, as fully as I can, the views of the Legislature of Scotland, at the introduction of this process; with the history of the action down to the present day.

In the Roman law, the creditor of an insolvent debtor might, instead of adopting the ordinary execution of the judicial pledge, apply for the 'missio in possessionem,' and judicial sale. This was given by a double decree: the first of which authorised the creditor to enter into possession, or placed the estate under the management of an administrator for the general behoof: the second was pronounced after the elapse of a certain interval, and authorised the land to be publicly exposed to sale. When sold, the price was divided, by decree of the court, according to certain rules, the creditors being distributed into five classes. Dig. lib. xlii. tit. 4. & 5. *

In France, the ordinary execution for single debts, seems to have been, from the first, mingled with the general remedy calculated for a case of insolvency. The 'saisie réelle,' or attachment of lands by an individual creditor in execution of a sentence pronounced in his favour, was a proper sequestration. The lands were immediately put under the care of a commissaire, to be held and administered by him for the common benefit. It was his duty, within six months, to record, in the register of the College of Commissaires, the saisie réelle; and the creditor, in the mean while, proceeded, under the authority of a warrant from the judge, to

* Of these rules, I shall take occasion to speak hereafter, at present, I attend merely to the form of the distribution

to denounce the lands publicly for sale, both upon the ground, and at the church door at the dismissing from mass. These intimations were made at proper intervals; and, being reported to the judge, he gave authority for a public sale within forty days. During this term, offers were received by the clerk of court; and, at the day of sale, they were opened and read in court, and the highest preferred. The lands were adjudged, by decree, to belong to this highest offerer, on payment of the price: and this title was considered as, in many respects, very advantageous and secure. The price was divided by the judge, according to a scheme of ranking and division, settled upon full discussion *.

We have already marked the early and strong repugnance of our Legislature to any institution which might irretrievably deprive a landholder of his estate. We have seen, that, under the influence of this feeling, the power of redemption was first introduced into the common execution by apprizing, which originally was an absolute sale—that the consequence of this change in the nature of the apprizing, combined with other circumstances, was to annihilate the sale altogether; to reduce the effect of the apprizing, to that of a judicial mortgage, general over the whole of the debtor's lands; and to involve subsequent creditors, as well as the debtor, in great distress. Notwithstanding the anxiety shown by the Legislature, in redressing the evils which had thus arisen; first, by declaring apprizers, who should enter into possession, liable for their intromissions; afterwards, by the introduction of the pari passu preference; and, finally, by the substitution of adjudications in place of apprizings—still the diligence, thus reformed, was unfit for cases of insolvency. Instead of a creditor having it in his power, at once, to bring to sale the estate of his debtor, all that he could do, if he held a real security, by infeftment of annualrent, or infeftment in security, was, to get into possession, and draw the rents: he could, in no shape convert his redeemable into an irredeemable right. If he was merely a personal creditor, he had no resource, but to adjudge; and an adjudger could do nothing more than endeavour to get into possession, or to get a share of the rent,

* V de M. Pothier, Trait. de la Procedure Civile, p. 205. 278.

rent, and calmly wait, till the expiry of the legal term should permit him to convert his redeemable security into a right of property.

This imperfect and rude state of the law, was attended with two enormous evils. 1. Although the pari passu preference put all adjudgers within year and day, upon an equal footing, as if the first effectual adjudication had been a general diligence for the behoof of them all; yet, during the legal, however numerous the adjudgers might be, and however inadequate the estate or rents, nothing else could be done, than to have the estate sequestrated by authority of the Court, and put under the management of a factor, who should draw the rents, and pay them rateably to the creditors. It is plain, that the smallest excess of the interest above the rents occasioned thus an annual loss to the creditors; and the expence of management added considerably to the defalcation. The creditors, who were not entitled to a pari passu preference, were, in such a situation, entirely deprived of the interest of their debts during the legal. 2. But this was not all. Even after expiry of the legal, matters were not easily settled. The creditors who held real securities, were no doubt entitled, by common consent, to have the lands exposed to sale; but, to this, there were many obstacles. On the one hand, it was difficult to get them to agree; for some would naturally hope, that, by keeping the lands unsold, and tiring out the rest of the creditors, they might, perhaps, be able to pick up for trifles debts which might operate strongly to their own advantage. On the other hand, it was not to be expected, that a full price should be got for an estate, about which there were so many concerned, and to the sale of which the debtor, perhaps, might refuse his concurrence, and disturb the purchaser by after challenges.

These evils called for a Legislative remedy, but it was applied with a delicate and timorous hand. Instead of adopting, at once, the judicial sale of the Roman, or of the French law, the Legislature seemed to forget that they were providing for a case of insolvency, and still suffered their reluctance against depriving the debtor of his power of redemption, to palsy those exertions which were necessary for redressing the injustice of the law. They, indeed, allowed a creditor holding a real security over land, to bring the land to sale, before the Court of Session, without the consent of the other creditors; but, while the term for redeeming was unexpired, no such measure was competent, without the debtor's consent. The statute 1681, c. 17. which introduced the judicial sale, proceeds on this preamble: 'That when the estate and lands of 'bankrupts are affected with adjudications, comprizings, and other 'real rights, exceeding their value, it oftentimes falls out, that 'the creditors do not agree to sell the lands; whereby such as 'have small sums upon such securities, cannot command any part 'thereof, and such estates do oftentimes become ineffectual to 'many creditors.' Therefore, the Court of Session is authorised, upon a process raised at the instance of any creditor having a real right, to cognosce and try the value of such estate, where the heritor is notoriously bankrupt, and the creditors in possession of the estate; and to value the same; and to commission persons to sell it by public roup, at an upset price fixed by the Court; but not without consent of the debtor, unless the legal was expired. Rules are laid down for securing the due intimation of the roup, and citation of all the creditors; and, finally, it is declared, that the sale so made, and reported to the Court, and, by their warrant, registered in the books of Session, shall be as effectual, upon payment of the price, as if the same were made by the debtor, and all the apprizers, adjudgers, and other creditors; the price being distributable among the creditors proportionally, by the commissioner, or by the purchaser, as the creditors shall be ranked by the Court, whether the creditors have appeared or not.

Under this imperfect law, the sales of bankrupt estates were conducted for nine years only. The proof of the value of the estate, and of the amount of the debts, was taken before the Court of Session; a commissioner was named, (commonly one of the Judges), before whom the sale was conducted; the lands being exposed at the price affixed by the Court. If no purchaser offered, the pursuer of the action got the lands at the upset price. The purchaser's purchaser's title was completed by a conveyance signed by the commissioner, approved of by the Court, and by them ordered to be recorded; the concurrence of the bankrupt being also necessary, where the right of reversion was unexpired. The distribution of the price was made in an action raised by the commissioner, or by the purchaser, stating the fund in his hands, and calling upon the creditors to appear for their interests, that he might pay safely, and be discharged; and a conveyance by each creditor of his debt and diligence to the purchaser, with a warrandice binding the creditor to refund, in case of the estate being evicted, fortified the title, and closed the whole.

This may be regarded as the first stage of the remedy by judicial sale. The improvements made by the statute 1690, c. 20, form the second stage.* The Legislature ventured now to act more freely, than in the first attempt. They, in the true spirit of bankrupt law, made the reformed judicial sale a remedy competent to all real creditors, in cases of bankruptcy, without regard to any right of redemption in the debtor's person. They improved, and made more simple, the title to be offered to the purchaser; moulding it into the form

* 'Our Sovereign Lord and Lady, and the Estates of Parliament, considering, That by the 17th act, 3d Parliament, K. Charles Second, intituled, Act concerning the Sale of Bankrupts Lands: it is statute, That the Lords of Session shall commissionate persons to sell the lands and estates of bankrupts, with consent of the debitor, where there is a legal reversion competent to him, or without his consent, where there is no legal; whereby the said useful act is made ineffectual, no person being willing to dispone other mens lands, neither will the bankrupt ever consent with any such person. For remeid whereof, their Majesties, with consent of the said Estates, statute, enact, and declare, That the buyers of bankrupts estates shall have right thereto, by the decreet of sale to be pronounced by the Lords, adjudging the lands sold, to the buyer, for the price decerned; and that the buyer shall thereupon be infeft, in the same way as upon other adjudications; and that the sale may proceed so soon as it shall be found that the debitor is bankrupt, and utterly insolvent, whether the legal be expired, or not: And if no buyer be found at the rate determined by the Lords, it shall be leisume to the said Lords to divide the lands and other rights amongst the creditors, according to their several rights and diligences: And because the sale may be obstructed by donatars of liferent-escheat, the said Lords are hereby impowered to determine the price and value of the said liferent-escheats, and to sell lands for the price thereof, according as the said rights shall be found to have preference.'

form of a general and irredeemable adjudication. The purchaser's right was declared to depend upon a decree of sale to be pronounced by the Lords, adjudging to him the lands sold, and ordering that he should thereupon be infeft, in the same way as in other adjudications. Besides this, conveyances by the creditors were still to be given as a fortification of the purchaser's title. Where there were no purchasers, the Legislature, instead of allowing the lands to be given up to the pursuer of the action, ordered them to be divided among the creditors, according to their rights and diligences; a thing which was found so impracticable, that the Court of Session introduced, in practice, the obvious remedy of lowering the upset price.

Five years after the passing of this law, the Legislature, in providing against the frauds of apparent heirs, bestowed upon them the privilege of bringing to sale the estate of their predecessor, when burdened with debts; 1695, c. 24.: and this distinction was made between these sales, and sales by creditors, that the apparent heir, being the only person interested in the reversion, should be entitled to bring the action, 'whether the estate was bankrupt or 'not.'

As the law now stood, an estate might be brought to sale in two ways: 1. By a real creditor, provided it was bankrupt; and, 2. By an apparent heir, in case of the debtor's death, whether it was bankrupt or not.

But although, originally, the action was directed merely to the sale of the lands, it came gradually to be extended, so as to include in it an action also of ranking. The ranking of the creditors was originally carried on in a separate action, called an action of multiplepoinding. This action proceeded on an allegation, that the pursuer, being possessed of a fund belonging to the common debtor, was in danger of being distressed for payment of it by several competitors; and, therefore, all those having claims, were called to settle their preferences, that the pursuer might pay safely. Instead of this separate action, the practice was introduced, of includ-

ing,

ing, in the summons of sale, a conclusion for ranking the creditors on the price; with certification, that the creditors who neglected to apply, should not afterwards be suffered to challenge the sale, or the division of the price. But as the security of the purchaser greatly depended on the production of all the claims, and his assignation to them all; and as the action proceeded only in case of insolvency, it was thought necessary to adopt some method of forcing the creditors to appear; or, at least, of disburdening the estate of their debts, if they did not choose to do so. For this purpose, the best expedient which occurred to the practitioners of those days was afforded by the action of reduction-improbation. The reduction-improbation is a form of action, by which a deed that is forged and objectionable is declared null, the action proceeding upon an allegation of forgery; to remove which, the deed must be produced within an assigned term, under the penalty of the forgery being held as proved. In applying that action to the purpose of the judicial sale, the summons charged the securities, and vouchers, and diligences, of all the creditors, as false and forged; and the decree of certification operated as a complete exclusion of all who had not produced their rights. The necessity of this separate action of reduction-improbation, was taken away by act of sederunt, 17th January 1756; and it now makes a part of the combined action of ranking and sale.

The action of ranking and sale, as thus established, afforded a plain remedy to any of the creditors of an insolvent debtor, wishing to bring the estate to sale for his payment. But, hitherto, an important object was left unprovided for. No remedy was yet afforded to the debtor or the creditors, against the necessity of all the creditors proceeding with adjudications to attach the estate. Indeed, not only did the action of ranking and sale still want that character, of a general attachment for behoof of all the creditors, which could enable it to supersede the use of individual diligence; but things had taken a turn still more unfortunate. The title of the purchaser, in a judicial sale, being corroborated by an assignation to the debts of the creditors, it was necessary, in order to connect these debts with the estate, and to give them effect as a confirmation

firmation of the title, that every creditor should adjudge, even when he was beyond the term of the pari passu preference; and, unless he did so, the purchaser was entitled to retain his proportion of the price. Thus, the law itself compelled creditors to adjudge; wasting the debtor's reversion with useless proceedings, or consuming the fund of division, which belonged to the postponed creditors. This absurdity was avoided in the sale by an apparent heir: for it was held, that the apparent heir was a trustee for the general body of creditors; that, by his action of sale, he adjudged the estate for the behoof of them all; and that this adjudication not only precluded the necessity of postponed creditors adjudging, in order to draw their shares, but admitted all the creditors to the benefit of the pari passu preference, provided the decree of sale was pronounced within the year. But there was no principle, upon which a similar construction was thought applicable to the case of a sale by a creditor. He was not, in law, held as a trustee for others, but as an individual, prosecuting legal diligence for his own advantage; and the only relief from the accumulation of separate diligences, was afforded by a provision in the act of sederunt, 23d November 1711, by which the factor, who should be appointed by the Court for managing the estate previous to the sale, was empowered, upon the application of the creditors, to lead one adjudication for many creditors. It was not till the year 1794, that the sale, at the instance of a creditor, was put, in this respect, upon the same footing with that at the instance of an apparent heir. By an act of sederunt, passed upon the 11th July 1794, under the powers vested in the Court by the 33 Geo. III. c. 74, it was declared, That a decree of sale, at the instance of a creditor, should operate as a common decree of adjudication, in favour of all the creditors who should be included in the decree of ranking.

Although great improvements have thus gradually been made upon the judicial sale, as a general process of attachment, something still remains to be done, in order to give it full effect. The law of pari passu preference, entitles those creditors only to an equality with the first effectual adjudication, who shall have adjudged within the year; and, under it, none has been held entitled,

whose

whose decree of adjudication has not been pronounced before the expiry of that term. But as it can seldom happen, that the decree of sale should be pronounced within the year from the date of the first effectual adjudication, creditors feel it still necessary to proceed with their separate adjudications, in order to secure themselves from injury. This defect, it is to be hoped, will be remedied in the renewal of the law.

In commenting upon the proceedings in the action of ranking and sale, it will be natural to divide a subject so extensive, into distinct heads; and the following seem to comprehend every thing of importance:

1. Of the Sequestration and Intermediate Management.
2. Of the Nature and Description of the Action of Ranking and Sale, by a Creditor, and by an Apparent Heir.
3. Of the Election of a Common Agent—his Duty and Powers.
4. Of the Sale of the Estate.
5. Of the Title of the Purchaser: And,
6. Of the Ranking of the Creditors.

SECTION I.

Of the Sequestration and Intermediate Management.

Before the action of judicial sale was introduced, the sequestration afforded the only relief to creditors, during the term of redemption, where the estate of the debtor was insolvent. A creditor, instead of being excluded from the possession by a prior adjudger, or by any other real creditor, as under the older law, was entitled to apply to the Court of Session, after the statute of 1661, c. 62, to have the possession vested in a factor, accountable to all the competitors. At present, the sequestration is used during the dependance of the ranking and sale, in order to preserve the rents, and have the estate properly managed for the common advantage.

Sequestration is a judicial assumption of the possession of a subject, which is in competition before a Court; that it may be placed in the custody of a neutral person, accountable for his management, and sufficiently responsible; to be by him preserved, and properly managed, for the benefit of those who shall be found to have the best right to it.

The circumstance which gives power to the Court to sequestrate is the competition: where all are before the Court, who have a claim to the property: where either the entire subject belongs to them in common; or there is a contest, who shall have it preferably; or the estate is attached by diligence to its full extent· and where, during the contest, no one of the competitors has attained possession, or has an exclusive right to it. If an estate, therefore, which is attached by creditors, be not bankrupt, it should follow, that the debtor cannot be deprived of the possession by a sequestration, so long as he continues to pay the interests of the

debts.

debts. But when the rents come to fall short of the debts, or when there is reason to fear that there may be any interruption to the regular payment of the interests, or any confusion or encroachment on the rights of the real creditors, by the forwardness of individuals wishing to acquire the possession; it is competent for any real creditor, not only to raise an action of ranking and sale, and to apply to the Court for sequestration, but even to apply without such action of ranking and sale: IV. Stair, Inst. xxxv 26.

The effect of the sequestration is, to vest the possession and the accruing rents in the person of a factor, for the benefit of those whose diligence covers the estate; and to stop all diligence that might otherwise have been competent against the right of possession; as, the attachment of rents, &c.

1. OF THE AWARDING OF THE SEQUESTRATION.

Sequestration is applied for by petition to the Court in which the contested rights depend. In ranking and sale, which is an action competent only to the Court of Session, the petition is presented to the whole Lords. It states the dependence of the action, and prays that the estate should be sequestrated, and a factor appointed, to manage the rents, and take care of the estate. In an old case, it was found, that personal creditors had no right to petition for sequestration—24th Dec. 1702, Sir James Hall against Sir Alexander Bruce's creditors, II. Fount. 168., but there seems to be reason to believe, that now, as a ranking and sale is held to be a process of general attachment and distribution, to all the benefits of which, every one of the creditors is entitled, a petition for sequestration would be competent, (an action of ranking and sale being in dependence), though applied for by a personal creditor.

The application may be opposed by the proprietor of the estate, by creditors in possession, or by any one having an interest to keep the rents, &c. open to diligence.

1. The proprietor of the estate can oppose the sequestration, by denying the bankruptcy, and the deficiency of the rents. Thus, where an apparent heir has raised an action of judicial sale, and is in possession of the estate, the creditors cannot insist for sequestration, unless it can also be shown, that the diligence covers the whole estate, and makes it bankrupt; for, as the creditors could not themselves have brought the action of sale in such a case, and consequently could have had no pretence for applying for a sequestration, if the debtor had not voluntarily interfered, so neither should it seem, that they can be entitled to insist for his being dispossessed in the course of that action which he himself has brought, unless by showing an interest in consequence of insolvency. It seems, indeed, at one time, to have been held, that a sequestration was not in any circumstances competent, where the ranking and sale was at the instance of an apparent heir; upon this ground, that 'a competition of rights can alone authorize the Court to take 'subjects into their possession by sequestration;' 24th July 1781, Blackwoods petitioners, VI. Fac. Coll. lxxv. 129.; but, in a subsequent case, 'the Lords considered the ancestor's estate, by the depending process of sale, to be equally in manibus curiæ, with one 'brought to sale by creditors in virtue of the statutes 1681 and '1690; and, therefore, awarded sequestration.' 15th June 1782, Campbell, VII. Fac. Coll. xliv. 71.

2. If a creditor have actually attained possession, he cannot be excluded by sequestration. Thus, two creditors, by heritable bonds, having attained possession of the lands belonging to their debtor, an adjudging creditor raised an action of ranking and sale of the lands, and a process of accounting, against the possessors. He stated several objections to the heritable bonds, and affirmed, that the debts were already paid off by intromission. In these circumstances, he applied for sequestration. But the Court listened to the plea of the heritable creditors in possession, viz. that their debts must be held valid, till, in a proper discussion, shown to be bad, and that neither is it just to deprive creditors in possession under fair deeds of security; nor is it necessary, since they are answerable to all concerned for the due management of the property.

Sequestration was refused: 3d August 1782, Buchanan, VII. Fac. Coll. lxi. 97. And, indeed, this seems to have been long the established understanding and practice: 7th June 1707, Catenach; Dalr. lxxviii. 99.

3. A creditor, though he neither has attained possession, nor even can found upon an heritable security over the lands, may have an interest to oppose sequestration, and is permitted to do so. Thus, Gartshore of Gartshore, having concurred with some of his creditors in applying for sequestration, a creditor, who had not been informed of these proceedings, was found entitled to go on with diligence; for, till the subject be completely affected, so as to entitle the Court to take the custody of it, for behoof of those who have right to it, the title to proceed with ordinary diligence must be left unrestrained: Winter Session, 1745 *. Again, a petition was presented, for sequestration of the estate of Auchtertyre, by a very great number of creditors, with concurrence of the debtor, Sir Patrick Murray; in which it was stated, that a trust-deed had been granted for the general behoof; and that it was necessary, to prevent a repetition of certain expensive proceedings which had taken place; some of the creditors having arrested the rents, and raised forthcomings, &c. The outstanding creditors contended, that this demand goes beyond the true purpose of a sequestration: that a sequestration is intended, not to stop diligence, but merely to secure the subject after it has been fully affected by diligence; and that, here, sequestration is demanded, with a view to prevent the outstanding creditors from attaching the rents as they fall due: that when a term's rent is attached, and brought into Court by an action of forthcoming, or of multiplepoinding, it may be sequestrated, wherever there is a competition, in order to prevent it from perishing in the tenant's hands; but there is no instance of sequestrating a subject not yet in Court, in order to prevent future diligence: that the common law gives preference according to priority, and that, to sequestrate a subject, which is not regularly in Court, nor fully affected already, is to prejudge this common-law right. The Lords were of opinion, that there could

* This case was quoted in a paper, in Graham of Balgowan's case, by Lord Pitfour.

could be no sequestration, if any creditors opposed: 13th Feb. 1745, Graham of Balgowan, &c. against Frazers; I. Falc. lx. 75.; Sess. Pap. Adv. Lib.

2. OF THE FACTOR.

In the interlocutor awarding sequestration, the Court appoint a factor, or steward, to manage the estate. This is a point of chief importance in the sequestration.

I. The factor is appointed by the Court: he is to act in the place of the Court; for in their hands is the estate held to be. But the recommendation of the creditors is followed in this appointment; and the factor finds sureties for his faithful administration, according to the rules appointed for his conduct by the Court: Act of sederunt, 22d Nov. 1711. There does not seem to be any absolute and peculiar disqualification for holding this office; that of the act of sederunt, 23d Nov. 1710, not being in observance. An extract of the act of sequestration and factory, vests the factor with all the powers which belong to his office.

II. As the factor is appointed to take the full intermediate management of the estate, for the best advantage of those concerned, his duties and his powers may, in general, be described as those of an administrator. But it may not be improper to enter a little into detail.

1. He must take up the rents; both those which are in arrear, and those which arise during his factory; and he must take the proper legal measures for procuring payment. In particular, he must take the proper steps for removing tenants who are in arrear, or forcing them to find security, as pointed out in the act of sederunt, 1756.

2. In removing tenants, whose leases are expired, he has all the powers which belong to a proprietor infeft: 9th July 1757, Thomson against Elderson, II. Fac. Coll. xli. 74.

3. Where

3. Where the lands are let at a reasonable rent, and the tenant is willing to con. .ue at that rent, the factor must allow him to continue from year to year, unless there be good grounds for believing, that, upon exposing them to public auction, a rent would be got for them so much higher, as to recompence the additional expence. Thus, the Court refused to allow a factor to remove tenants, who had taken tacks from him for a year, although they had bound themselves to remove without warning; they having punctually paid their rents, and being abundantly solvent; and having even offered more rent than was to have been paid by the persons who were to supplant them. The factor maintained, that they cut the wood and destroyed it; but this seems to have been but a pretence: 22d July 1714, Edgar against Whitehead, Forb. MS. Adv. Lib.

4. Where the lands will not let at the former rent, though exposed to public auction, the factor must apply to the Court for authority to let them at a lower rate; and this the Court permit to be done, on short leases of two or three years. 19th June 1750, Shaw, Kilk. 185.

5. In all cases of difficulty, with respect to the management, the factor should take the advice of those who are elected by the creditors as their committee of management, and apply to the Court for authority, where any extraordinary act of administration becomes necessary.

6. The factor is bound, by act of sederunt 22d November 1711, to make up a rental of the estate, stating the arrears, within six months after the extracting of his factory; and to lodge it with the clerk of the process, to serve as the rule of charge against him; to make such alterations on this rental as may be necessary, from any increase or diminution of the rents, within three months of the change; and to make up a yearly account of charge and discharge, and lodge it with the clerk, that the creditors may be enabled to check it properly: § 6. 7. 8.

7. The factor is, of course, entitled to pay the necessary expences of management; but he cannot make payments to creditors, without a special warrant from the Court.

8. Before leaving this subject, it may be observed, that it is peculiarly the business of the factor, to show the lands, or, at least, to appoint proper persons to show them, that those intending to purchase, may have a fair opportunity of understanding all the advantages which the purchase may hold out. And, although the situation which he holds, cannot incapacitate him from becoming a purchaser at the sale of the lands, there seems little room to doubt, on the principle of the determination in the House of Lords upon the late case of M'Kenzie, that, if the factor has betrayed his trust, and misled persons intending to purchase, or concealed any of the advantages of the purchase from their inquiry, he will be exposed to a reduction of any purchase which he may have made.

III. When the lands are sold, the factor's duties are at an end. He has then only to account for his intromissions, to have his allowance settled, his accounts approved of, the balance paid over and discharged, and an act of exoneration pronounced in his favour, authorising also the delivery of the bond of caution.

If the factor should become insolvent, legal measures must of course be taken to recover, from his funds, any balance which he may be due; and a warrant will be given for recording the bond of caution, that diligence may be done against his sureties.

SECTION II.

Description and Nature of the Action of Ranking and Sale—Cases in which it is Competent—Legal Effects of the Commencement of the Action.

In the introductory view of this action, we have seen how it gradually, from a simple action of sale, grew into a complicated action of sale, reduction-improbation, and division. These are the three essential features of the action, as known in our day; and they are blended into one mass, that they may mutually assist each other, for the benefit of the creditors, and the security of the purchaser; and accomplish, in one course of proceedings, the double object of bringing the property into a divisible shape, and having it equally distributed among the creditors, according to legal proportion.

The complicated nature of the action gives little interruption, in practice: for the business of each separate part of it proceeds, independently of the others. Thus, the steps necessary for bringing the estate to the market, the proof of its value, the fixing of the upset price, the preparing of the articles of roup, the advertisements, the sale itself, go on, uninterrupted by the proceedings which are necessary with a view to the ranking. This enables us to consider the subject in two distinct views: taking, first, the judicial sale; and, next, the ranking or division of the price: while the action of reduction-improbation, as it bears a mutual relation to both the sale and the division, will of course be fully explained in discussing these two subjects. But there are some general considerations, applicable to the whole action, which must be attended to, before descending to this more minute detail; and these it shall be the business of this and the next Section to discuss. In the present Section, I shall contrast the two actions, at the instance of a creditor, and at the instance of an apparent heir, in these three points: 1. The nature and conclusions of the summons: 2. The cases in which the action is competent: and, 3. The effect of the commencement of the proceedings. In the next Section, I shall consider the office and duty of a common agent.

§ 1. NATURE OF THE ACTION.

1. The summons of ranking and sale, at the instance of a creditor, proceeds upon a recital of the statutes permitting bankrupt estates to be sold judicially; of the ground of debt, and real security or diligence in the person of the pursuer; of the bankruptcy of the debtor; and of the circumstance, of the creditors being in possession. The conclusion is thence deduced thus: 1mo, That, as the pursuer cannot procure payment of his debt otherwise, the whole lands and heritable rights of the debtor should be sold judicially, for that purpose; that a proof of their value should be taken on the one hand, and a proof of the debts on the other; that an upset price should be fixed, and the lands exposed (after due intimation) to public roup and sale; that they should be adjudged heritably and irredeemably to the purchaser; and that, upon payment of the price, the purchaser should be discharged, the lands declared free of the debts, and the superiors ordered to receive the purchaser, and infeft him in the lands: 2do, That the whole creditors should be ordered to produce their claims, under the penalty of their being held as false and forged, in all questions with the other creditors, and with the purchaser: and, 3tio, That the price should be divided among the creditors, according to the respective rights and interests; that the creditors should be ordained, upon payment of the sums assigned to them in the division, to convey their respective rights and diligences to the purchaser, in order to be held by him as securities and corroborations of his right as purchaser.

2. Where the action is raised, not by a creditor, but by the debtor's apparent heir, there is a considerable difference upon the form

form of the summons: for, it will be remembered, not only that it is under a different statute that the apparent heir is authorised to bring his ancestor's estate to sale, but that he may do so, whether there be a bankruptcy, or not. The summons therefore recites the statute of 1695, c. 24.; declares the pursuer's intention, as apparent heir, to take advantage of it; and concludes as the other summons of sale does; with this difference, that there is no necessity for a proof of the bankruptcy; and that there is not, in general, any conclusion of reduction-improbation.

It is to the whole Court that the power of ordering a sale is committed: and therefore, the Lord Ordinary, when he authorizes the proof of the value, &c. acts in a ministerial capacity merely; preparing the cause for decision by the whole Court, to whom, when the proof is concluded, he reports it. The first step of the proceedings taken before the Lord Ordinary, is, to obtain a warrant from him to take the proof, and to order the production of the claims. But, what are his powers of judging whether this warrant ought to be issued? The statute 1681 authorises a sale, only where the debtor is 'notoriously insolvent:' May not the debtor therefore appear, and oppose the issuing of a warrant, which must be disgraceful to him as a landholder, by denying that he is insolvent, far less notoriously so?—A case of this kind was tried in 1781. A creditor, by heritable bond and infeftment, raised an action of sale. The debtor appeared before the Lord Ordinary, and opposed the issuing of the warrant for proving, upon the grounds, that he was not bankrupt, the estate not affected by adjudication, and the creditor not in possession. The pursuer answered, That the summons of sale stated the bankruptcy, the possession of the creditors, and the real burden in the pursuer's person; and that it was the very object of the proof which was asked, to establish, by evidence, those facts which the debtor had denied. The Lord Ordinary repelled the objection, and granted warrant for proving. and the Court confirmed the judgment. 23d December 1780, Cunningham & Co. against Marshal, VI. Fac. Coll. Part II. xiii. 23.

§ 2. CASES IN WHICH THE ACTION IS COMPETENT.

The cases in which the action is competent, may be distinguished by their relation to the title of the pursuer of the action; to the condition of the debtor; or to the nature of the property.

I. TITLE OF THE PURSUER.—1. In a sale by a creditor, no person can appear as pursuer, who does not hold a real security over the subjects to be sold. The remedy of a judicial sale was devised for the benefit of those creditors who had already proceeded as far as the common law allowed them to go with individual diligence. A creditor who held, either by voluntary deed or by adjudication, a real security over the lands, could do nothing more than attempt to get into possession; and as that was often unavailing to him, the extraordinary remedy of the judicial sale was given. But, to personal creditors, no such remedy was open. Not having yet exhausted the execution which the common law allowed, they were denied the benefit of the extraordinary remedy, intended merely for supplying the defects of that execution. A real creditor is, strictly speaking, one who is infeft in the lands: yet, sales have been allowed to proceed, at the instance of creditors whose rights were not thus completed. Thus, in the sale of Balcomie, several objections were taken to the action of sale; and, among others, this was stated against the pursuer's title—' That ' it was only an infeftment of annualrent, which is but a servi' tude; whereas, none can pursue a sale, but a creditor having a ' right of property.' The pursuer, however, contended, that an annualrent right was, strictly speaking, a real right: and a former case was cited, from the sale of the estate of Nicolson, where that had been sustained. ' The Lords repelled the defence, in respect ' of the answer.' 11th July 1699, Learmont; II. Fount. 58.—An adjudication, with a charge against the superior, has also been sustained as sufficient: January 1729, Newton against Anderson. Nay, even without a charge or infeftment, a mere decree of adjudication was sustained: July 1731, Creditors of Robertson against his Children; 7th February 1738, Auchterlony against Sir George M'Kenzie of Grandvile; Clerk Hume, 136. See also 27th

January

January 1714, Duke of Gordon against M'Pherson; Forbes, MS. Although, therefore, a personal creditor cannot bring an action of sale directly; the road, by which he may reach his object, is not very circuitous. If the debt be ascertained by a written document, he may, at once, raise adjudication; and he will, after completing the adjudication, be entitled to raise an action of ranking and sale.

2. In sales by apparent heirs, the apparency alone is a sufficient title to pursue. The statute 1695, c. 24. declares, 'That 'the said APPARENT HEIR may bring the said estate to a roup,' &c. But as this is a privilege given to an apparent heir, it was questioned, on one occasion, whether the heir did not deprive himself of it, where, by 'behaviour as heir,' he had made himself liable, as the proper debtor, for all his predecessor's debts? The Court decided in the negative, finding the heir still entitled to pursue a sale: 28th February 1733, Blair against Stewart.—It was next doubted, whether a service, as heir in general 'cum beneficio inventarii,' did not take the heir out of the description of the statute of 1695? This question came to decision, upon a search of precedents on the 27th February 1751. Two precedents were brought forward: One, on the 14th July 1742, M'Dowal against Creditors of Kelton; where a disponee from the heir served cum beneficio, was 'found 'entitled to bring the subjects of the inventory to a sale, on the 'act 1695.' The other was on the 30th July 1748; where, Andrew Rutherford having raised a sale, as apparent heir to his father, the creditors objected, that he had been served cum beneficio, and was excluded from the privilege of the statute; but the Court found, 'that, notwithstanding the pursuer was served heir 'in general cum beneficio to his father, yet it was competent to 'him to carry on the sale, on the act 1695.' And in conformity with these precedents, the Court decided, 27th February 1751, Blair Petitioner; Kilk. 241.

But another difficulty remained, whether the heir could, if actually entered and infeft as heir cum beneficio inventarii, bring a judicial sale of the estate? Where an heir thus enters, the com-

mon

mon course is, to bring an action of valuation of the estate given up in the inventory—that, on payment of the value, which is thus judicially ascertained, he may be free from the representation. And if, in this action, he meet with no opposition, his payment of the value fairly to creditors, as they appear, or under a multiplepoinding, is a full exoneration to him; or, if he find it convenient to sell, rather than to keep the property, he may do so voluntarily, and distribute the price: III. Esk. viii. 69.—A case occurred, in which an heir, who had entered cum beneficio inventarii, and been infeft in the lands, brought an action of declarator of sale, containing a conclusion of ranking against the ancestor's creditors. The Court doubted, whether such an action was competent, as it was unusual, seemed to be unprecedented, and was unnecessary; the heir himself having sufficient power, without judicial authority, to sell. A search of precedents was ordered; and, in a memorial, the heir stated the above cases from Lord Kilkerran: and, in particular, with regard to the case of M'Dowal (quoted as a precedent in Blair's case), it was stated, that the person, whose disponee was there pursuing the sale, had been not only served heir, but infeft in the lands, as appeared from the records. The memorial was lodged 8th March 178. How the question was decided, I cannot discover. The minute-book of the Court of Session is not printed of so early a date, and although I have examined the record of decrees, I can find no decision of it. But I see, that the estate was afterwards sold at the instance of the creditors, 7th February 1785. Rec. of Decreets.

3. But as, on the one hand, it has been made a question, whether an apparent heir, served in general cum beneficio inventarii, could bring a sale under the statute of 1695? on the other, the judgements of the Court have varied upon the point, whether the creditors were entitled to bring an estate, given up in the inventory, to sale, or were bound to take it at the value that should judicially be put upon it, in an action of valuation at the instance of the heir? The Court found, in one case, that the heir was entitled to persist in such action, and that the creditors had no

option

option of taking the subjects, and making the most of them: 6th July 1733, Gray against M'Caul.—Again, it was found, that such an action was a complete bar to a judicial sale by the creditors: 17th February 1736, Murray against Pilmuir's creditors.—But, in the next case that occurred of this kind, a solemn pleading was ordered; when these decisions were overturned, and the creditors found entitled to proceed with a sale: 12th July 1738, Strachan's Heirs against his Creditors; Kilk. 239.

4. If the pursuer should die during the course of the action, there is a distinction between the sale by creditors, and the sale by an apparent heir In a sale by creditors, any other creditor may apply for leave to take it up; and this the Court will grant of course: Kilk. 472.—It is held to have been with a particular view to the sale, at the instance of a creditor, that the Court, in the 4th section of the act of sederunt, 23d November 1711, provided, that 'if the pursuer of a process of sale and ranking shall, 'during the dependence, die, or forbear to insist, or if his title and 'interest shall happen to be satisfied and extinguished, the factor, 'if any be, or, otherwise, any other real creditor, may, upon special 'warrant from the Lords, take up the process where it left, and 'carry it on, to its final issue, for the common behoof of the whole 'creditors.' In a sale, by an apparent heir, the Court refused to authorise creditors to interfere: 29th June 1749, Creditors of Hamilton; Kilk. 472.

5. If the action have been begun against the original debtor, and he have happened to die during its dependance, the action does not fall; it proceeds as before, after his heir has been called to appear for his interest. 'If the debtor, or any of the 'creditors defenders,' says the act of sederunt, 23d November 1711, 'shall happen to die, the process thereupon shall stop no 'longer than till the apparent heir be cited to compear, upon a 'diligence, without any necessity of waiting the year of delibera-'tion, or transferring the process passivè against them so that if 'no person appear, in the place of the common debtor or creditor 'deceased, the Lords declare, they will proceed in the process

'where

'where it last left, and to the discussing thereof, in such manner 'as where parties alive do not compear.'

II. CONDITION OF THE DEBTOR.—An apparent heir may bring the estate of his ancestor to sale, whether it be bankrupt or not. He is the only person interested in objecting to a sale; for, if the estate be bankrupt, a sale is conducted with less expence at his instance; and if there be a reversion, it is to him alone that it falls. But it is otherwise in a sale by creditors. There, the debtor must be bankrupt; otherwise the sale cannot proceed without his concurrence. The original view of the law was, to enable creditors to bring to sale the heritable estate of their debtor, only when it was insufficient for answering, from the rents, the interest of the debts really secured on it; or inadequate, upon a division, after expiry of the legal, to satisfy the creditors who, by their real securities, were entitled to shares. The law took no account of personal debts in this matter; personal creditors being left to the common remedy of adjudication. But, as the law now stands, even personal debts must be taken into the account. It is not necessary that the debts should be made real, in order to enter into this computation; since the decree of sale realizes them, by operating as an adjudication for all creditors whose debts are included in it. It is with a view to the question of competency, that the comparison of the value of the lands, and of the amount of the debts, is made the first step in the action of sale, at the instance of a creditor. That the comparison may be fair, the most effectual means are taken for including the whole heritable property of the debtor, on the one hand, and for securing production of all claims, on the other.

1. In order to secure the inclusion of all the heritable estate of the debtor, in the action of sale, it was formerly a rule, that they should all be specially named, and that the omission of any of them should be fatal to the sale. Thus, in the case of Sir Harry Monro, 6th January 1749, the Court found, 'That a sale could 'not proceed, on a summons not containing the debtor's whole 'lands, though those omitted were lands to which he had only suc-

'ceeded,

‘ ceeded, but not entered:’ Kilk. 471. The remedy, for such an omission, was, to raise a new action of sale, and have it conjoined with the former. This the Court allowed, though not without some hesitation, in a case, where a coal-work, belonging to a common debtor, in the hands of another heritor, was omitted, and not discovered till after the proof was taken in the sale. 1st February 1751, Creditors of Mrs Margaret Balfour; Kilk. 474. To put an end to all the delays and inconveniences attending this state of the law, it was provided, by act of sederunt 17th January 1756, § 12, that, ‘ in respect it may happen, that a bankrupt may be
‘ possessed of an heritable estate, which either does not admit of
‘ infeftment, or where the bankrupt is not actually infeft, and
‘ thereby such estate may possibly escape the knowledge of the
‘ raiser of the process of ranking and sale, and this hath proved
‘ very inconvenient to the creditors; every summons of ranking
‘ and sale shall contain a general clause, mentioning all other lands
‘ and heritable estate belonging to the bankrupt, or to which he
‘ may succeed as heir to any of his predecessors; and it shall
‘ be competent to the raiser and carrier on of such process of
‘ ranking and sale, upon his discovering any heritable estate be-
‘ longing to the bankrupt, during the course of the ranking and
‘ sale, to bring a proof of the rental and value of such lands, and
‘ other heritable estates, so discovered, notwithstanding they were
‘ not specially libelled: providing always, that, upon such disco-
‘ very, and before granting warrant for a proof of the rental and
‘ value of the newly discovered estate, application shall be made
‘ to the Lord Ordinary in the ranking, and he shall give directions
‘ to give notice of the estate being discovered to belong to the
‘ bankrupt, and that the same is to be sold,’ &c.

No subject, which is included in the rights of the creditors, and mentioned in the summons of sale, can be dropped out of the action, and neglected in the proof, without the clearest evidence that it does not belong to the debtor.—In the ranking and sale of Borlum, a reversionary right in a wadset, was adjudged, along with the other heritage, and mentioned in the summons of sale; but it was disregarded, and no proof taken of its value, in consequence of of very strong claims made upon it by three competitors,—the superior under a quinquennial retour—the wadsetter, under adjudications fortified by prescription—and the heirs of line of the family, as preferable to the common debtor, the heir-male. But the Court found, 'That the sale could not proceed, till it was determined, whether the lands of Benchar, or the reversion thereof, 'did belong to the common debtor:' 25th December 1784, Macpherson against Tod; VII. Fac. Coll. clxxxix. p. 297 *.

It has been thought proper, by act of sederunt 11th July 1794, to appoint it, as a part of the duty of the common agent, 'to 'take the most effectual means for ascertaining the nature and extent of the subjects belonging to the common debtor, together 'with the incumbrances affecting them; in order to which, he 'shall, if necessary, cause search the public registers, and apply 'to the Lord Ordinary for letters of first and second diligence against havers:' § 6.

2. That a due investigation might be made of the debtor's condition, it was necessary to insure production of the claims. This is done, by the conclusion of reduction-improbation, contained in the summons of ranking and sale. By act of sederunt 17th January 1756, § 1. when the Lord Ordinary pronounces an act or order, for proving the rental and value of the bankrupt's estate, he is directed, 'at the same time, to assign a term for the whole creditors of the bankrupt to produce all their claims, rights, and 'diligences, competent to them, respectively, against the bankrupt, or his estate; with certification, as in a reduction-improbation.' Provision is likewise made, for the proper advertisement of this term, and for supplying the creditors with diligence for recovering their documents and securities. When the first term expires, a second is appointed, upon the application of the common agent; and the decree of certification is extracted ten days

* The proof of the rental, with the deductions, and whole process for ascertaining the value, shall be afterwards detailed, in treating of the steps preliminary to the sale of the lands.

days after the elapse of it, excluding all creditors who have not *then produced their claims.*

In ascertaining the bankruptcy, by the comparison of the debts and funds, the rule established by the bankrupt statute of 1793 is, 'That a judicial sale at the instance of creditors may in all 'cases proceed, where the interest of the debts, and the other 'annual burdens, exceed the yearly income of the subjects under 'sale.' And as, in mercantile bankruptcies, the creditors have an option of selling the heritable estate by judicial sale, rather than by voluntary roup under direction of the trustee, it is provided, that the sale may proceed, where sequestration has taken place, 'without other proof of bankruptcy or insolvency:' § 10.

Before leaving this point, it may be observed, that, by the statute 1681, c. 17, it is required, in a sale by a creditor, that the creditors should be in possession of the estate. This expression in the statute, seems fairly deducible, from the view which the Legislature at that time had, of the nature of the remedy, which, as a boon, they were offering to creditors. As already observed, it was only after creditors had done every thing within the reach of the common law, that the Legislature intended them to have recourse to this extraordinary remedy; and the attainment of possession, was one of the most obvious means of recovering payment at common law. This expression, relating to the possession of the creditors, is not repeated in the statute of 1690, c. 20, nor in any of the acts of sederunt made for regulating this action; yet it is generally held to be necessary. The requisite is easily complied with, by any of the creditors getting into the natural possession of the lands, or by the civil possession of an action of mails and duties against the tenants, for forcing them to pay their rents to the creditor who pursues it; or by a sequestration of the rents, as already explained.

III. NATURE OF THE PROPERTY.—In discussing what particular description of property may be thus brought to sale, we must recur to the occasion for which this remedy was introduced. The attachment of moveables was effected by arrestments and poinding, both operating directly for payment of the debtor: the latter, by a public sale of the poinded goods; the former, by a forthcoming of the cash arrested, or by a sale of the goods, similar to that in poinding. But it was to moveables only, that these forms applied. Against heritage, the creditor had no other resource, but adjudication; and it was to supply the imperfections of that diligence, that the judicial sale was introduced. Naturally, therefore, every subject which is adjudgeable, is capable of being brought to a judicial sale. If the subject, indeed, be of the nature of a debt, where, for example, the bankrupt is creditor by heritable bond, or by adjudication over another estate, the most direct and obvious course for the creditors to take, is, after adjudging the heritable security, to force the debtor in the bond to pay, or to bring his estate to a sale, as if it were the estate of their own debtor. But, in the case of leases, liferents, or other inferior or limited rights upon land, the creditors have no other way of obtaining the value of them, than by means of a judicial sale

§ 3. Effect of the Commencement of the Action.

The commencement of the action of ranking and sale, considered as a general process of attachment, ought to have the double effect, of preventing any voluntary alienation or security, and stopping all diligence by individuals.

1. Without entering, at present, into the general doctrine of litigiosity, which is the legal bar against the disappointment of real actions by voluntary deed, I shall merely observe, in this place, that the creditors are, by the effect of the inchoated ranking and sale, not only guarded against alienations of the property of the lands, but against all acts of administration, by which the principal or accessary rights may be injured. From the preamble of the act of sederunt, 24th February 1692, it appears, that the advantage taken by bankrupts, in embezzling their rents, and destroying their land, after the commencement of the action, was such, as to

call

call for some remedy *; but the only remedy provided, was, to give to the action of sale the benefit of summary discussion. It must, however, be evident, that, where there is no sequestration, material harm may be done to the creditors, by mere acts of administration. Thus, in the case of Carlyle against Lowther, a tack was granted, or at least renewed, at a low rent, prior to sequestration, but after the ranking and sale was in Court It was challenged, by the factor under the sequestration, as an act of extraordinary administration, to the detriment of the creditors, after litigiosity begun. The Lords reduced the tack, as granted during the dependence of the ranking and sale: 27th February 1766, Select Decisions, ccxlii. 316. A similar decision was pronounced in the case of the York Buildings Company, who, being insolvent, had given long leases after the ranking was begun, and a petition to sequestrate was presented. In particular, they had renewed a lease, for thirty-seven years, to Mr Fordyce. 'The 'Court was of opinion, that, in the circumstances of the Company at the time, they had no power to grant the lease in question; and, that the long endurance of the lease, is sufficient objection to it, though the rent might be adequate. It was observed on the Bench, that, after a process of sale is brought, the debtor, even before a petition for sequestration, cannot grant leases, for any length of time; for, such leases must have a bad effect on the sale. and it was said, that the edictal citation is sufficient intimation to all and sundry, of the debtor's situation.' The lease was reduced: 7th July 1778, Creditors of York Building Company against Fordyce. Affirmed in the House of Lords, 16th April 1779.

2. As to the effect of the action, in stopping the diligence of individuals, I have, in the preliminary sketch, hinted, that, hitherto, it remains in some degree imperfect. Mr Erskine, in speaking of the litigiosity consequent upon the dependence of an action of ranking and sale, expresses himself thus—' No diligence, car- ' ried

* 'Seeing bankrupts do ordinarily imbazle their estates, uplift their rents, destroy their planting, policy, and houses, until the sale be expede'—

'ried on or perfected while the sale is pendent, in order to create 'a new preference to the user of it, in competition with other 'creditors, ought to have any legal effect.' B. II. tit. 12. § 65. But this doctrine was far from being sound or accurate, in Mr Erskine's time, and is not, at present, to be much regarded. At the time that Mr Erskine wrote, there was a very marked distinction between the sale by an apparent heir, and the sale by a creditor. The former was regarded, as a general adjudication by a trustee, for the benefit of all the creditors: the latter was held to be merely a form of law, by which an individual creditor might bring his debtor's estate to the market, in order to procure payment of his own debt. A corresponding difference took place in their effects. The former superseded the necessity of diligence by individual creditors: the latter could have no effect in supplying, to other creditors, the place of individual adjudications for affecting the estate. In the very case, to which Mr Erskine refers in illustration of his doctrine, this distinction was acknowledged; for the ground of decision, in that case, was, 'that the decree of sale 'is to be considered as an adjudication for the benefit of the whole 'creditors, when obtained by the apparent heir, who is empower'ed by law to act as trustee for them and himself:' 29th January 1748, Irvine against Maxwell, I. Falc. ccxxxiii. 319.—Kilk. 469. The contrast is completed, by the case of Massey against Smith, in which 'the Lords found, that the maxim, "pendente lite nihil "innovandum," applies only to things done by the debtor or de'fender in the action, which tend to make the right of the creditor 'or pursuer worse, but cannot hinder the creditor or pursuer from 'making his right better, even in competition with another credi'tor or pursuer; and that, in this case, one of the creditors, by 'raising a process of sale, cannot hinder the other creditors from 'using the diligence of the law, to make their rights effectual:' 12th July 1785, Massey against Smith, VII. Fac. Coll. ccxxi. 347.—Sales by creditors, are now, however, by act of sederunt, 11th July 1794, put upon a footing, nearly similar to that of sales by apparent heirs: 'Whereas,' says the act, 'it has been found, that, 'in the case of judicial sales, at the instance of apparent heirs, the 'decree of sale has the effect of an adjudication for behoof of the

'whole

'whole creditors, it shall be, in like manner, a rule, in time coming, that, in processes of sale and ranking at the instance of creditors, the decree of sale shall have the same effect, and shall operate as a common decree of adjudication in favour of all the creditors who shall be included in the decree of ranking and division; and it shall not be necessary, in time coming, for any of the creditors ranking as aforesaid, to lead separate adjudications against the estate, in order to entitle them to receive payment; neither shall such adjudications be necessary for the security of the purchaser, the decrees of sale, ranking and division, being, in effect, an adjudication of the estate, for all the debts therein contained:' § 15.

But, further, it will be observed, that, neither the sale at the instance of an apparent heir, nor, under the act of sederunt, the sale by a creditor, can have any effect in preventing adjudications from being led by individuals; nor can either of them prevent preferences from being acquired by those adjudgers, unless the decree of sale shall be pronounced within year and day from the date of the decree in the first effectual adjudication. In the above case of Irvine against Maxwell, the decree of sale was within the year and day of the first effectual adjudication; and the judgement found, that the sale by the apparent heir, as trustee, 'being within year and day of the first adjudication, it ought to be beneficial to all, whether they had adjudged subsequent to it, or not; and that the whole creditors on the estate were to be ranked pari passu.' But, in a late case, a very different decision was given, where the decree of sale was beyond the year. In June 1775, a process of sale was begun by an apparent heir. In September, decree of adjudication was obtained by a creditor. The decree of sale was not pronounced for several years after; and it was argued by the general body of the creditors, (some of whom had adjudged after the year and day), against a preference contended for on the part of the first effectual adjudgers, that the summons of sale was to be held as an adjudication for all the creditors. 'The Lords unanimously found, that, in the circumstances of this case, the creditors were preferable, according to the diligences used by them respectively:

15th

15th November 1791, Haldane against Palmer, VIII. Fac. Coll. clxxxix. 394.

It is clear, therefore, that, neither in sales by apparent heirs, nor in sales by creditors, is there any stop to the acquisition of preferences by adjudication, unless the decree of sale shall be pronounced (which it is scarcely possible to expect) within the year and day of the first effectual. Had the Legislature, or had the Court of Session, under the powers delegated by the 33. Geo. III., declared, that the effect of the decree of sale, as a general adjudication, should draw back to the date of the summons of sale, and be considered as a general adjudication of that date, debtors would have been shielded from much oppression, and much expence saved to the fund. There have, of late, occurred, several bankruptcies of landholders; and in two, particularly, which I have occasion to be well acquainted with, the torrent of adjudications has poured impetuously on in full stream, during the whole course of the action of ranking and sale. In one of these cases, the debtor would have had a very handsome reversion, could it have been possible to stop the creditors from proceeding with adjudications; but now, his estates are reduced, by these accumulated expences, very far indeed below the amount of his debts.

SEC.

SECTION III.

Of the Election of a Common Agent—His Powers and Duties.

The judicial sale, though a measure, begun perhaps by a single creditor, and with no other view than for the recovery of his particular debt, is a general remedy for bringing the estate to a sale; for forcing production of all claims; for dividing the produce of the estate, according to legal proportion, among the creditors. It is necessary, therefore, to the true constitution of such a remedy, that proper means should be taken for managing the common interest, with a strict impartiality. For this purpose, a common agent is appointed, who, while the agents of the individual creditors are striving for preferences to his own client, has the duty devolved upon him, of watching over the general interest—conducting all the steps of the proceedings—seeing that the proper intimations are made—the proofs of value fairly taken—the estate brought to sale—and the price divided. Officers of this kind, may either be permanently appointed, like the clerks of Court, or elected by the creditors themselves, under the controul of the Court, in case of difference. In the Court of Session, a middle course is taken. The College of Justice contains several classes; of whom the writers to the signet, and agents or solicitors, are intrusted with the conducting of causes before the Court. As members of the College of Justice, they are under the peculiar jurisdiction of the Senators or Judges of the Court. as practitioners in the Court, they are amenable to its Bar, for their conduct in any cause. They are properly, therefore, officers of Court. But, from these great bodies, the creditors have the right of electing the person in whom they choose to place their confidence.

The right of electing agents, factors, trustees, and managers of all kinds, is one of the most important which belong to a body

of

of creditors; and it has been much the object of all the regulations in such cases, to establish, upon good principles, this right of election; to fix such a criterion of the qualification to elect, as may prevent undue elections; and to impose such restraints upon eligibility, as may guard against the admission of men, who may be induced to act with partiality or favour to individuals, against the general interest.

1. OF THE RIGHT OF ELECTING A COMMON AGENT.—The first regulation of the right of electing a common agent was made by act of sederunt of the Court of Session, 17th January 1756. To secure the right of the true creditors, it was ordered, that the election should not proceed, till after the expiry of the first term appointed for the creditors to produce their claims. A meeting was then to be appointed by the Lord Ordinary, for the election. The title to vote, was fixed at 30l. of principal debt, (excluding interest and expences, except when accumulated by adjudication), where the yearly rent of the estate was under 300l.; and 50l., where it exceeded that sum. It was declared, that the majority should decide the election; which being reported to the Lord Ordinary, he was to approve of it, and give authority to the common agent to proceed in the execution of his office.

The elections carried on under this act of sederunt, having been frequently attended with litigation and disputes, to the great prejudice of the creditors, and delay of the proceedings, new regulations were thought necessary by the Court, when, under the bankrupt act of 1793, they were called upon to deliberate on the 'necessary regulations for carrying the act into effectual execution.' By act of sederunt, 11th July 1794, they ordered, 1. That the Lord Ordinary should appoint intimation of the time and place of meeting, for the choice of the common agent, to be made in the minute-book, and by one advertisement in the Edinburgh Gazette, at least fourteen days previous to the meeting. 2. The nature of the election was very materially altered. Instead of a majority of creditors in debts of 30l. or of 50l., every creditor is admitted to vote, (by himself or his agent), who 'shall have produced his 'ground

'ground of debt, with an oath of verity upon the same, (by him-'self, if in Britain, or, if out of the country, with an oath of 'credulity by his agent), twenty-four hours, at least, previous to 'the election.' And the election is decided by 'a majority in 'value, exclusive of penalties, and bygone or current interest, '(unless in so far as bygone interest shall have been accumulated 'by a decree of adjudication); and it is declared, that, in com-'puting the amount of such debts as consist of annuities or life-'rents, they shall be estimated at ten years purchase of the annui-'ty or liferent.'

2. ELIGIBILITY AS COMMON AGENT.—It is only in the act of sederunt, of 11th July 1794, that any thing is said upon this subject; and yet, it is not without its importance. Watched, as the proceedings of a common agent are, a thousand opportunities occur, for favouring particular creditors, and throwing interruptions in the way of others, almost imperceptibly, or, at least, with every appearance of the fairest conduct. It is, therefore, of much importance, to guard, if possible, against every chance of partiality; and the Judges have acted properly, as the guardians of creditors, in wiping away as many of the motives of partiality, as could legally come within the reach of a general rule. They have declared, 1. 'That no person shall be capable of being elected as common a-'gent, who is himself one of the creditors.' 2. That, being 'a 'conjunct or confident person, with respect to the common debt-'or,' shall be a disqualification. 3. That if, after his appointment as common agent, the person named 'shall act, either by 'himself, or by a confidential person, or clerk, as private agent 'of any creditor, or class of creditors, or of the common debtor, 'in any matter relative to the ranking, or to the division of the 'price, while the same are in dependence before the Court,' it shall be an ipso facto disqualification: § 3.

3. DISPUTES CONCERNING THE ELECTION.—To abridge the litigation upon such questions, and the ruinous stoppage of proceedings during their dependence, without depriving the creditors of the benefit of discussing a matter which may be important, it is

declared, that the judgement of the Lord Ordinary shall be subject to review only of the whole Court, and that only once; the person approved of by the Lord Ordinary being, in the mean time, entitled to act; and the person, who is ultimately unsuccessful, being liable in costs: § 4.

4. OFFICE AND DUTY OF THE COMMON AGENT.—The person officiating as clerk to the meeting for election, is directed, by the act of sederunt 11th July 1794, to 'report the person duly chosen 'common agent;' and the common agent, when chosen, 'shall 'take an oath de fideli administratione, before the Lord Ordinary, 'at the first calling of the cause after his election is confirmed.' In this faithful administration, he is bound to attend to the following particulars: 1. 'After his nomination is confirmed by the Lord 'Ordinary, he shall take the most effectual steps for ascertaining 'the nature and extent of the subjects belonging to the common 'debtor, together with the incumbrances affecting the same; in 'order to which, he shall, if necessary, cause search the public 'registers, and apply to the Lord Ordinary for letters of first 'and second diligence *:' Act of sederunt, 11th July 1794, § 6. 2. In the conduct of the sale, he must be particularly careful in clearing up all obscurities, and supplying all defects in the debtor's titles —in making complete searches, to satisfy the minds of the creditors, his constituents, that they are safe from future questions of relief—and giving such confidence to the public, as may induce purchasers to wish for so unexceptionable a title. He must not only take care that all the prescribed publications be scrupulously made, but that the lands be advertised in such newspapers as the creditors, or the committee of management, may think most likely to promote the sale. 3. In the view of the ranking and division, he must, immediately after his being confirmed, apply to the Lord Ordinary 'to assign 'a second term for the whole creditors of the bankrupt to produce 'their claims, with the vouchers thereof, with certification, that 'what

* The first diligence, is a warrant for citing a person, who is to be examined as a witness, or who is suspected to be possessed of writings, to appear for examination If it be not obeyed, a second warrant is issued, of the nature of a caption, to force appearance.

'what shall not be produced, shall be held false and forged:' Act of sederunt, 17th January 1756, § 3. By this act, too, it was appointed, that 'notice should be given of the said interlocutor to all 'parties concerned, by inserting it in the Edinburgh Evening 'Courant, weekly, for three successive weeks, immediately following the date of the foresaid interlocutor; and that, the notification 'being reported to the Lord Ordinary, a minute should be made 'thereon, and which should be held as sufficient evidence of the 'said notice against all parties concerned.' By the late act of sederunt, these notices so appointed or ordered, are, 'in time coming, 'to be given by advertisement in the newspaper called the Edinburgh Gazette, in place of the other two newspapers before 'mentioned:' § 1. 3dly, Upon elapsing of the second term so assigned, he must apply to the Lord Ordinary for decree of certification contra non producta, and have the extract made as soon as possible after the expiry of ten days from the date of the judgement: Act of sederunt, 17th January 1756, § 4. 4thly, He must then make up a full state of the debts and claims of the creditors, and of the objections thereto, and the questions thereon; distinguishing those objections or questions which go to the enlargement of the common fund, or to prevent its diminution, from those which only affect the interest of particular creditors, or classes of creditors, in competition with one another, and also suggesting the order of ranking; which state shall be printed, &c.; and, if any new interest, or new objections, arise, a supplementary state is to be made up, pointing out the variations thereby occasioned; and he shall, in these states, set forth, whether there is any probability of a reversion to the common debtor; and in what view, or different views, such a prospect arises: Act of sederunt, 11th July 1794, § 7. 5thly, The common agent is required to keep a minute-book of his proceedings, and of his official correspondence, open to the inspection of all concerned: § 5. These are all the particulars specified in the acts of sederunt, relating to the office and duty of the common agent. What remains, may be comprehended in one general proposition, viz. that his duty is, to superintend, for the common interest, all the proceedings in the action—to conduct the sale—to call the factor (if there be a sequestration) to account—to prevent

prevent any of the creditors from gaining an advantage to the prejudice of the general interest—to prevent undue delays—and to discuss all questions in which the creditors, or the funds, are concerned.

With a view to have a more complete superintendance over the common agent, the act of sederunt of 1794 establishes a new office. 'In order,' says the act, 'to prevent, as far as possible, 'any undue delays in carrying on judicial sales and rankings, the 'creditors, or their agents, at the meeting for election of a com- 'mon agent, shall name a committee of three of their number, if 'they think fit so to do, whose duty it shall be, if the proceed- 'ings are not finally closed within two years after commence- 'ment of them, to inquire into the reasons thereof; and the com- 'mon agent shall, at any rate, with or without the concurrence of 'such a committee, print, and give in to the Court, and distribute 'among the other agents concerned, a short minute, stating the 'then situation of the process, and what have been the causes of 'the delay; and a similar minute shall be given in at the end of 'every year thereafter, till the proceedings are closed, unless dis- 'pensed with by the Court:' § 14. The object and intention of these periodical minutes, have been ill understood in practice. It has been the custom to print most voluminous states, which do not, in truth, serve the purpose of explaining clearly the situation of the process, and the causes of delay; while the expence upon the funds is enormous. Some new regulation of this point will, most probably, be made soon. It is declared, by § 5, that the common agent shall, at all times, be amenable to answer for his conduct, by summary application to the Court, at the instance of any party interested; the Court being entitled, upon cause shown, either to remove him from the office of common agent, and to appoint a meeting of the creditors to choose another, or to give such other redress, as the circumstances of the case may require.

Before

Before leaving this subject, one question of some importance must be taken notice of, viz. the power of a common agent to become an offerer at the sale, for his own behoof. This question was fully tried, in the late case of the common agent for the York-Building Company. Upon a search of the records in that case, it was found, that, since the year 1756, common agents had been offerers in no less than one hundred and thirty-five sales, and had become purchasers in eighteen instances. But it was contended, 1. That a common agent, as being himself the seller, could not become the purchaser: 2. That it were most dangerous and inexpedient to permit him to do so, as too strong an inducement to his misleading the creditors. The Court first judged, that, 'in respect 'the defender was common agent, when the sale of the two lots 'of Seaton in question took place, the sale must be reduced.' They afterwards decided in his favour, on the ground, that there was no legal disability in his situation as common agent. In the House of Peers, the sale was reduced. The view taken up there, was, that, in their two judgements, the Court of Session had taken the extremes; that truth lay in the middle; that equity and expediency required, from a common agent, the strictest and most impartial attention to the best interest of the creditors, and forbade his taking the slightest advantage which he could have prevented; and, in the application of this rule, their Lordships found reason for reducing the sale: 8th March 1793, York-Building Company against M'Kenzie, IX. Fac. Coll. No. 47. p. 97. Appeal Cases, 13th May 1795.

SECTION IV.

OF THE JUDICIAL SALE.

THE judicial sale is naturally the first object of attention, in considering this combined action of sale and ranking.

I. We have already seen, that all the estate of the debtor must be included in the summons, and made the subject of proof, in order to establish the bankruptcy. But, are the creditors bound to bring the whole estate to sale? Once it seems to have been the practice, to expose the whole estate in the lump; and it must therefore have been an object of considerable importance, to avoid the injuring of the sale of the clear property, by any combination with questionable rights. Thus, the creditors of Ramsay of Leuchars applied to the Court, representing, that their debtor had an heritable right on the lands of Crimon-Megget, but had never attained possession, being always excluded by preferable rights, though, he contended, they were nearly paid by their intromissions; yet this being a very dubious, uncertain plea, it might hinder the sale of his other uncontroverted property, if they were exposed together: therefore, craved allowance to leave them out of the roup, lest they should mar the whole, and scare buyers from bidding and offering for the rest. 'The Lords saw, that the acts of Parliament ordained the bankrupt's whole estate to be rouped; but thought this could be only understood of his clear, liquid, and undoubted property, but not of uncertain claims and clampers he might have on other mens estates; and therefore, allowed the roup to go on, without including these lands; or else, that they might be exposed to sale separately by themselves. And here, a new difficulty occurred, what price or value could be put on such dubious claims; for it was not to be expected they could sell at eighteen, nineteen, or twenty years purchase, as clear lands did:'

22d February 1712, II. Fount. 729. But the dangers which were dreaded in this case, cannot threaten creditors now, since the practice has been introduced of exposing the estate in such divisions or lots as seem to promise the most advantageous sale. The rule now is, that all the debtor's property, whether of doubtful, or of clear right, must be exposed to auction, to bring what it may. In the ranking of Borlum, already quoted upon the question of bankruptcy, it was questioned, whether any part of the estate could be neglected in the sale, from an opinion that it was not the property of the debtor; or whether the sale of the other lands must not be stopped, till it was determined whether the neglected subject really was the debtor's property or not. In that case, indeed, the omission affected the question of bankruptcy; for the subject neglected, though included in the adjudications, and in the summons of sale, was not attended to in the proof of the value of the estate. But the opinion delivered from the Bench, is good law, as applicable to the question which we are now discussing. 'The 'pursuers of a judicial sale are not obliged, indiscriminately, to follow out every claim suggested to them by the debtor himself, or 'by his creditors; but, where an estate has been comprehended 'in the adjudications led by the creditors themselves, and enumerated in the action of sale, as belonging to the debtor, it is incumbent on them, either to bring it to sale, along with the other 'lands, or to shew, in the clearest manner, that in truth it does 'not belong to him:' 25th December 1783, Macpherson against Tod, VII. Fac. Coll. clxxxix. 297.

II. PROOF OF THE VALUE.—The proof of the value of the estate, for the double purpose of ascertaining the bankruptcy, and fixing the upset price, is one of the first steps in the action. The days of citation being elapsed, * and the returns of the execution recorded, the summons is, in common form, called in Court; and when it comes before the Lord Ordinary, he pronounces an interlocutor, allowing a proof to be taken of the rental and value of the

* The debtor, and all his real creditors in possession, must be cited specially, as defenders are in common actions, and an edictal citation must be made at the market cross of Edinburgh, pier and shore of Leith, and at the doors of the parish church where the lands lie, after divine service.

the estate, and of the bankruptcy of the debtor; and granting a commission to the Judge Ordinary, or some respectable person, to take the proof; and this he accompanies with a warrant for letters of diligence for enforcing the attendance of witnesses, and of persons possessed of papers and documents. Act of Sed. 17th Jan. 1756, § 1. To prevent collusion in the proof of the rental and value of the estate, it is provided, by act of sederunt 24th February 1692, that any creditor appearing and producing a real right, shall be allowed to concur with, and insist in the action, along with the creditor who pursues it. The common debtor himself may also appear and adduce witnesses; as, in the sale of Lord Dundonald's estates, he did with respect to the woods of Culross, and the old walls of the Abbey.

In order to prove the value of the lands, it is necessary that the feu-duties, and other deductions to be made from the rental, should be known; and for this purpose, it is necessary that the pursuers of the sale should have possession of the title deeds. Indeed, this is necessary also, on another account: for they must be put in good order, and all defects supplied, that the purchaser may be satisfied, and the estate may have a fair chance for drawing a full price at the sale. To get possession of the title deeds was, however, in the days of Lord Fountainhall, a matter of considerable difficulty. 'The great difficulty' (says he) 'which creditors meet 'with, is, to recover the charter chest, and writs of the lands, to 'instruct the holding and reddendo, and to satisfy a buyer of the 'sufficiency of the progress: for bankrupts abstract the writs, and 'lodge them in obscure corners, till they make their bargain, and 'get a sum of money from the creditors to produce them:' II. 729. It is by the force of the first and second diligence, for which the Lord Ordinary grants warrant, in the interlocutor allowing the proof, that the title deeds, as well as the documents of the creditors claims, are recovered. Where the title deeds are in the repositories of a person deceased, a warrant for opening the repository is given: 11th January 1750, Kilk. 473. And where they are in the hands of an agent, the Court will order him to deliver them up, under a reservation of his right of hypothec.

The

The proof of the rental is naturally attended with very little difficulty The evidence of the tenants, the tenor of the leases, &c. are the materials from which the yearly rent is to be stated. But attention must be paid to any peculiarity in the leases, as grassums, and the common agent must consider himself as bound to a be very accurate, and perfectly impartial, in attaining, if possible, clear proof of the present value of the rental. He should not restrict himself to the rents actually given for the lands; but endeavour to discover, by the value of lands in the neighbourhood, whether they be not possessed at an inadequate value. Lord Fountainhall makes the following remarks upon this subject, vol. II. p. 729. 'There is no such difficulty in constituting the rental, as in recovering the title deeds: for the tenants oaths, or tacks, do that, 'unless where the estate is in the debtor's own hand; for that 'puts creditors to prove the sowing and increase; what it might 'produce, if laboured; and if grass, how many soums of cattle 'it could hold? As to the price which such lands may give in 'that part of the country, the Lords have very justly refused to 'allow any witnesses to depone upon it, but only landed gentlemen 'in that shire, what lands of that holding used to give betwixt 'buyer and seller· and by their testimonies, they (the Lords) set 'a price, even somewhat within, to encourage bidders.' After the rental is fixed, the value of the land, and the number of years purchase at which it may be expected to sell, are commonly ascertained, by the evidence of respectable men of business, acquainted with the part of the country in which the lands lie, and whose attention has, by their profession, been naturally directed to such kind of information. Where there are coals, lime, &c. professional men are examined, who, from a general knowledge of the value of such subjects, can ascertain the probable worth of that in question: Where houses or manufactories are to be valued, tradesmen, accustomed to estimate such subjects, are the most natural and the best judges.

Difficulties may sometimes, however, occur in the valuation of particular subjects. The following rules are delivered by Lord

 Kilkerran,

Kilkerran, 471. 2. 1. Services due to the debtor, by his tenants, &c. are never to be valued, unless the debtor has, in the tack, an option of requiring money: the like judgement was pronounced as to poultry, even where the tenant was in use of paying a conversion for them, (23d February 1749): and also, as to coal-leading, shearing, harrowing, tilling, (27th July 1749, Cochran); 'though the tilling particularly,' says Lord Kilkerran, 'be of a considerable and determinate value.' 2. 'Where teinds are not saleable, and not in tack, no value at all is put upon them, in a sale, on account of the kindly right to obtain a tack: but where teinds are saleable, though not in tack, five years purchase is put upon the kindly right: and where unsaleable teinds are in tack, the value is according to the endurance of the tack; that is, the tack is supposed to be worth three years free teind; and the years to run are rated at a proportion thereof: and so it was found,' 23d February 1749. In the valuation of tacks, there can be no difficulty. In that of liferents, the value must be taken according to the market price of a liferent of the same extent, equally well secured, according to the tables of life.

The holdings and reddendos are stated from the title-deeds, and the necessary deductions made from the rental. We shall afterwards have occasion to inquire into the effect of an erroneous deduction; whether it makes the deduction be reserved as a separate estate unsold; or, whether the purchaser be entitled to claim the benefit of the mistake, and to hold the subject free from the deduction. At present, we have only to inquire into the true criterion of value; and this is so obvious, with regard to the deductions, that nothing need be said upon the subject.

If, in an action at the instance of creditors, the value of the estate, as proved, should exceed the amount of the debts, the sale cannot proceed, as there is no bankruptcy: but if the apparent heir should bring the lands to sale, after the creditors have abandoned their action, Is all the expensive proof already taken, to go for nothing?—In a case which occurred in 1771, Brownlee, an apparent heir, raised a sale of lands, which the creditors had attempted

tempted to sell, but the value of which having been proved to exceed the amount of the debts, they were obliged to abandon the proceedings. The apparent heir applied to the Court, to be allowed to use the proof formerly taken; and the Court had no difficulty in allowing the proof to be held as repeated in the apparent heir's action.

III. UPSET PRICE.—The proof of the value is stated, along with the amount of the claims, in a memorial and abstract, which is reported to the Court by the Lord Ordinary. At the enrolment before the Lord Ordinary, for the purpose of his taking the cause to report, parties may appear and show, either that the bankruptcy is not established, when the action must fall, or, that the value is not fairly estimated, so as to be a fair criterion of the upset price. This they might properly do, even were the proof concerning facts and circumstances; but as it is a proof of opinion, merely, in so far at least as regards the number of years purchase, much more must the parties have a right to argue upon that proof, for the information of the Court, in forming their judgement. The price is fixed at the number of years purchase, which the proof fairly entitles the Court to take, as the reasonable value to be put upon the lands.

But it may happen, that the price may have been fixed too high: ignorance, on the part of the witnesses, may have led to this; or accidents, happening between the fixing of the price and the sale, may prevent the lands from selling at the upset price. The statute of 1690, c. 24, provides only one remedy for the accident of a purchaser not being found; which is, to divide the lands among the creditors, according to their respective preferences and rights. This was nearly to leave things to all the evils of the common law. Lord Stair says, (B III. tit. ii. § 55.), 'In case there be a division, the creditors have the choice of the lands effeiring to their share; but the Lords will not allow fractions, but whole rooms (farms) to be chosen; the excresce to make up the price, being

'paid

'paid out, to be divided proportionally; the choice to be made by 'the apprizers and adjudgers, according to the date of their ap-'prizings and adjudications: but if there be more persons, who 'have right to the same apprizing or adjudication, they must have 'preference of their choice by lot; and none may choose in the 'middle of contiguous lands, but at a side.' While the Court thought themselves bound to follow this course, the evils with which it was attended were found almost insurmountable. Lord Fountainhall tells us, 'that where a buyer cannot be got, then the 'act of Parliament ordains the lands to be divided among the cre-'ditors, according to their respective preferences on their dili-'gences; and which happened in the case of Bruce of Kennet's 'creditors: but such inextricable difficulties arose, that it is not 'adjusted to this hour, seeing particular rooms will not answer to 'particular creditors sums; so they are forced to stay in an invo-'luntary communion, by dividing the rents of the lands, without 'getting the property ascertained and parcelled out to them, con-'form to their preferences:' II. Fount. 729.

The evils of this situation induced the Court to listen to the only proposal which could relieve the creditors, viz. the lowering of the upset price. In the sale of Cleland, the Lords had fixed the upset price at 19 years purchase, but no offerers appeared, for the price was thought high, and the holding was not eligible. The creditors, therefore, applied to have the price lowered. They were opposed, upon the ground, 1. That the minimum being 'consti-'tuted and established, in a probation led, of what lands of that 'kind may give between buyer and seller, the same cannot now be 'altered, without reviewing and reconsidering the probation, which 'the Lords are not in use to do.' 2dly, 'That where lands can-'not get a buyer, the act of Parliament, introducing sales, has pro-'vided a remedy, by dividing the lands among the creditors.'— 'But the Lords remembered, that this division had been attempted 'in the case of Bruce of Kennet and others, and was found utterly 'impracticable, and then observed, that the probation of the va-'lue of lands was only founded on credulity and opinion, some 'neighbouring gentlemen deponing, they thought the land's worth

'20

'so many years purchase, wherein the Lords themselves were as 'good judges as they, and finding, here, from the holdings and 'other motives, a just ground of abatement, they brought down 'the price to 18 years purchase: but, for intimation to the lieges, 'they ordained new letters of publication to be executed, before 'they should be again exposed to sale at that price:' 8th July 1709, Hamilton of Wishaw, II. Fount. 512. Afterwards (729.), in speaking of this decision, Lord Fountainhall says, 'it was a 'great step,' meaning, that it was a stretch of power, to reduce the upset price; but this will scarcely be thought by any one now-a-days, who examines, with attention, the grounds stated in the above decision, for such interposition. The reduction of the upset price is a step of daily practice now, care being always taken to advertise, with the same precision as at the first, the adjournment of the sale, and reduction of the price.

IV. PLACE OF SALE.—Judicial sales always proceed in presence of the Lord Ordinary, in the New Session House at Edinburgh. Sometimes it may appear, that it would be more advantageous for all parties to expose the lands elsewhere; but it never is done. An application to have this done was made, and refused.—'The estate of Colquhoun of Kenmore and Wardrobe of Dalmar-'nock being bankrupt, the creditors gave in a bill to the Lords, re-'presenting, that the lands lie within two miles of Glasgow, and 'the creditors concerned live all in the neighbourhood; and that 'it will be most convenient for all bidders, that the roup be at 'Glasgow, before the Baillie of the regality, or any other they 'shall appoint to oversee it, the articles of roup being adjusted 'here.—The Lords considered this was the first time ever such a 'thing was demanded, since the act introducing the sale of bank-'rupt lands, in 1681; and that they have been all uniformly before 'one of their own number, and still at Edinburgh; and, whatever 'semblance of ease this had, at the first view, yet, the yielding to 'such a novelty might draw inconveniences with it; for, by the 'same rule, they might be craved to be held in Orkney or Inverness:

'and

'and, though they doubted not, but, on specialties, they had 'power to appoint them at any place, and before any gentleman 'they should commissionate for Judge, it was never yet done: 'and Edinburgh being the communis patria for all Scotchmen, the 'purchase was little worth, if it would not bear the offerers ex'pence to come to Edinburgh; and, for their small conveniency, 'such a novelty was not to be introduced, &c.—The Lords refused 'the desire of the petition.' 22d February 1712, II. Fount. 729.

V. TIME OF THE SALE.—The sale will be fixed at the time most likely to give the fairest chance for a good market. This, of course, will be, during the time of session, when men of business are in town, and attentive to matters of this kind. There seems not to be any absolute incompetency in a sale during vacation, since it always proceeds before the Lord Ordinary on the Bills: and this, in fact, once happened, and was, I believe, sustained. But the Court was struck with the danger of such proceedings; and, although no act of sederunt was made against the practice, it was very seriously resolved, that it should never be repeated *. If it be considered, that, as the law stands at present, an advertisement of the sale in the Edinburgh Gazette (a paper which has little circulation in the country) is sufficient to validate the sale, the danger of allowing the possibility of proceeding during the vacation, when the town is empty, will be strongly felt.

VI. INTIMATION TO THE PUBLIC.—When the report of the Lord Ordinary upon the bankruptcy, and the upset price, is received, and advised by the whole Lords, and the sale allowed to proceed, a warrant is issued by the Court, for letters of publication to pass the signet. This is a writ in the King's name, signed by a clerk of Session, and containing an order upon messengers at arms, to make intimation to all and sundry, of the intended sale. The

* This case is not reported, nor, indeed, do I know the name of the estate, in the sale of which it occurred; but it happened some time about the year 1781

The form of publication, as laid down in the original statute of 1681, is thus:—The sale was to be published at the head burgh of the shire where the lands lay; at the kirk of the parish, and at six other parish kirks, (to be named by the Court), at the dissolving of the congregation after the forenoon's sermon, and at the market cross of Edinburgh, pier and shore of Leith. Special intimation was also necessary to the creditors holding real rights. The publication at the market cross, pier and shore, was ordered to be made sixty days before the sale; and the personal citation to real creditors twenty-one days before it. Copies also of the intimation, must have been left at the different places.

But these forms of publication were found to be enormously expensive, proportioned to the benefit derived from them, and the Legislature, by 33. Geo. III. c. 74, directed that the Court of Session should devise some more effectual publication, at less expence. Accordingly, by act of sederunt 13th November 1793, the Court of Session 'appointed and ordained, that, in time coming, it shall be sufficient to execute the letters of publication at 'the market cross of Edinburgh, and pier and shore of Leith; and 'to intimate the interlocutor of the Court, granting warrant for 'such letters, by an advertisement in the newspaper, intituled, 'The Edinburgh Gazette.'

This is all the advertisement of the sale that is required by law; but the practice is, to advertise the sale very carefully in all the Edinburgh, sometimes even in the English newspapers, and especially in any newspaper published in the part of the country where the lands ly. This, it is much the interest of the creditors to order the common agent to do, that the market may be more extensive, and that they themselves, and the purchaser, may be better secured against any claim of eviction.

VII. SALE.—In preparing for the sale, it is the duty of the common agent to have every thing in such order, as may, to persons

sons intending to purchase, give the most complete information respecting the situation of the estate, the state of the title-deeds, &c.: and he must have the articles of roup prepared, that they may examine the conditions upon which their offers are to be made.

1. Plans of the estate are proper, or necessary rather; in which the lots must be distinguished, as they are to be exposed to sale. A purchaser may, in this way, see the situation of the part for which he wishes to offer; and has an opportunity of examining, whether the title-deeds be correctly applicable to the arbitrary division that may have been made of the lands.

2. Inventories of the title-deeds of each lot must be made up, to be signed by the Lord Ordinary, stating the whole progress of the titles, so as to enable a purchaser to satisfy himself of his safety. The title-deeds themselves must also be accessible to purchasers.

3. The articles of roup are made out by the clerk to the process of sale, and revised by the common agent. They are generally drawn up in one uniform style; and it is unnecessary to recite them. But there is one article generally inserted, upon the interpretation of which there has been much dispute. It is that article, by which a term is assigned for the highest offerer to give security for the price, under the penalty of a devolution of the right upon the next offerer, and a claim of damages against the person who fails. By one article, the highest offerers are taken bound to find security for the price, and interest from the term of entry, within thirty days after the sale; and, by another, it is provided, 'That in case the highest offerer for any of the said lots, 'should fail to find caution within the foresaid space, then the 'next immediate preceding offerer is to be preferred to the pur-'chase; he always granting bond, with a sufficient cautioner, for 'payment of the price offered by him, in the terms above written, 'within thirty days after the failure of the next immediate highest 'offerer: and, in case he likewise fails to find caution within the 'limited time, then the other offerers to be preferred in their

'order,

'order, they finding caution, as said is; without prejudice to 'the creditors to insist against the several offerers for the surplus 'price offered by them respectively, more than the price of- 'fered by the offerers who shall find caution; as also the pe- 'nalty aforesaid, for not finding caution; intimation being al- 'ways made to the preceding offerers, on the several offerers above 'them failing to find caution, and that within ten days after the 'purchase has devolved upon them respectively.'

There are rights arising out of this condition, to the creditors, on the one hand, and to the subsequent offerers, on the other; and both deserve attention.

If no such article were inserted in the conditions of the sale, but it were simply a sale to the highest offerer, there can be no doubt, that, upon failure of that offerer to pay the price, or to find security for it, the exposers would have a right to annul the sale; to expose the estate again; and to claim from the offerer, the damage arising from his breach of contract. But the delay and expence, and anxiety and danger, arising from such a measure, are, if possible, to be avoided; and the above condition has been adopted for this purpose; declaring every offerer, in his turn, liable to have the purchase fixed upon him, at the sum offered by him; the difference, and the expences, being claimable from the offerer who fails to perform. This is an expedient, adopted evidently for the benefit of the exposers alone; but it is one, attended with no inconsiderable hardship to the lower offerers. Even the second highest offerer must, in this way, be precluded from safely offering for any other estate, for at least forty days, and the offerers under him, must each have their hands tied from the free employment of their capital, for still a longer time. The fair inference would seem to be, that, although the condition is meant for the benefit of the exposers, yet, being attended with sacrifices and inconveniences so great to the offerers, their right of devolution ought to be absolute, and not entirely dependent upon the will of the exposers. When the terms of the contract are considered, (for articles of roup are nothing else than a contract between the exposers and the offerers), it seems to accord most perfectly with this idea of the mutual right. The jus devolutum is declared in simple and absolute terms—'In case the highest offerer shall fail to find caution within 'the foresaid space, then the next immediate preceding offerer is 'to be preferred to the purchase.' There, no doubt, is afterwards added, a clause, expressing, 'that intimation is always to 'to be made to the preceding offerers, on the several offerers a-'bove them failing to find caution, and that within ten days, af-'ter the purchase has devolved upon them.' But it does not appear to be a fair inference, from this clause, that the right is intended to be made optional to the creditors insisting for the devolution, or refusing it. The clause seems rather to be intended with a view to the claim of damage by the creditors, against the several offerers. In this view, the true meaning of the condition would seem to be this; that, upon the failure of the highest offerer, the right to the purchase should devolve upon the next; so that, either he should be entitled to insist for fulfilment of the bargain against the creditors, within ten days from the devolution, or they to call upon him for fulfilment, by intimation within the ten days. that if the second offerer should insist upon his purchase, in due time, the only resource for the creditors would be, a claim against the first offerer, for the difference, or damage occasioned by failure and that, if the creditors should call upon the second offerer, in due time, they would have a good claim, upon his failure, against the next, claiming the second difference, as they did the first. This interpretation, however, is not confirmed by the judgements which appear in our books of reports; they would rather seem to support a different doctrine—to establish, that the right of the second offerer is not absolute, but depends upon the choice of the exposers.

The first question that occurred upon this article, in a judicial sale, was in 1787; and the question was, Whether the right of the second highest offerer was absolute, upon failure of the highest? Mr Gavin was highest offerer at the sale of Mainsmel, Mr Walker was the second. By some omission, Mr Gavin allowed the

the thirty days to elapse, and did not present his bond till the thirty-first day, and after Mr Walker had insisted on his jus devolutum. The question was reported to the Inner-House, upon minutes of debate, when the Lords preferred Mr Gavin, the highest bidder: 10th February 1787, Walker against Gavin, VII. Fac. Coll. cccxii. 481. The year after the decision of the above case, there occurred, in the sale of Newlaw, a question, which differed from the above, in the circumstance only, of intimation having been given to the preceding offerer, on failure of the highest. Mr Hannay, the highest offerer, had, by some accident, failed to get his security ready; and the common agent, two days after the expiry of the thirty days, made intimation to the preceding offerer; but, before any proceedings in consequence of it, the highest offerer presented his bond, and petitioned the Court to have it received; urging the extreme hardship of the situation, as he was liable, both for the difference between the price offered by himself and that offered by the immediately preceding offerer, and also for a penalty of a fifth part more. 'The Court,' (says the Reporter), 'in giving judgement against Mr Hannay, were principally moved 'by the intimation that had been made to the immediately preceding offerers. It was observed, that, although the readiness which 'Mr Hannay had shown to rectify the error into which he had 'fallen, might have the effect, in a question with the exposers, to 'relieve him from the penal consequences, those, whose offers 'were next to his, by being called on to perform their part of the 'agreement, had thus acquired a right to demand reciprocal performance, which no equitable consideration, in favour of third 'parties, could take away:' 15th July 1788, Hannay against Stotherd, &c. VIII. Fac. Coll. xxxv. 58.

Another case occurred in 1799, similar to that of Walker. In the sale of the unentailed property of Mr Boswell of Auchinleck, certain lands were purchased by Mr Boswell, and the Earl of Dumfries was the immediately preceding offerer. Mr Boswell signed the bond for the price, at London; but the cautioner having left London for Scotland, it could not be signed by him, but was sent

down

down to Edinburgh, to wait his arrival. He did not arrive till the thirty days were expired, having made some visits in England, on his way down. Immediately on his arrival, he signed the bond, but the clerk refused to receive it, as it was beyond the term; and an application was made to the Court, for their authority to its being received. The application was opposed by the Earl of Dumfries, who claimed his right, as second purchaser. One of the Judges observed, upon the moving of the petition, that, if he was not much mistaken, the Court proceeded, in the case of Hannay, upon the general principle, that this clause, in articles of roup, forms a proper contract or condition, not a penalty; and, that failure to perform, gives a double right—1. To the creditors, to have a new sale, if that shall be thought beneficial for them; or, to call upon the second offerer as purchaser, and upon the highest offerer for the difference between the offers—2. To the second offerer a right, if the old sale should be adhered to, of insisting upon being preferred as purchaser, leaving it to the creditors to claim the difference from the highest offerer. His Lordship also said, that, in so important a question, it was proper to have a full discussion, and moved for an additional petition and answers; which was ordered, and the parties desired to examine the precedents. But the cause was compromised, and no papers were ever given in.

The right of the creditors, to call upon the highest offerer, to pay them the difference between his offer and the second, may, at first sight, appear to be of the nature of a penalty. It is now, however, fixed clearly, that it is not so, but a proper debt arising by contract. The question already taken notice of, as occurring in the ranking of Newlaw, where the second offerer insisted on his right to be preferred to the purchaser, in consequence of the intimated failure of the first, was followed by an action, at the instance of the creditors, against the highest offerer, for the difference between the highest and the second offer, which was no less than 290l. Mr Hannay, the highest offerer, argued chiefly upon the ground of this being a claim of damage, or penalty, which is demandable only, if an actual loss can be shown to have arisen; whereas, the truth was, that, by his interference, the price of the lands was very much advanced. * But the answer to all this was, that this was a fair and proper contract, by which the exposers were to be assured of the highest price offered at the sale; the highest offerer being bound, upon failure, to pay, at least, the difference occasioned by that failure, so that the exposers should be no losers. The cause having been reported to the Court, they gave judgement for the difference: 13th December 1791, Currie's Creditors against Hannay, VIII. Fac. Coll. cxcv. 405.

It is plainly deducible, from this state of the law, that each offerer, at a judicial sale, has a strong interest to insist upon the offer that precedes his, being taken down; for, if it be not, and an intermediate offer omitted, he may, upon failure to find caution, be called upon to pay a difference much greater than is due.

---

4. SECURITY FOR THE PRICE.—The purchaser grants bond, with cautioners for the price, or he consigns it.

As no man purchasing a large estate, can be supposed to have the money ready to be immediately paid down, it is necessary that the exposers should accept of security, till it be possible for the purchaser to command his money. The clerks of Session are bound to satisfy themselves with the security offered, and are liable, if they take a man who is not at the time sufficient for the price. But, even if the cautioner should afterwards fail, and the purchaser be unable to pay; still, the creditors are not deprived of all security for the price: the land itself still continues bound to them, till the price be paid, and the debts of the creditors discharged. On the one hand, the statute of 1681, c. 17, declares the sale effectual, only upon payment of the price; and, by 1695, c.

* To prove this, he printed an analysis of the offers; by which he showed, that the sums at which the competition ceased with all but him, were, 2[illegible],[illegible]40l., whereas, the amount of the offers preferred by his failure, was 23,210l., making a difference, by his offering, of 2270l.

c. 6, the lands are declared disburdened of the price, upon payment to the creditors, or upon consignment. Upon the other hand, it is a fixed point, that a 'sale does not purge the estate of the debts 'and diligences affecting the same, but that they remain a burden 'upon the estate, until the purchaser make payment of the price.' 24th July 1739, Donator of Ward against Creditors of Bonhard, II. Dict. 312. If, therefore, the purchaser and his cautioner should fail, the creditors are entitled to sell the lands again. This was done in a very late case, 27th November 1793, Murray, &c. against the postponed creditors of Rae, IX. Fac. Coll. lxxvii. 170. The purchaser and his cautioner having both become bankrupt, the estate was again exposed by the creditors, but at a reduced price, which gave occasion to a question in the division, upon whom the defalcation should fall, whether upon all the creditors proportionally, or only upon those postponed? a question, which will demand our attention afterwards, in treating of the rules of distribution. It was observed, from the Bench, that 'the 'estate does not effectually belong to the purchaser, till he pay 'the price. Till then, the securities of the creditors remain entire, 'and, of consequence, the subject continues pledged to the pre-'ferable creditors, to the full amount of their debts.'

The creditors, or the cautioner, or even the purchaser himself, may wish to have the price consigned. It is declared, by the act of 1695, c. 6. to be lawful for purchasers, after a year from the decree of sale, to consign the price, with the annualrent due at the time of consignation, in the hands of the Magistrates and Town-Council of Edinburgh, and their treasurer for the time; but this is, by the statute of 33. Geo. III. c. 74. § 7, changed to a consignation with the Royal Bank, to be made at any Whitsunday or Martinmas after the term of payment; the purchaser being freed from his obligation, by intimating the consignation to the common agent. The creditors are entitled, at any term subsequent to the term of payment, to insist for consignation. It may be added, as a kind of appendix to this rule of consignation, that, 'because purchasers of lands affected with liferents, have re-'tention of a share of the price, the purchaser is allowed to con-

'sign

' sign what remains in his hand after the decease of the liferenter,' in the same way with the rest of the price, ' he always making due ' intimation of the consignation to the creditors, who got the rest ' of the price:' 1695, c. 6, and the other statutes.

5. DISCHARGE OF THE PRICE.—By 1695, c. 6, the purchaser paying the price to the creditors as ranked, or consigning it in terms of law, ' shall be for ever exonered; and the security given ' for the price shall be delivered up, to be cancelled; and the lands ' and others purchased and acquired, disburdened of all debts or ' deeds of the bankrupt or his predecessors, from whom he had ' right; and that the bankrupt, or his heirs, or apparent heir or ' creditors, without exception of minority, not compearing, or con- ' ceiving themselves to be prejudged, shall only have access to ' pursue the receivers of the price and their heirs, and reserving ' to the minor lesed, his relief as accords.' For these purposes, a petition is given in to the Court, praying to have the bond delivered up, and the purchaser discharged of the price

SECTION V.

OF THE TITLE AND RIGHT OF THE PURCHASER AT A JUDICIAL SALE.

QUESTIONS of great difficulty and importance have occurred, with respect both to the title, and to the extent of right acquired by the purchaser at a judicial sale; and the common notions upon the subject are so dangerously erroneous, that I have thought it proper to consider them in a separate Section.

I. TITLE OF THE PURCHASER.

A decree of judicial sale, when properly completed as a feudal right, has ever been regarded as the best and most eligible title that

a

a purchaser can receive: and yet, perhaps, many talk of the goodness of such a title, without knowing precisely in what its virtue consists. The title by judicial sale, may be defined a feudal right, proceeding upon an irredeemable decree of adjudication;—secured against all objection on the part of the debtor, and those deriving right from him, by its judicial nature as a decree, and by the declarations in the acts of Parliament which establish it;—against all claims of creditors by the decree of certification, which, to the effect of securing the purchaser, holds every debt not produced as false and forged;—and, finally, against any claim of eviction from other quarters, by the conveyances to the debts of the creditors, and by the right of recalling from each the sum paid to him.

This seems to comprehend all the circumstances of extraordinary security which the purchaser enjoys from this sort of title. Yet it was vehemently contended once, nay, actually decided by the Court, that a judicial sale gives a title of a much stronger kind, that, being so public an act, so carefully and anxiously in every shape advertised, not only by citations, both special and edictal, to all who may be interested, but also by advertisements in the newspapers, and publications of every possible kind, a purchaser should not be subjected to the claims of strangers, in the character of proprietors, since they ought to have appeared before the sale; and that the only remedy for them should be, an action against those to whom the price had been paid. This plea was first maintained, and with success, in the case of Cooper against Sir Andrew Myreton, 21st June 1720. Sir Andrew purchased, at a judicial sale, the estate of Gogar. The son of the bankrupt, then an infant, was fiar of the estate, the father having nothing but a mere right of liferent. An action was afterwards brought by the son, for having the sale reduced; and he founded his claim upon his own radical right to the land, independently of his father; the statutes authorising the sale only of what belonged to the bankrupt. He urged strongly, in support of his claim, his unprotected state as an infant, deserted by his natural guardian. Sir Andrew Myreton, the purchaser, founded upon the sacred nature of that title under which

which he understood himself to have acquired the lands, contending, that purchasers at judicial sales relied upon the public faith, pledged to them upon every point that could secure their purchase, first, against all defects in the proceedings, as those proceedings were reviewed and considered by the Judges, before pronouncing the decree of sale, which was a pledge to the public of their accuracy; secondly, against all latent claims, in consequence of the anxiety shown, in every step of the proceedings, to bring forward those claims, by intimations, advertisements, &c. And, in corroboration of his plea, he cited a case of one Murray, who, having purchased Scotscraig, and having, for his further security, examined the records, and found there some rights affecting the purchase, preferable to those ranked, applied to have them purged away, before he should be forced to pay the price; but the Court refused his application, and ordered him to pay the price, propter fidem publicam; judging that, however preferable the debt on record might be, the purchaser was secure *. The Lords found, that the decree of sale was sufficient to exclude the pursuer's title of challenge against Sir Andrew Myreton's right as purchaser President Dalrymple, clxxxii. 250. A similar judgement seems also to have been pronounced in the year 1739, where the claim by the pursuer of the reduction, was founded on a right flowing from the bankrupt's father, from whom the bankrupt's title, which was merely revocable, was also derived. Thomas Wylie acquired right to a tenement, by a deed from his father, granted to him, not as heir, but as singular successor, and containing a power to alter. This power the father exercised in favour of another son, Henry Wylie. The creditors of Thomas proceeded to bring the tenement to sale judicially; and it having been bought by Mr Dundas, his right, as purchaser, was challenged by Lady Rollo, who had acquired, by

 adjudication,

* It will be observed upon this case, that the burdens discovered in the records seem to have been debts of the bankrupt; but perhaps, as it was under the old form, where there was no decree of certification, but merely a process of multiplepoinding, the case is not essentially different from that of a claim by one not founding upon the bankrupt's right

adjudication, Henry's right. The Lords found Mr Dundas's right as purchaser secured by 1695, c. 6. †

But another view came to be taken of this question, and the true principles to be better understood. Urquhart of Meldrum purchased, at a judicial sale of Sir Kenneth M'Kenzie's estate, a right of patronage. A claim for this patronage was made, on the part of the Crown; and the general question, of the effect of a judicial sale, against the right of a person not called as a party in the sale, was debated. The Court found, that the right of the Crown was not barred by the decree of sale. 28th July 1753, Urquhart of Meldrum against the Officers of State, I. Fac. Coll. lxxxiv. 122. This decision is highly approved of by Mr Erskine; for, 'though 'the purchaser acquires (says he) all right vested in, or descendible to, the bankrupt, from his ancestors, or authors, it cannot 'hurt third parties, who may have had a right preferable to that 'of the bankrupt, and who, not being called as defenders, had no 'access to know of the sale, and, upon that account, no opportunity of appearing for their interest:' II. xii. 63. It is no longer then to be questioned, that a judicial sale gives no protection against the claims of third parties, whose right is not derived from the bankrupt, and who were not parties in the action of sale; and there seems to be as little doubt, that, upon the emerging of any claim which undermines the right that was in the bankrupt, the purchaser would be entitled to suspend the payment of the price, until he were relieved from it.

The effect of a decree of sale, then, being confined thus far in its operation, let us consider in what its real strength consists.

1. Against the bankrupt, and all deriving right to the lands from him, it is protected by its judicial nature as a decree; by the peculiarity of the proceedings in the action upon which the decree proceeds, and by the declarations of the statutes establishing it. It is of importance, that all judgements should be secured against the arts, or the undue

† This case is not to be found in any of our books of reports. It was quoted as a precedent in the case to be immediately taken notice of, between Urquhart of Meldrum and the Officers of State.

undue neglect of those, who, although properly parties to the cause, and having good objections to the proceedings, may omit to state them, or, having stated them, and taken the judgement of the Court upon them, may choose, after every thing is settled by decree, to insist for a reconsideration of the cause. In all actions, therefore, it is established as a rule, that claims, which might have been brought forward by the parties, but were not, and pleas stated and judged of, are to be rejected as grounds of suspension or reduction, under the names of 'competent and omitted,' and 'proponed and repelled.' (See regulations for the Session, 1672, c. 16, § 19) These rules apply, with peculiar force, to judicial sales. No plea competent and omitted, or proponed and repelled, will be allowed to shake the strength of the decree of sale, let them be ever so well founded and strong. Thus, an objection having been moved to a decree of ranking and sale, founded upon the circumstance of the action having been inadvertently carried on in the name of one of the adjudgers who was dead, the Court, in respect that the creditor objecting had discovered a new document, opened up the decree of ranking, so far as to allow him to be heard, but 'found the reason of reduction noways to affect the decree of 'sale:' 4th January 1749, Blackwood of Pitreavie, Kilk. 436., II. Falconer, 31.

In common cases, the rule applies to no plea which arises from facts unknown at the time, 'res noviter venientes ad notitiam:' IV. Stair, i. 44.; IV. Ersk iii. 3. Is the same exception admitted in a judicial sale? This question was debated, but not determined, in the above case of Blackwood of Pitreavie. In considering such a question, it would be of importance to remember, how strong the line of distinction is between a common decree, and a decree of sale. A common decree, is but a judgement of right between the parties; but, in a judicial sale, a third party, otherwise uninvolved, is drawn in to risk his money upon the faith of a public sale.

If the right of any of the parties appearing in the action suffer, it is not the purchaser who gains, as in the common case, where the victorious party has the benefit of a decree; for the purchaser pays a full price for the right which he receives. The creditors alone, who have received the price in payment of debts due by the bankrupt, gain by any error; and against them, therefore, the remedy and recourse must ly.

The same reasoning is applicable to the case of a decree of sale pronounced in absence of any person who holds a real burden upon the estate sold. In common cases, a decree in absence may be opened up, upon paying the expence of the former proceedings; but it would be of dangerous consequence, upon the principles already explained, to allow to decrees of sale no stronger effect. All that the law can do, is to insure the best possible chance of intimation, to all concerned, that a sale is going on. Perhaps, in this respect, the late regulations requiring the intimations (which, under the acts of sederunt of 1756 & 1783, were ordered to be made in the Caledonian Mercury and Edinburgh Evening Courant) to be made only in the Edinburgh Gazette, are no improvements; since the Edinburgh Gazette has no wide circulation among the body of the people, especially in the country. But, with all the personal citations, and modes of intimation which have been thought compatible with the œconomy to be observed in such institutions, the law has given to a decree of sale this peculiar strength and security, more than is indulged to common decrees; that although it be pronounced in absence of the debtor, and of those deriving right from him, and so having an interest to appear and object to the proceedings, it shall be secure against all challenge; 'the bankrupt, or his heirs, or 'apparent heirs or creditors, without exception of minority, not 'compearing, or conceiving themselves to be prejudiced, only having access to pursue the receivers of the price, and their heirs; 'and reserving to the minor lesed his relief as accords..' 1695 c. 6.

So far the law has given effect to those principles of expediency and justice, which may be urged in favour of a bona fide purchaser at a judicial sale, and endeavoured to reconcile his security with the

rights

rights of those who may be interested to reduce the sale. The claim of relief has been turned against those who have received the benefit; and the purchaser has been, in a considerable degree, shielded from danger. But no law which encroaches on the rights of individuals, can be entitled to a liberal or extended interpretation. If, therefore, it should happen, that a person having an interest to object to a sale, had been prevented from doing so, while the action was in dependence, by insanity, or any other incapacity not expressly mentioned (as minority is) in the statute; I should conceive that there were no slight grounds for doubting whether he would not be entitled to reduce the sale, leaving it to the purchaser to seek for relief under the warrandice of the conveyances from the creditors. On this account, a purchaser should be exceedingly careful to insist upon searches being made, with almost as much scrupulousness as if he were engaging in a voluntary purchase; and, on the other hand, it is materially the interest of the creditors, to see that their common agent order such searches to be made, as may leave them as little as possible exposed to danger, and, by giving additional confidence to purchasers, make the title to the lands more eligible, and worthy of a higher price.

The peculiar strength with which the decree of sale is endowed, as it rests chiefly upon the accuracy of the intimations ordered in the statutes, must fail, wherever any fundamental defect of that kind can be proved. It would not, I apprehend, be sufficient to argue, (as was done in the case of Sir Andrew Myreton), that a peculiar provision is made in the very forms of proceeding for a revisal of the whole, prior to the pronouncing of the decree of sale. The purchaser should be bound to see, that the proceedings are, at least, ex facie, regular and unobjectionable.

2. Against the creditors of the bankrupt, the purchaser is protected by the decree of certification. We have already seen, that the terms for producing claims are assigned successively; the first, in the same interlocutor which orders the proof of bankruptcy, the second, under the strongest declaration, immediately on the

expiry

expiry of the first, and the election of the common agent: and that, after a further indulgence of ten days, the decree of certification is extracted. It has the double effect of protecting the purchaser against all latent claims from creditors, and of freeing the field of competition, for the other creditors, of all who have not appeared. It is the first of these effects only, that we at present consider. It cannot safely be said, that a decree of sale, even though guarded by a previous decree of certification, is absolutely and irrevocably sacred; for instances have occurred, of decrees of sale having been opened up. But this, at least, may be said, that there does not appear to be any case, where this has been done, in which some peculiar circumstances of connivance, or interested conduct on the part of the purchaser, were not established. As, for example, in the case of Mortimer against Hay of Mountblairy, where the pursuer of the sale was himself the purchaser, and contrived to lull the children of the bankrupt from appearing, till the decree was extracted in his favour: November 1757.

3. We have seen, that the purchaser has no protection in the strength of his title, against claims of eviction from third parties, whose rights are preferable to that of the bankrupt; that his right is in nothing better, than that of the bankrupt himself; and that the Legislature, by introducing a mode of selling the property of the bankrupt, had no design of creating a new estate for him. All that the purchaser, therefore, has to trust to, as a defence against eviction, is, on the one hand, a strict search of the records, and a scrupulous examination of the title deeds; and, on the other, the obligation of warrandice contained in the conveyances from the creditors. That, in the common case, where there is no peculiar stipulation, the purchaser has a right, upon discovering any defect in the titles, or any ground of eviction, to suspend the payment of the price, is certain. But sometimes, where the debtor's titles are not clear, nor such as the creditors can answer for, it is necessary to expose the lands, under a qualification, that they may bring what they can, with the least possible risk of a call upon the creditors to refund. In such a case, the bargain is made in the articles of roup, that the purchaser shall accept of the titles as they stand. A sale

of

of this kind was made by a trustee for creditors, not indeed judicially; but that seems to make no difference on the principle. A provision was inserted in the articles of roup, that the creditors should assign their debts and rights, with warrandice, to the extent of the price; and that the purchaser should accept of such titles as the creditors had to give, which were specified in an inventory. The purchaser finding, on more minute examination, that really there was no right vested in the common debtor, presented a suspension, in order to get quit of the sale. The Lord Ordinary (Alva) decided in his favour—'finding him not barred, by the articles of roup, from objecting, that no right whatever, in the 'person of the common debtor, is produced, or, though such title 'were produced, from objecting the nullity thereof, if such should 'appear.' But the Court altered this judgement, and found the sale binding. It was observed on the Bench, that 'a purchaser is 'not, in the common case, obliged to pay, before the seller has 'delivered to him a sufficient progress to the property of the sub-'ject sold. Here, however, it has been agreed, that eviction 'alone should entitle the purchaser to recourse against the sellers, 'and no reason occurs, why this practice should not be effectual.' 10th July 1783, Hay against Panton, VII. Fac. Coll. cxii. 175. I do not see a good ground for doubting, that the principle of this decision should be carried further, so as to support an article in the agreement, declaring, that the creditors should not be bound in warrandice to the purchaser. Creditors will often take a smaller sum, rather than risk a call for the refunding of what they have received: and it seems much more eligible to them, that they should pay (by receiving a smaller price) the insurance of a defective title, than that they should remain in continual apprehension of a claim of eviction. The warrandice, implied in the conveyances of the debts, is, no doubt, a security at common law, against the eviction of the estate; but, as an implied obligation, it is capable of being transacted—it is not inseparably connected with the nature of the sale, or distribution of the price.

The nature of the conveyances, by the creditors to the purchaser, and the extent of the warrandice which they imply, are

declared

declared and regulated by act of sederunt, 31st March 1685. It requires 'the creditors, who are preferred to the price of the lands, 'upon payment, to dispone their rights and diligences, used at 'their instances, in favour of the purchaser, with warrandice quoad 'the sums received by them; so that, in case of eviction of the 'lands disponed, they shall be liable to refund those sums, in whole 'or in part, effeiring to the eviction, and the sums paid to them, 'with annualrents thereof, from the time of the sentence; provid-'ing, always, intimation be made to the creditors of the process of 'eviction, before litiscontestation in the cause.' It belongs, more strictly, to another part of the subject, to inquire into the effect of such conveyances; whether it be to extinguish the debts, or to keep them up as burdens upon the estate: it may, here, only be intimated, that they are to be regarded rather as extinguished and discharged debts, in so far as regards the estate, although they are still good and subsisting debts, to the effect of claiming against the creditors upon eviction. See afterwards, Book VI.

II. RIGHT ACQUIRED BY THE PURCHASER.

Questions have often arisen, respecting the extent of the right acquired by the purchaser, as affected by the value, descriptions, &c. in the proven rental, or letters of publication, and advertisements. In all such cases, there seems to be room for a material distinction, between the description of the subject itself, and the statement of its value and advantages.

DESCRIPTION OF THE SUBJECT.—The purchaser is entitled to have warranted to him, every thing which is described in the judicial rental, as part of the lands sold; and, on the contrary, he is not entitled to claim any thing which is by that description excluded.

That he is entitled to have every thing which the description includes, or a deduction proportioned to its value, is proved by the case of Wilson against the creditors of Sir James Campbell of Auchinbreck, 14th Nov. 1764, in which the teinds, having been in-

cluded

cluded in the rental, and exposed and sold, along with the lands, it was afterwards discovered, that one fourth of them did not belong to the seller. The Court 'found the purchasers entitled to deduc- 'tion of a fourth part of the teinds:' III. Fac. Coll. clxviii. 351. But if the subjects have been valued and sold in cumulo, and no separate value put upon the subject which is evicted or lost to the purchaser, then he must either renounce the bargain altogether, or keep it without any abatement. 13th Feb. 1782, Lloyds against the apparent heir and creditors of Paterson, VII. Fac. Coll. xxxi. 52.

That the purchaser can claim nothing which is excluded by the description, is proved by the case of Blair of Balthayock against Murray. The lands of Overdurdie, part of the estate of Balthayock, were originally held of the abbots of Scoon in feu, for payment of certain quantities of bear, &c. amounting in value to about 20l. a year of present money. They belonged, at the beginning of last century, to Sir Robert Ayton: he obtained a signature from the Crown, empowering him to purchase up the feu-duty and superiority, at the same rate which, by the decree-arbitral concerning teinds, was declared optional to the Crown; but in this charter, a power of redemption was reserved to the Crown. Sir Robert accordingly purchased up the feu-duties and superiority; and received a conveyance of them from the Viscount of Stormont, under the condition of reversion in favour of his Majesty. This right contained a procuratory for resigning the lands, to be holden of the Crown in blench; but with a condition, that Sir Robert should, in case of the Crown choosing to redeem the feu-farms, resign the lands, and receive a renewal of the holding in feu, for payment of the feu-farms, &c. as before. Sir Robert's charter was, however, taken out, to be held, not blench, but in feu, for payment of the duties in the old investitures; and, in narrating the right from Viscount Stormont, it was provided, that Sir Robert and his heirs, &c. should have retention of the feu-duties, &c. until they should be redeemed by the Crown. In this form the titles continued, though, by statute 1707, c. 11, the power of redemption by the Crown was renounced, 'that the feu-duties might remain with the Lords of 'erection, and those having right from them, irredeemably, and 'for ever.' When these lands of Overdurdie were exposed to judicial sale by the creditors of Mr Blair, they were stated, in the prepared state, &c. at a gross rent of 122l. 9s. 7d., but as holding feu of the Crown for payment of the feu-duties, as in the old titles, which, being converted at certain rates, amounted to 16l. 3s. 1d., leaving, after other deductions, a free rental of 96l. 1s. 5d. And, in the act of roup, it was found proved by charters, &c. 'that the said 'lands of Overdurdie do hold feu of the Crown, for payment of the 'above duties,' &c. The purchaser of these lands claimed right to them, unburdened with the feu-duties; and an action was brought against him by the heir of Balthayock, to whom a clear reversion had arisen from the sale of his father's estates. Lord Eskgrove Ordinary, having 'considered mutual memorials, found, that the de- 'fender Daniel Murray, being, by the decree of sale, declared to 'have as valid and effectual a right to the lands of Overdurdie, 'teinds and pertinents, as if they had been sold and disponed to 'him by the deceased John Blair of Balthayock, whose titles to the 'land included the right of retention of the ancient feu-duties 'thereof; and that the defender should hold them, sicklike and as 'freely in all respects as the said John Blair, or any of his prede- 'cessors or authors, held or might have held the same; the said 'defender is thereby entitled to the retention of the said feu-duties, 'as a part of, or accessory to his purchase: Finds, that as the said 'lands and others have been sold judicially to the defender, as the 'highest bidder at the public roup, where the same were exposed 'to sale, not conform to any rental, but at a slump, or total upset 'price; he cannot now be obliged to pay a higher price than his 'last offer, on account of any deductions erroneously made in the 'rental, taken up by this Court, before the said judicial sale: and 'assoilzies the defender, and decerns: But, in respect of the na- 'ture of the case, as meriting the most deliberate discussion, su- 'persedes,' &c. When the question came before the Court, upon a petition and answers, the other Judges took a different view of it. They held the case to come simply to this, that the right to the feu-duty, standing upon the right of retention and the statute, formed a separate estate; which was neither exposed to sale, nor intended to be purchased: and accordingly this judgement was pro-

nounced—

nounced—'The Lords find, that the defender must either give up 'the purchase of the lands of Overdurdie, or pay an additional 'price, corresponding to the value of the feu-duty in question, de-'ducted from the rental; and remit to the Lord Ordinary to pro-'ceed accordingly; and, in particular, to ascertain the additional 'price to be paid, in the event of the defender agreeing to hold the 'purchase:' 16th July 1790, Blair of Balthayock against Murrays.— In the case of Campbell of Blythswood, some years before, the Court had decided in the same way against the purchaser, although the circumstances were much more favourable for him. Some burgh acres, in the neighbourhood of Renfrew, were purchased by Mr Campbell at a judicial sale; but it was discovered, before the decree was pronounced, that a mistake had been committed in fixing the upset price, according to the proven rental of 2½ acres, although the subject really consisted of 7 acres. The Court found, that no more than 2½ acres were sold, the rest remaining unsold; and they put it in Mr Campbell's option, to retain or to reject the purchase. Yet, here, the different parcels, composing the seven acres, were all specially enumerated in the summons of sale; and in the letters of publication, and minutes and articles of roup, all the unentailed acres were said to be exposed: 4th July 1781, Hepburn & Sommervile against Campbell of Blythswood, VI. Fac. Coll. Part II. lxix. 113.

STATEMENTS OF VALUE, ADVANTAGES, &c.—In private sales, it may sometimes be a question of some nicety, what is to be held as a description implying warrandice But, in judicial sales, the general rule is, that the purchaser is entitled to trust to no statement of value, or of peculiar advantages. His business is, to examine every thing himself, and to proceed only upon the information which he so acquires. The measurements and values stated in the proven rental, are not intended for the information of purchasers, but for the purpose, merely, of serving as data to the Court, in deciding upon the question of bankruptcy, and in fixing the upset price. Even when stated, as they generally are, in the newspaper advertisements, they are to be taken rather as hints, to direct the inquiries of the purchaser, than as solid information,

upon

upon which he is ultimately to rely, in deciding upon the propriety of purchasing. Every judicial sale, therefore, is a slump bargain.—In Hay of Drummelzier's case, the purchasers of part of the estate, having discovered some material errors, in stating the rental and upset price, they applied to have a rectification and allowance. 'The Lords would not receive any errors in the testimonies of the 'witnesses, or the probation; but, if there was any material error in calculo, or in the misapplication of the probation, the plurality inclined to reconsider the same; as, where a house in 'Dunse is given up to belong to Sir James Cockburn in superiority, and it is proven to hold of the Magistrates of Edinburgh; 'and the like.' 'But this latitude,' says Lord Fountainhall, 'may be of a very bad preparative:' 20th July 1697, I. Fount. 788. Many cases have occurred, in which, upon the same principle, deductions have been refused, on account of falls in the value of subjects, between the time of taking the proof, and the date of the sale. The first case of this kind, seems to have been, that of the creditors of Hallgreen, 15th January 1725, where this general point was decided, that the purchaser can have no deduction, on account of the rents falling lower after the proof, and before the sale. The next case was, that of the creditors of Cockpen, where, after the proof of the rental, a tenant having quitted his possession, the judicial factor set the farm by roup, (after full advertisement, but without any warrant from the Court), at a loss of 100l. below the proven rental. The lands were exposed, of course, at the proven rental, and sold at twenty-seven years purchase. The purchaser claimed a deduction on account of this enormous discrepancy between the proved rental and real value. The creditors pleaded, that all such bargains were slump—the purchaser, that they were plainly not slump, but by a rental. The Lords found, that the purchaser was not entitled to any abatement of the price, on account of any diminution of the rental between the time of the judicial proof of the rental and the purchase: 22d December 1732, II. Dict. 312. A similar decision was pronounced in the case of Wilson against the Creditors of Sir James Campbell of Auchinbreck, already quoted. The proof of the rental was taken in 1739; and the sale did not proceed till twenty-one years afterwards. The purchasers discovered,

discovered, that some houses, which, in the judicial rental, were stated as yielding a considerable sum, had, since the proof was led, become entirely ruinous, and of no value; and, that some of the lands had been overrated, yielding a rent considerably lower than that at which they were stated in the judicial rental. On account of these things, they claimed a deduction from the price. But 'the Lords repelled the claim of deduction:' 14th November 1764, Wilson against Creditors of Sir James Campbell, III. Fac. Coll. cxlviii. 351. Again, the question occurred in the sale of Skibo. Between the year 1780, when the estate of Skibo was valued, and 1786, when it was sold, the rents had fallen about a sixth part. The purchaser claimed deduction, or liberty to renounce the bargain. 'The Court, however, was unanimously of 'opinion, agreeably to many former determinations, that the plea 'here urged for the purchaser, was inadmissible; as it was known, 'that the chief object of the judicial rental was, to ascertain the 'bankruptcy; and that, in the interval which preceded the actual 'sale, many alterations would necessarily happen: it was the business of intending purchasers to make a proper inquiry into the 'matter; and, nothing but an undue concealment of the facts, 'could annul a judicial sale, otherwise unexceptionable.' The Court refused the claim of the purchaser: 27th June 1788, Inglis against Dempster, VIII. Fac. Coll. xxvi. 43.

A measurement, which enters into the description of the lands, will, as in the case of Campbell of Blythswood, be held as a bounding description; but a measurement, which is merely spoken of in the advertisements, or which appears upon a plan or survey of the estate, is to be considered only as intended to give information as to the probable extent of the estate, or as a mere relation of apparent advantages, which the purchaser is not entitled to consider as a condition, or as taking away the obligation upon him to satisfy himself by his own inquiries. In the advertisements publishing the judicial sale of Bargaly, the estate was said to consist of 1710 acres: 146 were covered with wood; and reference was made to a plan and measurement in the hands of the common agent. Mr Hannay, the purchaser, offered

to

to prove a deficiency of 96 acres, of which 46 were woodlands; and he claimed a proportional deduction from the price, upon the footing, that there was a fraud or error in the description. The creditors answered, that the value put upon the estate, and the articles of roup, which alone formed the contract between the creditors and the purchaser, were fixed, in this case, without any regard to the measurement; which was referred to, merely as descriptive of the subject, and by no means as making these dimensions an essential condition of the bargain. The Lords refused to give the deduction: 26th January 1785, Hannay against Creditors of Bargaly, VII. Fac. Coll. cxcv. 306.

SECTION VI.

OF THE RANKING.

THE sale is useful to the creditors, only as it converts the estate of the debtor into a distributable fund. To distribute it among them, is the business of the ranking. At present, we are to consider merely the forms of the ranking; reserving the rules and principles of division for future discussion. The great object of any judicial form of distribution, is, to have the debts properly scrutinized, that no person may draw as a creditor, who has no title to that character, and that none may acquire a preference, to which he is not entitled—to secure to those, who choose to come forward, a safe payment of whatever may fall to them in the division—to have the adequacy, or deficiency, of the funds clearly pointed out, and the distribution regulated accordingly—to have all these proceedings carried on under the eye of a Court, and subject to its review—and to have them all accomplished in the shortest time, and at the least expence.

The ranking, as a mode of distribution, may be considered as totally independent of the action of sale. It is a process, in which, for the accomplishment of the above purposes, a common agent or

trustee

trustee is appointed, to take measures of exclusion against all who do not, within a certain time, produce their claims, and to make up a state of the debts, containing such objections as occur, and classing them according to those preferences which have been legally acquired;—in which, this state is ordered to be seen and answered by all concerned, so that they may have a full opportunity of correcting any errors or omissions of the common agent, or of removing any objections to their debts, which are capable of being removed;—in which, the whole of these states, objections, answers, &c. are judged of, and determined by the Court, and the interests of the creditors fixed;—and in which, finally, a scheme of division is made up, containing a fair statement of the price of the lands, rents, interests, &c. on the one hand; and striking the dividend payable to each creditor, according to the previously fixed order of ranking, on the other. But, though the ranking may be considered, in one sense, as a separate process from the sale, the law has varied considerably, in regulating their relation to each other. When the action of sale was first introduced, it was merely an action of sale, not of ranking. The ranking was settled in a process of multiplepoinding, after the sale was concluded. See Sir George M'Kenzie's Observations, 463. This continued to be the practice, after the reform of the action, in some particulars, by the statute of 1690, c. 20. But, one great evil was found to spring from it. The purchaser contrived, by purchasing up debts, &c. to throw such difficulties in the way of the ranking, that, often, many years passed away before it was settled, while he retained the price in his own hands. To remedy this evil, it was enacted, in the Regulations for the Session, 29th April 1695, art. 26, 'That in all actions of sale of bankrupts' lands, upon late acts of 'Parliament, either depending, or to be hereafter raised, the rank-'ing of the creditors, and others concerned, shall proceed, and 'first be concluded by decree, at least to the avail of the price of 'the lands, found and stated by the Lords of Session, before the 'said lands be exposed to roup and sale.' At the time that these regulations were made, there was not, as yet, any provision for enabling apparent heirs to bring the estates of their ancestors to sale; and accordingly, this regulation, of the respective date of the

the sale and ranking, never has been understood to apply to actions of sale raised by apparent heirs; but, on the contrary, the sale has always, in those cases, preceded the ranking. The first alteration made upon the rule, that the ranking should precede the sale, was by a private statute, empowering the Court of Session to depart from it, in the very peculiar case of the York Building Company's bankruptcy. The ranking of the complicated claims against the estates of that Company, had depended for more than forty years; and it was found necessary, in 1777, to apply to Parliament for authority to sell the estates, without waiting the issue of so tedious a process. It was not till 1783, that any alteration was made upon the rule, as applicable to common rankings and sales. The loss and inconvenience to creditors, was found, in many cases, to be great. The estate, during the long period of the contest among the creditors, continued under sequestration, and a factor was paid for his management and care. There was a great risk, rather perhaps an absolute certainty, that, during the short leases which a factor could give, the lands, instead of being improved, would fall back in cultivation, and in value, to a purchaser: there was a danger, that, during the dependence of the ranking, the best, and most favourable opportunity for selling to advantage, might be lost: there was even a possibility, that the debtor himself, or his friends, flattering themselves with some favourable turn, might retard the ranking, by objecting to debts: and, it is perfectly plain, that, wherever the price exceeded twenty years purchase, there would have arisen from a sale an annual advantage to the fund, by the excess of the interest of the price over the rents, even supposing it possible to levy rents without expence or deduction. These, with other reasons, not perhaps so well founded, were stated by the proposers of the law of 1783, as the inductive causes of an alteration upon the old rule. It was proposed, and approved of by the Legislature, 'that all actions of sale of 'lands, or other heritable subjects, raised, or to be raised, and 'pursued at the instance of creditors, before the Court of Session, upon any of the statutes in that behalf made, shall proceed, and be carried on to a conclusion, by actual sale, as soon 'as the necessary previous steps of a sale are taken, whether

'the

'the ranking of the creditors is concluded, or not; unless the 'Court, upon application of the creditors, or any of them, shall 'find sufficient cause to delay the sale, any law or practice to 'the contrary notwithstanding.'—And, to avoid the evil which led to the establishment of the old law, viz. the interested interference of the purchaser, in picking up debts, and delaying the ranking, the Court of Session was authorised, upon application of the creditors, to order consignation in the hands of a Bank. This law is continued by the statute of 1793. What the effect of the rule is upon the funds, and upon the debts, shall be an object of future inquiry.

All the explanations which appear to be necessary, concerning this action of ranking, may be given, under these few heads. 1. The effect of the decree of certification, in clearing away all claims not produced within ten days after the expiry of the second term. 2. The state of interests, and order and decree of ranking. 3. The scheme of division, or statement of the funds, and application of the decree of ranking to them. 4. The effect of the draught made by the creditors, and of the conveyances which they are bound to give to the purchaser, upon the personal claim against the bankrupt.

1. EFFECT OF THE DECREE OF CERTIFICATION.—We have already considered the effect of this decree, as a guard and protection to the right of the purchaser, in which view, we have seen it to be nearly absolute, preventing any creditor from challenging the decree of sale, or disturbing that title, which it is highly the interest of all the creditors to have considered as the most unexceptionable a purchaser can hold. But there is obviously less danger in permitting the decree to be so far opened as to admit a creditor to claim his dividend of the fund. Notwithstanding the anxiety of the law to secure the best possible intimation to all the creditors, it is within the bounds of possibility, that a creditor may not have heard of the proceedings; and it would be unjust to exclude him absolutely, when he may not be in fault. It was therefore provided,

 by

by act of sederunt 23d November 1711, § 6, that a creditor should be allowed to produce his claim, upon payment of 'a certain 'pecuniary mulct, to be modified by the Lord Ordinary, not under 'twenty shillings Sterling; and to be increased according to the 'delay the producer is guilty of; and this mulct to be paid in to 'the factor or clerk, towards defraying the charge of the process.' By the act of sederunt of 1794, this rule is altered; and it is provided, that 'in case, at any time hereafter, a creditor shall, 'upon cause shown, be reponed against a decree of certification 'in a ranking and sale, he shall be obliged to pay the whole expence 'occasioned by the delay, and by the production of a new interest, 'as the same shall be ascertained by the Court, or by the Lord 'Ordinary.' Under this clause, the general creditors have a good right to object to this expence, if it should be charged in the accounts of the common agent, whose business it is to insist upon it from the creditor reponed. The effect of a decree of certification, then, is to make every claim, not produced in due time, be held as false and forged, unless upon cause shown, and payment of the expence incurred.

2. STATE OF INTERESTS, AND DECREE OF RANKING.—The decree of certification having closed the chequer against the production of claims, the common agent may sit down, without interruption, to consider the documents and vouchers of debt, and to propose his scheme of ranking, according to what appears to be the just rights and preferences of the creditors. The act of sederunt, 11th July 1794, appoints the common agent 'to make up 'a full state of the interests of the creditors, and of the objections 'thereto, and the questions arising thereon; distinguishing those 'objections or questions, which go to the enlargement of the com'mon fund, or to prevent its diminution, from those which only 'affect the interest of particular creditors, or classes of creditors, 'in competition with one another; and also suggesting the order 'of ranking: which state shall be printed, and copies of it put 'into the Lords boxes, and distributed among the creditors, or 'their known agents.' And provision is made for the production of new interests, or the occurrence of any additional objections,

&c,

&c. He is also required, 'in these states, to set forth, whether 'there is any probability of a reversion to the common debtor; 'and in what view, or different views, there may be a prospect of 'such reversion.' § 7.

The scrutiny to which a claim is subjected in a ranking, is, in this way, very strict. 1. The common agent is bound, by the duties of his office, to investigate each claim accurately; and to state every possible objection to it, which may either strike it out of the division, and so benefit the common fund; or postpone it in the ranking, and so benefit particular creditors. 2. He is bound to state the particulars of each claim, in a report, which is laid before all the other creditors for their inspection; so that any omission of the common agent may be corrected. And, 3dly, The claimant must swear to the truth of his claim, before he can be admitted to draw a dividend upon it.

The creditor, whose claim is objected to, has a full opportunity of being heard in answer—the common agent being bound to support the objection, if for the common behoof—the individuals interested being left to maintain, at their own expence, such objections as may tend only to their advantage, as regulating their place in the ranking: Act of Sed. 11th July 1794, § 8.—By art. 9. & 10. of the act of sederunt, 17th January 1756, the Lord Ordinary is directed to name days, for lodging objections, answers, and replies; and then to order a pleading, and pronounce judgement, unless he please to order the point to be stated before the whole Lords. This is altered by the act of sederunt of 1794, and, either written, or viva voce pleadings, declared to be sufficient, at the option of the Lord Ordinary. Much care is taken, in these regulations, to ensure dispatch:—No representation to the Lord Ordinary is allowed; but the party dissatisfied must carry the cause, at once, before the whole Lords. And, to prevent the splitting of the ranking into many parts, it is, by the 11th section of the act of 1756, ordered, that all the points, upon which the judgement of the Inner-house is sought, are to be decided at once—those which are brought under review from the judgement

of

of the Lord Ordinary, and upon which the petition is not at once refused, and those which are taken to report by him, being ordered to be brought before the Court on the same day.

The whole objections being determined finally, the clerk to the process is ordered to draw up a decree, including all the particular judgements, and ranking and preferring those claims which are sustained as good, according to the preferences to which they are found entitled by the scheme of ranking, as acquiesced in, or as settled by the judgements of the Court. This interlocutor being signed by the Lord Ordinary, the decree of ranking is extracted.

The effect of an extracted decree of ranking, when considered with relation to those who have actually appeared in the action, is, to settle their claims and preferences. But still, the judgements must, of course, be subject to appeal, and also liable to be reduced, upon facts newly emerging, 'res noviter venientes ad notitiam:' 4th January 1749, Blackwood against Sir Geo. Hamilton, Kilk. 436.—Considered in relation to those who have not appeared in the action, the effect of the decree of ranking, as an exclusion, will be understood, by remembering, that those who, under the express declaration of the law, are prevented from disturbing the purchaser, are still entitled to have their relief against the creditors, even after the division of the fund: much more, consequently, must they be entitled to such relief before the fund is divided: and accordingly, it is established, that creditors are entitled to appear, and claim a share in the division, without the necessity of reducing the decree of ranking: Kilk. 468.

3. SCHEME AND DECREE OF DIVISION.—The decree of ranking ascertains the claims of the creditors who are entitled to share the price; the scheme of division is, as it were, the point of union of the two actions of sale and ranking, in which the produce of the sale, or fund to be divided, is stated, on the one hand, and the shares or dividends due to each creditor, according to the rights fixed by the decree of ranking, are struck, upon the other.

The

The explanation of the principles and rules, by which schemes of division in ranking and sales, in sequestrations, and in voluntary trusts, are to be made, is the subject of the Fifth Book; where it will be found, that, not only are there many difficult and intricate questions to be settled, in ascertaining the dividends due to each creditor, according to the different relations in which he stands with others; but questions, also, of no mean importance, respecting the period of accumulation of the funds, on the one hand, and the debts on the other; and the effect of accidental defalcations, bankruptcy of purchasers, factors, &c. as they touch the general interest, or the postponed creditors. It is commonly to an accountant that the making up of the scheme of division is remitted. When made out, it is lodged with the clerk, to be examined by the creditors, and objected to, if there be cause. It is then approved of by the Lord Ordinary, if there be no objection, or if the objections be repelled; or with alteration, if the objections be good. A decree of division is pronounced, containing a warrant upon the purchaser to pay the price; and upon this, as upon any other decree for payment, diligence may proceed.

4. RECOVERY OF THE PRICE.—The common agent is bound to take the proper steps for recovering, from the purchaser, the price of the lands, to be distributed. For this purpose, all the diligence of the law is open to him. If the purchaser should fail, the bond for the price is to be recorded, so that diligence may proceed against the cautioner: and if, in no way, the price can be recovered, the common agent must proceed to have the sale annulled, and the lands re-exposed.

5. When the creditors receive their dividends, they are bound to aſſign to the purchaser their debts and securities. But this is nothing more than an aſſignation of the real security, to the amount of the dividend received, so as to be a security to the purchaser. Still the creditors are entitled to proceed in diligence against the person and moveables of the debtor, in order to recover the balance which may remain unpaid. The extract of the decree of division, and the payment of the dividends in consequence of

it,

it, operate not as an insuperable bar to any subsequent claim by a creditor who has not been included in the division. If the division should proceed, for example, during the five years allowed for appealing to the House of Lords, the creditor aggrieved is not thereby precluded from his right of appealing. Again, if he shall have discovered new evidence, sufficient to establish his claim; or if he shall be able to show, that he was, by minority, or other incapacity, prevented from attending to his interest in the ranking, he is not to be for ever deprived of his share of the funds, by the mere circumstance of its having been distributed among the other creditors, however hard it may be for them to repay what they had bona fide received. Relief will be given to him, in an action calling the other creditors for indemnification: and the Court will make a new remit to an accountant, to proportion the dividend upon the different creditors whose former draught it may affect.

CHAP.

CHAP. II.

Of the Processes of Distribution of the Moveable or Personal Estate, where the Debtor is not a Trader.

When, in 1783, the Legislature thought fit to alter the original plan of the sequestration law, and to restrict the benefit of this institution to the bankruptcies of those engaged in trade or manufactures, the personal estates of other insolvent debtors were left to be attached by the ordinary forms of individual diligence, and to be distributed in the processes which were already established by the common law.

The statutes, by which a pari passu preference is established among creditors doing diligence against moveables, have corrected many of the evils and hardships of the old law; but still, as we have seen in the Third Book, some evils remain, for which, it were surely to be wished that a remedy could be devised. It is still possible, we have seen, that a creditor may be unable to render the debtor bankrupt, or to complete his own diligence within the appointed terms; and it is much to be regreted, that equality is to be attained only by the accumulation of diligences, and heaping up of expence. These evils were too great, to be suffered in the bankruptcies of traders; but although they are, in a national point of view, of comparatively little importance in common cases, still they are frequently attended with great hardship. The provision, indeed, is ample for securing a pari passu preference, where the creditors observe the first step of diligence taken against their debtor. If it be an arrestment, and the debtor insolvent, all the creditors

creditors may, with great ease, and by the assistance of a trustee, at no great expence, get their arrestments ready in time—if a poinding, they may, within six weeks, even have their debts liquidated, and the poinder summoned *. But it may happen, that a debtor may be rendered bankrupt, a considerable time before the creditors think of taking steps for securing themselves against preferences; that much time may be consumed in proposals for voluntary arrangements; and that the creditors may be roused from their security by a poinding, executed when the four months are almost expired. No expedition, on the part of those whose debts are unliquidated, can save them in such a situation: the Court of Session has no power to dispense with the legal induciæ, or to hurry on all the actions of constitution, so as to enable the creditors to take the benefit of the pari passu preference.

Whether it may be thought expedient, in the renewal of the bankrupt law, to devise any general form of attachment, which could prevent these evils—save the expence of accumulated diligences—prevent the danger of preferences, thus hurriedly acquired—and enable the creditors, coolly and deliberately, to take measures, in concert, for arranging the affairs, and settling the distribution, it is not proper, in this place, to inquire. I have stated, what appears to be the great defect of the law, as it stands at present; and shall proceed to explain, shortly, the nature and use of the processes of distribution, as applicable to the various attachments which may be made of the moveable funds.

There are three processes, in which the moveable funds of a debtor, who is not a trader, may, at common law, be distributed among his creditors; the MULTIPLEPOINDING, the FORTHCOMING, and the ACTION AGAINST POINDERS.

SEC-

* In treating of the pari passu preference of poinders, I ought to have observed, that, upon the analogy of the cases of adjudications, and upon the plain principles of equity, there seems to be no question, that the Court would interpose in these actions of constitution, as in those which are to be followed by adjudication, to abridge, as much as possible, the proceedings, and, in particular, to reserve the defences, to be stated in the shape of objections.

SECTION I.

OF THE ACTION OF MULTIPLEPOINDING.

THE multiplepoinding is a very old form of action in Scotland. It proceeds, as its name intimates, upon the idea of double distress, either actually begun, or threatened, against a person holding the moveable property of another. It is directed against those who have intimated to the holder, that they have received conveyances of the fund, or who have used legal measures, for attaching the fund, for their payment. These creditors are called into the field to debate their preferences, and have it settled, by a judgement, to whom the fund is to be paid over; and this must, of course, be attended with this penalty, that, if they do not appear, their claims shall be disregarded, and the fund distributed. One great view of the law, in the institution of this action, was, to save the expence of all the various actions and counteractions that, in the common course of things, might be necessary for settling the rights of the creditors. It is therefore held to be a congeries of all the actions which may be necessary for explicating the competition; and not only the holder of the fund himself, but any creditor interested, or even the common debtor himself, may bring the action, though it must always proceed in the name of him who holds the fund, and against whom the warrant for payment is ultimately to proceed.

I shall not attempt to detail, formally, the proceedings in this action; but shall rather confine my attention to those points, which are of real importance, in understanding its true nature and effect.

1. As the object of the action is, to dispose, finally, of a disputed fund, it is necessary to call, as parties to it, every creditor,

 who,

who, by voluntary or judicial act, has any real right constituted in his person, upon the fund. This is done by citation, as in any common action; and the effect of overlooking such creditors in the citation, must, of course, be, to entitle them to repetition from the creditors, who shall be preferred, of such part of the fund as they would have drawn in the competition, and to indemnification from the holder of the fund.

When all who have real rights over the funds, are called, the decree of multiplepoinding, which orders payment to those who are preferred, is a shield to the holder, who under such authority pays, against any future challenge by creditors who have not appeared. This decree is to be considered as a part of the creditors' diligence, or legal execution, similar in its effect to a decree of forthcoming. It must be obeyed, and, of consequence, must operate as a complete discharge to him who pays under its command: Sir Geo. M'Kenzie's Observ. 9 James VI. c. 3.; IV. Ersk. iii. 23.

To the creditors preferred, the decree of multiplepoinding is no absolute protection. By 1584, c. 3, one who can show a necessary cause of absence, or a minor without tutors or curators, is entitled to reduce the decree, and, although he was expressly called in the action, to claim from those preferred, repayment of what he should have drawn. Those who were not summoned, must have a right to show that the decree was erroneous, and that the fund should be repaid to them. It is a matter of great importance, to guard, as completely as possible, against the probability of creditors coming forward after the fund is divided: and therefore, it is often the practice to insert advertisements in the newspaper, intimating the dependance of the multiplepoinding, and requiring all having claims upon the fund to appear. These intimations, too, contain, in general, a declaration, that those who do not appear shall be excluded from any share in the division. But no such declaration can deprive a creditor of his legal right of redress, should he afterwards bring a reduction of the decree of multiplepoinding.

In

In all competitions, it is held as a rule, that, while the fund is still in medio, undisposed of, any creditor interested may appear and claim: and thus, in the multiplepoinding, any creditor of the common debtor may appear, though not called; and, on producing his ground of debt, enter into the competition, object to the claims of other creditors, maintain the superiority of his own, and contend for a place in the division, as if he had been an original party to the cause.

The pursuer of the action has little further interest, than to see that such citations have been given as may secure the efficacy of the decree as a discharge to him—to abide the orders of the Court, respecting the intermediate disposal of the fund, and the ultimate payment of it—and to get the necessary expences of the common action allowed as a deduction from his debt. The first interlocutor, in a multiplepoinding, accordingly, finds the raiser of the action liable only in single payment, and, if the action be well founded, entitled to the expence of raising it: the subsequent proceedings concern the competition of the creditors, and settlement of their rights alone; and the whole is closed with the decree of division, and for payment.

Thus, the action is of such a nature as to infer a judicial discharge to the holder of the fund; while it is a congeries of all the actions necessary for settling the disputed preferences among the creditors. What, then, is the effect of the action upon the diligence of individuals?

1. One thing is certain, that no individual, who has appeared in the action, can proceed with personal diligence against the holder of the fund. His claim is properly under suspension, as to that fund; and he will expose himself to an action of damages, by using diligence against the holder of it: 13th February 1772, White against Brown, V. Fac. Coll. vi. 10. Should any other creditors, not called in the multiplepoinding, proceed with diligence against the holder of the fund, the multiplepoinding will afford a complete ground of suspension.

2. The

2. The multiplepoinding is certainly to be regarded as making the fund litigious, to the effect of preventing the common debtor, to whom that fund originally belonged, from giving any voluntary conveyances to it, while the action is in dependance.

3. There does not seem to be any good ground for thinking, that the multiplepoinding either supersedes the necessity of proceeding with diligence, in order to attach the fund; or has the effect of preventing creditors from going on with their diligences, in order to acquire preferences. If it be supposed, for example, that an arrestment has been used and the debtor rendered bankrupt, the other creditors must also, under the statute, arrest within the four months, in order to have the benefit of the pari passu preference.—It would not appear to be sufficient for this purpose, to produce a claim in a multiplepoinding raised by the arrestee· in the statute 23 Geo. III. it was indeed provided, that this should be sufficient, § 2.; but no such provision is made in the last statute. Again, let it be supposed, that a creditor has arrested, and the arrestee has raised a multiplepoinding, no one will question, that a creditor, who is not a party to that action, must be allowed to proceed with every diligence that can attach the fund: he may, for example, as I conceive, carry it off by poinding, if the subject be poindable, just as effectually, as if the action in dependence were a forthcoming. The only difficulty seems to be, where the person proceeding with diligence is a party to the action. Let it be supposed, for example, that a creditor, appearing in an action of multiplepoinding, sees fatal objections to the diligence of his rivals; can he proceed to arrest, or do other diligence, to the effect of acquiring a preference? We have seen, that even an action of ranking and sale has no effect in stopping diligence; that, not only before the late act of sederunt, was it necessary to proceed with adjudication, during the course of a sale by creditors; but that, even at present, although a ranking and sale by an apparent heir is held to be an action of distribution by a trustee, and a ranking and sale by creditors has received a similar effect, it still is perfectly competent to proceed with adjudication, to the effect of acquiring

preferences prior to the decree of sale *. But an action of multiplepoinding is in no shape entitled to the same strong effects with a ranking and sale. It is not a general diligence or attachment for behoof of all the creditors; it is merely a suspension of personal diligence against the holder of the fund, and a form of distributing what is given up, among those who can show the best right to it; and as it does not supersede the necessity of using diligence, it cannot have the effect of stopping it.

The creditors, who, by this action, are brought together to dispute and settle their preferences, are not indeed formed into a deliberative body, as in the sequestration; but they may apply to the Judge for the appointment of a factor, to manage the common property; or of a common agent, to attend to the general interest of the creditors.

In the common case, however, there is little occasion for a factor. Where the fund is money, the general course is, to order it to be consigned in a bank, upon a promissory note, payable to the order of Court. Where the fund consists of goods that need to be disposed of, the Court gives, of course, such orders respecting the sale, as may insure the best price, and greatest advantage to all concerned.

It is only in cases which are much involved, that a common agent is ever appointed. The clerk of the process is, in general, the person who makes up the state of the interests, and order of ranking. This duty does not differ from that of the common agent in the ranking and sale. 1. The funds are stated as ascertained: 2. The claims are arranged into classes, and detailed with the proper objections: and, 3. A scheme of the order of ranking is subjoined. This state is allowed to be seen and objected to, and the discussion proceeds among such of the creditors as find themselves engaged. The great use of the appointment of a common agent is, to prevent these individual discussions from putting the action out of its proper shape,

* See above, p. 370. & seq.

shape, and to keep the parties from unduly delaying the division of the fund.

When the preference is settled by a final interlocutor of ranking, effect is given to it in a scheme of division; which, after being seen by all concerned, and either acquiesced in, or corrected and approved of, is the foundation of the final decree settling the distribution of the fund, and finally discharging the raiser of the multiplepoinding.

The action, which has now been treated of, is the most general process of distribution of moveable funds at common law. It is commonly raised as an original action; but very often also it is repeated (as we call it in the language of the bar) in the course of an action of forthcoming. The action of forthcoming itself is also convertible into a process of competition and distribution. We proceed, therefore, to consider it as an occasional substitute for the multiplepoinding.

SECTION II.

Of the Forthcoming, considered as a Process of Distribution.

We have already considered the nature and proceedings in this action, as a part of the common attaching diligence, used by individuals against moveables. When several creditors concur with such diligence, and have raised forthcomings, it is unnecessary to multiply proceedings by raising an action of multiplepoinding, where there are no other creditors in the field. The separate actions of forthcoming are conjoined into one; and the competition determined, as if it were a multiplepoinding.

In such combined action, the Court will give the necessary orders for preserving the common fund, and will make the proper remits to the clerk, or to an accountant, after the points of preference are determined, to make up a scheme of division. Simple as, in the abstract, a competition of arrestments may seem to be, it often becomes, especially in the arrestment of the rents of an extensive estate by many creditors, a matter of very great difficulty, to bring out an intelligible view of the effect of the different arrestments, and of the places to which they are entitled in the division of the fund.

It seems to be quite unnecessary, after what has already been said upon multiplepoinding, to add any thing further respecting the combined action of forthcoming, as a process of distribution.

SECTION III.

Of the Process of Distribution of the Price of Poinded Goods.

The statute, introducing the pari passu preference amongst poinders, requires, that creditors, who wish to take the benefit of it, shall 'summon' the poinder, within four months from the bankruptcy. This expression has not been rigidly interpreted by the Court; and, indeed, it could not be the intention of the Legislature, absolutely and precisely, to require an action at the instance of every creditor wishing to take the benefit of the statute. It has, accordingly, been found competent for other creditors, instead of raising each of them an action, to appear in the action raised by any one creditor against the poinder, and produce their interests there: 16th January 1788, Finlay against Bertram Gardner & Co. VIII. Fac. Coll. xv. 27.—I have also taken occasion, formerly, to observe, that, in the case of M'Lellan against Hog, the Court held the statute to be fulfilled, though the action, in which the pari passu preference was sought, was not at the instance of the creditor claiming the benefit of the statute, but at the instance of the poinder against that creditor, for the purpose of cutting him off from a conjunction with the original poinding, to which he had been improperly admitted by the messenger: 2d January 1797, X. Fac. Coll. xxxii. 74. There seems to be no doubt, that a multiplepoinding, brought by a creditor in the name of the first poinder, would be held regular and effectual, to entitle that creditor, and all who should appear in it within the four months, to the benefit of the statute.

PART THE SECOND.

Of the Sequestration, or Process of Distribution of the Estates of those engaged in Trade or Manufactures.

The explanation of this subject, will require a considerable detail; and as the sequestration is strictly analogous to the English commission of bankruptcy, it will be proper to keep the contrast of the two institutions constantly in view. I shall therefore endeavour, in an introductory chapter, to present a general view of them, before proceeding to the consideration of particulars.

INTRODUCTORY CHAPTER.

General Contrast of the English Commission of Bankruptcy with the Scotish Sequestration—History of the Sequestration—Progressive Improvement of the Law.

The great view of the Legislature, both of England and of Scotland, in instituting a peculiar system of distribution for the estates of those who are engaged in trade and manufactures, has been, 1. To provide more severe laws against fraud, on the one hand, and, on the other, a greater indulgence to innocent misfortune. 2. To form the creditors into a deliberative body, capable of consulting upon their common interests. And, 3. To reduce the estate into money, and have it quickly and economically divided among the creditors, by trustees acting under the superintendance of a court of justice.

For the attainment of these purposes in England, a very peculiar institution has been devised. When, amidst the increasing commerce of the country, the imperfections of the common law, considered as applicable to cases of insolvency, called for the interference of the Legislature, it was found necessary to depart so widely from all the old maxims and rules of law, and so largely to encroach upon what had been considered as the personal privileges both of debtors and of creditors, that, in the first statute respecting bankruptcy, it was thought proper to take the jurisdiction in this matter out of the hands of the courts of common law, and to vest it in certain commissioners. The powers to be given to these commissioners, were so unusual, and so extensive, that none seemed fit for bearing the commission, but men of the first consideration in the country, and on whom the public had entire reliance. By the 35. Henry VIII. c. 4, the Lord Chancellor, or Lord Keeper, the Lord Treasurer, the Lord President, the Lord Privy Seal, and others of the Privy Council, with the two Chief Justices, were named as commissioners, to proceed 'against such 'as do make bankrupt.' Their powers were, to take orders and directions, at their own wisdom and discretion, with the bodies of insolvents, and their real and personal estate—and to cause the said estates and property to be viewed, rented, and appraised, and to make sale thereof—or, otherwise, to order the same, for the satisfaction and payment of the creditors, rateably, and in proportion to the quantities of their debts. They were also vested with very high powers for the prevention and punishment of frauds, concealments, &c. In the 13th of Elizabeth, the system was changed—and, a distinction having been marked out between insolvents and bankrupts, the Legislature, instead of the great Judges to whom the former law had entrusted these extraordinary powers, substituted such wise, discreet, and learned persons, as to the Lord Chancellor should seem good, to be appointed by his commission

under

under the Great Seal—these commissioners being always bound, upon request made to them by the bankrupt, to make a true declaration to him, of the manner in which his estates and property had been employed and disposed of, and to pay the overplus to him. The powers delegated to this new court of commissioners, were similar to those vested in the judges of the former commission. But it were useless to trace all the changes upon the bankrupt laws of England. It is enough for our present purpose, to observe, that, down to the fourth and fifth years of Queen Anne, the commissioners continued to be the sole managers and distributors of the bankrupt's estate, combining, in their official character, that of judges and of trustees. But, by a statute passed at that period, the commissioners were ordered to give notice in the Gazette, of the commission being issued; and to appoint, in the same advertisement, a day for the creditors to meet and choose assignees, in whom the estate should be vested, by assignment from the commissioners—a power of naming provisional assignees, for the intermediate management, being given to the commissioners. The assignees named under this law, and under the successive laws which have since been made amending and improving upon this plan, are properly trustees, for recovering and liquidating the estate, that it may be ready for dividing. The commissioners themselves examine the accounts of the proceeds of the estate, and, comparing them with the debts which are entitled to a dividend, strike that dividend, and order it to be paid.

The general idea, then, of the English system, is this—

1. A court is constituted pro re nata, consisting of five commissioners, named by the Lord Chancellor; and the charter of their jurisdiction and powers, is the commission, issued under the Great Seal, directed to them. To the jurisdiction of this court of commissioners, belong the proof of the debts, and all questions arising upon them; the examinations of the bankrupt; and the order for the distribution of the funds in dividends, till the whole be exhausted; with the power of judging of the bankrupt's title to a certificate.

2. All

2 All the orders and decisions of the commissioners are subject to review and controul by the Lord Chancellor himself.

3. The creditors are so much of a deliberative body, that they have the choosing of the assignees, who are to be vested with the estate, for the purpose of managing and distributing it; and they have the power of deciding, in the first instance, upon the debtor's title to a discharge. And,

4. The assignees, chosen by the creditors themselves, are vested with the estate, and entrusted with the care of recovering and distributing it, in dividends, according to the order fixed by the commissioners.

The Scotish system is somewhat different.

1. Instead of a commission from the King, appointing a court of commissioners pro re nata, the course of the common law of Scotland is followed, and the estate sequestrated in the hands of the Court of Session, for the common behoof.

2. A trust is vested in a person, chosen by the creditors themselves: he holds the titles to the estate and effects: he is bound, with the advice of three commissioners, chosen also by the creditors, out of their own number, to manage and recover the estate; to receive the grounds of debt from the creditors; to arrange them; to judge of them, in the first instance, rejecting all such claims as are exposed to objections ex facie, and to state such objections, as cannot be decided without investigation, for the decision of the Court; to regulate the order of preference; to strike the dividend, and, upon its being approved of, to pay it to the creditors.

3. The proceedings of the trustee and commissioners, are subject, in some instances, to the controul of general meetings of the creditors, as in questions relating to the sale of particular estates, submissions to arbitration, &c. The creditors decide, in the first instance, as in England, of the bankrupt's title to a discharge.

4. The

4. The proceedings of the trustee, and his judgements respecting debts, are subject to review of the Court of Session, upon complaint by any of the creditors; and if objections be stated to particular debts, which he has not the means of deciding, they are determined summarily by the Court, on petition by the creditors interested to support them, or by the trustee as acting for the general body unless those interested shall agree to a submission or compromise.

Thus, in Scotland, the law has endeavoured to provide for the easy and economical distribution of the estate, under the immediate eye and controul of the Court of Session, but without its direct interference, except in cases where that is absolutely required. But it is proper to enter a little more fully into the history of this part of our law: We shall thus see the motives which first led to this institution, and the course and spirit of the improvements which have been made upon it.

About thirty years ago, speculation of all kinds had risen to an alarming height in Scotland. The rage for improving the land, and extending the commerce of the country, gave occasion, indeed, to the institution of a bank, the object of which was to supply, upon a plan the most extravagant and impolitic, the unnatural demand of the times. To all thinking men, the prospect of an interruption to those extraordinary supplies was terrible, for not only had they to fear the evils, naturally attendant on the bankruptcies which such an interruption threatened, but they had also this melancholy reflection to heighten their anxiety, that there was no law in the country, by which, in cases of bankruptcy, it was possible to prevent the acquisition of preferences, according to the priority of diligence, or to force a concurrence in common measures, for distributing the estates. To such anxieties, we owe the statute of 1772, establishing sequestration in personal estates.

The first sequestration law was, comparatively, very imperfect. The great objects were, to remedy these two evils. *First*, The want of of an equalizing law for diligence against moveables, by which a disgraceful race of diligence, and acquisition of unfair preferences in that way, might be prevented: And, *secondly*, The want of a general process for distributing the personal or moveable estates of bankrupts. Both these evils had been in some degree obviated, with respect to the heritable estate, but they were left totally without a remedy in the case of moveables. It was not to be expected, that creditors should concur in a voluntary plan of distribution, when, by starting aside, individuals might have a chance of acquiring a preference: nor was the validity of a trust-deed to be depended on, surrounded by so many grounds of objection, as the statutes of 1621, and of 1696, afforded. It was, therefore, enacted, that upon a petition to the Court of Session, by any creditor, on his debtor's bankruptcy, a sequestration of the personal estate of the debtor should be awarded; and that it should be vested in a factor, proposed by the creditors, to be distributed by him according to the direction and judgement of the Court; or, if it should seem more eligible to the creditors, that the distribution should proceed extrajudicially (as under a private voluntary deed of trust), by a trustee elected by the creditors. It was also declared, that no arrestment nor poinding, used within thirty days of the date of the application to the Court, should give any preference, in the event of a sequestration taking place.

This statute of 1772 was temporary. When it was about to expire, there was some contest, whether it ought to be renewed; at least, the objections against many parts of the law were loudly supported. The truth I believe is, that the universality of its application to all ranks, and even to the most inconsiderable bankruptcies, was found to be productive of many inconveniences and frauds. But the benefits, which, in an experiment of ten years, the law had produced to the mercantile part of the country, called forth all their interest and abilities in support of its renewal, with such amendments as experience had pointed out to be proper; and they met with the powerful support of the most eminent of our Judges and lawyers. It was affirmed as a fact, to which every merchant could bear testimony, that, in the many instances of

mercantile

mercantile bankruptcy, which had occurred since the act of 1772, some of them in the very moment of passing the act, the sequestration had proved a most salutary remedy; that, indeed, it had been the very salvation of their trade, and that ruin would have fallen upon them, had it not fortunately been established at that critical period. A new law was therefore proposed, in which the most glaring defects of the first were remedied, and great progress made towards that state of improvement, which the institution has at last attained. I shall endeavour, shortly, to explain the improvements of this second sequestration act, by contrasting it with the first.

1. In the statute of 1772, the equalizing of diligence, in all cases, was made to depend upon the sequestration: in the new law, it was made to depend upon the bankruptcy. If it had been expedient to continue the sequestration, as applicable to all ranks of men, the former was strictly proper; but the restriction required a separation of the equalizing rule for diligence, from the other effects of the sequestration. Till this was accomplished, the Legislature could not restrict the sequestration, without leaving the rest of the country to all the evils of the old rule of preference by priority, from which they had just escaped. It was therefore enacted, that all arrestments, used within thirty days before, or four months after bankruptcy, as defined in the statute of 1696, should be pari passu preferable; and that no poinding, executed within the same period, should bestow a preference on the poinding creditor. The effect of this alteration was, that the sequestration was left simple and pure, as a plan of management and distribution, in those cases for which the Legislature might think it peculiarly adapted, and, at the same time, the general provisions of the law were completed; by which the effect of individual diligence is, upon a bankruptcy, to be stopt, and all the creditors brought to a level.

2. The Legislature, being left untrammelled, found it perfectly safe, and thought it expedient, to restrict the sequestration, both in respect of the class of debtors, and in respect of the extent of the

bankruptcy.

bankruptcy. In bringing about the first of these restrictions, the example of the law of England had a very powerful effect. In a memorial prefixed to the draught of the bill, which was afterwards passed into a statute in 1783, it is said for the merchants, by whom this bill was proposed, that 'they are not ignorant, that, in other 'countries, the positive laws made with respect to bankruptcy, 'are confined to those classes of men who are connected with 'trade. The original meaning of the word goes no further; and 'the principle upon which bankrupt laws are founded, are applicable to them alone.—" The laws of England (we are told by a " late learned author) provide at once against the inhumanity of " the creditor, who is not suffered to confine an honest bankrupt, " after his effects are delivered up; and at the same time take care, " that all his just debts shall be paid, so far as the effects will extend: But still they are cautious of encouraging prodigality and " extravagance, by this indulgence to debtors; and, therefore, " they allow the benefit of the laws of bankruptcy to none but actual traders, since that set of men are, generally speaking, the " only persons liable to accidental losses, and to an inability of " paying their debts, without any fault of their own. If persons, " in other situations in life, run in debt, without the power of payment, they must take the consequences of their own indiscretion, " even though they meet with sudden accidents, that may reduce " their fortunes: For the law holds it to be an unjustifiable practice, for any person but a trader to incumber himself with debts " of any considerable value. If a gentleman, or any one in a liberal profession, at the time of contracting his debts, has a sufficient fund to pay them, the delay of payment is a species of dishonesty, and a temporary injustice to his creditor; and if, at " such time, he has no sufficient fund, the dishonesty and injustice is the greater: he cannot therefore murmur, if he suffers " the punishment which he has voluntarily drawn upon himself. " But in mercantile transactions, the case is far otherwise. Trade " cannot be carried on, without mutual credit on both sides; the " contracting of debts is therefore, here, not only justifiable but " necessary. And if, by accidental calamities, as by the loss of a " ship in a tempest, the failure of brother traders, or by the non-

" payment

" payment of persons out of trade, a merchant or tradesman become incapable of discharging his own debts, it is his misfortune, " and not his fault. To this misfortune, therefore, of debtors, " the law has given a compassionate remedy, but denied it to their " faults; since, at the same time that it provides for the security " of commerce, by enacting, that every considerable trader may be " declared a bankrupt, for the benefit of his creditors as well as " himself, it has also, to discourage extravagance, declared, that " no one shall be capable of being made a bankrupt, but only a " trader; nor capable of receiving the full benefit of the statutes, " but only an industrious trader:" 2. Blackst. 473. The memorialists afterwards say, in speaking of that clause of the bill, which restricts the sequestration to the case of those connected with trade and commerce—' The distinctions which it aims ' at, are founded on the presumption above noticed, that bank' rupt laws are chiefly useful, and in other countries practised, ' for regulating the case of those, who, from the nature of their ' dealings, are exposed to sudden and accidental losses, and to be ' reduced, by unforeseen misfortune, to the situation of bank' rupts.' But it may not be improper to observe, that the strict confinement of the bankrupt law of England to traders, arose from peculiar circumstances, to which nothing analogous was to be found in the Scotish law. The English, attached, with indiscriminating fondness, to their ancient common law, had admitted no remedy, even where the debtor was insolvent, against the evils of individual execution for debts: And the old common law rights of the debtor, on the one hand, and of the individual creditor, on the other, remaining thus unaltered, when the Legislature interfered, to provide for the case of bankruptcy, every thing was to be done. The new code appeared as a system of extraordinary constraint, of rapid execution, and of provision against fraud, so opposite to the common law, that the necessities of commerce alone could palliate it. Instead of the action of debt, which, even when followed with a judgement, led only to the alternative of the imprisonment of the debtor's person, or the attachment of his estate, it was made lawful to hurry a bankrupt, by a commission of bankruptcy, immediately to prison,—his house which, against the diligence of the common law, is his castle and defence, was allowed to be broken open—his shop to be shut—his property and effects to be thrown into confusion, without previous notice, or possibility of preventing the blow. These are indeed evils, against which any man would anxiously struggle. On the other hand, the commission of bankruptcy gave, to the unfortunate debtor, a hope of escape from that perpetual imprisonment, in which, at common law, the creditor has a right to persevere, and which it requires the special interference of the Legislature, by an insolvent act, to take away. In whatever way, in short, this system be taken, it was, in England, one which so widely departed from all the rules and maxims of the common law, that it was natural to confine it strictly to the case of mercantile bankruptcy. But there are no such peculiarities in the sequestration of the Scotish law, to stand in the way of its universal adoption. It is not by the sequestration, as it is in England by the commission of bankruptcy, that the hands of individual creditors are tied up from procuring partial preferences: the Scotish statutes in that behalf, have an universal application to all ranks and classes of men. Neither do creditors depend upon the sequestration alone, for bringing the estate to sale and distribution; for that may be done, as we have seen, under laws and statutes which also have universal application. The debtor does not depend upon it even for liberation, the cessio bonorum being open to him at common law. Finally, the execution, both against the person and against the property of the debtor, is as rapid at common law, as under the sequestration; so that the suddenness and secrecy which, in England, attends the taking out of the commission of bankruptcy, is not necessary nor permitted, in the plan of our sequestration. In short, all those evils, which are in England provided for by the commission of bankruptcy, after so violent a manner, and so totally opposite to the spirit of the common law, are, in Scotland, guarded against, without violence, or hardship, or injustice, independently altogether of the sequestration; and the only peculiarity of the sequestration is, that, instead of the tedious and expensive forms of distribution at common law, and under the statutes respecting judicial sales, the whole estate is vested in a trustee,

to

to be distributed by him under the controul of the Court, the debtor being entitled, by consent of four-fifths of his creditors, (with concurrence of the trustee), to an absolute discharge, after the period assigned for the second dividend from his estate. When not abused, therefore, the sequestration is a form of distribution beneficial to all concerned, and hurtful to none: and no analogy should have been admitted from the law of England to disturb the system of our bankrupt law. The propriety of restricting the sequestration, should have been made to rest upon the basis of expediency alone. But, at the time that the statute was to be renewed, the cry was strong against sequestrations; and it may perhaps have been thought that commercial expediency, as in England, could alone support it against the opposition that was made. Whether, now, that the terror of the innovation is gone, the restriction is, in its full extent, wise or proper to be continued—or what regulations should be adopted for supplying the want of a general process of attachment, and saving expence to creditors in common bankruptcies, this is not the proper place to inquire.

3. The sequestration law of 1772, reached only to personal property: In that of 1783, the whole estate, heritable and personal, was included. In a first experiment, it was perhaps not to be expected that the remedy should go further than to remove that evil which more immediately pressed upon the attention of the Legislature; and the distribution of heritable property was already provided for. But while the sequestration system was found, on the whole, beneficial, the delay, the expence, and the involved proceedings of a ranking and sale, were found to be very unfit for a case of mercantile bankruptcy; and the separation of the estate into two processes of distribution, the judicial sale and ranking, and the sequestration, was felt as a gross impropriety, and great inconvenience. But the inclusion of heritable property under the sequestration law was opposed; chiefly upon the ground, that there might be a danger in making any change upon the known feudal forms of attaching and conveying real property, and that the security of the title by judicial sale was a point of great consequence to the creditors, as well as to purchasers. These difficulties were,

however,

however, overcome. It was urged, in answer to them, that there was no wish nor intention to subvert the feudal forms of conveyance that, in the cessio bonorum, a precedent was afforded of a form for obliging the debtor to invest his estate in a trustee; and, in the judicial sale, a precedent of an irredeemable adjudication to the highest offerer: that heritage might, therefore, be included in the sequestration, without any outrage upon feudal forms or principles—without any ipso facto transmission, but by requiring a disposition and seisine from the debtor to the trustee, or by transferring the estate to him, by an irredeemable decree of adjudication and feudal titles; leaving it still in the option of the creditors to adopt the old form of the judicial sale.

4. By the act of 1772, a double system of distribution, optional to the creditors, was introduced—one, of the nature of the old sequestration at common law, in which a factor was appointed to manage the estate, under the direction of the Court, and in which the competition of the creditors, and the division of the funds, was made by the Court, in the same way as in a ranking and sale—the other, a system of private trust, sanctioned by the Legislature, provided the creditors, when met, after proper advertisement by the factor, should (by a majority of two-thirds in value of those present) prefer the appointment of a trustee to the continuance under the sequestration. The faults of these two systems were, that, in the former, every thing was done by the Court, and, consequently, at much expence, and with all the delays necessarily attendant on litigation, while the factor did comparatively nothing, but manage the estate—and that, in the latter, the delays, which are ever to be dreaded in a private trust, not under the controul of the Court, were scarcely to be avoided. By the act of 1783, these were corrected, and one uniform system of trust and controul devised, by which the estate might be managed and disposed of—the competition of the creditors decided—and the dividends struck, by a private and extrajudicial operation, and with little expence, while the Court was open for the trial, in a summary manner, of every objection which the parties concerned had to state against the decision of the trustee, and for a continual

tinual interference with its controuling power, upon all proper occasions. This great design was attained by the combination of the sequestration, and of the statutory trust. The sequestration was to serve as an universal diligence, for attaching the whole estate, and enabling the creditors to pursue a systematic plan for calling the rest together, in order to constitute the trust in some proper person. The trust was to be rendered effectual by a proper conveyance of the whole estate to the trustee, to be liquidated and distributed fairly among the creditors, under the controul of the Court, upon complaint made.

These are the great lines of distinction between the spirit of the statute 1772, and that of 1783. The renewal of the law in 1793, was attended with many important improvements; but these, being made after the spirit of the former law, it may be more proper to reserve for consideration, till we come to discuss the particular parts of the system. The sequestration, then, as established in this last act, is a system of distribution by means of a trust, (under the sanction and controul of the Court of Session), of the whole estate, real and personal, of bankrupts engaged in trade, or in manufactures. It is well fitted for the easy, expeditious, and economical distribution of the estate—freed, on the one hand, from the tedious, expensive, and multifarious litigation, attendant on the forms of distribution at common law—and from the uncontrouled decision of a private trustee, on the other. It contains provisions equally for the benefit of the creditors, and of the debtor; it forms the creditors into a deliberative body, that they may easily consult upon their common interest; and it entitles them to have the bankrupt, and those of his household, and connected with his trade, examined in the strictest manner, in presence of a Judge; while, to the debtor himself, it goes, in this respect, beyond the indulgence of the common law—that, instead of a mere liberation from diligence, which is all that the cessio bonorum bestows, it permits, in two several cases, a complete discharge, so as to enable the debtor to begin the world again a free man.

CHAP.

CHAP. I.

Of Sequestration—its Nature and Effects—Recal—Election, Powers, and Duties of the Factor.

In the Introductory Chapter, it was observed, as the great peculiarity of the improved law, that, instead of being a mere sequestration, the plan of management and distribution came to be a combination of the sequestration, and of the statutory trust—the sequestration being a measure merely preparative and intermediate, intended to serve as an universal diligence for attaching the estate in the name of all the creditors, and to enable those who applied for the sequestration, to take proper measures for calling the creditors together, in order to constitute the trust, and for preserving and managing the estate during the necessary interval, till the trust should be constituted. In this view, then, it is here to be considered:—and the object of this chapter shall be, to explain the nature and effect of the petition, and of the act of sequestration—the cases in which it is competent, or in which it may be recalled—and the nature of the proceedings previous to the constitution of the trust.

SECTION I.

Of the Petition for Sequestration, and of the Objections which may be stated against it.

'Whereas,' says the statute 33 Geo. III. c. 74. 'it is for the 'interest of commerce, that the estates of those concerned in 'trade and manufactures, when they are unable to answer the de- 'mands upon them, shall be disposed of, and distributed among their 'creditors, in the most expeditious manner, without abiding the 'ordinary forms of law;' therefore, it is made 'lawful to the cre- 'ditors of such person, being bankrupt, or to himself, with con- 'currence of his creditors, to apply to the Court of Session, for 'sequestration of his whole estate, real and personal, heritable 'and moveable.' This application is to be made by summary petition. If it be made by the debtor himself, sequestration is immediately awarded; if without his concurrence, the petition is ordered to be served upon him, and a day is appointed for him to answer it; when, if he have no good objection against the awarding of sequestration, it is awarded.

Such is the general scope of the law, respecting the cases in which sequestration may be applied for, and the form in which the application is to be made. But it is necessary to descend minutely into the particulars of the law, and explain the practice founded upon it. In considering the requisites of the application, it may be proper to discuss, in the *first* place, those which must accompany the petition, in order to entitle it to be received by the Court; and, *secondly*, those which more properly form the ground of opposition to the sequestration, and the object of subsequent inquiry.

§ I.

§ I. Of the primary Requisites of a Petition for Sequestration.

In entering upon the enumeration of those circumstances, which are requisite to entitle the application to be received or heard by the Court, it is necessary, so far, to anticipate the doctrines of the next Section, as to explain, that these become the more important, as it is from the date of the first deliverance upon the petition, that the whole effect of the sequestration, as an universal diligence, is declared to commence. It is enacted, That, 'from 'the date of the first deliverance, the petition for sequestration 'shall be held equivalent to an inhibition against the debtor, for 'behoof of the whole creditors, in case the sequestration is finally 'awarded,' § 19.; and the decree of adjudication, which is pronounced in favour of the trustee, is to have the same effect 'as 'if it had been a common decree of adjudication, obtained and 'rendered effectual at the date of the first deliverance on the 'petition for sequestration;' and it is to operate as a 'complete at-'tachment and transfer of the moveable or personal estate, for 'behoof of all the creditors, at the date of the first deliverance 'aforesaid;' § 24.

The petition may be presented either by the debtor himself, with concurrence of his creditors to a certain extent; or by creditors to a certain extent, without the debtor's concurrence. The first point, therefore, to which the attention should be directed, is, the description of the debtor and of the petitioning creditor.

I. Description of the Debtor.—There are two points in the description of those whose estates are liable to sequestration: First, That they must be bankrupt (which is, however, dispensed with, when the debtor himself concurs): And, Secondly, That they must be merchants, or traders, or manufacturers. No petition will be received, which does not bear a description of the debtor (whether concurring in the application or not), corresponding with the character required in the statute. The remedy of

sequestration

sequestration is restricted, by the Legislature, to a particular class of bankrupts; and the Court of Session holds it to be pars judicis, to see the law precisely executed.

1. The BANKRUPTCY required by the statute, to validate a petition for sequestration, where the debtor does not himself concur, differs a little from that description of bankruptcy which, under the statute 1696, c. 5, as reformed by the late statutes, is necessary in reductions of voluntary deeds of preference. Insolvency is not required to be proved in support of a petition for sequestration, though it makes an essential ingredient in the bankruptcy of the act 1696. The 13th section of the statute 33 Geo. III. c. 74. requires, 1st, That the debtor 'shall be under diligence, by horning 'and caption, for debt:' and, 2dly, That he 'shall either, in 'virtue thereof, be imprisoned, or retire to a sanctuary, or flee 'or abscond for his personal safety, or defend his person by force, 'or being out of Scotland, or not liable to be imprisoned, by rea'son of privilege or personal protection, shall be under diligence, 'by charge of horning, attended with arrestment not loosed or 'discharged within fifteen days; or poinding of any part of his 'moveables; or adjudication of any part of his estate, for pay'ment or security of debt, at the instance of any creditor.'

The first of these requisites, the diligence of horning and caption, the petitioning creditor will be able to establish, at the first presenting of his petition, if the diligence have proceeded at his own instance. But as diligence used by any one creditor, establishes a part of the legal character of the debtor, of which every other creditor is entitled to take advantage, the Court, when they pronounce the order for citation, issue also 'the usual authority for 'recovering written evidence of the said diligence;' and, under this authority, the creditor recovers and produces it, when the days of citation, on the petition of sequestration, are expired.

Although the law has not permitted a debtor to be deprived of the management of his affairs, and his estate to be sequestrated, except in cases of bankruptcy, it has not refused to award sequestration

tration with his own consent, even where no bankruptcy has taken place: at the same time, as debtors sometimes abuse their creditors, by means of sequestrations, the Court will naturally be more rigid in attending to the other parts of the description, where the debtor himself applies, and where, consequently, no evidence of bankruptcy is necessary. It has not unfrequently happened, that debtors, though not bankrupt, have attempted, by means of a sequestration, to throw their whole affairs into the management of some of their own friends, for the very purpose of disappointing the common diligence of the law; and that, after tiring out the creditors with the proceedings, and frightening them with the expence of a sequestration, they have got them to accede to a composition and discharge, for a small part of their debts.

2. The OCCUPATION of the debtor forms the other part of the legal description.

In this matter, there is an essential distinction between the English and the Scotish law. In England, the commission of bankruptcy is open to the creditors of a trader only. 'I take the 'term trading,' said Lord Chancellor Loughborough, in the case of Parker v. Wells, 'to be essential to the description of a bank-'rupt; and that the bankrupt laws are framed only for the con-'venience of trade; and that no person, who cannot be said to 'carry on trade, is the subject of these laws, otherwise than by 'special provision.'—'The case of Port v. Turton,' continued his Lordship, 'I think, very well states the probable principle 'why the Legislature has subjected traders to the bankrupt law, 'and not suffered other people to be included in them. A trader 'gains, as Lord Cambden says, an extensive credit, upon an un-'certain and invisible capital; that credit will be in proportion to 'the extent of his dealings, and can be measured by nothing else; 'his real means are not visible; and, from the very nature of his 'trade, he is liable to unforeseen losses, by the failure of those 'persons to whom he is obliged to give credit, and with whose 'credit his is interwoven. In his behalf, the law, in these sta-'tutes of bankruptcy, relieves him, in consequence of his large

'engagements,

'engagements, on a fair distribution of what he has; and, on the 'behalf of the creditors, they permit them to have an immediate 'execution, in the first instance, and force him to produce his 'accounts, and then make an equal distribution of his effects. 'But, with respect to those persons, whose principal business is 'not buying and selling, but only bringing to market the produce 'of the lands, they are in a different situation from a trader; their 'capital is open; it is permanent; it is limited; and their deal-'ings are necessarily confined: their credit rests upon their own 'endeavours and industry, and can rarely be involved with the 'credit of other persons: they are, therefore, not entitled to re-'lief from all their engagements, and to those benefits, which, 'for the sake of commerce, are given to persons to carry on trade. 'As there is no necessity, with regard to them, to introduce the 'execution, in the first instance, the summary process for seizing 'and distress, is not necessary; the common course of law, in 'common cases, being sufficient. It is plain, that the same occu-'pation may bring one man within the statutes, the other not. 'There cannot be a plainer one, than the case of a tailor, the 'working and the merchant tailor; one only purchasing his 'instruments and necessaries to carry on the work; the other 'buying and selling the cloth: the one is a labourer, and there-'fore not liable to bankruptcy; the other introduces all those 'consequences of extensive credit and connexions with other 'persons.' I. Cook's B. L. 52. 56.—Thus, the strong bent of the common law of England, against the principles and practice of the bankrupt system, has confined its coercion and its benefits to one peculiar set of cases; where the debtor carries on his trade by credit. But happily, with us, the spirit of our general law has given a mildness to the whole system, which makes the danger of its abuse, as a form of distribution, the only reason for excluding sequestration in any case. The description of persons who fall within the reach of the sequestration law, has therefore been made much more comprehensive in Scotland. 'The chief diffi-'culty,' (say the proposers of the law, in which the sequestration was restricted from a universal remedy), 'is, to draw the line 'between those classes of people, which ought certainly to be in-

'cluded

'cluded in such a law, and others that may, with propriety, be 'omitted. We have endeavoured to simplify this as much as pos- 'sible, by taking in traders and manufacturers in general, even 'those commonly known by the name of mechanics, without at- 'tending to the nice distinctions in the law of England, between 'those who buy their materials and sell their work, and others 'who do not: because we apprehend, that a man, employed in 'any sort of mechanical occupation, cannot well carry on his busi- 'ness, to any extent, without buying and selling; and, if he is a 'very small dealer, he will, at any rate, by excluded by the ex- 'tent of the sum necessary to found the application. We like- 'wise thought it necessary to make a special exception of such 'landholders and tenants as are not bona fide under the foregoing 'descriptions; because it was chiefly with regard to these, and 'particularly tenants, that the abuse of the late law (of 1772) was 'experienced. The reasons for excepting holders of India stock, 'as well as of Bank stock, is obvious: and with regard to the In- 'surance Company at Edinburgh against Fire, it stands on a pe- 'culiar footing; the parties engaged in it being both insurers and 'insured, and consisting of a very numerous body, of all ranks 'and occupations, many of whom do not consider themselves as 'traders in any respect.' Remarks prefixed to the proposed Bill in 1783.

The description in the statute, was accordingly made to include, not merely merchants and traders in gross or wholesale, bankers, brokers, and underwriters; but traders by retail, manufacturers, artificers, and mechanics, (unless they be merely common labourers for hire), and all persons who, either for themselves, or as agents, or factors, for others, seek their living by buying and selling, or by the workmanship of goods or commodities, or hold a share in any such undertaking. There are, however, exceptions made, of 'holders of India stock, or stock in the Banks establish- 'ed by public authority, or in the Friendly Insurance Company at 'Edinburgh against fire, the Forth or Clyde Navigation, or other 'inland navigation Companies, or the British fisheries.' These are not qualifications sufficient to entitle a person to be considered

as

as within the description, unless otherwise he be included in it. All 'landholders' are likewise excluded, and 'tenants of land, or 'husbandmen,' and 'common labourers, or workmen for hire.' These characters are not, however, regarded as disqualifications, if, in other respects, the description apply.

Few questions have occurred relative to this description: but there are some points, arising from the exceptions in the statute, on which it is necessary to make a few remarks. The law, in excluding from the sequestration, 'landlords, tenants of land, husbandmen,' &c. is intended to comprehend those cases only, 'where such persons are not otherwise bona fide under one 'or other of the foregoing descriptions;' and, of course, where sequestration is awarded in a case of this kind, the creditors, whose debts have arisen from the debtor's dealings as a landlord, tenant, or husbandman, must come in along with the others. But the difficulty is, to distinguish what ought to be held as entitling any of these excluded persons to the independent and separate character of a trader or manufacturer, so as to support the petition. Thus, a tenant of land may have occasion to deal extensively, both as a buyer and a seller of corn; or the grazing farmer to buy and to sell great quantities of cattle or of sheep. But, if the one is to be held as a corn-merchant, and the other as a cattle-dealer, there is an end of their exclusion from the statute. and accordingly, in England, says Lord Loughborough, in the case of Parker v. Wells, 'by the construction of the statute originally 'describing a bankrupt, and referring its description to a trading, 'a farmer, who, though no trader, buys and sells considerably, 'was held not to be within the intent and meaning of these statutes.' A statute was afterwards made, declaring a drover not to be a bankrupt; of which his Lordship speaks thus:—'The question, 'since that statute, was determined in the King's Bench, whether 'a particular person was a drover, within the meaning of it: the 'dealing was stated to be, buying at one fair, and selling at another; but the circumstance of the case was likewise, that he had 'land, and upon that land he fed his cattle. The Court held that 'he was a drover, within the spirit and exception of the statute:

'he

'he was a person described having connexion with land; this 'made the distinction between him and the salesman *:' I. Cook, 55.—'But though a farmer, merely as such,' (says Mr Espinasse, vol. 2. p. 549,), 'is not an object of the bankrupt law; yet, if 'he buys any great quantities of things, such as are the produce 'of his farm, and sells them, he shall be liable to a commission 'of bankruptcy; as, where a special verdict found one R. Baxter 'had occupied a farm of 300l. a year, and annually planted it 'with many acres of potatoes, which he sold for gain; and like-'wise bought from others large quantities of potatoes, which he 'kept in warehouses, and sold again at different markets; his deal-'ing so extensively, and in such manner, was held to make him a 'trader, within the meaning of the bankrupt laws:' Mayo v. Archer, I. Stra. 513.—'So, where a plaintiff was assignee of one 'Davies, who, it appeared, rented a considerable farm at Whit-'church, and kept two or three teams of horses, and had, previous 'to his taking the farm, lived with an uncle, during which time he 'attended fairs, and bought and sold several horses, and, after he took 'the farm, he occasionally attended fairs, and bought horses, which 'were not calculated for the farming business, and which he al-'ways sold again for some profit;—on this evidence, the Judge left 'it to the Jury to decide, whether the dealing in horses was not dis-'tinct from the farming business, and done with a view to profit? 'The Jury found Davies a bankrupt; which verdict, on a motion 'for a new trial, was afterwards confirmed by the Court:' Bartholomew v. Sherwood, I. Term Rep. 573—We have not, in Scotland, had many cases upon these questions; but, of late, several petitions have been presented for the sequestration of the estates of grazing farmers and drovers, which have called the attention of the Court to the subject: and perhaps the true distinction is to be taken between mere graziers who fatten cattle for the market, and, so, may be considered as merely reaping, in this way, the produce of their farm;—and cattle-dealers, or drovers, who carry on a trade in cattle; speculating upon the state of the country,

* The case to which Lord Loughborough alludes, seems to be, that of Mills v. Hughes.—Buller's N. P. 39.

country, and the demand for cattle; regulating their purchases, not by the extent of their farm, but by the appearances of the markets; and buying cheap at one market, with a view to the profit to be gained at another.

It is in general laid down by English writers on bankruptcy, that the buying and selling, which is necessary to bring a man under the bankrupt law of England, must be in the way of a merchant, and of goods and merchandize. 'The buying and selling land,' (says Cook), 'or an interest in land, is not a buying and selling 'within the statute, which must be restrained to things personal.' I. Cook, B. L. 78. And in this opinion he is followed by Mr Cullen, who says—'Buying and selling of land, or an interest in 'land, or land-jobbing, is not within the statutes.' Principles of the Bankrupt Law, p. 17.—Whether this opinion goes beyond the case of Port v. Turton, which was the case of a purchase of a mine of coals, for the purpose of selling the produce, it were presumptuous in me to say. But, in the following case, which is includeable within the general doctrine laid down by Cook and Cullen, the question has been otherwise settled with us.—An agent or solicitor before the Court of Session, having 'engaged in the trade of build-'ing houses for sale, failed, and presented a petition for sequestra-'tion under the statute of 1783. Some of his creditors objected 'that the application was not warranted by the statute, the peti-'tioner being by profession a writer, and not, according to its terms, 'either a merchant, or a manufacturer, artificer, or mechanic. 'The Court, however, considered the petitioner, notwithstanding 'the different nature of his original profession *, as within the de-'scription of the statue; and therefore the Lords awarded seque-'stration: and, upon advising a reclaiming petition, with answers, 'adhered to that judgement.' 9. February 1790, Scot; VIII. Fac. Coll. cx. 206.

But

* In the report of this case in the Faculty Collection, the expression is not perfectly accurate. It would lead to the idea, that the Court decided thus, although convinced that the profession of a writer was his 'principal' profession But the truth is, that the Court really understood him to have, in a great measure, abandoned this his original profession, for that of a trading builder

But supposing the debtor to have relinquished trade or manufactures, is it a sufficient objection to the petition, that, although formerly a trader, he is not now under the description in the law? The law was evidently intended for the case of those who, being engaged in trade or manufactures, have failed; and every principle upon which it rests, seems to concur in extending it to those who, though they have relinquished their trade, or been forced out of it by their failure, have not been able to pay off, or settle with their creditors.

It is natural to doubt, whether married women, carrying on merchandize, be subject to the law of sequestration. In England, this is left for a question of construction; and so it also was in Scotland, till the year 1793. The courts of England rest the liability of a married woman to the statute execution of a commission of bankruptcy, upon the same principle on which the common execution of the law is held to be competent against her; viz. 1. That, where a woman has a separate estate, and acts, and receives credit, as a 'femme sole,' she shall be liable as such: 2. That, even without such separate estate, where her husband is absent from the country, and she is necessarily considered as a femme sole, she is also liable, both to common execution, and to the bankrupt law: I. Cook, B. L. xxix. 45. In Scotland, it seemed proper to clear this matter by Legislative declaration; and it is accordingly provided, by section 61. of the 33d Geo. III. c. 74, that this act 'shall be construed to comprehend unmarried women 'and widows, coming within any of the descriptions above mentioned, and also married women, carrying on trade or merchandize, independent of their husbands.'

The evidence which is primarily required on these two points, the bankruptcy, and the occupation of the debtor, is the description given of the debtor in the petition, and an oath of credulity by the petitioning creditors, that 'they believe the party, against 'whom the application is made, to be a merchant, or otherwise

'within

'within one or other of the descriptions, and not within the excep-'tions aforesaid:' § 13.—This oath of credulity, however, does not preclude any subsequent inquiry in consequence of the opposition of the debtor, or of other creditors. It is merely prima facie evidence, without which no deliverance will be given on the petition, but which may be redargued by proper evidence, when the Court comes to determine whether the sequestration should be awarded.

II. OF THE PETITIONING CREDITOR.—In distinguishing the requisite qualifications of the petitioning creditor, there are three points, to which our attention must be directed. 1. The amount of the debt. 2. The nature of the debt. And, 3, The proof of its existence.

1. AMOUNT OF THE DEBT.—It has been an object of much anxiety with the Legislature in both countries, to limit the remedy, in mercantile cases, to the more considerable bankruptcies; and this has been done, by requiring a particular amount of debt, as a qualification to petition. It has been sometimes doubted, whether this be a good criterion of such limitation. One great objection to the sequestration, in small bankruptcies, is the expence of the proceedings; and this is to be taken in reference to the amount of the funds, rather than of the debts. It has accordingly been proposed, to qualify the law, by requiring the Court to discuss the sequestration, if, within a certain period, the funds do not amount to such a sum as may, to the Legislature, seem fit to bear the expence. Perhaps it might be still better, were it possible to devise some plan for saving expence, in the more inconsiderable bankruptcies, without excluding them from the benefit of such a law.

As the law stands at present, both in England and in Scotland, the qualification to petition as a creditor, is regulated by the amount of the debt of the petitioner. As it is impossible to know what the ultimate amount either of the debts or of the funds

 may

may be, till the commission has been issued, or the sequestration awarded, and till the creditors have been called upon to produce their claims, and the extent of the funds has been investigated, it was thought necessary to take the petitioner's debt as a test, à priori, of the probable importance of the bankruptcy. This test was first adopted in England, long before the sequestration law was introduced into this country; and when, in 1783, the sequestration came to be restricted from an universal to a partial remedy, the rule was adopted in our statute, and is still continued. In both countries, if a single creditor have a debt of 100l against the bankrupt, it is taken as evidence of a bankruptcy, sufficiently important to fall under the law. But, as there may be considerable bankruptcies, where no single creditor's debt amounts to 100l., such cases are provided for, by requiring a higher sum, divided among several claimants. L. 150l. due to two creditors, in whatever proportions, will authorise their application—or 200l. of debt, divided among three or more creditors.

The creditor must state the amount of his debt particularly, and not in one general slump sum. The 13th section of the statute requires, that he shall produce the grounds of debt, or a certified copy of the amount, with an oath of verity, of the debt—a specification, which is quite sufficient to enable the Court to judge, whether the claim be not overrated. In the statement of the debt, the petitioning creditor is not obliged to restrict himself to the principal sum due; he may include interest to the date of the petition, and the expences already incurred—with exchange and re-exchange, if the debt arise upon a foreign bill of exchange.

If the debt of the petitioning creditor be a future debt, (for such, we shall immediately see, is sufficient to support an application), the amount of interest, between the date of the application, and the day of payment, must be discounted; for the petitioner is to be considered as a creditor for the balance only. Where the term is one which, though it must arrive, is uncertain in point of time, (as, where a sum is payable upon the death of a third party), there may be some difficulty in the estimation; but I should apprehend,

apprehend, that the computation would, in such a case, be made by the common tables of life, upon which annuities and liferents are calculated.

All partial payments must be deducted. We shall hereafter see, that, if the proper deduction have not been made, the debtor, or any other creditor, by establishing such a partial payment as would, if deducted, have reduced the debt below the sum required by statute for validating the application, will succeed in opposing the petition. But, at present, we are considering only the *prima facie* requisites of the application, in which view, it is absolutely necessary, that allowance be given for the payments which appear from the grounds of debt themselves.

2. NATURE OF THE DEBT.—Debts are of three kinds; pure, future, and contingent.

A PURE DEBT, is one, of which the term of payment is arrived; and of which, consequently, payment may immediately be enforced. These are the proper subjects of all kinds of diligence; and, among others, of sequestration. Yet there are claims of such a nature, that it seems doubtful, whether they can be admitted as the foundation of such an application: e. g. claims of unliquidated damages. There are, in such cases, no data for fixing, as an absolute debt, the sum of damage. It remains in arbitrio judicis, whether any damage is due at all, and whether, if due, it may not be fixed at a sum far within the amount required by law for the qualification of a petitioning creditor. whereas, a common debt, at law, if it be due at all, is due without deduction. the ground of the debt cannot be true, and yet the debt itself fallacious. The English make such ground of action a contingent debt merely, and absolutely exclude it even from being proved as a debt, so as to draw a dividend: I. Cook, 235.

We have already considered, at some length, the question of FUTURE and CONTINGENT DEBTS—and seen, that, by the common law of Scotland, neither the one nor the other are excluded, in the

the distribution of an insolvent debtor's estate. Doubts had indeed been moved, prior to the statute 33d Geo. III, whether such debts could be held as legally includeable under the sequestration law, without an express declaration of the Legislature; and the analogy of the English law was, by sòme, thought entitled to much consideration. But although there seems to be no ground for these doubts, in the true principles of the common law of Scotland, it was thought proper to put an end to all question, by declaring, that both future and contingent debts are included within the statute. It was, however, thought necessary, to make this distinction between them, that future creditors should not only be admitted to prove their debts, and draw under the sequestration, but also to petition for sequestration—while contingent creditors should not be admitted to petition, but only to prove their debts, and have their dividends consigned. By § 37. it is enacted, That 'in all questions upon this act, persons, to whom the debtor is 'under obligation to pay money at a certain future time, shall be 'accounted creditors de præsenti, for the amount of the money, 'discounting the interest to the term of payment specified in the 'obligation.'—And by § 38, That 'where a claim is entered by a 'creditor, upon any obligation, the existence or amount of which 'depends upon a contingency which is still unascertained at the 'period of lodging the claim, the trustee shall rank the claimant, 'as if the condition were purified; but the dividend, or sum, 'which the claimant would be entitled, in that case, to draw, shall 'again be deposited, &c. and the interest thereupon arising, shall 'belong to the creditors, &c. until the contingency, upon which 'the obligation depends, shall be declared, &c.; but that such 'contingent claims shall not be sufficient to authorise a petition 'for sequestration; unless in so far as the amount of them is 'clearly ascertained, and the condition purified, before presenting 'the petition.'

3. PROOF OF THE DEBT.—In proof of the petitioner's debt, the statute requires, that 'the grounds of debt shall be produced, 'or a certified copy of the account, and a deposition by the credi'tor or creditors, at whose instance the application is made, taken

'by

'by any Judge-Ordinary, or Justice of the Peace, to the verity of 'the debt or debts:' § 13.

The difference in the general plan and spirit of the laws of the two countries, is perceptible at every point. In England, the circumspection necessary in authorising the commission of bankruptcy, which proceeds without inquiry, or opportunity given to the debtor to oppose it, has, among other consequences, led to this, that in no case, where the creditor does not himself, personally, make affidavit to his debt, can a commission issue upon his petition. An infant, therefore, cannot be a petitioning creditor: I. Atk. 218.; Cullen, Princip. of B. L. 67.—In Scotland, the same strict precautions not being necessary, since time is given for a fair inquiry, the guardians of an infant are not prevented from taking the benefit of the law, for the protection of his interest. By § 42. it is declared, that an oath of credulity by the guardian, managers, &c. of persons under age, or incapable to give an oath, or absent from Great Britain or Ireland, shall be sufficient.

It was questioned, under the statute of 1783, whether a diligence, so alarming as sequestration, could issue upon a debt, of the existence of which there was not evidence. The expressions of the statute left room for the doubt; but the Court, upon the question being tried, decided, that there was no good principle for rejecting an illiquid claim, as a ground for supporting the petition.—David Dale & Co., merchants in Glasgow, and other creditors of John Yool, manufacturer at Manderston, had claims to the extent of 201l.; but they rested upon open accounts, unsupported by any evidence, except to the extent of 55l., which was constituted by bill. Upon these debts they petitioned, and were met by an objection on the part of the debtor, who argued, that the statute, requiring production 'of the grounds of debt,' seemed anxiously intended to guard against the possibility of a sequestration being taken out by a person not having a real and true debt; that open accounts are not, in terminis, grounds of debt; neither are they evidence, in any shape, of the truth of the claim; and that, of the debts, in this case, some were not due to the extent claimed; and, in others, the term of payment was not come. The Bench was divided upon the question, Whether open accounts were sufficient grounds of debt, in the meaning of the statute, to support the petition? Some of the Judges thought them insufficient, because the statute, in requiring production of the grounds of debt, with an oath to the verity of it, seems to show great anxiety, that no creditor should be admitted to apply, who did not hold a true debt; that the Legislature must be understood, in this expression, to have required evidence of the truth of the debt, by production of a voucher, and of its subsistence, by the oath of the creditor; that the anxiety was the greater, because, bad effects had resulted, under the former law, from permitting an application to be made without the concurrence of true creditors;—and yet, the evil would subsist in full force, if claims, upon open unvouched accounts, were held sufficient to authorise an application. But the rest of the Court, admitting that there was an ambiguity in the expression of the statute, ('grounds of debt,'), and that it ought to be cleared up, held the proof of the bankruptcy as the point of chief importance; and that it was comparatively a matter of little consequence, who should apply for the sequestration. Sequestration was accordingly awarded: 26th January 1792, Dale, &c. against Yool.—I have taken notice of this case, more for the sake of the instruction to be derived from it, respecting the principle which ought to determine such questions, than from its value, strictly considered, as a precedent; since the statute of 1793 removed the doubt which came there into question, by declaring, that the petitioning creditor's debt should be sufficient to support the peitition, 'whether liquidated by formal vouchers, or standing upon open 'account:' § 13.

A question of considerable nicety occurs, where the debt is not merely illiquid, but the former evidence of its existence is cut off by prescription. The long negative prescription of forty years, is a legal discharge and extinction of the debt; while the shorter prescriptions operate as an extinction of the evidence on which the debt formerly rested, and as a præsumptio juris of the debt having been paid. But these ways of extinguishing a debt, are not abso-

lute,

lute. Their operation, for example, is prevented by the minority of the creditor; but the shorter prescriptions, even where not interrupted, leave the debt still unextinguished, although the original evidence of it be destroyed. There is, indeed, some distinction between our shorter prescriptions, and the English statute of limitations; but, in the present question, that difference does not seem to be essential. The least hint revives a debt which has fallen under the statute of limitations, and the courts do not even presume the debt (though the six years have elapsed) to be barred, to the effect of entitling any other person than the debtor himself, to plead this objection (II. Espinasse, 563.): neither does the statute extinguish the debt, nor take away any other remedy, but that by action, mentioned in the act itself—on which ground, Lord Mansfield held the statute of limitation to be no bar to the creditor taking out a commission of bankruptcy: (Fowler v. Brown, I. Cook, B. L. 12.) The short prescriptions of our law, not only bar the action, but extinguish the former evidence, unless legally supported. By 12 Geo. III. c. 72, bills and promissory notes are declared 'to be of no force 'or effect to produce any diligence or action, unless such diligence 'shall be raised and executed, or such action commenced thereon, '*within* the space of six years,' &c.; it being however 'lawful 'and competent, at any time after the expiry of the six years, to 'prove the debts contained in the said bills, &c. and that the same 'are resting owing, by the oath or writ of the debtor.' The statute 1579, c. 83, provides, that 'all actions of debt, for merchants accounts, &c. not founded upon written obligations, 'must be pursued within three years, otherwise the creditor sall 'have nae action, except he either prove, by writ or oath of the 'party.' But as both the one debt and the other, the sum in the bill, and the amount of the account, still subsist as legal claims; and as a creditor may petition upon an open and unliquidated debt; it would appear, that a creditor, by bill more than six years old, or by open account which has stood over for more than three, may lawfully petition for sequestration.

I

I have already observed, that the petition for sequestration proceeds either in the name of the creditor, without the concurrence of the debtor; or in the name, or with the concurrence of the debtor himself, along with the requisite number of qualified creditors.

1. Where the debtor falls within the description of the statute, and is a *native* of Scotland, and *resident within it*, his concurrence to the petition is not necessary. His creditors, qualified as the law directs, may apply without his knowledge, or against his will: but then it is necessary, in such a case, to serve the petition upon the debtor, that he may have an opportunity of opposing it. Upon the presenting of a regular petition, without the debtor's concurrence, the Court pronounces an order, to serve the petition upon the debtor, 'by delivering to him personally, or by leaving, 'at his dwellinghouse, a copy of the said petition; or, if the said 'debtor is out of Scotland, by affixing copies upon the market 'cross of Edinburgh, pier and shore of Leith; and also, leaving 'a copy at the dwellinghouse, or house of business, in Scotland, 'last occupied by such debtor, to appear in Court, within a time 'specified in the warrant of citation, not being less than six, nor 'more than forty days from the date of citation, to show cause, 'why sequestration should not be awarded:' (§ 13.)—In the case of a copartnership, the citation is directed to be made, by leaving a copy at the house or shop where their business is, or was carried on, or where any of their acting partners resides; and, if the houses and shop be shut, or deserted, by affixing copies to the market cross, pier and shore of Leith: (§ 18.)

It is impossible to consider this part of the law, without a glance of comparison at the law of England. The English commission of bankruptcy is applied for in secrecy, and falls, with a sudden violence, upon the debtor. The English lawyers themselves declaim against this as a monstrous defect. One of them represents the commission as secretly applied for; the commissioners as meeting at at a coffee-house; the affidavits taken as in a conspiracy; and, with all imaginable privacy, the debtor declared bankrupt. 'This,' says he, 'is succeeded by a warrant, directed to the messenger, authorizing and commanding him to enter and break open the 'house of the bankrupt, and any place where his property 'is, or may be suspected to be, to seize and detain all his ready 'money, furniture, goods, property, and books of accounts, 'and it is likewise followed by a summons, directed to the bankrupt, requiring him to attend at Guildhall, on the three days 'appointed for his appearance.'—'The whole of the process' (he continues) 'is mysterious. To the bankrupt himself, of all others 'the most interested party, no notice is given: the first information he can receive, is, by the arrival of the messenger, and 'his attendant, at his house *.' After enlarging upon the evil consequences of such proceedings, he says, that, 'for all this, 'the debtor can have no other remedy, than a petition to the 'Great Seal, to supersede the commission, or an action at law 'to recover damages.' He adds, too, that, 'during the long 'vacation, when the courts are shut for three months, no petition against such proceedings can be heard, nor action tried: 'and the debtor remains without relief; without a vindication of 'his character: his effects are in the hands of his enemies; he 'continues subject to all the severe penalties of the bankrupt 'law.' That the most improper advantages have been taken of this state of the law, the author very positively affirms; nay, he tells us, that the oppressions which he describes, have been committed even against country gentlemen wholly unconnected with trade, p. 326, 7. The whole system of the English bankrupt law seems to require this dangerous secrecy in the taking out of commissions, as upon it depends the accomplishment of two important objects of the bankrupt statutes—rapidity of execution, and the prevention of frauds. But, in Scotland, there is ample provision made for the prevention of fraud, and for rapid execution, independently of the sequestration; and no harm can arise, with us, from allowing the question to be fairly discussed before the

* Considerations on the Law of Insolvency, by Sir J. Bland Burgess, second edition, p 324.

sequestration be awarded, whether it be a fair step of diligence, or a malicious attack, and unnecessary piece of cruelty.

2. In all cases, the debtor himself may concur in the application; in some, that concurrence is absolutely necessary. The effect of his voluntary concurrence, in those cases, where, even without his consent, sequestration might be obtained, is to make the service of the petition unnecessary, and to entitle the Court instantly to award the sequestration. The cases, in which his concurrence is absolutely necessary, are, where he is not bankrupt in terms of the 13th section of the statute; or where, 'at the time 'of the application, he does not reside in Scotland, and has no 'dwellinghouse, or house of business, there; or, at least, has had 'no such residence, or dwellinghouse, or house of business, with-'in a year previous to the application.'—In these cases, by the 16th and 17th sections of the statute, sequestration may be awarded, if the debtor shall make a joint application, along with creditors qualified as above; or if he shall, by himself, or those acting for him, (he not being in the country), concur in the application.

What, then, shall be deemed a legal concurrence in the petition for sequestration? It is the rule of the Court of Session, that an advocate, appearing for a party, is presumed to have a mandate. (I. Stair, Inst. xii. 12.) But it may seem not unworthy of attention, whether, in so peculiar a case as this of sequestration, where the effect of a concurrence by the bankrupt, renders a citation to him unnecessary, and, consequently, precludes opposition in the first stages of proceedings so important, it should not be required, either that the bankrupt himself should sign the petition, along with his Counsel, or, at least, that a mandate from him should be produced. When he is out of the country, I should conceive this to be necessary; and the only difficulty in such a case, must rest upon the letter, in which the concurrence is given. When the debtor, in the precipitation of his anxiety to prevent unfair preferences, writes ambiguously to his man of business in this country, it may be doubtful, whether his letter goes the full length of a mandate to apply for sequestration. Thus, in the case of Flammaire & Sons,

which

which occurred under the statute of 1772, two questions occurred. 1. As no provision was hitherto made for the case where the debtor was not in Scotland, it was doubted whether sequestration was competent, where the debtor was an Englishman, residing in England, and where the only estate to be sequestrated, was a parcel of silks, which he had sent down with a factor to be sold here? 2. It was doubted, whether an application by the debtor himself, was sufficiently authorised by a letter from him, informing the institor of his having committed an act of bankruptcy, and of an English creditor's having left London, with the intention of attaching the silks; and concluding thus—' Have the opinion of the ' most able advocate; and, if you have not given up the goods, ' APPLY DIRECTLY?'—In support of this, as an authority for applying for sequestration in the name of the bankrupt, powers of attorney, posterior to the application, were produced. ' The letter was considered to be sufficient; and the Court found the presenting of the petition, in the name of Samuel Cole the debtor, ' sufficiently authorised by him: Repelled the objections to the ' competency of the application, so far as in the name of Samuel ' Cole; and therefore sequestrated,' &c. 4th August 1772.

Thus, the primary requisites of a petition for sequestration, without which it will not even be entertained by the Court, are, 1. That the debtor be a trader, or manufacturer: 2. That he either be bankrupt, or concur in the application: 3. That the petitioning creditor shall hold a debt of 100l. against the bankrupt, if he be the sole petitioner; or, if there be two petitioners, their debts shall amount to 150l.; or if three or more, to 200l.: that these debts shall not be contingent at the date of the petition, and if future, they shall suffer an abatement of interest: And, 4. That the petitioner shall prove his debt, by producing the vouchers, or grounds thereof, and swearing to its verity. We now proceed to consider the application in another view, in which the circumstances of the debtor's situation, and of the creditor's claim, are subjected to a more strict inquiry.

§ 2.

§ 2. Of the Grounds of Opposition to the Awarding of Sequestration.

The awarding of sequestration may be opposed, either on the part of the debtor, or on the part of the creditors. The debtor has a plain interest to oppose an act which involves his whole affairs, puts his estate under expensive management, deprives him of the capacities which belong to a solvent man, and proclaims him as a bankrupt through every country of Europe. Creditors, on the other hand, may have a strong interest to oppose such a measure; either if they have reason to dread the effects of a stop in their debtor's trade, or if, as individuals, they have the view of acquiring preferences, which the sequestration will level to the ground. Thus, the sequestration is an adjudication for all the creditors as at the date of the first deliverance, and, so, communicates with the first effectual, if within year and day: It bestows also a pari passu preference along with all poinders or arresters, provided the first deliverance is dated within four months from the bankruptcy. If, therefore, any creditor interested in the previous diligence, can prevail in cutting down the sequestration, he will save the preference from reduction.

In supporting this opposition, the attention of the opponent must be directed to some one of the points already taken notice of, in speaking of the primary requisites of the petition;—either to show, that the debtor does not really come within the description of the statute; or that the petitioning creditors are not true creditors; or, at least, that their debts are not of such a nature or amount, as can ground a legal application. For this purpose, a strict scrutiny may be made into the circumstances of the debtor, and the ground of the debts.

The situation of the debtor, we have already considered as fully as seems to be in any degree necessary. But, with regard to the debt of the petitioning creditor, there are several cases which seem to require consideration.

1. It would not appear to be a good objection to the petitioner's debt, nor to entitle the opposer of the sequestration to insist for its being restricted, that the claim had been purchased for less than the sum claimed. In England, it has been determined, (though the case has not occurred, that I know of, in this country), that a creditor, by notes bought in at 10s. in the pound, is a creditor for the full sum, and entitled to take out a commission: I. P. Williams, 783.—I. Cook, B. L. 17.

2. Neither would it seem t be a good objection, to restrict the debt of the petitioner, that he had agreed to take a composition payable by instalments. This also, though it has not occurred in Scotland, has been determined in England, by Lord Hardwicke, upon sound principles:—'For, where a creditor agrees to take 'less than his debt, so that it be paid precisely at the day, if the 'debtor fails of payment, he cannot be relieved in equity:'—Ex parte Bennet, II. Atk. 528.—Cullen's Principles of Bankrupt Law, 104.

3. Deduction, we have seen, must be given of all partial payments; and unless the debt, after all these deductions, amount to the sum specified in the statute, the sequestration must fall. But questions may arise here of some nicety. 1. If, in payment of the whole, or of such part of the debt of the petitioning creditor, as would reduce his sum below the legal standard, the debtor have indorsed to him a bill, and it has been dishonoured, and the creditor has not, as he might have done, enforced payment by due negotiation; the debtor, or any creditor having an interest to oppose the sequestration, is entitled to insist that this shall form a deduction from the debt. I scruple not again to refer to the English law, in illustration of this point.—A debtor was due to the petitioning creditor more than 100l. He gave him a bill for a part, which reduced the debt within 100l.; but the bill, having been drawn on one who held no funds of the debtor, was not accepted. The petitioning creditor kept the bill, without giving notice of the non-acceptance, and sued out a commission on the whole debt. The question having been moved, whether this was a good commission? the Court held, that,

in

in this special case, there could be no extinguishment of the amount of the bill, notice being unnecessary, as the drawee had no funds in his hands, so that the drawer could suffer no prejudice for want of notice: Bickersdike v. Bolman, II. Espinasse, 561.—I. Cook, B. L. 13.—I. Term Rep. 405. But the opinions of the Judges clearly show, that, if there had been funds in the hands of the drawee, the judgement would have been reversed—the debt so far extinguished—and the commission held bad, as proceeding on a debt below the legal standard. 2. If the partial payment be such as the general body of creditors are entitled to reduce, it cannot be held to diminish the debt of the petitioning creditor in this question. Thus, if one who is a prior creditor receive, within sixty days of the debtor's bankruptcy, an indorsation to a bill in part payment of his debt; or receive from the bankrupt, within that period, delivery of goods in liquidation of part of his claim, these are preferences subject to reduction; and if, by way of objection to the petitioner, they be stated as deductions which ought to have been made from the debt of the petitioning creditor when he applied, the answer is good, that they are ineffectual to extinguish the debt, or any part of it. This point also has been decided in England, where the petitioning creditor having, after an act of bankruptcy, received 50l. of his debt, (which reduced it under 100l.), sued out the commission notwithstanding; it was held that the payment was void; and, therefore, the original debt remaining undiminished, the commission was good: Mann, assignee of Stevens, v. Shepherd, VI. Term Rep. 680.—II. Espinasse, 562. 3. Where the debtor, although he has made no payment to account of the debt, has counter-claims against the petitioning creditor, there seems to be little doubt, that these counter-claims will be held to diminish the debt, if instantly verified or admitted, but, where unliquidated, they will not; as compensation is no extinction of a debt, ipso jure.

4. Where the petitioning creditor's debt is under suspension, can he apply for sequestration? In England, (where a decree-arbitral, or award by arbitrators, is subject to review in the Court of Chancery), a sum awarded by arbitrators, is held to support a commission,

mission, notwithstanding a bill filed to set aside the award; for the arbitration bond is a debt at law, and binds the parties, until it is set aside for corruption or partiality, &c.: Ex parte Lingwood, I. Atk. 241.; I. Cook, B. L. 20.—But, perhaps, a different judgement would be pronounced upon the effect of a suspension with us. The object of a suspension is, to put a stop to execution; but sequestration is the highest of all civil executions, the most active of all diligences, and that which is least of all susceptible of reparation. If, indeed, a creditor were, in this country, without any resource, at common law, for securing himself against the effects of the activity of other creditors—if no attachment were competent—if there were no inhibition, nor adjudication, nor arrestment, to which he might have recourse—it might be equally hard to deny him the benefit of applying for sequestration, as I conceive it to be in England, to deny the power of applying for the commission. But a suspension does not preclude him from arrestment, so as to acquire a pari passu preference on the personal estate, along with other arresters; nor does it prevent him from summoning a poinder, or raising a multiplepoinding in his name, so as to acquire a right to a communication of the benefit of that diligence, if his claim shall ultimately be sustained: and as to the heritable estate, he may raise inhibition, or he may adjudge, so as to secure himself a place in the ranking. All these are compatible with the idea of a claim being under suspension; but a sequestration, which tends, not merely to the security of the creditor, but to the active seizure of his estate and person, and its final distribution, is not to be issued at the call of a creditor, whose debt is under the express suspension of a Court, and who enjoys, by other means, the protection of the law.

5. Another doubt may be moved, respecting the time of contracting the debt of the petitioning creditor. Although the debt was contracted before the bankrupt entered into trade, it still may entitle the creditor to petition; for, by entering into trade, the debtor's funds are universally subjected to all the perils and mischances which were in the view of the Legislature, as the induc-

tive

tive cause of the enactment. The law of England, as laid down by Mr Cook, may, I apprehend, be assumed as good doctrine also in Scotland. 'A creditor, before the party entered into trade, 'may, on account of such debt, sue out a commission; but a cre-'ditor for a debt contracted after leaving off trade, cannot. But, 'when a commission is sued out, those creditors, who have become 'such since the quitting trade, may come in and share the divi-'dend with those who were creditors before, or during the trad-'ing:' I. Cook, B. L. 21. and cases there cited.

SECTION II.

OF THE FIRST DELIVERANCE—AND OF THE JUDGEMENT AWARDING SEQUESTRATION.

IT is an important point, in the law of sequestration, to ascertain the nature and effect of the petition, and of the judgement, or act of sequestration; for, upon these must depend the whole force of this, as an universal diligence against the bankrupt's e-state.

The 'first deliverance' upon the petition of sequestration, is the interlocutor, or order of Court, which is pronounced at the first moving of the petition in Court; and any order whatever, whether for service, or superseding the consideration of the petition for a few days, is deemed a deliverance, in the sense of the statute. It is declared by the statute, that the date of the first deliverance, is the point of time to which the effect of the sequestration is referable. Thus, the petition of sequestration, and the first deliverance, being duly recorded, is declared to have the effect of an inhibition, as from the date of the first deliverance: § 19. The judgment for vesting the estate in the trustee, is declared to have the effect of 'a common decree of adjudication, obtained, 'and rendered effectual, at the date of the first deliverance on the 'petition for sequestration, accumulating the whole debts of the

'bankrupt,

'bankrupt, principal and interest, as at that period, and adjudging 'for security or payment thereof' § 24.—And it is also declared to operate 'as a complete attachment and transfer of the move-'able or personal estate, for behoof of all the creditors, at the 'date of the first deliverance aforesaid.' Ibid.—The importance of having a deliverance given upon a petition of sequestration, and the particular care necessary in guarding against any such objections to its form and requisites, as may induce the Court to refuse pronouncing an order upon it, must therefore be very evident. The petition and deliverance must 'be recorded in the ge-'neral register of inhibitions, within fifteen days after the said de-'liverance is pronounced.' And this publication would appear to be necessary, not merely for the purpose of giving to the proceeding the effect of an inhibition, (which would be unnecessary, in bankruptcies where there was no heritable estate), but it is requisite in every sequestration; for the act declares, 'That the pro-'ceedings shall be of no effect, if such registration be omit-'ted:' § 19.—This is the only publication of the proceedings, till the judgement be pronounced awarding sequestration; it is the only one which it would not have been cruel and unjust to authorise, before time had been allowed to the debtor for objecting to the publication as improper and unnecessary. The first thing done after the awarding of sequestration, is to advertise it in the newspapers.

The days of citation to the debtor being expired; 'if he shall 'not appear, either in person, or by his Counsel or agent; or, so 'appearing, shall not instantly pay, or produce written evidence 'of the debt or debts being satisfied, upon which the diligence 'proceeded; and also pay, or satisfy the debt, or debts, due to 'the petitioner, or petitioners, or show other reasonable cause 'why further proceedings should not be had; the Court shall im-'mediately award sequestration of the debtor's whole estate and 'effects, heritable and moveable, real and personal, for the benefit 'of his whole just and lawful creditors:' § 13.—'If the applica-'tion be with the debtor's own concurrence, sequestration is im-'mediately awarded, on the petition being presented:' § 16.—

 And

And 'the whole deliverance' (which the statute also orders to contain the appointment of certain days for electing a factor and a trustee) 'the petitioning creditor, or creditors, shall forthwith 'cause to be advertised in a paper called the Edinburgh Gazette, 'otherwise the whole proceedings to be null and void.' § 14.

The judgement awarding sequestration puts the estate and effects under the management of the Court, to be by them delegated to a proper person as judicial factor, until the creditors shall have an opportunity of choosing a trustee. But the effect of the sequestration ought to be carefully distinguished from that of the disposition or adjudication, by which the estate is vested in the trustee. The judgement awarding sequestration makes no transference of the property, either heritable or moveable:—it deprives the bankrupt, indeed, of the adminstration of his funds; it takes away all his powers of conveyance, or even of paying off debt, (though, at the same time, the rights of bona fide purchasers from him, at a fair price, are saved, and those of debtors who have, bona fide, made payments to him); but the right of property is left untouched; and the bankrupt, to all intents and purposes, undivested. The law does, indeed, declare, that the adjudication, in favour of the trustee, shall, with respect both to the heritable and to the moveable estate, draw back to the date of the first deliverance; but it will be observed, in the *first* place, that this in no shape rests upon the nature of the award of sequestration: *Secondly*, that it forms no bar to the completion of former voluntary rights between the date of the deliverance and the decree of adjudication, or disposition to the trustee.

This doctrine was fully established in a case which occurred in May 1797. An assignation of a personal bond was granted before bankruptcy, but not completed by intimation till after the date of the deliverance awarding sequestration. A competition arose between the assignee and the trustee for the creditors, whose title, under the bankrupt's disposition, was not completed till after the assignation was intimated. Some of the Judges were at first inclined to consider the act of sequestration as an arrestment; not indeed

indeed as transferring the subject, but as fixing and securing it, and having, like an arrestment, the effect of superseding and cutting down any assignation unintimated at the date of the sequestration But it was suggested, that the first deliverance on the petition of sequestration was no bar whatever to a creditor's proceeding to complete a voluntary right fairly granted to him before bankruptcy; and that the completeness, or incompleteness of that right depended on the competition of priority between it and the vesting of the estate in the trustee. The notion of a litigiosity, created by the mere force of the sequestration, to the effect of tying up the hands of real creditors from completing their rights, was held to be unwarranted; for, although the sequestration does indeed tie up the hands of the bankrupt himself, and renders it impossible for any creditor to acquire, ab origine, a preferable right to which he had no claim before, it puts no check or interruption in the way of those who had already obtained from the bankrupt all that he had to give, and had only to complete and render effectual, either by their own act, or by the course of law, a right which they already possessed in substance. The Court, therefore, held the common rule to apply in this situation, just as in any other, that the conveyance of an heritable right, first completed, is preferable; whether it be in the person of one whose right was incomplete at the date of the sequestration, or of the trustee who represents the whole community of creditors—unless, in so far as the same may be struck at by that clause of the act 1696, which holds real securities to be of the date of the seisine: That, as to the case of an assignation unintimated till after the deliverance on the petition of sequestration, the same general doctrine holds good; a person being entitled to complete that right by intimating, as well after the sequestration, as before; and that this would secure his preference, provided the intimation preceded the conveyance by which the whole bankrupt estate was vested in the trustee; which, being a public assignation, does not need intimation, and is preferable without it. In this particular case, it appeared, that the individual creditor had intimated before the trustee was vested, though after the deliverance on the petition of sequestration; and therefore, the Court held his right to be good. But it was further observed, that, though this

was

was the law, as standing upon the statute of 1793, it was plainly inequitable, in so far as the statute tied up the hands of the creditors, by preventing them from poinding or arresting for sixty days before the bankruptcy, while it left those who had unintimated assignations (which, at common law, and in ordinary cases, might have been cut down by either of these diligences) entirely at liberty to complete them, and thus to secure a preference over those who were disabled from contending in the course of diligence. It was therefore thought, that the statute ought to be extended to unintimated assignations, so as to prevent them from being made effectual any more than arrestments or poindings 24th May 1797, Buchan against Farquharson. I shall have occasion to say more upon this subject afterwards.

SECTION III.

OF THE RECALL OF A SEQUESTRATION IMPROPERLY AWARDED.

WHEN the nature of the English commission of bankruptcy is compared with that of the sequestration in this country; the application for the former being secret, and the evidence of the debt and of the bankruptcy being conducted in a private tribunal, unknown to the person whose existence as a trader is at stake; while, in the latter, every thing is fair and open, full opportunity being given for inquiry before the sequestration be awarded, it will appear a matter of infinitely greater importance, in England, to provide for the recall of a commission erroneously or maliciously taken out, than it possibly can be in Scotland. As there is a possibility, however, of a fraudulent application being made, even in Scotland, which may never come to the ear of the person against whom the petition is directed, as it may be pretended, that he has concurred in the application, when he has not, so as to procure an immediate award of sequestration; and as creditors may be interested to oppose, who never hear of the proceedings till sequestration

be

be awarded; the Legislature has not neglected, in our sequestration statute, to provide the necessary remedy.

The English commission is recalled, by a writ issuing under the Great Seal, at the discretion of the Lord Chancellor, ordering the commission to be superseded. The application may be made, either by the bankrupt, or by the creditors. If the commission appear to have been taken out fraudulently and vexatiously, the Court will not only at once supersede it, but give a remedy against the petitioning creditor. For making effectual this remedy, it is enacted, by 5. Geo. II. c. 30. § 23. that the petitioning creditor shall give bond to the Lord Chancellor in the penalty of 200l.: and if his debt shall turn out not to be really due, or if the party be not bankrupt, but the commission has been taken out maliciously and fraudulently, the Lord Chancellor may assign the bond to the person who is aggrieved by the taking out of the commission. The remedy may therefore be had either in this way, or by action at law for damages, in the election of the party.

The Scotish bankrupt statute has provided, 'That if the debtor, against whom sequestration has been awarded without his own concurrence, or if any creditor who has not concurred in, or consented to the' application, shall apprehend that the party against whom it is awarded, does not come within the description before given, or falls under any of the exceptions therefrom, or that there is any other good ground for recalling the sequestration, and annulling the whole proceedings; such debtor or creditor shall be at liberty, at any time within thirty days after sequestration is awarded, to apply to the Court of Session, setting forth the grounds upon which the sequestration ought to be recalled: and this petition being intimated to the party or parties at whose instance the sequestration was obtained, or their known agent, and a reasonable time given to make answers thereto, and to adduce the necessary proofs on either side, the Court shall determine upon the same, and either recall or confirm the sequestration, as the justice of the case may require: but, in the mean time, until this matter is finally decided, the proceedings under

'the

'the sequestration shall go on, as if no such application had been 'made:' § 19.

In this law, it has been thought sufficient to allow the term of thirty days from the advertisement of the sequestration, (the advertisement must be made forthwith) for any one to appear and object nullity or irregularity in the proceedings; and, on the other hand, it has been deemed proper to prevent any interruption to the business, after it has been fairly begun, by excluding all application for a recall, after the thirty days. In the interpretation of this part of the statute, the Court has given it a liberal construction, for supporting the sequestration as an universal diligence in favour of all the creditors:—31. January 1787, Beadie against Higgie's Creditors.

SECTION IV.

OF THE MANAGEMENT, PREVIOUS TO THE ELECTION OF A FACTOR.

IN England, as well as in this country, the trustees, or, as they are called there, the assignees, are elected by the creditors themselves; but, as some time is necessary for the creditors to hear of the commission, and to bring in their debts, so as to qualify themselves for electing, it is necessary that some means should be provided for intermediate management. This is done, in England, by the nomination of a provisional assignee; who takes such steps as are necessary for preserving the estate to the creditors, until the proper assignees shall be elected. The factor under the sequestration, corresponds properly with the provisional assignee of the English law; but as the factor's office, shortlived as it is, may be of much importance, he also is elected by the creditors themselves: and as, in the mean while, many things may be necessary, the law has provided, that 'any creditor may call upon the Sheriff-depute 'or substitute, upon cause shown, at any time after sequestration,

'and

'and before the meeting for the election of the factor, to seal up, 'and cause to be put under safe custody, the books and papers of 'the bankrupt, and to lock up his or her shop, warehouse, or other 'repositories, and to keep the keys thereof, till a factor is nam-'ed, or the custody and care devolved upon the Sheriff-clerk; sub-'ject, in the mean time, to such orders and directions, as either 'the Court of Session, or Sheriff, may think proper to give, on 'the application of any party concerned, for preservation of the 'effects:' § 14.

Where it is necessary immediately to procure delivery of cargoes, &c. to avoid the danger of their being stopped in transitu—where measures are to be taken for stopping, in transitu, goods sent by the bankrupt to persons who have failed—where there is danger of any commodity spoiling, by being kept, or a necessity for proceeding in any operation of art, which is in the course of completion at the time of the petition for sequestration being presented—wherever, in short, any incidental act requires to be done, before the election of a factor, it is accomplished by presenting, in the name of the bankrupt, or of the petitioning creditors, a petition to the Sheriff of the county; or to the Judge of the High Court of Admiralty, in matters under his jurisdiction, or to the Court of Session, or, in vacation, to the Lord Ordinary on the Bills.

SECTION V.

OF THE ELECTION OF THE FACTOR—HIS DUTIES AND POWERS.

To complete this system of sequestration, as a preliminary stage to the vesting of the estate in a trustee, in order to be recovered and distributed, it is necessary that there should be a factor appointed, to conduct the intermediate management; receive the claims of the creditors; make the proper arrangements; and prepare every thing for the immediate and effectual commencement of the trustee's office.

1. ELECTION.—The first sequestration statute in 1772, it has been seen, was a double system, optional to the creditors, of sequestration or of private trust. If the sequestration was adhered to, the whole business was conducted by a factor. The Court, at the time of awarding sequestration, named as factor, 'the person presented by the majority of the creditors concurring in the application for sequestration, or producing their 'grounds of debt in the hands of the clerk to the sequestration.' This factor was not, indeed, continued without inquiry, as the sole factor, through the whole of the sequestration: an advertisement for a meeting, at the distance of at least thirty days, was ordered to confirm his election, or to choose a new one. But the factor, thus appointed by the petitioning creditors, stood exactly in the place of the interim factor of the present law; and this, it must be obvious, left much room for fraud. All diligence was stopped—the factor got the administration of the whole estate—the opportunity of collusion with the bankrupt, by a man whose election might have been managed between the bankrupt and the concurring creditors, was manifest, and almost inscrutable. It was from the consideration of such dangers, that the Legislature adopted the plan at present in force; ordering a day to be appointed, 'not more than three weeks, and as much sooner as circum-'stances may permit, for the creditors to meet and elect an inte-'rim factor, if they should think fit, or to leave the interim ma-'nagement to the Sheriff-clerk.' This meeting is ordered to be advertised, so that all having interest may appear at the election; and a Magistrate is appointed to attend at the meeting, in order to receive the grounds of debt and oaths of verity, and to sign the minutes of the meeting along with the preses whom the creditors shall elect: § 14.

AS A QUALIFICATION TO VOTE, nothing more is necessary than the production of a claim of debt, (with its grounds and vouchers, if founded upon documents), and of an oath of verity. There plainly is not time for an inquiry into the real merit of the claims; and all the security that can be had against an unfair election, is, to make each voter specify the nature and extent of his claim,

claim, and swear to its truth. It cannot be supposed, that many will run the risk of the penalties of false swearing, for an object so trivial.

The election is determined by a majority of the creditors in value, or extent of debt, appearing at the said meeting, by themselves, or authorised by others, and whose grounds of debt, and oaths thereon, are so produced: § 14. And it may be added, that the act provides, respecting authorities and mandates, given to agents, &c. to vote in any meeting, that a commission, either general or 'special,' shall be sufficient: § 20. This commission, however, must be in writing.

'The factor, if required, shall find security for his intromis-'sions, to such extent as the said majority shall think reasonable:' § 15. The Sheriff-clerk is not bound to find caution, other than the general security he gives for the faithful administration of his office as Sheriff-clerk.

2. FACTOR'S TITLE OF ACTING.—The factor, or the Sheriff-clerk (if the management devolves upon him) is ordered 'to engross 'the minutes of the meeting at which he is appointed, in a book 'of sederunt properly authenticated, which shall be kept by him, 'as his warrant of acting:' and 'the bankrupt, if required by 'him, or by the creditors at said meeting, shall grant powers of 'attorney, or other deeds which may be deemed necessary or pro-'per, for the recovery of the estate and effects situated in foreign 'parts, under the pain of fraudulent bankruptcy, and of being 'deprived of all benefit from the statute:' § 15.

3. DUTY AND POWERS OF THE FACTOR.—The general description of his duties and powers is, that they are those of an administrator and manager; the object of whose appointment is, to preserve and recover, as far as possible, the estate of the debtor, and prepare it for being, to the best advantage, converted into a divisible fund.

1. He

1. He is entitled 'to take possession of the bankrupt's whole 'estate and effects,' § 15. Without any warrant but his act of election, he may demand delivery of goods consigned to the bankrupt; he may stop in transitu; he may demand payment of bills when due; receive the money, and grant a valid discharge. The money which he recovers, he must lodge in a bank; for, though there is no special provision to this effect in the statute, except with regard to the trustee, (who is required to lodge all the money he receives in such bank, or with such banking company as four-fifths of the creditors in number and value, at any general meeting, shall appoint, &c. § 34.), yet the same rule is held to apply to the factor; for, in a case upon the statute of 1783, the meeting for choosing a factor, having ordered the money that should be recovered to be lodged in the hands of any six merchants in Dundee, to be named by the creditors, the Court found, 'that the 'lodging of the money in the hands of the persons mentioned in 'the complaint, was not warranted by the statute; though they 'did not determine whether such money could be lodged in the 'hand of an individual carrying on the trade of a banker:' 24th December 1788, Playfair against Walker, &c. The factor may use such steps of diligence as may be necessary for enforcing payment, or for securing a share of the debtor's fund, in case of his failure; but he has no power of discretionary acting, as, of entering into submissions, of compromising claims, &c. He acts under the strict rules of the law; and is bound to follow, in the recovery of the estate, the ordinary steps of legal diligence. He has power to draw the rents of the estate, like a factor in the sequestration previous to a ranking and sale; and to remove tenants; and do other acts of administration necessary.

2. He is entitled 'to take possession of all the bills, notes, and 'and whole other vouchers, title-deeds, and instructions of the 'bankrupt's estate, and also of his books and papers,' § 15. Where these are in the possession of the bankrupt's agent, he may insist for possession of them, reserving the agent's preference, in consequence of the right of retention. Thus, in Bertram Gardner & Co.'s bankruptcy, the affairs were managed, for some time, un-

der

der a voluntary plan of trust; and Mr Thomson acted as agent for the creditors. In this capacity, he received possession of all the books and papers, grounds of debt, and oaths of verity, lodged by the creditors. When a sequestration was applied for, Mr Hotchkis, having been named interim factor, applied for the papers. Mr Thomson was willing to give inspection of the bankrupts papers, in his own hands, but refused to deliver them up, till an account due to him for business done, was paid, or at least an obligation granted for payment of it; and, as to the grounds of debt, he contended that these were the property of the creditors, which the interim factor was not entitled to demand possession of. A petition was presented by the interim factor to the Court; and, on considering it, with answers, the Lords 'authorised the said Richard Hotchkis, as interim factor on the sequestrated estate of 'Bertram Gardner & Co. &c., and the trustee acting for the time 'upon the said estate, to make payment to the said David Thomson, out of the funds in their hands, of the amount of his accounts, as soon as the same are finally liquidated and adjusted; 'and, in the mean time, ordained the said David Thomson instantly to deliver to the said Richard Hotchkis, the whole writings, 'vouchers, documents, books and papers, of every kind, both of 'the creditors and of the bankrupts, or connected with their affairs:' 16th January 1794, Interim Factor on Bertram Gardner & Co.'s estate against Thomson.

3. As manager of the estate, the factor is entitled to pay all demands of expences, &c. necessary in carrying through his acts of administration; and all those debts, without payment of which, he cannot insist for implement of any obligation due to the bankrupt. He is entitled, for example, to pay freight, carriage, &c. of goods, which are sent to the bankrupt from a distance. He is entitled to pay also the expence of manufacturing commodities, which the bankrupt had put into the hands of workmen, and for which, as the counterpart of the contract, they are entitled to retain the commodities. He is also, I apprehend, entitled to allow, out of the rents, &c. which may be due to the bankrupt, the expence of such repairs as the bankrupt was bound to pay, for those also are secured

by

by a direct retention under the contract. But he is not entitled to make any other payments, without an express warrant of Court. Of claims of compensation, and of general retention, not arising out of the obligation itself, for implement of which he is insisting, he is not entitled to judge. These he must leave to the Court, and to the creditors themselves.

4. It may be necessary for a factor, in the course of his management, to appear in the meetings of the creditors of those who are indebted to the funds. What his powers in such meetings are, is not laid down in the statute; and is to be judged of by the analogy of his other powers. He cannot accede to any compromise; nor agree to any submission; nor do any other act of extraordinary or discretionary power, without the express authority of his constituents. But I should apprehend, that, as the voting for a factor, or trustee, is an act of common administration, the factor's vote could not be objected to, as unauthorised by his general warrant.

5. The duties of the factor may be ascertained from his powers. Having all the power which can enable him to manage the estate, and to recover it for the general benefit, he is bound to do so; and, in a particular manner, he is bound to supply the defects of the sequestration itself, by taking the proper means, under letters of attorney, or whatever other form of authority may be necessary, for recovering those funds which may be situated beyond the jurisdiction of the Court. He must forward, as much as possible, the discovery of the estate. He must take care to prevent prescriptions from running against any claims to which the bankrupt may be entitled. To enumerate every particular of his duty, were endless; they must vary infinitely with the circumstances of the bankruptcy; and a factor will be valuable, and respected, in proportion as he is diligent and sagacious in attending to all the points of his duty, for the benefit of the creditors. If negligent, he will not only be guilty of sporting with the interest of others, but he will subject himself to the hazard of the worst constructions, and to claims of damage of a very disagreeable kind.

SECTION VI.

Exoneration and Discharge of the Factor.

The sequestration, properly so called, is at an end, when the trustee is elected, and the estate vested in him. The statute provides, that, at the meeting for choosing a trustee, 'the interim 'manager shall exhibit the book of sederunt, containing the minute of his appointment, together with a state of his intromis- 'sions, and the books and papers in his possession; which state 'shall be engrossed in the said book of sederunt.'—'And the book 'of sederunt, and title-deeds of the heritable estate, shall be de- 'livered to the trustee; and the other papers to the interim ma- 'nager, to be kept by him, until the same are duly taken off his 'hand by the trustee, upon being discharged of his intromissions, 'and satisfied of all demands which he has against the estate, for 'advances of money, commission, or trouble.' § 20. & 21.—When the trustee's nomination is confirmed, (as it must be by the Court, before he can act), 'he then has a right to take into his custody 'all books, accounts, vouchers of debt, securities, and other pa- 'pers and documents, &c. and to account with, and discharge the 'interim manager:' § 22.

If there be any dispute about the accounting with the interim factor, it must proceed before the Court of Session. To that Court (by § 15.) is delegated, the modification of the gratuity which the majority of creditors may assign to him; and (by § 59.) it is before them that the interim manager and trustee shall, on all occasions, be called to answer for their conduct, and account for their intromissions. If the accounting with the factor is likely to require any time to discuss, the trustee will obtain an order upon the factor to deliver up the papers, under a reservation of his preference for payment of any claim he may have against the estate.

CHAP.

CHAP. III.

Of the Trust—Disposal of the Estate—Distribution among the Creditors—and Winding up of the Sequestration.

Having considered the sequestration, properly so called, the first, or preliminary part of the proceedings, in cases of mercantile bankruptcy; I shall, in this Chapter, endeavour to explain, methodically, the system of trust which has been devised, for the purpose of distributing the estate and funds of the bankrupt. The subject may be discussed in the following order:

1. The powers of the trustee—of the commissioners—of the assembled creditors—and of the Court of Session.

2. The vesting of the estate in the trustee.

3. The bankrupt's examination.

4. The management, recovery, and disposal of the estate.

5. The distribution of the funds among the creditors. And,

6. The disposal of the debtor's person—his allowance, and his discharge.

SECTION I.

Powers of the Trustee—of the Commissioners—of the Assembled Creditors—and of the Court of Session.

The settlement of the bankruptcy, requires the co-operation of several powers. The estate is to be recovered, managed, and distributed; questions of prudence, in the settlement of disputes, and in the disposal of property, are to be considered; the propriety of accepting or refusing proposals for a composition, is to be judged of; the justice of concurring in applications for a personal protection, or a discharge, is to be determined; and many points of law, in respect to the claims of creditors, or to the order of ranking, or to questionable proceedings in the sequestration, are to be decided; so that a combination of jurisdictions, and of powers, becomes necessary, which may not, at first sight, seem to be required. For these various purposes, a trustee is appointed, by the election of the creditors—a committee of creditors is named as his council—the creditors themselves are subject to a general call, upon emergencies—the rules of their proceedings and votes being duly ascertained; and the Court of Session is ever open to all the necessary applications, and ever ready to decide, summarily, the questions of law which may occur in the course of the business.

§ 1. Of the Trustee—His Powers and Duties—Election—Removal—Discharge and Exoneration.

It is the interest and the duty of creditors, on the one hand, and of trustees, upon the other, to have a comprehensive and clear view of the office of a trustee in a sequestration; that the one may be apprized of the power which they are consenting to delegate, and the other have a due sense of the burden of duties for which he ought to be qualified. In entering upon the explanation of this subject, I find myself called upon to say, that, plain and clear as the law is, there seems to have been the most unaccountable misapprehension of the nature of this office; so that the Court of Session have daily been pestered with applications, and the creditors loaded with expence, which the law never meant to sanction or allow.

I. OFFICE AND DUTIES OF THE TRUSTEE.—The office of trustee in a sequestration, combines in the same person, the powers and duties of the English assignee, with many of the powers of the commissioners of bankruptcy. He is the assignee of the estate and funds—to hold them for the creditors; to manage them; to dispose of them; and to distribute the produce, when the interests of all the claimants are settled. His powers partake of those of the English commissioners, so far as he receives the claims of the creditors—examines them as a judge—admits or rejects them—and settles the whole scheme of ranking, marshalling the creditors according to his opinion of their legal rights. All this is done, indeed, under the controul of the Court of Session; but, unless in cases of necessity, or where the proceedings of the trustee are thought objectionable, or his judgment erroneous, the whole is settled without any appeal to their decision *. Many other duties the trustee has to perform, of a more ambiguous nature, neither in the character of a mere trustee, nor in that of a judge. It is his business to call the creditors together—to have the debtor brought up for examination, when necessary—and to apply to the Court of Session for all the necessary and incidental warrants.

But this general enumeration is far from being sufficient. It is necessary to descend a little into particulars.

I.

* It is in Glasgow, the first commercial city in Scotland, that the duties and powers of a trustee, under a sequestration, seem to be best understood, and most ably discharged. The gentlemen, who are commonly confided in as trustees, enjoy so entirely the confidence of the public—are so well versed in the principles upon which, according to mercantile ideas, the division of such estates should be conducted—and so sensible of the infinite advantage of a quick distribution, and of the danger of throwing the affairs into a court of law, that their decisions are seldom challenged, or the sequestration ever heard of in the Court of Session, but when the applications, necessary in point of form, are presented.

i. The trustee is the person in whom, as the representative of all the creditors, the estate is to be vested; and as he is, from the moment of his election, the active person in the management of the common interest, one important part of his duty is, to have his titles to the estate and effects completed instantly after his election, that the general right may not be affected by the prior completion of the rights of individual creditors. In the performance of this duty, the trustee has not only to attend to those parts of the funds which are immediately under his eye, but to those also which may be situated abroad, and those which may, in the course of the sequestration, devolve upon the bankrupt.

ii. To the trustee is committed the management, disposal, and recovery of the property and funds. The duties which, in this view, he has to perform, are manifold, as the circumstances of the bankrupt's estate may require. His first business is, to settle with the factor; to examine his accounts, his states, rentals, and inventories; to pay, or allow retention of the proper charges; to require a clear delivery of all papers, documents, books, &c.; and to prosecute the factor and his sureties for any deficit in the money which may have come into his hands. He must direct a most anxious and scrutinizing investigation into the possibility of concealment of funds on the part of the bankrupt, in which the examination of the bankrupt, his wife, and family, and those connected with his business, will much assist him. He must prosecute all claims competent to the debtor; unless the Commissioners, or the creditors, shall authorize him to submit, or compound, or neglect such claims. He must keep a watchful eye on such contracts as may be in dependence, so as to take instant delivery of goods imported for the bankrupt. He must direct the proper proceedings to be taken, for claiming and making effectual, in other countries, such property as may belong to the bankrupt there. He must attend the meetings of creditors, or authorize agents, &c. to do so, where any of the debtors to the estate are bankrupt. In such meetings, he is entitled, without the concurrence of his commissioners, or the authority of a general meeting, to exercise all the acts of ordinary administration; though certainly not to consent

 to

to submissions, compositions, discharges, &c. In disposing of the estate, he must take the advice of the meeting of creditors, held after the last examination of the bankrupt, whether the heritable subjects shall be sold by public voluntary roup, or judicial sale; and, according to such advice, he must proceed, either in accomplishing the voluntary sale, or in bringing the action of judicial sale into Court. He must also convert into money the moveables, in the way most for the interest of the creditors. There is no provision, that he shall consult the commissioners on this subject; but, if one-fourth of the creditors in value choose to require him, he must call a general meeting, to consult upon the interest of the creditors (§ 32.). All the money which the trustee receives, he must lodge in such Bank, or with such Banking Company, as four-fifths of the creditors, in number and value, at any general meeting, shall appoint, &c.; and 'never retain, in his own hands, a-'bove the sum of 50l. Sterling, for the space of ten days, other-'wise to be liable for 7½ per cent. on whatever exceeds the 50l., 'in name of interest and damages:' (§ 34.)

iii. To the trustee is committed the important duty of settling the whole distribution of the estate; in which he acts more in the capacity of a Judge, than in that of a mere trustee. This great and important part of the duty of a trustee, may be considered under three heads—as it regards the admission or rejection of claims; as it regards the settlement of preferences among the creditors, and as it regards the division of the fund.

1. The trustee is appointed to receive and mark the claims of the several creditors, and their vouchers, or grounds of debt, with the oaths of verity; and to make a minute, or entry thereof, and of the date of production, in the book of sederunt: § 35. In this way, the creditors have an opportunity, by examining the sederunt book, to make their inquiries with respect to the various claims, and to state objections. In the examination of these claims, the trustee is judge, in the first instance, whether the claim be sufficiently established, to be admitted. His judgement of admission or rejection, receives effect in striking the dividend; but, to satisfy the

creditors,

creditors, and enable them to sue for redress, if so advised, he makes up a state of the claims, subjoining to each debt which he deems objectionable his reason for rejecting it, or reserving it for subsequent investigation. Claims may be liable to radical objections, which are palpable at first sight, and which, by law, are competent, via exceptionis; or they may be such as, although exposed to objection, require reduction—or to be annulled by the decree of a Court, after due investigation and proof. In the former case, the onus probandi lies upon the claimant, and the trustee is entitled, if he think the objection sufficient, to reject the claim: In the latter case, although the onus probandi lies upon the general body of creditors, the trustee is entitled to state the grounds of challenge, and to refuse payment of the dividend, till the challenge shall regularly be discussed, or settled by arbitration or compromise. The judgement of the trustee, rejecting a claim as objectionable, or admitting it as good, is subject to review of the Court of Session, upon a petition, either presented by the claimant in support of his claim, or by any creditors interested to have the claim rejected. Grounds of challenge or reduction, stated by the trustee, if not submitted or compromised, are to be tried by the Court; and if a judicial trial is resolved on, the trustee, in the name of the creditors, presents a petition, stating to the Court of Session the question which has occurred for investigation; and praying, that it may be summarily discussed before the Lord Ordinary. In either case, whether the trustee find himself called upon to reject a claim, or only to state grounds of challenge against it, he is, in justice, bound to reserve the dividends, subject to future determination. Unless he do so, he may chance to preclude the creditors altogether from their remedy; and so, indirectly, to make his own decision final; for the subsequent dividends may happen to turn out very poorly.

2. The trustee, in stating grounds of challenge, or in rejecting claims, acts as the preserver of the general fund against those who have no right to a share in it; but, in settling the scheme of ranking, he is more properly the arbiter of the contending creditors, for ascertaining their respective interests against each other. It is

his

his duty to class the creditors in the order of their legal preferences; and, in doing so, he must decide as judge in the first instance. He is not to refer to the judgement of the Court of Session, any of the principles of the ranking; nor to force the creditors into a litigation, which it is the very spirit and intention of the law to avoid. He must act as if he were the trustee and arbiter named in a voluntary trust-deed and submission, signed by all the creditors, leaving it to those creditors, who may be affected by the order of ranking which he adopts, to petition the Court for an alteration of his judgement.

3. The trustee must, in order to prepare for the distribution of the estate, make up, within ten months from the sequestration, accurate states of the funds, and of his own accounts, to be laid before the commissioners, and by them be audited and settled, and the sum ascertained, which, after a reasonable deduction for contingent expences, is to form the fund of division. At the stated intervals for each dividend, he must make the same preparations. Each state is to be accompanied with an account of the unrecovered estate, and of the money in bank, after the sum to be divided. The trustee must strike the dividend, applying the state of debts, and the scheme of ranking to the fund, which, from the above audited state, shall appear to be divisible at the time appointed by law; retaining what shall be sufficient to answer the objectionable debts, should the objections be overruled by the Court, and the creditors found entitled to their share, § 35.

In paying the dividends to the creditors, the trustee must be careful to take vouchers for his exoneration.

iv. The trustee must take the proper measures for obtaining personal protections for the bankrupt, when authorised by the creditors—especially for the purpose of bringing him forward for examination; and, in general, it is his duty to make all the incidental applications to the Court, which are absolutely necessary for extricating the affairs.

These seem to be the great lines of the trustee's duty, and of his powers. The emoluments which he is to expect, are in the way of commission only. The use of the money he is debarred from taking, under the penalty of an interest of 7½ per cent.; but as, at some moments, the accommodation of money, even at that high interest, is a great object, this is not the ultimate resource of the creditors for preventing a practice so dangerous. It is a breach of trust, either to keep the money unlodged in the appointed bank, or to draw it out again, after it is lodged, for any other purposes than those of the trust; and so justly delicate is the Court in this matter, that a complaint of irregularity of this kind, will procure the trustee's instant removal. The allowance, or commission, to be given to the trustee, is, previous to each dividend, to be fixed by the commissioners elected by the creditors: (of whom afterwards). § 22.

II. ELECTION OF THE TRUSTEE.—When all these powers and duties are considered, the election of the trustee must appear to be a matter of great importance in every sequestration. As he is to be vested with the whole estate, and charged with the recovery of the debts—as he is to check all the claims, and be the judge of them in the first instance, rejecting or admitting them—and as he is to rank, in the first instance, all the creditors, so that there may be no proceedings at law, unless his principles of ranking be erroneous, he must be a man of fidelity, abilities, and knowledge in such affairs; in whose honour and judgement the creditors may have confidence. The election of an officer so important as this, is not therefore to be proceeded in, without giving the creditors a full opportunity of voting in the deliberation; and, to this end, the law has provided the intermediate office of a factor, for managing the occurrences of a commencing sequestration.

i. TIME ALLOWED FOR CREDITORS TO QUALIFY FOR THE ELECTION.—It has been thought enough, to allow the space of six weeks for creditors, who choose to take any concern in the election of trustee, to appear and qualify. And although this term cannot, indeed, be sufficient, in many cases, for those creditors who may happen to be abroad; yet, as it might be of the worst consequence to postpone this matter too long, the only remedies which are given by law, in case of an improper trustee having been elected, are, that he may, at any time, be removed by the Court, upon cause shown; and that the majority in value may, at a meeting called for the purpose, remove him, and name another in his room (§ 59.) In England, where the commissioners appoint a day, as early as circumstances will permit, for the term of election of assignees, it was ruled by Lord Hardwicke, that it is not enough, in order to have a new election, for creditors to show that they were precluded from voting by their distance; they must also give good and cogent reasons for having the trustee removed. (Ex parte Gregnier, Atk. 91.) The day of election is fixed, by the judgement awarding sequestration, at not less than four, nor more than six, weeks from the date of the judgement. The place of meeting is to be fixed, as near as possible, to the place where the bankrupt's business was carried on, (§ 14.); and this deliverance is to be advertised in the newspaper called the Edinburgh Gazette, the publication of which is regulated by act of sederunt, 29th June 1793.

ii. QUALIFICATION OF ELECTORS.—The 20th section of the statute declares, that to entitle a creditor to vote, he 'shall have, 'at this meeting, or formerly, exhibited not only an oath of verity 'on his debt, but also the grounds or vouchers thereof, and got 'the same marked or entered in the book of sederunt;' agents for creditors being admitted to vote upon commissions general or special.

However careful the Legislature has been, to arrange matters, in such a manner, as to avoid the possibility of the trustee doing great injury to the creditors in the administration of his office, it must

still

still be an object of some importance, to prevent the powers with which, after every check, he must be invested, from coming into the hands of a person collusively proposed by the bankrupt, and elected by the votes of pretended creditors. And yet, there can be no opportunity for discussing the intrinsic merit and truth of the claims, either at the meeting for election, or previous to it. The only possible precaution, is that which the law has adopted to require the production of the grounds and vouchers of each debt, with an oath of verity to its subsistence. The expression, 'grounds and vouchers,' evidently implies, that, where there are vouchers, they must be produced; and that, where the debt is unliquidated, it must be specified, in the claim, what are the grounds and nature of the demand. In this way, should the election be contested, although the meeting of creditors cannot determine objections to claims, the materials are furnished for stating objections to the Court, in order to overturn the election. The way in which the contest is brought on in the Court, is, by the unsuccessful candidate, or creditors, opposing the application of the person named as trustee, from being confirmed; for, after election, the trustee must be confirmed judicially by the Court of Session. As, during this contest, the trustee cannot proceed to act, the interim factor should be ordered to proceed in the recovery of the estate. This should either be done by the creditors themselves, or, upon their application, the Court will do it.

Objections to the qualifications of voters, must turn either upon the nature of the debt—its existence and extent—or the defect of some formality in the lodging of the claim, or of the oath.

1. The nature of the debt seems to afford an objection, no further than as it may affect the extent of it. A contingent debt, we have seen, to be insufficient for supporting a petition for sequestration. But a creditor in such a debt, may vote in the election of a trustee. It must, however, be confessed, that, in some cases, persons who are, strictly speaking, entitled to be considered as contingent creditors, may have a very undue influence in an election. The bankrupt, it ſhall be supposed, has been in the custom of

of doing business at a particular bank, who have taken care, however, never to receive from him paper which was not of the first credit. Upon his failure, this bank is, no doubt, strictly entitled to the character of a contingent creditor, upon such bills as are not yet due. The acceptors, and all the indorsers previous to the bankruptcy, may fail; but, even should this be next to impossible, the bank is entitled to vote at the election of the trustee; and perhaps, by the value of the bills which they hold, (although upon those bills they never shall have occasion to claim), they place the trustee by their own vote alone. To a single creditor, it is a thing of very little consequence indeed, who shall be trustee: the object of real importance is, to enable the body of the creditors to have the sway in the election. An individual may have private and interested views: the body can have no object but the common interest. It were no great sacrifice, then, were contingent creditors deprived of the right of voting at elections. In England, no contingent creditor can even claim, or bring in his debt to be proved, unless the contingency take effect before an act of bankruptcy committed: I. Cook, 233. This has been thought in this country unjust, as indeed it is; but the interest which fairly belongs to a contingent creditor, is to have a share reserved for him, in case the contingency should happen: he should have no right to take an active part, or to thwart the measures of the actual creditors.

2. The election of the trustee is not the occasion upon which the scrutiny into the merits or amount of the debt, is to be made. At the same time, every obvious objection must receive effect, not to exclude the claim, or to bar the creditor from proving it, and receiving his dividend, if he can succeed in doing so, but to prevent him from voting in an important step of the proceedings, when he has, in reality, no interest in the fund. The objections, for example, of prescription, of compensation, &c. if either they appear from the face of the grounds of debt, or from the creditor's acknowledgement in the oath of verity, will, I should apprehend, exclude his vote. They will exclude the debt entirely, if they affect the whole claim; they will reduce it in value, as a qualification to vote for trustee, if only partial: for, in this election, it is by

by strength, not numbers, that the victory is decided. 'The majority of creditors in value or extent of debt, (says the statute), 'present at this meeting, shall determine who is to be trustee:' § 20.

In treating of the ranking and sale, we have seen particular regulations established, for estimating the value of debts, with a view to the election of the common agent—1. That interest is not allowed to be included, in reckoning the debt, unless it has been accumulated by decree of adjudication—2. That penalties are excluded—and, 3. That liferents and annuities are estimated at ten years purchase of the annuity or liferent. But there are no such rules established, with a view to the election of a trustee in a sequestration. The amount of the debt, in this case, is left entirely to the common law; and as there can be no doubt, that the interest, up to the date of the sequestration, and the expences actually incurred, form a debt as completely, and for which the creditor has as solid and as true a claim, as for the principal itself, he will be entitled to have his vote held as valuable, to the extent of principal, interest, and expences actually incurred. As to penalties, the law does not seem to be clear. Perhaps a distinction may be admitted, that although, to the effect of enlarging his dividend, a creditor is entitled to rank for penalties; yet, his real interest in the funds being no more than his debt, with interest, and the expences truly incurred, he should not, in a case like this, be allowed to assume a power higher than that which regularly belongs to his actual debt. In the votes of liferenters and annuitants, the market value of the annuity or liferent, must, I apprehend, be taken. In one set of cases, it is provided, that if a creditor hold a preferable security over the debtor's estate or effects, he shall be considered as a creditor only for the balance, after deducting it. This is in questions about 'compounding with, or discharging the bankrupt:' § 51.—The natural effect of an exception in these peculiar cases would seem to be, that, in all others, a creditor, holding such security, shall be entitled to vote, to the value or extent of his debt, without any deduction.

3. Defects of formality, in lodging the claim or oath, are disqualifications so obvious, that the meeting of creditors, I apprehend, may, upon their being stated and proved, reject the vote of the creditor. What these may be, it is unnecessary to point out.

III. QUALIFICATION TO BE ELECTED TRUSTEE.—There seem to be no absolute disqualifications, except, *first*, such as disqualify a man from holding any office—youth or imbecility of mind, for example—so as to unfit him for the conduct of affairs; and, *secondly*, such a connexion with the bankrupt, as law has pointed out, in the term 'conjunct and confident.' By the 20th section of the statute, it is declared to be incompetent, in any case, to appoint the debtor himself, or any conjunct or confident person, to be trustee. Perhaps it should also be held a good objection, that the person appointed is bankrupt. Mere insolvency seems not to be enough; for it is an indefinite and ambiguous condition, against which, the security given by the trustee, may be held sufficient. But a bankrupt cannot be considered as his own master. He is hourly liable to be deprived of his personal freedom, and prevented from attending to the management of the estate. In England, bankruptcy is a good ground for removing an assignee, (I. Cook, 339.—see also I. Atk. 88. 90.); but, perhaps, it may have some influence upon the question, that the English assignee does not seem to be bound to find security.

It is not a good objection, that the trustee is not acquainted with the particular trade or profession of the bankrupt, and that he is opposed by a person who is versant in it. That is a question of prudence, for the consideration of the creditors themselves, and to be decided by a fair majority, in terms of law. The Court never can interfere, but upon legal grounds of objection.

Neither is it a good objection, that the trustee is himself a creditor. In England, the same rule prevailing as in this country, a single creditor may, if his debt be large enough to form a majority in value, elect himself to be trustee: I. Cook, 316. Where a creditor is candidate for the trusteeship, he votes for himself; and it is not in this, as in some other elections, where the candidates choose to vote for each other; since a vote is valuable, not as the voice of an individual, but as that of a share of the interest in the common fund, proportioned to the debt of the voter.

IV. SECURITY must be given by the trustee, to the extent required by the majority which elects him, (§ 22.); subject, no doubt, to the review and correction of the Court of Session, upon cause shown, on account of the trustee's situation, and the extent of the funds.

V. CONFIRMATION OF THE ELECTION.—The trustee having accepted, and found surety, applies by petition to the Court of Session, under the 22d section of the statute, to have his election confirmed. If no good objection be made, he is confirmed accordingly; and a judgment pronounced, declaring every right, title and interest, which was formerly in the bankrupt, to be now in the trustee; adjudging, decerning, and declaring the whole lands and heritable estate to pertain and belong to the trustee, for behoof of the creditors; and ordering the bankrupt to deliver to him all the proper conveyances: § 22, 23.

VI. OF ELECTING A SUCCESSION OF TRUSTEES.—In England, several assignees may be named; but, in Scotland, one trustee, and no more, can act at a time. In England, the great object, in the choice of assignees, is their ability in point of credit; and the creditors must, of course, be secure, in proportion to the number of assignees. But the trustee's office, in Scotland, is of much greater activity than that of the English assignees; and it seems to have been thought, that, while a multiplicity of trustees might lead only to delay and interruption, the safety of the creditors, in a pecuniary point of view, could be as well insured, by requiring sureties for the trustee's faithful management. But though only one trustee can act at a time, the creditors may, to prevent interruption, and save the expence of new meetings, name a succession of trustees. The 20th section of the statute declares, that they may choose 'two or more trustees, to act in succession, one

'failing

'failing the other, by death, resignation, or removal; but that 'only one trustee shall act at a time.'—Of the manner in which the rights to the estate are to be transferred to a new trustee, I shall speak, in a subsequent section.

III. OF THE REMOVAL OF TRUSTEES.—By § 59, the trustee is declared 'amenable to the Court, to answer for his conduct:' and, in particular, it is declared 'competent, at any time, for one-fourth 'of the creditors in value to apply summarily to the Court of Session, for having the trustee removed, upon cause shown. A majority of creditors in value, at any meeting to be advertised for 'the purpose, shall likewise be entitled to remove, or to accept of 'any trustee: and, in either of these cases, or in the event of the 'trustee's death, the next in succession shall be entitled to act; 'and, upon failure of the several trustees originally named, by 'death or otherwise, it shall be competent to any two of the creditors, &c. to apply to the Court for a meeting to be held, on 'due advertisement, in order to elect a new trustee: and, in any 'of these cases, the new acting trustee shall immediately call to 'account his predecessors in office, or their heirs and representatives; and shall be vested with the same powers, and subject to 'the same rules and regulations, as any former acting trustee.'

IV. DISCHARGE OF THE TRUSTEE.—When a final division is made among the creditors in a sequestration, or when a trustee intends to resign his office, it is competent for him to apply, by petition, to the Court of Session, craving to be discharged of the trust; and the Court shall appoint the petition to be advertised in the Edinburgh Gazette: and at the end of fourteen days from the date of the advertisement, if no valid objection is stated, the Court shall grant the desire of the petition, but if any objection is stated, the Court shall proceed to determine the same summarily: § 60.

§ 2. OF THE COMMISSIONERS—THEIR ELECTION, AND POWERS.

The commissioners form a standing committee of the creditors, named for the purpose of assisting the trustee in the management of the affairs, and of authorising him to submit disputes to arbitration, or to enter into compositions and transactions. This institution was first brought into the sequestration law by the statute of 1793. Under the statute 1772, the place of the trustee was filled up by the factor; but he had not even the powers of a trustee. By the second statute in 1783, the trustee, who took the factor's place, was left much to his own discretion. He was indeed bound 'to follow the directions and rules, with regard to the recovery, management, and sale of the estate, real and personal, which were laid down by a majority of the creditors in value, convened at the meeting by which he was appointed, or any subsequent meeting.' He was also bound to call, 'if required, at any time, by three-fourths of the creditors in value,' a general meeting; and he was also authorised, upon any emergency, to call such meeting: (23d Geo. III. c. 18. § 26.) But a standing committee was still wanting, to direct the trustee, amidst the difficulties and intricacies of a bankruptcy, without the expence and trouble of continual meetings, or the danger which ever must attend the giving of general directions, by a great assembled body of creditors. The statute of 1793 therefore provided, that 'at the meeting immediately after the bankrupt's last examination,' (by which time, full opportunity is given for all the creditors to appear, and for them completely to understand the state of the bankrupt's property), 'the majority, in value, of creditors present, shall also name any three of the creditors as commissioners.' And the purpose of their nomination is thus expressed.—They are 'to audite the trustee's accounts—settle his commission or allowance—concur with him in submissions and compromises—and give their advice and assistance to him in any other matters; subject always to the controul of general meetings.' § 28.

Of

Of the election of the commissioners, little needs to be observed. The same title which qualifies a creditor to vote in the election of a trustee, gives him a voice in this election; or rather, to speak more properly, entitles his debt to be estimated for or against the candidates. The incapacities also, which prevent a person from acting as trustee, will disqualify him from being a commissioner. But there is this farther qualification necessary in a commissioner, that he must be a creditor. It is as a committee of the creditors, and to represent them, that the commissioners are named. Under this description, however, is included, a person who acts as agent for a creditor, properly authorised to sit and vote in the meetings of the creditors—at least, so it is understood in practice. It seems not to be clear, whether, if such a person should cease to be agent for the creditor he acted for at first; or if a creditor, elected as commissioner, should receive payment from another source, (as, where his ground of debt is a bill indorsed by the bankrupt), the cessation of his interest as a creditor, and of his right to sit in the meetings, would furnish a good ground of removal.

If any of the commissioners refuse to act, or, after having accepted, think proper to resign, it would rather seem, that the whole nomination should fall. The creditors may have confidence in a particular combination of knowledge, alacrity and prudence, in the commissioners they name, which is destroyed by the failure of any one. In Bertram Gardner & Co.'s bankruptcy, this was the opinion of a majority of the creditors. Three commissioners were chosen; but one of them having declined to act, a new meeting was called; and a difficulty occurred, whether the whole nomination was to be renewed, or whether only the single vacancy was to be supplied. The majority of the creditors was of opinion, that the whole nomination fell; and accordingly elected three new commissioners. The minority protested, and elected only a successor to the person who declined to act. The person chosen by the minority, and one of those originally named, gave in voluntary resignations; but the other original nominee, conceiving the election of THREE new commissioners to be irregular, would not sanction

sanction the measure by a voluntary resignation, though he declined making any opposition to the prayer of the petition given in by the trustee, for having the new nomination approved of. The Court confirmed the nomination: 14th May 1794, Petition of Mr Hotchkis. This is not, indeed, to be regarded as a decision of the Court upon the question of law: the petition was refused, because there was no opposition, and without entering into any consideration of the point; but it seems probable, that, upon the principle of the law, had the question been discussed, the decision would have been the same.

The duties of the commissioners are laid down so plainly in the statute, that it can be necessary only to enumerate them from it.

1. They are, by the vote of a majority, to give authority to the trustee to compound and transact, either by submission or private compromise, all doubtful claims which the bankrupt may have against others; or all debts due to the estate out of other bankrupt subjects; and likewise all doubtful claims or demands made against the estate, or questions of ranking and preference; and all contingent debts and securities due to or by the estate, the value of which it may be expedient to settle in that manner, in order that a final distribution may the sooner take place. § 44.

2. A majority of them, with the trustee, is to fix the upset price of any property which the general meeting of creditors shall order to be sold by public voluntary sale. § 33.

3. They, or a majority, are to audite the trustee's accounts; and, by a minute under their hand, to fix the allowance for commission to the trustee, and ascertain the net proceeds of the estate recovered, at the end of the first ten months; and they are, in the same way, to prepare for each dividend. § 35. & 36.

4. They are to ascertain the sum of contingent expence, to be left in the Bank at each dividend, for the purpose of carrying on the affairs. § 35.

5. If

5. If authorized by four-fifths of the creditors, at a general meeting, to give any allowance to the bankrupt, the commissioners and trustee may allow and pay to him, in terms of the act, from time to time, as they shall think fit, such sums out of the proceeds of his own estate, as they shall think proper, towards the subsistence and support of himself and family, till the period assigned for the second dividend, not exceeding two guineas per week, from the date of the sequestration to the period aforesaid, and so as not to amount, upon the whole, to more than 5l. per cent. of the net produce of the estate: § 51.

Such being the office of the commissioners, and such the powers of the trustee, with their aid and concurrence, it is plain, that the creditors can be bound by any act of the trustees, to which such concurrence is declared to be necessary, only if there shall be legal evidence of such concurrence. In the meetings, therefore, of the creditors, of those indebted to the estate, the trustee can be entitled to concur in any measure of compromise, discharge, submission, &c. only by a minute of the concurrence of his own commissioners; and in all transactions with individuals, they require, for their own safety, a similar security.

Before leaving this subject, it may be proper to observe, that the office of commissioner is entirely gratuitous; that the commissioners are entitled to no salary, nor commission, nor allowance of any kind. The statute does not, indeed, contain any express declaration to this effect; but no allowance is appointed for commissioners, as there is for the factor or trustee, and as there would have been, had the Legislature intended to make any. Accordingly, the Court of Session, in a late case, disapproved, in very strong terms, of a claim made for an allowance to commissioners.

---

§ 3. OF

§ 3. Of the Creditors in their Deliberative Capacity.

The creditors, assembled in their deliberative capacity, may be considered, in some cases, as judges, in the first instance; in others, as a court of review.

1. They determine, in the first instance, the election of the factor, of the trustee, and of the commissioners. They determine, also, whether the heritable estate shall be sold by public voluntary roup, or by judicial sale, where the money recovered is to be lodged, whether the outstanding debts may be sold; whether the bankrupt is entitled to a personal protection, to an allowance, and, finally, to a discharge; and whether any proposal of composition is to be accepted of.

2. As a court of review, they may be called upon to consider the determinations of the trustee, and of the commissioners, respecting the upset price of heritable subjects, which the creditors have resolved to sell by public voluntary roup; respecting submissions, compositions, and transactions of all kinds; respecting the amount of the allowance to the bankrupt, and of the commission to the trustee.

They deliberate upon different footings, according to the nature of the question before them. In electing the factor, the trustee, and the commissioners; in determining, whether the heritable estate is to be sold by judicial, or by voluntary roup; and in giving, at the meeting after the last examination, or at any meeting called for the purpose, directions respecting the recovery and disposal of the estate; a majority, in value, of the creditors assembled, decides the question. The votes of each party are taken down by the sum of their debts; and the balance on the contract gives the superiority. But, in determining where the money is to be lodged by the trustee when recovered—whether the outstanding debts are to be sold—whether the bankrupt's application for a personal protection, or for a discharge, is to be acceded to—or whether the trustee and commissioners are to be authorized to make him an allowance, another

mode

mode of decision is taken: Instead of the majority in value, the votes of four-fifths in number and value are required, to make an effectual decision. In one particular case, viz. the receiving of a proposal from the bankrupt for a composition, and the deciding upon it, a majority of no less than nine-tenths in number and value is required. The majority of value is easily taken: that of value and numbers united, requires an additional regulation, fixing the amount of the sum that shall be held equal to one vote. Accordingly, it is fixed, in the 52d section of the statute, 1. That, in counting numbers, no creditor shall be reckoned, whose debt is below 20l.: 2. That if under 20l., he shall be counted in value; and if more than 20l., the balance shall be reckoned in value: 3. That the whole value of each side of the division shall be reckoned at a vote to each 20l.; but that, in all questions of composition or discharge with the bankrupt, no creditor shall be reckoned as a creditor for more than the free balance, after deducting the value of any collateral security which he may hold.

§ 4. OF JURISDICTION IN SEQUESTRATIONS.

To conduct the affairs of a bankruptcy, independently of voluntary measures, it must often be necessary to apply for the interposition of judicial authority. The authority of a Court is necessary for sequestrating the estate, and vesting it in the creditors, or in a trustee for them, so as to restrain separate measures, and force the creditors to union; for protecting the bankrupt's person from diligence; for taking his examination, and that of his family, upon oath; for judging of the bankrupt's title to a discharge, when applied to by the legal majority in his favour; and for discharging the trustee, if he shall petition for a judicial exoneration. It is also necessary, to have recourse to a court of law, on many occasions, during the course of the management; both for issuing warrants and interdicts, and for trying disputed claims; for reviewing the proceedings and resolutions of the trustee and commissioners, upon complaints made; for calling the trustee to account; and for removing him, when unfit, or when guilty of any misdemeanour.

Of

Of these occasions for judicial interference, some are so much a matter of course, that it is of little consequence to whose superintendance they are entrusted;—others form so essential a part of the jurisdiction, under which the whole estate is sequestrated, or are in themselves so truly important, that the Supreme Court alone has been entrusted with them.

Of the former kind, are the necessary warrants of execution, and of interdict. These are entrusted to the Sheriff, or to the Judge Admiral, if within his jurisdiction. The examinations always are in presence of the Sheriff of the county, where the bankrupt resided, or carried on his business; and who is required, upon the application of the trustee, to name days for the examination; being entitled to a fee of one guinea for each sitting, and authorized to issue his warrant for apprehending the bankrupt, § 26. On application to the Sheriff, also, warrant will be issued for shutting the bankrupt's shop, &c. § 14.

Of the more important subjects of judicial interference, almost every other occasion for the interposition of a court, in the whole course of the sequestration, affords an example.

1. The Court of Session judges summarily, in all challenges in which a judicial investigation is necessary, the burden of which lies upon the creditors, and where the parties interested have not agreed to settle it amicably, or by arbitration. The form of applying to the Court, in such cases, is, by petition from the trustee, recapitulating the grounds of challenge, as contained in his state, and praying for a remit to a Lord Ordinary, to discuss them summarily. In the first instance, also, the Court of Session, at the request, or with the concurrence of a particular number of the creditors, decide whether a sequestration shall be recalled? whether a composition shall be received? whether the bankrupt shall receive his discharge?

2. As a Court of review, the Court of Session decides, at the request of creditors conceiving themselves to be aggrieved, all objections

jections to claims which the trustee may have sustained, or which he may have rejected; and they also determine, when appealed to by any party interested, the justness of the principles of ranking, which the trustee may have assumed. As a Court of review, also, the Court judges of the proceedings and resolutions of the creditors relative to elections, compositions, discharge to the bankrupt, &c. The Court cannot, indeed, give a discharge, or compel the acceptance of a composition, when the creditors have negatived the proposal; but they may, on cause shown, refuse to confirm a resolution, which the creditors may have passed, in the affirmative.

For all the irregular and occasional, as well as the regular applications, the Court of Session is at all times open. While the session continues sitting, the whole Court is the proper judicature to be applied to by petition. During the vacation, there is always one Judge officiating, as Lord Ordinary, in the Bill-chamber; and in him, by the 54th section of the statute, the full powers of the Court are vested, for ordering and following out the different steps of procedure appointed by the act. In case of an appeal being entered to the House of Lords, the Court, or the Lord Ordinary, are authorised to order such proceedings, in the mean while, as may be necessary for preventing embezzlement, &c., and for carrying on the management and recovery of the estate, in all points, not injurious to the interest of the party appealing.

Such is the system of co-operating powers, which the Legislature has appointed for conducting and regulating the concerns of a mercantile bankruptcy: and, amidst all the complication of acts to be performed, and all the variety of necessary provisions for the due performance of them, there is an admirable simplicity and unity of design, and of effect, for the accomplishment of the great objects in the view of the Legislature; a plan of private management and distribution, to the satisfaction of the creditors, under the controul of the Supreme Court, but without the necessity of its interference.

SECT.

SECTION II.

OF THE VESTING OF THE ESTATE IN THE PERSON OF THE TRUSTEE.

ON occasion of the renewal of the sequestration law, in 1783, much discussion took place concerning the methods in which the estate of the bankrupt should be vested in the creditors; and an alarm was taken, lest the proposal of including the heritable estate, should subvert the feudal principles of transmission, upon which the whole of our system of heritable conveyances is built. These alarms naturally occasioned a great degree of caution, in this part of the law: all idea of an ipso facto transmission, departing from the analogy of other conveyances, was utterly disclaimed; and the alternative of a voluntary conveyance, by disposition, from the bankrupt, or a judicial adjudication, by express decree of the Court, were declared to be the only modes of vesting the estate. At the same time, the best precautions were taken to prevent the possibility of the conveyance to the creditors, in general, being anticipated or interrupted by the voluntary deeds of the bankrupt, or by the effect of individual proceedings. For this end, 1. It was ordered, that the sequestration should be recorded as an inhibition, to have the full effect of that diligence, § 19. 2. The effect of all individual adjudications was declared to be swallowed up in the general adjudication to be pronounced in the course of the sequestration; no other adjudication, led or made effectual after the date of the first deliverance, having any effect, in competition with the right of the creditors, under the sequestration, § 33. And, 3. Poindings and arrestments, within sixty days of sequestration, were declared to give no preference, but for 10l. per cent., and the fair expence of the diligence, § 31. By these precautions, every security was given, that advantage should not be taken of the creditors in general, while the deeds of transmission, and decree of adjudication, were unfinished, or as yet uncompleted by the proper forms required by law, for fully vesting the

property,

property. There was only one danger, against which the creditors were left unprotected, viz. the possibility of an incomplete voluntary right, constituted before the bankruptcy, being completed into an effectual conveyance, before the completion of the trustee's right. This danger, however, was fully guarded against, in respect to conveyances of heritage, by the statute of 1696, c. 5, which, by declaring that such conveyances were to be held as of the date of their completion by seisine, made them directly subject to reduction, as granted within sixty days of bankruptcy. The remedy is still defective as to moveable conveyances; they not being held as of the date of their being completed by intimation, but as of the proper date of their being granted, however secretly. This will probably be corrected in the next statute; for it has been taken notice of by the Court, as a defect which ought to be supplied.

1. VESTING OF THE HERITABLE PROPERTY.—The principles upon which the inclusion of the heritable estate, under the sequestration law, was reconciled with the feudal forms, were these: 1. That, in the cessio bonorum, 'the debtor is compelled, under 'the pain of perpetual imprisonment, to grant a disposition omnium bonorum to his creditors, whatever the nature of the estate may be, whether personal or real:' And, 2dly, That 'if, 'either from wilfulness, or from any additional circumstance, a 'bankrupt does not convey his heritable estate to his creditors, 'the law, as at present (independently of the sequestration statutes) it stands, will convey it, whether he will or not, by a process of judicial sale, before the Court of Session, at the instance of any real creditor. A decree of sale, is an adjudication of the estate, by the Court of Session, in favour of the 'highest bidder, that the price may be divided among the creditors, according as they are ranked. We have, therefore, the 'form of compelling a bankrupt debtor to dispone his heritable 'estate, and we have the form of adjudging it from him irredeemably, if he decline to do it voluntarily *.' Upon these principles,

* Observations upon the proposed Bankrupt Bill of 1783.

principles, the transmission and vesting of the bankrupt's heritable estate were settled. It is enacted, in the 23d section of the statute of 1793, that the Court 'shall ordain the bankrupt to execute and deliver, within a certain reasonable time, to be specified in the interlocutor, a disposition, or other proper deed or deeds of conveyance or assignment, making over to the trustee, or trustees, in their order, his whole estate and effects, heritable and moveable, real and personal, wherever situated; and which shall specially describe and convey the premises, so far as they are known, or so far as the trustee shall think it necessary, and be in such form and style as may effectually vest the right in him, with full powers of recovery and sale, for behoof of the creditors; and if the bankrupt shall, without reasonable cause, neglect or refuse to obey such order, the Court may punish him by imprisonment.' And it is further declared, 'That, in all events, whether such deed or deeds be executed or not, it is hereby statuted and declared, that the said whole estate and effects of whatever kind, and wherever situated (in so far as may be consistent with the laws of other countries, when the effects are out of Scotland), shall be deemed and held to be vested in the said trustee, or trustees in succession, for behoof of the creditors: and the Court shall, in the act or order above mentioned, declare every right, title or interest, which was formerly in the bankrupt, to be now in the trustee, for the purposes aforesaid; and particularly, shall adjudge, decern, and declare the whole lands, and other heritable estate, belonging to the bankrupt, within the jurisdiction of the Court, and which, as far as known, shall be specially enumerated and described, to pertain and belong to the trustee or trustees, in succession, absolutely and irredeemably, to the end that the same may be sold, levied, and recovered, and converted into money, for the payment of the creditors: which adjudication being of the nature of an adjudication in implement, as well as for payment or security of debt, shall be subject to no legal reversion,' § 23. This adjudication being recorded within fifteen days, has effect as a decree of adjudication of the date of the first deliverance; 'and upon the disposition, or decree of adjudication, the feudal titles re-

'quisite,

'quisite, by the law of Scotland, to vest heritable property, shall 'and may be made up, either in the person of the trustee, or in 'the person of the purchaser from the trustee, in virtue of his 'conveyance, agreeably to the forms of the law of Scotland; the 'superior being obliged to enter either of them, in the same man-'ner as he is directed by 20 Geo. II. for abolishing wardholdings.' Where the titles of the bankrupt himself have not been completed, 'the trustee is to take the most safe and eligible method of com-'pleting them, in such way and manner as the law requires; 'which title shall accresce to that already acquired by the trustee, 'in the same way as if it had been completed prior to the dispo-'sition by the bankrupt, or adjudication against him,' § 25.

The same methods are to be followed respecting all newly discovered estates, which belonged to the bankrupt at the date of the first deliverance.

2. VESTING OF THE MOVEABLE PROPERTY.—The disposition to the bankrupt, is directed to contain a right also to all the personal or moveable property; and it is declared, that, failing such conveyance, the adjudication by the Court 'shall operate as a com-'plete attachment and transfer of the moveable or personal estate, 'for behoof of all the creditors, at the date of the first deliver-'ance aforesaid:' § 24.—It appears anomalous, to speak of an adjudication of moveables; but this is really in strict analogy with the common law. The apprizing, it will be recollected, (to which the adjudication is the legitimate successor), comprehended, at one period, moveables, as well as heritage; and the two forms of diligence against moveables at the present day, the arrestment and forthcoming, and the poinding, are nothing but adjudications. Nay, Lord Stair blames the use of the term 'forthcoming' as improper, proposing rather that the term 'adjudication of move-'ables' should be used in its stead, as more truly expressing the nature of the diligence.

The right to the moveables, as thus vested in the trustee, needs no intimation, as in the case of a private assignation. It is a pub-

lic

lic conveyance, which implies intimation in its very nature; so that the trustee's right is complete without intimation.

Thus far, of property situated within the jurisdiction of the Court of Session. But many valuable funds may be in other countries; and it is the business of the trustee, with the advice of a commissioner, to order such proceedings as may be necessary for making them effectual, and for bringing home the proceeds, as part of the fund of division.

Although, in other countries, the same effect will not be given to the sequestration, as in Scotland; yet, the title acquired by the trustee, will, of course, be sufficient to establish in him a right to claim, in any other country, as an assignee of the bankrupt; though, no doubt, the accomplishment of his right must be subject to the peculiar regulations of the municipal law. If the bankrupt refuse to convey, or if he be abroad, the law declares the decree of the Court of Session to have the same effect, wherever the funds may be situated, in so far as may be consistent with the laws of the countries in which they happen to be: § 23.

It is a matter of great difficulty, to reconcile the rights of the creditors under the sequestration in this country, with those of creditors abroad, who may have attached the foreign funds. The only title, under which the trustee can claim the funds, is that of assignee, coming into the bankrupt's place; and, under that title, his right must, of course, be subject to the fair claims of the foreign creditors, according to the law of the country in which the fund is situated. It often happens, for example, that many of our Scotish merchants have connexions in America, and much property, as well as many debts, due by them there. The trustee may find, on sending out his claim to America, that the funds have been attached. The law of America is liberally attentive, in cases of death or bankruptcy, to prevent premature payments—delaying, for a year, the satisfying of any claims, upon which attachments

 have

have been used; and, in this way, the trustee has a chance of coming in time to the competition. But he cannot pretend to the whole fund, or deprive the American creditors of the benefit of their proceedings, and bring them over to this country, to claim as creditors under the sequestration. He must be contented with such proportion of the funds, as may, according to the law of the country, and the steps he has used, fall to him in the division. The only thing, which it has been in the power of the Legislature in Scotland to do, is to declare, 1. That no creditor, who shall have obtained a preference or payment abroad, after the first deliverance in the sequestration, shall be allowed to claim under the sequestration, without assigning or communicating the same to the trustee; and, 2. That, should it happen not to be necessary for him, after such preference, to claim under the sequestration, the trustee may bring an action against him, if the jurisdiction of the Court of Session can reach him, for forcing him to communicate the foreign payment to the other creditors: § 40.

But it seems doubtful, whether this clause can apply to any other case, than where the creditor, who has received such payment, was under the jurisdiction of this country at the date of the sequestration? Let it be supposed, for example, that a person, settled in America, has attached, in America, the property of a Scottish merchant, his debtor; that, in consequence of that attachment, he has received payment; and that, having left off trade, he comes to this country to enjoy the fruits of his industry, and is called in an action before the Court of Session, to relinquish the payment which he, fairly and bona fide, obtained in America; on the ground, that, some time previous to that payment being made, his debtor had been rendered bankrupt, and his affairs were under sequestration. This is a case, to which the spirit and intention of the statute does not seem to apply. The intention of the law appears to have been, to prevent creditors in this country, from disturbing the course of the Scottish law respecting bankrupts, and from taking an unfair advantage over the other creditors, by sending out to attach funds abroad, in order to constitute a pre-

ference

ference for themselves, which they could not have obtained at home.

Still less should I apprehend the law to include such a case as the following. The Legislature has provided, that sequestration may be awarded, even where the debtor is a foreign trader, who happens to have funds situated in this country. A merchant in London, for example, may have funds in this country; and although, when a commission of bankruptcy issues in England, his assignees are entitled to claim his funds here; yet these funds may be attached, so that it may be necessary or prudent to apply for sequestration. In such a case as this, it would not appear that a creditor, receiving payment of his debt in England, or elsewhere, would (on coming to this country, or if he should happen to be native here) be exposed to an action, for having the payment made to him recalled, and converted into a divisible fund under the sequestration. The property of the bankrupt should strictly be considered as with himself; subject to the distribution of the law of his domicile, where he has carried on his trade, and contracted his debts: but as this rule is not strong enough to withdraw, from the jurisdiction of our courts, lands situated in this country, or moveables which have been attached here, the law of Scotland has allowed sequestration of such partial estate, in order to provide for the equal distribution of what actually is here subject to our laws, but not to disturb the distribution made by the law of the bankrupt's domicile.

What has hitherto been said, relates only to such property as belonged to the bankrupt at the date of the sequestration. No estate nor effects falling to him after that date, can be touched by the sequestration. They must be legally vested in the trustee, by the proper forms and proceedings, otherwise they will be exposed to the diligence of individual creditors. The hands of the bankrupt himself are tied up, by the statute of 1696, c. 5., so that he can give no voluntary conveyance to particular creditors, to the prejudice of the general interest. But, against legal diligence, there is no protection, except by taking immediate measures for vesting the

new

new property in the trustee. It would appear, however, that this is not to be done merely by a private conveyance from the bankrupt. The case is precisely the same, with respect to this new estate, as if no sequestration of the other property had taken place at all; and, of consequence, the debtor can no more grant an effectual disposition, or conveyance of it, in trust, than he might have given of the sequestrated property before sequestration. At least it is plain, that the act 1696, c. 5. would fully apply to such a case, and that the trustee acting under such a deed, would be no other than a private trustee. Neither would it appear, that the Court has power to pronounce, in this case, an adjudication, such as is authorised by the sequestration statute. So that the only regular way seems to be, to apply for a new sequestration, to be conjoined with that already awarded, by which all undue preferences may be prevented, and an effectual conveyance made to the trustee, as under the sequestration law. The 30th section of the statute provides the proper means of discovering such newly devolved estates, and requires the trustee to take such steps as are necessary, and to give notice thereof to the creditors, either at the next general meeting, or by advertising a meeting for the purpose; but nothing is said of the steps that are proper to be taken.

TRANSMISSION OF THE ESTATE TO A NEW TRUSTEE.—'Each 'trustee succeeding a prior trustee, through death, resignation, or 'removal, (unless substituted at the first nomination, in which 'case no other form is necessary), shall be vested in the right, either by disposition from the former trustee, or by adjudication 'obtained by the new trustee, on a summary application to the 'Court of Session.' § 25.

SEC.

SECTION III.

Of the Examination of the Bankrupt and others.

It is an object of no mean consideration, in a system of bankrupt law, to provide means for discovering fraudulent debts, and concealments, and partial preferences. This is the source from which the most prominent evils of a bankruptcy flow. If a debtor wish, under pretence of a failure, to take advantage of his fair creditors, and so to manage matters, as to have it in his power to begin the world anew, discharged from his debt, his plan will probably be conducted by concealment of funds, and by confidential conveyances, and fraudulent transactions, and false debts. In this way, he may be able, on the one hand, to secrete a fund; while, on the other, by means of his confidents, and of the debts which they seem legally to hold, he may acquire a great influence in the management of the bankruptcy. To prevent evils so gross as these, provision has been anxiously made, both in the English and in the Scotish laws.

In England, measures of terrible severity are provided for forcing the debtor to appear before the commissioners, within a certain time, to be examined, upon oath, respecting his estate and funds, his whole transactions, conveyances, and debts, and every particular, in short, which may throw light upon any fraudulent plan of concealment he may have practised. The punishment of death, as a felon, has been pronounced against his disobedience; and that of perjury, against his falsely answering: and the commissioners have been vested with a power of calling upon, and examining others than the bankrupt. On the other hand, inducements have been held out for fair discovery; and those who have accepted trusts, for the purpose of facilitating concealments, and do not appear to disclose them, are declared liable to forfeit 100l., with

with double the value of the property concealed. The bankrupt can obtain personal protection and discharge, only on condition of a full and fair discovery. Rewards have been offered to others, who voluntarily come forward to prove concealments: I. Cook, B. L. 460—491.; Cullen, Prin. of B. L. 323—370.

In Scotland, the provisions are somewhat different. It was thought sufficient, at first, that the bankrupt should be ordered 'to produce his books and papers, and to make a full and fair discovery of his, her, or their whole estate, heritable and moveable, wherever situated, upon oath, if required by the petitioners, or other creditors appearing:' 12. Geo. III. c. 72. But, when the act came to be renewed, it had been felt that this was not sufficient; that it was necessary to have not only an absolute appointment and term fixed for the examination of the bankrupt, without the necessity of an application for that purpose; but also a power of examining his family, and those concerned in carrying on his business. It was therefore enacted, by § 15. of the statute 1783, that the factor should, immediately after his appointment, apply to the Sheriff of the county where the debtor resided, or carried on his business, to appoint a day in each of the four succeeding weeks, to be set apart for the public examination of the bankrupt, and of his family, or others acquainted with his business. These meetings were to be advertised, and the whole creditors invited to be present, that they might have an opportunity of putting such questions as should be judged of importance for rendering the discovery and surrender more complete. The Sheriff was also authorised to issue warrants of apprehension against the bankrupt, his family, and others who were to be examined; and, if without his jurisdiction, the factor was to apply for the warrant of the Court of Session. This power of coercion was qualified with a declaration, that the Court should grant, upon application of the factor, or trustee, a personal protection, for such time as might be necessary for the bankrupt attending the examinations. The punishments for not appearing to be examined, or for concealing funds, &c. are declared to be those of fraudulent bankruptcy; that the debtor shall, as such, be punished, and rendered for ever incapable of holding any office of public trust or emolument, and deprived of the benefit of the sequestration statute, and accounted infamous, and incapable of giving evidence in any court of justice, or of sitting or acting in any assize or jury; and if, appearing, he shall swear falsely, the penalties of perjury are superadded to these. These provisions were renewed by the statute of 1793, with some alterations of no great importance. Instead of a day in each of the four weeks following the factor's appointment, the days of examination are to be one day, not less than fourteen days, nor more than three weeks, after the election of the trustee; and another at the same distance from the first one.

As this power of examining, which extends to others, as well as to the bankrupt himself, is a matter of infinite delicacy; and of great importance to the creditors, as interested in the estate; and to the bankrupt, and those who are subject to examination, as exposed to a very disagreeable scrutiny, in which they may be involved in suspicion, or proved to be guilty of fraud; it may be proper to bestow some attention on the subject.

1. JURISDICTION IN EXAMINATIONS.—This is a judicial, not a private investigation. In England, it proceeds before the commissioners of bankruptcy, who appear to have little of the character of a court of justice, but rather to act in a ministerial capacity alone. In Scotland, it proceeds before the Sheriff of the county where the debtor resides, or where his trade was carried on, who, instead of acting as in an office merely ministerial, sits in his proper character of a judge, holding a regular court, and entitled to the exercise of all the concomitant powers, which, at common law, a judge possesses in matters of evidence.

He is empowered to issue his warrant, if necessary, for apprehending the bankrupt, or any of his family, or those connected with his business, in order to force their appearance at the diets of examination; and, if without his jurisdiction, a warrant is granted

granted by the Court of Session, on the application of the trustee, for apprehending them, and bringing them before him. If those to be examined, cannot, from indisposition, &c. attend; the Sheriff, or the Court of Session, give directions for examining them elsewhere. The Court of Session will grant a personal protection, to enable those cited for examination, to attend. A protection for the bankrupt himself, is, by the statute, directed to be given; and, at common law, every other person so called upon, is entitled to it.

---

2. OF THOSE WHO MAY BE EXAMINED.—The means of discovering collusive transactions and embezzlements, would be very imperfect, if the power of examination were restricted to the bankrupt himself; and therefore, it has been thought proper to extend it to others, who may be connected with his business, and have had an opportunity of becoming acquainted with his transactions and schemes of concealment. The act of 1783 speaks of 'the 'bankrupt, his family, or others acquainted with his business.' The statute of 1793 speaks of 'the bankrupt, his wife, and others 'of his family, or connected with his business.'

By the common law, both of England and of Scotland, a wife is not a competent witness against, or for her husband; and as there was not, at first, in the English bankrupt laws, any exception of a wife, the commissioners could not call upon her for examination; but this was supplied by the 21. James I. c. 19.; and she may now be examined for the discovery of the estate and effects concealed, kept, or disposed of by her: Cullen, Prin. of B. L. 331. Our statute of 1793, expressly authorises the examination of the bankrupt's wife. It is a harsh provision, but perhaps necessary in a situation of so peculiar a kind, where the presumption of concealment is so strong, and the crime itself of so secret a nature.

Another

Another question was much doubted, prior to the statute of 1793, viz. Whether the character of creditor, in the debt which is the subject of investigation, will save a person from an examination, to which otherwise he would be forced to submit? The Court decided in the affirmative: M'Lae against M'Lehose, 4th December 1792. These were the circumstances:—David Robb & Co. ſtopt payment in January 1792. William Robb, one of the partners, absconded, and the trustee wished to have an uncle of William's (who appeared as an heritable creditor, in circumstances which the trustee thought suspicious) examined. He accordingly appeared, and gave written answers to certain interrogatories; but refused to submit to any examination more particular, or to swear. The trustee applied for a warrant from the Court of Session, to have him examined. The question was argued at some length, and well considered. The trustee, founding on the expressions of the statute of 1783, authorizing the examination of the bankrupt's 'family, and others acquainted with his business,' contended, that he was entitled to examine this uncle of William's; who was not only a conjunct and confident person, but the only person who could give information respecting some very suspicious transactions, between him and the bankrupt William Robb—a knowledge of which was absolutely necessary, for understanding the bankrupt's affairs: That the great and important object of the examination, authorized by the statute, was to discover collusive claims; a purpose which would be defeated entirely, if a pretended interest in a claim were sufficient to protect those best able to give information from being examined: That the circumstance, of a conjunct and confident person having acquired a conveyance, or being enabled to assume the appearance of a creditor, should, instead of abating, strengthen the necessity for hearing him examined: That this man, though said to be a creditor, had truly a double character; being a pretended creditor, who had been engaged in the traffic of accommodation bills with the bankrupt: That as the bankrupt himself may be examined, respecting transactions into which he may have entered; so also should the other persons, whom the statute subjects to the necessity of undergoing an examination: That, accordingly, in the Sheriff Court of Glasgow, where there are more ex-

 aminations

aminations than in all the rest of Scotland, it is the practice, to examine all who have had transactions with the bankrupt, in which there appears any thing suspicious, or requiring investigation: and the mere circumstance, of the person being a creditor on the estate, has never been thought an objection to the examination proceeding. It was, on the other hand, maintained by the creditors, That, independently of the statute, there is no power by which a creditor can be called upon to submit to examination: That, although judicial examination is lawful, where issue is joined in an action, a right to insist for a general and vague examination, in which a creditor is to be called, unprepared, into the presence of an inferior Judge, and ordered to answer, upon oath, before all the creditors who choose to attend, such interrogatories as may be put to him; to produce his papers, and to open his books; is a right dangerous to be placed in any man, or body of men: That it is liable to the grossest abuse, and most apt to be converted into an instrument of injustice and oppression: That the statute does not authorize such a right in the creditors, nor in the trustee; and that the only way in which a creditor can be legally examined, is in consequence of an objection moved to his debt by the trustee, and made the subject of an application to the Court for discussion: That issue being thus fairly joined upon the question of debt, as in a common action, the creditor may be called upon, in the common course of judicial procedure, to undergo an examination: That the examination of a bankrupt and his family, and those acquainted with his business, has been provided for, because the law applies to traders; and it is in a manner necessary, that the family, the clerks, and the servants of a trader, should be subject to examination, as well as himself, in order to get at a full discovery. The Court was much divided upon this question; but at last refused the petition of the trustee: thus declaring the examination incompetent. Those of the Judges who favoured the examination, said, that they could see no harm in it to the creditors, if all was fair; and rested a good deal upon this, that frequently truth is very unexpectedly brought to light, in the course of examining the parties in an action: They considered the bankrupt law as, in this point of examination, analogous to the vesting act of 1745—In the case

of

of attainder, it was naturally suspected, that the friends and relations of the criminal would conspire to secrete his fortune: to prevent which, a general power of examination was given; not an examination, as upon a reference to oath, but merely 'ad rimendam 'veritatem;' so that instances occurred, even of debts, which had stood the test of such examinations, being afterwards cut down, in consequence of a legal proof of collusion: The suspicions against the relations and friends of a bankrupt were said to be similar; and the clause in the statute ought to be so explained, as to give a similar remedy and means of detection. The prevailing opinion rested upon these grounds, that the judicial examination of a party, even in a depending action, is not competent in the general case, but is merely a remedy in the hand of the Judge, to be applied in particular circumstances; and where it is used, the person to be examined, does not come to answer the vague questions of the other party, but to explain fully, the points proposed to him in concerted interrogatories, and which the Court thinks it his duty to explain: That the right contended for by the trustee is dangerous, laying every creditor at his mercy; and that neither the Judicature, before which he may be called, nor the form of procedure, can afford him any protection against the capricious abuse of this power: That such examinations are contrary to the common law, and totally unauthorized by the statute, which confines the precognition to the family of the bankrupt, and those acquainted with his business; and that, in so far as relates to the particular debts of the person who is to be examined, a full opportunity of investigating it is given, when the claim entered upon it comes to be discussed, with a view to the dividing of the funds.

This case occurred between the date of the statute 1783 and that of 1793; and the only alteration which (with this question in view) was made upon the expression of the statute, was that which has already been marked. As the law, therefore, stands at present, it would seem to be held, that the expression, 'all others connected with his business,' is restrictive; that none can be examined, but those who have acted as clerk, manager, assistant, workman, &c. to the bankrupt; and who,

who, by such connexion, are presumed to know the secrets of his affairs. Whether this provision, assisted by the inducements held out to those acquainted with any concealment, and by the penalties enacted against those who have accepted of a secret trust, and who do not disclose it, be sufficient for attaining the object aimed at by the Legislature, it would be presumptuous in me to inquire; but I may observe, that, in England, the commissioners may examine 'all and every person, duly summoned 'before, or present at any meeting of the commissioners, or major 'part of them, touching all matters relating to the person, trade, 'dealings, estate, and effects of all and every such bankrupt,' &c. 5. Geo. II. c. 30. § 16.

It is to secure the examination of the bankrupt himself, that the Legislature has been chiefly solicitous, and, as each creditor is entitled to see this investigation fully made, the trustee can have no right, even with the assistance of the commissioners, nay, the most decided majority of the creditors could not agree, to protect the bankrupt from an examination. A question of this kind was very fully tried in England, in the case of Nerot *v.* Wallace & others, assignees of Reilly & Colliers: 3 Term. Rep. 17. A transaction was made by Colliers, one of the bankrupts, and by Nerot as his friend, by which they agreed to pay the assignees certain sums received by Colliers, on the partnership account, and concerning which Colliers was called upon to be examined, provided they would dispense with the examination. Nerot afterwards drew back, however, and refused to pay, on the grounds, 1. That the consideration was nugatory, as the assignees had no power to dispense with the examination: and, 2. That the transaction was illegal, and contrary to the spirit of the bankrupt law. A verdict was given against Nerot for 852l. A motion in arrest of judgement was refused; and a writ of error was then brought, when the Court decided in favour of Nerot. All the Judges (Lord Kenyon, and Judges Ashburton, Buller, and Grose) were clear, that each creditor had an absolute right to insist for the examination proceeding; of which they could be deprived, neither by the assignees, nor by the commissioners, nor even by the rest of the

creditors;

creditors: Even the public were thought to have an interest strong enough, to entitle the commissioners to disregard such collusive agreement, though not objected to by any creditor. But that interest has not been held to be so powerful, as to prevent the bankrupt from settling the bankruptcy, by paying off the debts with the assistance of his friends: Kaye & Bolton, 6 Term. Rep. 134.; Cullen, Prin. of B. L. 337. 8. In Scotland, the law has permitted compositions to be proposed, and voted by the creditors, only at the meeting after the second examination; though this does not seem to proceed from any view to the public interest, but merely from a wish to prevent the danger of fraudulent evasions by bankrupts, of that fair investigation into the state of their affairs, which it is the object of the examination to accomplish.

3. OF THE MANNER OF THE EXAMINATION.—The examination of the bankrupt is to be confirmed by a general oath to the truth of the states which he has given up, and to the fullness of the discovery he has made. § 27. This oath is engrossed in the sederunt-book, after all the states and particulars of his examination.* The other persons who may, by law, be examined, may also, if required, be put upon oath; § 26.—the affirmation of Quakers

"* I A B do, in the presence of Almighty God, and as I shall answer to God at the great day of judgement, solemnly swear, That the state of my affairs, engrossed in this book, contains a full and true account of all the debts, of whatever nature, due to me, and of all my estate and effects, heritable and moveable, real or personal, (the necessary wearing apparel of myself, my wife and family, only excepted), as well as of all claims which I am entitled to make against any person or persons whatsoever, and of all estate in expectancy, or means of whatever kind, which I have an eventual right to by contract of marriage, deed of entail, or otherwise, to the best of my knowledge, and that the said state likewise contains a full and true account of all the debts due by me, or demands upon me, so far as I know, or can remember, and that I have delivered up the whole books, documents, accounts, and papers, of every kind, belonging to me, which in any way relate to my affairs, and which were in my possession, or under my power; and have made a full disclosure of every particular relating to my affairs And further, I swear, That I shall forthwith reveal all and every other circumstance or particular relative to my affairs, or which may tend to increase or diminish my estate, or in which my creditors may be interested, directly or indirectly, which may, at any time hereafter, come to my knowledge. So help me, GOD."

Quakers being admitted, in all cases under the statute, as an oath: § 27.

The statute allows the examination of others than the bankrupt, only 'upon all proper interrogatories;' but the bankrupt may be examined without interrogatories. In England, at first, the examination, both of the bankrupt and of others, was directed to be by interrogatories; 1. Ja. I. c. 15. § 7.: and these interrogatories were delivered to the bankrupt, and time given him to consider them, and prepare his answer: Cullen, Princ. of B. L. 326. But, afterwards, the system was completely changed; and now, by 5. Geo. II. c. 30. § 16, the commissioners are empowered 'to 'examine, as well by word of mouth, as on interrogatories in writing,' both the bankrupt, and all others.

4. OF THE ANSWER.—The bankrupt is ordered 'to exhibit, 'at the meeting for choosing the trustee, a state of his affairs, spe- 'cifying the whole estate and effects, heritable and moveable, real 'and personal, wheresoever situated, belonging to him, and debts 'due to him, including any estate in expectancy, which he may 'have an eventual right to by contract of marriage, entail, or o- 'therwise; and specifying also the debts due by him, and demands 'upon him, so far as they are known to him; and also a rental of 'his lands, and an inventory or list of his books, papers, accounts, 'bills, notes, and title-deeds, or other documents of his estate:' § 21.—At his examination, 'he shall be allowed to make such ad- 'ditions or alterations upon the state of his affairs, exhibited at 'the meeting when the trustee was chosen, as have occurred to 'him since said meeting, and are necessary to be set forth, to give 'a perfect view of his affairs;' and he is bound to authenticate all the information which he thus gives, and all the answers to particular interrogatories, by an oath, as detailed in the statute, § 27. Upon these states, and every point relating to the estate and affairs, the bankrupt himself, and the other persons whom the law allows to be examined, must answer every legal question, to the best of their knowledge.

1. OF THE BANKRUPT'S ANSWER.—The hold which the law takes of the bankrupt, is alternative. If he refuse to answer, or to make a full discovery, he is to be held as a fraudulent bankrupt; if he answer falsely, he is indictable for perjury. It is only when he is open and fair and honest, in his answer, that he is entitled to hope for the benefit of the statute, and the protection of the law: 33. Geo. III. c. 74. § 27. In England, the punishment of refusing to answer, or not answering fully and satisfactorily, is, that the commissioners may send the persons to jail, there to remain, without bail or mainprize, till they shall submit, and full answer make: 5. Geo. II. c 30. § 16. In England, then, it is a question for the decision of the commissioners, whether the bankrupt has FULLY and SATISFACTORILY answered: In Scotland, this is rather to be considered as a point in the bankrupt's trial for fraudulent bankruptcy. In both countries, it is a point of the trial for perjury, whether he has TRULY answered.

But, although the question, of the fullness of the answer, comes thus into a different shape, in the two countries, the principles of decision must be nearly the same; and, in this view, the frequent trials that have occurred in England, respecting the bankrupt's answer, may not be altogether useless to us.

1. A general answer by a bankrupt, to a question, which requires and admits of a full and particular answer, is held sufficient in England to justify a commitment, and would, I apprehend, if obstinately persisted in, be deemed, in Scotland, a concealment sufficient to bring the debtor within the description of a fraudulent bankrupt, as in § 27. of the statute. Thus, in Langhorne's case in England, a question was in this form proposed—'As you do 'admit, that, since the month of October 1771, being the time 'you entered into trade, to the time of your bankruptcy, there is 'a deficiency of the sum of 2751l., although your books do not 'show such deficiency; give a true and particular account what 'has become of the same, and how, and in what manner, you 'have applied and disposed thereof?'—The bankrupt answered—'My expences, in sundry journeys to establish trade, amount to

' 150l.;

'150l.; the amount of discount, noting, interest on bills and 'notes, and premiums given to me, is 200l.; I have lost 15l. by a 'horse; I have spent 500l. in housekeeping; and I have lost 1886l. 'by selling goods under prime cost. and the reason why such de-'ficiency does not appear in my books, is, that my brother, who 'was in the capacity of a shopman with me, might not be ac-'quainted with the nature of my dealings, and hurt my credit by 'divulging the same.'—This answer was signed; but, not being thought satisfactory, a warrant was prepared for committing the bankrupt, when he acknowledged to have lent John Crofts, the Kendal carrier, 100l.; to have deposited with Bailiff, a grocer, hose to the value of 15l., to indemnify him for being bail; to have delivered to Alison, a boot-catcher at a certain inn, a note of Crawford & Co., to be received to his use; and to have sent a quantity of hosiery goods, to the value of 22l., to R. Estwick, to be kept for his use. The Court was clearly of opinion, that these answers were not satisfactory: Langhorne's case, II. Black. Rep. 919.

There is another case of one Perrot, who was afterwards executed for concealing his effects, illustrative of the obligation which the bankrupt lies under of speaking distinctly and particularly. The question was, 'As you admit that you have spent the last 'week, previous to this your examination, with Mr Maynard, one 'of your assignees, to settle and adjust your accounts, and to draw 'out a true state thereof, to enable you to close your examina-'tion; and do likewise admit, that, upon such state thereof, it 'appears, that, after giving you credit for all sums of money paid 'by you, and making you debtor for all goods sold and delivered 'to you, from your first entering into trade, to the time of your 'bankruptcy, it appears, that there is a deficiency of the sum of '13,513l.: give a true and particular account, what is become of the 'same, and how, and in what manner, you have applied and dispos-'ed thereof.' To this question, Perrot would give no other than this general one: 'On goods sold this year, I have lost upwards of '2000l.; and by mournings, I have lost upwards of 1000l.; and 'for nine or ten years, I have, and I am sorry to say it, been ex-'tremely extravagant, and spent large sums of money.' He was

committed;

committed; and the Court held the question to be legal, the answer unsatisfactory. Afterwards, the bankrupt gave a further answer; and gave an account of the manner in which he had disposed of 15,030l., in sixteen general articles; one of which was, 'Expences 'attending my connexion with the fair sex, 5500l.' In answer to the question formerly proposed to him, he particularized one woman, to whom, in the year 1759, he gave 5000l.; and also particularized the times of sending and giving it to her: 'That no o'ther person was privy to this: that the woman, Sarah Powel, is 'since dead, as he understands: that she knew him to be a bank'rupt, and never returned the money, or any part of it: that he 'gave it her for her maintenance and expences, and not for a 'fund for her future support, or wherefrom he could draw any 'advantage: that he knew, when he gave her these sums, that 'he was not worth any thing, and that he was remitting her the 'money of his creditors: that he was acquainted with her five or 'six years, but cannot recollect what he gave her during the se'cond, third, or fourth year of their acquaintance; nor did he 'keep any particular account or memorandum thereof, either in 'those years, or in the year 1759; but speaks from memory only: 'that he did not take any of this money from his banker, but 'from Mr Thomson, since deceased, who used to sell goods for 'him: that all letters between him and this woman, except one 'or two, are burnt or destroyed.' Perrot's counsel argued, that he ought now to be discharged, as having given a full and complete answer; which, whether true or false, or whether his conduct was prudent or imprudent, satisfies the law respecting his examination. It was contended, on the other hand, that the answer was incomplete, and unsatisfactory, and such as cannot found a prosecution for perjury: that there was a great deficiency proved, which the bankrupt was bound to account for in a satisfactory manner: that his account was not satisfactory: that it was grossly improbable, that five, six, seven hundred pounds in a month, should be paid to this woman for her maintenance, especially as it appeared, from the bankrupt's own account, that she had only a man servant and two maids, while at Bath. that he gave the commissioners no kind of trace, by which to follow this money, or discover what had become of it. The Court held the answer incomplete and unsatisfactory, and ordered him to be remanded: Rex v. Perrot, II. Burr. 1122.

2. But what shall be said to a want of recollection? Under this cloke may, no doubt, often be hid a fraudulent intention of concealment: but all that can be said is, that wherever the circumstances and nature of the case admit a reasonable probability of forgetfulness or inattention, an answer according to belief will be held sufficient. A case of this kind occurred in England. The object of the examination was, to discover whether two bales of silk were, or were not the property of the bankrupt? Miller, who was the person under examination, was asked, 1. 'Did you purchase, by a broker, the two bales of silk?' his answer was, 'I cannot positively recollect, whether I bought them of a broker or not.' 2. 'Can you form any belief, whether you bought them by a broker or not?' his answer was, 'I should rather believe, I bought them by a broker.' 3. 'Whether or not do you believe you bought them by a broker?' 'I cannot give any other answer.' 4. 'Whether, by the words, "I should rather believe I bought them by a broker," you mean, that you do believe the two bales of silk were bought by a broker, or whether you mean to say, you do believe, that the said two bales of silk were not bought by a broker?' Miller refused to answer. Lord Chief Justice de Grey said, 'That Miller had only two ways or means to enable him to answer the question put to him, either by recollection or belief. The first is knowledge, and must imply consciousness. But, in some cases, no trace of a fact remains in a man's memory, whereby he can recollect the fact; it is possible he may have lost all knowledge of it; and if he have, he can only answer, that he does not know, or does not recollect the fact. A man may recollect to a certain degree; and although he cannot recollect at one time, he may at another. Suppose I cannot recollect, yet I may and can believe I did a certain fact: you may tell me, you saw me do it, and I give credit to you, as a person of veracity. How is it, in courts of justice, where a man swears, he neither recollects nor believes

'that

'that he did such a fact, or that he did, or did not do such a fact, 'to the best of his knowledge, remembrance and belief? It is 'certainly a full answer. A subscribing witness to a bond may 'swear, he has totally forgot that he subscribed his name as a 'witness thereto; and he may not be able to swear, positively, he 'saw the obligor seal and deliver the bond; but, seeing his own 'handwriting subscribed as a witness to the execution thereof, 'he may swear he believes he saw the obligor execute the bond: 'and such answer would be satisfactory to the Court. Suppose 'a banker was, upon examination, asked, Whether he paid such 'a bill by cash or notes? and he answers, he cannot tell, but his 'books may inform him, or his books may be lost, and his clerks 'gone away from him: if, on looking into his books, he saw, by 'the handwriting of his clerks, that the bill appears to be paid by 'cash or notes, he then swears to his belief accordingly: but, if 'his books be lost or destroyed, and his clerks be dead or gone, 'and he thus swears he cannot tell, or does not know, whether 'the bill was paid by cash or notes, his answer is full, and ought 'to be taken as satisfactory.' Having said this much, in general, his Lordship said, of Miller's answer to the second interrogatory, 'I think this answer amounts to a degree of belief, sufficient to 'answer civil purposes. If an heir at law, in a court of equity, 'were to swear, in his answer, that he rather believes his ances-'tor made and left a will, the Court would hold him to it. I 'think, in this case, Miller would be liable to be convicted of per-'jury, if it could be proved that he bought the silk himself, and 'not by a broker: After he had said, he rather believed he had 'bought the silk by a broker, the commissioners might have pro-'ceeded to ask him, who was his broker, &c. I am of opinion, 'Miller must be discharged out of custody.' The three other Judges were of the same opinion, and he was discharged. Miller's case, III. Wils. 427.; II. Blackst. 881.

2. OF THE ANSWER OF OTHERS THAN THE BANKRUPT.—The other persons whom the law allows to be examined, are to be considered in the same light with any other witnesses in courts of justice, and to be proceeded with accordingly. The Sheriff has, at common law,

law, powers to punish prevarication, and to enforce a fair answer. He may, if required, take the examination upon oath, to be the ground of a prosecution for perjury: § 27.

The intention of the examination being merely investigation, and not ultimate evidence, what comes out from the bankrupt, and the other persons thus examined, is not to be held as conclusive, although upon oath. It is to be regarded, in respect to others, as a declaration, or precognition merely; which, if necessary, is to be followed up by legal evidence. It is taken upon oath, because that may be necessary, as a compulsitory upon the bankrupt to speak truth, from a knowledge that his falsehood may be punished with the pains of perjury.

SECTION IV.

OF THE MANAGEMENT, RECOVERY, AND DISPOSAL OF THE ESTATE.

IN this section, I shall endeavour to mark out the features which may seem to be important in the course of management, and in the recovery and disposal of the estate.

By the 28th section of the statute, the meeting, after the bankrupt's last examination, is to give general directions respecting the recovery and disposal of the estate; and with these, so far as they go, the trustee must comply; but, by § 32, the trustee is ordered 'to proceed in recovering and converting into money, in the 'speediest and most effectual manner, the whole estate under his 'management or power, whether at home, or in foreign parts,' &c.

1. MANAGEMENT OF THE ESTATE.—Particular circumstances may require, that, in the course of the management, the trade of the

the bankrupt should be continued, as the most likely way of realizing a fund for payment of the debts, and for enabling the debtor himself again to begin the world, after his creditors are paid. A shop in a centrical situation, and well established; or a manufactory, of which the instruments and workhouses are of very inconsiderable value in themselves, but of very great value, if the work be continued; it may be truly for the advantage of the creditors to carry on. But in a matter of so much importance as this, where something is to be risked in order to gain, it is to the creditors themselves that the decision must be left. The meeting for choosing an interim factor, will, of course, give directions for the intermediate management; and the fuller meeting for the choice of the trustee, will decide what is to be done. The natural way is, to employ the bankrupt himself, at an allowance, if the creditors have confidence in him; or any confidential clerk or manager, who is able, and has been accustomed to the management of the concern. In the common course of management, there can be little difficulty—none which the trustee and commissioners cannot easily solve. The creditors may be called together by the trustee, at any time, to consider all matters of difficulty and importance, and to give directions, when he and the commissioners are at a loss, or where they are divided in opinion.

2. RECOVERY OF THE ESTATE.—The trustee is, with the advice of the commissioners, to raise such actions as may be necessary for bringing in the funds, or deciding disputed claims; unless it shall appear to them better to compound, or submit them: § 44. In particular, a trustee must be careful to prevent the running of prescription against the claims.

In questions between trustees on a sequestrated estate, and third parties, it sometimes comes to be doubted, whether there really be any difference between the situation of the creditors, and that of the bankrupt himself; but this is a question which I shall need hereafter to discuss, in a more extended view, as a general question, applicable to all sorts of bankruptcies;—and to that discussion, I shall here beg leave to refer.

3.

3. DISPOSAL OF THE ESTATE.—In disposing of the heritable property, the creditors have their choice of a judicial sale, (according to the forms already explained in the first part of this Fourth Book), or a public voluntary sale. In determining which should be preferred, the great points to which the attention of the creditors must be turned, are, the comparative expence and delay, and the comparative goodness of the purchaser's title. 1. In respect of delay and expence, the judicial sale must yield to the voluntary. We have already considered the subject of judicial sales very minutely, and seen, that the expence is very considerable, and the delay great: whereas, in the voluntary roup, the trustee and commissioners, after the proper inquiries, settle the upset price, and the most eligible time for disposing of the property, and, at once, bring it to sale, and throw the price (so far as not exhausted by real securities) into the divisible fund. 2. In respect of the security of the title offered to the purchaser, there will not appear to be much difference, as the law at present stands. The judicial sale affords a title of absolute security against the bankrupt, and all deriving right from him; but so does the voluntary sale under sequestration. There is not, indeed, a decree of certification in the sequestration, as in the ranking and sale; but there are proceedings which produce an effect equally strong. Those who claim, as in right of the bankrupt, must either have real securities over the land to be sold; or they must be personal creditors only. As to the former, their rights must appear in the record; and the purchaser has, of course, an opportunity of retaining the share of the price necessary for paying them off; and although, prior to 1793, there might have been some danger of real creditors claiming to an extent greater than the price, that danger is now, by the statute of that year, done away, it being declared, that the sale shall 'be valid and effectual, with and under the burden of all real 'securities, or other liens upon the estate, so far as the same are 'preferable to the disposition or decree vesting the estate in the 'trustee; but which burden shall go no further than to the extent 'of the price:' § 33. As to personal creditors, the adjudication and conveyance vest the whole funds in the trustee, as their sole representative: his deeds, properly authorised, are therefore most

completely

completely effectual in giving a title to the purchaser; excluding, on the one hand, all who do not choose to appear in the sequestration; and including, on the other, all who do appear. The title of the trustee forms, thus, a solid basis for a conveyance, that shall be unobjectionable by any personal creditor; and the statute declares, 'that the purchaser shall be entitled to a discharge from 'the trustee, which shall have the effect completely to disencumber 'the subject acquired:' § 33. The conveyances which the purchaser is entitled to have, not from the trustee only, but from the real creditors, whose debts are paid from the price, afford, to the voluntary title, as complete a fortification, as the analogous conveyances under a judicial sale possess: and the only point in which the voluntary sale seems to be inferior to the judicial sale, is this, that there is a possibility of a real burden affecting the property, which does not appear from the record; and the creditor in which, not being forced to appear in the sequestration, as in the judicial sale, may, if neglected, have a claim against the purchaser for the share of the price corresponding with his debt. But, to balance this, the greater degree of care to make effectual searches of incumbrances, where the voluntary sale is to be adopted, may confidently be set in opposition to the declarations of the older statutes relating to judicial sales.

If, however, the majority of the creditors in value, determine for a JUDICIAL SALE, the trustee is obliged, forthwith, to proceed in the same, and is entitled to carry it on, as to a part of the estate, without including the whole, and without any other proof of bankruptcy, than the act of sequestration. It is enough, too, that the bankrupt himself, and his real creditors in possession, be called upon a citation of fifteen days, whether they are within the kingdom or not: the edictal citation is dispensed with: § 33. But if no such judicial sale has been begun, and if the majority of the creditors in value shall not have resolved upon a voluntary sale, any real creditor may follow out his privilege of bringing a judicial sale, under the statutes in that behalf: § 33. In the event of a judicial sale, it is provided by the same section, that 'the balance 'of the price, if there be any, after satisfying the preferable securities,

'rities, shall be paid into the hands of the trustee, as a part of 'the funds of division to be made by him amongst the creditors 'in general; the purchaser being always entitled, whether the 'lands have been sold in the one way or in the other, to a dis-'charge from the trustee, which shall have the effect completely 'to disencumber the subject acquired; and the creditors shall be 'entitled to draw their shares of the price, in virtue of the dispo-'sition and adjudication in favour of the trustee, without the ne-'cessity of any other adjudication.'

If the majority in value of the creditors, shall prefer a VOLUNTARY SALE, the sale, when made after such advertisement, and at such upset price, and upon such articles and conditions as shall be fixed by the trustee, with the consent of a majority of the said commissioners, shall be valid and effectual, with and under the burden of all real securities, &c. § 33. By § 62, it is declared, that no duty imposed on sales by auction, shall be exigible upon sales under this statute.

In disposing of the MOVEABLE PROPERTY, public voluntary roup is the way which is generally adopted, and perhaps the most beneficial. The only moveable subject, over which any thing like a real right can extend, is a ship. There may be an hypothec upon it for repairs in a foreign port; and the creditor who holds such real security, must, of course, be entitled, out of the first of the price, to receive his payment; the purchaser, on the other hand, being no doubt entitled to see it applied, or to retain a share of the price, as in heritage, for answering it.

If, at the expiration of a year and a half (formerly three years) from the date of the sequestration, any of the personal effects of the bankrupt, or any debts, whether heritable or moveable, due to him, remain still unrecovered, it shall be in the power of four-fifths of the creditors in number and value, convened at any general meeting called for the purpose, (after an advertisement two weeks

weeks previous to the meeting in the Gazette), to direct, that such outstanding debts and effects, and also any contingent or future interest, which the creditors at large may have in dividends deposited in bank, or lent out, be sold off by public auction, upon three months previous notice published in the Gazette, the sale either to be in whole, or in lots, as a majority in value of the creditors shall direct: § 45.

It is scarcely necessary to repeat the regulations for lodging the produce of the estate in a bank. The 34th section of the statute declares, that four-fifths of the creditors in number and value, at any general meeting, shall appoint the bank, in which such depositation is to be made; that, failing of such appointment, the Royal Bank, or Bank of Scotland, shall be the place of depositation; and that the trustee shall never keep more than 50l. in his hands at once, for the space of ten days, without being liable for 7½ per cent. interest on the excess.

Upon this clause, it was questioned, in the case already mentioned, of Playfair against Walkers, &c. 24th Dec. 1788, whether a majority of the creditors could authorize the money to be lodged in the hands of private merchants, who dealt in taking up money upon promissory notes, but who were not properly bankers? The Court did not precisely determine, whether, in such cases, money could be deposited in the hands of an individual, carrying on the trade of a banker; but it was thought, that the persons, suggested by the creditors, not being bankers, the resolution complained of was unauthorized by the statutes; 'and they refused to authorize 'the money so to be lodged.'

SECTION V.

Of the Proof of Debts.

No debt is to be refused a place in the division, whatever its nature be, if the proof of it be clear: whether pure, or future, or contingent, whether a debt at law, or a claim in equity, and for damage, it is proveable under the sequestration, and entitled to its place. In England, it is otherwise. The general rule there, is, that no debt, which is not due at the time of the bankruptcy, can be proved under the commission: and although several exceptions have been admitted; as, of future debts payable at a certain day, by 7 Geo. I. c 31.; of bills and promissory notes, though not due at the time of the commission, by the same statute; and of bottomry and respondentia bonds, by 19 Geo. II. c. 32. § 2.; yet still the rule applies to all contingent debts, and even to annuities, unless the annuitant can claim as upon the forfeiture of the penalty before the bankruptcy. All claims of damages, and in equity also, they hold to be contingent, and not proveable under the commission.

I. In lodging his claim under a sequestration, a creditor must not only produce all the evidence, in support of it, which can be produced, and specify it so particularly, as to furnish every possible means of checking it, but he must also swear to its truth: § 41, 42.

1. The specification of the grounds and nature of the claim, with the production of such documents as are intended to support it, is necessary to enable the trustee, and the other creditors, to scrutinize the claim, and perceive what is objectionable. The trustee receives the claim and grounds of debt, which he is bound carefully to keep, if the creditor do not wish them returned; and if

if he do, the trustee must mark them as received, and return them but he must make a particular minute, or entry in the book of sederunt, specifying the nature of the claim, and the documents produced in support of it; and this must at all times be open to the creditors, that they may examine the claims, and state objections to them, or suggest them to the trustee (§ 35.) The production of the claim, and grounds of debt, is declared (by § 41.) to have the same effect, in all questions of interruption of prescription, as if a proper action had been raised on the said grounds of debt, against the bankrupt and the trustee.

2. The oath of verity is taken before any Judge Ordinary, or Justice of the Peace. It is in no shape to be regarded as an oath upon reference; nor, in any degree, as strengthening the evidence of the claim against any objection. The statute says, that the oath, 'either by the party himself, or any person acting for him, 'shall not supersede the necessity of bringing legal evidence of 'the debt, if the same is objected to as unliquidated, or where evi-'dence appears to be necessary in the circumstances of the case:' § 42. In short, the effect of it is nothing more, than to deter, by the pains of perjury, from the making of false claims. The 43d section denounces the punishment of perjury, to be prosecuted by the trustee, or any of the creditors, and his Majesty's Advocate; with forfeiture of all the dividend which the true debt would have drawn. The oath of verity must be made by the creditor himself, if in circumstances which admit of it; but if not, 'if he be out 'of Great Britain and Ireland, or under age, or incapable of giv-'ing an oath; in all such cases, an oath of credulity by the agent, 'factor, guardian, or other manager, taken in the same manner, 'shall be sufficient:' § 42. The statute says nothing of companies, corporations, &c. But I apprehend, that, in the former case, the acting partner, or any of the partners giving their oath, is sufficient to satisfy the view of the law; and, in the latter, the oath of the clerk or treasurer of the corporation. The creditor, in his oath, must 'specify every security which he holds for his 'debt, whether on the estate of the debtor, or other obligants; 'and he shall swear, that he holds no other security than is men-

'tioned

'tioned in his oath, otherwise his oath shall not be received by the 'trustee as sufficient, nor his claim be sustained:' § 42. This section is subservient to the 39th and 40th sections, by which it is declared, that the value of all preferable securities, obtained over the bankrupt's estate prior to sequestration, shall be deducted from the debt; that the creditor shall be ranked, and draw only for the balance after such deduction, and that the creditor shall be bound to communicate the benefit of any payment or security, obtained after the date of the sequestration, without the jurisdiction of the Court.

II. We have already seen, that it is the duty of the trustee, to judge, in the first instance, of all objections to claims, and to admit them into the ranking, or absolutely to reject them, as he shall conceive to be the fair judgement in law.

When any claim is thus rejected, as unliquidated or unproved, the creditor must take the proper measures for establishing his debt at law If there be no occasion to apply to the Court of Session on any other account; as, for the discussion of grounds of challenge, which requires investigation, or for the reviewing of some judgement of the trustee complained against; the creditor, whose debt is rejected as unconstituted, must bring a separate action. But if any of the proceedings are brought into the Court, either upon an application from the trustee, or by any creditor dissatisfied with his scheme of ranking, &c. it is provided by § 35. that 'it shall be 'competent for any creditor, to produce his interest, and to have 'his debt proved and constituted, if necessary, without raising a 'separate action for the purpose.'

III. It only remains, upon this subject, to observe, that no creditor is cut off from his dividend, from the accident of being later than others in producing his claim. He is indeed cut off from the share of any dividend which shall be made before producing his ground of debt; but, then, 'he is entitled, in the next distribution 'which happens after the grounds of debt are so produced and 'proved, to draw out of the first of the remaining fund in the

'trustee's

'trustee's hands, a sum equal to the former dividend or dividends 'on his debt, with deduction of 5 per cent. on the said dividends; 'which is to be retained by the trustee for the common behoof, on 'account of the creditor's delay:' § 36.

SECTION VI.

OF THE MANNER OF DISTRIBUTING THE FUNDS AMONG THE CREDITORS.

THE idea of the statute is, to preclude, as much as possible, the necessity for proceedings at law; and, therefore, it is the business of the trustee, to make up an accurate state of the funds, and of the debts; to ascertain, to the best of his abilities, with all the assistance he can procure, the places of the different creditors in the ranking; and to calculate the scheme of division in a form so complete, that if the creditors do not object to it, the division may proceed upon it, and be finished. The Court is, indeed, open for the revisal of the trustee's scheme of division; but they are not to be called upon, to arrange the ranking in the first instance.

In calculating the dividend, every debt must be taken into the account, however objectionable. It would prejudge the merit of the objection, were the trustee to exclude any debt; for the necessary effect is, to refuse setting apart the dividend, and so to risk the total exclusion of that debt from any share in the division: but where the claim is unaccompanied with an oath of verity, the trustee is not entitled to include it; even should there be no chance of another dividend. The act absolutely requires the oath of verity, to entitle the claim to be ranked (§ 26.); and this was found to exclude a creditor neglecting it: 8th March 1787, Humphrey against Crawford.

In fixing the division, the trustee must regulate himself by the principles of law; which, in the ascertainment of the fund, in the marshalling

marshalling of the debts, and in the calculation of redraughts, and of the effects of securities, come, in many cases, to be of very difficult application. All these are the proper object of the FIFTH BOOK: and here it is necessary only to take notice of some regulations, particularly laid down in the sequestration statute.

1. FUNDS.—The whole estate and effects belonging to the bankrupt, at the period of sequestration, or the produce thereof, after paying all charges, is the fund of division. This is declared to include all payments made by the debtor to any of his creditors, after the date of the first deliverance; and all rights which the bankrupt may have alienated after that date. While these parts of the estate are preserved for the creditors by the sequestration, the effect of the statute of 1696, c. 5, guards against all transactions within sixty days of the bankruptcy, the effect of which would be to confer a preference upon prior creditors.

2. DEBTS.—Those debts only are to be included in the distribution, which were due at the date of the first deliverance: among these, all future debts, of which the term of payment, 'etsi non-'dum venerit, cessit,' are, at common law, includeable. Contingent debts, also, are included, by this statute, to the effect of having a sum set apart for their payment. The debts are to be taken, with interest on each, up to the date of the first deliverance; except future debts, which suffer an abatement, or discount of interest, for the time to expire before the term of payment come. Contingent debts and annuities are to be ascertained by compromise, arbitration, or process at law, as may be agreed on by the party and the trustee, with consent of the commissioners, (§ 44.)

3. RANKING.—The rules for ranking, of which it seems proper to take notice here, are these, 1. That the preferences acknowledged, in the law of Scotland, are to be observed, in so far as they have been obtained, by conveyances or diligence, before the first deliverance; excepting the effects of poinding and arrestment, which are, in part, restrained by the sequestration statute (§ 36. 29. 31.) 2dly, That all debts, merely personal, and not covered by

by any security, are to be ranked pari passu; it being always observed, that those creditors who hold preferable securities, can be ranked among the personal creditors, only, for the balance of their debt, after deducting the value of the security. This is to be ascertained, in case of dispute, by the trustee and commissioners; the creditor having it in his option to deduct the value from his claim, reserving the full effect of his security; or to draw the said value, in the first place, out of the sum to be divided, and his share of the remainder of the divisible fund, corresponding to the balance; in which case, he must convey his security (§ 39.) In the same way, if the claimant have, after the date of the first deliverance, got payment or security, from any subject belonging to the bankrupt, beyond the jurisdiction of the Court, he must communicate it, before being allowed to draw. 3dly, Future and contingent debts are to be ranked according to the place to which they would be entitled, if pure; the directions of the statute being observed with regard to the draughts to be made for them (§ 37. 8.)

4. DIVIDENDS.—The superintendance of the Court has not been thought a sufficient restraint upon the delays which might occur in the settlement of a bankruptcy. The statute has, therefore, fixed down certain terms, at which the dividends are required to be made. The *first* dividend is to be made at the end of 'one complete year from the date of the first deliverance on the 'petition for sequestration,' § 35. The *second*, at the end of a year and a half from the date of the first deliverance; and a dividend, at the end of every six months thereafter, till the whole division be finished, § 36. Provision is made for the possibility of the funds being ready for a dividend being made, earlier than these appointed terms. It is declared, that four-fifths of the creditors, in number and value, present at the meeting after the last diet of the bankrupt's examination, or at any other meeting called for the purpose, may direct the trustee to apply for the authority of the Court of Session, to make the first dividend at an earlier period than the end of the first year, but not earlier than six months from the date of the first deliverance aforesaid, if, upon cause shown, it shall be found expedient to do so; and also to accelerate the time

for

for making the second and other dividends. It is also provided, that, after a second dividend, a majority of the creditors in value, at any general meeting called for the purpose, may determine that future dividends shall be made after a shorter interval, and the affairs of the trust brought to a more speedy close, § 36.

A creditor, we have seen, is not excluded from the distribution, in consequence of neglecting to lodge his claim before the first dividend. He is, of course, kept out of that dividend, but he is entitled to reimbursement (except to the extent of 5 per cent. on his debt) from the next dividend, § 36.

The dividend payable to a creditor in a future debt, is the share corresponding with the debt, taken at a discount of the interest to the term of payment. The dividend upon a contingent debt, is to be set apart, and deposited in the bank chosen by the creditors; or lent out, on heritable security, by the trustee, at the sight of the claimant, at such rate of interest as can be got for the same: and the interest thereupon arising shall belong to the creditors, and be included in the fund for their dividends; until the contingency, whereupon the obligation depends, shall be declared; when the dividend so deposited shall belong to the claimant, or the other creditors, according to the terms of the obligation (§ 38). Provision is also made for the sale of the contingent interest which the creditors have in the sum so deposited, after the expiration of a year and a half from the date of the sequestration, if it shall be thought prudent so to do, by four-fifths of the creditors in number and value, assembled at a general meeting called for the purpose, § 45.

5. ALLOWANCE TO THE BANKRUPT.—By § 51, four-fifths of the creditors in number and value at the meeting after the last examination, may authorise the trustee and commissioners to allow and pay the bankrupt such sums as they shall think fit, for the subsistence and support of the bankrupt and his family, till the period assigned for the second dividend, not exceeding two guineas

per

per week, and, in all events, not to amount to more than 5 per cent. of the net produce of the estate.

SECTION VII.

OF WINDING UP THE SEQUESTRATION, AND DISCHARGING THE BANKRUPT.

IN considering this subject, there are two situations, which demand attention.

1. If the fund be more than adequate to pay off the debts, principal, interest, and expences, with the charges of the trust, the debtor is entitled to call the trustee to account, and to oblige him instantly to bring the matter to a conclusion, and pay over the balance, (§ 46); the trustee being, on the other hand, entitled to a discharge and exoneration of his trust.

2. If the funds be inadequate, the trustee may apply to the Court, after the final dividend, to be discharged of his trust; and, after this application has been properly advertised in the newspapers, the Court grants the desire of the petition, if there be no objection, and orders the bond of caution to be delivered up; or, if there be objections, the question is summarily decided. As to the debtor, if his creditors judge him worthy of a discharge, by a vote of four-fifths in number and value, he may apply, by petition, for a discharge. This may be done, even before the winding up of the sequestration, any time after the second dividend. But, of this subject, I shall treat more at large hereafter, in speaking of the disposal of the debtor's person.

CHAP. IV.

Of Compositions after Sequestration is begun.

Although a fair proposal for a composition, is often the most beneficial measure, both for the creditors, and the bankrupt himself, yet it sometimes happens, that such proposals are the instruments of dishonesty. If a bankrupt can contrive, while he keeps his funds concealed, to magnify, in the eyes of the creditors, the difficulties, the delays, and the expence of persevering in the sequestration; and to follow this up with a proposal for a composition, to be paid without trouble or expence; what more likely means are there for escaping detection, and being allowed to enjoy, unmolested, the fruits of his deceit? What greater encouragement to fraudulent bankruptcies?

It has been, therefore, a great object with the Legislature, in the last statute, to guard against the dangers incident to such proposals: *First*, To prevent the delays, expence and litigation, which collusive and ineffectual plans of composition, were found formerly to occasion: *Secondly*, To prevent the creditors from being exposed to the temptation of accepting proposals of this kind, before a full opportunity was given, of investigating whether the debtor had fairly disclosed his funds: and, *Thirdly*, To prevent the bankrupt, and others, when a proposal does come forward, from purchasing the consent of particular creditors, by gratuities, or higher compositions.

1. To attain the two first of these objects, it was enacted, in the 48th section of the statute, that a proposal for a composition might

might be made, after the second examination of the bankrupt, when the creditors have had a full opportunity of seeing how the affairs stand—that it should be received, only upon an offer of caution, to the satisfaction of nine-tenths of the creditors in number and value assembled at the meeting after the examination—that the proposal should then be considered in another meeting, at the distance of at least three weeks, to give time to creditors to appear, and then only on due advertisement—that the dependance of these proposals should make no interruption to the proceedings—and that it should require the consent of nine-tenths of the whole creditors in number and value, to validate the proposal, so far as to entitle it to be laid before the Court for their approbation. The approbation of the Court, is the final acceptance of the proposal, and is accompanied with a discharge to the bankrupt, except as to payment of the composition.

2. For the attainment of the third object, it is enacted in the 49th section, that all private proposals, &c. for a composition, shall be null and void; and that any creditor, proved to have accepted of a gratuity, or higher composition, for giving his concurrence, shall forfeit his debt, and be liable in restitution of what he has received; and the bankrupt is, if required, to make oath, that there has been no private transaction, or undue influence used.

In all questions, upon the effect of the discharge which accompanies the acceptance of the composition, it is a material consideration, that this transaction takes place at an early period of the bankruptcy—before all the creditors may have found it convenient to appear, and produce their claims. On this consideration, it does not seem to be necessary, in order to entitle a creditor to draw a share of that composition, with the burden of which the discharge is qualified, that he shall have produced his claim in the sequestration. The statute requires the composition to be 'upon 'the whole debts;' and, all that seems to be requisite for any creditor claiming the composition, is, that he shall be able to establish his debt, by legal evidence, to have been due.

PART THE THIRD.

OF THE DISTRIBUTION OF THE ESTATE OF A BANKRUPT, BY VOLUNTARY TRUST AND ACCESSION.

THE great object of creditors, in attempting to accomplish the distribution of their debtor's estate privately, is, to avoid the expence, litigation, and delay inseparable from judicial proceedings. For mercantile cases, we have seen that a system of distribution has been devised, which, by a happy union of private and judicial proceedings, leaves scarcely any thing to be wished for, on the part of the creditors, or of the debtor, to promote their mutual benefit. But we have also seen, that, in other cases, the proceedings at law are tedious and expensive, while the danger of partial preferences being acquired by superior alacrity is not inconsiderable. In these cases, then, a plan of private distribution, which should save creditors from the expence and delay of proceedings at law, and prevent the acquisition of partial preferences, is greatly to be wished : and it shall be our object, in this Part, to inquire how far such a plan is practicable, as the law now stands—what are the obstacles and dangers to which it is exposed—and how these are to be avoided, and the distribution accomplished.

1. This inquiry, will naturally begin with a deduction of the law, and history of the cases relating to the debtor's powers of constituting an effectual trust-deed, independently of the accession of his creditors.

2. It w be proper next to inquire, in what way creditors, willing to agree in common measures, may secure themselves against those who do not accede—and what shall be held to amount to an accession. And,

3. A representation of the leading features of an agreement between the debtor and the creditors, on the supposition that all the creditors accede, and of the proper methods of giving effect to the agreement, will close the subject.

CHAP. I.

Of the Power of the Debtor to make an Effectual Trust-Deed, for behoof of his Creditors, independently of their Accession.

Trust-deeds, for the benefit of creditors, are of two kinds: a simple conveyance of the debtor's funds to his creditors, or to a trustee, in their name, to be distributed among them, according to their respective rights; or a conveyance, burdened with conditions, relative to the rights of the creditors, or to the management and distribution of the funds, or to the debtor's own discharge, &c. To make the explanation of the subject as simple as possible, it may be proper to consider, separately, the powers which these two classes of acts require.

§ I. Of Unqualified Trust-Deeds.

Every debtor, who grants a voluntary deed of trust, for behoof of his creditors, must be in one or other of these three situations. He must either be simply insolvent; or diligence must have begun against him, without being carried the length of making him bankrupt; or he must be rendered bankrupt within the prescribed period. And the object of the present inquiry must be, to determine, whether the same rules are applicable to trust-deeds, as to deeds granted in favour of individual creditors, of which, in the Second Book, we have treated so much at large.

We shall find, that, as the law now stands, these rules are precisely applicable; so that, on the one hand, in the case of mere insolvency, the debtor's conveyance, in trust, will be good, provided it it be first completed; and, on the other, that however just and expedient the conveyance in trust may be, it will fall under the statutes of 1621, and of 1696.

1. A trust-deed by a debtor insolvent, but not bankrupt, and against whom no diligence has proceeded, is not reducible. The great principle, upon which it has ever been contended that a debtor in this situation is barred from making an effectual trust-deed in favour of his creditors, is, that although he remains vested with his property, even after insolvency, he holds it, not as absolute proprietor, but merely as trustee for his whole creditors; or rather as negotiorum gestor, bound to take care of the subject which he has under charge, but not entitled to do any act, by which the situation of those who have the radical right to it, can in any shape be altered, or their legal privileges destroyed. Such was the ground-work of a very ingenious and excellent pleading upon this question, by one of the first of our commercial lawyers, in the case of Hutchinson against Wright. But it is a principle, which, in fair legal reasoning, cannot support the argument of which it is the foundation. Conveyances by a proprietor are, at common law, reducible only where fraudulent; it is with no other view, than to prevent fraud, that his powers suffer, upon insolvency, any sort of limitation. Now, fraud can be committed, only by the unfair diminution of the funds, in consequence of embezzlement, alienation, or the rearing of false debts; or by the constitution of unfair preferences in favour of particular creditors. Although, therefore, every act done by an insolvent debtor, which has any of these objects in view, is, at common law, fraudulent and reducible; yet, where no such fraud is committed; where the debtor, acting for the common benefit, steps forward only to do that very thing, which, if he refused, the law would force him to do, he can in no shape be held as guilty of fraud. Even in the rudest period of our law, while no means were as yet provided for securing creditors against preferences by execution, a deed, anticipating the diligence of the creditors, could not have been objected to as an illegal invasion of the privilege competent to individual creditors. On the contrary, it is very certain, that prior to the statute of

1621,

1621, it was held to be perfectly competent, for a debtor, to give security or payment to a true creditor, even after the diligence of another creditor was actually begun; and, at common law, the competition depended upon the priority of the voluntary, or of the judicial right. But the question here is not whether a debtor can entirely disappoint the right of an individual creditor?—it is, whether the funds, which yet remain legally in him, and which, without challenge, he may sell for a price, can, by his voluntary conveyance, be legally vested in the whole body of his creditors, to be divided among them according to the rights which stand constituted in their persons? That no objection of fraud can be moved against such an exercise of the debtor's powers, is plain; since the very object and wish of the law is, to produce this very effect, and bring the whole creditors to an equality.

The first time that this question seems to have been tried, was in 1744, in the case of Snodgrass against the trustee and creditors of David Bett. Bett the debtor was insolvent, but not bankrupt, in terms of the act 1696. He made a trust-deed in favour of his whole creditors, and it was challenged as ineffectual, in competition with posterior arrestments. The arresters maintained the right of creditors, to proceed with their diligence uncontrouled by the debtor; and complained, that the appearance of equality, which such deeds were made to assume, was a mere cloke, to cover the injustice of bringing in, upon the same footing, those creditors who had parata executio, and those who had not even constituted their debts. Lord Kilkerran, in his report of the case, says, 'Where there lies *no ground of reduction on the statute*, there 'appears to be no foundation, in the common law, upon which a 'disposition by a man, however insolvent, to all his creditors equal-'ly among them, can be reduced. And, accordingly, in this case, 'where David Bett the debtor, though insolvent, was not bank-'rupt in terms of the statute, a disposition by him in favour of 'trustees, for the behoof of his whole creditors, duly intimated, 'was preferred to posterior arrestments, and the alledgeance repel-'led, that a person insolvent had it not in his power, by such dis-'positions, to deprive his creditors of their right of obtaining a

'preference

'preference over each other, vigilantia:' 13th November 1744, Kilk. 51. 2.

This decision was confirmed three years afterwards, in the case of the Corporation of Shoemakers of the Canongate. The affairs of the incorporation having gone into disorder, but no diligence having been done, a trust-deed was executed in favour of the creditors of the incorporation. One of the creditors afterwards proceeded to arrest, and claimed a preference over the trustee, both upon the act 1696, (they having offered to prove circumstances equivalent to the bankruptcy of an individual), and upon the common law. 'The 'Court was clear,' says Lord Kilkerran, 'that no reduction could 'lie upon the act 1696, as the incorporation, a body politic, was 'not capable of the personal diligence requisite by that statute; 'and that no equivalent circumstances are ever admitted to bring a 'debtor under the description of it*. And they were no less 'clear, that as a reduction at common law had no other effect 'than to bring in all the creditors equally, there could be no re-'duction, at common law, of a disposition, which gave the credi-'tors the very same thing which they could obtain by the reduc-'tion; and so the Lords have uniformly found; and lately in the 'case between Snodgrass and the Creditors of Bett:' 5th June 1747, Grant, Kilk. 52.

Again, in the case of M'Kell against the trustees of Anthony M'Lurg, 'the Lords were unanimous, that where the case of an 'insolvent person comes not under either of the bankrupt statutes, 'a disposition by him to trustees, for his whole creditors, must 'be effectual in law:' and, in support of this judgement, the above mentioned case of Snodgrass was referred to: 30th July 1766, Kames's Sel. Dec. p. 321. A similar decision was also given, 24th February 1769, Watson against Orr and others: IV. Fac. Coll. Part ii. No. lxxxix. 340.; and another on the 15th June 1773, in the case of Ramsay of Barra against Kenneth M'Kenzie's trustees.

* It would seem to be otherwise now, since the late sequestration laws See above, p 50.

The last decision which I shall mention, was pronounced in a case to which I have already alluded: Hutchison against Gibson's creditors, 8th December 1791. In that case, Gibson was insolvent, but not bankrupt. He offered to make over his funds to his creditors in a body. To which proposal, those present at a meeting having agreed, he executed a trust-deed; and the trustees having sold his furniture, a creditor, who had not acceded, arrested the price. A competition arose between the trustees and the arresting creditor; and the Court, holding this decision to be of importance as a precedent, ordered memorials, that they might have a full view of former cases. On advising these memorials, they were 'unanimously of opinion, that the conveyance in question was 'valid and effectual; and therefore, they dismissed the claim of 'the arresting creditor, and found him liable in expences.' VIII. Fac. Coll. cxciii. 401.

It is then to be held as a settled point, that a debtor, though insolvent, may make an effectual trust-deed for the benefit of all his creditors; and that, unless there be room for challenge on the statutes of 1621 and 1696, the question between the body of creditors founding upon the trust-deed, and those who choose to pursue separate measures, comes to a proper competition between the priority of completion of the two rights.

---

2. But although it is not a sufficient ground for reduction of a trust-deed, that the debtor was insolvent at the time of granting it; yet, if diligence have been commenced by any creditor, in order to attach the estate real or personal of the debtor, a right of challenge is competent to the creditor whose diligence is injured by the deed. It was in this respect that the statute of 1621 produced those unforeseen and unfortunate consequences, which formerly I took occasion to remark, (p. 111, 112.) The principles of bankrupt law were imperfectly understood in this early age; and the attention of those who framed the law, was confined entirely to the object of protecting individual creditors, who had be-

gun

gun diligence, against the fraudulent attempts of the debtor to disappoint them. The statute, once enacted in the broad terms which it bears, and with a total disregard to any deeds which might be intended for the benefit of all, and the effecting of a general distribution, was held to strike equally against trust-deeds as against deeds in favour of individuals. It was thought enough, if the creditor who had begun diligence, could say, that, by a voluntary deed, his diligence was interrupted. It was held to be a complete answer to every argument of expediency or of justice, in favour of trust-deeds for equalizing the rights of the creditors and distributing the funds, that the law had provided means for attaching the property of a debtor, and that, after insolvency, no debtor could interfere to destroy, what the law had begun to rear. In all this reasoning, it was forgot, that the law had not yet provided for the case of insolvency; that the measures which creditors were permitted to take for attaching their debtors estates, were constituted only with a view to individual debtors and creditors; and that the obvious effect of the prosecution of such individual measures, being directly unjust, the law ought not to vindicate and support the right of individuals against a deed not fraudulent, but for the common benefit of all.

By one judgement, indeed, the Court found the statute inapplicable to the case of a trust-deed for the general behoof The case to which I allude, is that of Farquharson against Cumming's creditors in 1729, where a disposition in trust was sustained, although challenged by a creditor who had given a charge of horning prior to the deed: I. Dict. 85. But, in the case of Dawson & Lupton against Anderson, 26th July 1734, this judgement was reversed, and the trust-deed cut down: and again, in the case of Mansfield against Brown, 28th January 1735, the same judgement was pronounced. Mansfield had raised a horning prior to the disposition in trust; the other creditors had raised horning also, but had stopped their diligence upon the disposition being granted, which Mansfield proceeded to arrest. He claimed a preference; and the Court reduced the deed: 28th January 1735, I. Dict. 85.

In

In a subsequent case, Wardrobe against Fairholme and Arbuthnot, the Lords found a trust-assignation ' reducible on the act ' 1621, there being diligence by horning, at the instance of Fair' holme and Arbuthnot, and of Arbuthnot & Co., prior to the ' granting of the assignation :' 19th December 1744, I. Falc. 30.

There is only one case, then, in which it has been found that the statute in 1621 did not apply to such deeds. In all the others, the reduction has been found competent, both when the challenge proceeded on the statute of 1621, and when it proceeded on both statutes. The necessary effect of this was, that every creditor who had commenced his diligence before the date of a voluntary deed of trust, however equal and beneficial for the whole the plan of trust might have been, had it in his power to counteract its operation, and proceed with his separate diligence, so as either to acquire a preference, to force the other creditors to follow similar measures, or to oblige them to purchase his concurrence, by paying off his debt.

3. But although, by the second branch of the statute of 1621, a creditor, who has begun diligence, has a right to challenge even a trust-deed, however equal and just, this is a right merely personal to him. If he choose to acquiesce in the trust-deed, none of the other creditors have a right to pursue separate measures, or to challenge the trust, unless they have also begun diligence before the granting of the deed. But under the statute of 1696, c. 5, a general right of challenge was given to all creditors whose debts were prior to a deed of preference granted within sixty days of bankruptcy. After many fluctuations of opinion, it has at last been fixed, that, under this statute, all trust-deeds may be objected to: and this judgement has been confirmed as law in the House of Peers.

Instead of any disquisition upon this question, I shall confine myself to a short analysis of the cases; for, where the opinions have varied so much, it will not only be satisfactory to see the reasons of those changes, as they appeared at the time, but something

thing may, from such an analysis, be learnt of the progress of our commercial law.

In a case which occurred immediately before the passing of the statute, a debtor insolvent, and in the Sanctuary, having made a trust-deed in favour of his creditors, the Court found, that 'being 'a notour bankrupt at the time of his granting his disposition, '(though it was in favour of his whole creditors), the same was 'null in law, being now quarrelled by adjudgers, and could not 'defend against them.' 9th January 1696, Creditors-adjudgers of Drysdale against the other Creditors, I. Fount. 697. This may be taken, therefore, as the law immediately prior to the enacting of the statute 1696, c. 5; and no case seems to have been tried under the statute for eight-and-twenty years. Whether this arose from a conviction that the statute was not intended to apply to the case of a fair and equal trust-deed, for behoof of all the creditors, (as seems to be intimated by no less an authority than the late Lord President Craigie, when at the Bar, in a case to be immediately taken notice of); or, whether it was not rather conceived, that the statute so strongly confirmed the above judgement, as to leave no room for the question, it is of no great importance, perhaps, to inquire. But, if the latter was the case, it was natural to expect, that, with the increasing commerce of the country, and amidst the inconveniences of a total want of equalizing measures in arrestments and other diligence against moveables, attempts should be made to obtain redress by means of trust-deeds.

The failure of Mr Watson, who was clerk of the Bills, gave occasion to two questions, in which the effect of the statute was very fully discussed; and although the Court found the deeds, which he had granted to his creditors, reducible, the judgements proceeded upon special circumstances, and are, in reality, to be regarded as judgements deciding that the statute was not applicable to any simple trust-deed in favour of creditors. The first case was this: Mr Watson having become insolvent, and diligence by horning and caption having been taken out against him, he made a trust-disposition in favour of all his creditors, for payment of their

their debts, according to their former rights and securities, and, ten days afterwards, retired to the Sanctuary. The conveyance included his heritable and moveable estate; and having sold his office in the Bill-Chamber, he took the price payable to all the creditors, in terms of the disposition. Two of the creditors, particularly named in the disposition, arrested the price of the office in the hand of the purchaser, who immediately raised an action of multiplepoinding, calling into Court all having interest. On the first hearing of the cause, the Court preferred the arresters, but without expressing the ground of the judgement. Upon reconsidering the case, as most admirably stated in a petition and answers,* the Court 'adhered to their former interlocutor, especi-'ally

* The case is reported only in the Dictionary I have therefore subjoined an abstract of the argument

Mr CRAIGIE, for the general body of the creditors, contended, That as Mr Watson's having taken a bond for the price of his office, payable to the creditors in general, was equal to his having taken the bond, first to himself, and afterwards assigned it to the creditors, and intimated the assignation, by which he would have been legally denuded of the right to the price, (Stair, Restitution, § 14), the creditors are entitled to state themselves as holding an intimated assignation, which, in the common case, would unquestionably be preferable to the posterior arrestment. Therefore, the simple question is, Whether this assignation be reducible? It is not reducible upon the statute of 1621, for, no diligence had been begun when it was granted. Neither is it reducible upon the statute of 1696, which was intended not to preclude a bankrupt from doing justice, but to prevent him from fraudulently alienating his property in prejudice of creditors But this is a deed, which gives the debtor's funds among them all equally, without preference, and without expence. It is a deed, agreeable to equity, and to the analogy of law. 1 It is agreeable to equity, because all creditors should be brought in equally, in so far as diligence has not already been done, or preferences acquired, upon which principle, the pari passu rule for adjudications, and that established for the creditors of a deceased person, rest A jus quæsitum to do diligence, so as to obtain preference, by priority in execution, is against all equity It is even against law: for, if acts of sederunt be declaratory of the law, and not introductory of new law, the act of sederunt, which establishes an equality among the creditors of a deceased person, is demonstration that a right to persist in diligence is not acknowledged by the law. On the very same principle which is embodied in this act of sederunt, might the Court legally regulate the right of proceeding with diligence, in cases of bankruptcy, and establish a pari passu ranking among all creditors doing diligence within a limited time. 2. This deed is agreeable to the analogy of law. for, as a debtor may safely pay to a creditor,

' ally upon this medium, that the bond was conditional, depend-
' ing upon the acceptance of the creditors, and that, during the
' dependance

creditor using arrestment, or, where a precept of poinding has been raised, payment may as effectually be made, as if the creditor had proceeded to complete his poinding so, a voluntary disposition ought to be, and has been sustained, as equal to an adjudication, where there is no prior diligence, and where the pari passu preference competent to adjudgers, is not injured. Voluntary rights, in short, are equal to legal diligence, wherever the debtor has not been interpelled, and where no undue preference is bestowed. Reductions, in cases where the reducer had not done diligence, had no other effect, prior to 1696, than to bring in the reducers equally with the disponee, but the statute of that year, though it established the marks and characters of bankruptcy, altered not its effect, and it is only deeds of preference that fall by it. Many a trust-deed accordingly has been made since 1696, but they never have been challenged, where an equal partition was made, the act not being thought to apply to such a case.

To this argument, Mr BOSWELL, for the arresting creditors, answered, 1. That the bond not only pre-supposes the use of diligence by the creditors, since the price is made payable to the creditors, as they shall be ranked by the Lords of Session; but it is conditional, till the acceptance by the creditors of the deed, as qualified with the obligation to grant a full discharge, and it was while the right was in suspense, that the arrestments were used—which therefore must be effectual. 2. The interpretation put upon the statute, is bad, in supposing it to strike only against deeds granted to individual creditors. By the common law, and this statute, creditors have a right to use diligence, and the bankrupt has no power to prevent them, for, by the very making of a deed, whose effect shall prevent their diligence, he acts 'in their prejudice;' which the statute forbids him to do. Independently of a general consent among the creditors, there is no strength in such a deed; and therefore, where the creditors wish to make a trust-deed effectual, and are suspicious that some one creditor may proceed with separate measures, every possible means are taken to prevent the debtor from being rendered bankrupt, or, if that cannot be prevented, to adjudge, and do diligence, for behoof of the whole creditors. Here, all the creditors are indeed included in the bond, but without any regard to the different degrees of right which each is entitled to, the parata executio of some, and the unascertained claims of others. 3. On the footing of a voluntary right, the affairs are inextricable, for, as each creditor has a share pro indiviso, all must concur in the disposal of the fund, and any one, refusing to do so, may stop their operations. 4. The statute, and act of sederunt, establishing pari passu rankings in adjudications and confirmations, show, that provisions are carefully made for cases that really deserve them; while others are left to the common line of the law, strengthened by the exception. 5. By the statute of 1621, no deed granted to a prior onerous creditor, was reducible, unless in prejudice of diligence already begun. Creditors holding assignations, therefore, were entitled, under that law, to a preference over those who had done no diligence. But, at that time, a bankrupt was not described and defined by the law: now,

he

'dependance of the condition, before the creditors acceptance, the 'subject had been arrested; but, if the bond had been simple, 'and equally to all the creditors, the Lords would have preferred 'the creditors, though the bond had been taken in their names, 'after the debtor's notour bankruptcy:' 3d July 1724, Creditors of Watson competing, I. Dict. 85. Sess. Pap. Adv. Lib.

The second case which arose upon the failure of Mr Watson, illustrates the decision in the above case. It occurred the year after, between other two sets of that gentleman's creditors, concerning the right to a bond due to Mr Watson, and assigned by him, among other funds, to his creditors. The assignation was duly completed by intimation; and afterwards, a creditor of Mr Watson's used arrestment, and pursued an action of forthcoming. The general argument was not essentially different from that maintained in the former case, and is well reported, I. Kames, lxi. 160—4. But, in this report, his Lordship neither marks clearly the distinction which was taken between the two cases, nor gives the judgement of the Court fully. Mr Craigie, who was lawyer also in this case, stated the former decision as having proceeded entirely on specialties, and on this, in particular, that the bond was declared to be conditional, on acceptance of it with the qualification annexed; and the arrestment was used before the conveyance was completed by acceptance: whereas, the assignation here was simple. The answer was general upon this point: but other specialties were pointed out in this deed, which ought, it was said, to be fatal to it. 1. Mr Watson excepts from the conveyance to his creditors, one half of the emoluments of his office: and, 2. He declares, that any creditor proceeding to diligence, shall forfeit his right. These conditions proved fatal to the deed, in the opinion of the Court; for, although it was said in reply, that the emoluments of the office were not alienable, and that all the

he is. The law did not venture to deal harshly with creditors, who might transact with debtors, while yet there was no criterion of mala fides established; but, since the statute of 1696, there can be no mistake. Before 1696, deeds done by bankrupts, were not good to all effects: they were reducible, to the effect of correcting inequalities, and undue preferences, but, if the act produce no further effects, it does nothing, the debtor could do was, to draw them, and account to his creditors, for which it was necessary that he should receive a subsistence; and that, as to the declaration respecting diligence, it was only what would otherwise be implied: yet the Court 'found, 'that a disposition, simple and unqualified, and completed by a 'bankrupt in favour of his whole creditors, is not reducible upon the act 1696, at the instance of a posterior arrester; but that 'this deed is not simple and unqualified, and therefore is reducible:' 17th November 1725, Muirhead's Representatives against Watson's Creditors, Sess. Pap. Adv. Lib.

In these two cases, then, although the deeds were reduced, the judgements really were in support of a simple conveyance by a bankrupt to his creditors; and accordingly, we find a case decided in 1726, in which the hypothetical judgements in these cases were confirmed. Wyndrum of Eymouth disponed his estate to a trustee, for behoof of all his creditors. Most of them, neglecting this conveyance, led adjudications; and, after the expiry of the year and day, a competition arose between the adjudgers, and those of the creditors who had relied on the disposition. The adjudgers sought to reduce the disposition on the act 1696; the other creditors maintained it to be beyond the reach of that law, and argued strongly upon their bona fides in trusting to it, and the hardship of cutting them entirely out of the competition. The Court sustained the disposition, and ranked the personal creditors and adjudgers pari passu: 15th July 1726, Competition of Eymouth's creditors, Sess. Pap. Adv. Lib.

Hitherto, the statute of 1696 had been thought inapplicable to the case of a fair and equal disposition by a debtor to his whole creditors, provided it was not clogged with any improper condition; but now, the tide began to set the other way. The first case, in which the change of opinion appeared, was in the competition of Barclay's creditors in January 1727. An estate was disponed to Barclay, under the burden of the disponer's debts. Barclay having become bankrupt, disponed this estate to trustees for his creditors. The trust-deed took no notice of the ancestor's cre-

 ditors,

ditors, and contained a submission by the creditors to arbiters of the bankrupt's nomination. Bell of Craigfordy, a creditor of the ancestor, proceeded to adjudge, and was strenuously opposed by Barclay's trustee. The Court supported the adjudication. This case, however, is too much involved in circumstances, to be considered as any thing more than an indication of the changing opinion of the Court. It was founded upon in the subsequent competition of Merchieston's creditors, two years afterwards; when the one party said, that the circumstances were so peculiar, as to take away the general question altogether: the other maintained, that there was no peculiarity, since the disposition in trust left to the creditors of the ancestor all their rights unimpaired, with full power to claim upon those rights before the arbiter as preferable; and that the decision proceeded entirely on the ground, that a creditor is entitled rather to entrust his rights to the law, than to the deed of his debtor.

But, whatever, may have been the ground of decision in Barclay's case, that of the next judgement upon the question was clear. A bankrupt having granted a disposition omnium bonorum, to his creditors; one of them, dissatisfied, proceeded to adjudge. This was opposed by the other creditors. But the Court found the trust-deed ineffectual to stop the adjudication. This judgement (as appears from the petition presented against it, on the part of the creditors), proceeded on these general grounds: That it is every creditor's privilege to take the assistance of the law, for enforcing and securing his debt: that he is not bound to accede to measures proposed by another, nor to entrust his affairs to one not of his own choosing, but is 'rei suæ moderator et arbiter;' and that Judges have no power to grant or to refuse diligence. It was against these, as the grounds of the decision, that the creditors directed their argument *; but it was unavailing. The Court

* They contended, that no man should be allowed obstinately to insist upon his own right, when only in æmulationem vicini. that, to sanction diligence in such a case, is, to involve all parties in destructive expences; whereas, the deed gives to the creditors themselves the whole management: that Judges do, and are entitled to interfere

Court refused the petition, without answers. January 1729, Cheyne against Merchieston's Creditors, I. Dict. 85. Sess. Pap. Adv. Lib.

A similar judgement was pronounced in the case of Snee & Co. against Anderson's trustee, in 1734. Bogle, as factor for Snee & Co., English creditors of Michael Anderson, raised a reduction of a trust-deed, made by him for behoof of his creditors. This reduction was, however, abandoned, as it proceeded upon a bond of corroboration, which was reduced, as falling under the act of 1696. But Bogle brought an action, and arrested; and the question was tried in a competition between the arrestment and the trust-deed. Lord Elchies, as Ordinary, took the cause to report. The general argument for the arresters was much the same as in the former cases; and certain peculiarities were objected, as, 1. That the trustees were named by the bankrupt himself: 2. That they were empowered to assume other creditors, and, as arbiters, to divide the funds, according to a scheme of division to be signed by them: 3. That the assignations of the debts, &c. due to the bankrupt, not being special, they could not be intimated; so that the creditors had no security against the bankrupt's privately taking up the money: 4. That the trustees were declared free from omissions: and, 5. That there was a declaration of forfeiture against any creditor proceeding to diligence. The answer of the creditors, upon the general question, was also similar to that urged in former cases. And as to the specialties, they said, that no trust-deed could be perfectly simple: that objectionable conditions may be challenged on the statute of 1621, not on that of 1696: that the grounds of challenge of such deeds are

fere in stopping the diligence of inhibition and arrestment, upon equitable grounds, and do not scruple to interfere in contests among annualrenters, adjudgers, pounders of the ground, &c. by sequestration: that the highest equity calls for an interruption to diligence here, since the creditors of a bankrupt are as people caught in a storm, who must give up a little, to preserve the whole; they constitute a society, and the estate is the debtor, the bankrupt nothing: that adjudication is a legal disposition, made by the Judge, upon the debtor's refusal to dispone, but here, there is no refusal, since the debtor has already disponed all.

are either in respect of undue preference, which proceeds upon the act 1696, or in respect of the injustice and hardship of the conditions imposed, which proceeds on the act 1621. But the mere existence of conditions, is no ground of objection; they must be unjust, which these are not: For, 1. the naming of the trustee here, is necessary to give form and effect to the deed; and the creditors are not prevented from changing him, if they think fit. 2. Instead of being empowered to assume other creditors, all that is done, is, to give the trustees a power of communicating the benefit of the deed to such creditors as may appear within a certain time, though they be not named in the deed; the time being limited, that things may be extricable. 3. The forfeiture, upon using diligence, is not reducible on the statute 1696, since it applies to all the creditors; but if it be illegal, it will be held pro non scripto, and 'utile per inutile non vitiatur.' 4. As to freedom from omissions, there have been none; and, besides, it is a clause necessary to induce trustees to accept.

The Court found the reasons of reduction relevant; and the case having been brought again under review, they 'adhered to 'their former judgement; and further found, that no disposition 'by a bankrupt debtor can disable creditors from doing diligence:' 12th July 1734, Snee & Co. against Anderson's trustee, I. Dict. 85. Sess. Pap. Adv. Lib.

A similar judgement was pronounced, 3d February 1736, in the case of the Earl of Aberdeen against Trustees for the Creditors of Blair. And the law, at this period, may be summed up in the words of Lord Kilkerran, who says, in his report of the case of Snodgrass, in 1744: 'The Lords have come and gone upon the question, how far, where one is bankrupt, in terms of 'the statute, he can, by a general disposition to his creditors, tie 'them up from after diligence? and, by the latest decisions, it is 'found that he cannot:' Kilk. 51.

Strongly, however, as the opinion seemed now to be fixed in favour of the application of the statute; yet, of six cases which

occurred

occurred in the thirty years which followed the judgement in the cases of Snee and of Blair's creditors, three were decided in the one way, and three in the other. It is worthy of inquiry, what peculiarities there were in these cases, that could occasion such changes of opinion.

In the first case, between the Trustee for the creditors of Jacksons and Alexander Simson, Jacksons having become bankrupt, their creditors proceeded with diligence, and carried off the greater part of their effects, a meeting was called, at which almost all the creditors, but Simson, appeared; and, at this meeting, the bankrupts executed a disposition of the remainder of their effects, to a trustee for all the creditors. The disposition was simple and unqualified; reserved the several rights and preferences of the creditors; enumerated them all; referred to a signed inventory of the effects; and contained none but the most common and ordinary clauses necessary for the execution of the trust. But there was one peculiarity in this case, which induced the Court to support the deed. All the creditors, except Simson, had begun diligence, by which they would unquestionably have affected the whole subject of the conveyance, to his utter exclusion; and having ceased their diligence only, upon this deed being granted, the deed, in reality, had given Simson an advantage, which otherwise he would not have enjoyed. In treating of the second branch of the statute of 1621 *, I had occasion to mention a case, in which a peculiarity of this kind occurred, and where the Court refused to sustain the challenge of a creditor, who had begun diligence before the deed challenged, because the person to whom the deed was granted, though later of beginning his diligence, had, at the date of the deed, made greater progress in acquiring a preference. I have not had an opportunity of seeing the papers in this case of Jackson's creditors, nor do I know whether that old decision was founded on; but it appears to me most likely, that the Court proceeded upon this ground in supporting the deed: 16th November 1757, II. Fac. Coll. 102.

In

* See above, p. 130

In the next case, the trust-deed was, consistently with the decision in Snee's case, cut down; although prepared at a meeting of the creditors, and although the trustees were named by the creditors themselves. It had been founded upon as a ground for stopping adjudications against the estate; but the Court refused to sustain it, decerned in the adjudication, and remitted to the several Lords Ordinary, before whom other adjudications against the debtor were depending, to decern also in them: 25th July 1759, John Forbes Leith & others against Livingston, II. Fac. Coll. cxciii. 346.

In two years afterwards, a trust-deed was supported, to the effect of preventing a creditor from arresting, although there appears, in the Faculty Collection, no mark of peculiarity in the case: 15th February 1762, Wilson against M'Vicar. But there was a very distinguishing peculiarity, upon which, in a great degree, the decision, I believe, proceeded. The son of the arresting creditor had attended at a full meeting, previous to the execution of the trust disposition, and tacitly acquiesced in a resolution, taken by that meeting, to follow common measures. This circumstance I learn from the papers in the subsequent case of Dr Heriot against Farquharson, trustee for Fairholme's creditors, in which a very full discussion took place, upon the question of accession to a trust-deed.

The next case which occurred was, that of Digges the comedian, in which it is easy to see a good reason for supporting the trust. Indeed, the judgement of the Court expresses it—' The ' Lords having considered the terms of the trust-disposition, the ' particular state of the fund assigned, depending entirely on the ' creditors acting in concert *, and David Bett's letter,' (agreeing that this was the only hope of getting payment) ' they prefer Mr ' Jameson the trustee, he being accountable to the whole creditors ' of Digges pari passu:' 16th Nov. 1763, Jamieson, trustee for the creditors of Digges, against Coutts Brothers & Co. III. Fac. Coll. cxx. 280.

With

* It was a conveyance of four guineas weekly, of Digges's salary as an actor.

With these deviations, all of which are easily accounted for, the Court, in 1764, returned to the judgement pronounced in Snee's case, and the others alluded to by Lord Kilkerran. Strachan made a trust-deed within sixty days of his bankruptcy; but one of his creditors chose rather to proceed with his diligence, than to accede to it. In a competition, the Court 'found the bankruptcy proven, reduced the disposition, and preferred the arrester:' 4th Nov. 1764, Mudie against Dickson & Mitchell, trustees for Strachan's creditors, III Fac. Coll. cxlix. 353.

Still the point was not ultimately fixed—doubts were entertained—there was much division of opinion on the Bench; and, upon a question of power, which the imperfection of the law, relative to diligence, made so truly important, it is not wonderful that many trials should have occurred; it is not surprising, that the opinions of our Judges should have fluctuated exceedingly, while the force of the statute on the one hand, and the sense of justice, and views of expediency on the other, must have operated strongly upon every mind. Lord Kames was not a man who could look unconcerned upon so interesting a question. In reporting the case of M'Kell against M'Lurg, in 1766, he takes occasion to remark, that 'every trust-deed by a bankrupt ought to be sustained, as far 'as to operate a division of the bankrupt's effects, equally and proportionally among his creditors.'—'That where such disposition 'is made, it remedies a gross defect in the bankrupt statutes, viz. 'permitting creditors to take, by force of legal execution, what 'they are not permitted to take by the bankrupt's voluntary deed.' And he goes on to remark, that 'it seems to be settled, that an insolvent person, who is not in the terms of either of the bankrupt 'statutes, has it in his power to do justice to all his creditors, by 'dividing his effects equally among them: And as it was never 'intended, by either of the bankrupt statutes, to bar the exercise 'of this equitable power, it is probable, that, when the principles 'of equity are better understood than at present, the Court will 'sustain every disposition of this kind, though even made by a notour bankrupt:' Kames, Sel. Dec. ccxlix. 321.

In 1767, a case occurred, in which, first, the Court of Session, *and afterwards the House of Lords, decided against the validity of* trust-deeds by bankrupts. In November 1763, Dunlop executed a trust-disposition; and, a few days afterwards, the trustees, to prevent undue preferences, officiously made him bankrupt in terms of law. This extraordinary caution proved fatal to the deed; for Peters, a creditor, taking advantage of it, raised an action for his debt, and arrested on the dependance. In the forthcoming, the trustees appeared, and were preferred; but Peters immediately raised a reduction of the trust deed, and had it conjoined with the forthcoming. The Lord Ordinary pronounced this judgement: 'In respect it is not 'denied, that the conveyance to the trustees was granted after James 'Dunlop became bankrupt, for the behoof of his creditors, and that 'the Messrs Peters are neither parties, nor have acceded to it, they 'are not thereby barred from the benefit of their diligence; there-'fore, alters the former interlocutor, and prefers them upon their 'arrestment,' &c. In the argument, the expediency and justice of such deeds was insisted upon on the one hand; and, on the other, the experience of their inutility; and Snee's case and Mudie's were founded on as decisive. 'The Lords adhered to the 'Lord Ordinary's interlocutor.' And the judgement was affirmed upon appeal: 27th Jan. 1767, T. & A. Peters against Spiers & Blackbourn, trustees for Dunlop's creditors, IV. Fac. Coll. lviii. 98; Appeal Cases, 18th Dec. 1767.

Five years prior, then, to the sequestration law, this judgement was settled—that imperfect and ruinous to those concerned, as the power of acquiring preferences at common law then was; although it was impossible, by any means, but by a trust-deed, to attain any thing like equality among the creditors doing diligence; although a bankruptcy was almost necessarily a scene of horrible confusion, of monstrous extravagance and expence in diligence, and of most shameful contests for priority; yet no trust deed could be effectual, even to the extent of vesting the funds in the creditors, and putting a stop to diligence, if the grantor was rendered bankrupt within the sixty days. In one view, the sequestration law might be expected to strengthen this opinion, with regard to vo-

luntary

luntary trust-deeds; since the hardship of the reduction of a trust-deed was much decreased, the other creditors having it now in their power, by applying for sequestration, to bring all to an equality. But, in another view, the individual creditors had not so strong an interest to insist in the reduction, since they were now deprived of that preference for which they had formerly to strive. We have seen, that by the later statutes, the Legislature, in restricting the remedy of sequestration to mercantile cases, has provided against the worst of those evils, which trust-deeds were intended to avoid, by making the equality of diligence, in all cases, to depend upon the bankruptcy itself. I do not know any case, in which the effect of the statute of 1696, upon a trust-deed, has been tried, since the introduction of these laws; and shall only observe, that, in the case of Hutcheson against Gibson, 8th December 1791, it was taken for granted incidentally, that, had the act of 1696 applied, the trust-deed would have been reducible.

This long deduction may be summed up, then, in these three propositions:

1. That a debtor, merely insolvent, but not bankrupt, and against whose person or estate no diligence has been begun, may grant a trust-right for the benefit of all his creditors equally, to the effect of vesting his funds in them; so that, if completed before the diligence of any of the creditors, and if he shall not be rendered bankrupt within the sixty days, it will be effectual and preferable.

2. That if diligence have been begun by any of the creditors, which, if completed, would attach the estate, it cannot be defeated by any such trust-deed.

3. That if the debtor be rendered bankrupt, according to the directions of the act 1696, c. 5. he cannot, by any trust-deed, how-

ever simple or unqualified, tie up the hands of his creditors from diligence.

II. Hitherto, we have considered the trust-deed merely in the view of its vesting the estate in the creditors, so as to prevent partial preferences on the one hand, and expensive steps of diligence on the other. But the dangers of partial preferences, and of a ruinous concourse of diligence, although the most prominent, are not the only evils which a trust-deed is fitted to prevent. We have seen, that, prior to the sequestration law, there were no proper means for distributing the funds of a bankrupt, and, at present, for cases beyond the reach of that law, the means of distribution are expensive and tedious. It was, therefore, not unnatural, to attempt, by means of trust-deeds, to supply this defect also; by making the trustee the distributor of the estate, by bestowing upon him the powers of an arbiter, and so rendering unnecessary all judicial proceedings, and by adding such other regulations and conditions, as might secure the recovery and distribution of the estate, and the discharge of the debtor, when the funds should be divided. But, however defective the common law might be, these are powers, with which it would be in the highest degree dangerous to intrust a bankrupt or insolvent debtor, and, although the Court has supported simple trust-deeds, vesting the funds in the creditors, or in a trustee for their behoof, where neither of the two statutes apply, they have never held it among the legal powers of a debtor, in any situation, to impose such conditions upon his creditors. Lord Kames, in reporting the case of M'Kell, says, 'In 'this case, the Court had no occasion to determine, whether creditors are bound to submit to the management of trustees named 'by their insolvent debtor. A bankrupt may and ought to convey 'to his creditors his whole effects for their payment; but he cannot legally bind them down to any particular form of management, whether by trustees or otherwise: Therefore, every trust-'deed of this kind, when brought under reduction, whether upon 'the bankrupt statutes, or upon common law, ought to be reduced,

'as

'as far as concerns the bankrupt's nomination of trustees: but, on 'the other hand, any such trust-deed ought to be sustained, as far 'as to operate a division of the bankrupt's effects, equally and 'proportionally among his creditors. The reason is, that neither 'by the bankrupt statutes, nor by the common law, can there ly 'any objection against a disposition by a bankrupt to his whole 'creditors nominatim, nor against a disposition to a single person 'for behoof of the whole creditors; the person being named, not 'as a trustee, to manage for the creditors independent of them, 'but merely as a name, to hold the subject for the creditors:' Kames, Sel. Dec. p. 321.

To descend to particulars, seems to be almost unnecessary. There is no doubt, that even the nomination of the trustee, is a power which belongs, not to the debtor, but to the creditors themselves, who have the true and radical right in the fund: And if the deed should be executed privately, (perhaps with a view of preventing alarm, till the sixty days elapse), the trustee named may be rejected by the creditors, and another chosen in his room: See Kilk. 52. 54. If the creditors cannot agree in the choice of a trustee, it will naturally be the business of the person named in the trust-deed, considering himself as the legal holder of the fund, to raise an action of multiplepoinding, in which the creditors may be forced to appear; and the Court may sequestrate the estate under the common law, and name a factor, accountable under the rules of Court, which have already been explained.

CHAP.

CHAP. II.

Of the Manner in which the Creditors are to Secure themselves against Non-accession, and of the Nature and Proof of Accession.

When creditors are assembled, to deliberate upon the propriety of following common measures, the subject of their deliberation naturally divides itself into these two questions: 1. Whether ought the creditors to agree to the superseding of individual diligence, and the vesting of the estate in a trustee for the common behoof? And, 2dly, Whether ought they to leave the distribution of the funds so vested, to the legal processes of ranking and sale, multiplepoinding, &c. or ought they to settle a plan of private and extrajudicial distribution? These questions are very different, in point of prudence, and never ought to be confounded. A creditor will often be willing to forego any probable chance of preference, which, by standing out, he might, after an expensive struggle, be able to acquire, for the consideration, that all the rest forego their chance likewise. But he will have much more hesitation in agreeing to delegate to a trustee, even though superintended by a committee of the creditors, the extraordinary powers which are necessary to supersede the judicial processes of division. It may be proper to follow this obvious distinction, in treating of this subject—to consider, in the first place, what is necessary and safe, in respect to the superseding of diligence and renunciation of all individual attempts to acquire preferences; and afterwards, to consider the question of distribution.

§ 1.

§ 1. OF THE RENUNCIATION OF INDIVIDUAL DILIGENCE.

I. It sometimes happens, that a person, conscious of his insolvency, and fearful lest the vindictive or anxious disposition of some of his creditors should interrupt any plan of voluntary trust, and open the funds to a destructive torrent of diligence, has fortitude enough to call his friends together secretly, before his condition is known, and, by their advice, to execute a simple trust-deed in favour of his whole creditors. If this be done before any creditor have begun diligence against the debtor, and if the deed can be completed by seisine in the heritable property, and by the traditions and intimations necessary to carry a right to the moveables, and the execution of it can be kept secret for sixty days, so that no creditor can take measures for laying it open to a challenge on the statute of 1696, c. 5. the debtor may meet his creditors with confidence; convince them that separate diligence is out of the question; and leave it to their determination, whether the distribution shall be made at law, or privately.

II. But it is not often that things are managed in this way. It commonly happens, that a meeting is called, to which the debtor lays open his situation, and offers to convey every thing to trustees named by the creditors. The propriety of agreeing to such a proposal, and concurring in common measures, is, of course, to be judged of from the circumstances of each case; but it may be proper to consider, what are the dangers which creditors have to fear; and how a debtor, or his friends, anxious to get them to agree in common measures, are to give them satisfaction against every possible chance of danger. We have already seen, in the first chapter, that there are only two cases, in which it is possible for individuals to persist in separate measures, so as to destroy the effect of a simple trust for behoof of the creditors; either where a creditor has, under the statute 1621, c. 18, a right to persist in diligence once begun, or where the trust-deed is objectionable, on the statute 1696, c. 5.

1. Let

1. Let us take first the supposition, that there is no creditor, who, at the time of the meeting, has a right to object on either of the statutes; the question is, how are the creditors to be satisfied of this?

To give any creditor a right of challenge, on the second branch of 1621, c. 18, these things are necessary: 1. That he shall have begun diligence, which, if carried on to completion, will effectually attach the funds; and, 2. That the diligence shall not have been unreasonably and improperly delayed. These points we have already considered, in commenting upon this statute, (p. 118. & seq.) Now, in order to afford complete satisfaction, (though, in practice, creditors do not proceed so very circumspectly), it may be necessary to produce searches of diligence against the property. The cases, in which settlements of this kind are most frequently proposed, and in which they are chiefly necessary, are those of landed proprietors, whose moveable property is comparatively of little consequence. Perfect satisfaction may be given with regard to the heritable estate; since all diligence against it, must appear, either in the register of inhibitions, or in the register of abbreviates of adjudication; * or in the minute-book of the Court of Session, where every first adjudication must be entered, in order to be effectual; or in the signet-rolls, where all letters of inhibition, not yet recorded in the register of inhibitions, must appear. A search of these records, will at once bring to the knowledge of the creditors, any diligence which can be a ground for challenging the trust, on the statute of 1621, and thus set their minds at ease with respect to the dangers which they might otherwise dread from this quarter. Searches of diligence against moveables, where the moveable fund appears to be of sufficient importance, though not susceptible of the same complete check, may

* In one case, recourse would be necessary to the Sheriff-court; viz where there had been room for adjudications contra hereditatem jacentem. See above, p 264.

may yet be made sufficiently satisfactory for all the purposes of such a transaction. If arrestments and poindings were required to be registered, as under the act of sederunt of 1754, the check might be complete. As things are, it cannot be difficult to trace, in the signet-rolls, or in the record of the jurisdiction where the fund lies, any diligence of importance which may have been begun.

The creditors are next to be satisfied, that there is no objection competent upon the statute 1696, c. 5. This is a matter of considerable importance; for, if the trust-deed be liable to challenge on that statute, the heritable estate of the debtor is open to the diligence of adjudication, and the rents to that of arrestment; while the moveable estate may be carried off by arrestment and poinding. If the creditors be satisfied, that, at the time of the meeting, the debtor is not bankrupt, and at the same time convinced, that no diligence has been begun against the heritable estate, they need not (in so far as that estate at least is concerned) be under any apprehension, but may wait calmly, to see whether any creditor shall proceed, within sixty days of the trust-deed, to make the debtor bankrupt. Should this be done, they can then proceed to take the proper steps for securing themselves against preferences, since the term of the pari passu preference in adjudications, is long enough to afford them full time for doing so. If the debtors be possessed of any moveable funds of importance, the creditors cannot be secured by a search of diligence, showing that the debtor is not bankrupt at the time of the meeting; for, if any diligence has been used to attach those funds, they will be completely opened to its operation, by rendering the debtor bankrupt within sixty days after the execution of the trust-deed. A search of diligence against moveables should therefore, in strictness, be required to satisfy the creditors, that they run no risk by waiting for the completion of the term necessary to validate the trust-deed. If no diligence against moveables has been executed prior to the completion of the trust-deed, then the creditors may rest in security till the sixty days expire; for if the debtor be not, within that time, rendered bankrupt, the trust-deed will be preferable; and, if he be, the creditors

ditors have still four months in which to provide for the pari passu preference.

Now, to obtain satisfaction with respect to the debtor's freedom from that diligence, which law has appointed as the criterion of bankruptcy, is sometimes attended with difficulty. The debtor must himself know, in general, the steps of diligence that have been used against him, but, in some cases, his information must be received with caution. One absolute security there is, that no man can be rendered bankrupt, without a horning denounced against him appearing in the record of hornings, since that is necessary previous to caption *. If any denounced horning shall appear in the register, the creditor who holds the diligence can be easily traced, and a certificate from him may be obtained, in evidence that the debtor has not been rendered bankrupt on his diligence.

2. But let us now vary the supposition, and take the case, that there are creditors entitled to challenge the trust-deed, how are the acceding creditors to secure themselves against them, and take away all interest, on their part, to stand out?

Where the danger arises from the act 1621 alone, as only those creditors, who have begun diligence before the trust-deed, can move the objection, the creditors can easily satisfy themselves, how far this danger extends; and, in trying to get quit of it, they have this alternative: 1. If the estate be heritable, and adjudication have been begun, the creditors have a year, within which they may come in upon a footing of equality; and in the case of moveables, if the diligence be not yet completed, or if it have been completed so lately, that the other creditors, by rendering the debtor bankrupt,

* Unless he has been under personal protection. A Peer, or member of the House of Commons, or one judicially protected, or within the Sanctuary, may be made bankrupt by a charge of horning, (without denunciation), followed by poinding, or adjudication, or arrestment unloosed for fourteen days In such cases, the signet rolls will show the horning, and recourse must be had for evidence to the holder of the diligence

bankrupt, can subject it to the *pari passu* preference of the act 1793; they will have a shorter term, it is true, but one which will probably be sufficient for bringing themselves to the same level. He will be a very unreasonable creditor, who refuses, in either of these cases, to settle upon the same terms of preference which the statutes allow to the creditor who first does diligence; but, if he cannot be brought into the general measure, it will then remain for the acceding creditors to consider, whether they should not take steps for adjudging the estate, in the one case, and for rendering the debtor bankrupt, and constituting their debts, in the other. 2. If the diligence be completed beyond the reach of the pari passu preferences of the statutes of 1661 and 1793, the creditors must submit to the preference, and can do themselves no good by refusing to accede, more than if no such creditor were in the field.

Where the danger arises from the act 1696, that is to say, where the debtor has already been made bankrupt, it is in the power of every creditor, whose debt existed prior to the trust-deed, to challenge that deed, and to proceed at any time with diligence. In such a case, then, a trust-deed can afford no absolute security to the creditors; for if the non-acceding creditors choose to adjudge, the others must adjudge also, unless they can accommodate matters; and, as to moveable diligence, should the four months be allowed to expire after the debtor's bankruptcy, the old law of preference by priority takes place, and any creditor who has not acceded, may proceed with diligence, beyond the reach of interruption.

The expence and confusion of attempts, thus to guard against preferences, often induce creditors to rely upon the appearance of unanimity, and to allow the term given by law, for establishing equality, to expire unused. In this way, it not unfrequently happens, that creditors find themselves involved in questions with individuals, who choose insidiously to ly by till this advantage is secured, and then suddenly proceed with their diligence, in order to seize a preference, which, by attention, the other creditors might have prevented. The acceding creditors have now no resource, unless they can show, that the creditors who thus strive for a preference, have, by their own conduct, barred their right of challenge.

In considering what circumstances shall be deemed an accession, strong enough to bar a creditor's right of challenging a trust-deed, it will not be forgotten, that, on the one hand, the only effect of holding a creditor to have acceded to a simple trust, is, that he is prevented from acquiring a preference, and that the equality is maintained among creditors, which it is the object of all bankrupt laws to establish; while, on the other, a very serious loss is suffered by the general body of creditors, deceived, by a seeming acquiescence, into a neglect of those measures which might have protected them against preferences. At common law, a person who, by acts of homologation or acquiescence, leads others to believe that he holds a contract as effectual, and, on the faith of this, to alter their circumstances, is held bound: 17th November 1779, Lombe against Scott; 7th January 1752, Gordon against Drummond, Kilk. 341.—Of such a plea, creditors, in the situation which we are now considering, are well entitled to avail themselves. They suffer by the acquiescence of the creditor, against whom they might, if put upon their guard, have easily protected themselves. But it is a question, not without difficulty, what circumstances shall be held to infer this kind of acquiescence? There are only three cases, which appear in our books, upon this subject: that of Wilson, trustee for Baillie's creditors, against Niel M'Vicar, in 1762—that of Dr Heriot against Fairholme's creditors, in 1766—and a late case, Croll's trustees against Robertson, in 1791.

In the first of these cases, Robert Baillie, merchant in Edinburgh, having become bankrupt, a very numerous meeting of his creditors was held, at which it was resolved to concur in common measures. At this meeting, the son of Neil M'Vicar, a creditor, attended as agent for his father, and tacitly acquiesced in the general resolution. * In consequence of this resolution, a trust-deed was executed by Baillie, in favour of a trustee for his creditors; and the trustee entered to possession. M'Vicar having afterwards proceeded to do diligence, a competition arose between him and the trustee. The Court preferred the trustee, and found that M'-Vicar was not entitled to be preferred upon his diligence: 18th February 1762. In the subsequent case of Dr Heriot, in which M'Vicar's was much canvassed, it was stated, as the ground of that decision, that the Court held the son to have attended as agent for his father, that the silence was deceitful; and that, having amused the meeting by a seeming acquiescence, M'Vicar was barred, personali exceptione, from disturbing the equality established by the trust-deed.

In the case of Dr Heriot, a great complication of circumstances was founded upon in support of the personal exception. On the bankruptcy of Messrs Thomas & Adam Fairholmes, who carried on business as merchants and bankers, to a great extent, in Edinburgh, a trust-deed was executed in favour of the late Mr Farquharson, for behoof of all the creditors, with power to dispose of the property, and divide the proceeds among the creditors according to their rights and interests. The trustee was also declared liable only for actual intromissions. This deed was accepted of by the trustee, and great diligence used in getting it intimated to the debtors of the bankrupts. A meeting was called, and the trust-deed communicated to the creditors present; but the matter was referred to a fuller meeting, as the creditors had not had time to determine what they should do. The second meeting was very full; and a deed of accession, containing a submission to the trustee, and supersedere of diligence, having been proposed, and read over, it was agreed to, without any dissentient voice. A minute to this purpose was signed by the preses of the meeting; and the deed lay for the signatures of the creditors. Dr Heriot never signed

* This circumstance is entirely omitted in the Faculty Collection. It is, on the contrary, stated there, 'That he had neither acceded to joint measures, nor to the 'trust disposition.' III Fac. Coll. lxxx. 177.

signed the deed of accession; but the circumstances from which his accession was inferred by the creditors, were these—That Dr Heriot, being at London, wrote thus to his agent here—'I expect 'you'll exert yourself for me, with the rest of the creditors, so 'as to come in, share and share alike, according to the nature of 'my debt:'—That the agent having reported to Dr Heriot the nature of the trust-deed, and the propriety of following common measures, he wrote to him—'I impower you to act for me in the 'best manner you can, jointly with the rest of the creditors, 'which is all I apprehend we can do now.' And again—'I shall 'agree to your signing the deed of accession for me, with the rest 'of the majority of the creditors, or any thing else which they 'may deem for the good of the whole concerned:'—That the agent attended the meeting, at which the resolution to accede was expressed without dissenting: That he, in consequence of advertisements issued by the trustee, lodged the Doctor's claim and grounds of debt; and that the Doctor himself, when he came down to Edinburgh, attended a meeting concerning the connexion of the English and Scotish Companies, without intimating any dissent from the common measures. The Court was clear, that Dr Heriot was not bound by the deed of accession, but that he was barred from taking separate measures. It was observed from the Bench, that, in a question of this kind, a Court is at liberty to consider the nature and effect of the contract to which the creditor is said to have acceded: that the circumstances, from which accession is attempted to be inferred, will naturally be taken with more scruple, if the contract said to have been acceded to, is attended with hardship: that, here, the only effect of the contract was to introduce equality among the creditors, and to prevent unjust preferences: that, if Dr Heriot had fairly said, at first, or given notice, at least, before proceeding with his diligence, other creditors might have taken measures for their own security; but that, having lulled them into security, and made them believe that he was an acceding creditor, he was not afterwards entitled to pursue separate measures: 27th June 1766, Heriot against Farquharson, trustee for Fairholme's creditors.

The

The case of Croll's trustees, is thus stated in the 4th volume of the Dictionary: 'Accession to a trust was found sufficiently 'proved, by the creditor having attended a roup of the bankrupt's 'effects, called by the trustees, bought several articles, and given 'his bill, payable to the trustees, for the price; though the cre-'ditor contended, that he had openly expressed his disapproba-'tion of the trust, and that, seeing the bankrupt himself at the 'roup, he conceived it was held solely under his authority: 7th 'May 1791, Trustees of Croll against Robertson,' IV. Dict. 160.

§ 2. OF ACCESSION TO THE PLAN OF PRIVATE DISTRIBUTION.

The delay and expence of proceedings at law, in dividing the funds, are not nearly so formidable as those which accompany the attempts of individuals to acquire, or to prevent, preferences. Still, they are very great; and it is much the interest of creditors to avoid them, if possible, by the settling of a beneficial plan of private distribution. But, to the accomplishment of this object, delegations of so important a kind are necessary, that creditors do not always agree. In particular, unless the trustee, or some other person in whom the creditors have confidence, be made the arbiter and judge of their claims, and of their preferences, the plan of private distribution cannot proceed. But such an agreement as this, and such a delegation of power, is not lightly to be presumed. Hardly, indeed, would it appear, that any thing short of an express and written accession should be strong enough to bind a creditor to conditions so extraordinary. The Court have always held the distinction between the accession necessary in this case, and that which is sufficient to bar a creditor from taking separate measures, as very different. In the above case of Dr Heriot against Fairholme's creditors, the Court found, that 'there 'was sufficient evidence that Dr Heriot did accede to the trust-'right and disposition granted by Messrs Fairholmes to their cre-'ditors; but found no evidence that he acceded to the deed of ac-

'cession

'cession relative to the said trust-deed, or that he is bound there-
'by:' 27th June 1766.

But, at the same time, there may be cases of this, as of every other contract, in which accession will be inferred from circumstances. These are cases, in which the general creditors, or particular individuals, have been induced to forego an advantage, for the sake of gaining the benefit of the accession, and in which, consequently, things are no longer entire. Thus, it sometimes happens, that the friends of the bankrupt have such confidence in him, or such interest in his welfare, as to agree to relinquish securities, or to forego the opportunity of doing diligence, in order to procure the consent of the rest to an amicable settlement. Creditors who hear, and acquiesce in this proposal at a meeting, and who take partial benefit, as by drawing dividends under the concert proceeding on it, would scarcely be entitled to plead, that the deed of accession had not been subscribed by them.

No person can review the difficulties, which, on all hands, surround those who are anxious to attain an easy and economical distribution by private trust, and to avoid tedious and expensive proceedings at law, without regreting deeply the necessity of restricting the sequestration to mercantile cases, and wishing, at least, that it could be possible to devise some method of preventing the confusion and disturbance which are at present incident to all plans of private distribution. When the situation of a landed gentleman, who finds his circumstances involved, is considered, this will appear in its true colours. He is willing, perhaps, to constitute a trust for behoof of his creditors, in the reasonable expectation of saving, by such a plan, the wreck of his fortune, and avoiding the disgrace of legal proceedings, continued for years in a public court. The generality of his creditors are, perhaps, convinced of the prudence of such a plan, and of the mutual benefit to be derived from it to all concerned; but some vindictive or timorous creditor, without taking the trouble of coolly examining the subject, or incapable of sympathy, perhaps, with a gentleman reduced to distress,

distress, insists on what he calls the 'plain beaten path of the law.' What is the consequence? Instead of the estate being at once vested in a trustee elected by the creditors—instead of its being quickly sold, the price recovered, and a dividend paid—instead of the creditors receiving their money quickly, and the debtor having the comfort of seeing the confusion dissipating, and his creditors paid—the alarm is taken, the unanimity of the creditors is dissolved, and each rushes forward with his adjudication, accumulating enormous expence, to the benefit of the practitioners of the law, but to the ruin of all besides. Even that fund, which, if prudently managed, would have paid every fraction of the debt, is encroached upon; while the unfortunate debtor himself is left, with his family, miserable and helpless, amidst the general confusion. Even if the debtor should have been so fortunate as to complete his trust conveyance beyond the reach of objection or competition, still, in the tedious and expensive discussion of an intricate ranking in the Court, his chance of reversion is lost, while he is kept a hanger on for years, with all the terrors of personal diligence impending over him.

Similar evils, though in a less degree, are experienced with regard to the moveable estate. A pari passu preference is indeed eſtablished; but, without concurrence in common measures, equality is to be attained only by a most expensive accumulation of legal proceedings.

I hope for excuse, if a view of this situation should lead me to any presumptuous suggestion of improvements. But it seems to me, that much relief might be given in such cases, without any wide departure from the course and principles of the present law. To facilitate the adoption of plans of private distribution, it is only necessary to remove the interest which individual creditors may have to persist in separate measures, and to protect those, who are willing to accede, from the danger of partial preferences.

Even if the Legislature were to declare an action of ranking and sale to have the effect of a general adjudication, as of the date of the citation,

citation, the acceding creditors could at once remove many of the obstacles to the acceptance of the trust, so far as respected heritable property. But perhaps something more might be done safely. The statutes of 1621 and 1696 were intended merely to prevent fraudulent preferences, and not to stand as obstacles in the way of that equality which it should be the object of all bankrupt laws to establish. There would be no dangerous novelty, therefore, in declaring, that a fair trust-deed, unqualified with conditions, but intended merely for vesting the estate in a trustee for the general benefit of the creditors, according to their respective interests at its completion, should not be challengeable upon either of these statutes. The necessary effect of this would be, that if the creditors could not agree in any plan of private distribution, at least a debtor, willing to do justice, would not be reduced to the unfortunate condition of beholding his creditors striving for preferences, and dissipating, in idle disputes, the only fund from which they could expect their payment.

But as a debtor might be enabled, with such a power as this exclusively in his person, to stand upon terms with his creditors, it might perhaps be expedient, to open up to the creditors a judicial process similar to sequestration, modified according to the wisdom of the Legislature; by which a stop should at once be put to all individual attempts to acquire preferences; leaving the distribution to be made by the common legal processes, or by extrajudicial operation, as the creditors should agree upon.

Some such provisions would seem to promise the introduction of a mild spirit of forbearance and moderation, in the discussion of all proposals for private distribution; and could not fail to be beneficial to all concerned. No creditor could have any interest to refuse his accession to common measures, since his hopes of acquiring preference by separate diligence would be extinguished. None could fear unknown dangers, since the vesting of the estate in the trustee, for the common behoof, would be proof against all attempts at inequality.

CHAP.

CHAP. III.

Of the Trust-Deed, and Deed of Accession.

Having considered what are the powers of the debtor in making an unchallengeable trust-deed for the benefit of his creditors; and how the objection is to be done away, where the deed is exposed to challenge, we have only to observe a few of the leading features of such an arrangement. In order to take the most simple view of the principles by which the doctrine of trust-rights is regulated, it may be proper to consider the conveyance of the estate, and the plan of management and distribution, separately. The one is properly the object of the trust-deed—the other is to be accomplished by a deed of accession.

§ 1. Of the Trust-Deed.

I shall, in treating of this subject, disregard altogether the objections that may be competent on the statutes of 1621 or 1696, and take the question, on the supposition that these statutes do not apply, or that the objections competent upon them have been renounced. The object of inquiry is, What are the objects to be attained by a trust-deed? and, how are these to be safely accomplished?

The great object of the trust-conveyance plainly is, to convert the debtor's estate into a fund, peculiar to those who already have claims against him, and divisible among them equally, according to their respective rights. This complex object includes the following particulars: 1. The estate must be secured in such a manner to the creditors, as to prevent the debtor from selling it for a price, which he may dissipate to their prejudice: 2. The creditors must be stopped from contentions about preferences: and 3. The debtor must be so far divested of his property, that no future creditor of his can claim a share with those for whose benefit the trust is intended. These objects are to be attained only by the force of deeds; for we have already seen, that bankruptcy alone has no effect in annihilating a debtor's powers as proprietor, or preventing him from selling his property; nor in stopping the diligence of creditors; nor in debarring those who shall afterwards become creditors, from claiming a share of the funds.

By what kind of a deed then is it, that these effects are to be produced? and how is that deed to be completed and made effectual? These are questions, which an inattention to principle sometimes involves in obscurity, but which do not seem to be attended with much real difficulty.

1. That a deed, conceived in the form of a conveyance directly to the creditors, by name, vests the real right of property in their persons, as joint proprietors pro indiviso, is a position which admits of no question: Kilk. 518. But the danger of mistakes in names, or in the method of disponing to those holding, as heirs, &c. the right of the original creditor *, and the difficulty of remembering each creditor, where there are many, condemn this as an improper method of vesting an estate voluntarily in creditors. The preferable way, and that which is in common use, is, to convey the estate to a trustee for the behoof of the grantor's creditors, according to their respective rights and interests. These trust-deeds sometimes contain a particular enumeration of the creditors,

* Kilkerran, 503.

ditors, and a specification of the amount of their debts; with a declaration, that these shall not be exclusive of fair creditors, nor restrictive of the amount of the debts. But, such enumeration is not to be held as essential to the constitution of an effectual trust-deed, for the accomplishment of the purposes already explained. The debtor is fully denuded, by a conveyance legally completed in favour of a trustee, for uses and purposes. He has indeed the faculty still remaining in his person, of calling the trustee to account, after the purposes of the conveyance are executed; and this reversionary right his future creditors may attach; but he has no power of recalling the trust, nor can any one coming in his place have a right of touching the property, till those purposes have been fulfilled. From this it follows, that the debtor cannot sell the property—that no future creditor can affect it—and that those who are already creditors, must, when they take the benefit of the trust, take it with its qualifications, each being entitled to a share, according to the rights already constituted in his person

A trust-deed, whether it enumerate the creditors and their debts, or express only, in general, the trust to be for selling the estate, and dividing it among the creditors, cannot be held to constitute a real burden upon the estate in favour of the individual creditors, whatever may be its effect on the debts in point of succession. Although it might seem to be much safer for the creditors, that their debts were thus constituted as real burdens upon the estate, it will be remembered, how inconsistent this would be with the easy and quick disposal of the estate, for the purpose of distributing the price; how infinitely preferable it is, to have the whole right delegated to a trustee, with powers to sell, under a declaration that the purchaser shall have no concern with the application of the price. And as for dangers from unfaithfulness, they are easily to be prevented, by a prudent choice of a trustee, or by requiring caution from him. The Court have accordingly held, that it is not the purpose of a trust-deed for creditors, even where the creditors are named, and their debts specified, to make the debts

real

real burdens on the estate, but only to enable the creditors to turn the estate into money, and to obtain payment out of the price; there being no difference between such a case, and that of a simple general conveyance to trustees, with power to sell, and apply the price in payment of certain debts, of which a list is given to the trustee. Upon this opinion the Court proceeded, in the case of M'-Ewan against Thomson, 18th June 1793, where the question respected the succession to one of the debts enumerated in a trust-deed for creditors. *

2. Such being the nature and effect of the trust-deed for creditors, the next question is, How the right of the trustee is to be completed, and the debtor denuded of all right? Where the estate is heritable, seisine must pass in favour of the trustee, in order to divest the debtor, to stop him from alienating; to prevent preferences by diligence; or to exclude future creditors. Where there is a moveable estate, the right of the trustee must be completed by tradition of the corporeal subjects, and by intimation of the assignation or conveyance to those indebted to the truster. The competition between the trustee, as representing the general body of the creditors, and any individual who shall have proceeded to separate measures, must be regulated by the date of completion of the trust conveyance.

It has been sometimes doubted, whether a trust-deed requires acceptance, in order to make it effectual? 1. There may indeed be

* A decision to this effect had been pronounced in the ranking of M'Kenzie of Redcastle's creditors; but the case was not without specialties The trust-deed was declared to be for the purpose of paying certain debts, enumerated in a list, which was subscribed by the grantor, as relative to the trust-deed, and ordered to be registered along with the infeftment The trustees were infeft, and the list was recorded along with the seisine. The trust deed contained a power to the trustees of giving it up, which they having done, the estate was brought to judicial sale In the ranking, a preference was claimed by the creditors in the list; but the Court, 'in respect the debts were not rendered 'real burdens on the lands by the trust-right, and in respect that the trust-right has 'been given up, and abandoned,' found that the trust-creditors were entitled to no preference. 27th January 1791.

be some doubt, where the trust-deed is qualified with any condition to which the creditors are, by acceptance, to be held as bound, whether the trust be effectual, till accepted by the creditors. But we are here considering the case of a simple unconditional trust, to which no objection on the statutes applies, or where it has been renounced. 2. The acceptance of the trustee does not seem to be absolutely necessary. The essential purpose of the trust is for the benefit of the creditors; and theirs is the radical interest, which a court will not suffer to be defeated by the will of the trustee. His name will, I apprehend, be sufficient to support the conveyance, even where there is no substitution of trustees; and the analogy of the cases of Dallas against Leishman, 21st November 1710, II. Fount 599.; and Campbell against Lord Monzie, 26th June 1752, Kilk. 518., seem strongly to support this conclusion. In the former of these cases, a person had filled up his friend's name in a bond, as his trustee, without his knowledge; and the Court found him under an obligation of denuding, when required: And in the latter, the trustees in a mortification having failed, the Court found, that the mortification did not fall or become void, but that it was competent to the Court to nominate and appoint persons to carry on the trust.

I do not mean to enter here into the several conditions and minutiæ of trust-deeds. I aim only at a general indication of the leading principles by which the detail is to be regulated. It is common to insert in the trust-deed, among the provisions and conditions, the declarations of uses and purposes, the general outlines of the trustee's powers of management, disposal and distribution. Perhaps the better and the simpler way is, to keep the trust-deed as general as possible; to qualify the trustee's right with the general obligation of paying off the grantor's creditors, according to their respective rights and preferences, established at the completion of the trust-right; and to declare, among the uses and purposes of the trust, that those special regulations, which the creditors shall, by their deed of accession, establish, shall be binding on the trustee, and be held the regulators of his powers and duties. To

prevent

prevent confusion and interruption in the management and sale of the estate, it is generally declared, that purchasers from the trustee shall have no concern with the application of the price; and that a discharge from the trustee for the price shall be sufficient, without requiring conveyances from the creditors themselves.

When a trust-deed is simple, and unclogged with conditions, it is effectual in preventing preferences, and protecting the creditors against future debts or alienations, even should no deed of accession be agreed to; and should it be necessary to carry on the distribution judicially, by bringing a multiplepoinding into Court in the name of the trustee.

§ 2. OF THE DEED OF ACCESSION.

The great purpose of the deed of accession, is, to settle a plan of management, disposal, and distribution of the estate; and as no creditor can be bound by the extraordinary conditions which are necessary for accomplishing such a purpose, without his own consent; so, the deed of accession must, on the other hand, be considered as a mutual contract, by the terms and conditions of which, no creditor is bound, till the rest have acceded.

As I have not ventured to descend to particulars in treating of the trust-deed, neither shall I pretend to enter here into the minute discussion of all the arrangements necessary for regulating the management and disposal of the estate, or for accomplishing the extrajudicial distribution of a bankrupt estate. They are to be found digested in almost every form of a private trust-deed and deed of accession. They seem to be reducible to these heads.

1. The power of arbitration, either to the trustee, or to some one chosen by the creditors, to determine their claims and their preferences. Without this, it is plain that judicial proceedings are scarcely to be avoided. The deed of accession includes, with this view, a proper submission, by which the creditors mutually bind

bind themselves to submit to the final sentence and decree-arbitral of the trustee, or whoever else shall be chosen; and the clause of registration, bearing a consent to the registration also of the decree-arbitral, gives it the full efficacy and force of a judgement by a court of law.

2. The powers of management and sale, are generally regulated in the deed of accession; and a committee of advice is named to act along with the trustee, if that be thought necessary.

3. In respect to the dividends, there is sometimes a provision that they shall be made within a determinate time; and a power is given of calling upon the trustee, at the end of that period, to denude of his trust, if a dividend shall appear to have been unduly delayed.

4. The creditors generally consent to a supersedere of diligence; or they consent to delegate their power over the debtor's person to the trustee.

5. Sometimes the creditors agree, that, after a fixed period, provided a certain proportion of the debts be then paid up, the debtor shall be entitled to a discharge, as to his person and future acquisitions.

6. In mercantile cases, where trust-deeds are agreed to, it is with the intention of saving expence; and the arrangement is commonly settled, as nearly as possible, upon the footing of the statute. Indeed, as this statute is constructed upon principles of equity and expediency, it is perhaps, in all cases, one of the best regulators that can be taken by creditors, in arranging their plan of trust and accession.

END OF THE FIRST VOLUME.

PRINTED BY D. WILLISON,
EDINBURGH.

Lightning Source UK Ltd.
Milton Keynes UK
UKOW05f1822230616

276949UK00005B/105/P

9 781240 011018